The Adventures of Huckleberry Finn

Webster's Chinese Simplified Thesaurus Edition

for ESL, EFL, ELP, TOEFL®, TOEIC®, and AP® Test Preparation

Mark Twain

ICON CLASSICS

Published by ICON Group International, Inc.
7404 Trade Street
San Diego, CA 92121 USA

www.icongrouponline.com

The Adventures of Huckleberry Finn: Webster's Chinese Simplified Thesaurus Edition for ESL, EFL, ELP, TOEFL®, TOEIC®, and AP® Test Preparation

This edition published by ICON Classics in 2005
Printed in the United States of America.

ISBN 0-497-26056-5

Contents

PREFACE FROM THE EDITOR

Webster's paperbacks take advantage of the fact that classics are frequently assigned readings in English courses. By using a running English-to-Chinese Simplified thesaurus at the bottom of each page, this edition of *The Adventures of Huckleberry Finn* by Mark Twain (Samuel Clemens) was edited for three audiences. The first includes Chinese Simplified-speaking students enrolled in an English Language Program (ELP), an English as a Foreign Language (EFL) program, an English as a Second Language Program (ESL), or in a TOEFL® or TOEIC® preparation program. The second audience includes English-speaking students enrolled in bilingual education programs or Chinese Simplified speakers enrolled in English speaking schools. The third audience consists of students who are actively building their vocabularies in Chinese Simplified in order to take foreign service, translation certification, Advanced Placement® (AP®)[1] or similar examinations. By using the Webster's Chinese Simplified Thesaurus Edition when assigned for an English course, the reader can enrich their vocabulary in anticipation of an examination in Chinese Simplified or English.

Webster's edition of this classic is organized to expose the reader to a maximum number of difficult and potentially ambiguous English words. Rare or idiosyncratic words and expressions are given lower priority compared to "difficult, yet commonly used" words. Rather than supply a single translation, many words are translated for a variety of meanings in Chinese Simplified, allowing readers to better grasp the ambiguity of English, and avoid them using the notes as a pure translation crutch. Having the reader decipher a word's meaning within context serves to improve vocabulary retention and understanding. Each page covers words not already highlighted on previous pages. If a difficult word is not translated on a page, chances are that it has been translated on a previous page. A more complete glossary of translations is supplied at the end of the book; translations are extracted from Webster's Online Dictionary.

Definitions of remaining terms as well as translations can be found at www.websters-online-dictionary.org. Please send suggestions to websters@icongroupbooks.com

The Editor
Webster's Online Dictionary
www.websters-online-dictionary.org

[1] TOEFL®, TOEIC®, AP® and Advanced Placement® are trademarks of the Educational Testing Service which has neither reviewed nor endorsed this book.

CHAPTER I

I DISCOVER MOSES AND THE BULRUSHES

YOU don't know about me *without* you have read a book by the name of The Adventures of Tom Sawyer; but that ain't no matter. That book was made by Mr. Mark Twain, and he told the **truth, mainly**. There was things which he **stretched**, but mainly he told the truth. That is nothing. I never seen **anybody** but lied one time or another, without it was Aunt Polly, or the **widow**, or **maybe** Mary. Aunt Polly--Tom's Aunt Polly, she is--and Mary, and the Widow Douglas is all told about in that book, which is **mostly** a true book, with some **stretchers**, as I said before.

Now the way that the book **winds** up is this: Tom and me found the money that the robbers **hid** in the **cave**, and it made us **rich**. We got six **thousand dollars apiece**--all **gold**. It was an **awful sight** of money when it was piled up. Well, Judge Thatcher he took it and put it out at interest, and it fetched us a dollar a day apiece all the year round-- more than a body could tell what to do with. The Widow Douglas she took me for her **son**, and **allowed** she would sivilize me; but it was **rough living** in the house all the time, considering how **dismal regular** and **decent** the widow was in all her ways; and so when I couldn't stand it no **longer** I **lit** out. I got into my old **rags** and my sugar-hogshead again, and was free and **satisfied**. But Tom Sawyer he hunted me up

Chinese Simplified

allowed: 允许.
anybody: 任何人.
apiece: 各自, 各自地.
awful: 可怕, 可怕的.
cave: 洞穴, 洞, 穴.
decent: 像样, 合适, 像样的, 正经.
dismal: 暗淡, 忧郁的.
dollar: 元.
gold: 金, 黄金.
hid: 躲藏.
lit: 点燃.
living: 活泼的.
longer: 较长的.
mainly: 主要地.
maybe: 或许, 也许, 或者, 说不定, 可能, 不一定.
mostly: 大多, 多半, 大部份.
rags: 碎布.
regular: 固定, 正常, 通常, 端正, 正规的, 常例的, 定期的, 整齐的, 有秩序的, 正规, 经常.
rich: 富有, 丰富, 富有的, 充实.
rough: 粗暴, 大概, 粗糙, 粗鲁.
satisfied: 满意, 乐意, 心满意足的.
sight: 视觉, 景象, 情景, 目光, 视力, 视线.
son: 儿子.
stretched: 伸展.
stretchers: 担架.
thousand: 千.
truth: 真理, 实话.
widow: 寡妇.
winds: 风.

and said he was going to start a band of robbers, and I might join if I would go back to the widow and be **respectable**. So I went back.

The widow she cried over me, and called me a poor lost **lamb**, and she called me a lot of other names, too, but she never meant no **harm** by it. She put me in them new clothes again, and I couldn't do nothing but **sweat** and sweat, and feel all **cramped** up. Well, then, the old thing commenced again. The widow **rung** a **bell** for **supper**, and you had to come to time. When you got to the table you couldn't go right to **eating**, but you had to wait for the widow to **tuck** down her head and **grumble** a little over the victuals, though there warn't really anything the matter with them,--that is, nothing only everything was **cooked** by itself. In a **barrel** of **odds** and **ends** it is different; things get **mixed** up, and the **juice kind** of swaps around, and the things go better.

After supper she got out her book and learned me about Moses and the Bulrushers, and I was in a sweat to find out all about him; but by and by she let it out that Moses had been dead a considerable long time; so then I didn't care no more about him, because I don't take no stock in dead people.

Pretty soon I wanted to smoke, and asked the widow to let me. But she wouldn't. She said it was a mean practice and wasn't clean, and I must try to not do it any more. That is just the way with some people. They get down on a thing when they don't know nothing about it. Here she was a-bothering about Moses, which was no kin to her, and no use to anybody, being gone, you see, yet finding a power of fault with me for doing a thing that had some good in it. And she took **snuff**, too; of course that was all right, because she done it herself.

Her sister, Miss Watson, a **tolerable slim** old **maid**, with **goggles** on, had just come to live with her, and took a set at me now with a **spelling-** book. She worked me **middling** hard for about an hour, and then the widow made her **ease** up. I couldn't stood it much longer. Then for an hour it was **deadly dull**, and I was **fidgety**. Miss Watson would say, "Don't put your feet up there, Huckleberry;" and "Don't **scrunch** up like that, Huckleberry--set up straight;" and pretty soon she would say, "Don't gap and **stretch** like that, Huckleberry--why don't you try to behave?" Then she told me all about the bad place, and I said I

Chinese Simplified

barrel: 桶，大桶.
bell: 钟，铃.
cooked: 煮熟.
cramped: 逼仄，难懂的.
deadly: 死亡，致死，致命的.
dull: 索然，板滞，沉闷的，干燥，拙，深沉.
ease: 缓解，减轻，容易，悠，舒适.
eating: 吃.
ends: 末端.
fidgety: 烦躁.
goggles: 护目镜.
grumble: 抱怨，诉苦，发牢骚.
harm: 伤害，损害，坏处，害处，祸害.
juice: 汁，汁液，液.
kin: 亲属，骨肉.
lamb: 小羊，羔羊.
maid: 女佣，侍女，少女，姑娘.
middling: 中级品.
mixed: 混合，混合的，错杂.
odds: 可能性，差距.
respectable: 可尊敬，可尊敬的.
rung: 响铃.
scrunch: 碾碎.
slim: 瘦长，纤细，苗条的.
snuff: 鼻烟，用鼻子使劲吸.
spelling: 拼字，斯佩林，拼写检查.
stretch: 张开，拉紧，伸展，伸.
supper: 晚饭，晚餐.
sweat: 汗，出汗，流汗.
tolerable: 可容忍，可容忍的.
tuck: 挤进，塞进.

wished I was there. She got **mad** then, but I didn't mean no harm. All I wanted was to go somewheres; all I wanted was a change, I warn't particular. She said it was **wicked** to say what I said; said she wouldn't say it for the whole world; she was going to live so as to go to the good place. Well, I couldn't see no advantage in going where she was going, so I made up my mind I wouldn't try for it. But I never said so, because it would only make trouble, and wouldn't do no good.

Now she had got a start, and she went on and told me all about the good place. She said all a body would have to do there was to go around all day long with a **harp** and **sing**, **forever** and ever. So I didn't think much of it. But I never said so. I asked her if she reckoned Tom Sawyer would go there, and she said not by a considerable sight. I was **glad** about that, because I wanted him and me to be together.

Miss Watson she kept pecking at me, and it got **tiresome** and **lonesome**. By and by they **fetched** the niggers in and had prayers, and then everybody was off to bed. I went up to my room with a piece of **candle**, and put it on the table. Then I set down in a chair by the window and tried to think of something **cheerful**, but it warn't no use. I felt so lonesome I most wished I was dead. The **stars** were **shining**, and the leaves rustled in the **woods** ever so **mournful**; and I heard an **owl**, away off, who-whooing about somebody that was dead, and a whippowill and a dog **crying** about somebody that was going to die; and the wind was trying to **whisper** something to me, and I couldn't make out what it was, and so it made the cold **shivers** run over me. Then away out in the woods I heard that kind of a sound that a **ghost** makes when it wants to tell about something that's on its mind and can't make itself **understood**, and so can't rest easy in its **grave**, and has to go about that way every night grieving. I got so down-hearted and scared I did wish I had some company. Pretty soon a **spider** went **crawling** up my **shoulder**, and I flipped it off and it lit in the candle; and before I could **budge** it was all **shriveled** up. I didn't need anybody to tell me that that was an awful bad sign and would fetch me some bad **luck**, so I was scared and most **shook** the clothes off of me. I got up and turned around in my **tracks** three times and crossed my **breast** every time; and then I tied up a little

Chinese Simplified

breast：奶子，乳房，胸，胸部.
budge：微微一动，改变态度，羔皮.
candle：蜡烛.
cheerful：愉快，愉快的.
crawling：爬行.
crying：叫喊的，嚎哭的，显著的.
fetch：拿，取，带来.
forever：永远，永久.
ghost：鬼，鬼魂，幽灵.
glad：高兴，高兴的.
grave：严重，庄重，坟墓，墓穴，深重.
harp：竖琴.
lonesome：寂寞，寂寞的.
luck：运气，幸运.
mad：狂，发怒，发狂，生气，疯狂的.
mournful：悲切，悲恸，悲恸的.
owl：猫头鹰，枭.
shining：彪炳，发亮.
shivers：颤抖.
shook：摇动.
shoulder：肩，肩膀，担负.
shriveled：瘪.
sing：唱，歌唱，唱歌.
spider：蜘蛛.
stars：星.
tiresome：使人疲惫的.
tracks：轨道.
understood：明白.
whisper：耳语，低语.
wicked：邪恶，邪恶的，恶性.
woods：树林，森林.

lock of my **hair** with a **thread** to keep witches away. But I hadn't no **confidence**. You do that when you've **lost** a **horseshoe** that you've found, **instead** of nailing it up over the door, but I hadn't ever **heard** anybody say it was any way to keep off **bad** luck when you'd **killed** a spider.

I set down again, a-shaking all over, and got out my **pipe** for a **smoke**; for the house was all as still as death now, and so the widow wouldn't know. Well, after a long time I heard the **clock** away off in the town go boom--boom--boom--twelve licks; and all still again--stiller than ever. **Pretty** soon I heard a **twig snap** down in the **dark** amongst the **trees**-- something was a **stirring**. I set still and **listened**. Directly I could just **barely** hear a "me-yow! me-yow!" down there. That was good! Says I, "me-yow! me-yow!" as **soft** as I could, and then I put out the **light** and **scrambled** out of the **window** on to the **shed**. Then I **slipped** down to the ground and crawled in among the trees, and, **sure** enough, there was Tom Sawyer **waiting** for me.

Chinese Simplified

bad：坏，糟糕，不良，不善，淘气，坏的．
barely：仅仅，仅．
clock：钟，时钟，钟表．
confidence：信心，自信．
dark：暗，黑暗，夜．
hair：头发．
hear：听见，听取，听．
horseshoe：马蹄铁．
instead：代替，反而．
killed：被屠宰的，被杀死的．
light：光，轻，灯，光纤，燃放，灯光，点燃，亮光．
listened：听．
lock：锁，撞锁．
lost：遗失．
pipe：管，管子，筒，喉管．
pretty：漂亮，美丽的，秀丽．
scrambled：攀登，扰频．
shed：散出，棚子，流出，脱落．
slipped：滑落．
smoke：烟，抽烟，烟雾，硝烟，吸烟，熏．
snap：折断，抢夺，猛咬．
soft：柔软，柔和，柔软的．
stirring：活跃的，激动人心的，忙碌的．
sure：肯定．
thread：线，线索，细线，运作．
trees：树木．
twig：嫩枝．
waiting：等候，等待．
window：窗口，窗户，窗，窗子．

CHAPTER II

OUR GANG'S DARK OATH

WE went tiptoeing along a **path** amongst the **trees** back towards the end of the widow's ***garden***, **stooping** down so as the **branches** wouldn't **scrape** our **heads**. When we was **passing** by the **kitchen** I **fell** over a **root** and made a **noise**. We scrouched down and **laid still**. Miss Watson's big nigger, named Jim, was **setting** in the kitchen door; we could see him pretty **clear**, because there was a light behind him. He got up and stretched his **neck** out about a minute, **listening**. Then he says:

"Who dah?"

He listened some more; then he come tiptoeing down and stood right between us; we could a touched him, nearly. Well, likely it was minutes and minutes that there warn't a sound, and we all there so close together. There was a place on my **ankle** that got to **itching**, but I dasn't **scratch** it; and then my ear **begun** to itch; and next my back, right between my **shoulders**. Seemed like I'd **die** if I couldn't scratch. Well, I've noticed that thing **plenty** times since. If you are with the quality, or at a **funeral**, or trying to go to **sleep** when you ain't sleepy--if you are anywheres where it won't do for you to scratch, why you will itch all over in **upwards** of a thousand **places**. Pretty soon Jim says:

Chinese Simplified

ankle: 脚踝，踝，脚脖子.
begun: 开始.
branches: 分支.
die: 逝世，不讳，死.
ear: 耳朵，耳.
fell: 采伐，伐，跌落.
funeral: 葬礼.
garden: 花园.
heads: 头.
itch: 发痒，痒.
itching: 痒的.
kitchen: 厨房.
laid: 放.
listen: 听，倾听.
listening: 听.
neck: 颈项，脖子，颈.
noise: 噪音，噪声，响声，吵闹声，吵声.
passing: 经过的，短暂的，目前的，及格的.
path: 道，道路，路径，小径，走道.
places: 地方.
plenty: 丰富，许多.
root: 根，根本，根源.
scrape: 刮掉，削刮.
scratch: 抓伤，抓，搔刮.
setting: 排字，设定.
shoulders: 肩，双肩.
sleep: 梦寐，睡觉，睡眠，睡.
stooping: 弯腰.
till: 直到.
tree: 树.
upwards: 向上地，向上.

"Say, who is you? Whar is you? Dog my **cats** ef I didn't hear sumf'n. Well, I know **what** I's gwyne to do: I's gwyne to set down here and listen tell I hears it agin."

So he set down on the ground **betwixt** me and Tom. He **leaned** his back up against a tree, and stretched his legs out till one of them most touched one of **mine**. My **nose** begun to itch. It itched till the **tears** come into my eyes. But I dasn't scratch. Then it begun to itch on the inside. Next I got to itching **underneath**. I didn't know how I was going to set still. This miserableness went on as much as six or seven minutes; but it seemed a sight longer than that. I was itching in **eleven** different places now. I reckoned I couldn't stand it more'n a minute longer, but I set my **teeth** hard and got ready to try. Just then Jim begun to **breathe** heavy; next he begun to snore--and then I was pretty soon **comfortable** again.

Tom he made a sign to me--kind of a little noise with his mouth--and we went creeping away on our hands and **knees**. When we was ten foot off Tom **whispered** to me, and wanted to **tie** Jim to the tree for **fun**. But I said no; he might **wake** and make a **disturbance**, and then they'd find out I warn't in. Then Tom said he hadn't got **candles** enough, and he would **slip** in the kitchen and get some more. I didn't want him to try. I said Jim might wake up and come. But Tom wanted to resk it; so we **slid** in there and got three candles, and Tom laid five cents on the table for pay. Then we got out, and I was in a sweat to get away; but nothing would do Tom but he must **crawl** to where Jim was, on his hands and knees, and play something on him. I waited, and it seemed a good while, everything was so still and lonesome.

As soon as Tom was back we cut along the path, around the garden **fence**, and by and by fetched up on the **steep** top of the hill the other side of the house. Tom said he slipped Jim's hat off of his head and **hung** it on a **limb** right over him, and Jim stirred a little, but he didn't wake. **Afterwards** Jim said the witches be witched him and put him in a **trance**, and **rode** him all over the State, and then set him under the trees again, and hung his hat on a limb to show who done it. And next time Jim told it he said they rode him down to New Orleans; and,

Chinese Simplified

afterwards：后来，然后，以后，此后，後，然後，后，过后，底下，此後，後来.
betwixt：中间，在…之间.
breathe：呼吸.
candles：蜡烛.
cats：猫.
comfortable：舒服，舒服的.
crawl：爬，爬行.
disturbance：风波，骚动，干扰，骚乱.
eleven：十一.
fence：篱笆，栅栏，栏位，栏.
fun：娱乐.
hat：帽子.
hung：挂.
knees：膝盖.
leaned：倾斜.
limb：肢，肢体.
mine：矿，我的，矿山，矿井.
nose：鼻子.
rode：骑.
slid：滑行.
slip：滑倒，溜走，溜.
steep：险峻，峭壁，浸，泡，陡峭的.
tears：泪，泪水，眼泪.
teeth：牙齿，牙.
tie：不分胜负，打结，束缚，轨枕，绑，领带.
trance：恍惚.
underneath：在下面，下面的.
wake：醒来，醒觉.
whispered：耳语.

after that, every time he told it he spread it more and more, till by and by he said they rode him all over the world, and **tired** him most to death, and his back was all over saddle-boils. Jim was **monstrous proud** about it, and he got so he wouldn't hardly notice the other niggers. Niggers would come **miles** to hear Jim tell about it, and he was more looked up to than any nigger in that country. Strange niggers would stand with their **mouths** open and look him all over, same as if he was a **wonder**. Niggers is always talking about witches in the dark by the kitchen fire; but **whenever** one was talking and letting on to know all about such things, Jim would happen in and say, "Hm! What you know 'bout witches?" and that nigger was corked up and had to take a back seat. Jim always kept that five-center piece round his neck with a **string**, and said it was a **charm** the **devil** give to him with his own hands, and told him he could **cure** anybody with it and fetch witches whenever he wanted to just by saying something to it; but he never told what it was he said to it. Niggers would come from all around there and give Jim anything they had, just for a sight of that five-center piece; but they wouldn't touch it, because the devil had had his hands on it. Jim was most **ruined** for a **servant**, because he got **stuck** up on account of having seen the devil and been rode by witches.

Well, when Tom and me got to the edge of the **hilltop** we looked away down into the village and could see three or four **lights twinkling**, where there was **sick** folks, maybe; and the stars over us was sparkling ever so fine; and down by the village was the river, a **whole** mile **broad**, and awful still and grand. We went down the hill and found Jo Harper and Ben Rogers, and two or three more of the boys, hid in the old tanyard. So we unhitched a **skiff** and pulled down the river two mile and a half, to the big **scar** on the **hillside**, and went **ashore**.

We went to a **clump** of **bushes**, and Tom made everybody **swear** to keep the **secret**, and then showed them a hole in the hill, right in the thickest part of the bushes. Then we lit the candles, and crawled in on our hands and knees. We went about two hundred **yards**, and then the cave opened up. Tom poked about amongst the **passages**, and pretty soon **ducked** under a wall where you wouldn't

Chinese Simplified

ashore：岸上，上岸.
broad：宽，宽广.
bushes：灌木.
charm：魅力，迷人.
clump：土块.
cure：治疗，防治，药，治愈，医治.
devil：魔鬼，妖怪，鬼.
ducked：鸭.
hillside：山坡.
hilltop：山顶.
hole：洞，漏洞，孔，穴，洞穴，窟窿.
lights：灯火.
mile：英里.
monstrous：怪物似，似怪物的.
mouths：口.
passages：通路.
proud：傲岸，骄矜，骄傲的，自豪的.
ruined：破败，毁坏.
scar：疤痕，痕，疤，瘢痕，伤痕.
secret：秘密，机密.
servant：仆人，佣人，用人.
sick：生病.
skiff：小船，小艇.
string：绳子，串，线，细线，弦.
stuck：黏贴.
swear：立誓，发誓.
tired：疲倦，疲乏，疲倦的.
twinkling：闪烁，闪烁的.
whenever：无论何时，每当.
wonder：奇迹，惊奇.
yards：场地.

a noticed that there was a hole. We went along a **narrow** place and got into a kind of room, all **damp** and sweaty and cold, and there we stopped. Tom says:

"Now, we'll start this band of robbers and call it Tom Sawyer's Gang. **Everybody** that wants to join has got to take an **oath**, and write his name in blood."

Everybody was **willing**. So Tom got out a **sheet** of paper that he had wrote the oath on, and read it. It **swore** every boy to **stick** to the band, and never tell any of the **secrets**; and if anybody done anything to any boy in the band, **whichever** boy was ordered to **kill** that person and his family must do it, and he mustn't eat and he mustn't sleep till he had killed them and hacked a **cross** in their **breasts**, which was the sign of the band. And **nobody** that didn't **belong** to the band could use that mark, and if he did he must be sued; and if he done it again he must be killed. And if anybody that belonged to the band told the secrets, he must have his **throat** cut, and then have his **carcass burnt** up and the **ashes scattered** all around, and his name blotted off of the list with blood and never mentioned again by the **gang**, but have a **curse** put on it and be **forgot** forever.

Everybody said it was a real beautiful oath, and asked Tom if he got it out of his own head. He said, some of it, but the rest was out of pirate-books and robber-books, and every gang that was **high**-toned had it.

Some thought it would be good to kill the *families* of boys that told the secrets. Tom said it was a good idea, so he took a **pencil** and wrote it in. Then Ben Rogers says:

"Here's Huck Finn, he hain't got no family; what you going to do 'bout him?"

"Well, hain't he got a father?" says Tom Sawyer.

"Yes, he's got a father, but you can't never find him these days. He used to lay **drunk** with the hogs in the tanyard, but he hain't been seen in these parts for a year or more."

They **talked** it over, and they was going to rule me out, because they said every boy must have a family or somebody to kill, or else it wouldn't be **fair** and

Chinese Simplified

ashes: 灰烬.
belong: 属于.
breasts: 乳房.
burnt: 烧伤的，烧过的，烧.
carcass: 残骸.
cross: 交叉，十字架，越过，相交，渡过，穿过.
curse: 咒骂，诅咒，咒.
damp: 潮湿，潮湿的.
drunk: 喝了，喝醉.
everybody: 每个人，各位.
fair: 公平，博览会，清澈，公正，公道，展，直.
forgot: 忘记.
gang: 一群，帮.
high-toned: 调子高的，高尚的.
kill: 打死，杀害，杀死.
narrow: 狭窄，窄，逼仄，狭，小气，狭隘，狭窄的.
nobody: 没有人，没人.
oath: 誓言，誓词，宣誓.
pencil: 铅笔，笔套，笔帽.
scattered: 零落，散播，散乱的，分散的.
secrets: 秘密.
sheet: 片，一张，床单，纸张.
stick: 棍，棒子，棍子，插入，棒，黏贴，手杖.
swore: 立誓.
talked: 谈话.
throat: 嗓子，喉咙，喉头，咽喉.
whichever: 任何，视何者为.
willing: 愿意，高兴，情愿的.

square for the others. Well, nobody could think of anything to do--everybody was stumped, and set still. I was most **ready** to **cry**; but all at once I thought of a way, and so I offered them Miss Watson--they could kill her. Everybody said:

"Oh, she'll do. That's all right. Huck can come in."

Then they all stuck a **pin** in their fingers to get **blood** to **sign** with, and I made my **mark** on the paper.

"Now," says Ben Rogers, "what's the line of business of this Gang?"

"Nothing only **robbery** and murder," Tom said.

"But who are we going to rob?--houses, or **cattle**, or--"

"**Stuff! stealing** cattle and such things ain't robbery; it's burglary," says Tom Sawyer. "We ain't burglars. That ain't no sort of **style**. We are highwaymen. We **stop** stages and carriages on the road, with masks on, and kill the people and take their watches and money."

"Must we always kill the people?"

"Oh, **certainly**. It's best. Some **authorities** think different, but mostly it's **considered** best to kill them--except some that you **bring** to the cave here, and keep them till they're ransomed."

"Ransomed? What's that?"

"I don't know. But that's what they do. I've seen it in **books**; and so of **course** that's what we've got to do."

"But how can we do it if we don't know what it is?"

"Why, **blame** it all, we've *got* to do it. Don't I tell you it's in the books? Do you want to go to doing different from what's in the books, and get things all **muddled** up?"

"Oh, that's all very **fine** to *say*, Tom Sawyer, but how in the **nation** are these fellows going to be ransomed if we don't know how to do it to them? --that's the thing I want to get at. Now, what do you **reckon** it is?"

"Well, I don't know. But per'aps if we keep them till they're ransomed, it means that we keep them till they're dead."

Chinese Simplified

authorities: 当局.
blame: 责备, 咎, 非难, 责任, 罪, 责怪, 归咎.
blood: 血, 血液, 鲜血.
books: 图书, 书籍, 书, 篇.
bring: 带, 带来, 携带.
cattle: 家畜, 牛.
certainly: 一定, 保管, 当然, 理所当然, 岂不, 肯定地.
considered: 被尊重的, 考虑过的.
course: 课程, 经过, 进程, 路程, 路线, 学科, 过程.
cry: 喊, 叫, 哭, 哭泣.
fine: 罚款, 罚金, 良好, 要得, 美好, 精美, 纤小, 纤细, 不赖, 优美, 美好的.
mark: 标记, 印, 符号, 标明, 标识, 迹, 迹象, 标志, 成绩, 马克, 做记号.
muddled: 糊涂, 懵懂.
nation: 国家.
pin: 别针, 个人鉴别码.
ready: 就绪, 愿意, 准备, 妥当.
reckon: 估计, 计算.
robbery: 掠夺, 抢劫.
sign: 符号, 标记, 署名, 牌子, 迹象, 标志, 签署, 手势, 旗.
square: 正方形, 平方, 四方形.
stealing: 偷垒, 偷窃.
stop: 停止, 终止, 截止, 站.
stuff: 材料, 填塞, 职员.
style: 方式, 风格, 式样, 样式, 试样, 笔调, 模样, 作风.

"Now, that's something *like*. That'll answer. Why couldn't you said that before? We'll keep them till they're **ransomed** to death; and a **bothersome** lot they'll be, too--eating up everything, and always trying to get **loose**."

"How you talk, Ben Rogers. How can they get loose when there's a **guard** over them, ready to **shoot** them down if they move a peg?"

"A guard! Well, that *is* good. So **somebody's** got to set up all night and never get any sleep, just so as to **watch** them. I think that's **foolishness**. Why can't a body take a club and ransom them as soon as they get here?"

"Because it ain't in the books so--that's why. Now, Ben Rogers, do you want to do things regular, or don't you?--that's the idea. Don't you reckon that the people that **made** the books **knows** what's the **correct** thing to do? Do you reckon *you* can **learn** 'em anything? Not by a good **deal**. No, sir, we'll just go on and ransom them in the regular way."

"All right. I don't mind; but I say it's a fool way, **anyhow**. Say, do we kill the women, too?"

"Well, Ben Rogers, if I was as **ignorant** as you I wouldn't let on. Kill the women? No; nobody ever saw anything in the books like that. You fetch them to the cave, and you're always as **polite** as **pie** to them; and by and by they fall in love with you, and never want to go home any more."

"Well, if that's the way I'm agreed, but I don't take no **stock** in it. **Mighty** soon we'll have the cave so **cluttered** up with women, and fellows waiting to be ransomed, that there won't be no place for the **robbers**. But go **ahead**, I ain't got nothing to say."

Little Tommy Barnes was **asleep** now, and when they waked him up he was scared, and cried, and said he wanted to go home to his ma, and didn't want to be a robber any more.

So they all made fun of him, and called him cry-baby, and that made him mad, and he said he would go **straight** and tell all the secrets. But Tom give him five cents to keep **quiet**, and said we would all go home and meet next week, and rob somebody and kill some people.

Chinese Simplified

ahead：前头，前方，前面的.
anyhow：无论如何，反正.
asleep：睡着，睡着的.
bothersome：淘神，麻烦的，伤脑筋.
cluttered：混乱.
correct：正确，拨正，不错，对，端正，纠正，对头，改正，对了.
deal：处理.
fool：呆子，笨蛋，傻子，笨人，愚人.
foolishness：愚蠢.
guard：警卫，警备，把守，保守，守卫，防卫，警戒.
ignorant：愚昧，无知的，茫然.
knows：知道.
learn：学，学习.
loose：松开，松弛的.
ma：妈，马，文学硕士.
mighty：伟大，强势，强大的.
pie：馅饼.
polite：有礼貌，客气，有礼貌的，斯文，和气.
quiet：安静，寂静，安定，安生，沉静，宁静的.
ransom：赎金.
rob：抢劫.
robber：强盗.
shoot：射击，芽，射门.
somebody：某人，有人.
stock：存货，股票，股份，库存.
straight：直，海峡，迳直，直接，笔直，一直.
watch：观看，手表，监视.

Ben Rogers said he couldn't get out much, only Sundays, and so he wanted to **begin** next Sunday; but all the **boys** said it would be **wicked** to do it on Sunday, and that **settled** the thing. They agreed to get together and **fix** a day as **soon** as they could, and then we **elected** Tom Sawyer first **captain** and Jo Harper second captain of the Gang, and so **started** home.

I clumb up the **shed** and **crept** into my **window** just before day was breaking. My new **clothes** was all greased up and clayey, and I was **dog- tired**.

Chinese Simplified

begin：开始，开创，发起，掀起，兴办.
boys：哥儿，男孩.
captain：队长，舰长，领队.
clothes：衣服，服装，西装，件，衣裳.
crept：爬行.
dog：狗，犬.
elected：被选.
fix：安装，奠定，固定，修理.
settled：安定.
shed：散出，棚子，流出，脱落.
soon：不久，最近，眼看，快，近期，早，早日.
started：开始.
tired：疲倦，疲乏，疲倦的.
wicked：邪恶，邪恶的，恶性.
window：窗口，窗户，窗，窗子.

CHAPTER III

WE AMBUSCADE THE A-RABS

Well, I got a good going-over in the morning from old Miss Watson on account of my **clothes**; but the **widow** she didn't **scold**, but only cleaned off the **grease** and **clay**, and looked so **sorry** that I thought I would **behave awhile** if I could. Then Miss Watson she took me in the **closet** and *prayed*, but nothing come of it. She told me to pray every day, and **whatever** I asked for I would get it. But it warn't so. I tried it. Once I got a fish-line, but no **hooks**. It warn't any good to me without hooks. I tried for the hooks three or four times, but **somehow** I couldn't make it work. By and by, one day, I asked Miss Watson to try for me, but she said I was a **fool**. She never told me why, and I couldn't make it out no way.

I set down one time back in the **woods**, and had a long think about it. I says to **myself**, if a body can get anything they pray for, why don't Deacon Winn get back the money he **lost** on **pork**? Why can't the widow get back her **silver** snuffbox that was **stole**? Why can't Miss Watson **fat** up? No, says I to my self, there ain't nothing in it. I went and told the widow about it, and she said the thing a body could get by praying for it was "spiritual gifts." This was too many for me, but she told me what she meant--I must help other people, and do everything I could for other people, and look out for them all the time, and never

Chinese Simplified

awhile: 一会儿.
behave: 举止，表现，行为.
clay: 泥土，黏土.
closet: 壁橱.
clothes: 衣服，服装，西装，件，衣裳.
fat: 档案分配区，肥，油脂，肥胖，脂肪.
fool: 呆子，笨蛋，傻子，笨人，愚人.
grease: 油脂.
hooks: 钩.
lost: 遗失.
myself: 我自己.
pork: 猪肉.
pray: 祈祷.
scold: 责骂.
self: 自己，自，自我，我.
silver: 银，白银.
somehow: 不知何故.
sorry: 遗憾，对不起.
stole: 偷了.
whatever: 无论如何，无论何事，不拘，任何.
widow: 寡妇.
woods: 树林，森林.

think about myself. This was including Miss Watson, as I took it. I went out in the woods and turned it over in my mind a long time, but I couldn't see no **advantage** about it--except for the other people; so at last I reckoned I wouldn't **worry** about it any more, but just let it go. Sometimes the widow would take me one side and **talk** about Providence in a way to make a body's **mouth** water; but maybe next day Miss Watson would take **hold** and **knock** it all down again. I judged I could see that there was two Providences, and a poor **chap** would **stand considerable** show with the widow's Providence, but if Miss Watson's got him there warn't no help for him any more. I thought it all out, and reckoned I would belong to the widow's if he wanted me, though I couldn't make out how he was a-going to be any better off then than what he was before, **seeing** I was so ignorant, and so kind of **low**-down and ornery.

Pap he hadn't been seen for more than a year, and that was comfortable for me; I didn't want to see him no more. He used to always **whale** me when he was **sober** and could get his hands on me; though I used to take to the woods most of the time when he was around. Well, about this time he was found in the **river** drownded, about **twelve** mile above town, so people said. They judged it was him, **anyway**; said this drownded man was just his **size**, and was **ragged**, and had **uncommon** long hair, which was all like pap; but they couldn't make nothing out of the face, because it had been in the water so long it warn't much like a face at all. They said he was **floating** on his back in the water. They took him and **buried** him on the bank. But I warn't comfortable long, because I **happened** to think of something. I knowed mighty well that a drownded man don't float on his back, but on his face. So I knowed, then, that this warn't pap, but a woman dressed up in a man's clothes. So I was **uncomfortable** again. I judged the old man would turn up again by and by, though I wished he wouldn't.

We played robber now and then about a month, and then I **resigned**. All the boys did. We hadn't robbed nobody, hadn't killed any people, but only just pretended. We used to **hop** out of the woods and go **charging** down on hog-drivers and women in carts taking garden stuff to market, but we never hived

Chinese Simplified

advantage: 好处，裨益，优点．
anyway: 无论如何，反正．
buried: 埋下．
chap: 家伙，皴裂．
charging: 收费，充电．
considerable: 可观，相当多的．
float: 漂浮．
floating: 漂浮的，移动的，浮动的，飘浮．
happened: 发生．
hold: 握住，持有，把握，包容，认为，保持．
hop: 跳跃，三级跳远．
knock: 敲，敲撞．
low-down: 非常低的，下作．
mouth: 口，嘴巴，嘴，吻．
ragged: 破烂，衣著褴褛的．
resigned: 忍从的．
river: 河，江，川，河流，条．
seeing: 有鉴于．
size: 大小，尺寸，纤度，个子，个儿．
sober: 清醒，清醒的．
stand: 站住，主张，架子，站立，耐，站，架．
talk: 谈话，报告，言语，谈．
twelve: 十二．
uncomfortable: 不舒适，不舒适的，拘束，别扭．
uncommon: 稀有，稀有的．
whale: 鲸鱼．
worry: 担心，使烦恼，缠绕，担忧，心事，担，烦恼，着急．

any of them. Tom Sawyer called the hogs "ingots," and he called the **turnips** and stuff "julery," and we would go to the cave and **powwow** over what we had done, and how many people we had killed and marked. But I couldn't see no profit in it. One time Tom sent a boy to run about town with a blazing stick, which he called a **slogan** (which was the sign for the Gang to get together), and then he said he had got secret news by his spies that next day a whole **parcel** of Spanish **merchants** and rich A-rabs was going to camp in Cave Hollow with two hundred **elephants**, and six hundred camels, and over a thousand "sumter" **mules**, all **loaded** down with di'monds, and they didn't have only a guard of four hundred soldiers, and so we would lay in **ambuscade**, as he called it, and kill the lot and **scoop** the things. He said we must **slick** up our **swords** and **guns**, and get ready. He never could go after even a turnip- **cart** but he must have the swords and guns all **scoured** up for it, though they was only **lath** and broomsticks, and you might scour at them till you rotted, and then they warn't worth a **mouthful** of ashes more than what they was before. I didn't believe we could lick such a crowd of Spaniards and A-rabs, but I wanted to see the camels and elephants, so I was on hand next day, Saturday, in the ambuscade; and when we got the word we rushed out of the woods and down the hill. But there warn't no Spaniards and A-rabs, and there warn't no camels nor no elephants. It warn't anything but a Sunday-school **picnic**, and only a primer-class at that. We busted it up, and chased the children up the **hollow**; but we never got anything but some doughnuts and **jam**, though Ben Rogers got a **rag doll**, and Jo Harper got a hymn-book and a **tract**; and then the teacher charged in, and made us drop everything and cut. I didn't see no di'monds, and I told Tom Sawyer so. He said there was **loads** of them there, anyway; and he said there was A-rabs there, too, and elephants and things. I said, why couldn't we see them, then? He said if I warn't so ignorant, but had read a book called Don Quixote, I would know without asking. He said it was all done by **enchantment**. He said there was hundreds of soldiers there, and elephants and **treasure**, and so on, but we had **enemies** which he called **magicians**; and they had turned the whole thing into an **infant** Sunday-school, just out of **spite**. I said, all right; then the thing for us to do was to go for the magicians. Tom Sawyer said I was a numskull.

Chinese Simplified

ambuscade: 伏击，伏兵.
cart: 手拉车，手推车.
doll: 洋娃娃，玩偶.
elephants: 象.
enchantment: 魔法，迷惑.
enemies: 敌人.
guns: 枪支.
hollow: 凹陷，中空的，空心，空虚.
infant: 婴儿.
jam: 果酱，干扰.
lath: 板条.
lick: 舔，舐.
loaded: 载入.
loads: 装载.
magicians: 魔法师.
merchants: 商人.
mouthful: 满口的.
mules: 骡子.
parcel: 包裹，包，邮包.
picnic: 野餐.
powwow: 巫师.
rag: 破布，碎布.
scoop: 杓子，勺子，勺.
scour: 擦洗，擦亮，搜索.
slick: 油头滑脑.
slogan: 口号，标语.
spite: 恶意.
swords: 剑.
tract: 地域.
treasure: 爱护，爱惜，宝贝，宝物，宝贵，宝藏，珍惜.
turnip: 芜菁，萝卜.
turnips: 萝卜.

"Why," said he, "a **magician** could call up a lot of genies, and they would **hash** you up like nothing before you could say Jack Robinson. They are as **tall** as a tree and as big around as a church."

"Well," I says, "s'pose we got some genies to help *us*--can't we lick the other **crowd** then?"

"How you going to get them?"

"I don't know. How do *they* get them?"

"Why, they **rub** an old **tin lamp** or an **iron ring**, and then the genies come **tearing** in, with the **thunder** and **lightning** a-ripping around and the smoke a-rolling, and everything they're told to do they up and do it. They don't think nothing of **pulling** a shot-tower up by the **roots**, and **belting** a Sunday-school **superintendent** over the head with it--or any other man."

"Who makes them tear around so?"

"Why, **whoever rubs** the lamp or the ring. They belong to whoever rubs the lamp or the ring, and they've got to do whatever he says. If he tells them to build a **palace** forty miles long out of di'monds, and **fill** it full of chewing-gum, or whatever you want, and fetch an emperor's daughter from China for you to **marry**, they've got to do it--and they've got to do it before sun-up next morning, too. And more: they've got to **waltz** that palace around over the country **wherever** you want it, you understand."

"Well," says I, "I think they are a **pack** of flat-heads for not **keeping** the palace themselves 'stead of fooling them away like that. And what's more--if I was one of them I would see a man in Jericho before I would **drop** my business and come to him for the **rubbing** of an old tin lamp."

"How you talk, Huck Finn. Why, you'd *have* to come when he **rubbed** it, whether you wanted to or not."

"What! and I as high as a tree and as big as a church? All right, then; I *would* come; but I lay I'd make that man **climb** the **highest** tree there was in the country."

Chinese Simplified

belting：带类.
climb：爬，攀登.
crowd：人群.
drop：落，水滴，衰退，掉落，降，点子.
fill：添补，补足，装满，填满，填充.
hash：剁碎.
highest：最高.
iron：铁，熨斗，鐵.
keeping：保管，保持.
lamp：灯.
lightning：闪电.
magician：魔术师，妖人，魔法师.
marry：结婚.
pack：包装，包扎，包，背包.
palace：宫殿，宫，皇宫.
pulling：拉.
ring：戒指，环，圈，篮圈，戒子，圈子，响铃，电话铃声.
roots：根.
rub：摩擦，擦.
rubbed：摩擦.
rubbing：研磨，拓片，摩擦.
rubs：摩擦.
superintendent：监督人.
tall：高大的，高大.
tear：眼泪，撕破，撕.
tearing：撕裂的.
thunder：雷，雷声，打雷.
tin：锡，罐头.
waltz：华尔滋舞.
wherever：无论何处，哪里.
whoever：无论何人.

"Shucks, it ain't no use to **talk** to you, Huck Finn. You don't **seem** to know anything, somehow--perfect saphead."

I thought all this over for two or three days, and then I reckoned I would see if there was anything in it. I got an old **tin lamp** and an **iron ring**, and went out in the **woods** and **rubbed** and rubbed **till** I **sweat** like an Injun, **calculating** to **build** a **palace** and **sell** it; but it warn't no use, **none** of the genies come. So then I judged that all that **stuff** was only just one of Tom Sawyer's **lies**. I reckoned he believed in the A-rabs and the **elephants**, but as for me I think different. It had all the marks of a Sunday-school.

Chinese Simplified

build: 建造，建立，兴建，筑，个子，造，建筑，建成，修筑，建.
calculating: 工于心计的.
elephants: 象.
iron: 铁，熨斗，鐵.
lamp: 灯.
lies: 谎言.
none: 无，没有.
palace: 宫殿，宫，皇宫.
ring: 戒指，环，圈，篮圈，戒子，圈子，响铃，电话铃声.
rubbed: 摩擦.
seem: 显得，看来，彷佛，好象.
sell: 销售，游说，贩卖，出售.
stuff: 材料，填塞，职员.
sweat: 汗，出汗，流汗.
talk: 谈话，报告，言语，谈.
till: 直到.
tin: 锡，罐头.
woods: 树林，森林.

CHAPTER IV

THE HAIR-BALL ORACLE

Well, three or four months run **along**, and it was well into the **winter** now. I had been to school most all the time and could **spell** and read and **write** just a little, and could say the **multiplication** table up to six times **seven** is thirty-five, and I don't reckon I could ever get any further than that if I was to **live** forever. I don't take no stock in **mathematics**, anyway.

At first I hated the school, but by and by I got so I could stand it. Whenever I got **uncommon** tired I played hookey, and the **hiding** I got next day done me good and cheered me up. So the longer I went to school the **easier** it got to be. I was getting sort of used to the widow's **ways**, too, and they warn't so **raspy** on me. Living in a house and **sleeping** in a **bed** pulled on me pretty **tight** mostly, but before the **cold weather** I used to **slide** out and sleep in the woods sometimes, and so that was a **rest** to me. I liked the old ways best, but I was getting so I liked the new ones, too, a little **bit**. The widow said I was **coming** along **slow** but sure, and doing very **satisfactory**. She said she warn't **ashamed** of me.

One morning I happened to **turn** over the salt-cellar at **breakfast**. I **reached** for some of it as **quick** as I could to **throw** over my left shoulder and keep off the bad luck, but Miss Watson was in ahead of me, and crossed me off. She says,

Chinese Simplified

along：沿着，沿，一同.
ashamed：惭愧，羞愧，惭愧的.
bed：床，床铺.
bit：位元，咬.
breakfast：早餐，早饭，早点.
cold：冷，感冒，寒冷，寒，冷淡.
coming：未来，到来.
easier：更容易.
hiding：隐匿.
live：住，活，居住.
mathematics：数学.
multiplication：乘法，增加.
quick：快，玲珑，敏捷的，迅速的.
raspy：易怒的.
reached：到达.
rest：休息，安息，其余.
satisfactory：满意的，称心，圆满.
seven：七.
sleeping：睡眠，睡着.
slide：滑落，滑行，滑.
slow：慢，缓慢，迟慢，迟钝，迟迟，迟缓.
spell：拼写，咒语，符咒.
throw：扔，丢掉，丢，投.
tight：严格，严密，紧，紧的，严竣，狭隘.
turn：转动，转弯.
uncommon：稀有，稀有的.
ways：方法.
weather：天气.
winter：冬天，冬季，冬.
write：撰写，写，编着，写作，写信给，书写，书写器，写字，作曲.

"Take your hands away, Huckleberry; what a **mess** you are always making!" The widow put in a good word for me, but that warn't going to keep off the bad luck, I knowed that well enough. I started out, after breakfast, **feeling worried** and **shaky**, and wondering where it was going to **fall** on me, and what it was going to be. There is ways to keep off some kinds of bad luck, but this wasn't one of them kind; so I never tried to do anything, but just poked along low-spirited and on the watch-out.

I went down to the **front** garden and clumb over the stile where you go through the high **board** fence. There was an **inch** of new **snow** on the ground, and I seen somebody's tracks. They had come up from the **quarry** and **stood** around the stile a while, and then went on around the garden fence. It was **funny** they hadn't come in, after **standing** around so. I couldn't make it out. It was very **curious**, somehow. I was going to **follow** around, but I **stooped** down to look at the tracks first. I didn't **notice** anything at first, but next I did. There was a cross in the left boot-heel made with big nails, to keep off the devil.

I was up in a second and shinning down the **hill**. I looked over my shoulder every now and then, but I didn't see nobody. I was at Judge Thatcher's as quick as I could get there. He said:

"Why, my **boy**, you are all out of **breath**. Did you come for your interest?"

"No, sir," I says; "is there some for me?"

"Oh, yes, a half-yearly is in last night--over a hundred and **fifty** dollars. Quite a **fortune** for you. You had better let me **invest** it along with your six thousand, because if you take it you'll **spend** it."

"No, sir," I says, "I don't want to spend it. I don't want it at all-- **nor** the six thousand, nuther. I want you to take it; I want to give it to you--the six thousand and all."

He looked **surprised**. He couldn't seem to make it out. He says:

"Why, what can you mean, my boy?"

I says, "Don't you ask me no **questions** about it, please. You'll take it --won't you?"

Chinese Simplified

board: 木板，包饭，板，板子，板纸，牌匾，部，木版，委员会.
boy: 男孩，男孩子，男孩儿，小子.
breath: 气息，鼻息，呼吸，气流.
curious: 有好奇心，好奇，好奇的.
fall: 跌落，落下，衰退，下跌，覆亡，沈落，跌倒，沉落.
feeling: 感觉，情绪，感情，情感，思绪.
fifty: 五十，半白.
follow: 跟进，跟从，接着，跟随，遵照.
fortune: 幸运，命运，运气.
front: 前面，正面，跟前，战线，阵地.
funny: 有趣的.
hill: 小丘，山坡，山岗，陵.
inch: 英寸.
invest: 投资，投产.
mess: 杂乱，混乱.
nor: 也不.
notice: 通知，注意，布告，注意到，启事.
quarry: 采石场.
questions: 问题.
shaky: 动摇不稳，震动的.
snow: 雪.
spend: 度过，花费，支出，耗费.
standing: 站立，地位.
stood: 站了.
stooped: 弯腰.
surprised: 惊讶.
worried: 担心，不安，优虑.

He says:

"Well, I'm **puzzled**. Is something the matter?"

"**Please** take it," says I, "and don't ask me nothing--then I won't have to tell no lies."

He studied a while, and then he says:

"Oho-o! I think I see. You want to *sell* all your property to me--not give it. That's the correct idea."

Then he **wrote** something on a paper and read it over, and says:

"There; you see it says 'for a consideration.' That means I have **bought** it of you and **paid** you for it. Here's a dollar for you. Now you sign it."

So I signed it, and left.

Miss Watson's nigger, Jim, had a hair-ball as big as your **fist**, which had been took out of the **fourth stomach** of an **ox**, and he used to do **magic** with it. He said there was a **spirit** inside of it, and it knowed everything. So I went to him that night and told him pap was here again, for I found his tracks in the snow. What I wanted to know was, what he was going to do, and was he going to **stay**? Jim got out his hair-ball and said something over it, and then he held it up and **dropped** it on the **floor**. It fell pretty **solid**, and only **rolled** about an inch. Jim tried it again, and then another time, and it acted just the same. Jim got down on his knees, and put his ear against it and listened. But it warn't no use; he said it wouldn't talk. He said sometimes it wouldn't talk without money. I told him I had an old slick **counterfeit quarter** that warn't no good because the **brass showed** through the silver a little, and it wouldn't **pass** nohow, even if the brass didn't show, because it was so slick it felt **greasy**, and so that would tell on it every time. (I reckoned I wouldn't say nothing about the dollar I got from the judge.) I said it was pretty bad money, but maybe the hair-ball would take it, because maybe it wouldn't know the **difference**. Jim **smelt** it and bit it and rubbed it, and said he would **manage** so the hair-ball would think it was good. He said he would **split** open a **raw** Irish **potato** and stick the quarter in between and keep it there all night, and next morning you couldn't see no brass, and it

Chinese Simplified

bought: 买了.
brass: 黄铜.
counterfeit: 仿造，仿造的.
difference: 差异，差，差别，区别，分歧，分别，误差.
dropped: 落下.
fist: 拳头.
floor: 地板，地面.
fourth: 第四，第四的.
greasy: 泥泞的，油性的.
magic: 魔术.
manage: 符合，管理，处理.
ox: 牛.
paid: 支付.
pass: 隘口，及格，传递，度过，要隘.
please: 请，使高兴.
potato: 马铃薯，土豆.
puzzled: 惑.
quarter: 四分之一.
raw: 生的，未加工的，阴冷的.
rolled: 卷.
showed: 展示.
smelt: 熔炼，溶解.
solid: 固体，立体，固体的，坚硬，扎实，实心的，坚固的，坚实.
spirit: 神，精神，灵魂，气概，白干儿，白乾儿.
split: 均分，分裂，裂片，拆分，捧腹，裂开.
stay: 延缓，逗留，停留.
stomach: 胃，肚子.
wrote: 写了.

wouldn't feel **greasy** no more, and so **anybody** in **town** would take it in a **minute**, let **alone** a hair-ball. Well, I knowed a **potato** would do that before, but I had **forgot** it.

Jim put the **quarter under** the hair-ball, and got down and **listened** again. This time he said the hair-ball was all right. He said it would tell my whole **fortune** if I wanted it to. I says, go on. So the hair-ball **talked** to Jim, and Jim told it to me. He says:

"Yo' ole father doan' know yit what he's a-gwyne to do. Sometimes he spec he'll go 'way, en **den** agin he spec he'll stay. De bes' way is to res' easy en let de ole man take his own way. Dey's two **angels** hoverin' roun' 'bout him. One uv 'em is white en **shiny**, en t'other one is black. De white one gits him to go right a **little** while, den de black one **sail** in en **bust** it all up. A body can't tell yit which one gwyne to **fetch** him at de las'. But you is all right. You gwyne to have considable **trouble** in yo' life, en considable **joy**. Sometimes you gwyne to git **hurt**, en sometimes you gwyne to git **sick**; but every time you's gwyne to git well agin. Dey's two gals flyin' 'bout you in yo' life. One uv 'em's light en t'other one is **dark**. One is **rich** en t'other is po'. You's gwyne to **marry** de po' one fust en de rich one by en by. You wants to keep 'way fum de water as much as you **kin**, en don't run no resk, 'kase it's down in de bills dat you's gwyne to git hung."

When I lit my **candle** and went up to my room that night there **sat** pap--his own **self**!

Chinese Simplified

alone: 独自, 单独, 单纯, 单独地.
angels: 天使.
anybody: 任何人.
bust: 半身像, 逮捕, 破产.
candle: 蜡烛.
dark: 暗, 黑暗, 夜.
de: 可选择丢弃.
den: 窝.
easy: 容易, 轻而易举, 简易, 安逸, 便利, 便当, 容易的, 纵横.
fetch: 拿, 取, 带来.
forgot: 忘记.
fortune: 幸运, 命运, 运气.
greasy: 泥泞的, 油性的.
hurt: 伤害, 使受伤.
joy: 乐趣, 快乐, 高兴, 喜悦.
kin: 亲属, 骨肉.
listened: 听.
lit: 点燃.
marry: 结婚.
minute: 分钟, 详细, 分, 微小的, 渺小.
potato: 马铃薯, 土豆.
quarter: 四分之一.
rich: 富有, 丰富, 富有的, 充实.
sail: 帆, 帆船, 航行, 航海.
sat: 坐了, 星期六.
self: 自己, 自, 自我, 我.
shiny: 发亮, 闪亮, 发亮的.
sick: 生病.
talked: 谈话.
town: 城镇, 城市, 市镇.
trouble: 麻烦, 难度, 难处.

CHAPTER V

PAP STARTS IN ON A NEW LIFE

I *had* **shut** the door to. Then I turned around and there he was. I used to be scared of him all the time, he tanned me so much. I reckoned I was scared now, too; but in a **minute** I see I was mistaken--**that** is, after the first **jolt**, as you may say, when my **breath** sort of **hitched**, he being so **unexpected**; but right away after I see I warn't scared of him **worth** bothring about.

He was most fifty, and he looked it. His hair was long and tangled and **greasy**, and **hung** down, and you could see his eyes **shining** through like he was behind vines. It was all black, no **gray**; so was his long, mixed-up **whiskers**. There warn't no **color** in his face, where his face showed; it was white; not like another man's white, but a white to make a body **sick**, a white to make a body's **flesh** crawl--a tree-toad white, a fish-belly white. As for his clothes--just **rags**, that was all. He had one **ankle resting** on t'other **knee**; the **boot** on that **foot** was busted, and two of his toes **stuck** through, and he worked them now and then. His hat was laying on the floor--an old black slouch with the **top** caved in, like a **lid**.

I stood a-looking at him; he set there a-looking at me, with his **chair tilted** back a little. I set the **candle** down. I noticed the window was up; so he had clumb in by the **shed**. He **kept** a-looking me all over. By and by he says:

Chinese Simplified

ankle：脚踝，踝，脚脖子．
boot：长靴，靴子．
breath：气息，鼻息，呼吸，气流．
candle：蜡烛．
chair：椅子．
color：颜色，彩色．
flesh：肉，血肉，肌肉．
foot：脚，足，步兵，英尺，呎．
gray：灰色，灰．
greasy：泥泞的，油性的．
hat：帽子．
hitched：蹒跚．
hung：挂．
jolt：颠簸，摇晃．
kept：收存．
knee：膝盖，膝．
lid：盖子．
minute：分钟，详细，分，微小的，渺小．
rags：碎布．
resting：静止的．
shed：散出，棚子，流出，脱落．
shining：彪炳，发亮．
shut：关闭．
sick：生病．
stuck：黏贴．
tilted：倾斜的．
top：顶，盖，尖峰，顶端，顶部，树梢，最高的．
unexpected：意想不到，意外，不虞，突然，出现意外，没意料到的．
whiskers：胡子．
worth：价值，值，值得．

"Starchy clothes--very. You think you're a good deal of a big-bug, *don't* you?"

"**Maybe** I am, maybe I ain't," I says.

"Don't you give me **none** o' your lip," says he. "You've put on **considerable** many frills since I been away. I'll take you down a **peg** before I get done with you. You're **educated**, too, they say--can read and write. You think you're better'n your father, now, don't you, because he can't? *I'll* take it out of you. Who told you you might **meddle** with such hifalut'n **foolishness**, hey?--who told you you could?"

"The **widow**. She told me."

"The widow, hey?--and who told the widow she could put in her **shovel** about a thing that ain't none of her business?"

"**Nobody** never told her."

"Well, I'll **learn** her how to meddle. And looky here--you **drop** that school, you hear? I'll learn people to bring up a boy to put on airs over his own father and let on to be better'n what *he* is. You lemme **catch** you fooling around that school again, you hear? Your mother couldn't read, and she couldn't write, nuther, before she died. None of the family couldn't before *they* died. I can't; and here you're a- **swelling yourself** up like this. I ain't the man to **stand** it--you hear? Say, lemme hear you read."

I took up a book and **begun** something about General Washington and the **wars**. When I'd read about a half a **minute**, he fetched the book a **whack** with his hand and knocked it across the house. He says:

"It's so. You can do it. I had my **doubts** when you told me. Now looky here; you stop that putting on frills. I won't have it. I'll **lay** for you, my smarty; and if I catch you about that school I'll tan you good. First you know you'll get **religion**, too. I never see such a son."

He took up a little **blue** and yaller **picture** of some **cows** and a boy, and says:

"What's this?"

"It's something they give me for **learning** my lessons good."

Chinese Simplified

begun: 开始.
blue: 蓝, 蓝色, 青.
catch: 捕捉, 捕捞, 捕拿, 捉.
considerable: 可观, 相当多的.
cows: 母牛.
doubts: 怀疑.
drop: 落, 水滴, 衰退, 掉落, 降, 点子.
educated: 受过教育的.
foolishness: 愚蠢.
lay: 产卵, 安放, 放, 凡俗.
learn: 学, 学习.
learning: 学问, 学术, 学习.
maybe: 或许, 也许, 或者, 说不定, 可能, 不一定.
meddle: 干预, 干涉.
minute: 分钟, 详细, 分, 微小的, 渺小.
nobody: 没有人, 没人.
none: 无, 没有.
peg: 木钉, 衣夹, 栓.
picture: 图画, 照片, 图像, 图片, 画, 画儿, 拍摄, 图象, 像.
religion: 宗教.
shovel: 铲子, 铲, 铁锹.
stand: 站住, 主张, 架子, 站立, 耐, 站, 架.
swelling: 肿胀, 增大, 膨胀.
tan: 黄褐色, 鞣, 棕黄色.
wars: 战争.
whack: 重打.
widow: 寡妇.
yourself: 你自己.

He **tore** it up, and says:

"I'll give you something **better**--I'll give you a cowhide."

He set there a-mumbling and a-growling a **minute**, and then he says:

"*Ain't* you a **sweet**-scented **dandy**, though? A bed; and **bedclothes**; and a look'n'-glass; and a **piece** of **carpet** on the floor--and your own father got to **sleep** with the hogs in the tanyard. I never see such a son. I bet I'll take some o' these frills out o' you before I'm done with you. Why, there ain't no end to your airs--they say you're **rich**. Hey?--how's that?"

"They **lie**--that's how."

"Looky here--mind how you talk to me; I'm a-standing about all I can **stand** now--so don't gimme no **sass**. I've been in town two days, and I hain't **heard** nothing but about you bein' rich. I heard about it away down the **river**, too. That's why I come. You git me that money to-morrow--I want it."

"I hain't got no money."

"It's a lie. Judge Thatcher's got it. You git it. I want it."

"I hain't got no money, I tell you. You ask Judge Thatcher; he'll tell you the same."

"All right. I'll ask him; and I'll make him pungle, too, or I'll know the **reason** why. Say, how much you got in your **pocket**? I want it."

"I hain't got only a **dollar**, and I want that to--"

"It don't make no difference what you want it for--you just **shell** it out."

He took it and bit it to see if it was good, and then he said he was going down town to get some **whisky**; said he hadn't had a **drink** all day. When he had got out on the **shed** he put his head in again, and cussed me for putting on frills and **trying** to be better than him; and when I reckoned he was gone he come back and put his head in again, and told me to mind about that school, because he was going to **lay** for me and **lick** me if I didn't **drop** that.

Chinese Simplified

bedclothes：被褥，床上用品.
bet：打赌，赌.
carpet：地毯.
dandy：花花公子，纨绔子弟.
dollar：元.
drink：喝，饮用，饮，饮料.
drop：落，水滴，衰退，掉落，降，点子.
heard：听见.
lay：产卵，安放，放，凡俗.
lick：舔，舐.
lie：谎言，谎话，躺，撒谎，说谎.
minute：分钟，详细，分，微小的，渺小.
piece：片，部分，一块，一片，块，部份，份.
pocket：口袋，衣袋，兜儿，窟窿.
reason：理由，道理，原因，缘故，缘由，情理.
rich：富有，丰富，富有的，充实.
river：河，江，川，河流，条.
sass：顶嘴.
shed：散出，棚子，流出，脱落.
shell：壳，部份，贝壳，贝，盖子，炮弹，剥，外壳.
sleep：梦寐，睡觉，睡眠，睡.
stand：站住，主张，架子，站立，耐，站，架.
sweet-scented：香味好的.
tore：撕扯.
trying：难捱，设法.
whisky：威士忌酒.

Next day he was drunk, and he went to Judge Thatcher's and bullyragged him, and tried to make him give up the money; but he couldn't, and then he swore he'd make the law force him.

The **judge** and the widow went to law to get the court to take me away from him and let one of them be my **guardian**; but it was a new judge that had just come, and he didn't know the old man; so he said courts mustn't **interfere** and **separate families** if they could help it; said he'd druther not take a child away from its father. So Judge Thatcher and the widow had to **quit** on the business.

That **pleased** the old man till he couldn't rest. He said he'd cowhide me till I was black and blue if I didn't **raise** some money for him. I borrowed three dollars from Judge Thatcher, and pap took it and got drunk, and went a-blowing around and cussing and whooping and **carrying** on; and he kept it up all over town, with a tin **pan**, till most **midnight**; then they jailed him, and next day they had him before court, and jailed him again for a week. But he said *he* was satisfied; said he was **boss** of his son, and he'd make it **warm** for *him*.

When he got out the new judge said he was a-going to make a man of him. So he took him to his own house, and dressed him up **clean** and **nice**, and had him to breakfast and **dinner** and supper with the family, and was just old pie to him, so to **speak**. And after supper he talked to him about **temperance** and such things till the old man cried, and said he'd been a fool, and fooled away his life; but now he was a-going to turn over a new **leaf** and be a man nobody wouldn't be ashamed of, and he hoped the judge would help him and not look down on him. The judge said he could **hug** him for them words; so he cried, and his wife she cried again; pap said he'd been a man that had always been **misunderstood** before, and the judge said he believed it. The old man said that what a man wanted that was down was **sympathy**, and the judge said it was so; so they cried again. And when it was **bedtime** the old man **rose** up and held out his hand, and says:

"Look at it, **gentlemen** and **ladies** all; take a-hold of it; **shake** it. There's a hand that was the hand of a **hog**; but it ain't so no more; it's the hand of a man that's started in on a new life, and'll **die** before he'll go back. You mark them

Chinese Simplified

bedtime：就寝时间.
boss：老板，上司，头子，浮雕.
carrying：运送的，运输的.
clean：清洁，擦拭，乾净，刷，清洗，干净.
dinner：晚餐，正餐.
families：家庭.
gentlemen：绅士.
guardian：监护人.
hog：猪.
hug：紧抱，拥抱.
interfere：干涉，干扰，妨碍.
judge：法官，裁判，判定，判断，审判员.
ladies：女洗手间.
leaf：叶子，箔.
midnight：午夜，半夜.
misunderstood：误会.
nice：和蔼，可亲，好，尼斯.
pan：平锅.
pleased：满意，高兴的.
quit：退出，退离.
raise：升起，提高，筹措，增加，抚育，举起.
rose：蔷薇，玫瑰，升起.
separate：脱离，另外，分别，分离，别.
shake：摇动，震动，摇，震荡，颠簸.
speak：说，讲.
sympathy：同情.
temperance：节制.
warm：暖，暖和，温暖，热烈，温暖的.

words--don't **forget** I said them. It's a **clean** hand now; **shake** it--don't be afeard."

So they **shook** it, one after the other, all around, and cried. The **judge's wife** she kissed it. Then the old man he signed a pledge--made his mark. The judge said it was the holiest time on **record**, or something like that. Then they tucked the old man into a **beautiful** room, which was the **spare** room, and in the night some time he got **powerful thirsty** and clumb out on to the **porch**-roof and **slid** down a **stanchion** and traded his new **coat** for a **jug** of forty-rod, and clumb back again and had a good old time; and towards **daylight** he crawled out again, **drunk** as a fiddler, and **rolled** off the porch and **broke** his left **arm** in two places, and was most froze to death when somebody found him after sun-up. And when they come to look at that spare room they had to take soundings before they could **navigate** it.

The judge he felt kind of **sore**. He said he reckoned a body could **reform** the old man with a **shotgun**, maybe, but he didn't know no other way.

Chinese Simplified

arm: 手臂，膀子，臂膀，臂，膀臂，胳膊，肩膀，武器.
beautiful: 漂亮，美，美丽，菲菲，锦绣，美丽的，秀丽，美观.
broke: 打破.
clean: 清洁，擦拭，乾净，刷，清洗，干净.
coat: 外套，上衣.
daylight: 日光，白天.
die: 逝世，不讳，死.
drunk: 喝了，喝醉.
forget: 忘记，忘，忘却.
judge: 法官，裁判，判定，判断，审判员.
jug: 细颈瓶，罐.
navigate: 航行.
porch: 阳台，门廊.
powerful: 强大，有力，强劲，强有力的.
record: 记录，记载，档案，唱片，笔录，纪录.
reform: 改革.
rolled: 卷.
shake: 摇动，震动，摇，震荡，颠簸.
shook: 摇动.
shotgun: 猎枪.
slid: 滑行.
sore: 疼痛，疮，疼痛的.
spare: 备用，饶恕.
stanchion: 坚强，支柱，标柱.
thirsty: 渴的.
wife: 妻子，太太，爱人，媳妇儿，妻，老婆.

CHAPTER VI

PAP STRUGGLES WITH THE DEATH ANGEL

WELL, pretty **soon** the old man was up and around again, and then he went for Judge Thatcher in the courts to make him give up that money, and he went for me, too, for not **stopping** school. He catched me a couple of times and thrashed me, but I went to school just the same, and dodged him or outrun him most of the time. I didn't want to go to school much before, but I **reckoned** I'd go now to **spite** pap. That law **trial** was a **slow** business--appeared like they warn't ever going to get **started** on it; so every now and then I'd **borrow** two or three dollars off of the **judge** for him, to keep from getting a cowhiding. Every time he got money he got **drunk**; and every time he got drunk he **raised** Cain around **town**; and every time he raised Cain he got jailed. He was just suited--this kind of thing was right in his line.

He got to hanging around the **widow's** too much and so she told him at last that if he didn't **quit** using around there she would make **trouble** for him. Well, wasn't he **mad**? He said he would show who was Huck Finn's **boss**. So he watched out for me one day in the **spring**, and catched me, and took me up the **river** about three **mile** in a **skiff**, and crossed over to the Illinois **shore** where it was **woody** and there warn't no **houses** but an old **log hut** in a place where the **timber** was so **thick** you couldn't find it if you didn't know where it was.

Chinese Simplified

borrow: 借.
boss: 老板, 上司, 头子, 浮雕.
drunk: 喝了, 喝醉.
houses: 房屋.
hut: 茅舍, 棚屋.
judge: 法官, 裁判, 判定, 判断, 审判员.
log: 圆形木材, 圆木, 木头.
mad: 狂, 发怒, 发狂, 生气, 疯狂的.
mile: 英里.
quit: 退出, 退离.
raised: 凸起的, 浮雕的.
reckon: 估计, 计算.
river: 河, 江, 川, 河流, 条.
shore: 岸, 滨, 岸边, 海岸, 海滨.
skiff: 小船, 小艇.
slow: 慢, 缓慢, 迟慢, 迟钝, 迟迟, 迟缓.
soon: 不久, 最近, 眼看, 快, 近期, 早, 早日.
spite: 恶意.
spring: 弹簧, 泉, 春天, 绷簧, 春季, 水源, 跳.
started: 开始.
stopping: 停止.
thick: 厚, 密, 浓厚.
timber: 木料, 木材, 木头.
town: 城镇, 城市, 市镇.
trial: 审讯, 测试.
trouble: 麻烦, 难度, 难处.
widow: 寡妇.
woody: 木制的, 木质的.

He kept me with him all the time, and I never got a chance to run off. We lived in that old **cabin**, and he always locked the door and put the key under his head nights. He had a **gun** which he had stole, I reckon, and we fished and hunted, and that was what we lived on. Every little while he locked me in and went down to the **store**, three miles, to the **ferry**, and traded fish and game for whisky, and fetched it home and got drunk and had a good time, and licked me. The widow she found out where I was by and by, and she sent a man over to try to get hold of me; but pap **drove** him off with the gun, and it warn't long after that till I was used to being where I was, and liked it--all but the cowhide part.

It was kind of **lazy** and **jolly**, laying off comfortable all day, **smoking** and **fishing**, and no books nor study. Two months or more run along, and my clothes got to be all rags and **dirt**, and I didn't see how I'd ever got to like it so well at the widow's, where you had to **wash**, and **eat** on a **plate**, and **comb** up, and go to bed and get up regular, and be forever **bothering** over a book, and have old Miss Watson pecking at you all the time. I didn't want to go back no more. I had **stopped** cussing, because the widow didn't like it; but now I took to it again because pap hadn't no **objections**. It was pretty good times up in the woods there, take it all around.

But by and by pap got too **handy** with his hick'ry, and I couldn't stand it. I was all over welts. He got to going away so much, too, and **locking** me in. Once he locked me in and was gone three days. It was **dreadful** lonesome. I judged he had got **drowned**, and I wasn't ever going to get out any more. I was scared. I made up my mind I would fix up some way to leave there. I had tried to get out of that cabin many a time, but I couldn't find no way. There warn't a window to it big enough for a dog to get through. I couldn't get up the chimbly; it was too narrow. The door was thick, solid **oak** slabs. Pap was pretty **careful** not to leave a **knife** or anything in the cabin when he was away; I reckon I had hunted the place over as much as a hundred times; well, I was most all the time at it, because it was about the only way to put in the time. But this time I found something at last; I found an old **rusty** wood-saw without any **handle**; it was laid in between a **rafter** and the clapboards of the **roof**. I greased it up and went to

Chinese Simplified

bothering: 打扰.
cabin: 小屋, 船舱.
careful: 小心, 仔细, 不苟, 慎重, 周密, 小心的, 精细, 细心, 细致.
comb: 梳, 梳子.
dirt: 污垢.
dreadful: 可怕, 恐怖的.
drove: 驾.
drowned: 淹死.
eat: 吃.
ferry: 摆渡, 渡口, 渡船, 渡轮.
fishing: 钓鱼.
gun: 枪, 炮, 长枪.
handle: 柄, 把手, 把柄, 处理, 辫子, 耳子, 把子, 弄, 对付, 加以, 处置.
handy: 灵巧, 便当, 顺手, 方便的, 简便.
jolly: 痛快, 开心的.
knife: 刀子, 刀, 餐刀.
lazy: 懒惰, 懒惰的.
locking: 锁紧.
oak: 橡树, 橡.
objections: 反对.
plate: 碟, 盘子.
rafter: 椽.
roof: 屋顶, 顶部, 顶板.
rusty: 腐蚀, 生锈的.
smoking: 冒烟, 抽烟.
stopped: 停止.
store: 商店, 储藏, 商号, 贮藏, 店铺.
wash: 洗涤, 洗刷, 洗.

work. There was an old horse-blanket nailed against the logs at the far end of the cabin behind the table, to keep the **wind** from **blowing** through the chinks and putting the candle out. I got under the table and raised the **blanket**, and went to work to saw a **section** of the big **bottom** log out--big enough to let me through. Well, it was a good long job, but I was getting **towards** the end of it when I heard pap's gun in the woods. I got **rid** of the signs of my work, and dropped the blanket and hid my saw, and pretty soon pap come in.

Pap warn't in a good humor--so he was his **natural** self. He said he was down town, and everything was going **wrong**. His **lawyer** said he reckoned he would win his **lawsuit** and get the money if they ever got started on the trial; but then there was ways to put it off a long time, and Judge Thatcher knowed how to do it. And he said people allowed there'd be another trial to get me away from him and give me to the widow for my guardian, and they guessed it would win this time. This shook me up considerable, because I didn't want to go back to the widow's any more and be so cramped up and sivilized, as they called it. Then the old man got to cussing, and cussed everything and everybody he could think of, and then cussed them all over again to make sure he hadn't skipped any, and after that he **polished** off with a kind of a general cuss all round, including a considerable parcel of people which he didn't know the names of, and so called them what's-his-name when he got to them, and went right along with his cussing.

He said he would like to see the widow get me. He said he would watch out, and if they tried to come any such **game** on him he knowed of a place six or seven mile off to **stow** me in, where they might **hunt** till they dropped and they couldn't find me. That made me pretty **uneasy** again, but only for a minute; I reckoned I wouldn't stay on hand till he got that **chance**.

The old man made me go to the skiff and fetch the things he had got. There was a fifty-pound **sack** of **corn meal**, and a side of **bacon**, **ammunition**, and a four-gallon jug of whisky, and an old book and two **newspapers** for **wadding**, **besides** some tow. I toted up a **load**, and went back and set down on the **bow** of the skiff to rest. I thought it all over, and I reckoned I would **walk** off with the

Chinese Simplified

ammunition: 弹药.
bacon: 熏肉，咸肉，熏猪肉.
besides: 此外，另外，除了，并且，再说，况且.
blanket: 毛毯，被子.
blowing: 吹.
bottom: 底部，屁股，底.
bow: 弓.
chance: 机会.
corn: 玉蜀黍，包谷，玉米.
game: 游戏，把戏.
hunt: 打猎，狩猎.
lawsuit: 诉讼，官司，讼诉案.
lawyer: 律师，法人.
load: 包袱，负载，装满，担子，装载，负荷，载重.
meal: 餐，膳食，饭.
natural: 自然，天然，自然的，天生.
newspapers: 报章，报纸.
polished: 优美的，精练的，擦亮的.
rid: 摆脱.
sack: 大袋子，开除.
section: 部分，部，部门，段，股，部份，章节，阶段，科.
stow: 装载.
tow: 拖船，拖车，牵引，拖.
uneasy: 不安，担心，不安的.
wadding: 填塞物，填料，絮.
walk: 行走，步行，走，走道，散步.
win: 博得，赢得，胜，赢.
wind: 风，弯曲，上弦，缠绕.
wrong: 不对，不平，错误的，错误.

gun and some **lines**, and take to the woods when I run away. I guessed I wouldn't stay in one place, but just **tramp** right across the country, mostly night times, and hunt and **fish** to keep **alive**, and so get so far away that the old man nor the widow couldn't ever find me any more. I judged I would saw out and **leave** that night if pap got **drunk** enough, and I reckoned he would. I got so full of it I didn't notice how long I was **staying** till the old man hollered and asked me whether I was asleep or drownded.

I got the things all up to the **cabin**, and then it was about dark. While I was **cooking** supper the old man took a **swig** or two and got sort of warmed up, and went to ripping again. He had been drunk over in town, and laid in the **gutter** all night, and he was a sight to look at. A body would a thought he was Adam--he was just all **mud**. Whenever his **liquor** begun to work he most always went for the govment, this time he says:

"Call this a govment! why, just look at it and see what it's like. Here's the law a-standing ready to take a man's son away from him--a man's own son, which he has had all the trouble and all the **anxiety** and all the **expense** of raising. Yes, just as that man has got that son raised at last, and ready to go to work and begin to do suthin' for *him* and give him a rest, the law up and **goes** for him. And they **call** *that* govment! That ain't all, nuther. The law **backs** that old Judge Thatcher up and **helps** him to keep me out o' my **property**. Here's what the law does: The law **takes** a man worth six thousand dollars and up'ards, and jams him into an old **trap** of a cabin like this, and **lets** him go round in clothes that ain't fitten for a **hog**. They call that govment! A man can't get his **rights** in a govment like this. Sometimes I've a **mighty notion** to just leave the country for good and all. Yes, and I *told* 'em so; I told old Thatcher so to his face. Lots of 'em heard me, and can tell what I said. Says I, for two cents I'd leave the blamed country and never come a-near it agin. Them's the very words. I says look at my hat--if you call it a hat--but the **lid raises** up and the rest of it goes down till it's **below** my **chin**, and then it ain't **rightly** a hat at all, but more like my head was shoved up through a jint o' stove-pipe. Look at it, says I-- such a hat for me to wear--one of the wealthiest men in this town if I could git my rights.

Chinese Simplified

alive：活着，活，活泼的，活着的．
anxiety：焦急，忧虑，担．
backs：支持．
below：下面，以下．
cabin：小屋，船舱．
call：喊，称呼，叫，号召，召唤．
chin：下巴，颊．
cooking：烹调．
drunk：喝了，喝醉．
expense：花费，费用，支出．
fish：鱼，捕鱼．
goes：去．
gutter：排水沟，沟，水槽，贫民区．
helps：帮助．
hog：猪．
leave：别离，动身，离开，起身．
lets：让我们，让．
lid：盖子．
lines：行数．
liquor：酒，酒精饮料，液体．
mighty：伟大，强势，强大的．
mud：泥，泥浆．
notion：观念．
property：财产，属性，特性，资产，财物，产业，地产．
raises：加薪．
rightly：正确地．
rights：权力．
staying：停留．
swig：痛饮．
takes：拿，取走．
tramp：沉重脚步．
trap：圈套，陷阱，阱．

"Oh, yes, this is a **wonderful** govment, wonderful. Why, looky here. There was a free nigger there from Ohio--a mulatter, most as white as a white man. He had the **whitest shirt** on you ever see, too, and the **shiniest** hat; and there ain't a man in that town that's got as fine clothes as what he had; and he had a gold watch and **chain**, and a silver- **headed** cane--the awfulest old gray-headed **nabob** in the State. And what do you think? They said he was a p'fessor in a **college**, and could talk all kinds of **languages**, and knowed everything. And that ain't the wust. They said he could VOTE when he was at home. Well, that let me out. **Thinks** I, what is the country a-coming to? It was 'lection day, and I was just about to go and **vote** myself if I warn't too drunk to get there; but when they told me there was a State in this country where they'd let that nigger vote, I drawed out. I says I'll never vote agin. Them's the very words I said; they all heard me; and the country may **rot** for all me --I'll never vote agin as long as I live. And to see the **cool** way of that nigger--why, he wouldn't a give me the road if I hadn't shoved him out o' the way. I says to the people, why ain't this nigger put up at **auction** and **sold**?--that's what I want to know. And what do you reckon they said? Why, they said he couldn't be sold till he'd been in the State six months, and he hadn't been there that long yet. There, now--that's a **specimen**. They call that a govment that can't sell a free nigger till he's been in the State six months. Here's a govment that calls itself a govment, and lets on to be a govment, and thinks it is a govment, and yet's got to set **stock**-still for six whole months before it can take a hold of a prowling, **thieving**, **infernal**, white-shirted free nigger, and--"

Pap was a-going on so he never noticed where his old **limber** legs was taking him to, so he went head over heels over the **tub** of **salt** pork and barked both shins, and the rest of his **speech** was all the **hottest** kind of language--mostly hove at the nigger and the govment, though he give the tub some, too, all along, here and there. He hopped around the cabin considerable, first on one leg and then on the other, holding first one shin and then the other one, and at last he let out with his left foot all of a **sudden** and fetched the tub a rattling **kick**. But it warn't good **judgment**, because that was the boot that had a couple of his toes leaking out of the front end of it; so now he raised a **howl** that **fairly** made a

Chinese Simplified

auction: 拍卖.
chain: 链，链子，连锁.
college: 学院.
cool: 凉，镇静，镇定，凉爽，凉爽的.
fairly: 相当，比较，公平地.
headed: 有头的.
hottest: 最热的，热烈的.
howl: 狂吠，号叫.
infernal: 地狱，地狱的.
judgment: 判决，裁判，报应，判定，判断，裁.
kick: 踢.
languages: 语言.
leg: 腿，脚.
limber: 可塑.
nabob: 富翁，大财主.
rot: 腐坏，腐烂，腐化.
salt: 盐.
shin: 外小腿，胫.
shirt: 衬衫，衬衣.
sold: 卖了.
specimen: 标本，样品，样本.
speech: 演说，言语，报告.
stock-still: 静止的.
sudden: 突然，急剧，突然的.
thieving: 偷.
thinks: 想.
tub: 浴盆，桶.
vote: 投票，表决，表决权.
whitest: 苍白的.
wonderful: 奇妙，奇妙的.

body's hair raise, and down he went in the dirt, and rolled there, and held his toes; and the cussing he done then laid over anything he had ever done **previous**. He said so his own self afterwards. He had heard old Sowberry Hagan in his best days, and he said it laid over him, too; but I reckon that was sort of **piling** it on, maybe.

After supper pap took the jug, and said he had enough whisky there for two drunks and one **delirium** tremens. That was always his word. I judged he would be **blind** drunk in about an **hour**, and then I would **steal** the **key**, or saw myself out, one or t'other. He **drank** and drank, and tumbled down on his **blankets** by and by; but luck didn't run my way. He didn't go **sound** asleep, but was uneasy. He groaned and moaned and thrashed around this way and that for a long time. At last I got so **sleepy** I couldn't keep my eyes open all I could do, and so before I knowed what I was about I was sound asleep, and the candle burning.

I don't know how long I was asleep, but all of a sudden there was an awful **scream** and I was up. There was pap looking **wild**, and **skipping** around every which way and **yelling** about snakes. He said they was crawling up his legs; and then he would give a **jump** and scream, and say one had bit him on the cheek--but I couldn't see no snakes. He started and run round and round the cabin, hollering "Take him off! take him off! he's biting me on the neck!" I never see a man look so wild in the eyes. Pretty soon he was all **fagged** out, and fell down **panting**; then he rolled over and over wonderful **fast**, kicking things every which way, and **striking** and grabbing at the air with his hands, and screaming and **saying** there was devils a-hold of him. He **wore** out by and by, and laid still a while, moaning. Then he laid stiller, and didn't make a sound. I could hear the **owls** and the wolves away off in the woods, and it seemed **terrible** still. He was laying over by the **corner**. By and by he raised up part way and listened, with his head to one side. He says, very **low**:

"Tramp--tramp--tramp; that's the **dead**; tramp--tramp--tramp; they're coming after me; but I won't go. Oh, they're here! don't **touch** me-- don't! hands off--they're cold; let go. Oh, let a **poor** devil alone!"

Chinese Simplified

blankets: 毛毯.
blind: 瞎，盲，百叶窗，盲目，盲的.
corner: 角落，隅，棱，角，转角.
dead: 死.
delirium: 神志昏迷，谵妄.
drank: 喝了.
fagged: 累坏了的.
fast: 快，禁食，快速，迅速，速.
hour: 小时，钟头，钟点，现在.
jump: 跳，跳跃.
key: 钥匙，关键，题解，键，主要的.
low: 低，卑下，低廉，浅的，低的.
owls: 猫头鹰.
panting: 气吁吁.
piling: 打桩，打桩工程，桩材.
poor: 差，贫穷，穷，差劲，贫瘠，贫穷的，贫苦，困苦.
previous: 前，以前，过去，先前的，过急的.
saying: 名言，说.
scream: 叫喊，呐喊，呼啸.
skipping: 跳跃，跳过.
sleepy: 想睡，眼睡的.
sound: 声音，音.
steal: 偷窃，盗窃，偷，窃取.
striking: 引人注目，引人注目的.
terrible: 可怕，糟糕，可怕的.
touch: 触摸，笔锋，触，联系，碰，接触.
wild: 野，猖披，猖獗，野生，野性的.
wore: 穿了.
yelling: 叫声，叫喊.

Then he went down on all fours and crawled off, **begging** them to let him alone, and he **rolled** himself up in his **blanket** and **wallowed** in under the old **pine** table, still a-begging; and then he went to **crying**. I could hear him through the blanket.

By and by he rolled out and **jumped** up on his **feet** looking wild, and he see me and went for me. He chased me round and round the place with a clasp-knife, calling me the Angel of Death, and saying he would kill me, and then I couldn't come for him no more. I **begged**, and told him I was only Huck; but he **laughed** *such* a screechy laugh, and roared and cussed, and kept on **chasing** me up. Once when I turned **short** and dodged under his arm he made a **grab** and got me by the **jacket** between my shoulders, and I thought I was **gone**; but I **slid** out of the jacket quick as **lightning**, and saved myself. Pretty soon he was all tired out, and dropped down with his back against the door, and said he would rest a minute and then kill me. He put his **knife** under him, and said he would sleep and get **strong**, and then he would see who was who.

So he **dozed** off pretty soon. By and by I got the old split-bottom chair and clumb up as easy as I could, not to make any noise, and got down the gun. I **slipped** the **ramrod** down it to make sure it was **loaded**, then I **laid** it across the **turnip barrel**, **pointing** towards pap, and set down behind it to **wait** for him to **stir**. And how slow and still the time did **drag** along.

Chinese Simplified

barrel：桶，大桶.
begged：乞求.
begging：行乞.
blanket：毛毯，被子.
chasing：追逐.
crying：叫喊的，嚎哭的，显著的.
dozed：打瞌睡.
drag：曳，拖拉，阻力，拖动.
feet：英尺.
gone：去.
grab：抓住，攫取，抓斗.
jacket：夹克，上衣，短上衣，外套.
jumped：跳跃.
knife：刀子，刀，餐刀.
laid：放.
laugh：笑.
laughed：笑.
lightning：闪电.
loaded：载入.
pine：松树.
pointing：指，瞄准.
ramrod：推弹杆.
rolled：卷.
short：短，矮，小结，短暂.
slid：滑行.
slipped：滑落.
stir：轰动，搅拌，鼓动.
strong：轰轰烈烈，健全，霸道，坚强，强有力，强大，强烈，强大的，扎实，干，强烈的.
turnip：芜菁，萝卜.
wait：等待，等，伺候.
wallowed：喷出.

CHAPTER VII

I FOOL PAP AND GET AWAY

"Git up! What you 'bout?"

I **opened** my eyes and looked around, **trying** to make out where I was. It was after sun-up, and I had been **sound asleep**. Pap was **standing** over me looking **sour** and **sick**, too. He says:

"What you doin' with this gun?"

I judged he didn't know nothing about what he had been doing, so I says:

"Somebody tried to get in, so I was laying for him."

"Why didn't you roust me out?"

"Well, I tried to, but I couldn't; I couldn't **budge** you."

"Well, all right. Don't stand there palavering all day, but out with you and see if there's a **fish** on the **lines** for **breakfast**. I'll be **along** in a minute."

He unlocked the door, and I cleared out up the **river**-bank. I noticed some pieces of limbs and such things **floating** down, and a sprinkling of **bark**; so I knowed the river had **begun** to **rise**. I reckoned I would have great times now if I was over at the **town**. The June rise used to be always **luck** for me; because as **soon** as that rise **begins** here **comes** cordwood floating down, and pieces of log

Chinese Simplified

along: 沿着，沿，一同.
asleep: 睡着，睡着的.
bark: 吠.
begins: 开始.
begun: 开始.
breakfast: 早餐，早饭，早点.
budge: 微微一动，改变态度，羔皮.
comes: 来.
fish: 鱼，捕鱼.
floating: 漂浮的，移动的，浮动的，飘浮.
lines: 行数.
luck: 运气，幸运.
opened: 打开.
rise: 升起，上升，上涨，兴起，增大.
river: 河，江，川，河流，条.
sick: 生病.
soon: 不久，最近，眼看，快，近期，早，早日.
sound: 声音，音.
sour: 酸，酸味.
stand: 站住，主张，架子，站立，耐，站，架.
standing: 站立，地位.
town: 城镇，城市，市镇.
trying: 难捱，设法.

rafts--sometimes a **dozen** logs together; so all you have to do is to catch them and sell them to the wood-yards and the sawmill.

I went along up the **bank** with one **eye** out for pap and t'other one out for what the rise might fetch along. Well, all at once here comes a **canoe**; just a **beauty**, too, about **thirteen** or **fourteen** foot long, riding high like a **duck**. I **shot** head-first off of the bank like a **frog**, clothes and all on, and **struck** out for the canoe. I just **expected** there'd be somebody laying down in it, because people often done that to fool folks, and when a chap had pulled a **skiff** out most to it they'd raise up and laugh at him. But it warn't so this time. It was a drift-canoe sure enough, and I clumb in and paddled her **ashore**. Thinks I, the old man will be glad when he sees this--she's worth ten dollars. But when I got to shore pap wasn't in sight yet, and as I was **running** her into a little creek like a **gully**, all hung over with vines and willows, I struck another idea: I judged I'd **hide** her good, and then, 'stead of taking to the woods when I run off, I'd go down the river about fifty mile and **camp** in one place for good, and not have such a rough time tramping on foot.

It was pretty **close** to the **shanty**, and I thought I heard the old man coming all the time; but I got her hid; and then I out and looked around a **bunch** of willows, and there was the old man down the path a piece just **drawing** a **bead** on a **bird** with his gun. So he hadn't seen anything.

When he got along I was **hard** at it taking up a "trot" line. He abused me a little for being so slow; but I told him I fell in the river, and that was what made me so long. I knowed he would see I was **wet**, and then he would be asking questions. We got five **catfish** off the lines and went home.

While we laid off after breakfast to sleep up, both of us being about wore out, I got to **thinking** that if I could fix up some way to keep pap and the widow from trying to follow me, it would be a certainer thing than trusting to luck to get far enough off before they missed me; you see, all kinds of things might **happen**. Well, I didn't see no way for a while, but by and by pap raised up a minute to drink another barrel of water, and he says:

Chinese Simplified

ashore: 岸上，上岸.
bank: 银行，岸.
bead: 珠子，小珠.
beauty: 美人，美丽，美.
bird: 鸟.
bunch: 束，串.
camp: 阵营，营，露营，安营.
canoe: 独木舟.
catfish: 鲇鱼.
close: 关闭，闭合，密切，相近，结束，截止，亲密，关.
dozen: 一打，打.
drawing: 图，图画，画儿，绘画，并条，图纸，画.
duck: 鸭，鸭子.
expected: 预期.
eye: 眼睛，目，鼻儿.
fourteen: 十四.
frog: 青蛙，蛙.
gully: 山沟，溪谷.
happen: 发生.
hard: 硬，坚固，沉重，辛苦，艰苦，坚硬.
hide: 躲藏，暗藏，掩饰，藏，隐瞒，隐藏.
running: 一连.
shanty: 棚屋.
shot: 射击.
skiff: 小船，小艇.
struck: 敲打.
thinking: 思想，思维.
thirteen: 十三.
wet: 湿.

"Another time a man comes a-prowling round here you roust me out, you hear? That man warn't here for no good. I'd a shot him. Next time you roust me out, you hear?"

Then he dropped down and went to sleep again; but what he had been saying give me the very idea I wanted. I says to myself, I can fix it now so nobody won't think of following me.

About twelve o'clock we turned out and went along up the bank. The river was coming up pretty fast, and lots of driftwood going by on the rise. By and by along comes part of a log **raft**--nine logs fast together. We went out with the **skiff** and towed it ashore. Then we had dinner. Anybody but pap would a waited and seen the day through, so as to catch more stuff; but that warn't pap's style. Nine logs was enough for one time; he must **shove** right over to town and sell. So he locked me in and took the skiff, and started off towing the raft about half-past three. I judged he wouldn't come back that night. I waited till I reckoned he had got a good start; then I out with my saw, and went to work on that log again. Before he was t'other side of the river I was out of the hole; him and his raft was just a **speck** on the water away off **yonder**.

I took the sack of corn meal and took it to where the **canoe** was hid, and shoved the vines and branches **apart** and put it in; then I done the same with the side of bacon; then the whisky-jug. I took all the **coffee** and **sugar** there was, and all the **ammunition**; I took the **wadding**; I took the **bucket** and **gourd**; I took a **dipper** and a tin **cup**, and my old saw and two **blankets**, and the **skillet** and the coffee-pot. I took fish-lines and matches and other things--everything that was worth a **cent**. I cleaned out the place. I wanted an **axe**, but there wasn't any, only the one out at the **woodpile**, and I knowed why I was going to leave that. I fetched out the gun, and now I was done.

I had wore the **ground** a good deal **crawling** out of the hole and **dragging** out so many things. So I **fixed** that as good as I could from the **outside** by **scattering** **dust** on the place, which covered up the smoothness and the **sawdust**. Then I fixed the piece of log back into its place, and put two **rocks** under it and one against it to hold it there, for it was **bent** up at that place and didn't quite touch

Chinese Simplified

ammunition: 弹药.
apart: 分别, 分开.
axe: 斧子, 斧, 削减.
bent: 曲, 弯, 弯曲, 弯折.
blankets: 毛毯.
bucket: 水桶, 桶.
canoe: 独木舟.
cent: 一分钱, 分.
coffee: 咖啡.
crawling: 爬行.
cup: 杯, 茶杯, 杯子.
dipper: 舀水杓.
dragging: 拖, 拖动, 拖曳.
dust: 灰尘, 土, 尘, 尘土, 粉末.
fixed: 固定, 确定, 一定, 固定的.
gourd: 葫芦.
ground: 地, 地面, 地皮, 理由, 土地.
outside: 外面, 外表, 表面, 面儿, 外来, 外部的, 外面的, 外头, 之外, 外边.
raft: 筏, 木排, 槎, 桴.
rocks: 岩石.
sawdust: 木屑.
scattering: 散射.
shove: 推.
skiff: 小船, 小艇.
skillet: 长柄锅.
speck: 斑点, 点子.
sugar: 糖.
wadding: 填塞物, 填料, 絮.
woodpile: 柴堆.
yonder: 那边.

ground. If you stood four or five foot away and didn't know it was **sawed**, you wouldn't never notice it; and besides, this was the back of the cabin, and it warn't likely anybody would go fooling around there.

It was all **grass** clear to the canoe, so I hadn't left a **track**. I followed around to see. I stood on the bank and looked out over the river. All **safe**. So I took the gun and went up a piece into the woods, and was **hunting** around for some **birds** when I see a wild **pig**; hogs soon went wild in them **bottoms** after they had got away from the **prairie farms**. I shot this **fellow** and took him into camp.

I took the axe and smashed in the door. I **beat** it and hacked it considerable a-doing it. I fetched the pig in, and took him back nearly to the table and hacked into his throat with the axe, and laid him down on the ground to **bleed**; I say ground because it was ground--hard **packed**, and no **boards**. Well, next I took an old sack and put a lot of big rocks in it--all I could drag--and I started it from the pig, and **dragged** it to the door and through the woods down to the river and dumped it in, and down it **sunk**, out of sight. You could easy see that something had been dragged over the ground. I did wish Tom Sawyer was there; I knowed he would take an interest in this kind of business, and throw in the **fancy touches**. Nobody could **spread** himself like Tom Sawyer in such a thing as that.

Well, last I pulled out some of my hair, and **blooded** the axe good, and stuck it on the back side, and slung the axe in the corner. Then I took up the pig and held him to my breast with my jacket (so he couldn't **drip**) till I got a good piece below the house and then dumped him into the river. Now I thought of something else. So I went and got the **bag** of meal and my old saw out of the canoe, and fetched them to the house. I took the bag to where it used to stand, and ripped a hole in the bottom of it with the saw, for there warn't no knives and **forks** on the place-- pap done everything with his clasp-knife about the cooking. Then I carried the sack about a hundred yards across the grass and through the willows east of the house, to a **shallow lake** that was five mile wide and full of rushes--and **ducks** too, you might say, in the **season**. There was a slough or a creek **leading** out of it on the other side that went miles away, I don't know where, but it didn't go to the river. The meal sifted out and made a little track all

Chinese Simplified

bag：袋子，袋，手提包，提包，囊．
beat：打，击败，拍击，敲打，拍子，敲．
birds：禽，禽类，鸟．
bleed：流血．
blooded：纯种的．
boards：纸板．
bottoms：底．
dragged：拖拉，拖曳．
drip：滴下，滴．
ducks：鸭．
fancy：花俏，想像力．
farms：农场．
fellow：同伴，伙伴．
forks：叉子．
grass：草，青草．
hunting：狩猎．
lake：湖，湖泊．
leading：领导．
packed：挤得满满的．
pig：猪．
prairie：大草原，草原．
safe：安全，保险，安全的，稳妥，保险箱．
sawed：锯．
season：季节，季，时节．
shallow：粗浅，浅，鄙陋，浅的．
spread：扩散，流传，传播，散播，敷，撒．
sunk：沉没．
touches：接触．
track：跑道，径赛，迳迹，轨道，行踪，履带，踪迹．

the way to the lake. I dropped pap's **whetstone** there too, so as to look like it had been done by **accident**. Then I tied up the **rip** in the meal sack with a string, so it wouldn't **leak** no more, and took it and my saw to the canoe again.

It was about dark now; so I dropped the canoe down the river under some **willows** that hung over the bank, and waited for the **moon** to rise. I made fast to a willow; then I took a **bite** to eat, and by and by laid down in the canoe to smoke a pipe and lay out a **plan**. I says to myself, they'll follow the track of that **sackful** of rocks to the shore and then drag the river for me. And they'll follow that meal track to the lake and go **browsing** down the creek that **leads** out of it to find the robbers that killed me and took the things. They won't ever hunt the river for anything but my dead carcass. They'll soon get tired of that, and won't **bother** no more about me. All right; I can stop **anywhere** I want to. Jackson's Island is good enough for me; I know that **island** pretty well, and nobody ever comes there. And then I can **paddle** over to town nights, and slink around and **pick** up things I want. Jackson's Island's the place.

I was pretty tired, and the first thing I knowed I was asleep. When I **woke** up I didn't know where I was for a minute. I set up and looked around, a little scared. Then I remembered. The river looked miles and miles across. The moon was so **bright** I could a counted the **drift** logs that went a-slipping along, black and still, **hundreds** of yards out from shore. **Everything** was dead quiet, and it looked **late**, and *smelt* late. You know what I mean--I don't know the words to put it in.

I took a good **gap** and a stretch, and was just going to **unhitch** and start when I heard a sound away over the water. I listened. Pretty soon I made it out. It was that dull kind of a regular sound that comes from oars working in rowlocks when it's a still night. I peeped out through the willow branches, and there it was--a skiff, away across the water. I couldn't tell how many was in it. It kept a-coming, and when it was **abreast** of me I see there warn't but one man in it. Thinks I, maybe it's pap, though I warn't expecting him. He dropped below me with the **current**, and by and by he came a-swinging up shore in the easy water,

Chinese Simplified

abreast：并肩，并排，并列．
accident：事故，不测，变故，失事，意外．
anywhere：无论何处．
bite：咬，辣，咬伤．
bother：烦扰，打扰，理会．
bright：聪明，光明，光亮，光明的，鲜明．
browsing：浏览．
current：潮流，现时，现在，这次，本届，当今，当前，当前的，水流，电流，现在的．
drift：漂游，漂移，漂．
everything：一切事物，应有尽有，一切，事事．
gap：差距，空白点，间隔，间隙．
hundreds：百．
island：岛．
late：晚，迟，迟慢，迟了，迟迟．
leads：铅．
leak：漏洞，会漏，泄露，漏．
moon：月亮，月球，月．
paddle：桨．
pick：掐，采摘，挑选，挑，鹤嘴锄，采，选择．
plan：计划，方案，规划，设计，主意，计画，擘画，打算，设计图．
rip：扯裂，撕破，裂口．
sackful：满袋．
unhitch：解开．
whetstone：磨刀石．
willow：柳树．
woke：醒觉．

and he went by so **close** I could a reached out the gun and touched him. Well, it *was* pap, sure enough--and **sober**, too, by the way he laid his oars.

I didn't lose no time. The next minute I was a-spinning down **stream** soft but quick in the **shade** of the bank. I made two **mile** and a half, and then **struck** out a quarter of a mile or more towards the **middle** of the river, because pretty soon I would be passing the **ferry landing**, and people might see me and **hail** me. I got out amongst the driftwood, and then laid down in the bottom of the **canoe** and let her **float**. I laid there, and had a good rest and a smoke out of my **pipe**, looking away into the **sky**; not a **cloud** in it. The sky **looks** ever so **deep** when you lay down on your back in the moonshine; I never knowed it before. And how far a body can hear on the water such nights! I heard people talking at the ferry landing. I heard what they said, too--every **word** of it. One man said it was getting towards the long days and the short nights now. T'other one said *this* warn't one of the short ones, he reckoned--and then they laughed, and he said it over again, and they laughed again; then they waked up another **fellow** and told him, and laughed, but he didn't laugh; he ripped out something **brisk**, and said let him alone. The first fellow said he 'lowed to tell it to his old woman--she would think it was pretty good; but he said that warn't nothing to some things he had said in his time. I heard one man say it was **nearly** three o'clock, and he hoped **daylight** wouldn't wait more than about a week longer. After that the talk got further and further away, and I couldn't make out the words any more; but I could hear the **mumble**, and now and then a laugh, too, but it seemed a long ways off.

I was away below the ferry now. I rose up, and there was Jackson's Island, about two mile and a half down stream, **heavy** timbered and standing up out of the middle of the river, big and dark and solid, like a **steamboat** without any lights. There warn't any signs of the **bar** at the head--it was all under water now.

It didn't take me long to get there. I shot past the head at a ripping **rate**, the current was so **swift**, and then I got into the dead water and **landed** on the side towards the Illinois **shore**. I run the canoe into a deep dent in the bank that I

Chinese Simplified

bar: 酒廊，酒吧，柜台.
brisk: 活泼，活泼的.
canoe: 独木舟.
cloud: 云.
daylight: 日光，白天.
deep: 深，深深，深刻，深厚，浓厚，深沉，奥秘.
fellow: 同伴，伙伴.
ferry: 摆渡，渡口，渡船，渡轮.
float: 漂浮.
hail: 冰雹，雹，雹子，欢呼.
heavy: 重，沉重，笨重，沈重，沉闷.
landed: 着陆.
landing: 着陆.
looks: 样子，姿容，神态，看.
lose: 丢失，丧失，失掉，遗失.
middle: 中央，中间，半中腰，中间的，中部，中央的.
mile: 英里.
mumble: 嘀咕.
nearly: 几乎，差不多，将近.
pipe: 管，管子，筒，喉管.
rate: 比率，速度，率，速率，流量，等级.
shade: 荫，荫凉，阴影，树阴.
shore: 岸，滨，岸边，海岸，海滨.
sky: 天空，天.
sober: 清醒，清醒的.
steamboat: 汽船，轮船.
stream: 溪流，河流，流，小溪，川.
struck: 敲打.
swift: 迅速的.
word: 字，词，单词，誓言.

knowed about; I had to part the **willow branches** to get in; and when I made **fast nobody** could a seen the **canoe** from the outside.

I went up and set down on a **log** at the head of the **island**, and looked out on the big **river** and the black driftwood and away over to the **town**, three **mile** away, where there was three or four **lights twinkling**. A **monstrous** big lumber-raft was about a mile up **stream**, **coming along** down, with a **lantern** in the **middle** of it. I watched it come creeping down, and when it was most **abreast** of where I **stood** I **heard** a man say, "Stern oars, there! **heave** her head to stabboard!" I heard that just as **plain** as if the man was by my side.

There was a little **gray** in the **sky** now; so I stepped into the **woods**, and **laid** down for a **nap** before **breakfast**.

Chinese Simplified

abreast：并肩，并排，并列．
along：沿着，沿，一同．
branches：分支．
breakfast：早餐，早饭，早点．
canoe：独木舟．
coming：未来，到来．
fast：快，禁食，快速，迅速，速．
gray：灰色，灰．
heard：听见．
heave：举起，波荡，喘气．
island：岛．
laid：放．
lantern：灯笼．
lights：灯火．
log：圆形木材，圆木，木头．
middle：中央，中间，半中腰，中间的，中部，中央的．
mile：英里．
monstrous：怪物似，似怪物的．
nap：瞌睡．
nobody：没有人，没人．
plain：平原．
river：河，江，川，河流，条．
sky：天空，天．
stood：站了．
stream：溪流，河流，流，小溪，川．
town：城镇，城市，市镇．
twinkling：闪烁，闪烁的．
willow：柳树．
woods：树林，森林．

CHAPTER VIII

I SPARE MISS WATSON'S JIM

The sun was up so high when I waked that I judged it was after eight o'clock. I **laid** there in the **grass** and the **cool shade** thinking about things, and feeling rested and ruther **comfortable** and **satisfied**. I could see the sun out at one or two **holes**, but **mostly** it was big trees all about, and **gloomy** in there amongst them. There was freckled places on the ground where the light sifted down through the leaves, and the freckled places swapped about a little, showing there was a little **breeze** up there. A couple of **squirrels** set on a **limb** and jabbered at me very friendly.

I was powerful **lazy** and comfortable--didn't want to get up and **cook** breakfast. Well, I was **dozing** off again when I **thinks** I hears a deep sound of "**boom**!" away up the river. I rouses up, and **rests** on my **elbow** and **listens**; pretty soon I hears it again. I hopped up, and went and looked out at a hole in the leaves, and I see a **bunch** of **smoke** laying on the water a long ways up--about **abreast** the **ferry**. And there was the ferryboat full of people **floating** along down. I knowed what was the matter now. "Boom!" I see the white smoke **squirt** out of the ferryboat's side. You see, they was firing **cannon** over the water, trying to make my **carcass** come to the top.

Chinese Simplified

abreast: 并肩，并排，并列.
boom: 景气，繁荣，吊杆，盛旺.
breeze: 和风.
bunch: 束，串.
cannon: 大炮.
carcass: 残骸.
comfortable: 舒服，舒服的.
cook: 厨子，厨司，厨师，炊事员，烹调，煮，烹煮.
cool: 凉，镇静，镇定，凉爽，凉爽的.
dozing: 打瞌睡.
elbow: 肘，手肘.
ferry: 摆渡，渡口，渡船，渡轮.
float: 漂浮.
floating: 漂浮的，移动的，浮动的，飘浮.
gloomy: 阴郁，暗淡，阴郁的.
grass: 草，青草.
holes: 洞.
laid: 放.
lazy: 懒惰，懒惰的.
limb: 肢，肢体.
listens: 听.
mostly: 大多，多半，大部份.
rests: 休息.
satisfied: 满意，乐意，心满意足的.
shade: 荫，荫凉，阴影，树阴.
smoke: 烟，抽烟，烟雾，硝烟，吸烟，熏.
squirrels: 松鼠.
squirt: 喷出.
thinks: 想.

I was pretty **hungry**, but it warn't going to do for me to start a **fire**, because they might see the smoke. So I set there and watched the **cannon**- smoke and listened to the boom. The river was a mile **wide** there, and it always looks pretty on a **summer** morning--so I was having a good enough time seeing them hunt for my remainders if I only had a bite to eat. Well, then I happened to think how they always put **quicksilver** in loaves of **bread** and **float** them off, because they always go right to the drownded **carcass** and stop there. So, says I, I'll keep a **lookout**, and if any of them's **floating** around after me I'll give them a show. I **changed** to the Illinois **edge** of the island to see what luck I could have, and I warn't **disappointed**. A big **double loaf** come along, and I most got it with a long stick, but my foot slipped and she floated out further. Of course I was where the current set in the closest to the shore--I knowed enough for that. But by and by along comes another one, and this time I **won**. I took out the **plug** and shook out the little **dab** of quicksilver, and set my teeth in. It was "baker's bread"--what the quality eat; none of your **low**-down corn-pone.

I got a good place amongst the **leaves**, and set there on a log, munching the bread and watching the ferry-boat, and very well satisfied. And then something struck me. I says, now I reckon the widow or the **parson** or somebody prayed that this bread would find me, and here it has gone and done it. So there ain't no **doubt** but there is something in that thing-- that is, there's something in it when a body like the widow or the parson prays, but it don't work for me, and I reckon it don't work for only just the right kind.

I lit a pipe and had a good long smoke, and went on watching. The **ferryboat** was floating with the current, and I allowed I'd have a chance to see who was **aboard** when she come along, because she would come in close, where the bread did. When she'd got pretty well along down towards me, I put out my pipe and went to where I fished out the bread, and laid down behind a log on the bank in a little open place. Where the log forked I could **peep** through.

By and by she come along, and she drifted in so close that they could a run out a **plank** and **walked ashore**. Most everybody was on the boat. Pap, and Judge Thatcher, and Bessie Thatcher, and Jo Harper, and Tom Sawyer, and his

Chinese Simplified

aboard：船上，在车，上.
ashore：岸上，上岸.
boat：小船，船，帆船，乘务员.
bread：面包.
cannon：大炮.
carcass：残骸.
changed：改变.
dab：轻拍，少量，轻抚.
disappointed：败兴，失望的，惘.
double：双重，双，加倍.
doubt：怀疑，疑.
edge：边缘，边，边沿，棱，沿儿.
fire：火，射击，失火，火灾，发射，火力.
float：漂浮.
floating：漂浮的，移动的，浮动的，飘浮.
hungry：饥饿，饿，饥饿的.
leaves：离开.
loaf：一块面，游荡.
lookout：眺望，伸出窗口观看.
low-down：非常低的，下作.
parson：牧师.
peep：偷看，窥，张望.
plank：板，木板，木版，板子.
plug：插头，板烟，插.
quicksilver：水银.
summer：夏天，夏季.
walked：步行.
wide：宽阔，广阔，开阔，宽广的，宽广.
won：圜，胜.

old Aunt Polly, and Sid and Mary, and plenty more. Everybody was talking about the **murder**, but the captain broke in and says:

"Look **sharp**, now; the current **sets** in the closest here, and maybe he's washed **ashore** and got tangled amongst the **brush** at the water's edge. I **hope** so, anyway."

"I didn't hope so. They all **crowded** up and leaned over the **rails**, **nearly** in my face, and kept still, watching with all their might. I could see them first-rate, but they couldn't see me. Then the captain **sung** out:

"Stand away!" and the **cannon** let off such a **blast** right before me that it made me deef with the noise and pretty near blind with the smoke, and I judged I was gone. If they'd a had some **bullets** in, I reckon they'd a got the **corpse** they was after. Well, I see I warn't hurt, **thanks** to **goodness**. The boat floated on and went out of sight around the shoulder of the island. I could hear the **booming** now and then, further and further off, and by and by, after an hour, I didn't hear it no more. The island was three mile long. I judged they had got to the foot, and was **giving** it up. But they didn't yet a while. They turned around the foot of the island and started up the **channel** on the Missouri side, under **steam**, and booming once in a while as they went. I crossed over to that side and watched them. When they got **abreast** the head of the island they **quit shooting** and dropped over to the Missouri shore and went home to the town.

I knowed I was all right now. Nobody else would come a-hunting after me. I got my traps out of the **canoe** and made me a nice camp in the thick woods. I made a kind of a **tent** out of my **blankets** to put my things under so the **rain** couldn't get at them. I catched a **catfish** and haggled him open with my saw, and towards **sundown** I started my camp fire and had supper. Then I set out a line to catch some fish for breakfast.

When it was dark I set by my camp fire smoking, and feeling pretty well satisfied; but by and by it got sort of **lonesome**, and so I went and set on the bank and listened to the current swashing along, and counted the stars and drift logs and **rafts** that come down, and then went to bed; there ain't no better way to put in time when you are lonesome; you can't stay so, you soon get over it.

Chinese Simplified

abreast: 并肩，并排，并列.
ashore: 岸上，上岸.
blankets: 毛毯.
blast: 疾风，爆破，爆炸.
booming: 繁荣.
brush: 刷，毛刷，洗刷，刷子，拂，擦.
bullets: 子弹.
cannon: 大炮.
canoe: 独木舟.
catfish: 鲇鱼.
channel: 频道，通道，途径，海峡，渠.
corpse: 尸体.
crowded: 拥挤的.
giving: 慷慨，给予物.
goodness: 美德.
hope: 期望，希望，指望.
lonesome: 寂寞，寂寞的.
murder: 谋杀，杀人案件，杀害.
near: 近，靠近，接近，比邻.
quit: 退出，退离.
rafts: 木排.
rails: 铁路，铁路股票，轨道.
rain: 雨，下雨.
sets: 装置.
sharp: 尖锐，锐利，锋利的，锋利.
shooting: 射击，猎场.
steam: 蒸汽，热气，废气，蒸.
sundown: 日落.
sung: 唱歌.
tent: 帐篷，帐蓬，篷帐.
thanks: 感谢，谢谢.

And so for three days and nights. No difference--just the same thing. But the next day I went **exploring** around down through the island. I was boss of it; it all belonged to me, so to say, and I wanted to know all about it; but mainly I wanted to put in the time. I found plenty **strawberries**, **ripe** and **prime**; and **green** summer grapes, and green razberries; and the green blackberries was just **beginning** to show. They would all come **handy** by and by, I judged.

Well, I went fooling along in the deep woods till I judged I warn't far from the foot of the island. I had my gun along, but I hadn't shot nothing; it was for **protection**; thought I would kill some game nigh home. About this time I **mighty** near stepped on a good-sized **snake**, and it went **sliding** off through the grass and **flowers**, and I after it, trying to get a shot at it. I clipped along, and all of a sudden I bounded right on to the **ashes** of a camp fire that was still **smoking**.

My **heart** jumped up amongst my **lungs**. I never waited for to look further, but uncocked my gun and went **sneaking** back on my tiptoes as fast as ever I could. Every now and then I stopped a second amongst the thick leaves and listened, but my breath come so hard I couldn't hear nothing else. I slunk along another piece further, then listened again; and so on, and so on. If I see a **stump**, I took it for a man; if I trod on a stick and broke it, it made me feel like a person had **cut** one of my **breaths** in two and I only got half, and the short half, too.

When I got to camp I warn't feeling very **brash**, there warn't much **sand** in my **craw**; but I says, this ain't no time to be fooling around. So I got all my traps into my **canoe** again so as to have them out of sight, and I put out the fire and **scattered** the ashes around to look like an old last year's camp, and then clumb a tree.

I reckon I was up in the tree two **hours**; but I didn't see nothing, I didn't hear nothing--I only *thought* I heard and seen as much as a thousand things. Well, I couldn't stay up there forever; so at last I got down, but I kept in the thick woods and on the **lookout** all the time. All I could get to eat was berries and what was left over from breakfast.

By the time it was night I was pretty hungry. So when it was good and dark I slid out from **shore** before moonrise and paddled over to the Illinois bank--about

Chinese Simplified

ashes: 灰烬.
beginning: 开头，初，开端，开始.
berries: 莓.
brash: 胃灼热，无礼的，傲慢的.
breaths: 呼吸.
canoe: 独木舟.
craw: 嗉子.
cut: 采伐，切，刀口，伤口，割，截，剪切，切口.
exploring: 探索.
flowers: 花.
green: 绿色，碧瓦，青，绿色的，未成熟的.
handy: 灵巧，便当，顺手，方便的，简便.
heart: 心、心脏，中心，胸，内心.
hours: 小时.
lookout: 眺望，伸出窗口观看.
lungs: 肺脏.
mighty: 伟大，强势，强大的.
prime: 首要的.
protection: 保护，通行证.
ripe: 熟，成熟.
sand: 沙，沙子.
scattered: 零落，散播，散乱的，分散的.
shore: 岸，滨，岸边，海岸，海滨.
slid: 滑行.
smoking: 冒烟，抽烟.
snake: 蛇.
sneaking: 鬼鬼祟祟的.
strawberries: 草莓.
stump: 树桩，残肢.

a quarter of a **mile**. I went out in the **woods** and **cooked** a **supper**, and I had about made up my mind I would stay there all night when I hear a *plunkety-plunk, plunkety-plunk,* and says to myself, horses coming; and next I hear people's voices. I got everything into the **canoe** as quick as I could, and then went creeping through the woods to see what I could find out. I hadn't got far when I hear a man say:

"We better **camp** here if we can find a good place; the horses is about beat out. Let's look around."

I didn't wait, but shoved out and **paddled** away easy. I tied up in the old place, and reckoned I would sleep in the canoe.

I didn't sleep much. I couldn't, somehow, for thinking. And every time I waked up I thought somebody had me by the neck. So the sleep didn't do me no good. By and by I says to myself, I can't live this way; I'm a- going to find out who it is that's here on the island with me; I'll find it out or **bust**. Well, I felt better right off.

So I took my paddle and **slid** out from **shore** just a **step** or two, and then let the canoe drop along down amongst the **shadows**. The **moon** was **shining**, and outside of the shadows it made it most as light as day. I poked along well on to an hour, everything still as **rocks** and sound **asleep**. Well, by this time I was most down to the foot of the island. A little ripply, **cool breeze** begun to **blow**, and that was as good as saying the night was about done. I give her a turn with the paddle and brung her nose to shore; then I got my gun and **slipped** out and into the edge of the woods. I sat down there on a **log**, and looked out through the leaves. I see the moon go off watch, and the **darkness** begin to **blanket** the river. But in a little while I see a **pale streak** over the treetops, and knowed the day was coming. So I took my gun and slipped off towards where I had run across that camp fire, **stopping** every minute or two to listen. But I hadn't no **luck** somehow; I couldn't seem to find the place. But by and by, sure enough, I catched a **glimpse** of fire away through the trees. I went for it, **cautious** and slow. By and by I was close enough to have a look, and there **laid** a man on the ground. It most give me the fantods. He had a blanket around his head, and his

Chinese Simplified

asleep: 睡着，睡着的.
blanket: 毛毯，被子.
blow: 吹，打击.
breeze: 和风.
bust: 半身像，逮捕，破产.
camp: 阵营，营，露营，安营.
canoe: 独木舟.
cautious: 谨慎，仔细，慎重，警慎的.
cooked: 煮熟.
cool: 凉，镇静，镇定，凉爽，凉爽的.
darkness: 黑暗.
glimpse: 一瞥，瞥见.
laid: 放.
log: 圆形木材，圆木，木头.
luck: 运气，幸运.
mile: 英里.
moon: 月亮，月球，月.
paddle: 桨.
pale: 苍白，苍白的.
rocks: 岩石.
shadows: 影子.
shining: 彪炳，发亮.
shore: 岸，滨，岸边，海岸，海滨.
slid: 滑行.
slipped: 滑落.
step: 步骤，步伐，措施，一步，步调，步子，级，脚步，踏.
stopping: 停止.
streak: 斑纹，线条.
supper: 晚饭，晚餐.
woods: 树林，森林.

head was nearly in the fire. I set there behind a **clump** of **bushes** in about six foot of him, and kept my eyes on him **steady**. It was getting **gray daylight** now. Pretty soon he gapped and **stretched** himself and hove off the **blanket**, and it was Miss Watson's Jim! I **bet** I was **glad** to see him. I says:

"Hello, Jim!" and skipped out.

He bounced up and stared at me **wild**. Then he drops down on his **knees**, and **puts** his **hands** together and says:

"Doan' **hurt** me--don't! I hain't ever done no **harm** to a ghos'. I alwuz liked dead people, en done all I could for 'em. You go en git in de river agin, whah you b'longs, en doan' do nuffn to Ole Jim, 'at 'uz awluz yo' fren'."

Well, I warn't long **making** him **understand** I warn't dead. I was ever so glad to see Jim. I warn't **lonesome** now. I told him I warn't **afraid** of *him* telling the people where I was. I **talked** along, but he only set there and looked at me; never said nothing. Then I says:

"It's good daylight. Le's get **breakfast**. Make up your **camp** fire good."

"What's de use er makin' up de camp fire to **cook** strawbries en sich **truck**? But you got a **gun**, hain't you? Den we kin git sumfn better **den** strawbries."

"**Strawberries** and such truck," I says. "Is that what you live on?"

"I couldn' git nuffn else," he says.

"Why, how long you been on the **island**, Jim?"

"I come heah de night arter you's killed."

"What, all that time?"

"Yes--indeedy."

"And ain't you had nothing but that kind of rubbage to eat?"

"No, sah--nuffn else."

"Well, you must be most **starved**, ain't you?"

"I reck'n I could eat a hoss. I think I could. How long you ben on de islan'?"

"Since the night I got killed."

Chinese Simplified

afraid：危惧，恐怕，害怕.
bet：打赌，赌.
blanket：毛毯，被子.
breakfast：早餐，早饭，早点.
bushes：灌木.
camp：阵营，营，露营，安营.
clump：土块.
cook：厨子，厨司，厨师，炊事员，烹调，煮，烹煮.
daylight：日光，白天.
den：窝.
glad：高兴，高兴的.
gray：灰色，灰.
gun：枪，炮，长枪.
hands：手.
harm：伤害，损害，坏处，害处，祸害.
hurt：伤害，使受伤.
island：岛.
kin：亲属，骨肉.
knees：膝盖.
lonesome：寂寞，寂寞的.
puts：放.
starved：饥饿.
steady：稳定，坚定，平稳，平稳的.
strawberries：草莓.
stretched：伸展.
talked：谈话.
truck：卡车.
understand：了解，明白，理解，领会.
wild：野，猖披，猖獗，野生，野性的.

"No! W'y, what has you lived on? But you got a **gun**. Oh, yes, you got a gun. Dat's good. Now you **kill** sumfn en I'll make up de fire."

So we went over to where the **canoe** was, and while he **built** a fire in a **grassy** open place amongst the trees, I fetched **meal** and **bacon** and **coffee**, and coffee-pot and frying-pan, and **sugar** and **tin** cups, and the nigger was set back considerable, because he reckoned it was all done with **witchcraft**. I catched a good big **catfish**, too, and Jim cleaned him with his **knife**, and **fried** him.

When **breakfast** was ready we lolled on the grass and eat it **smoking hot**. Jim **laid** it in with all his might, for he was most about **starved**. Then when we had got **pretty** well stuffed, we laid off and lazied.

By and by Jim says:

"But looky here, Huck, who wuz it dat 'uz **killed** in dat **shanty** ef it warn't you?"

Then I told him the whole thing, and he said it was **smart**. He said Tom Sawyer couldn't get up no better plan than what I had. Then I says:

"How do you come to be here, Jim, and how'd you get here?"

He looked pretty **uneasy**, and didn't say nothing for a **minute**. Then he says:

"Maybe I better not tell."

"Why, Jim?"

"Well, dey's reasons. But you wouldn' tell on me ef I uz to tell you, would you, Huck?"

"Blamed if I would, Jim."

"Well, I b'lieve you, Huck. I--I *run off*."

"Jim!"

"But mind, you said you wouldn' tell--you know you said you wouldn' tell, Huck."

"Well, I did. I said I wouldn't, and I'll **stick** to it. Honest *injun*, I will. People would call me a **low**-down Abolitionist and **despise** me for **keeping** mum--but

Chinese Simplified

bacon: 熏肉，咸肉，熏猪肉.
breakfast: 早餐，早饭，早点.
built: 建了.
canoe: 独木舟.
catfish: 鲇鱼.
coffee: 咖啡.
despise: 鄙视，轻视，不齿，鄙薄，蔑视，看不起.
fried: 炸.
grass: 草，青草.
grassy: 如草，长满草的.
gun: 枪，炮，长枪.
hot: 热.
keeping: 保管，保持.
kill: 打死，杀害，杀死.
killed: 被屠宰的，被杀死的.
knife: 刀子，刀，餐刀.
laid: 放.
low-down: 非常低的，下作.
meal: 餐，膳食，饭.
minute: 分钟，详细，分，微小的，渺小.
pretty: 漂亮，美丽的，秀丽.
shanty: 棚屋.
smart: 高明，时髦的.
smoking: 冒烟，抽烟.
starved: 饥饿.
stick: 棍，棒子，棍子，插入，棒，黏贴，手杖.
sugar: 糖.
tin: 锡，罐头.
uneasy: 不安，担心，不安的.
witchcraft: 巫术.

that don't make no difference. I ain't a-going to tell, and I ain't a-going back there, anyways. So, now, le's know all about it."

"Well, you see, it 'uz dis way. Ole missus--dat's Miss Watson--she pecks on me all de time, en **treats** me pooty **rough**, but she awluz said she wouldn' sell me down to Orleans. But I noticed dey wuz a nigger **trader** roun' de place considable **lately**, en I begin to git oneasy. Well, one night I **creeps** to de do' pooty late, en de do' warn't quite shet, en I hear old missus tell de widder she gwyne to sell me down to Orleans, but she didn' want to, but she could git **eight** hund'd dollars for me, en it 'uz sich a big **stack** o' money she couldn' resis'. De widder she try to git her to say she wouldn' do it, but I never waited to hear de res'. I **lit** out **mighty quick**, I tell you.

"I **tuck** out en **shin** down de hill, en 'spec to **steal** a skift 'long de sho' som'ers 'bove de town, but dey wuz people a-stirring yit, so I **hid** in de ole tumble-down cooper-shop on de bank to wait for **everybody** to go 'way. Well, I wuz dah all night. Dey wuz somebody roun' all de time. 'Long 'bout six in de mawnin' skifts begin to go by, en 'bout eight er **nine** every skift dat went 'long wuz talkin' 'bout how yo' pap come over to de town en say you's killed. Dese las' skifts wuz full o' **ladies** en genlmen a-goin' over for to see de place. Sometimes dey'd **pull** up at de sho' en take a res' b'fo' dey started acrost, so by de talk I got to know all 'bout de killin'. I 'uz powerful sorry you's killed, Huck, but I ain't no mo' now.

"I **laid** dah under de shavin's all day. I 'uz **hungry**, but I warn't afeard; bekase I knowed ole missus en de widder wuz goin' to start to de camp-meet'n' right arter breakfas' en be gone all day, en dey knows I goes off wid de **cattle** 'bout **daylight**, so dey wouldn' 'spec to see me roun' de place, en so dey wouldn' miss me tell arter dark in de evenin'. De yuther servants wouldn' miss me, kase dey'd shin out en take **holiday** soon as de ole folks 'uz out'n de way.

"Well, when it come dark I tuck out up de river road, en went 'bout two **mile** er more to whah dey warn't no houses. I'd made up my **mine** 'bout what I's a-gwyne to do. You see, ef I kep' on tryin' to git away **afoot**, de **dogs** 'ud **track** me; ef I **stole** a skift to **cross** over, dey'd miss dat skift, you see, en dey'd know 'bout

Chinese Simplified

afoot：徒步．
cattle：家畜，牛．
creeps：爬行．
cross：交叉，十字架，越过，相交，渡过，穿过．
daylight：日光，白天．
dogs：狗．
eight：八．
everybody：每个人，各位．
hid：躲藏．
holiday：假日，节日，假期．
hungry：饥饿，饿，饥饿的．
ladies：女洗手间．
laid：放．
lately：近来，一向，最近．
lit：点燃．
mighty：伟大，强势，强大的．
mile：英里．
mine：矿，我的，矿山，矿井．
nine：九．
pull：拉，牵引．
quick：快，玲珑，敏捷的，迅速的．
rough：粗暴，大概，粗糙，粗鲁．
shin：外小腿，胫．
stack：堆，栈，垛，堆叠，堆积，堆置．
steal：偷窃，盗窃，偷，窃取．
stole：偷了．
track：跑道，径赛，径迹，轨道，行踪，履带，踪迹．
trader：商人．
treats：对待．
tuck：挤进，塞进．

whah I'd **lan'** on de yuther side, en whah to pick up my track. So I says, a raff is what I's arter; it doan' *make* no track.

"I see a light a-comin' roun' de p'int bymeby, so I **wade'** in en **shove'** a **log** ahead o' me en swum more'n half way acrost de river, en got in 'mongst de drift-wood, en kep' my head down low, en kinder swum agin de current tell de raff come along. Den I swum to de **stern** uv it en **tuck** a- **holt**. It **clouded** up en 'uz pooty dark for a little while. So I clumb up en laid down on de planks. De men 'uz all 'way **yonder** in de middle, whah de **lantern** wuz. De river wuz a-risin', en dey wuz a good current; so I reck'n'd 'at by fo' in de mawnin' I'd be twenty-five mile down de river, en **den** I'd slip in **jis** b'fo' **daylight** en **swim** asho', en take to de woods on de Illinois side.

"But I didn' have no luck. When we 'uz mos' down to de head er de islan' a man begin to come **aft** wid de lantern, I see it warn't no use fer to wait, so I **slid** **overboard** en struck out fer de islan'. Well, I had a notion I could lan' mos' anywhers, but I couldn't--bank too **bluff**. I 'uz mos' to de foot er de islan' b'fo' I found' a good place. I went into de woods en jedged I wouldn' fool wid raffs no mo', long as dey **move** de lantern roun' so. I had my pipe en a **plug** er dog-leg, en some matches in my **cap**, en dey warn't wet, so I 'uz all right."

"And so you ain't had no **meat** nor bread to eat all this time? Why didn't you get mud-turkles?"

"How you gwyne to git 'm? You can't slip up on um en **grab** um; en how's a body gwyne to **hit** um wid a **rock**? How could a body do it in de night? En I warn't gwyne to show mysef on de bank in de daytime."

"Well, that's so. You've had to keep in the woods all the time, of course. Did you hear 'em **shooting** the cannon?"

"Oh, yes. I knowed dey was arter you. I see um go by heah--watched um thoo de bushes."

Some young birds come along, **flying** a **yard** or two at a time and **lighting**. Jim said it was a sign it was going to rain. He said it was a sign when young **chickens flew** that way, and so he reckoned it was the same way when young

Chinese Simplified

aft: 在船尾.
bluff: 虚张声势, 吹牛.
cap: 便帽, 帽子, 套子, 鸭舌帽.
chickens: 小鸡.
clouded: 阴云密布的, 有暗影的.
daylight: 日光, 白天.
den: 窝.
flew: 飞.
flying: 飞行, 飞.
grab: 抓住, 攫取, 抓斗.
hit: 袭击, 命中, 击中, 打.
holt: 兽穴.
jis: 日本工业标准.
lan: 区域网络, 区域网路, 本地网络, 局域网.
lantern: 灯笼.
lighting: 灯光, 采光, 照明.
log: 圆形木材, 圆木, 木头.
meat: 肉.
move: 步骤, 搬家, 移动, 一举, 运动, 感动, 开动, 移.
overboard: 向船外.
plug: 插头, 板烟, 插.
rock: 岩石, 簸荡, 摇.
shooting: 射击, 猎场.
shove: 推.
slid: 滑行.
stern: 严竣, 严厉的, 船尾.
swim: 游泳.
tuck: 挤进, 塞进.
wade: 在水步行, 涉过, 蹚.
yard: 码, 厂, 厂子, 场地.
yonder: 那边.

birds done it. I was going to **catch** some of them, but Jim wouldn't let me. He said it was death. He said his father **laid mighty sick** once, and some of them catched a bird, and his old **granny** said his father would **die**, and he did.

And Jim said you mustn't **count** the things you are going to **cook** for **dinner**, because that would bring bad **luck**. The same if you **shook** the table-cloth after **sundown**. And he said if a man **owned** a **beehive** and that man died, the bees must be told about it before sun-up next morning, or else the bees would all **weaken** down and **quit** work and die. Jim said bees wouldn't **sting idiots**; but I didn't believe that, because I had tried them lots of times myself, and they wouldn't sting me.

I had heard about some of these things before, but not all of them. Jim knowed all kinds of signs. He said he knowed most everything. I said it looked to me like all the signs was about bad luck, and so I asked him if there warn't any good-luck signs. He says:

"Mighty few--an' *dey* ain't no use to a body. What you want to know when good luck's a-comin' for? Want to keep it off?" And he said: "Ef you's got **hairy arms** en a hairy breas', it's a sign dat you's a-gwyne to be rich. Well, dey's some use in a sign like dat, 'kase it's so **fur ahead**. You see, maybe you's got to be po' a long time fust, en so you might git **discourage'** en **kill** yo'sef 'f you didn' know by de sign dat you gwyne to be rich bymeby."

"Have you got hairy arms and a hairy **breast**, Jim?"

"What's de use to **ax** dat question? Don't you see I has?"

"Well, are you rich?"

"No, but I ben rich wunst, and gwyne to be rich agin. Wunst I had foteen dollars, but I **tuck** to specalat'n', en got busted out."

"What did you **speculate** in, Jim?"

"Well, fust I tackled stock."

"What kind of stock?"

Chinese Simplified

ahead：前头，前方，前面的.
arms：武器，武装，军备，兵戈，兵器，军火，兵戎.
ax：斧头，削减.
beehive：蜂箱，蜂窝.
bird：鸟.
birds：禽，禽类，鸟.
breast：奶子，乳房，胸，胸部.
catch：捕捉，捕捞，捕拿，捉.
cook：厨子，厨司，厨师，炊事员，烹调，煮，烹煮.
count：计数，伯爵，计算，有价值，认为.
die：逝世，不讳，死.
dinner：晚餐，正餐.
discourage：不鼓励.
fur：毛，软毛.
granny：婆婆，老大娘.
hairy：毛茸茸，多毛的，毛茸茸的.
idiots：白痴.
kill：打死，杀害，杀死.
laid：放.
luck：运气，幸运.
mighty：伟大，强势，强大的.
owned：拥有.
quit：退出，退离.
shook：摇动.
sick：生病.
speculate：推测，猜测，思索.
sting：刺，叮，螫.
sundown：日落.
tuck：挤进，塞进.
weaken：削弱，弱化.

"Why, **live stock**--cattle, you know. I put ten **dollars** in a **cow**. But I ain' gwyne to resk no mo' money in stock. De cow up 'n' died on my han's."

"So you **lost** the ten dollars."

"No, I didn't **lose** it all. I on'y los' 'bout **nine** of it. I **sole de hide** en taller for a dollar en ten cents."

"You had five dollars and ten cents left. Did you **speculate** any more?"

"Yes. You know that one-laigged nigger dat b'longs to old Misto Bradish? Well, he sot up a **bank**, en say **anybody** dat put in a dollar would git fo' dollars mo' at de en' er de year. Well, all de niggers went in, but dey didn't have much. I wuz de on'y one dat had much. So I **stuck** out for mo' dan fo' dollars, en I said 'f I didn' git it I'd start a bank mysef. Well, o' course dat nigger want' to keep me out er de business, bekase he says dey warn't business 'nough for two banks, so he say I could put in my five dollars en he pay me thirty-five at de en' er de year.

"So I done it. Den I reck'n'd I'd inves' de thirty-five dollars right off en keep things a-movin'. Dey wuz a nigger name' Bob, dat had ketched a wood-flat, en his marster didn' know it; en I **bought** it off'n him en told him to take de thirty-five dollars when de en' er de year come; but **somebody stole** de wood-flat dat night, en nex day de one-laigged nigger say de bank's busted. So dey didn' **none** uv us git no money."

"What did you do with the ten cents, Jim?"

"Well, I 'uz gwyne to spen' it, but I had a **dream**, en de dream tole me to give it to a nigger name' Balum--Balum's Ass dey **call** him for **short**; he's one er dem chuckleheads, you know. But he's **lucky**, dey say, en I see I warn't lucky. De dream say let Balum inves' de ten cents en he'd make a **raise** for me. Well, Balum he tuck de money, en when he wuz in church he **hear** de **preacher** say dat **whoever** give to de po' len' to de Lord, en boun' to git his money back a hund'd times. So Balum he tuck en give de ten cents to de po', en **laid low** to see what wuz gwyne to come of it."

"Well, what did come of it, Jim?"

Chinese Simplified

anybody：任何人.
bank：银行，岸.
bought：买了.
call：喊，称呼，叫，号召，召唤.
cow：母牛，牛.
de：可选择丢弃.
dollar：元.
dream：梦寐，梦见，做梦，梦想.
hear：听见，听取，听.
hide：躲藏，暗藏，掩饰，藏，隐瞒，隐藏.
laid：放.
live：住，活，居住.
lose：丢失，丧失，失掉，遗失.
lost：遗失.
low：低，卑下，低廉，浅的，低的.
lucky：幸运，幸运的，吉祥.
nine：九.
none：无，没有.
preacher：传道者.
raise：升起，提高，筹措，增加，抚育，举起.
short：短，矮，小结，短暂.
sole：唯一，单一，唯一的，惟一，跖，鞋底.
somebody：某人，有人.
speculate：推测，猜测，思索.
stock：存货，股票，股份，库存.
stole：偷了.
stuck：黏贴.
tuck：挤进，塞进.
whoever：无论何人.

"Nuffn never come of it. I couldn' **manage** to k'leck dat money no way; en Balum he couldn'. I ain' gwyne to len' no mo' money 'dout I see **de security**. Boun' to git yo' money back a hund'd times, de **preacher** says! Ef I could git de ten *cents* back, I'd **call** it squah, en be **glad** er de chanst."

"Well, it's all right **anyway**, Jim, long as you're going to be **rich** again some time or other."

"Yes; en I's rich now, come to look at it. I owns mysef, en I's wuth **eight** hund'd dollars. I wisht I had de money, I wouldn' want no mo'."

Chinese Simplified

anyway: 无论如何，反正.
call: 喊，称呼，叫，号召，召唤.
de: 可选择丢弃.
eight: 八.
glad: 高兴，高兴的.
manage: 符合，管理，处理.
preacher: 传道者.
rich: 富有，丰富，富有的，充实.
security: 安全，安全性.

CHAPTER IX

THE HOUSE OF DEATH FLOATS BY

I wanted to go and look at a place right about the middle of the **island** that I'd found when I was **exploring**; so we started and soon got to it, because the island was only three **miles** long and a **quarter** of a mile wide.

This place was a **tolerable** long, **steep hill** or **ridge** about **forty foot** high. We had a **rough** time getting to the top, the sides was so steep and the **bushes** so **thick**. We tramped and clumb around all over it, and by and by found a good big **cavern** in the **rock**, most up to the top on the side towards Illinois. The cavern was as big as two or three **rooms** bunched together, and Jim could stand up straight in it. It was **cool** in there. Jim was for putting our traps in there right away, but I said we didn't want to be **climbing** up and down there all the time.

Jim said if we had the **canoe hid** in a good place, and had all the traps in the cavern, we could **rush** there if **anybody** was to come to the island, and they would never find us without **dogs**. And, **besides**, he said them little **birds** had said it was going to **rain**, and did I want the things to get **wet**?

So we went back and got the canoe, and paddled up **abreast** the cavern, and lugged all the traps up there. Then we hunted up a place close by to **hide** the

Chinese Simplified

abreast: 并肩，并排，并列.
anybody: 任何人.
besides: 此外，另外，除了，并且，再说，况且.
birds: 禽，禽类，鸟.
bushes: 灌木.
canoe: 独木舟.
cavern: 大地洞，大山洞.
climbing: 攀登，上升的.
cool: 凉，镇静，镇定，凉爽，凉爽的.
dogs: 狗.
exploring: 探索.
foot: 脚，足，步兵，英尺，呎.
forty: 四十.
hid: 躲藏.
hide: 躲藏，暗藏，掩饰，藏，隐瞒，隐藏.
hill: 小丘，山坡，山岗，陵.
island: 岛.
mile: 英里.
quarter: 四分之一.
rain: 雨，下雨.
ridge: 脊，屋脊，山脊，背脊.
rock: 岩石，簸荡，摇.
rooms: 房间.
rough: 粗暴，大概，粗糙，粗鲁.
rush: 速行，匆匆.
steep: 险峻，峭壁，浸，泡，陡峭的.
thick: 厚，密，浓厚.
tolerable: 可容忍，可容忍的.
wet: 湿.

canoe in, amongst the thick willows. We took some fish off of the lines and set them again, and begun to get ready for dinner.

The door of the cavern was big enough to **roll** a hogshead in, and on one side of the door the floor stuck out a little bit, and was **flat** and a good place to build a fire on. So we built it there and cooked dinner.

We spread the blankets inside for a carpet, and eat our dinner in there. We put all the other things handy at the back of the cavern. Pretty soon it darkened up, and begun to thunder and **lighten**; so the birds was right about it. Directly it begun to rain, and it **rained** like all **fury**, too, and I never see the wind blow so. It was one of these regular summer **storms**. It would get so dark that it looked all **blue**-black outside, and **lovely**; and the rain would **thrash** along by so thick that the trees off a little ways looked **dim** and spider-webby; and here would come a blast of wind that would **bend** the trees down and turn up the pale **underside** of the leaves; and then a **perfect** ripper of a **gust** would follow along and set the branches to **tossing** their arms as if they was just wild; and next, when it was just about the bluest and blackest--FST! it was as bright as **glory**, and you'd have a little glimpse of tree-tops a-plunging about away off yonder in the storm, hundreds of yards further than you could see before; dark as sin again in a second, and now you'd hear the thunder let go with an awful **crash**, and then go **rumbling**, grumbling, **tumbling**, down the sky towards the under side of the world, like **rolling empty barrels** down **stairs**--where it's long stairs and they **bounce** a good deal, you know.

"Jim, this is nice," I says. "I wouldn't want to be **nowhere** else but here. Pass me along another hunk of fish and some hot corn-bread."

"Well, you wouldn't a ben here 'f it hadn't a ben for Jim. You'd a ben down dah in de woods widout any dinner, en gittn' mos' drownded, too; dat you would, **honey**. Chickens knows when it's gwyne to rain, en so do de birds, chile."

The river went on raising and raising for ten or twelve days, till at last it was over the banks. The water was three or four foot deep on the island in the low places and on the Illinois bottom. On that side it was a good many miles wide,

Chinese Simplified

barrels：桶．
bend：弯曲，弯折．
blue-black：深蓝色的．
bounce：乱跳，退票，弹跳，跳，弹回．
crash：粉碎，坠毁，相撞，毁坏，崩溃．
dim：阴暗，暗淡，暗淡的．
empty：空，空洞．
flat：平坦，平板，平坦的，平的，居室．
fury：暴怒，怒火，愤怒，气愤．
glory：荣耀，光荣，辉煌．
gust：阵风，狂风．
honey：蜂蜜，蜜，蜜糖．
lighten：照亮，减轻．
lovely：可爱，可爱的．
nowhere：无处．
perfect：完美，完善，完美的，无话可说，完备．
rained：下雨．
roll：滚动，簸荡，卷．
rolling：滚动，旋转的，起伏的，波动的．
rumbling：隆隆响．
sin：罪恶，罪行．
stairs：楼梯．
storm：暴风雨，暴风，风暴．
storms：暴风雨．
thrash：鞭打，击败．
tumbling：摔倒．
underside：下侧．

but on the Missouri side it was the same old **distance** across--a half a mile--because the Missouri **shore** was just a **wall** of high bluffs.

Daytimes we **paddled** all over the island in the **canoe**, It was **mighty cool** and **shady** in the deep **woods**, even if the **sun** was blazing outside. We went **winding** in and out amongst the trees, and sometimes the vines **hung** so thick we had to back away and go some other way. Well, on every old broken-down tree you could see **rabbits** and snakes and such things; and when the island had been overflowed a day or two they got so **tame**, on account of being **hungry**, that you could paddle right up and put your hand on them if you wanted to; but not the snakes and turtles--they would **slide** off in the water. The **ridge** our **cavern** was in was full of them. We could a had pets enough if we'd wanted them.

One night we catched a little section of a **lumber** raft--nice **pine** planks. It was twelve foot wide and about **fifteen** or **sixteen** foot long, and the top stood above water six or seven inches a solid, level floor. We could see saw-logs go by in the **daylight** sometimes, but we let them go; we didn't show **ourselves** in daylight.

Another night when we was up at the head of the island, just before daylight, here comes a frame-house down, on the west side. She was a two-story, and **tilted** over considerable. We paddled out and got aboard-- clumb in at an **upstairs** window. But it was too dark to see yet, so we made the canoe fast and set in her to wait for daylight.

The light begun to come before we got to the foot of the island. Then we looked in at the window. We could make out a bed, and a table, and two old **chairs**, and lots of things around about on the floor, and there was clothes hanging against the wall. There was something laying on the floor in the far corner that looked like a man. So Jim says:

"Hello, you!"

But it didn't **budge**. So I hollered again, and then Jim says:

"De man ain't asleep--he's dead. You hold still--I'll go en see."

He went, and **bent** down and looked, and says:

Chinese Simplified

bent: 曲，弯，弯曲，弯折.
budge: 微微一动，改变态度，羔皮.
canoe: 独木舟.
cavern: 大地洞，大山洞.
chairs: 椅子.
cool: 凉，镇静，镇定，凉爽，凉爽的.
daylight: 日光，白天.
distance: 距离.
fifteen: 十五.
hung: 挂.
hungry: 饥饿，饿，饥饿的.
lumber: 木料，木材.
mighty: 伟大，强势，强大的.
ourselves: 我们自己，我们.
paddle: 桨.
pine: 松树.
rabbits: 野兔.
ridge: 脊，屋脊，山脊，背脊.
shady: 暧昧，背阴，不三不四，阴凉，阴凉的.
shore: 岸，滨，岸边，海岸，海滨.
sixteen: 十六.
slide: 滑落，滑行，滑.
sun: 太阳，星期日，曝.
tame: 驯服，驯服的.
tilted: 倾斜的.
upstairs: 楼上，在楼上.
wall: 墙壁，墙.
winding: 曲折，弯曲.
woods: 树林，森林.

"It's a dead man. Yes, indeedy; **naked**, too. He's ben shot in de back. I reck'n he's ben dead two er three days. Come in, Huck, but doan' look at his face--it's too gashly."

I didn't look at him at all. Jim throwed some old rags over him, but he needn't done it; I didn't want to see him. There was heaps of old greasy cards scattered around over the floor, and old whisky **bottles**, and a couple of masks made out of black **cloth**; and all over the **walls** was the ignorantest kind of words and **pictures** made with **charcoal**. There was two old **dirty calico** dresses, and a sun-bonnet, and some women's **underclothes** hanging against the wall, and some men's **clothing**, too. We put the lot into the canoe--it might come good. There was a boy's old speckled **straw** hat on the floor; I took that, too. And there was a bottle that had had **milk** in it, and it had a rag **stopper** for a **baby** to **suck**. We would a took the bottle, but it was broke. There was a seedy old **chest**, and an old hair **trunk** with the hinges broke. They stood open, but there warn't nothing left in them that was any account. The way things was scattered about we reckoned the people left in a **hurry**, and warn't fixed so as to **carry** off most of their stuff.

We got an old tin lantern, and a butcher-knife without any handle, and a bran-new Barlow knife worth two **bits** in any store, and a lot of tallow candles, and a tin **candlestick**, and a gourd, and a tin cup, and a ratty old bedquilt off the bed, and a reticule with **needles** and **pins** and **beeswax** and buttons and thread and all such truck in it, and a **hatchet** and some nails, and a fish-line as thick as my little **finger** with some monstrous hooks on it, and a roll of buckskin, and a **leather** dog-collar, and a horseshoe, and some vials of **medicine** that didn't have no **label** on them; and just as we was leaving I found a tolerable good curry-comb, and Jim he found a ratty old fiddle-bow, and a **wooden** leg. The **straps** was broke off of it, but, barring that, it was a good enough leg, though it was too long for me and not long enough for Jim, and we couldn't find the other one, though we hunted all around.

And so, take it all around, we made a good **haul**. When we was ready to shove off we was a quarter of a mile below the island, and it was pretty broad

Chinese Simplified

baby：婴儿，宝宝，宝贝，娃娃.
beeswax：蜂蜡，蜜蜡.
bits：屑.
bottle：瓶，瓶子.
calico：白布，白棉布.
candlestick：烛台，蜡台.
carry：搬运，输送，携带，进位.
charcoal：木炭，炭.
chest：胸部，箱，胸膛.
cloth：布，布帛菽粟，布料.
clothing：服装，装束，衣服.
dirty：肮脏，脏脏，肮脏的，混浊.
finger：手指，指头.
hatchet：斧头，斧子.
haul：拖拉，曳.
hurry：仓促，匆忙，赶忙.
label：标签，取名.
leather：皮革，皮.
medicine：药物，药品，医学，药剂，医药，药.
milk：牛奶，乳.
naked：赤裸裸，裸体的.
needles：针.
pictures：图画.
pins：别针.
stopper：塞子，用塞子塞住.
straps：背带，带.
straw：稻草，吸管.
suck：吮吸，咂，吮.
trunk：躯干，主干，树干.
underclothes：内衣裤.
walls：墙壁.
wooden：木制，木制的.

day; so I made Jim **lay** down in the **canoe** and **cover** up with the **quilt**, because if he set up people could tell he was a nigger a good **ways** off. I paddled over to the Illinois **shore**, and drifted down most a half a **mile** doing it. I **crept** up the **dead** water under the **bank**, and hadn't no **accidents** and didn't see **nobody**. We got home all safe.

Chinese Simplified

accidents: 事故.
bank: 银行, 岸.
canoe: 独木舟.
cover: 盖子, 面儿, 包罗, 皮儿, 采访, 掩护, 遮盖.
crept: 爬行.
dead: 死.
lay: 产卵, 安放, 放, 凡俗.
mile: 英里.
nobody: 没有人, 没人.
quilt: 棉被, 被子.
shore: 岸, 滨, 岸边, 海岸, 海滨.
ways: 方法.

CHAPTER X

WHAT COMES OF HANDLIN' **SNAKESKIN**

After breakfast I wanted to **talk** about the **dead** man and **guess** out how he come to be **killed**, but Jim didn't want to. He said it would **fetch bad luck**; and **besides**, he said, he might come and ha'nt us; he said a man that warn't **buried** was more likely to go a-ha'nting around than one that was planted and **comfortable**. That sounded **pretty reasonable**, so I didn't say no more; but I couldn't keep from **studying** over it and **wishing** I knowed who **shot** the man, and what they done it for.

We rummaged the clothes we'd got, and found **eight** dollars in **silver sewed** up in the **lining** of an old **blanket overcoat**. Jim said he reckoned the people in that house **stole** the coat, because if they'd a knowed the money was there they wouldn't a left it. I said I reckoned they killed him, too; but Jim didn't want to talk about that. I says:

"Now you think it's bad luck; but what did you say when I fetched in the snake-skin that I found on the top of the **ridge** day before yesterday? You said it was the **worst** bad luck in the world to **touch** a snake-skin with my **hands**. Well, here's your bad luck! We've raked in all this **truck** and eight dollars besides. I wish we could have some bad luck like this every day, Jim."

Chinese Simplified

bad：坏，糟糕，不良，不善，淘气，坏的．
besides：此外，另外，除了，并且，再说，况且．
blanket：毛毯，被子．
buried：埋下．
coat：外套，上衣．
comfortable：舒服，舒服的．
dead：死．
eight：八．
fetch：拿，取，带来．
guess：猜测，臆测，猜谜儿，猜想，揣测，推测．
hands：手．
killed：被屠宰的，被杀死的．
lining：衬里，衬，内裙．
luck：运气，幸运．
overcoat：大衣．
pretty：漂亮，美丽的，秀丽．
reasonable：合理，合理的．
ridge：脊，屋脊，山脊，背脊．
sewed：缝．
shot：射击．
silver：银，白银．
snake：蛇．
stole：偷了．
studying：学习．
talk：谈话，报告，言语，谈．
touch：触摸，笔锋，触，联系，碰，接触．
truck：卡车．
wishing：恭祝．
worst：最坏的．

"Never you mind, honey, never you mind. Don't you git too **peart**. It's a-comin'. Mind I tell you, it's a-comin'."

It did come, too. It was a Tuesday that we had that talk. Well, after dinner Friday we was laying around in the grass at the **upper** end of the **ridge**, and got out of **tobacco**. I went to the **cavern** to get some, and found a **rattlesnake** in there. I killed him, and **curled** him up on the foot of Jim's **blanket**, ever so natural, thinking there'd be some fun when Jim found him there. Well, by night I forgot all about the snake, and when Jim flung himself down on the blanket while I struck a light the snake's **mate** was there, and bit him.

He jumped up **yelling**, and the first thing the light showed was the varmint curled up and ready for another spring. I laid him out in a second with a stick, and Jim grabbed pap's whisky-jug and begun to **pour** it down.

He was **barefooted**, and the snake bit him right on the **heel**. That all comes of my being such a fool as to not **remember** that wherever you leave a dead snake its mate always comes there and **curls** around it. Jim told me to **chop** off the snake's head and throw it away, and then **skin** the body and **roast** a piece of it. I done it, and he eat it and said it would help **cure** him. He made me take off the rattles and tie them around his **wrist**, too. He said that that would help. Then I **slid** out quiet and throwed the snakes clear away amongst the **bushes**; for I warn't going to let Jim find out it was all my **fault**, not if I could help it.

Jim sucked and sucked at the **jug**, and now and then he got out of his head and **pitched** around and **yelled**; but every time he come to himself he went to sucking at the jug again. His foot **swelled** up pretty big, and so did his leg; but by and by the **drunk** begun to come, and so I judged he was all right; but I'd druther been bit with a snake than pap's whisky.

Jim was laid up for four days and nights. Then the **swelling** was all gone and he was around again. I made up my mind I wouldn't ever take a-holt of a snake-skin again with my hands, now that I see what had come of it. Jim said he reckoned I would believe him next time. And he said that **handling** a snake-skin was such awful bad luck that maybe we hadn't got to the end of it yet. He said he druther see the new moon over his left shoulder as much as a thousand times

Chinese Simplified

barefooted: 赤足，赤足的.
blanket: 毛毯，被子.
bushes: 灌木.
cavern: 大地洞，大山洞.
chop: 劈，剁，砍，伐.
cure: 治疗，防治，药，治愈，医治.
curled: 卷曲.
curls: 卷曲.
drunk: 喝了，喝醉.
fault: 故障，过失，缺点，毛病，断层，短处，缺陷.
handling: 处理.
heel: 脚跟，踵，踝部.
jug: 细颈瓶，罐.
mate: 伴侣，配偶，伙伴.
peart: 快活的.
pitched: 沥青.
pour: 灌，奔流，倾倒，倒，注.
rattlesnake: 响尾蛇.
remember: 记忆，记得.
ridge: 脊，屋脊，山脊，背脊.
roast: 焙烧，烘烤，烤，烤肉，烘，炙，烧烤.
skin: 皮肤，剥皮.
slid: 滑行.
snake: 蛇.
swelled: 膨胀.
swelling: 肿胀，增大，膨胀.
tobacco: 烟草.
upper: 帮子，上面的.
wrist: 腕，腕部.
yelled: 叫喊.
yelling: 叫声，叫喊.

than take up a snake-skin in his hand. Well, I was getting to feel that way myself, though I've always reckoned that looking at the new moon over your left shoulder is one of the carelessest and foolishest things a body can do. Old Hank Bunker done it once, and bragged about it; and in less than two years he got drunk and fell off of the shot-tower, and spread himself out so that he was just a kind of a **layer**, as you may say; and they slid him **edgeways** between two **barn doors** for a **coffin**, and buried him so, so they say, but I didn't see it. Pap told me. But anyway it all come of looking at the moon that way, like a fool.

Well, the days went along, and the river went down between its banks again; and about the first thing we done was to **bait** one of the big hooks with a skinned **rabbit** and set it and catch a catfish that was as big as a man, being six foot two **inches** long, and weighed over two **hundred pounds**. We couldn't handle him, of course; he would a flung us into Illinois. We just set there and watched him rip and tear around till he drownded. We found a brass **button** in his stomach and a round **ball**, and lots of rubbage. We split the ball open with the **hatchet**, and there was a **spool** in it. Jim said he'd had it there a long time, to coat it over so and make a ball of it. It was as big a fish as was ever catched in the Mississippi, I reckon. Jim said he hadn't ever seen a **bigger** one. He would a been worth a good deal over at the **village**. They **peddle** out such a fish as that by the pound in the market-house there; everybody **buys** some of him; his meat's as white as snow and makes a good **fry**.

Next morning I said it was getting slow and dull, and I wanted to get a stirring up some way. I said I reckoned I would slip over the river and find out what was going on. Jim liked that notion; but he said I must go in the dark and look sharp. Then he studied it over and said, couldn't I put on some of them old things and **dress** up like a **girl**? That was a good notion, too. So we **shortened** up one of the **calico gowns**, and I turned up my trouser-legs to my knees and got into it. Jim hitched it behind with the hooks, and it was a fair **fit**. I put on the sun-bonnet and tied it under my chin, and then for a body to look in and see my face was like looking down a **joint** of stove-pipe. Jim said nobody would know me, even in the **daytime, hardly**. I **practiced** around all day to get the **hang** of

Chinese Simplified

bait：饵，诱饵.
ball：球，舞会.
barn：谷仓，仓，马厩.
bigger：更大，较大.
button：钮，扣子，按钮，钮扣，纽扣.
buys：购买.
calico：白布，白棉布.
coffin：棺材，寿材.
daytime：白天，白昼，日间.
doors：门.
dress：服装，打扮.
edgeways：从旁边.
fit：合适，适应，适合，适.
fry：用油炸.
girl：女孩，姑娘，女孩子.
gowns：长袍.
hang：挂，悬挂.
hardly：几乎不，毫不，辛苦地.
hatchet：斧头，斧子.
hundred：百，佰.
inches：英寸.
joint：关节，接合，共同，联合，接合点.
layer：层，一层.
peddle：贩卖，兜售，沿街叫卖，叫卖，零卖，挑卖.
pound：磅，敲击.
practiced：熟练.
rabbit：兔子，兔，野兔.
shortened：缩短.
spool：线轴.
village：村庄，农村，乡村，村子.

the things, and by and by I could do **pretty** well in them, only Jim said I didn't **walk** like a girl; and he said I must **quit pulling** up my **gown** to get at my britches-pocket. I took **notice**, and done better.

I **started** up the Illinois **shore** in the **canoe** just after **dark**.

I started across to the town from a little **below** the ferry-landing, and the **drift** of the **current** fetched me in at the **bottom** of the town. I tied up and started **along** the bank. There was a **light** burning in a little **shanty** that hadn't been lived in for a long time, and I wondered who had took up **quarters** there. I **slipped** up and peeped in at the **window**. There was a woman about **forty** year old in there **knitting** by a **candle** that was on a **pine** table. I didn't know her face; she was a **stranger**, for you couldn't start a face in that town that I didn't know. Now this was **lucky**, because I was **weakening**; I was getting **afraid** I had come; people might know my voice and find me out. But if this woman had been in such a little town two days she could tell me all I wanted to know; so I knocked at the door, and made up my mind I wouldn't **forget** I was a girl.

Chinese Simplified

afraid: 危惧，恐怕，害怕.
along: 沿着，沿，一同.
below: 下面，以下.
bottom: 底部，屁股，底.
candle: 蜡烛.
canoe: 独木舟.
current: 潮流，现时，现在，这次，本届，当今，当前，当前的，水流，电流，现在的.
dark: 暗，黑暗，夜.
drift: 漂游，漂移，漂.
forget: 忘记，忘，忘却.
forty: 四十.
gown: 长袍，女装长袍.
knitting: 编织.
light: 光，轻，灯，光纤，燃放，灯光，点燃，亮光.
lucky: 幸运，幸运的，吉祥.
notice: 通知，注意，布告，注意到，启事.
pine: 松树.
pretty: 漂亮，美丽的，秀丽.
pulling: 拉.
quarters: 住处，四分之一.
quit: 退出，退离.
shanty: 棚屋.
shore: 岸，滨，岸边，海岸，海滨.
slipped: 滑落.
started: 开始.
stranger: 陌生人，异乡人，生人.
walk: 行走，步行，走，走道，散步.
weakening: 削弱.
window: 窗口，窗户，窗，窗子.

CHAPTER XI

THEY'RE AFTER US!

"Come in," says the woman, and I did. She says: "Take a cheer."

I done it. She looked me all over with her little **shiny** eyes, and says:

"What might your name be?"

"**Sarah** Williams."

"Where 'bouts do you **live**? In this neighborhood?'

"No'm. In Hookerville, **seven mile below**. I've **walked** all the way and I'm all **tired** out."

"**Hungry**, too, I **reckon**. I'll find you something."

"No'm, I ain't hungry. I was so hungry I had to **stop** two miles below here at a **farm**; so I ain't hungry no more. It's what makes me so **late**. My mother's down **sick**, and out of money and **everything**, and I come to tell my **uncle** Abner Moore. He lives at the **upper** end of the **town**, she says. I hain't ever been here before. Do you know him?"

"No; but I don't know **everybody** yet. I haven't lived here quite two weeks. It's a **considerable ways** to the upper end of the town. You better **stay** here all night. Take off your bonnet."

Chinese Simplified

below: 下面，以下.
considerable: 可观，相当多的.
everybody: 每个人，各位.
everything: 一切事物，应有尽有，一切，事事.
farm: 农场，田间.
hungry: 饥饿，饿，饥饿的.
late: 晚，迟，迟慢，迟了，迟迟.
live: 住，活，居住.
mile: 英里.
reckon: 估计，计算.
sarah: 莎拉.
seven: 七.
shiny: 发亮，闪亮，发亮的.
sick: 生病.
stay: 延缓，逗留，停留.
stop: 停止，终止，截止，站.
tired: 疲倦，疲乏，疲倦的.
town: 城镇，城市，市镇.
uncle: 叔叔，伯伯，叔父，大爷，老大爷，姑夫.
upper: 帮子，上面的.
walked: 步行.
ways: 方法.

"No," I says; "I'll rest a while, I **reckon**, and go on. I ain't afeared of the dark."

She said she wouldn't let me go by **myself**, but her **husband** would be in by and by, **maybe** in a **hour** and a half, and she'd **send** him **along** with me. Then she got to talking about her husband, and about her **relations** up the **river**, and her relations down the river, and about how much better off they used to was, and how they didn't know but they'd made a **mistake coming** to our town, **instead** of letting well alone--and so on and so on, **till** I was afeard I had made a mistake coming to her to find out what was going on in the town; but by and by she **dropped** on to pap and the **murder**, and then I was **pretty willing** to let her clatter right along. She told about me and Tom Sawyer **finding** the six **thousand** dollars (only she got it ten) and all about pap and what a hard **lot** he was, and what a hard lot I was, and at last she got down to where I was murdered. I says:

"Who done it? We've heard **considerable** about these goings on down in Hookerville, but we don't know who 'twas that **killed** Huck Finn."

"Well, I reckon there's a right **smart chance** of people *here* that'd like to know who killed him. Some think old Finn done it himself."

"No--is that so?"

"Most **everybody** thought it at first. He'll never know how nigh he come to getting lynched. But before night they **changed** around and judged it was done by a **runaway** nigger named Jim."

"Why *he*--"

I **stopped**. I reckoned I better keep still. She run on, and never noticed I had put in at all:

"The nigger run off the very night Huck Finn was killed. So there's a **reward** out for him--three hundred dollars. And there's a reward out for old Finn, too--two hundred dollars. You see, he come to town the morning after the murder, and told about it, and was out with 'em on the ferryboat **hunt**, and right away after he up and left. Before night they wanted to lynch him, but he was gone, you see. Well, next day they found out the nigger was gone; they found out he

Chinese Simplified

along: 沿着，沿，一同.
chance: 机会.
changed: 改变.
coming: 未来，到来.
considerable: 可观，相当多的.
dropped: 落下.
everybody: 每个人，各位.
finding: 发现物，发现.
hour: 小时，钟头，钟点，现在.
hunt: 打猎，狩猎.
husband: 丈夫，爱人，老公.
instead: 代替，反而.
killed: 被屠宰的，被杀死的.
lot: 地皮，批量，地段.
maybe: 或许，也许，或者，说不定，可能，不一定.
mistake: 错误，差错.
murder: 谋杀，杀人案件，杀害.
myself: 我自己.
pretty: 漂亮，美丽的，秀丽.
reckon: 估计，计算.
relations: 关系.
reward: 报酬，酬劳，酬金，奖励，奖赏.
river: 河，江，川，河流，条.
runaway: 逃亡者，跑道.
send: 派遣，派出，送，发送，寄，投，派.
smart: 高明，时髦的.
stopped: 停止.
thousand: 千.
till: 直到.
willing: 愿意，高兴，情愿的.

hadn't ben seen sence ten o'clock the night the **murder** was done. So then they put it on him, you see; and while they was full of it, next day, back comes old Finn, and went boo-hooing to Judge Thatcher to get money to **hunt** for the nigger all over Illinois with. The judge gave him some, and that **evening** he got **drunk**, and was around **till** after **midnight** with a **couple** of **mighty** hard- looking **strangers**, and then went off with them. Well, he hain't come back sence, and they ain't looking for him back till this thing **blows** over a little, for people **thinks** now that he killed his boy and **fixed** things so folks would think robbers done it, and then he'd get Huck's money without having to **bother** a long time with a **lawsuit**. People do say he warn't any too good to do it. Oh, he's **sly**, I **reckon**. If he don't come back for a year he'll be all right. You can't **prove** anything on him, you know; everything will be quieted down then, and he'll walk in Huck's money as easy as nothing."

"Yes, I reckon so, 'm. I don't see nothing in the way of it. Has **everybody quit** thinking the nigger done it?"

"Oh, no, not everybody. A good many thinks he done it. But they'll get the nigger **pretty** soon now, and maybe they can **scare** it out of him."

"Why, are they after him yet?"

"Well, you're **innocent**, ain't you! Does three hundred dollars lay around every day for people to pick up? Some folks think the nigger ain't far from here. I'm one of them--but I hain't **talked** it around. A **few** days **ago** I was talking with an old couple that lives next door in the **log shanty**, and they happened to say hardly **anybody** ever goes to that island over **yonder** that they call Jackson's Island. Don't anybody live there? says I. No, nobody, says they. I didn't say any more, but I done some thinking. I was pretty near certain I'd seen **smoke** over there, about the head of the island, a day or two before that, so I says to myself, like as not that nigger's **hiding** over there; anyway, says I, it's worth the trouble to give the place a hunt. I hain't seen any smoke sence, so I reckon maybe he's gone, if it was him; but husband's going over to see-- him and another man. He was gone up the river; but he got back to-day, and I told him as soon as he got here two hours ago."

Chinese Simplified

ago: 前，之前，以前.
anybody: 任何人.
blows: 打击.
bother: 烦扰，打扰，理会.
couple: 一对，挂钩，连接，夫妇，一双.
drunk: 喝了，喝醉.
evening: 晚，黄昏，傍晚，晚上.
everybody: 每个人，各位.
few: 少数，很少.
fixed: 固定，确定，一定，固定的.
hiding: 隐匿.
hunt: 打猎，狩猎.
innocent: 无辜，无罪的，天真.
lawsuit: 诉讼，官司，讼诉案.
log: 圆形木材，圆木，木头.
midnight: 午夜，半夜.
mighty: 伟大，强势，强大的.
murder: 谋杀，杀人案件，杀害.
pretty: 漂亮，美丽的，秀丽.
prove: 证明.
quit: 退出，退离.
reckon: 估计，计算.
scare: 恐慌.
shanty: 棚屋.
sly: 隐密，狡猾.
smoke: 烟，抽烟，烟雾，硝烟，吸烟，熏.
strangers: 陌生人.
talked: 谈话.
thinks: 想.
till: 直到.
yonder: 那边.

I had got so **uneasy** I couldn't set **still**. I had to do something with my hands; so I took up a **needle** off of the table and went to **threading** it. My hands **shook**, and I was making a bad job of it. When the woman **stopped** talking I looked up, and she was looking at me **pretty curious** and **smiling** a little. I put down the needle and thread, and let on to be **interested** --and I was, too--and says:

"Three hundred dollars is a power of money. I **wish** my mother could get it. Is your **husband** going over there to-night?"

"Oh, yes. He went up-town with the man I was telling you of, to get a **boat** and see if they could **borrow** another **gun**. They'll go over after **midnight**."

"Couldn't they see better if they was to **wait** till daytime?"

"Yes. And couldn't the nigger see better, too? After midnight he'll likely be **asleep**, and they can **slip** around through the **woods** and **hunt** up his **camp** fire all the better for the **dark**, if he's got one."

"I didn't think of that."

The woman **kept** looking at me pretty curious, and I didn't feel a bit **comfortable**. Pretty soon she says"

"What did you say your name was, honey?"

"M--Mary Williams."

Somehow it didn't seem to me that I said it was Mary before, so I didn't look up--seemed to me I said it was Sarah; so I felt sort of cornered, and was afeared **maybe** I was looking it, too. I wished the woman would say something more; the **longer** she set still the uneasier I was. But now she says:

"Honey, I thought you said it was Sarah when you first come in?"

"Oh, yes'm, I did. Sarah Mary Williams. Sarah's my first name. Some calls me Sarah, some calls me Mary."

"Oh, that's the way of it?"

"Yes'm."

I was **feeling** better then, but I wished I was out of there, **anyway**. I couldn't look up yet.

Chinese Simplified

anyway：无论如何，反正.
asleep：睡着，睡着的.
boat：小船，船，帆船，乘务员.
borrow：借.
camp：阵营，营，露营，安营.
comfortable：舒服，舒服的.
curious：有好奇心，好奇，好奇的.
dark：暗，黑暗，夜.
feeling：感觉，情绪，感情，情感，思绪.
gun：枪，炮，长枪.
hunt：打猎，狩猎.
husband：丈夫，爱人，老公.
interested：有兴趣，感兴趣的.
kept：收存.
longer：较长的.
maybe：或许，也许，或者，说不定，可能，不一定.
midnight：午夜，半夜.
needle：针，缝针.
pretty：漂亮，美丽的，秀丽.
shook：摇动.
slip：滑倒，溜走，溜.
smiling：微笑的.
somehow：不知何故.
stopped：停止.
thread：线，线索，细线，运作.
till：直到.
uneasy：不安，担心，不安的.
wait：等待，等，伺候.
wish：愿望，希望，意愿，祝，祝愿，志愿.
woods：树林，森林.

Well, the woman fell to talking about how hard times was, and how poor they had to live, and how the **rats** was as free as if they **owned** the place, and so **forth** and so on, and then I got easy again. She was right about the rats. You'd see one stick his nose out of a hole in the corner every little while. She said she had to have things **handy** to **throw** at them when she was alone, or they wouldn't give her no **peace**. She showed me a bar of **lead** twisted up into a **knot**, and said she was a good shot with it generly, but she'd wrenched her arm a day or two ago, and didn't know whether she could throw **true** now. But she watched for a chance, and **directly** banged away at a rat; but she missed him wide, and said "Ouch!" it **hurt** her arm so. Then she told me to try for the next one. I wanted to be getting away before the old man got back, but of course I didn't let on. I got the thing, and the first rat that showed his nose I let **drive**, and if he'd a **stayed** where he was he'd a been a **tolerable sick** rat. She said that was first-rate, and she **reckoned** I would **hive** the next one. She went and got the **lump** of lead and fetched it back, and **brought** along a hank of **yarn** which she wanted me to help her with. I **held** up my two hands and she put the hank over them, and went on talking about her and her husband's **matters**. But she broke off to say:

"Keep your eye on the rats. You better have the lead in your **lap**, handy."

So she dropped the lump into my lap just at that moment, and I clapped my legs together on it and she went on talking. But only about a minute. Then she took off the hank and looked me straight in the face, and very **pleasant**, and says:

"Come, now, what's your real name?"

"Wh--what, **mum**?"

"What's your real name? Is it Bill, or Tom, or Bob?--or what is it?"

I reckon I shook like a **leaf**, and I didn't know hardly what to do. But I says:

"Please to don't **poke fun** at a poor girl like me, mum. If I'm in the way here, I'll--"

"No, you won't. Set down and stay where you are. I ain't going to hurt you, and I ain't going to tell on you, nuther. You just tell me your secret, and **trust** me.

Chinese Simplified

brought：携带.
directly：直接地，一头，索性.
drive：驱动器，精神，驾车，驾驶，志气，驾.
forth：向前.
fun：娱乐.
handy：灵巧，便当，顺手，方便的，简便.
held：握住.
hive：蜂房，蜂巢，蜂箱.
hurt：伤害，使受伤.
knot：结，打结，疙瘩，节.
lap：一段行程，大腿，山坳，被包住.
lead：领导，铅，带领，主角，率领.
leaf：叶子，箔.
lump：块状，块，疙瘩.
matters：事，事宜.
mum：妈妈.
owned：拥有.
peace：和平.
pleasant：愉快，愉快的，舒适的.
poke：戳，拨开，插入.
rat：老鼠，鼠.
reckon：估计，计算.
sick：生病.
stayed：停留.
throw：扔，丢掉，丢，投.
tolerable：可容忍，可容忍的.
true：真实，确实，确有其事，真正，属实，对头，真正的.
trust：信任，信赖，委托，信托，威信.
yarn：毛线.

I'll keep it; and, what's more, I'll help you. So'll my old man if you want him to. You see, you're a **runaway** 'prentice, that's all. It ain't anything. There ain't no **harm** in it. You've been treated bad, and you made up your mind to cut. Bless you, child, I wouldn't tell on you. Tell me all about it now, that's a good boy."

So I said it wouldn't be no use to try to **play** it any longer, and I would just make a clean **breast** and tell her everything, but she musn't go back on her **promise**. Then I told her my father and mother was dead, and the law had **bound** me out to a mean old **farmer** in the country **thirty mile** back from the river, and he treated me so bad I couldn't stand it no longer; he went away to be gone a couple of days, and so I took my chance and **stole** some of his daughter's old clothes and cleared out, and I had been three nights coming the thirty miles. I **traveled** nights, and **hid** daytimes and **slept**, and the bag of bread and meat I carried from home lasted me all the way, and I had a-plenty. I said I believed my uncle Abner Moore would take care of me, and so that was why I **struck** out for this town of Goshen.

"Goshen, child? This ain't Goshen. This is St. Petersburg. Goshen's ten mile further up the river. Who told you this was Goshen?"

"Why, a man I **met** at **daybreak** this morning, just as I was going to turn into the **woods** for my regular sleep. He told me when the **roads** forked I must take the right hand, and five mile would **fetch** me to Goshen."

"He was **drunk**, I **reckon**. He told you just **exactly** wrong."

"Well, he did act like he was drunk, but it ain't no **matter** now. I got to be **moving** along. I'll fetch Goshen before daylight."

"Hold on a minute. I'll put you up a **snack** to eat. You might want it."

So she put me up a snack, and says:

"Say, when a cow's laying down, which end of her gets up first? Answer up **prompt** now--don't stop to study over it. Which end gets up first?"

"The **hind** end, mum."

"Well, then, a horse?"

Chinese Simplified

bound：限，边际，弹回，范围.
breast：奶子，乳房，胸，胸部.
daybreak：黎明，破晓.
drunk：喝了，喝醉.
exactly：刚好，就是，确切地，就，恰恰，可不是.
farmer：农人，农夫.
fetch：拿，取，带来.
harm：伤害，损害，坏处，害处，祸害.
hid：躲藏.
hind：后面的.
matter：事情，事，物质，事项.
met：遇见了.
mile：英里.
moving：感动，动态，动人，活动，乔迁.
play：表演，戏剧，游戏，玩，演出，戏，剧本，扮演，悬念，弹奏，奏.
promise：答应，约定，承诺，誓言，诺言，允诺.
prompt：提示，立刻，迅速的，敏捷的.
reckon：估计，计算.
roads：道路.
runaway：逃亡者，跑道.
slept：睡了.
snack：小吃，快餐，点心.
stole：偷了.
struck：敲打.
thirty：三十.
traveled：旅客多的.
woods：树林，森林.

"The for'rard end, mum."

"Which side of a tree does the **moss grow** on?"

"North side."

"If fifteen **cows** is **browsing** on a **hillside**, how many of them eats with their heads **pointed** the same direction?"

"The whole fifteen, mum."

"Well, I reckon you *have* lived in the country. I thought maybe you was trying to hocus me again. What's your real name, now?"

"**George** Peters, mum."

"Well, try to remember it, George. Don't forget and tell me it's Elexander before you go, and then get out by saying it's George Elexander when I catch you. And don't go about women in that old **calico**. You do a girl **tolerable** poor, but you might **fool** men, maybe. Bless you, child, when you set out to **thread** a **needle** don't hold the thread still and **fetch** the needle up to it; hold the needle still and **poke** the thread at it; that's the way a woman most always does, but a man always does t'other way. And when you throw at a **rat** or anything, **hitch** yourself up a **tiptoe** and fetch your hand up over your head as **awkward** as you can, and miss your rat about six or seven foot. Throw stiff-armed from the shoulder, like there was a **pivot** there for it to turn on, like a girl; not from the **wrist** and **elbow**, with your arm out to one side, like a boy. And, mind you, when a girl tries to catch anything in her **lap** she throws her knees apart; she don't **clap** them together, the way you did when you catched the **lump** of lead. Why, I **spotted** you for a boy when you was threading the needle; and I contrived the other things just to make certain. Now **trot** along to your uncle, Sarah Mary Williams George Elexander Peters, and if you get into trouble you send word to Mrs. Judith Loftus, which is me, and I'll do what I can to get you out of it. Keep the river road all the way, and next time you **tramp** take shoes and **socks** with you. The river road's a **rocky** one, and your feet'll be in a **condition** when you get to Goshen, I reckon."

Chinese Simplified

awkward: 笨拙，尴尬，不得劲，拙，迟钝的.
browsing: 浏览.
calico: 白布，白棉布.
clap: 拍手，拍.
condition: 条件，制约，状况，情况，地步.
cows: 母牛.
elbow: 肘，手肘.
fetch: 拿，取，带来.
fool: 呆子，笨蛋，傻子，笨人，愚人.
george: 乔治.
grow: 生长，增长，成长，种植.
hillside: 山坡.
hitch: 拴住，蹒跚.
lap: 一段行程，大腿，山坳，被包住.
lump: 块状，块，疙瘩.
moss: 苔藓，苔.
needle: 针，缝针.
pivot: 枢轴，支点，枢，枢纽.
pointed: 尖锐.
poke: 戳，拨开，插入.
rat: 老鼠，鼠.
rocky: 岩石的.
socks: 袜子，短袜.
spotted: 有斑点的.
thread: 线，线索，细线，运作.
tiptoe: 趾尖，蹑手蹑脚.
tolerable: 可容忍，可容忍的.
tramp: 沉重脚步.
trot: 快步跑，小跑.
wrist: 腕，腕部.

I went up the bank about fifty yards, and then I **doubled** on my **tracks** and **slipped** back to where my **canoe** was, a good piece below the house. I **jumped** in, and was off in a **hurry**. I went up-stream far enough to make the head of the island, and then started across. I took off the sun- **bonnet**, for I didn't want no blinders on then. When I was about the middle I heard the **clock** begin to **strike**, so I **stops** and **listens**; the sound come **faint** over the water but clear--eleven. When I **struck** the head of the island I never waited to **blow**, though I was most winded, but I shoved right into the **timber** where my old **camp** used to be, and started a good fire there on a high and **dry** spot.

Then I jumped in the canoe and **dug** out for our place, a **mile** and a half below, as hard as I could go. I **landed**, and slopped through the timber and up the **ridge** and into the **cavern**. There Jim laid, sound **asleep** on the ground. I **roused** him out and says:

"Git up and **hump** yourself, Jim! There ain't a minute to lose. They're after us!"

Jim never asked no questions, he never said a word; but the way he worked for the next half an hour showed about how he was scared. By that time everything we had in the world was on our **raft**, and she was ready to be shoved out from the **willow** cove where she was **hid**. We put out the camp fire at the cavern the first thing, and didn't show a **candle** outside after that.

I took the canoe out from the **shore** a little piece, and took a look; but if there was a boat around I couldn't see it, for stars and **shadows** ain't good to see by. Then we got out the raft and slipped along down in the **shade**, past the foot of the island dead still--never saying a word.

Chinese Simplified

asleep: 睡着，睡着的.
blow: 吹，打击.
bonnet: 苏格兰帽，阀盖，无边有带的女帽.
camp: 阵营，营，露营，安营.
candle: 蜡烛.
canoe: 独木舟.
cavern: 大地洞，大山洞.
clock: 钟，时钟，钟表.
doubled: 双，加倍努力.
dry: 索然，干燥，乾，干旱，乾燥.
dug: 挖掘.
faint: 暗淡，隐约，昏厥，微弱.
hid: 躲藏.
hump: 驼背.
hurry: 仓促，匆忙，赶忙.
jumped: 跳跃.
landed: 着陆.
listens: 听.
mile: 英里.
raft: 筏，木排，槎，桴.
ridge: 脊，屋脊，山脊，背脊.
roused: 激昂.
shade: 荫，荫凉，阴影，树阴.
shadows: 影子.
shore: 岸，滨，岸边，海岸，海滨.
slipped: 滑落.
stops: 停止.
strike: 罢工，打，敲打，敲，打击.
struck: 敲打.
timber: 木料，木材，木头.
tracks: 轨道.
willow: 柳树.

CHAPTER XII

"**BETTER** LET BLAME WELL ALONE"

It must a been close on to one o'clock when we got below the **island** at last, and the **raft** did seem to go **mighty slow**. If a **boat** was to come along we was going to take to the **canoe** and **break** for the Illinois **shore**; and it was well a boat didn't come, for we hadn't ever thought to put the **gun** in the canoe, or a fishing-line, or anything to **eat**. We was in ruther too much of a **sweat** to think of so many things. It warn't good **judgment** to put *everything* on the raft.

If the men went to the island I just **expect** they found the **camp** fire I **built**, and **watched** it all night for Jim to come. Anyways, they **stayed** away from us, and if my building the fire never fooled them it warn't no **fault** of **mine**. I played it as low down on them as I could.

When the first **streak** of day began to show we tied up to a towhead in a big **bend** on the Illinois side, and hacked off cottonwood **branches** with the **hatchet**, and covered up the raft with them so she looked like there had been a cave-in in the bank there. A tow-head is a sandbar that has cottonwoods on it as **thick** as harrow-teeth.

We had mountains on the Missouri shore and **heavy timber** on the Illinois side, and the **channel** was down the Missouri shore at that place, so we warn't

Chinese Simplified

bend：弯曲，弯折.
bet：打赌，赌.
boat：小船，船，帆船，乘务员.
branches：分支.
break：破坏，断，打破，犯，中断，破，裂.
built：建了.
camp：阵营，营，露营，安营.
canoe：独木舟.
channel：频道，通道，途径，海峡，渠.
eat：吃.
expect：预期，期待.
fault：故障，过失，缺点，毛病，断层，短处，缺陷.
gun：枪，炮，长枪.
hatchet：斧头，斧子.
heavy：重，沉重，笨重，沈重，沉闷.
island：岛.
judgment：判决，裁判，报应，判定，判断，裁.
mighty：伟大，强势，强大的.
mine：矿，我的，矿山，矿井.
raft：筏，木排，槎，桴.
shore：岸，滨，岸边，海岸，海滨.
slow：慢，缓慢，迟慢，迟钝，迟迟，迟缓.
stayed：停留.
streak：斑纹，线条.
sweat：汗，出汗，流汗.
thick：厚，密，浓厚.
timber：木料，木材，木头.
watch：观看，手表，监视.

afraid of anybody running across us. We laid there all day, and watched the **rafts** and **steamboats spin** down the Missouri **shore**, and up- bound steamboats **fight** the big river in the middle. I told Jim all about the time I had jabbering with that woman; and Jim said she was a **smart** one, and if she was to start after us **herself** she wouldn't set down and watch a camp fire--no, **sir**, she'd **fetch** a dog. Well, then, I said, why couldn't she tell her husband to fetch a dog? Jim said he bet she did think of it by the time the men was ready to start, and he believed they must a gone up-town to get a dog and so they lost all that time, or else we wouldn't be here on a towhead sixteen or **seventeen** mile below the village--no, indeedy, we would be in that same old town again. So I said I didn't care what was the reason they didn't get us as long as they didn't.

When it was beginning to come on dark we poked our heads out of the cottonwood **thicket**, and looked up and down and across; nothing in sight; so Jim took up some of the top planks of the raft and built a **snug wigwam** to get under in blazing weather and **rainy**, and to keep the things dry. Jim made a floor for the wigwam, and raised it a foot or more above the level of the raft, so now the **blankets** and all the traps was out of **reach** of steamboat waves. Right in the middle of the wigwam we made a layer of **dirt** about five or six **inches** deep with a **frame** around it for to hold it to its place; this was to build a fire on in sloppy weather or **chilly**; the wigwam would keep it from being seen. We made an **extra** steering-oar, too, because one of the others might get broke on a **snag** or something. We fixed up a short forked stick to hang the old **lantern** on, because we must always light the lantern whenever we see a steamboat coming down-stream, to keep from getting run over; but we wouldn't have to light it for up-stream boats **unless** we see we was in what they call a "crossing"; for the river was pretty high yet, very low banks being still a little under water; so up-bound boats didn't always run the channel, but hunted easy water.

This second night we run between seven and eight hours, with a current that was making over four mile an hour. We catched fish and talked, and we took a **swim** now and then to keep off **sleepiness**. It was kind of **solemn**, drifting down the big, still river, laying on our **backs** looking up at the stars, and we didn't ever

Chinese Simplified

backs: 支持.
blankets: 毛毯.
boats: 船舶.
chilly: 寒冷的.
dirt: 污垢.
extra: 额外，额外的.
fetch: 拿，取，带来.
fight: 打，打仗，斗争，斗，打架，战斗，奋斗.
frame: 框，帧，架，画面，陷害，边框，诬陷，架子，框架.
herself: 她自己.
inches: 英寸.
lantern: 灯笼.
raft: 筏，木排，槎，桴.
rafts: 木排.
rainy: 下雨，多雨的.
reach: 抵达，到达，抵，到.
seventeen: 十七.
shore: 岸，滨，岸边，海岸，海滨.
sir: 先生，爵士.
sleepiness: 睡意.
smart: 高明，时髦的.
snag: 故障，钉子，残干，根株.
snug: 舒适，舒适的.
solemn: 严肃，俨然，岸然，隆重，庄严的，庄重.
spin: 纺，旋转.
steamboat: 汽船，轮船.
swim: 游泳.
thicket: 丛林，灌木丛.
unless: 除非.
wigwam: 帐篷，陋棚.

feel like talking **loud**, and it warn't often that we laughed--only a **little** kind of a low **chuckle**. We had **mighty** good weather as a general thing, and nothing ever happened to us at all--that night, nor the next, nor the next.

Every night we passed towns, some of them away up on black hillsides, nothing but just a **shiny** bed of lights; not a house could you see. The **fifth** night we passed St. **Louis**, and it was like the whole world lit up. In St. Petersburg they used to say there was **twenty** or thirty thousand people in St. Louis, but I never believed it till I see that wonderful spread of lights at two o'clock that still night. There warn't a sound there; everybody was **asleep**.

Every night now I used to **slip ashore** towards ten o'clock at some little village, and **buy** ten or fifteen cents' worth of meal or **bacon** or other stuff to eat; and sometimes I lifted a **chicken** that warn't roosting comfortable, and took him along. Pap always said, take a chicken when you get a chance, because if you don't want him yourself you can easy find somebody that does, and a good **deed** ain't ever **forgot**. I never see pap when he didn't want the chicken himself, but that is what he used to say, anyway.

Mornings before **daylight** I **slipped** into **cornfields** and **borrowed** a **watermelon**, or a mushmelon, or a punkin, or some new corn, or things of that kind. Pap always said it warn't no harm to borrow things if you was **meaning** to pay them back some time; but the **widow** said it warn't anything but a soft name for **stealing**, and no **decent** body would do it. Jim said he reckoned the widow was **partly** right and pap was partly right; so the best way would be for us to pick out two or three things from the **list** and say we wouldn't borrow them any more--then he reckoned it wouldn't be no harm to borrow the others. So we talked it over all one night, drifting along down the river, trying to make up our minds whether to drop the watermelons, or the cantelopes, or the mushmelons, or what. But towards daylight we got it all settled **satisfactory**, and **concluded** to drop crabapples and p'simmons. We warn't feeling just right before that, but it was all comfortable now. I was glad the way it come out, too, because crabapples ain't ever good, and the p'simmons wouldn't be **ripe** for two or three months yet.

Chinese Simplified

ashore：岸上，上岸.
asleep：睡着，睡着的.
bacon：熏肉，咸肉，熏猪肉.
borrow：借.
buy：买，采买，购买.
chicken：鸡，小鸡.
chuckle：咯咯笑，暗笑.
concluded：结束.
corn：玉蜀黍，包谷，玉米.
daylight：日光，白天.
decent：像样，合适，像样的，正经.
deed：契据，行为.
fifth：第五.
forgot：忘记.
list：名单，列举，开列，目录，编目，列出，列表.
lit：点燃.
loud：高声，大声，大声的.
louis：路易斯.
meaning：意义，意思，含义，含意，意味着.
mighty：伟大，强势，强大的.
mornings：早晨.
partly：部分地.
ripe：熟，成熟.
satisfactory：满意的，称心，圆满.
shiny：发亮，闪亮，发亮的.
slip：滑倒，溜走，溜.
slipped：滑落.
stealing：偷垒，偷窃.
twenty：二十.
watermelon：西瓜.
widow：寡妇.

We shot a water-fowl now and then that got up too early in the morning or didn't go to bed early enough in the evening. Take it all round, we lived pretty high.

The fifth night below St. **Louis** we had a big **storm** after **midnight**, with a power of **thunder** and **lightning**, and the rain poured down in a solid sheet. We stayed in the **wigwam** and let the **raft** take care of itself. When the lightning glared out we could see a big straight river ahead, and high, **rocky** bluffs on both sides. By and by says I, "Hel-*lo*, Jim, looky yonder!" It was a **steamboat** that had killed herself on a rock. We was drifting straight down for her. The lightning showed her very **distinct**. She was leaning over, with part of her upper **deck** above water, and you could see every little chimbly-guy clean and clear, and a chair by the big bell, with an old slouch hat hanging on the back of it, when the flashes come.

Well, it being away in the night and **stormy**, and all so mysterious-like, I felt just the way any other boy would a felt when I see that **wreck** laying there so **mournful** and **lonesome** in the middle of the river. I wanted to get **aboard** of her and slink around a little, and see what there was there. So I says:

"Le's land on her, Jim."

But Jim was dead against it at first. He says:

"I doan' want to go fool'n 'long er no wrack. We's doin' **blame'** well, en we **better** let blame' well alone, as de good book says. Like as not dey's a **watchman** on dat wrack."

"Watchman your grandmother," I says; "there ain't nothing to watch but the **texas** and the pilot-house; and do you **reckon** anybody's going to resk his life for a texas and a pilot-house such a night as this, when it's likely to break up and **wash** off down the river any minute?" Jim couldn't say nothing to that, so he didn't try. "And besides," I says, "we might **borrow** something worth having out of the captain's stateroom. Seegars, I bet you--and cost five **cents apiece**, solid **cash**. Steamboat captains is always rich, and get **sixty** dollars a **month**, and *they* don't care a cent what a thing **costs**, you know, long as they want it. Stick a

Chinese Simplified

aboard: 船上，在车，上.
apiece: 各自，各自地.
bet: 打赌，赌.
blame: 责备，咎，非难，责任，罪，责怪，归咎.
borrow: 借.
cash: 现金，现款，现钱.
cent: 一分钱，分.
costs: 成本，费用.
deck: 甲板.
distinct: 明显，不同，清楚，独特，独特的，清晰，鲜明.
lightning: 闪电.
lonesome: 寂寞，寂寞的.
louis: 路易斯.
midnight: 午夜，半夜.
month: 月，月份.
mournful: 悲切，悲恸，悲恸的.
raft: 筏，木排，槎，桴.
reckon: 估计，计算.
rocky: 岩石的.
sixty: 六十.
steamboat: 汽船，轮船.
storm: 暴风雨，暴风，风暴.
stormy: 暴风雨的.
texas: 德克萨斯，得克萨斯.
thunder: 雷，雷声，打雷.
wash: 洗涤，洗刷，洗.
watchman: 看守者，更夫.
wigwam: 帐篷，陋棚.
wreck: 破坏，摧毁，祸害，糟蹋.

candle in your pocket; I can't rest, Jim, till we give her a rummaging. Do you reckon Tom Sawyer would ever go by this thing? Not for **pie**, he wouldn't. He'd call it an adventure--that's what he'd call it; and he'd **land** on that **wreck** if it was his last act. And wouldn't he throw style into it? --wouldn't he spread himself, nor nothing? Why, you'd think it was Christopher C'lumbus **discovering** Kingdom-Come. I wish Tom Sawyer *was* here."

Jim he grumbled a little, but give in. He said we mustn't talk any more than we could help, and then talk **mighty** low. The **lightning** showed us the wreck again just in time, and we fetched the stabboard derrick, and made fast there.

The **deck** was high out here. We went **sneaking** down the **slope** of it to labboard, in the dark, towards the **texas**, feeling our way slow with our feet, and **spreading** our hands out to fend off the guys, for it was so dark we couldn't see no sign of them. Pretty soon we **struck** the **forward** end of the **skylight**, and clumb on to it; and the next step fetched us in front of the captain's door, which was open, and by Jimminy, away down through the texas-hall we see a light! and all in the same second we seem to hear low voices in **yonder**!

Jim whispered and said he was feeling powerful sick, and told me to come along. I says, all right, and was going to start for the **raft**; but just then I heard a voice **wail** out and say:

"Oh, please don't, boys; I **swear** I won't ever tell!"

Another voice said, pretty **loud**:

"It's a lie, Jim Turner. You've acted this way before. You always want more'n your **share** of the truck, and you've always got it, too, because you've **swore** 't if you didn't you'd tell. But this time you've said it **jest** one time too many. You're the meanest, treacherousest **hound** in this country."

By this time Jim was gone for the raft. I was just a-biling with **curiosity**; and I says to myself, Tom Sawyer wouldn't back out now, and so I won't either; I'm a-going to see what's going on here. So I dropped on my hands and knees in the little **passage**, and **crept** aft in the dark till there warn't but one stateroom **betwixt** me and the cross-hall of the texas. Then in there I see a man **stretched** on

Chinese Simplified

aft：在船尾．
betwixt：中间，在…之间．
candle：蜡烛．
crept：爬行．
curiosity：好奇心．
deck：甲板．
discovering：发现．
forward：向前，前言，在前，引言，前进的．
hound：猎犬．
jest：玩笑，笑话，戏弄，戏谑．
land：土地，着陆，陆地．
lightning：闪电．
loud：高声，大声，大声的．
mighty：伟大，强势，强大的．
passage：通道，通路，通过．
pie：馅饼．
raft：筏，木排，槎，桴．
share：部分，股，部份，股票，分享，共享，股份．
skylight：天窗．
slope：倾斜，坡，采场，斜坡．
sneaking：鬼鬼祟祟的．
spreading：撒，散布，传播，展开，扩展．
stretched：伸展．
swear：立誓，发誓．
swore：立誓．
texas：德克萨斯，得克萨斯．
truck：卡车．
wail：哀号，哀泣，哀鸣，呜咽．
wreck：破坏，摧毁，祸害，糟蹋．
yonder：那边．

the floor and tied hand and **foot**, and two men **standing** over him, and one of them had a **dim lantern** in his hand, and the other one had a **pistol**. This one kept **pointing** the pistol at the man's head on the floor, and saying:

"I'd *like* to! And I orter, too--a mean skunk!"

The man on the floor would **shrivel** up and say, "Oh, please don't, **Bill**; I hain't ever goin' to tell."

And every time he said that the man with the lantern would **laugh** and say:

"'Deed you *ain't*! You never said no truer thing 'n that, you **bet** you." And once he said: "Hear him **beg**! and yit if we hadn't got the best of him and tied him he'd a **killed** us both. And what *for*? Jist for noth'n. Jist because we stood on our *rights*--that's what for. But I lay you ain't a-goin' to **threaten nobody** any more, Jim Turner. Put *up* that pistol, Bill."

Bill says:

"I don't want to, Jake Packard. I'm for killin' him--and didn't he kill old Hatfield jist the same way and don't he **deserve** it?"

"But I don't *want* him killed, and I've got my reasons for it."

"**Bless** yo' heart for them words, Jake Packard! I'll never forgit you long's I live!" says the man on the floor, sort of blubbering.

Packard didn't take no **notice** of that, but **hung** up his lantern on a **nail** and started towards where I was there in the **dark**, and motioned Bill to come. I crawfished as **fast** as I could about two **yards**, but the **boat slanted** so that I couldn't make very good time; so to keep from getting run over and catched I crawled into a stateroom on the **upper** side. The man came a-pawing along in the dark, and when Packard got to my stateroom, he says:

"Here--come in here."

And in he come, and Bill after him. But before they got in I was up in the upper **berth**, cornered, and sorry I come. Then they stood there, with their hands on the **ledge** of the berth, and **talked**. I couldn't see them, but I could tell where they was by the **whisky** they'd been having. I was **glad** I didn't **drink** whisky;

Chinese Simplified

beg: 恳求，乞求，要求.
berth: 泊位，卧位，床位，卧铺.
bet: 打赌，赌.
bill: 法案，帐单，账单，发单.
bless: 保佑，庇佑，祝福.
boat: 小船，船，帆船，乘务员.
dark: 暗，黑暗，夜.
deserve: 应得.
dim: 阴暗，暗淡，暗淡的.
drink: 喝，饮用，饮，饮料.
fast: 快，禁食，快速，迅速，速.
foot: 脚，足，步兵，英尺，呎.
glad: 高兴，高兴的.
hung: 挂.
kill: 打死，杀害，杀死.
killed: 被屠宰的，被杀死的.
lantern: 灯笼.
laugh: 笑.
ledge: 壁架，矿脉.
nail: 钉，指甲，钉子.
nobody: 没有人，没人.
notice: 通知，注意，布告，注意到，启事.
pistol: 手枪.
pointing: 指，瞄准.
shrivel: 起皱纹.
slanted: 倾斜.
standing: 站立，地位.
talked: 谈话.
threaten: 威胁.
upper: 帮子，上面的.
whisky: 威士忌酒.
yards: 场地.

but it wouldn't made much difference anyway, because most of the time they couldn't a treed me because I didn't **breathe**. I was too scared. And, **besides**, a body *couldn't* breathe and hear such talk. They **talked** low and **earnest**. Bill wanted to **kill** Turner. He says:

"He's said he'll tell, and he will. If we was to give both our **shares** to him *now* it wouldn't make no difference after the **row** and the way we've served him. Shore's you're **born**, he'll turn State's evidence; now you hear *me*. I'm for putting him out of his troubles."

"So'm I," says Packard, very quiet.

"Blame it, I'd **sorter begun** to think you wasn't. Well, then, that's all right. Le's go and do it."

"Hold on a minute; I hain't had my say yit. You **listen** to me. Shooting's good, but there's quieter ways if the thing's *got* to be done. But what I say is this: it ain't good sense to go court'n around after a **halter** if you can git at what you're up to in some way that's jist as good and at the same time don't bring you into no resks. Ain't that so?"

"You **bet** it is. But how you goin' to **manage** it this time?"

"Well, my idea is this: we'll **rustle** around and **gather** up whatever pickins we've overlooked in the staterooms, and **shove** for **shore** and **hide** the **truck**. Then we'll wait. Now I say it ain't a-goin' to be more'n two hours befo' this wrack **breaks** up and **washes** off down the river. See? He'll be drownded, and won't have **nobody** to **blame** for it but his own **self**. I **reckon** that's a considerble sight better 'n killin' of him. I'm **unfavorable** to killin' a man as long as you can git aroun' it; it ain't good sense, it ain't good **morals**. Ain't I right?"

"Yes, I reck'n you are. But s'pose she *don't* break up and wash off?"

"Well, we can wait the two hours anyway and see, can't we?"

"All right, then; come along."

Chinese Simplified

begun: 开始.
besides: 此外, 另外, 除了, 并且, 再说, 况且.
bet: 打赌, 赌.
blame: 责备, 咎, 非难, 责任, 罪, 责怪, 归咎.
born: 出生, 天生的.
breaks: 中断.
breathe: 呼吸.
earnest: 认真.
gather: 集合, 聚集, 采集, 集聚, 集会, 召集, 搜集, 捡, 聚会.
halter: 缰绳.
hide: 躲藏, 暗藏, 掩饰, 藏, 隐瞒, 隐藏.
kill: 打死, 杀害, 杀死.
listen: 听, 倾听.
manage: 符合, 管理, 处理.
morals: 道德.
nobody: 没有人, 没人.
reckon: 估计, 计算.
row: 一排, 划, 行.
rustle: 瑟瑟.
self: 自己, 自, 自我, 我.
shares: 股.
shore: 岸, 滨, 岸边, 海岸, 海滨.
shove: 推.
sorter: 分类者.
talked: 谈话.
truck: 卡车.
unfavorable: 不利, 不利的.
wash: 洗涤, 洗刷, 洗.
washes: 洗涤.

So they **started**, and I **lit** out, all in a **cold sweat**, and **scrambled forward**. It was **dark** as **pitch** there; but I said, in a kind of a **coarse whisper**, "Jim !" and he **answered** up, right at my **elbow**, with a sort of a **moan**, and I says:

"Quick, Jim, it ain't no time for fooling around and moaning; there's a **gang** of murderers in **yonder**, and if we don't **hunt** up their **boat** and set her drifting down the **river** so these fellows can't get away from the **wreck** there's one of 'em going to be in a **bad fix**. But if we find their boat we can put *all* of 'em in a bad fix--for the **sheriff** 'll get 'em. Quick--hurry! I'll hunt the labboard side, you hunt the stabboard. You start at the **raft**, and--"

"Oh, my lordy, lordy! *raf*? Dey ain' no raf' no mo'; she done **broke loose** en **gone** I--en here we is!"

Chinese Simplified

answered：回答.
bad：坏，糟糕，不良，不善，淘气，坏的.
boat：小船，船，帆船，乘务员.
broke：打破.
coarse：粗劣，粗糙的，淫秽，粗鲁.
cold：冷，感冒，寒冷，寒，冷淡.
dark：暗，黑暗，夜.
elbow：肘，手肘.
fix：安装，奠定，固定，修理.
forward：向前，前言，在前，引言，前进的.
gang：一群，帮.
gone：去.
hunt：打猎，狩猎.
lit：点燃.
loose：松开，松弛的.
moan：悲叹.
pitch：沥青，投，音调.
raft：筏，木排，槎，桴.
river：河，江，川，河流，条.
scrambled：攀登，扰频.
sheriff：郡治安官，行政司法长官.
started：开始.
sweat：汗，出汗，流汗.
whisper：耳语，低语.
wreck：破坏，摧毁，祸害，糟蹋.
yonder：那边.

CHAPTER XIII

HONEST LOOT FROM THE *WALTER SCOTT*

Well, I catched my **breath** and most **fainted**. Shut up on a **wreck** with such a **gang** as that! But it warn't no time to be sentimentering. We'd *got* to find that **boat** now--had to have it for **ourselves**. So we went a-quaking and **shaking** down the stabboard side, and **slow** work it was, too--seemed a week before we got to the **stern**. No sign of a boat. Jim said he didn't believe he could go any further--so scared he hadn't hardly any strength left, he said. But I said, come on, if we get left on this wreck we are in a **fix**, sure. So on we prowled again. We **struck** for the stern of the **texas**, and found it, and then scrabbled along forwards on the **skylight**, **hanging** on from **shutter** to shutter, for the **edge** of the skylight was in the water. When we got **pretty** close to the cross-hall door there was the **skiff**, sure enough! I could just **barely** see her. I felt ever so **thankful**. In another second I would a been **aboard** of her, but just then the door **opened**. One of the men **stuck** his head out only about a couple of **foot** from me, and I thought I was gone; but he jerked it in again, and says:

"Heave that **blame lantern** out o' **sight**, Bill!"

He flung a **bag** of something into the boat, and then got in himself and set down. It was Packard. Then Bill *he* come out and got in. Packard says, in a low voice:

Chinese Simplified

aboard: 船上，在车，上.
bag: 袋子，袋，手提包，提包，囊.
barely: 仅仅，仅.
blame: 责备，咎，非难，责任，罪，责怪，归咎.
boat: 小船，船，帆船，乘务员.
breath: 气息，鼻息，呼吸，气流.
edge: 边缘，边，边沿，棱，沿儿.
fainted: 昏厥.
fix: 安装，奠定，固定，修理.
foot: 脚，足，步兵，英尺，呎.
gang: 一群，帮.
hang: 挂，悬挂.
lantern: 灯笼.
opened: 打开.
ourselves: 我们自己，我们.
pretty: 漂亮，美丽的，秀丽.
shaking: 摇动.
shutter: 百叶窗.
sight: 视觉，景象，情景，目光，视力，视线.
skiff: 小船，小艇.
skylight: 天窗.
slow: 慢，缓慢，迟慢，迟钝，迟迟，迟缓.
stern: 严竣，严厉的，船尾.
struck: 敲打.
stuck: 黏贴.
texas: 德克萨斯，得克萨斯.
thankful: 感谢，感谢的.
truck: 卡车.
wreck: 破坏，摧毁，祸害，糟蹋.

"All ready--shove off!"

I couldn't hardly **hang** on to the shutters, I was so **weak**. But Bill says:

"Hold on--'d you go through him?"

"No. Didn't you?"

"No. So he's got his share o' the cash yet."

"Well, then, come along; no use to take **truck** and leave money."

"Say, won't he **suspicion** what we're up to?"

"Maybe he won't. But we got to have it anyway. Come along."

So they got out and went in.

The door slammed to because it was on the careened side; and in a half second I was in the **boat**, and Jim come **tumbling** after me. I out with my **knife** and cut the **rope**, and away we went!

We didn't touch an **oar**, and we didn't speak nor **whisper**, nor hardly even **breathe**. We went **gliding swift** along, dead **silent**, past the **tip** of the paddle-box, and past the **stern**; then in a second or two more we was a hundred **yards** below the **wreck**, and the **darkness** soaked her up, every last sign of her, and we was safe, and knowed it.

When we was three or four hundred yards down-stream we see the **lantern** show like a little **spark** at the **texas** door for a second, and we knowed by that that the rascals had missed their boat, and was beginning to understand that they was in just as much trouble now as Jim Turner was.

Then Jim **manned** the oars, and we took out after our **raft**. Now was the first time that I **begun** to **worry** about the men--I **reckon** I hadn't had time to before. I begun to think how **dreadful** it was, even for **murderers**, to be in such a **fix**. I says to myself, there ain't no telling but I might come to be a murderer myself yet, and then how would I like it? So says I to Jim:

"The first light we see we'll land a hundred yards below it or above it, in a place where it's a good hiding-place for you and the **skiff**, and then I'll go and fix

Chinese Simplified

begun: 开始.
boat: 小船, 船, 帆船, 乘务员.
breathe: 呼吸.
darkness: 黑暗.
dreadful: 可怕, 恐怖的.
fix: 安装, 奠定, 固定, 修理.
gliding: 滑行的, 下滑.
hang: 挂, 悬挂.
knife: 刀子, 刀, 餐刀.
lantern: 灯笼.
manned: 由人操纵.
murderer: 凶手, 杀人犯.
oar: 桨.
raft: 筏, 木排, 槎, 桴.
reckon: 估计, 计算.
rope: 绳索, 绳子.
silent: 无声, 沉默的.
skiff: 小船, 小艇.
spark: 触发, 火花.
stern: 严竣, 严厉的, 船尾.
suspicion: 疑心, 怀疑, 嫌疑.
swift: 迅速的.
texas: 德克萨斯, 得克萨斯.
tip: 小费, 尖端, 尾端.
truck: 卡车.
tumbling: 摔倒.
weak: 衰弱, 瘫软, 脆弱, 薄弱, 虚弱, 虚弱的, 软弱, 微弱.
whisper: 耳语, 低语.
worry: 担心, 使烦恼, 缠绕, 担忧, 心事, 担, 烦恼, 着急.
wreck: 破坏, 摧毁, 祸害, 糟蹋.
yards: 场地.

up some kind of a **yarn**, and get somebody to go for that **gang** and get them out of their **scrape**, so they can be **hung** when their time comes."

But that idea was a **failure**; for pretty soon it begun to **storm** again, and this time **worse** than ever. The rain poured down, and never a light showed; everybody in bed, I **reckon**. We **boomed** along down the river, watching for lights and watching for our **raft**. After a long time the rain let up, but the clouds stayed, and the **lightning** kept whimpering, and by and by a **flash** showed us a black thing ahead, **floating**, and we made for it.

It was the raft, and **mighty** glad was we to get **aboard** of it again. We seen a light now away down to the right, on **shore**. So I said I would go for it. The **skiff** was half full of **plunder** which that gang had **stole** there on the **wreck**. We hustled it on to the raft in a **pile**, and I told Jim to float along down, and show a light when he judged he had gone about two mile, and keep it burning till I come; then I **manned** my oars and shoved for the light. As I got down towards it three or four more showed--up on a **hillside**. It was a village. I closed in above the shore light, and laid on my oars and floated. As I went by I see it was a **lantern** hanging on the jackstaff of a double-hull ferryboat. I skimmed around for the **watchman**, a-wondering **whereabouts** he **slept**; and by and by I found him roosting on the bitts forward, with his head down between his **knees**. I gave his shoulder two or three little shoves, and begun to cry.

He stirred up in a kind of a startlish way; but when he see it was only me he took a good gap and **stretch**, and then he says:

"Hello, what's up? Don't cry, bub. What's the trouble?"

I says:

"Pap, and mam, and sis, and--"

Then I broke down. He says:

"Oh, dang it now, *don't* take on so; we all has to have our **troubles**, and this 'n 'll come out all right. What's the matter with 'em?"

"They're--they're--are you the watchman of the boat?"

Chinese Simplified

aboard: 船上，在车，上.
boomed: 繁荣.
failure: 失败.
flash: 闪光，晃.
float: 漂浮.
floating: 漂浮的，移动的，浮动的，飘浮.
gang: 一群，帮.
hillside: 山坡.
hung: 挂.
knees: 膝盖.
lantern: 灯笼.
lightning: 闪电.
manned: 由人操纵.
mighty: 伟大，强势，强大的.
pile: 一堆，桩，堆.
plunder: 掠夺，抢劫，抢夺.
raft: 筏，木排，槎，桴.
reckon: 估计，计算.
scrape: 刮掉，削刮.
shore: 岸，滨，岸边，海岸，海滨.
skiff: 小船，小艇.
slept: 睡了.
stole: 偷了.
storm: 暴风雨，暴风，风暴.
stretch: 张开，拉紧，伸展，伸.
troubles: 坏处，麻烦.
watchman: 看守者，更夫.
whereabouts: 行踪，下落，所在之处.
worse: 更坏，更糟.
wreck: 破坏，摧毁，祸害，糟蹋.
yarn: 毛线.

"Yes," he says, kind of pretty-well-satisfied like. "I'm the **captain** and the **owner** and the **mate** and the **pilot** and **watchman** and head deck-hand; and sometimes I'm the **freight** and **passengers**. I ain't as **rich** as old Jim Hornback, and I can't be so **blame' generous** and good to Tom, Dick, and Harry as what he is, and **slam** around money the way he does; but I've told him a many a time 't I wouldn't **trade places** with him; for, says I, a sailor's life's the life for me, and I'm derned if *I'd* live two **mile** out o' town, where there ain't nothing ever goin' on, not for all his spondulicks and as much more on top of it. Says I--"

I **broke** in and says:

"They're in an **awful peck** of **trouble**, and--"

"*Who* is?"

"Why, pap and mam and sis and Miss Hooker; and if you'd take your ferryboat and go up there--"

"Up where? Where are they?"

"On the wreck."

"What wreck?"

"Why, there ain't but one."

"What, you don't mean the Walter Scott?"

"Yes."

"Good land! what are they doin' *there*, for **gracious** sakes?"

"Well, they didn't go there a-purpose."

"I **bet** they didn't! Why, great **goodness**, there ain't no **chance** for 'em if they don't git off **mighty quick**! Why, how in the **nation** did they ever git into such a scrape?"

"**Easy** enough. Miss Hooker was a-visiting up there to the town--"

"Yes, Booth's Landing--go on."

"She was a-visiting there at Booth's Landing, and just in the **edge** of the evening she **started** over with her nigger woman in the horse-ferry to **stay** all

Chinese Simplified

awful：可怕，可怕的．
bet：打赌，赌．
blame：责备，咎，非难，责任，罪，责怪，归咎．
broke：打破．
captain：队长，舰长，领队．
chance：机会．
easy：容易，轻而易举，简易，安逸，便利，便当，容易的，纵横．
edge：边缘，边，边沿，棱，沿儿．
freight：货物运输．
generous：大方，雍容大度，慷慨，慷慨的．
goodness：美德．
gracious：亲切，亲切的，有礼貌的．
mate：伴侣，配偶，伙伴．
mighty：伟大，强势，强大的．
mile：英里．
nation：国家．
owner：物主，业主，所有者，所有人，主人．
passengers：旅客．
peck：啄．
pilot：飞行员，驾驶员，飞机师．
places：地方．
quick：快，玲珑，敏捷的，迅速的．
rich：富有，丰富，富有的，充实．
slam：猛撞，猛力关．
started：开始．
stay：延缓，逗留，停留．
trade：贸易，商业，经贸．
trouble：麻烦，难度，难处．
watchman：看守者，更夫．

night at her friend's house, Miss What-you-may-call-her I disremember her name--and they lost their steering-oar, and **swung** around and went a- **floating** down, **stern** first, about two **mile**, and saddle-baggsed on the **wreck**, and the ferryman and the nigger woman and the horses was all lost, but Miss Hooker she made a **grab** and got **aboard** the wreck. Well, about an hour after dark we come along down in our trading-scow, and it was so dark we didn't notice the wreck **till** we was right on it; and so *we* saddle-baggsed; but all of us was saved but Bill Whipple--and oh, he *was* the best cretur !--I most wish 't it had been me, I do."

"My George! It's the beatenest thing I ever **struck**. And *then* what did you all do?"

"Well, we hollered and took on, but it's so wide there we couldn't make nobody hear. So pap said somebody got to get **ashore** and get help **somehow**. I was the only one that could **swim**, so I made a **dash** for it, and Miss Hooker she said if I didn't **strike** help sooner, come here and **hunt** up her **uncle**, and he'd **fix** the thing. I made the land about a mile below, and been **fooling** along ever since, trying to get people to do something, but they said, 'What, in such a night and such a current? There ain't no sense in it; go for the **steam** ferry.' Now if you'll go and--"

"By Jackson, I'd *like* to, and, **blame** it, I don't know but I will; but who in the dingnation's a-going' to *pay* for it? Do you **reckon** your pap--"

"Why *that*'s all right. Miss Hooker she tole me, *particular*, that her uncle Hornback--"

"Great **guns**! is *he* her uncle? Looky here, you break for that light over yonder-way, and turn out **west** when you git there, and about a quarter of a mile out you'll come to the **tavern**; tell 'em to **dart** you out to Jim Hornback's, and he'll foot the bill. And don't you fool around any, because he'll want to know the **news**. Tell him I'll have his **niece** all safe before he can get to town. Hump yourself, now; I'm a-going up around the corner here to roust out my engineer."

I struck for the light, but as soon as he turned the corner I went back and got into my **skiff** and bailed her out, and then pulled up shore in the easy water

Chinese Simplified

aboard: 船上，在车，上.
ashore: 岸上，上岸.
blame: 责备，咎，非难，责任，罪，责怪，归咎.
dart: 镖，投射.
dash: 冲撞，猛冲，短跑.
fix: 安装，奠定，固定，修理.
floating: 漂浮的，移动的，浮动的，飘浮.
fool: 呆子，笨蛋，傻子，笨人，愚人.
grab: 抓住，攫取，抓斗.
guns: 枪支.
hunt: 打猎，狩猎.
mile: 英里.
news: 新闻，信息，消息.
niece: 侄女，甥女.
reckon: 估计，计算.
shore: 岸，滨，岸边，海岸，海滨.
skiff: 小船，小艇.
somehow: 不知何故.
steam: 蒸汽，热气，废气，蒸.
stern: 严竣，严厉的，船尾.
strike: 罢工，打，敲打，敲，打击.
struck: 敲打.
swim: 游泳.
swung: 摇摆.
tavern: 客栈，酒馆.
till: 直到.
uncle: 叔叔，伯伯，叔父，大爷，老大爷，姑夫.
west: 西，西面，西方.
wreck: 破坏，摧毁，祸害，糟蹋.

about six hundred **yards**, and tucked myself in among some woodboats; for I couldn't rest easy **till** I could see the ferryboat start. But take it all around, I was feeling ruther **comfortable** on **accounts** of taking all this trouble for that **gang**, for not many would a done it. I wished the **widow** knowed about it. I judged she would be **proud** of me for **helping** these rapscallions, because rapscallions and dead **beats** is the kind the widow and good people takes the most interest in.

Well, before long here comes the **wreck**, **dim** and **dusky**, sliding along down! A kind of cold **shiver** went through me, and then I **struck** out for her. She was very deep, and I see in a minute there warn't much chance for anybody being **alive** in her. I pulled all around her and hollered a little, but there wasn't any **answer**; all dead still. I felt a little bit **heavy**-hearted about the gang, but not much, for I reckoned if they could stand it I could.

Then here comes the ferryboat; so I shoved for the middle of the river on a long down-stream **slant**; and when I judged I was out of eye-reach I **laid** on my oars, and looked back and see her go and **smell** around the wreck for Miss Hooker's remainders, because the captain would know her **uncle** Hornback would want them; and then pretty soon the ferryboat give it up and went for the **shore**, and I laid into my work and went a-booming down the river.

It did seem a powerful long time before Jim's light showed up; and when it did show it looked like it was a thousand **mile** off. By the time I got there the sky was beginning to get a little **gray** in the **east**; so we struck for an island, and **hid** the **raft**, and **sunk** the **skiff**, and turned in and slept like dead people.

Chinese Simplified

accounts: 据闻.
alive: 活着, 活, 活泼的, 活着的.
answer: 回答, 解答, 答案, 答复, 答, 响应, 适合, 负责, 符合.
beats: 节奏.
comfortable: 舒服, 舒服的.
dim: 阴暗, 暗淡, 暗淡的.
dusky: 昏暗, 昏暗的.
east: 东, 东方.
gang: 一群, 帮.
gray: 灰色, 灰.
heavy-**hearted**: 心情沉重.
helping: 帮助人的, 辅助的, 帮助.
hid: 躲藏.
laid: 放.
mile: 英里.
proud: 傲岸, 骄矜, 骄傲的, 自豪的.
raft: 筏, 木排, 槎, 桴.
shiver: 发抖, 颤抖, 哆嗦.
shore: 岸, 滨, 岸边, 海岸, 海滨.
skiff: 小船, 小艇.
slant: 倾斜.
slept: 睡了.
smell: 嗅, 臭, 香味.
struck: 敲打.
sunk: 沉没.
till: 直到.
uncle: 叔叔, 伯伯, 叔父, 大爷, 老大爷, 姑夫.
widow: 寡妇.
wreck: 破坏, 摧毁, 祸害, 糟蹋.
yards: 场地.

CHAPTER XIV

WAS SOLOMON WISE?

By and by, when we got up, we turned over the **truck** the **gang** had **stole** off of the **wreck**, and found **boots**, and **blankets**, and **clothes**, and all **sorts** of other things, and a lot of books, and a spyglass, and three boxes of seegars. We hadn't ever been this **rich** before in **neither** of our lives. The seegars was prime. We **laid** off all the **afternoon** in the **woods** **talking**, and me **reading** the books, and having a general good time. I told Jim all about what happened inside the wreck and at the ferryboat, and I said these kinds of things was **adventures**; but he said he didn't want no more adventures. He said that when I went in the **texas** and he crawled back to get on the **raft** and found her gone he nearly died, because he judged it was all up with *him* anyway it could be **fixed**; for if he didn't get saved he would get drownded; and if he did get saved, **whoever** saved him would send him back home so as to get the **reward**, and then Miss Watson would sell him South, sure. Well, he was right; he was most always right; he had an **uncommon** level head for a nigger.

I read considerable to Jim about **kings** and dukes and earls and such, and how **gaudy** they dressed, and how much style they put on, and called each other your **majesty**, and your **grace**, and your **lordship**, and so on, 'stead of **mister**; and Jim's eyes bugged out, and he was **interested**. He says:

Chinese Simplified

adventures：冒险．
afternoon：下午，午后．
blankets：毛毯．
boots：靴子．
clothes：衣服，服装，西装，件，衣裳．
fixed：固定，确定，一定，固定的．
gang：一群，帮．
gaudy：花哨，花里胡哨．
grace：优雅，恩典，天恩，魅力，宽限．
interested：有兴趣，感兴趣的．
king：国王，王．
kings：国王．
laid：放．
lordship：贵族身份．
majesty：威严．
mister：先生．
neither：也不，二者，两者都不是．
raft：筏，木排，槎，桴．
reading：读物，读数．
reward：报酬，酬劳，酬金，奖励，奖赏．
rich：富有，丰富，富有的，充实．
sorts：种类．
stole：偷了．
texas：德克萨斯，得克萨斯．
truck：卡车．
uncommon：稀有，稀有的．
whoever：无论何人．
woods：树林，森林．
wreck：破坏，摧毁，祸害，糟蹋．

"I didn' know **dey** was so many un um. I hain't **hearn** 'bout **none** un um, skasely, but ole King Sollermun, onless you counts dem **kings** dat's in a **pack** er k'yards. How much do a king git?"

"Get?" I says; "why, they get a **thousand** dollars a **month** if they want it; they can have just as much as they want; everything belongs to them."

"*Ain'* dat **gay**? En what dey got to do, Huck?"

"*They* don't do nothing! Why, how you **talk**! They just set around."

"No; is dat so?"

"Of course it is. They just set around--except, **maybe**, when there's a war; then they go to the war. But other times they just **lazy** around; or go hawking--just hawking and sp--Sh!--d' you hear a noise?"

We skipped out and looked; but it warn't nothing but the **flutter** of a steamboat's **wheel** away down, **coming** around the point; so we come back.

"Yes," says I, "and other times, when things is **dull**, they **fuss** with the parlyment; and if **everybody** don't go just so he whacks their **heads** off. But **mostly** they **hang** round the harem."

"Roun' de which?"

"Harem."

"What's de harem?"

"The place where he **keeps** his wives. Don't you know about the harem? **Solomon** had one; he had about a million wives."

"Why, yes, dat's so; I--I'd done **forgot** it. A harem's a bo'd'n-house, I reck'n. Mos' likely dey has **rackety** times in de nussery. En I reck'n de wives **quarrels** considable; en dat 'crease de racket. Yit dey say Sollermun de **wises'** man dat ever **live'**. I doan' take no **stock** in dat. Bekase why: would a wise man want to live in de mids' er sich a blim- blammin' all de time? No--'deed he wouldn't. A wise man 'ud take en buil' a biler-factry; en **den** he could shet *down* de biler-factry when he want to res'."

Chinese Simplified

coming：未来，到来.
de：可选择丢弃.
den：窝.
dull：索然，板滞，沉闷的，干燥，拙，深沉.
everybody：每个人，各位.
flutter：飘扬，颤动，振翅.
forgot：忘记.
fuss：大惊小怪.
gay：欢乐，快活，快乐的，基佬.
hang：挂，悬挂.
heads：头.
hear：听见，听取，听.
keeps：保持.
king：国王，王.
kings：国王.
lazy：懒惰，懒惰的.
live：住，活，居住.
maybe：或许，也许，或者，说不定，可能，不一定.
month：月，月份.
mostly：大多，多半，大部份.
none：无，没有.
pack：包装，包扎，包，背包.
quarrels：争吵.
racket：球拍，拍子.
rackety：喧闹的.
solomon：所罗门.
stock：存货，股票，股份，库存.
talk：谈话，报告，言语，谈.
thousand：千.
wheel：轮子，轮，车轮.
wise：高明，明智的，英明.

"Well, but he *was* the **wisest** man, anyway; because the **widow** she told me so, her own self."

"I doan k'yer what de widder say, he *warn't* no wise man nuther. He had some er de dad-fetchedes' ways I ever see. Does you know 'bout dat **chile** dat he 'uz gwyne to **chop** in two?"

"Yes, the widow told me all about it."

"*Well*, **den**! Warn' dat de beatenes' **notion** in de worl'? You jes' take en look at it a **minute**. Dah's de **stump**, dah--dat's one er de women; heah's you--dat's de yuther one; I's Sollermun; en **dish** yer **dollar bill's** de chile. Bofe un you claims it. What does I do? Does I **shin** aroun' mongs' de neighbors en fine out which un you de bill *do* b'long to, en han' it over to de right one, all **safe** en soun', de way dat **anybody** dat had any gumption would? No; I take en **whack** de bill in *two*, en give half un it to you, en de yuther half to de yuther woman. Dat's de way Sollermun was gwyne to do wid de chile. Now I want to **ast** you: what's de use er dat half a bill?--can't buy noth'n wid it. En what use is a half a chile? I wouldn' give a dern for a million un um."

"But **hang** it, Jim, you've **clean** missed the point--blame it, you've missed it a **thousand** mile."

"Who? Me? Go 'long. Doan' talk to me 'bout yo' **pints**. I reck'n I **knows** sense when I sees it; en dey ain' no sense in sich doin's as dat. De 'spute warn't 'bout a half a chile, de 'spute was 'bout a whole chile; en de man dat think he **kin** **settle** a 'spute 'bout a whole chile wid a half a chile doan' know enough to come in out'n de **rain**. Doan' talk to me 'bout Sollermun, Huck, I knows him by de back."

"But I tell you you don't get the point."

"**Blame** de point! I reck'n I knows what I knows. En **mine** you, de *real* pint is down furder--it's down deeper. It lays in de way Sollermun was **raised**. You take a man dat's got on'y one or two chillen; is dat man gwyne to be waseful o' chillen? No, he ain't; he can't 'ford it. *he* know how to **value** 'em. But you take a man dat's got 'bout five million chillen runnin' roun' de house, en it's diffunt. *He*

Chinese Simplified

anybody: 任何人.
ast: 虹志电脑.
bill: 法案，帐单，账单，发单.
blame: 责备，咎，非难，责任，罪，责怪，归咎.
chile: 智利.
chop: 劈，剁，砍，伐.
clean: 清洁，擦拭，乾净，刷，清洗，干净.
den: 窝.
dish: 菜，碟.
dollar: 元.
hang: 挂，悬挂.
kin: 亲属，骨肉.
knows: 知道.
mine: 矿，我的，矿山，矿井.
minute: 分钟，详细，分，微小的，渺小.
notion: 观念.
pint: 品脱.
rain: 雨，下雨.
raised: 凸起的，浮雕的.
safe: 安全，保险，安全的，稳妥，保险箱.
settle: 奠定，安家落户，澄清，解决.
shin: 外小腿，胫.
stump: 树桩，残肢.
thousand: 千.
value: 价值，值，宝贵，推崇，重视，估价，珍惜，计算结果.
whack: 重打.
widow: 寡妇.
wise: 高明，明智的，英明.

as **soon** **chop** a **chile** in two as a **cat**. Dey's **plenty** mo'. A chile er two, mo' er less, warn't no consekens to Sollermun, **dad** fatch him!"

I never see such a nigger. If he got a **notion** in his head once, there warn't no getting it out again. He was the most down on Solomon of any nigger I ever see. So I went to **talking** about other **kings**, and let Solomon **slide**. I told about Louis Sixteenth that got his head **cut** off in France long time **ago**; and about his little **boy** the **dolphin**, that would a been a king, but they took and **shut** him up in **jail**, and some say he died there.

"Po' little chap."

"But some says he got out and got away, and come to America."

"Dat's good! But he'll be pooty lonesome--dey ain' no kings here, is dey, Huck?"

"No."

"**Den** he cain't git no **situation**. What he gwyne to do?"

"Well, I don't know. Some of them gets on the police, and some of them learns people how to talk French."

"Why, Huck, doan' de French people talk de same way we does?"

"*No*, Jim; you couldn't **understand** a **word** they said--not a **single** word."

"Well, now, I be ding-busted! How do dat come?"

"I don't know; but it's so. I got some of their **jabber** out of a book. S'pose a man was to come to you and say Polly-voo-franzy--what would you think?"

"I wouldn' think nuff'n; I'd take en **bust** him over de head--dat is, if he warn't white. I wouldn't 'low no nigger to **call** me dat."

"Shucks, it ain't calling you anything. It's only **saying**, do you know how to talk French?"

"Well, den, why couldn't he *say* it?"

"Why, he *is* a-saying it. That's a Frenchman's *way* of saying it."

Chinese Simplified

ago：前，之前，以前.
boy：男孩，男孩子，男孩儿，小子.
bust：半身像，逮捕，破产.
call：喊，称呼，叫，号召，召唤.
cat：猫.
chile：智利.
chop：劈，剁，砍，伐.
cut：采伐，切，刀口，伤口，割，截，剪切，切口.
dad：爸爸.
de：可选择丢弃.
den：窝.
dolphin：海豚.
jabber：磨嘴皮子.
jail：班房，监牢，监狱.
king：国王，王.
kings：国王.
notion：观念.
plenty：丰富，许多.
saying：名言，说.
shut：关闭.
single：单一，单独的，单身的，唯一的，选拔.
situation：情况，形势，局面，局势，场合，事态，情形，气候，形式，状况.
slide：滑落，滑行，滑.
soon：不久，最近，眼看，快，近期，早，早日.
talk：谈话，报告，言语，谈.
understand：了解，明白，理解，领会.
word：字，词，单词，誓言.

"Well, it's a **blame** ridicklous way, en I doan' want to **hear** no mo' 'bout it. Dey ain' no sense in it."

"Looky here, Jim; does a **cat talk** like we do?"

"No, a cat don't."

"Well, does a **cow**?"

"No, a cow don't, nuther."

"Does a cat talk like a cow, or a cow talk like a cat?"

"No, dey don't."

"It's **natural** and right for 'em to talk different from each other, ain't it?"

"Course."

"And ain't it natural and right for a cat and a cow to talk different from us?"

"Why, mos' sholy it is."

"Well, then, why ain't it natural and right for a ***frenchman*** to talk different from us? You **answer** me that."

"Is a cat a man, Huck?"

"No."

"Well, **den**, dey ain't no sense in a cat talkin' like a man. Is a cow a man?--er is a cow a cat?"

"No, she ain't either of them."

"Well, den, she ain't got no business to talk like either one er the yuther of 'em. Is a Frenchman a man?"

"Yes."

"*Well*, den! Dad blame it, why doan' he *talk* like a man? You answer me *dat*!"

I see it warn't no use **wasting** words--you can't **learn** a nigger to **argue**. So I **quit**.

Chinese Simplified

answer：回答，解答，答案，答复，答，响应，适合，负责，符合.
argue：争辩，计较.
blame：责备，咎，非难，责任，罪，责怪，归咎.
cat：猫.
cow：母牛，牛.
den：窝.
frenchman：法国人.
hear：听见，听取，听.
learn：学，学习.
natural：自然，天然，自然的，天生.
quit：退出，退离.
talk：谈话，报告，言语，谈.
wasting：消耗.

CHAPTER XV

FOOLING POOR OLD JIM

WE judged that three nights more would **fetch** us to Cairo, at the **bottom** of Illinois, where the Ohio River comes in, and that was what we was after. We would **sell** the **raft** and get on a **steamboat** and go way up the Ohio amongst the free States, and then be out of trouble.

Well, the second night a **fog begun** to come on, and we made for a towhead to **tie** to, for it wouldn't do to try to run in a fog; but when I **paddled ahead** in the **canoe**, with the line to make **fast**, there warn't anything but little saplings to tie to. I passed the line around one of them right on the edge of the cut bank, but there was a **stiff** current, and the raft come **booming** down so **lively** she **tore** it out by the **roots** and away she went. I see the fog closing down, and it made me so **sick** and scared I couldn't **budge** for most a half a minute it seemed to me--and then there warn't no raft in **sight**; you couldn't see twenty **yards**. I **jumped** into the canoe and run back to the **stern**, and grabbed the paddle and set her back a **stroke**. But she didn't come. I was in such a **hurry** I hadn't **untied** her. I got up and tried to untie her, but I was so **excited** my hands **shook** so I couldn't hardly do anything with them.

As soon as I got started I took out after the raft, hot and heavy, right down the towhead. That was all right as far as it went, but the towhead warn't sixty

Chinese Simplified

ahead: 前头，前方，前面的.
begun: 开始.
booming: 繁荣.
bottom: 底部，屁股，底.
budge: 微微一动，改变态度，羔皮.
canoe: 独木舟.
excited: 兴奋，兴奋的，兴高采烈，激昂的.
fast: 快，禁食，快速，迅速，速.
fetch: 拿，取，带来.
fog: 雾.
hurry: 仓促，匆忙，赶忙.
jumped: 跳跃.
lively: 活泼，热闹，生气勃勃，生气勃勃地，轻快.
paddle: 桨.
raft: 筏，木排，槎，桴.
roots: 根.
sell: 销售，游说，贩卖，出售.
shook: 摇动.
sick: 生病.
sight: 视觉，景象，情景，目光，视力，视线.
steamboat: 汽船，轮船.
stern: 严竣，严厉的，船尾.
stiff: 僵硬，板滞，僵硬的.
stroke: 笔锋，冲程，打击，行程，敲打，笔划.
tie: 不分胜负，打结，束缚，轨枕，绑，领带.
tore: 撕扯.
untie: 解开.
yards: 场地.

yards long, and the minute I **flew** by the foot of it I shot out into the **solid** white **fog**, and hadn't no more idea which way I was going than a dead man.

Thinks I, it won't do to **paddle**; first I know I'll run into the bank or a towhead or something; I got to set **still** and **float**, and yet it's **mighty fidgety** business to have to hold your hands still at such a time. I **whooped** and **listened**. Away down there somewheres I hears a small whoop, and up comes my **spirits**. I went **tearing** after it, **listening** sharp to hear it again. The next time it come I see I warn't **heading** for it, but heading away to the right of it. And the next time I was heading away to the left of it--and not **gaining** on it much either, for I was **flying** around, this way and that and t'other, but it was going straight ahead all the time.

I did wish the **fool** would think to beat a **tin pan**, and beat it all the time, but he never did, and it was the still places between the whoops that was making the trouble for me. Well, I **fought** along, and directly I hears the whoop *behind* me. I was tangled good now. That was somebody else's whoop, or else I was turned around.

I throwed the paddle down. I heard the whoop again; it was behind me yet, but in a different place; it kept coming, and kept **changing** its place, and I kept **answering**, till by and by it was in front of me again, and I knowed the current had **swung** the canoe's head down-stream, and I was all right if that was Jim and not some other **raftsman** hollering. I couldn't tell nothing about voices in a fog, for nothing don't look natural nor sound natural in a fog.

The whooping went on, and in about a minute I come a-booming down on a cut bank with smoky **ghosts** of big trees on it, and the current throwed me off to the left and shot by, amongst a lot of snags that fairly roared, the currrent was tearing by them so **swift**.

In another second or two it was solid white and still again. I set **perfectly** still then, listening to my heart **thump**, and I **reckon** I didn't **draw** a breath while it thumped a hundred.

Chinese Simplified

answering: 回答.
changing: 变化.
draw: 画, 不分胜负, 描, 吸, 拉.
fidgety: 烦躁.
flew: 飞.
float: 漂浮.
flying: 飞行, 飞.
fog: 雾.
fool: 呆子, 笨蛋, 傻子, 笨人, 愚人.
fought: 打.
gaining: 赢得, 增益.
ghosts: 鬼.
heading: 标题, 朝向.
listened: 听.
listening: 听.
mighty: 伟大, 强势, 强大的.
paddle: 桨.
pan: 平锅.
perfectly: 完美, 完美地.
raftsman: 木排运送工人.
reckon: 估计, 计算.
solid: 固体, 立体, 固体的, 坚硬, 扎实, 实心的, 坚固的, 坚实.
spirits: 精神.
swift: 迅速的.
swung: 摇摆.
tearing: 撕裂的.
thump: 重击.
till: 直到.
tin: 锡, 罐头.
whoop: 呼叫声.
yards: 场地.

I just give up then. I knowed what the matter was. That cut bank was an island, and Jim had gone down t'other side of it. It warn't no towhead that you could **float** by in ten minutes. It had the big timber of a regular island; it might be five or six miles long and more than half a mile wide.

I kept quiet, with my **ears** cocked, about fifteen minutes, I reckon. I was **floating** along, of course, four or five miles an hour; but you don't ever think of that. No, you *feel* like you are laying dead still on the water; and if a little **glimpse** of a **snag** slips by you don't think to yourself how fast *you're* going, but you catch your breath and think, my! how that snag's **tearing** along. If you think it ain't **dismal** and **lonesome** out in a **fog** that way by yourself in the night, you try it once--you'll see.

Next, for about a half an hour, I **whoops** now and then; at last I hears the answer a long ways off, and tries to follow it, but I couldn't do it, and directly I judged I'd got into a **nest** of towheads, for I had little **dim** glimpses of them on both sides of me--sometimes just a narrow channel between, and some that I couldn't see I knowed was there because I'd hear the wash of the current against the old dead brush and **trash** that **hung** over the banks. Well, I warn't long **loosing** the whoops down amongst the towheads; and I only tried to **chase** them a little while, anyway, because it was worse than **chasing** a Jack-o'-lantern. You never knowed a sound **dodge** around so, and **swap** places so quick and so much.

I had to **claw** away from the bank pretty **lively** four or five times, to keep from knocking the **islands** out of the river; and so I judged the **raft** must be **butting** into the bank every now and then, or else it would get further ahead and clear out of hearing--it was floating a little **faster** than what I was.

Well, I seemed to be in the open river again by and by, but I couldn't hear no sign of a whoop nowheres. I reckoned Jim had fetched up on a snag, maybe, and it was all up with him. I was good and tired, so I laid down in the **canoe** and said I wouldn't bother no more. I didn't want to go to sleep, of course; but I was so **sleepy** I couldn't help it; so I thought I would take **jest** one little cat-nap.

But I reckon it was more than a cat-nap, for when I waked up the stars was **shining** bright, the fog was all gone, and I was **spinning** down a big **bend** stern

Chinese Simplified

bend: 弯曲，弯折.
butting: 扎接.
canoe: 独木舟.
chase: 追逐，驱赶.
chasing: 追逐.
claw: 爪.
dim: 阴暗，暗淡，暗淡的.
dismal: 暗淡，忧郁的.
dodge: 躲闪，躲避.
ears: 耳朵.
faster: 快些.
float: 漂浮.
floating: 漂浮的，移动的，浮动的，飘浮.
fog: 雾.
glimpse: 一瞥，瞥见.
hung: 挂.
islands: 岛屿，岛.
jest: 玩笑，笑话，戏弄，戏谑.
lively: 活泼，热闹，生气勃勃，生气勃勃地，轻快.
lonesome: 寂寞，寂寞的.
loosing: 松开.
nest: 窝巢，窝，巢.
raft: 筏，木排，槎，桴.
shining: 彪炳，发亮.
sleepy: 想睡，眼睡的.
snag: 故障，钉子，残干，根株.
spinning: 纺织，旋转.
swap: 交换.
tearing: 撕裂的.
trash: 垃圾，残馀物.
whoop: 呼叫声.

first. First I didn't know where I was; I thought I was **dreaming**; and when things began to come back to me they seemed to come up **dim** out of last week.

It was a **monstrous** big river here, with the tallest and the thickest kind of **timber** on both banks; just a **solid** wall, as well as I could see by the **stars**. I looked away down-stream, and seen a black **speck** on the water. I took after it; but when I got to it it warn't nothing but a couple of sawlogs made **fast** together. Then I see another speck, and chased that; then another, and this time I was right. It was the **raft**.

When I got to it Jim was **setting** there with his head down between his **knees**, **asleep**, with his right arm hanging over the steering-oar. The other **oar** was smashed off, and the raft was littered up with **leaves** and **branches** and **dirt**. So she'd had a **rough** time.

I made fast and **laid** down under Jim's **nose** on the raft, and began to **gap**, and **stretch** my **fists** out against Jim, and says:

"Hello, Jim, have I been asleep? Why didn't you **stir** me up?"

"**Goodness gracious**, is dat you, Huck? En you ain' dead--you ain' drownded--you's back agin? It's too good for true, **honey**, it's too good for true. Lemme look at you **chile**, lemme feel o' you. No, you ain' dead! you's back agin, 'live en soun', **jis** de same ole Huck--de same ole Huck, **thanks** to goodness!"

"What's the matter with you, Jim? You been a-drinking?"

"Drinkin'? Has I ben a-drinkin'? Has I had a chance to be a-drinkin'?"

"Well, then, what makes you talk so wild?"

"How does I talk wild?"

"*How*? Why, hain't you been talking about my coming back, and all that **stuff**, as if I'd been gone away?"

"Huck--Huck Finn, you look me in de eye; look me in de eye. *Hain't* you ben gone away?"

"Gone away? Why, what in the **nation** do you mean? I hain't been gone anywheres. Where would I go to?"

Chinese Simplified

asleep: 睡着，睡着的.
branches: 分支.
chile: 智利.
dim: 阴暗，暗淡，暗淡的.
dirt: 污垢.
dreaming: 梦见.
fast: 快，禁食，快速，迅速，速.
fists: 拳头.
gap: 差距，空白点，间隔，间隙.
goodness: 美德.
gracious: 亲切，亲切的，有礼貌的.
honey: 蜂蜜，蜜，蜜糖.
jis: 日本工业标准.
knees: 膝盖.
laid: 放.
leaves: 离开.
monstrous: 怪物似，似怪物的.
nation: 国家.
nose: 鼻子.
oar: 桨.
raft: 筏，木排，槎，桴.
rough: 粗暴，大概，粗糙，粗鲁.
setting: 排字，设定.
solid: 固体，立体，固体的，坚硬，扎实，实心的，坚固的，坚实.
speck: 斑点，点子.
stars: 星.
stir: 轰动，搅拌，鼓动.
stretch: 张开，拉紧，伸展，伸.
stuff: 材料，填塞，职员.
thanks: 感谢，谢谢.
timber: 木料，木材，木头.

"Well, looky here, **boss**, dey's sumf'n wrong, dey is. Is I *me*, or who *is* I? Is I heah, or whah *is* I? Now dat's what I wants to know."

"Well, I think you're here, **plain** enough, but I think you're a **tangle- headed** old **fool**, Jim."

"I is, is I? Well, you answer me dis: Didn't you tote out de line in de **canoe** fer to make fas' to de tow-head?"

"No, I didn't. What tow-head? I hain't see no tow-head."

"You hain't seen no towhead? Looky here, didn't de line **pull loose** en de raf' go a-hummin' down de **river**, en leave you en de canoe behine in de **fog**?"

"What fog?"

"Why, de fog!--de fog dat's been aroun' all night. En didn't you **whoop**, en didn't I whoop, tell we got **mix'** up in de **islands** en one un us got los' en t'other one was **jis'** as good as los', 'kase he didn' know whah he wuz? En didn't I **bust** up agin a lot er dem islands en have a turrible time en mos' git drownded? Now ain' dat so, boss ain't it so? You answer me dat."

"Well, this is too many for me, Jim. I hain't seen no fog, nor no islands, nor no **troubles**, nor nothing. I been **setting** here talking with you all night **till** you went to **sleep** about ten minutes ago, and I **reckon** I done the same. You couldn't a got **drunk** in that time, so of course you've been **dreaming**."

"**Dad fetch** it, how is I gwyne to dream all dat in ten minutes?"

"Well, **hang** it all, you did dream it, because there didn't any of it happen."

"But, Huck, it's all jis' as plain to me as--"

"It don't make no **difference** how plain it is; there ain't nothing in it. I know, because I've been here all the time."

Jim didn't say nothing for about five minutes, but set there **studying** over it. Then he says:

"Well, **den**, I reck'n I did dream it, Huck; but **dog** my **cats** ef it ain't de powerfullest dream I ever see. En I hain't ever had no dream b'fo' dat's **tired** me like dis one."

Chinese Simplified

boss: 老板，上司，头子，浮雕.
bust: 半身像，逮捕，破产.
canoe: 独木舟.
cats: 猫.
dad: 爸爸.
den: 窝.
difference: 差异，差，差别，区别，分歧，分别，误差.
dog: 狗，犬.
dream: 梦寐，梦见，做梦，梦想.
drunk: 喝了，喝醉.
fetch: 拿，取，带来.
fog: 雾.
fool: 呆子，笨蛋，傻子，笨人，愚人.
hang: 挂，悬挂.
headed: 有头的.
islands: 岛屿，岛.
jis: 日本工业标准.
loose: 松开，松弛的.
mix: 混，混杂，糅，混合，渗混.
plain: 平原.
pull: 拉，牵引.
reckon: 估计，计算.
river: 河，江，川，河流，条.
setting: 排字，设定.
sleep: 梦寐，睡觉，睡眠，睡.
studying: 学习.
tangle: 纠缠.
till: 直到.
tired: 疲倦，疲乏，疲倦的.
troubles: 坏处，麻烦.
whoop: 呼叫声.

"Oh, well, that's all right, because a **dream** does **tire** a body like everything sometimes. But this one was a staving dream; tell me all about it, Jim."

So Jim went to work and told me the whole thing right through, just as it happened, only he painted it up considerable. Then he said he must start in and "'terpret" it, because it was **sent** for a **warning**. He said the first towhead stood for a man that would try to do us some good, but the current was another man that would get us away from him. The whoops was warnings that would come to us every now and then, and if we didn't try hard to make out to understand them they'd just take us into bad **luck**, 'stead of keeping us out of it. The lot of towheads was **troubles** we was going to get into with **quarrelsome** people and all kinds of mean folks, but if we minded our business and didn't talk back and **aggravate** them, we would **pull** through and get out of the **fog** and into the big clear river, which was the free States, and wouldn't have no more trouble.

It had **clouded** up pretty dark just after I got on to the **raft**, but it was **clearing** up again now.

"Oh, well, that's all **interpreted** well enough as far as it goes, Jim," I says; "but what does *these* things stand for?"

It was the leaves and **rubbish** on the raft and the smashed **oar**. You could see them first-rate now.

Jim looked at the **trash**, and then looked at me, and back at the trash again. He had got the dream **fixed** so strong in his head that he couldn't seem to **shake** it **loose** and get the **facts** back into its place again right away. But when he did get the thing straightened around he looked at me **steady** without ever **smiling**, and says:

"What do dey stan' for? I'se gwyne to tell you. When I got all **wore** out wid work, en wid de callin' for you, en went to sleep, my heart wuz mos' broke bekase you wuz los', en I didn' k'yer no' mo' what become er me en de raf'. En when I **wake** up en fine you back agin, all safe en soun', de **tears** come, en I could a got down on my **knees** en **kiss** yo' foot, I's so **thankful**. En all you wuz thinkin' 'bout wuz how you could make a **fool** uv ole Jim wid a **lie**. Dat **truck** dah is

Chinese Simplified

aggravate: 加剧，激怒，恼火.
clearing: 清除.
clouded: 阴云密布的，有暗影的.
dream: 梦寐，梦见，做梦，梦想.
facts: 事实.
fixed: 固定，确定，一定，固定的.
fog: 雾.
fool: 呆子，笨蛋，傻子，笨人，愚人.
interpreted: 解释执行.
kiss: 吻，接吻，轻抚，轻触.
knees: 膝盖.
lie: 谎言，谎话，鞫，撒谎，说谎.
loose: 松开，松弛的.
luck: 运气，幸运.
oar: 桨.
pull: 拉，牵引.
quarrelsome: 喜欢吵架，喜爱争论的.
raft: 筏，木排，槎，桴.
rubbish: 废物，垃圾，废话.
sent: 送了.
shake: 摇动，震动，摇，震荡，颠簸.
smiling: 微笑的.
steady: 稳定，坚定，平稳，平稳的.
tears: 泪，泪水，眼泪.
thankful: 感谢，感谢的.
tire: 疲倦.
trash: 垃圾，残馀物.
troubles: 坏处，麻烦.
truck: 卡车.
wake: 醒来，醒觉.
warning: 警报，鉴戒，警告.
wore: 穿了.

trash; en trash is what people is dat **puts dirt** on **de** head er dey fren's en makes 'em ashamed."

Then he got up **slow** and **walked** to the **wigwam**, and went in there without **saying** anything but that. But that was enough. It made me feel so mean I could almost kissed *his* **foot** to get him to take it back.

It was **fifteen** minutes before I could work **myself** up to go and **humble** myself to a nigger; but I done it, and I warn't ever **sorry** for it **afterwards**, **neither**. I didn't do him no more mean **tricks**, and I wouldn't done that one if I'd a knowed it would make him feel that way.

Chinese Simplified

afterwards: 后来，然后，以后，此后，後，然後，后，过后，底下，此後，後来.
de: 可选择丢弃.
dirt: 污垢.
fifteen: 十五.
foot: 脚，足，步兵，英尺，呎.
humble: 谦逊，谦恭的.
myself: 我自己.
neither: 也不，二者，两者都不是.
puts: 放.
saying: 名言，说.
slow: 慢，缓慢，迟慢，迟钝，迟迟，迟缓.
sorry: 遗憾，对不起.
trash: 垃圾，残馀物.
tricks: 戏法，把戏.
walked: 步行.
wigwam: 帐篷，陋棚.

CHAPTER XVI

THE RATTLESNAKE SKIN DOES ITS WORK

We slept most all day, and started out at night, a **little** ways behind a **monstrous** long **raft** that was as long going by as a **procession**. She had four long sweeps at each end, so we judged she carried as many as **thirty** men, likely. She had five big wigwams **aboard**, wide **apart**, and an open **camp** fire in the middle, and a **tall** flag-pole at each end. There was a power of style about her. It *amounted* to something being a **raftsman** on such a **craft** as that.

We went drifting down into a big **bend**, and the night **clouded** up and got **hot**. The **river** was very wide, and was walled with **solid timber** on both sides; you couldn't see a **break** in it **hardly** ever, or a light. We **talked** about Cairo, and wondered whether we would know it when we got to it. I said likely we wouldn't, because I had heard say there warn't but about a **dozen** houses there, and if they didn't **happen** to have them lit up, how was we going to know we was **passing** a town? Jim said if the two big **rivers joined** together there, that would show. But I said maybe we might think we was passing the **foot** of an **island** and coming into the same old river again. That **disturbed** Jim--and me too. So the question was, what to do? I said, **paddle ashore** the first time a light showed, and tell them pap was behind, coming along with a trading-scow, and

Chinese Simplified

aboard：船上，在车，上.
apart：分别，分开.
ashore：岸上，上岸.
bend：弯曲，弯折.
break：破坏，断，打破，犯，中断，破，裂.
camp：阵营，营，露营，安营.
clouded：阴云密布的，有暗影的.
craft：手艺，狡诈，探测器，工艺.
disturbed：不安.
dozen：一打，打.
foot：脚，足，步兵，英尺，呎.
happen：发生.
hardly：几乎不，毫不，辛苦地.
hot：热.
island：岛.
joined：加入.
lit：点燃.
monstrous：怪物似，似怪物的.
paddle：桨.
passing：经过的，短暂的，目前的，及格的.
procession：行列，游行.
raft：筏，木排，槎，桴.
raftsman：木排运送工人.
river：河，江，川，河流，条.
rivers：河，河川.
solid：固体，立体，固体的，坚硬，扎实，实心的，坚固的，坚实.
talked：谈话.
tall：高大的，高大.
thirty：三十.
timber：木料，木材，木头.

was a green hand at the business, and wanted to know how far it was to Cairo. Jim thought it was a good idea, so we took a **smoke** on it and waited.

There warn't nothing to do now but to look out **sharp** for the town, and not **pass** it without **seeing** it. He said he'd be **mighty** sure to see it, because he'd be a free man the **minute** he seen it, but if he missed it he'd be in a **slave** country again and no more show for **freedom**. Every little while he **jumps** up and says:

"Dah she is?"

But it warn't. It was Jack-o'-lanterns, or **lightning** bugs; so he set down again, and went to watching, same as before. Jim said it made him all over trembly and **feverish** to be so close to freedom. Well, I can tell you it made me all over trembly and feverish, too, to hear him, because I **begun** to get it through my head that he *was* most free--and who was to **blame** for it? Why, *me*. I couldn't get that out of my **conscience**, no how nor no way. It got to troubling me so I couldn't rest; I couldn't stay still in one place. It hadn't ever come home to me before, what this thing was that I was doing. But now it did; and it **stayed** with me, and **scorched** me more and more. I tried to make out to myself that I warn't to blame, because I didn't run Jim off from his **rightful owner**; but it warn't no use, conscience up and says, every time, "But you knowed he was running for his freedom, and you could a paddled **ashore** and told somebody." That was so--I couldn't get around that noway. That was where it pinched. Conscience says to me, "What had poor Miss Watson done to you that you could see her nigger go off right under your eyes and never say one single word? What did that poor old woman do to you that you could **treat** her so mean? Why, she tried to learn you your book, she tried to learn you your **manners**, she tried to be good to you every way she knowed how. *that's* what she done."

I got to feeling so mean and so **miserable** I most wished I was dead. I fidgeted up and down the **raft**, **abusing** myself to myself, and Jim was fidgeting up and down past me. We **neither** of us could keep still. Every time he danced around and says, "Dah's Cairo!" it went through me like a **shot**, and I thought if it *was* Cairo I reckoned I would **die** of miserableness.

Chinese Simplified

abusing: 滥用.
ashore: 岸上，上岸.
begun: 开始.
blame: 责备，咎，非难，责任，罪，责怪，归咎.
conscience: 良心.
die: 逝世，不讳，死.
feverish: 发烧的.
freedom: 自由.
jumps: 跳跃.
lightning: 闪电.
manners: 礼貌.
mighty: 伟大，强势，强大的.
minute: 分钟，详细，分，微小的，渺小.
miserable: 悲惨，凄惨，困苦，凄惨的.
neither: 也不，二者，两者都不是.
owner: 物主，业主，所有者，所有人，主人.
pass: 隘口，及格，传递，度过，要隘.
raft: 筏，木排，槎，桴.
rightful: 正直的，合法的.
scorched: 焦.
seeing: 有鉴于.
sharp: 尖锐，锐利，锋利的，锋利.
shot: 射击.
slave: 奴隶.
smoke: 烟，抽烟，烟雾，硝烟，吸烟，熏.
stayed: 停留.
treat: 对待.

Jim **talked** out **loud** all the time while I was talking to myself. He was saying how the first thing he would do when he got to a free State he would go to **saving** up money and never spend a single **cent**, and when he got enough he would buy his wife, which was **owned** on a farm close to where Miss Watson lived; and then they would both work to buy the two children, and if their **master** wouldn't sell them, they'd get an Ab'litionist to go and **steal** them.

It most froze me to hear such talk. He wouldn't ever dared to talk such talk in his life before. Just see what a difference it made in him the minute he judged he was about free. It was **according** to the old saying, "Give a nigger an **inch** and he'll take an ell." Thinks I, this is what comes of my not thinking. Here was this nigger, which I had as good as helped to run away, coming right out flat-footed and saying he would steal his children--children that belonged to a man I didn't even know; a man that hadn't ever done me no **harm**.

I was sorry to hear Jim say that, it was such a **lowering** of him. My **conscience** got to **stirring** me up **hotter** than ever, until at last I says to it, "Let up on me--it ain't too late yet--I'll **paddle ashore** at the first light and tell." I felt easy and **happy** and light as a **feather** right off. All my **troubles** was gone. I went to looking out sharp for a light, and sort of **singing** to myself. By and by one showed. Jim **sings** out:

"We's safe, Huck, we's safe! Jump up and **crack** yo' heels! Dat's de good ole Cairo at las', I **jis** knows it!"

I says:

"I'll take the **canoe** and go and see, Jim. It mightn't be, you know."

He **jumped** and got the canoe ready, and put his old **coat** in the bottom for me to set on, and give me the paddle; and as I shoved off, he says:

"Pooty soon I'll be a-shout'n' for **joy**, en I'll say, it's all on accounts o' Huck; I's a free man, en I couldn't ever ben free ef it hadn' ben for Huck; Huck done it. Jim won't ever forgit you, Huck; you's de bes' fren' Jim's ever had; en you's de *only* fren' ole Jim's got now."

Chinese Simplified

according：根据.
ashore：岸上，上岸.
canoe：独木舟.
cent：一分钱，分.
coat：外套，上衣.
conscience：良心.
crack：裂缝，精干，崩裂，爆裂，裂开，空隙.
feather：羽毛.
happy：快乐，愉快，幸福，快活，美好，欢乐，高兴，快乐的，喜悦，舒畅，愉快的.
harm：伤害，损害，坏处，害处，祸害.
hotter：热，热烈的.
inch：英寸.
jis：日本工业标准.
joy：乐趣，快乐，高兴，喜悦.
jumped：跳跃.
loud：高声，大声，大声的.
lowering：昏暗的.
master：主，大师，主人，主人翁，师傅，万事达，硕士.
owned：拥有.
paddle：桨.
saving：节省.
singing：歌咏，歌唱.
sings：唱.
steal：偷窃，盗窃，偷，窃取.
stirring：活跃的，激动人心的，忙碌的.
talked：谈话.
troubles：坏处，麻烦.

I was paddling off, all in a **sweat** to tell on him; but when he says this, it seemed to kind of take the **tuck** all out of me. I went along **slow** then, and I warn't right down certain whether I was **glad** I started or whether I warn't. When I was **fifty yards** off, Jim says:

"Dah you goes, de ole true Huck; de on'y white genlman dat ever kep' his **promise** to ole Jim."

Well, I just felt **sick**. But I says, I *got* to do it--I can't get *out* of it. Right then along comes a **skiff** with two men in it with **guns**, and they **stopped** and I stopped. One of them says:

"What's that **yonder**?"

"A **piece** of a **raft**," I says.

"Do you **belong** on it?"

"Yes, sir."

"Any men on it?"

"Only one, sir."

"Well, there's five niggers run off to-night up yonder, above the head of the **bend**. Is your man white or black?"

I didn't answer up **prompt**. I tried to, but the words wouldn't come. I tried for a second or two to **brace** up and out with it, but I warn't man enough--hadn't the **spunk** of a **rabbit**. I see I was **weakening**; so I just give up trying, and up and says:

"He's white."

"I **reckon** we'll go and see for ourselves."

"I wish you would," says I, "because it's pap that's there, and maybe you'd help me **tow** the raft **ashore** where the light is. He's sick--and so is mam and Mary Ann."

"Oh, the **devil**! we're in a **hurry**, boy. But I s'pose we've got to. Come, **buckle** to your **paddle**, and let's get along."

Chinese Simplified

ashore：岸上，上岸.
belong：属于.
bend：弯曲，弯折.
brace：支柱.
buckle：带扣，扣子.
devil：魔鬼，妖怪，鬼.
fifty：五十，半白.
glad：高兴，高兴的.
guns：枪支.
hurry：仓促，匆忙，赶忙.
paddle：桨.
piece：片，部分，一块，一片，块，部份，份.
promise：答应，约定，承诺，誓言，诺言，允诺.
prompt：提示，立刻，迅速的，敏捷的.
rabbit：兔子，兔，野兔.
raft：筏，木排，槎，桴.
reckon：估计，计算.
sick：生病.
skiff：小船，小艇.
slow：慢，缓慢，迟慢，迟钝，迟迟，迟缓.
spunk：引火木柴.
stopped：停止.
sweat：汗，出汗，流汗.
tow：拖船，拖车，牵引，拖.
tuck：挤进，塞进.
weakening：削弱.
yards：场地.
yonder：那边.

I buckled to my **paddle** and they **laid** to their oars. When we had made a **stroke** or two, I says:

"Pap'll be **mighty** much obleeged to you, I can tell you. Everybody goes away when I want them to help me **tow** the **raft ashore**, and I can't do it by myself."

"Well, that's **infernal** mean. Odd, too. Say, boy, what's the matter with your father?"

"It's the--a--the--well, it ain't anything much."

They stopped **pulling.** It warn't but a mighty little ways to the raft now. One says:

"Boy, that's a **lie**. What *is* the matter with your pap? Answer up **square** now, and it'll be the better for you."

"I will, sir, I will, honest--but don't leave us, please. It's the--the --Gentlemen, if you'll only pull **ahead,** and let me **heave** you the **headline**, you won't have to come a-near the raft--please do."

"Set her back, John, set her back!" says one. They **backed** water. "Keep away, boy--keep to looard. Confound it, I just expect the wind has blowed it to us. Your pap's got the small-pox, and you know it **precious** well. Why didn't you come out and say so? Do you want to spread it all over?"

"Well," says I, a-blubbering, "I've told **everybody** before, and they just went away and left us."

"Poor **devil**, there's something in that. We are right down sorry for you, but we--well, **hang** it, we don't want the small-pox, you see. Look here, I'll tell you what to do. Don't you try to land by yourself, or you'll **smash** everything to pieces. You **float** along down about twenty miles, and you'll come to a town on the **left**-hand side of the river. It will be long after sun-up then, and when you ask for help you tell them your folks are all down with **chills** and **fever**. Don't be a **fool** again, and let people **guess** what is the matter. Now we're trying to do you a **kindness**; so you just put twenty miles between us, that's a good boy. It wouldn't do any good to land **yonder** where the light is--it's only a wood-yard.

Chinese Simplified

ahead: 前头，前方，前面的.
ashore: 岸上，上岸.
backed: 支撑.
chills: 寒冷.
devil: 魔鬼，妖怪，鬼.
everybody: 每个人，各位.
fever: 发烧，发热.
float: 漂浮.
fool: 呆子，笨蛋，傻子，笨人，愚人.
guess: 猜测，臆测，猜谜儿，猜想，揣测，推测.
hang: 挂，悬挂.
headline: 标题.
heave: 举起，波荡，喘气.
infernal: 地狱，地狱的.
kindness: 仁慈，好意.
laid: 放.
left-hand: 左手的.
lie: 谎言，谎话，躺，撒谎，说谎.
mighty: 伟大，强势，强大的.
paddle: 桨.
precious: 宝贵，珍贵，贵重，宝贵的.
pull: 拉，牵引.
pulling: 拉.
raft: 筏，木排，槎，桴.
smash: 捣碎，粉碎，破碎.
square: 正方形，平方，四方形.
stroke: 笔锋，冲程，打击，行程，敲打，笔划.
tow: 拖船，拖车，牵引，拖.
yonder: 那边.

Say, I **reckon** your father's poor, and I'm **bound** to say he's in **pretty** hard **luck**. Here, I'll put a twenty-dollar **gold** piece on this **board**, and you get it when it **floats** by. I feel **mighty** mean to leave you; but my **kingdom**! it won't do to **fool** with small-pox, don't you see?"

"Hold on, Parker," says the other man, "here's a twenty to put on the board for me. Good-bye, boy; you do as Mr. Parker told you, and you'll be all right."

"That's so, my boy--good-bye, **good**-bye. If you see any **runaway** niggers you get help and **nab** them, and you can make some money by it."

"Good-bye, sir," says I; "I won't let no runaway niggers get by me if I can help it."

They went off and I got **aboard** the **raft**, feeling bad and low, because I knowed very well I had done wrong, and I see it warn't no use for me to try to learn to do right; a body that don't get *started* right when he's little ain't got no show--when the **pinch** comes there ain't nothing to back him up and keep him to his work, and so he gets **beat**. Then I thought a minute, and says to myself, hold on; s'pose you'd a done right and give Jim up, would you felt better than what you do now? No, says I, I'd feel bad--I'd feel just the same way I do now. Well, then, says I, what's the use you **learning** to do right when it's **troublesome** to do right and ain't no trouble to do wrong, and the **wages** is just the same? I was **stuck**. I couldn't answer that. So I reckoned I wouldn't **bother** no more about it, but after this always do **whichever** come handiest at the time.

I went into the **wigwam**; Jim warn't there. I looked all around; he warn't **anywhere**. I says:

"Jim!"

"Here I is, Huck. Is dey out o' sight yit? Don't talk loud."

He was in the river under the **stern** oar, with just his **nose** out. I told him they were out of sight, so he come aboard. He says:

"I was a-listenin' to all de talk, en I slips into de river en was gwyne to **shove** for sho' if dey come aboard. Den I was gwyne to **swim** to de raf' agin when dey was gone. But lawsy, how you did fool 'em, Huck! Dat *wuz* de smartes' **dodge**! I

Chinese Simplified

aboard：船上，在车，上.
anywhere：无论何处.
beat：打，击败，拍击，敲打，拍子，敲.
bother：烦扰，打扰，理会.
bound：限，边际，弹回，范围.
dodge：躲闪，躲避.
floats：花车.
fool：呆子，笨蛋，傻子，笨人，愚人.
gold：金，黄金.
good-**bye**：再会.
kingdom：王国.
learning：学问，学术，学习.
luck：运气，幸运.
mighty：伟大，强势，强大的.
nab：逮捕.
nose：鼻子.
oar：桨.
pinch：捏，掐.
pretty：漂亮，美丽的，秀丽.
raft：筏，木排，槎，桴.
reckon：估计，计算.
runaway：逃亡者，跑道.
shove：推.
stern：严竣，严厉的，船尾.
stuck：黏贴.
swim：游泳.
troublesome：淘神，讨厌，麻烦，麻烦的，伤脑筋.
wages：工资，待遇，工钱.
whichever：任何，视何者为.
wigwam：帐篷，陋棚.

tell you, **chile**, I'spec it **save'** ole Jim--ole Jim ain't going to forgit you for dat, honey."

Then we **talked** about the money. It was a pretty good raise--twenty dollars **apiece**. Jim said we could take **deck** passage on a **steamboat** now, and the money would last us as far as we wanted to go in the free States. He said twenty **mile** more warn't far for the **raft** to go, but he wished we was already there.

Towards **daybreak** we tied up, and Jim was **mighty** particular about **hiding** the raft good. Then he worked all day **fixing** things in **bundles**, and getting all ready to **quit rafting**.

That night about ten we hove in sight of the lights of a town away down in a **left**-hand **bend**.

I went off in the **canoe** to **ask** about it. Pretty soon I found a man out in the river with a **skiff**, setting a trot-line. I **ranged** up and says:

"Mister, is that town **Cairo**?"

"Cairo? no. You must be a **blame'** fool."

"What town is it, mister?"

"If you want to know, go and find out. If you stay here botherin' around me for about a half a minute longer you'll get something you won't want."

I paddled to the raft. Jim was **awful disappointed**, but I said never mind, Cairo would be the next place, I reckoned.

We passed another town before **daylight**, and I was going out again; but it was high ground, so I didn't go. No high ground about Cairo, Jim said. I had **forgot** it. We laid up for the day on a towhead **tolerable** close to the left-hand bank. I begun to **suspicion** something. So did Jim. I says:

"Maybe we went by Cairo in the **fog** that night."

He says:

"Doan' le's talk about it, Huck. Po' niggers can't have no **luck**. I awluz 'spected dat rattlesnake-skin warn't done wid its work."

"I wish I'd never seen that snake-skin, Jim--I do wish I'd never laid eyes on it."

Chinese Simplified

apiece: 各自, 各自地.
ask: 问, 询问.
awful: 可怕, 可怕的.
bend: 弯曲, 弯折.
blame: 责备, 咎, 非难, 责任, 罪, 责怪, 归咎.
bundles: 捆.
cairo: 开罗.
canoe: 独木舟.
chile: 智利.
daybreak: 黎明, 破晓.
daylight: 日光, 白天.
deck: 甲板.
disappointed: 败兴, 失望的, 惆.
fixing: 定影, 固定.
fog: 雾.
forgot: 忘记.
hiding: 隐匿.
left-hand: 左手的.
luck: 运气, 幸运.
mighty: 伟大, 强势, 强大的.
mile: 英里.
quit: 退出, 退离.
raft: 筏, 木排, 槎, 桴.
rafting: 放排.
ranged: 排列.
save: 节约, 节省, 省得, 救, 援救, 挽救, 保存.
skiff: 小船, 小艇.
steamboat: 汽船, 轮船.
suspicion: 疑心, 怀疑, 嫌疑.
talked: 谈话.
tolerable: 可容忍, 可容忍的.

"It ain't yo' **fault**, Huck; you didn' know. Don't you **blame** yo'self 'bout it."

When it was **daylight**, here was the clear Ohio water **inshore**, sure enough, and outside was the old regular Muddy! So it was all up with Cairo.

We **talked** it all over. It wouldn't do to take to the shore; we couldn't take the **raft** up the **stream**, of course. There warn't no way but to wait for dark, and start back in the **canoe** and take the **chances**. So we **slept** all day amongst the cottonwood **thicket**, so as to be **fresh** for the work, and when we went back to the raft about dark the canoe was gone!

We didn't say a word for a good while. There warn't anything to say. We both knowed well enough it was some more work of the **rattlesnake**-skin; so what was the use to talk about it? It would only look like we was finding fault, and that would be bound to **fetch** more bad luck--and keep on **fetching** it, too, till we knowed enough to keep still.

By and by we talked about what we better do, and found there warn't no way but just to go along down with the raft till we got a chance to buy a canoe to go back in. We warn't going to **borrow** it when there warn't anybody around, the way pap would do, for that might set people after us.

So we shoved out after dark on the raft.

Anybody that don't believe yet that it's **foolishness** to handle a snake- skin, after all that that snake-skin done for us, will believe it now if they read on and see what more it done for us.

The place to buy **canoes** is off of **rafts** laying up at shore. But we didn't see no rafts laying up; so we went along during three hours and more. Well, the night got **gray** and ruther thick, which is the next meanest thing to **fog**. You can't tell the **shape** of the river, and you can't see no distance. It got to be very late and still, and then along comes a **steamboat** up the river. We **lit** the **lantern**, and judged she would see it. Up-stream **boats** didn't generly come close to us; they go out and follow the bars and **hunt** for easy water under the reefs; but nights like this they **bull** right up the channel against the whole river.

Chinese Simplified

blame: 责备，咎，非难，责任，罪，责怪，归咎.
boats: 船舶.
borrow: 借.
bull: 公牛.
canoe: 独木舟.
canoes: 独木舟.
chances: 机会.
daylight: 日光，白天.
fault: 故障，过失，缺点，毛病，断层，短处，缺陷.
fetch: 拿，取，带来.
fetching: 迷人的.
fog: 雾.
foolishness: 愚蠢.
fresh: 新鲜，新鲜的，新.
gray: 灰色，灰.
hunt: 打猎，狩猎.
inshore: 靠近海岸.
lantern: 灯笼.
lit: 点燃.
raft: 筏，木排，槎，桴.
rafts: 木排.
shape: 形状，形式，外形，型状，形态，塑造，使成形，成形.
shore: 岸，滨，岸边，海岸，海滨.
slept: 睡了.
snake: 蛇.
steamboat: 汽船，轮船.
stream: 溪流，河流，流，小溪，川.
talked: 谈话.
thick: 厚，密，浓厚.
thicket: 丛林，灌木丛.

We could hear her pounding along, but we didn't see her good till she was close. She aimed right for us. Often they do that and try to see how close they can come without **touching**; sometimes the wheel **bites** off a **sweep**, and then the pilot **sticks** his head out and **laughs**, and thinks he's **mighty** smart. Well, here she comes, and we said she was going to try and **shave** us; but she didn't seem to be sheering off a bit. She was a big one, and she was coming in a **hurry**, too, looking like a black cloud with rows of glow-worms around it; but all of a sudden she bulged out, big and **scary**, with a long row of wide-open **furnace** doors **shining** like **red**-hot teeth, and her **monstrous bows** and **guards** hanging right over us. There was a **yell** at us, and a jingling of **bells** to stop the **engines**, a **powwow** of cussing, and **whistling** of steam--and as Jim went **overboard** on one side and I on the other, she come smashing straight through the raft.

I dived--and I aimed to find the bottom, too, for a thirty-foot wheel had got to go over me, and I wanted it to have plenty of room. I could always stay under water a minute; this time I reckon I stayed under a minute and a half. Then I bounced for the top in a hurry, for I was nearly busting. I popped out to my armpits and blowed the water out of my nose, and puffed a bit. Of course there was a **booming** current; and of course that boat started her engines again ten **seconds** after she stopped them, for they never cared much for raftsmen; so now she was **churning** along up the river, out of sight in the thick weather, though I could hear her.

I **sung** out for Jim about a dozen times, but I didn't get any answer; so I grabbed a **plank** that touched me while I was "treading water," and struck out for shore, shoving it ahead of me. But I made out to see that the **drift** of the current was towards the **left**-hand shore, which meant that I was in a **crossing**; so I changed off and went that way.

It was one of these long, **slanting**, two-mile **crossings**; so I was a good long time in getting over. I made a safe landing, and clumb up the bank. I couldn't see but a little ways, but I went poking along over rough ground for a quarter of a mile or more, and then I run across a big old- **fashioned** double log-house before I noticed it. I was going to rush by and get away, but a lot of dogs jumped out

Chinese Simplified

bells：铃.
bites：咬伤.
booming：繁荣.
bows：弓.
churning：搅乳、一次提制的奶油.
crossing：路口，横越、交叉点.
crossings：横越.
drift：漂游，漂移、漂.
engines：发动机.
fashioned：方式.
furnace：熔矿炉，炉子，熔炉，极热的地方.
guards：警戒.
hurry：仓促，匆忙，赶忙.
laughs：笑.
left-hand：左手的.
mighty：伟大，强势，强大的.
monstrous：怪物似，似怪物的.
overboard：向船外.
plank：板，木板，木版，板子.
powwow：巫师.
red-hot：热烈的.
scary：引起惊慌.
seconds：秒.
shave：削，剃刮.
shining：彪炳，发亮.
slanting：倾斜的.
sticks：棍.
sung：唱歌.
sweep：席卷，打扫，扫描.
touching：动人.
whistling：吹口哨，吹笛.
yell：叫喊，呐喊.

and went to **howling** and **barking** at me, and I knowed better than to **move** another peg.

Chinese Simplified

barking: 叫声.
howling: 咆哮的, 啸声.
move: 步骤, 搬家, 移动, 一举, 运动, 感动, 开动, 移.

CHAPTER XVII

THE GRANGERFORDS TAKE ME IN

In about a **minute somebody spoke** out of a **window** without putting his head out, and says:

"Be done, **boys**! Who's there?"

I says:

"It's me."

"Who's me?"

"**George** Jackson, **sir**."

"What do you want?"

"I don't want nothing, sir. I only want to go **along** by, but the **dogs** won't let me."

"What are you prowling around here this time of night for--hey?"

"I warn't prowling around, sir, I **fell overboard** off of the steamboat."

"Oh, you did, did you? Strike a **light** there, somebody. What did you say your name was?"

"George Jackson, sir. I'm only a boy."

Chinese Simplified

along: 沿着，沿，一同.
boys: 哥儿，男孩.
dogs: 狗.
fell: 采伐，伐，跌落.
george: 乔治.
light: 光，轻，灯，光纤，燃放，灯光，点燃，亮光.
minute: 分钟，详细，分，微小的，渺小.
overboard: 向船外.
sir: 先生，爵士.
somebody: 某人，有人.
spoke: 辐条，说了.
window: 窗口，窗户，窗，窗子.

"Look here, if you're telling the truth you needn't be afraid--nobody'll **hurt** you. But don't try to **budge**; stand right where you are. Rouse out Bob and Tom, some of you, and **fetch** the **guns**. George Jackson, is there **anybody** with you?"

"No, sir, nobody."

I heard the people **stirring** around in the house now, and see a light. The man **sung** out:

"Snatch that light away, Betsy, you old fool--ain't you got any sense? Put it on the floor behind the front door. Bob, if you and Tom are ready, take your places."

"All ready."

"Now, George Jackson, do you know the Shepherdsons?"

"No, sir; I never heard of them."

"Well, that may be so, and it mayn't. Now, all ready. Step forward, George Jackson. And mind, don't you **hurry**--come **mighty slow**. If there's anybody with you, let him keep back--if he shows himself he'll be **shot**. Come along now. Come slow; **push** the door open yourself--just enough to **squeeze** in, d' you hear?"

I didn't hurry; I couldn't if I'd a wanted to. I took one slow **step** at a time and there warn't a sound, only I thought I could hear my heart. The **dogs** were as **still** as the humans, but they followed a little behind me. When I got to the three **log** doorsteps I heard them unlocking and unbarring and unbolting. I put my hand on the door and pushed it a little and a little more till **somebody** said, "There, that's enough--put your head in." I done it, but I judged they would take it off.

The **candle** was on the floor, and there they all was, looking at me, and me at them, for about a **quarter** of a **minute**: Three big men with guns **pointed** at me, which made me **wince**, I tell you; the **oldest**, **gray** and about **sixty**, the other two thirty or more--all of them fine and **handsome** --and the sweetest old gray-headed lady, and back of her two young women which I couldn't see right well. The old **gentleman** says:

Chinese Simplified

anybody: 任何人.
budge: 微微一动，改变态度，羔皮.
candle: 蜡烛.
dogs: 狗.
fetch: 拿，取，带来.
gentleman: 绅士.
gray: 灰色，灰.
guns: 枪支.
handsome: 英俊，慷慨的，英俊的.
hurry: 仓促，匆忙，赶忙.
hurt: 伤害，使受伤.
log: 圆形木材，圆木，木头.
mighty: 伟大，强势，强大的.
minute: 分钟，详细，分，微小的，渺小.
oldest: 最年长的.
pointed: 尖锐.
push: 推.
quarter: 四分之一.
shot: 射击.
sixty: 六十.
slow: 慢，缓慢，迟慢，迟钝，迟迟，迟缓.
somebody: 某人，有人.
squeeze: 压扁，压挤，榨.
step: 步骤，步伐，措施，一步，步调，步子，级，脚步，踏.
stirring: 活跃的，激动人心的，忙碌的.
sung: 唱歌.
till: 直到.
wince: 退缩，因疼痛退缩.

"There; I **reckon** it's all right. Come in."

As soon as I was in the old gentleman he locked the door and barred it and bolted it, and told the young men to come in with their **guns**, and they all went in a big **parlor** that had a new **rag carpet** on the floor, and got together in a corner that was out of the **range** of the front windows-- there warn't none on the side. They held the **candle**, and took a good look at me, and all said, "Why, *he* ain't a Shepherdson--no, there ain't any Shepherdson about him." Then the old man said he hoped I wouldn't mind being searched for arms, because he didn't mean no **harm** by it--it was only to make sure. So he didn't **pry** into my pockets, but only felt outside with his hands, and said it was all right. He told me to make myself easy and at home, and tell all about myself; but the old **lady** says:

"Why, **bless** you, Saul, the poor thing's as **wet** as he can be; and don't you reckon it may be he's hungry?"

"True for you, Rachel--I forgot."

So the old lady says:

"Betsy" (this was a nigger woman), "you **fly** around and get him something to eat as **quick** as you can, poor thing; and one of you girls go and **wake** up **Buck** and tell him--oh, here he is himself. Buck, take this little **stranger** and get the wet clothes off from him and **dress** him up in some of **yours** that's dry."

Buck looked about as old as me--thirteen or **fourteen** or along there, though he was a little **bigger** than me. He hadn't on anything but a **shirt**, and he was very frowzy-headed. He came in **gaping** and **digging** one **fist** into his eyes, and he was **dragging** a gun along with the other one. He says:

"Ain't they no Shepherdsons around?"

They said, no, 'twas a **false alarm**.

"Well," he says, "if they'd a ben some, I reckon I'd a got one."

They all **laughed**, and Bob says:

"Why, Buck, they might have scalped us all, you've been so slow in coming."

Chinese Simplified

alarm: 警报，惊动.
bigger: 更大，较大.
bless: 保佑，庇佑，祝福.
buck: 雄鹿.
candle: 蜡烛.
carpet: 地毯.
digging: 挖掘.
dragging: 拖，拖动，拖曳.
dress: 服装，打扮.
false: 假，虚伪，虚假.
fist: 拳头.
fly: 蝇，飞翔，苍蝇，飘扬，飞，飞行，飞跑.
fourteen: 十四.
gaping: 目瞪口呆.
gun: 枪，炮，长枪.
guns: 枪支.
harm: 伤害，损害，坏处，害处，祸害.
lady: 女士，夫人.
laughed: 笑.
parlor: 会客室.
pry: 刺探.
quick: 快，玲珑，敏捷的，迅速的.
rag: 破布，碎布.
range: 范围，靶场，射程，牧场，区域，距离，围范.
reckon: 估计，计算.
shirt: 衬衫，衬衣.
stranger: 陌生人，异乡人，生人.
wake: 醒来，醒觉.
wet: 湿.
yours: 你的.

"Well, **nobody** come after me, and it ain't right I'm always **kept** down; I don't get no show."

"Never mind, Buck, my boy," says the old **man**, "you'll have show enough, all in good time, don't you **fret** about that. Go 'long with you now, and do as your mother told you."

When we got up-stairs to his room he got me a **coarse shirt** and a **roundabout** and **pants** of his, and I put them on. While I was at it he asked me what my name was, but before I could tell him he started to tell me about a bluejay and a young **rabbit** he had catched in the **woods** day before **yesterday**, and he asked me where Moses was when the **candle** went out. I said I didn't know; I hadn't heard about it before, no way.

"Well, **guess**," he says.

"How'm I going to guess," says I, "when I never heard tell of it before?"

"But you can guess, can't you? It's just as easy."

"*Which* candle?" I says.

"Why, any candle," he says.

"I don't know where he was," says I; "where was he?"

"Why, he was in the ***dark***! That's where he was!"

"Well, if you knowed where he was, what did you ask me for?"

"Why, **blame** it, it's a **riddle**, don't you see? Say, how long are you going to stay here? You got to stay always. We can just have **booming** times--they don't have no school now. Do you own a **dog**? I've got a dog--and he'll go in the **river** and bring out chips that you **throw** in. Do you like to **comb** up Sundays, and all that kind of **foolishness**? You **bet** I don't, but ma she makes me. Confound these ole britches! I **reckon** I'd better put 'em on, but I'd ruther not, it's so **warm**. Are you all **ready**? All right. Come along, old hoss."

Cold corn-pone, cold corn-beef, **butter** and buttermilk--that is what they had for me down there, and there ain't nothing better that ever I've come across yet. Buck and his ma and all of them **smoked** cob pipes, **except** the nigger woman,

Chinese Simplified

bet: 打赌，赌.
blame: 责备，咎，非难，责任，罪，责怪，归咎.
booming: 繁荣.
butter: 牛油，黄油.
candle: 蜡烛.
coarse: 粗劣，粗糙的，淫秽，粗鲁.
cold: 冷，感冒，寒冷，寒，冷淡.
comb: 梳，梳子.
dark: 暗，黑暗，夜.
dog: 狗，犬.
except: 除了，除了之外.
foolishness: 愚蠢.
fret: 烦恼.
guess: 猜测，臆测，猜谜儿，猜想，揣测，推测.
kept: 收存.
ma: 妈，马，文学硕士.
nobody: 没有人，没人.
pants: 裤子.
rabbit: 兔子，兔，野兔.
ready: 就绪，愿意，准备，妥当.
reckon: 估计，计算.
riddle: 谜，谜语.
river: 河，江，川，河流，条.
roundabout: 曲线.
shirt: 衬衫，衬衣.
smoked: 熏.
throw: 扔，丢掉，丢，投.
warm: 暖，暖和，温暖，热烈，温暖的.
woods: 树林，森林.
yesterday: 昨天.

which was gone, and the two young women. They all **smoked** and **talked**, and I eat and talked. The young women had quilts around them, and their hair down their **backs**. They all asked me questions, and I told them how pap and me and all the family was living on a little farm down at the bottom of Arkansaw, and my **sister** Mary Ann run off and got **married** and never was heard of no more, and Bill went to **hunt** them and he warn't heard of no more, and Tom and Mort died, and then there warn't nobody but just me and pap left, and he was just trimmed down to nothing, on **account** of his **troubles**; so when he died I took what there was left, because the farm didn't **belong** to us, and started up the river, **deck** passage, and fell **overboard**; and that was how I come to be here. So they said I could have a home there as long as I wanted it. Then it was most **daylight** and everybody went to bed, and I went to bed with Buck, and when I waked up in the morning, drat it all, I had **forgot** what my name was. So I **laid** there about an hour trying to think, and when Buck waked up I says:

"Can you **spell**, Buck?"

"Yes," he says.

"I **bet** you can't spell my name," says I.

"I bet you what you **dare** I can," says he.

"All right," says I, "go ahead."

"G-e-o-r-g-e J-a-x-o-n--there now," he says.

"Well," says I, "you done it, but I didn't think you could. It ain't no slouch of a name to spell--right off without studying."

I set it down, **private**, because somebody might want *me* to spell it next, and so I wanted to be **handy** with it and **rattle** it off like I was used to it.

It was a **mighty** nice family, and a mighty nice house, too. I hadn't seen no house out in the country before that was so nice and had so much style. It didn't have an iron **latch** on the front door, nor a **wooden** one with a buckskin **string**, but a **brass knob** to turn, the same as houses in town. There warn't no bed in the **parlor**, nor a sign of a bed; but heaps of parlors in towns has **beds** in them. There was a big **fireplace** that was bricked on the bottom, and the **bricks** was kept

Chinese Simplified

account：帐户，账，帐，户口，重要性.
backs：支持.
beds：床.
belong：属于.
bet：打赌，赌.
brass：黄铜.
bricks：砖.
dare：敢.
daylight：日光，白天.
deck：甲板.
fireplace：壁炉.
forgot：忘记.
handy：灵巧，便当，顺手，方便的，简便.
hunt：打猎，狩猎.
knob：把手，球形捏手，旋钮.
laid：放.
latch：门闩.
married：已婚，已婚的.
mighty：伟大，强势，强大的.
overboard：向船外.
parlor：会客室.
private：私人，私营，私人的，私有，士兵.
rattle：发嘎嘎声，发出格格声响.
sister：姐妹.
smoked：熏.
spell：拼写，咒语，符咒.
string：绳子，串，线，细线，弦.
talked：谈话.
troubles：坏处，麻烦.
wooden：木制，木制的.

clean and **red** by pouring water on them and **scrubbing** them with another **brick**; sometimes they **wash** them over with red water-paint that they call Spanish-brown, same as they do in town. They had big **brass** dog-irons that could hold up a saw-log. There was a **clock** on the middle of the mantelpiece, with a picture of a town painted on the bottom half of the **glass** front, and a round place in the middle of it for the sun, and you could see the **pendulum** swinging behind it. It was beautiful to hear that clock **tick**; and sometimes when one of these peddlers had been along and scoured her up and got her in good shape, she would start in and strike a hundred and fifty before she got tuckered out. They wouldn't took any money for her.

Well, there was a big **outlandish parrot** on each side of the clock, made out of something like **chalk**, and painted up **gaudy**. By one of the **parrots** was a **cat** made of **crockery**, and a crockery dog by the other; and when you **pressed** down on them they squeaked, but didn't open their **mouths** nor look different nor interested. They squeaked through **underneath**. There was a couple of big wild-turkey-wing fans spread out behind those things. On the table in the middle of the room was a kind of a lovely crockery **basket** that had apples and oranges and peaches and grapes piled up in it, which was much redder and yellower and prettier than real ones is, but they warn't real because you could see where pieces had got chipped off and showed the white chalk, or whatever it was, underneath.

This table had a cover made out of beautiful **oilcloth**, with a red and blue spread-eagle painted on it, and a painted **border** all around. It come all the way from Philadelphia, they said. There was some books, too, piled up perfectly **exact**, on each corner of the table. One was a big family Bible full of pictures. One was Pilgrim's Progress, about a man that left his family, it didn't say why. I read considerable in it now and then. The **statements** was **interesting**, but **tough**. Another was Friendship's Offering, full of beautiful stuff and **poetry**; but I didn't read the poetry. Another was Henry Clay's Speeches, and another was Dr. Gunn's Family Medicine, which told you all about what to do if a body was **sick** or dead. There was a **hymn** book, and a lot of other books. And there was

Chinese Simplified

basket: 篮，篮子，笼，淘箩，筐，笼子.
border: 边界，边，疆界，边境，国界，缘.
brass: 黄铜.
brick: 砖，砖块.
cat: 猫.
chalk: 粉笔.
clock: 钟，时钟，钟表.
crockery: 瓦器.
exact: 确切，精密，准确，正确的.
gaudy: 花哨，花里胡哨.
glass: 玻璃，杯子.
hymn: 圣歌，圣诗.
interesting: 有趣，有意思，有兴趣，好玩儿，吸引人的.
mouths: 口.
oilcloth: 油布.
outlandish: 偏僻的，外国气派的，妄图.
parrot: 鹦鹉.
parrots: 鹦鹉.
pendulum: 钟摆.
poetry: 诗，诗歌.
pressed: 压.
red: 红，红色，红色的.
scrubbing: 擦洗.
sick: 生病.
statements: 声明.
tick: 壁虱，滴答声，勾.
tough: 强硬，坚韧的.
underneath: 在下面，下面的.
wash: 洗涤，洗刷，洗.

nice split-bottom chairs, and perfectly sound, too--not **bagged** down in the middle and busted, like an old basket.

They had pictures hung on the walls--mainly Washingtons and Lafayettes, and **battles**, and Highland Marys, and one called "Signing the Declaration." There was some that they called crayons, which one of the daughters which was dead made her own self when she was only fifteen years old. They was different from any pictures I ever see before-- **blacker**, mostly, than is common. One was a woman in a slim black dress, **belted** small under the armpits, with bulges like a **cabbage** in the middle of the **sleeves**, and a large black scoop-shovel **bonnet** with a black **veil**, and white slim **ankles** crossed about with black **tape**, and very **wee** black **slippers**, like a **chisel**, and she was leaning **pensive** on a **tombstone** on her right elbow, under a **weeping willow**, and her other hand hanging down her side holding a white **handkerchief** and a reticule, and underneath the picture it said "Shall I Never See Thee More Alas." Another one was a young lady with her hair all **combed** up straight to the top of her head, and knotted there in front of a comb like a chair-back, and she was crying into a handkerchief and had a dead bird laying on its back in her other hand with its heels up, and underneath the picture it said "I Shall Never Hear Thy Sweet Chirrup More Alas." There was one where a young lady was at a window looking up at the moon, and tears running down her cheeks; and she had an open **letter** in one hand with black **sealing wax** showing on one edge of it, and she was mashing a locket with a chain to it against her mouth, and underneath the picture it said "And Art Thou Gone Yes Thou Art Gone Alas." These was all nice pictures, I reckon, but I didn't somehow seem to take to them, because if ever I was down a little they always give me the fan-tods. Everybody was sorry she died, because she had laid out a lot more of these pictures to do, and a body could see by what she had done what they had lost. But I reckoned that with her **disposition** she was having a better time in the **graveyard**. She was at work on what they said was her **greatest** picture when she took sick, and every day and every night it was her **prayer** to be allowed to live till she got it done, but she never got the chance. It was a picture of a young woman in a long white gown, standing on the **rail** of a **bridge** all ready to jump off, with her hair all down her back, and looking up to

Chinese Simplified

ankles：脚脖子．
bagged：松弛下垂的．
battles：战斗．
belted：束带的，装甲的．
blacker：黑色，黑人．
bonnet：苏格兰帽，阀盖，无边有带的女帽．
bridge：网桥，桥梁，桥接器，桥，鼻梁．
cabbage：甘蓝菜，包菜．
chisel：凿子，凿．
comb：梳，梳子．
disposition：意向，性格，脾气，安排，部署．
graveyard：坟地，墓地．
greatest：莫大．
handkerchief：手帕，手绢．
letter：字母，信．
pensive：哀思，沉思的．
prayer：祷告，祈祷．
rail：铁路，轨道．
sealing：密封．
sleeves：袖子．
slippers：拖鞋，便鞋．
tape：卷带，胶带，磁带，录音带．
tombstone：墓碑．
veil：面罩，面纱．
wax：蜡．
wee：细小．
weeping：垂枝的．
willow：柳树．

the **moon**, with the tears running down her face, and she had two arms folded across her **breast**, and two arms **stretched** out in front, and two more **reaching** up towards the moon--and the idea was to see which **pair** would look best, and then **scratch** out all the other arms; but, as I was saying, she died before she got her mind made up, and now they kept this picture over the head of the bed in her room, and every time her **birthday** come they **hung** flowers on it. Other times it was **hid** with a little **curtain**. The young woman in the picture had a kind of a nice **sweet** face, but there was so many arms it made her look too spidery, seemed to me.

This young girl kept a scrap-book when she was alive, and used to **paste** obituaries and **accidents** and **cases** of **patient suffering** in it out of the Presbyterian Observer, and write **poetry** after them out of her own head. It was very good poetry. This is what she wrote about a boy by the name of Stephen Dowling Bots that fell down a well and was drownded:

Ode to Stephen Dowling Bots, Dec'd

And did young Stephen **sicken**,
And did young Stephen die?
And did the **sad hearts thicken**,
And did the mourners **cry**?
No; such was not the **fate** of Young Stephen Dowling Bots;
Though sad hearts round him **thickened**,
'Twas not from **sickness' shots**.

No whooping-cough did **rack** his frame,
Nor **measles** drear with spots;
Not these impaired the **sacred** name
Of Stephen Dowling Bots.

Despised love **struck** not with **woe**

Chinese Simplified

accidents: 事故.
birthday: 生日, 诞辰, 寿辰.
breast: 奶子, 乳房, 胸, 胸部.
cases: 情况.
cry: 喊, 叫, 哭, 哭泣.
curtain: 布帘.
fate: 命运.
hearts: 心.
hid: 躲藏.
hung: 挂.
measles: 麻疹.
moon: 月亮, 月球, 月.
pair: 对, 一对, 双.
paste: 糊, 软膏, 粘贴, 糊状物.
patient: 耐烦, 患者, 病号, 病员, 耐心, 忍耐, 病人.
poetry: 诗, 诗歌.
rack: 网架, 支架.
reaching: 到达.
sacred: 神圣, 神圣的.
sad: 悲伤, 哀愁, 不幸, 哀伤, 哀怨, 悲伤的, 悲哀的.
scratch: 抓伤, 抓, 搔刮.
shots: 射击.
sicken: 使作呕.
sickness: 病, 疾病.
stretched: 伸展.
struck: 敲打.
suffering: 痛苦, 熬煎, 苦难.
sweet: 甜, 甜食, 糖果.
thicken: 变厚.
thickened: 变厚.
woe: 悲哀, 悲痛.

That head of **curly knots**,
Nor **stomach troubles laid** him low,
Young Stephen Dowling Bots.

O no. Then list with **tearful** eye,
Whilst I his **fate** do tell.
His **soul** did from this cold world **fly**
By **falling** down a well.

They got him out and **emptied** him;
Alas it was too late;
His **spirit** was gone for to **sport aloft**
In the realms of the good and great.

If Emmeline Grangerford could make **poetry** like that before she was **fourteen**, there ain't no telling what she could a done by and by. Buck said she could **rattle** off poetry like nothing. She didn't ever have to stop to think. He said she would **slap** down a line, and if she couldn't find anything to **rhyme** with it would just **scratch** it out and slap down another one, and go **ahead**. She warn't particular; she could write about anything you **choose** to give her to write about just so it was sadful. Every time a man died, or a woman died, or a child died, she would be on hand with her "tribute" before he was cold. She called them tributes. The neighbors said it was the **doctor** first, then Emmeline, then the **undertaker**--the undertaker never got in ahead of Emmeline but once, and then she **hung** fire on a rhyme for the dead person's name, which was Whistler. She warn't ever the same after that; she never complained, but she kinder pined away and did not live long. Poor thing, many's the time I made myself go up to the little room that used to be **hers** and get out her poor old scrap-book and read in it when her **pictures** had been aggravating me and I had **soured** on her a little. I liked all that family, dead ones and all, and warn't going to let anything come between us. Poor Emmeline made poetry about all the dead people when she was **alive**, and it didn't seem right that there warn't **nobody** to make some about

Chinese Simplified

ahead：前头，前方，前面的.
alive：活着，活，活泼的，活着的.
aloft：在高处.
choose：挑选，选择，拣，推举，推选，选定，选取.
curly：卷曲，卷曲的.
doctor：医生，大夫，医师，博士.
emptied：空.
falling：落下的，落下.
fate：命运.
fly：蝇，飞翔，苍蝇，飘扬，飞，飞行，飞跑.
fourteen：十四.
hers：她的.
hung：挂.
knots：节.
laid：放.
nobody：没有人，没人.
pictures：图画.
poetry：诗，诗歌.
rattle：发嘎嘎声，发出格格声响.
rhyme：韵，押韵，压韵.
scratch：抓伤，抓，搔刮.
slap：掌击，拍.
soul：灵魂.
soured：酸味.
spirit：神，精神，灵魂，气概，白干儿，白乾儿.
sport：运动.
stomach：胃，肚子.
tearful：含泪的.
troubles：坏处，麻烦.
undertaker：承担人，殡仪馆.

her now she was gone; so I tried to **sweat** out a **verse** or two myself, but I couldn't seem to make it go **somehow**. They kept Emmeline's room **trim** and nice, and all the things **fixed** in it just the way she liked to have them when she was **alive**, and **nobody** ever **slept** there. The old lady took care of the room herself, though there was **plenty** of niggers, and she **sewed** there a good deal and read her Bible there mostly.

Well, as I was saying about the **parlor**, there was **beautiful** curtains on the **windows**: white, with **pictures** painted on them of castles with vines all down the **walls**, and **cattle** coming down to **drink**. There was a little old **piano**, too, that had **tin** pans in it, I **reckon**, and nothing was ever so **lovely** as to hear the young **ladies sing** "The Last Link is Broken" and play "The Battle of Prague" on it. The walls of all the **rooms** was plastered, and most had carpets on the **floors**, and the whole house was whitewashed on the outside.

It was a **double** house, and the big open place **betwixt** them was roofed and **floored**, and sometimes the table was set there in the middle of the day, and it was a **cool**, **comfortable** place. Nothing couldn't be better. And warn't the **cooking** good, and just bushels of it too!

Chinese Simplified

alive: 活着，活，活泼的，活着的.
beautiful: 漂亮，美，美丽，菲菲，锦绣，美丽的，秀丽，美观.
betwixt: 中间，在…之间.
cattle: 家畜，牛.
comfortable: 舒服，舒服的.
cooking: 烹调.
cool: 凉，镇静，镇定，凉爽，凉爽的.
double: 双重，双，加倍.
drink: 喝，饮用，饮，饮料.
fixed: 固定，确定，一定，固定的.
floored: 地板.
floors: 地板.
ladies: 女洗手间.
lovely: 可爱，可爱的.
nobody: 没有人，没人.
parlor: 会客室.
piano: 钢琴.
pictures: 图画.
plenty: 丰富，许多.
reckon: 估计，计算.
rooms: 房间.
sewed: 缝.
sing: 唱，歌唱，唱歌.
slept: 睡了.
somehow: 不知何故.
sweat: 汗，出汗，流汗.
tin: 锡，罐头.
trim: 修剪，笔挺.
verse: 诗，韵文，诗节，散文.
walls: 墙壁.
windows: 视窗.

CHAPTER XVIII

WHY HARNEY RODE AWAY FOR HIS HAT

Col. Grangerford was a **gentleman**, you see. He was a gentleman all over; and so was his family. He was well born, as the saying is, and that's worth as much in a man as it is in a **horse**, so the Widow Douglas said, and **nobody** ever denied that she was of the first **aristocracy** in our town; and pap he always said it, too, though he warn't no more **quality** than a mudcat himself. Col. Grangerford was very **tall** and very **slim**, and had a darkish-paly **complexion**, not a sign of red in it anywheres; he was **clean** shaved every morning all over his **thin** face, and he had the thinnest kind of **lips**, and the thinnest kind of nostrils, and a high **nose**, and heavy eyebrows, and the **blackest** kind of eyes, **sunk** so **deep** back that they seemed like they was looking out of caverns at you, as you may say. His **forehead** was high, and his hair was black and straight and **hung** to his **shoulders**. His hands was long and thin, and every day of his life he put on a clean **shirt** and a full **suit** from head to **foot** made out of **linen** so white it **hurt** your eyes to look at it; and on Sundays he **wore** a blue tail-coat with **brass** buttons on it. He carried a **mahogany cane** with a **silver** head to it. There warn't no frivolishness about him, not a bit, and he warn't ever **loud**. He was as kind as he could be--you could feel that, you know, and so you had **confidence**. Sometimes he smiled, and it was good to see; but when he straightened himself

Chinese Simplified

aristocracy: 贵族社会，贵族.
blackest: 黑人.
brass: 黄铜.
cane: 手杖，甘蔗，杖，鞭打.
clean: 清洁，擦拭，乾净，刷，清洗，干净.
complexion: 气色，脸色，肤色.
confidence: 信心，自信.
deep: 深，深深，深刻，深厚，浓厚，深沉，奥秘.
foot: 脚，足，步兵，英尺，呎.
forehead: 前额，额，额头.
gentleman: 绅士.
horse: 马.
hung: 挂.
hurt: 伤害，使受伤.
linen: 亚麻布.
lips: 嘴唇.
loud: 高声，大声，大声的.
mahogany: 桃花心木，红木.
nobody: 没有人，没人.
nose: 鼻子.
quality: 品质，质量，质，高低，档次，特质，粗细，优质的.
shirt: 衬衫，衬衣.
shoulders: 肩，双肩.
silver: 银，白银.
slim: 瘦长，纤细，苗条的.
suit: 适应，一套.
sunk: 沉没.
tall: 高大的，高大.
thin: 薄，疏，细，淡.
wore: 穿了.

up like a liberty-pole, and the **lightning** begun to **flicker** out from under his eyebrows, you wanted to **climb** a tree first, and find out what the matter was afterwards. He didn't ever have to tell anybody to mind their manners--everybody was always good-mannered where he was. Everybody loved to have him around, too; he was **sunshine** most always--I mean he made it seem like good weather. When he turned into a cloudbank it was **awful** dark for half a minute, and that was enough; there wouldn't nothing go wrong again for a week.

When him and the old lady come down in the morning all the family got up out of their **chairs** and give them good-day, and didn't set down again till they had set down. Then Tom and **Bob** went to the **sideboard** where the decanter was, and **mixed** a glass of **bitters** and **handed** it to him, and he held it in his hand and waited till Tom's and Bob's was mixed, and then they **bowed** and said, "Our **duty** to you, sir, and madam;" and *they* bowed the **least** bit in the world and said **thank** you, and so they **drank**, all three, and Bob and Tom poured a **spoonful** of water on the sugar and the mite of **whisky** or **apple brandy** in the bottom of their tumblers, and give it to me and Buck, and we drank to the old people too.

Bob was the **oldest** and Tom next--tall, beautiful men with very broad shoulders and **brown** faces, and long black hair and black eyes. They dressed in white **linen** from head to foot, like the old **gentleman**, and **wore** broad Panama hats.

Then there was Miss Charlotte; she was twenty-five, and tall and proud and **grand**, but as good as she could be when she warn't stirred up; but when she was she had a look that would make you **wilt** in your **tracks**, like her father. She was beautiful.

So was her sister, Miss Sophia, but it was a different kind. She was **gentle** and sweet like a **dove**, and she was only twenty.

Each person had their own nigger to wait on them--Buck too. My nigger had a **monstrous** easy time, because I warn't used to having anybody do anything for me, but Buck's was on the **jump** most of the time.

Chinese Simplified

apple：苹果，苹果.
awful：可怕，可怕的.
bitters：苦味.
bob：鲍勃.
bowed：有弓的.
brandy：白兰地.
brown：褐色，棕色，布朗.
chairs：椅子.
climb：爬，攀登.
dove：鸽.
drank：喝了.
duty：任务，义务，责任，关税，职责.
flicker：闪烁.
gentle：轻松，文雅的，斯文，柔和.
grand：堂皇，隆重，雄伟，盛大，宏大，大型的，宏伟.
handed：传递，有手的.
jump：跳，跳跃.
least：最少，至少，最少的.
lightning：闪电.
linen：亚麻布.
mixed：混合，混合的，错杂.
monstrous：怪物似，似怪物的.
oldest：最年长的.
sideboard：餐具柜.
spoonful：一匙，满匙的.
sunshine：阳光.
thank：感谢，谢谢.
tracks：轨道.
whisky：威士忌酒.
wilt：枯萎.
wore：穿了.

This was all there was of the family now, but there used to be more-- three **sons**; they got killed; and Emmeline that died.

The old gentleman **owned** a lot of **farms** and over a hundred niggers. Sometimes a **stack** of people would come there, **horseback**, from ten or fifteen mile around, and stay five or six days, and have such junketings round about and on the river, and **dances** and picnics in the **woods** daytimes, and **balls** at the house nights. These people was mostly kinfolks of the family. The men brought their **guns** with them. It was a **handsome** lot of quality, I tell you.

There was another **clan** of **aristocracy** around there--five or six families --mostly of the name of Shepherdson. They was as **high**-toned and well born and rich and grand as the **tribe** of Grangerfords. The Shepherdsons and Grangerfords used the same **steamboat landing**, which was about two mile above our house; so sometimes when I went up there with a lot of our folks I used to see a lot of the Shepherdsons there on their fine horses.

One day Buck and me was away out in the woods **hunting**, and **heard** a horse coming. We was **crossing** the road. Buck says:

"Quick! Jump for the woods!"

We done it, and then peeped down the woods through the leaves. Pretty soon a **splendid** young man come **galloping** down the road, setting his horse easy and looking like a **soldier**. He had his gun across his **pommel**. I had seen him before. It was young Harney Shepherdson. I heard Buck's gun go off at my ear, and Harney's hat tumbled off from his head. He grabbed his gun and **rode** straight to the place where we was **hid**. But we didn't wait. We started through the woods on a run. The woods warn't thick, so I looked over my shoulder to **dodge** the **bullet**, and **twice** I seen Harney cover Buck with his gun; and then he rode away the way he come--to get his hat, I **reckon**, but I couldn't see. We never stopped running till we got home. The old gentleman's eyes blazed a minute--'twas **pleasure**, mainly, I judged--then his face sort of **smoothed** down, and he says, kind of gentle:

Chinese Simplified

aristocracy：贵族社会，贵族．
balls：球．
bullet：子弹．
clan：氏族，家族．
crossing：路口，横越，交叉点．
dances：跳舞．
dodge：躲闪，躲避．
ear：耳朵，耳．
farms：农场．
galloping：迅速发展的．
guns：枪支．
handsome：英俊，慷慨的，英俊的．
hid：躲藏．
high-toned：调子高的，高尚的．
horseback：马背．
hunting：狩猎．
landing：着陆．
owned：拥有．
pleasure：欢乐、乐趣，愉快．
pommel：鞍头．
reckon：估计，计算．
rode：骑．
smoothed：平滑的．
soldier：士兵，战士，军人，兵家．
sons：儿子．
splendid：彪炳，卓越，辉煌，灿烂的，精彩，辉煌的．
stack：堆，栈，垛，堆叠，堆积，堆置．
steamboat：汽船，轮船．
tribe：部落，部族．
twice：两次．
woods：树林，森林．

"I don't like that **shooting** from behind a **bush**. Why didn't you **step** into the road, my boy?"

"The Shepherdsons don't, father. They always take advantage."

Miss Charlotte she held her head up like a **queen** while Buck was telling his **tale**, and her nostrils **spread** and her eyes **snapped**. The two young men looked **dark**, but never said nothing. Miss Sophia she turned **pale**, but the **color** come back when she found the man warn't hurt.

Soon as I could get Buck down by the corn-cribs under the **trees** by **ourselves**, I says:

"Did you want to **kill** him, Buck?"

"Well, I **bet** I did."

"What did he do to you?"

"Him? He never done nothing to me."

"Well, then, what did you want to kill him for?"

"Why, nothing--only it's on account of the **feud**."

"What's a feud?"

"Why, where was you **raised**? Don't you know what a feud is?"

"Never heard of it before--tell me about it."

"Well," says Buck, "a feud is this way: A man has a **quarrel** with another man, and **kills** him; then that other man's **brother** kills *him*; then the other **brothers**, on both sides, goes for one another; then the *cousins* **chip** in--and by and by everybody's **killed** off, and there ain't no more feud. But it's kind of **slow**, and takes a long time."

"Has this one been going on long, Buck?"

"Well, I should *reckon*! It started thirty year ago, or som'ers along there. There was trouble 'bout something, and then a **lawsuit** to **settle** it; and the suit went agin one of the men, and so he up and **shot** the man that **won** the suit--which he would **naturally** do, of course. Anybody would."

Chinese Simplified

bet：打赌，赌.
brother：弟兄，兄弟.
brothers：兄弟，哥儿.
bush：灌木，布什，丛林.
chip：碎片，芯片，晶片.
color：颜色，彩色.
dark：暗，黑暗，夜.
feud：世仇.
kill：打死、杀害，杀死.
killed：被屠宰的，被杀死的.
kills：杀死.
lawsuit：诉讼，官司，讼诉案.
naturally：自然，自然地.
ourselves：我们自己，我们.
pale：苍白，苍白的.
quarrel：拌嘴，争吵，吵嘴，是非.
queen：女王，王后，皇后.
raised：凸起的，浮雕的.
reckon：估计，计算.
settle：奠定，安家落户，澄清，解决.
shooting：射击，猎场.
shot：射击.
slow：慢，缓慢，迟慢，迟钝，迟迟，迟缓.
snapped：猛咬.
spread：扩散，流传，传播，散播，敷，撒.
step：步骤，步伐，措施，一步，步调，步子，级，脚步，踏.
suit：适应，一套.
tale：故事.
trees：树木.
won：圜，胜.

"What was the trouble about, Buck?--land?"

"I **reckon** maybe--I don't know."

"Well, who done the **shooting**? Was it a Grangerford or a Shepherdson?"

"Laws, how do I know? It was so long ago."

"Don't anybody know?"

"Oh, yes, **pa** knows, I reckon, and some of the other old people; but they don't know now what the row was about in the first place."

"Has there been many killed, Buck?"

"Yes; right **smart** chance of **funerals**. But they don't always kill. Pa's got a few buckshot in him; but he don't mind it 'cuz he don't **weigh** much, anyway. Bob's been carved up some with a bowie, and Tom's been **hurt** once or twice."

"Has anybody been killed this year, Buck?"

"Yes; we got one and they got one. 'Bout three months ago my **cousin** Bud, **fourteen** year old, was riding through the **woods** on t'other side of the river, and didn't have no **weapon** with him, which was **blame' foolishness**, and in a **lonesome** place he hears a horse a-coming behind him, and sees old Baldy Shepherdson a-linkin' after him with his **gun** in his hand and his white hair a-flying in the wind; and 'stead of jumping off and taking to the **brush**, Bud 'lowed he could out-run him; so they had it, **nip** and **tuck**, for five **mile** or more, the old man a-gaining all the time; so at last Bud seen it warn't any use, so he stopped and faced around so as to have the **bullet holes** in front, you know, and the old man he **rode** up and shot him down. But he didn't git much chance to **enjoy** his **luck**, for **inside** of a week our folks **laid** *him* out."

"I reckon that old man was a **coward**, Buck."

"I reckon he *warn't* a coward. Not by a blame' sight. There ain't a coward amongst them Shepherdsons--not a one. And there ain't no cowards amongst the Grangerfords either. Why, that old man kep' up his end in a fight one day for half an hour against three Grangerfords, and come out **winner**. They was all a-horseback; he **lit** off of his horse and got behind a little **woodpile**, and kep' his

Chinese Simplified

blame: 责备，咎，非难，责任，罪，责怪，归咎.
brush: 刷，毛刷，洗刷，刷子，拂，擦.
bullet: 子弹.
cousin: 表亲，表哥，堂表.
coward: 懦夫，胆小鬼.
enjoy: 享有，享受，喜欢.
foolishness: 愚蠢.
fourteen: 十四.
funerals: 葬礼.
gun: 枪，炮，长枪.
holes: 洞.
hurt: 伤害，使受伤.
inside: 里面，内部，里，里头，秘密的，在里面，在内，之内，之中.
laid: 放.
lit: 点燃.
lonesome: 寂寞，寂寞的.
luck: 运气，幸运.
mile: 英里.
nip: 咬，捏，掐.
pa: 爸爸.
reckon: 估计，计算.
rode: 骑.
shooting: 射击，猎场.
smart: 高明，时髦的.
tuck: 挤进，塞进.
weapon: 武器.
weigh: 权衡，秤.
winner: 胜利者.
woodpile: 柴堆.
woods: 树林，森林.

horse before him to stop the **bullets**; but the Grangerfords stayed on their horses and capered around the old man, and peppered away at him, and he peppered away at them. Him and his horse both went home pretty leaky and **crippled**, but the Grangerfords had to be *fetched* home--and one of 'em was dead, and another died the next day. No, sir; if a body's out **hunting** for cowards he don't want to **fool** away any time amongst them Shepherdsons, becuz they don't **breed** any of that *kind*."

Next Sunday we all went to church, about three mile, everybody a-**horseback**. The men took their **guns** along, so did Buck, and kept them between their knees or stood them **handy** against the wall. The Shepherdsons done the same. It was pretty **ornery** preaching--all about brotherly love, and such-like tiresomeness; but everybody said it was a good **sermon**, and they all talked it over going home, and had such a powerful lot to say about **faith** and good **works** and free **grace** and preforeordestination, and I don't know what all, that it did seem to me to be one of the roughest Sundays I had run across yet.

About an hour after dinner everybody was **dozing** around, some in their **chairs** and some in their rooms, and it got to be pretty **dull**. Buck and a dog was **stretched** out on the grass in the sun sound asleep. I went up to our room, and judged I would take a **nap** myself. I found that sweet Miss Sophia standing in her door, which was next to ours, and she took me in her room and shut the door very soft, and asked me if I liked her, and I said I did; and she asked me if I would do something for her and not tell anybody, and I said I would. Then she said she'd **forgot** her Testament, and left it in the **seat** at church between two other books, and would I **slip** out quiet and go there and fetch it to her, and not say nothing to nobody. I said I would. So I **slid** out and slipped off up the road, and there warn't anybody at the church, except maybe a **hog** or two, for there warn't any **lock** on the door, and hogs likes a **puncheon** floor in summer- time because it's cool. If you notice, most folks don't go to church only when they've got to; but a hog is different.

Says I to myself, something's up; it ain't natural for a girl to be in such a **sweat** about a Testament. So I give it a **shake**, and out drops a little piece of **paper** with

Chinese Simplified

breed：品种，繁殖，饲养．
bullets：子弹．
chairs：椅子．
crippled：瘫痪．
dozing：打瞌睡．
dull：索然，板滞，沉闷的，干燥，拙，深沉．
faith：信心，信仰，信任，信念．
fetch：拿，取，带来．
fool：呆子，笨蛋，傻子，笨人，愚人．
forgot：忘记．
grace：优雅，恩典，天恩，魅力，宽限．
guns：枪支．
handy：灵巧，便当，顺手，方便的，简便．
hog：猪．
horseback：马背．
hunting：狩猎．
lock：锁，撞锁．
nap：瞌睡．
ornery：低劣的．
paper：纸，论文，纸张．
puncheon：短柱．
seat：座位，位置，位子，席位，座．
sermon：传教．
shake：摇动，震动，摇，震荡，颠簸．
slid：滑行．
slip：滑倒，溜走，溜．
stretched：伸展．
sweat：汗，出汗，流汗．
works：作品，书籍，工作．

"*half-past two*" wrote on it with a **pencil**. I ransacked it, but couldn't find anything else. I couldn't make anything out of that, so I put the paper in the book again, and when I got home and **upstairs** there was Miss Sophia in her door waiting for me. She pulled me in and **shut** the door; then she looked in the Testament **till** she found the paper, and as soon as she read it she looked **glad**; and before a body could think she grabbed me and give me a **squeeze**, and said I was the best boy in the world, and not to tell **anybody**. She was **mighty** red in the face for a minute, and her eyes **lighted** up, and it made her powerful pretty. I was a good deal **astonished**, but when I got my **breath** I asked her what the paper was about, and she asked me if I had read it, and I said no, and she asked me if I could read **writing**, and I told her "no, only coarse-hand," and then she said the paper warn't anything but a book-mark to keep her place, and I might go and play now.

I went off down to the river, **studying** over this thing, and pretty soon I noticed that my nigger was following along behind. When we was out of sight of the house he looked back and around a second, and then comes a- running, and says:

"Mars Jawge, if you'll come down into de **swamp** I'll show you a whole **stack** o' water-moccasins."

Thinks I, that's mighty **curious**; he said that yesterday. He oughter know a body don't love water-moccasins enough to go around **hunting** for them. What is he up to, anyway? So I says:

"All right; **trot** ahead."

I followed a half a **mile**; then he **struck** out over the swamp, and waded **ankle** deep as much as another half-mile. We come to a little **flat** piece of land which was dry and very **thick** with trees and **bushes** and vines, and he says:

"You **shove** right in dah jist a few **steps**, Mars Jawge; dah's whah dey is. I's **seed** 'm befo'; I don't k'yer to see 'em no mo'."

Then he slopped right along and went away, and pretty soon the trees **hid** him. I poked into the place a-ways and come to a little open **patch** as big as a

Chinese Simplified

ankle：脚踝，踝，脚脖子．
anybody：任何人．
astonished：诧异．
breath：气息，鼻息，呼吸，气流．
bushes：灌木．
curious：有好奇心，好奇，好奇的．
flat：平坦，平板，平坦的，平的，居室．
glad：高兴，高兴的．
hid：躲藏．
hunting：狩猎．
lighted：点燃．
mighty：伟大，强势，强大的．
mile：英里．
patch：补缀，补丁，补．
pencil：铅笔，笔套，笔帽．
seed：种子，播种．
shove：推．
shut：关闭．
squeeze：压扁，压挤，榨．
stack：堆，栈，垛，堆叠，堆积，堆置．
steps：步骤．
struck：敲打．
studying：学习．
swamp：沼泽．
thick：厚，密，浓厚．
thinks：想．
till：直到．
trot：快步跑，小跑．
upstairs：楼上，在楼上．
writing：篇章，笔墨，着述，写，写作．

bedroom all **hung** around with vines, and found a man laying there asleep--and, by jings, it was my old Jim!

I waked him up, and I reckoned it was going to be a grand **surprise** to him to see me again, but it warn't. He nearly cried he was so **glad**, but he warn't **surprised**. Said he swum along behind me that night, and heard me **yell** every time, but dasn't answer, because he didn't want nobody to pick *him* up and take him into **slavery** again. Says he:

"I got **hurt** a little, en couldn't **swim** fas', so I wuz a considable ways behine you towards de las'; when you **landed** I reck'ned I could **ketch** up wid you on de lan' 'dout havin' to **shout** at you, but when I see dat house I begin to go **slow**. I 'uz off too **fur** to hearwhat dey say to you--I wuz 'fraid o' de **dogs**; but when it 'uz all quiet agin I knowed you's in de house, so I **struck** out for de **woods** to wait for day. Early in de mawnin' some er de niggers come along, gwyne to de fields, en dey tuk me en showed me dis place, whah de dogs can't track me on accounts o' de water, en dey **brings** me truck to eat every night, en tells me how you's a-gitt'n along."

"Why didn't you tell my Jack to **fetch** me here sooner, Jim?"

"Well, 'twarn't no use to 'sturb you, Huck, tell we could do sumfn--but we's all right now. I ben a-buyin' pots en pans en vittles, as I got a chanst, en a-patchin' up de raf' nights when--"

"*What* **raft**, Jim?"

"Our ole raf'."

"You mean to say our old raft warn't smashed all to flinders?"

"No, she warn't. She was **tore** up a good deal--one en' of her was; but dey warn't no great **harm** done, on'y our traps was mos' all los'. Ef we hadn' **dive'** so deep en swum so fur under water, en de night hadn' ben so dark, en we warn't so sk'yerd, en ben sich punkin-heads, as de sayin' is, we'd a **seed** de raf'. But it's **jis'** as well we didn't, 'kase now she's all **fixed** up agin mos' as good as new, en we's got a new lot o' stuff, in de place o' what 'uz los'."

"Why, how did you get hold of the raft again, Jim--did you **catch** her?"

Chinese Simplified

bedroom: 卧室，卧房.
brings: 带来.
catch: 捕捉，捕捞，捕拿，捉.
dive: 潜水，跳水.
dogs: 狗.
fetch: 拿，取，带来.
fixed: 固定，确定，一定，固定的.
fur: 毛，软毛.
glad: 高兴，高兴的.
harm: 伤害，损害，坏处，害处，祸害.
hung: 挂.
hurt: 伤害，使受伤.
jis: 日本工业标准.
ketch: 双桅船.
lan: 区域网络，区域网路，本地网络，局域网.
landed: 着陆.
raft: 筏，木排，槎，桴.
seed: 种子，播种.
shout: 叫喊，呼喊，呼唤，喊，喊叫.
slavery: 奴隶制度，奴隶制.
slow: 慢，缓慢，迟慢，迟钝，迟迟，迟缓.
struck: 敲打.
surprise: 使吃惊，惊奇，惊骇.
surprised: 惊讶.
swim: 游泳.
tore: 撕扯.
truck: 卡车.
woods: 树林，森林.
yell: 叫喊，呐喊.

"How I gwyne to **ketch** her en I out in de **woods**? No; some er de niggers foun' her ketched on a **snag** along heah in de ben', en dey **hid** her in a crick 'mongst de willows, en dey wuz so much jawin' 'bout which un 'um she b'long to de mos' dat I come to heah 'bout it pooty soon, so I **ups** en settles de trouble by tellin' 'um she don't b'long to none uv um, but to you en me; en I **ast** 'm if dey gwyne to **grab** a young white genlman's propaty, en git a hid'n for it? Den I **gin** 'm ten cents **apiece**, en dey 'uz **mighty** well **satisfied**, en wisht some mo' raf's 'ud come along en make 'm **rich** agin. Dey's mighty good to me, dese niggers is, en whatever I wants 'm to do **fur** me I doan' have to ast 'm **twice**, **honey**. Dat Jack's a good nigger, en pooty smart."

"Yes, he is. He ain't ever told me you was here; told me to come, and he'd show me a lot of water-moccasins. If anything **happens** *he* ain't **mixed** up in it. He can say he never seen us together, and it 'll be the truth."

I don't want to talk much about the next day. I **reckon** I'll cut it **pretty** short. I waked up about **dawn**, and was a-going to turn over and go to **sleep** again when I noticed how still it was--didn't seem to be **anybody stirring**. That warn't **usual**. Next I noticed that Buck was up and gone. Well, I gets up, a-wondering, and goes down stairs--nobody around; everything as still as a **mouse**. Just the same outside. Thinks I, what does it mean? Down by the wood-pile I comes across my Jack, and says:

"What's it all about?"

Says he:

"Don't you know, Mars Jawge?"

"No," says I, "I don't."

"Well, **den**, Miss Sophia's run off! **'deed** she has. She run off in de night some time--nobody don't know **jis'** when; run off to get married to dat young Harney Shepherdson, you know--leastways, so dey 'spec. De fambly foun' it out 'bout half an hour ago--maybe a little mo'--en' I *tell* you dey warn't no time los'. Sich another hurryin' up **guns** en hosses *you* never see! De women folks has gone for to stir up de relations, en ole Mars Saul en de boys **tuck** dey guns en **rode** up de

Chinese Simplified

anybody: 任何人.
apiece: 各自，各自地.
ast: 虹志电脑.
dawn: 黎明.
deed: 契据，行为.
den: 窝.
fur: 毛，软毛.
gin: 杜松子酒，陷阱.
grab: 抓住，攫取，抓斗.
guns: 枪支.
happens: 发生.
hid: 躲藏.
honey: 蜂蜜，蜜，蜜糖.
jis: 日本工业标准.
ketch: 双桅船.
mighty: 伟大，强势，强大的.
mixed: 混合，混合的，错杂.
mouse: 老鼠，滑鼠，鼠标器，鼠标.
pretty: 漂亮，美丽的，秀丽.
reckon: 估计，计算.
rich: 富有，丰富，富有的，充实.
rode: 骑.
satisfied: 满意，乐意，心满意足的.
sleep: 梦寐，睡觉，睡眠，睡.
snag: 故障，钉子，残干，根株.
stir: 轰动，搅拌，鼓动.
stirring: 活跃的，激动人心的，忙碌的.
tuck: 挤进，塞进.
twice: 两次.
ups: 电供衡常器.
usual: 通常，寻常，一般的.
woods: 树林，森林.

river road for to try to **ketch** dat young man en kill him 'fo' he **kin** git acrost de river wid Miss Sophia. I reck'n dey's gwyne to be **mighty** rough times."

"**Buck** went off 'thout **waking** me up."

"Well, I reck'n he *did*! Dey warn't gwyne to **mix** you up in it. Mars Buck he **loaded** up his gun en 'lowed he's gwyne to **fetch** home a Shepherdson or **bust**. Well, dey'll be plenty un 'm dah, I reck'n, en you bet you he'll fetch one ef he gits a chanst."

I took up the river road as hard as I could put. By and by I begin to hear **guns** a good ways off. When I came in sight of the **log** store and the **woodpile** where the **steamboats lands** I worked along under the trees and **brush** till I got to a good place, and then I clumb up into the **forks** of a cottonwood that was out of reach, and watched. There was a wood-rank four foot high a little ways in front of the tree, and first I was going to **hide** behind that; but maybe it was luckier I didn't.

There was four or five men cavorting around on their horses in the open place before the log store, cussing and **yelling**, and trying to get at a couple of young **chaps** that was behind the wood-rank **alongside** of the steamboat **landing**; but they couldn't come it. Every time one of them showed himself on the river side of the woodpile he got shot at. The two boys was **squatting** back to back behind the pile, so they could watch both ways.

By and by the men stopped cavorting around and yelling. They started riding towards the store; then up gets one of the boys, draws a **steady bead** over the wood-rank, and drops one of them out of his **saddle**. All the men **jumped** off of their horses and grabbed the hurt one and started to carry him to the store; and that minute the two boys started on the run. They got half way to the tree I was in before the men noticed. Then the men see them, and jumped on their horses and took out after them. They **gained** on the boys, but it didn't do no good, the boys had too good a start; they got to the woodpile that was in front of my tree, and slipped in behind it, and so they had the **bulge** on the men again. One of the boys was Buck, and the other was a **slim** young chap about **nineteen** years old.

Chinese Simplified

alongside：并肩，在旁边.
bead：珠子，小珠.
brush：刷，毛刷，洗刷，刷子，拂，擦.
buck：雄鹿.
bulge：胀起，肿胀.
bust：半身像，逮捕，破产.
chap：家伙，皴裂.
fetch：拿，取，带来.
forks：叉子.
gained：获利，赢得.
guns：枪支.
hide：躲藏，暗藏，掩饰，藏，隐瞒，隐藏.
jumped：跳跃.
ketch：双桅船.
kin：亲属，骨肉.
landing：着陆.
lands：陆地.
loaded：载入.
log：圆形木材，圆木，木头.
mighty：伟大，强势，强大的.
mix：混，混杂，糅，混合，渗混.
nineteen：十九.
pile：一堆，桩，堆.
saddle：鞍，鞍状物，马鞍.
slim：瘦长，纤细，苗条的.
squatting：蹲.
steady：稳定，坚定，平稳，平稳的.
steamboat：汽船，轮船.
waking：醒来，醒着的.
woodpile：柴堆.
yelling：叫声，叫喊.

The men **ripped** around **awhile**, and then **rode** away. As soon as they was out of sight I **sung** out to Buck and told him. He didn't know what to make of my voice coming out of the tree at first. He was **awful** surprised. He told me to watch out sharp and let him know when the men come in sight again; said they was up to some devilment or other-- wouldn't be gone long. I wished I was out of that tree, but I dasn't come down. Buck begun to **cry** and rip, and 'lowed that him and his **cousin** Joe (that was the other young **chap**) would make up for this day yet. He said his father and his two **brothers** was killed, and two or three of the **enemy**. Said the Shepherdsons **laid** for them in **ambush**. Buck said his father and brothers **ought** to waited for their relations--the Shepherdsons was too strong for them. I asked him what was become of young Harney and Miss Sophia. He said they'd got across the river and was safe. I was glad of that; but the way Buck did take on because he didn't manage to kill Harney that day he shot at him--I hain't ever heard anything like it.

All of a sudden, **bang**! bang! bang! goes three or four **guns**--the men had **slipped** around through the **woods** and come in from behind without their horses! The boys **jumped** for the river--both of them hurt--and as they swum down the current the men run along the bank **shooting** at them and **singing** out, "Kill them, kill them!" It made me so **sick** I most fell out of the tree. I ain't a-going to tell *all* that happened--it would make me sick again if I was to do that. I wished I hadn't ever come **ashore** that night to see such things. I ain't ever going to get shut of them--lots of times I dream about them.

I **stayed** in the tree till it begun to get dark, afraid to come down. Sometimes I heard guns away off in the woods; and twice I seen little gangs of men **gallop** past the **log** store with guns; so I reckoned the trouble was still a-going on. I was **mighty downhearted**; so I made up my mind I wouldn't ever go anear that house again, because I reckoned I was to **blame**, somehow. I judged that that piece of paper meant that Miss Sophia was to **meet** Harney somewheres at half-past two and run off; and I judged I ought to told her father about that paper and the **curious** way she acted, and then maybe he would a locked her up, and this awful **mess** wouldn't ever happened.

Chinese Simplified

ambush：埋伏，伏击.
ashore：岸上，上岸.
awful：可怕，可怕的.
awhile：一会儿.
bang：重击.
blame：责备，咎，非难，责任，罪，责怪，归咎.
brothers：兄弟，哥儿.
chap：家伙，皲裂.
cousin：表亲，表哥，堂表.
cry：喊，叫，哭，哭泣.
curious：有好奇心，好奇，好奇的.
downhearted：消沉，闷闷不乐的.
enemy：敌人.
gallop：疾驰，飞奔.
guns：枪支.
jumped：跳跃.
laid：放.
log：圆形木材，圆木，木头.
meet：遇见，见面，会合，会晤，聚会.
mess：杂乱，混乱.
mighty：伟大，强势，强大的.
ought：应该，活该.
rip：扯裂，撕破，裂口.
rode：骑.
shooting：射击，猎场.
sick：生病.
singing：歌咏，歌唱.
slipped：滑落.
stayed：停留.
sung：唱歌.
woods：树林，森林.

When I got down out of the tree I **crept** along down the river bank a piece, and found the two **bodies** laying in the edge of the water, and tugged at them **till** I got them **ashore**; then I covered up their faces, and got away as **quick** as I could. I cried a little when I was **covering** up Buck's face, for he was **mighty** good to me.

It was just dark now. I never went near the house, but **struck** through the **woods** and made for the **swamp**. Jim warn't on his island, so I tramped off in a **hurry** for the crick, and **crowded** through the willows, **red**-hot to **jump aboard** and get out of that **awful** country. The **raft** was gone! My **souls**, but I was scared! I couldn't get my breath for most a minute. Then I raised a **yell**. A voice not twenty-five foot from me says:

"Good lan'! is dat you, **honey**? Doan' make no noise."

It was Jim's voice--nothing ever sounded so good before. I run along the bank a piece and got aboard, and Jim he grabbed me and hugged me, he was so **glad** to see me. He says:

"Laws **bless** you, **chile**, I 'uz right down sho' you's dead agin. Jack's been heah; he say he reck'n you's ben shot, kase you didn' come home no mo'; so I's jes' dis minute a startin' de raf' down towards de mouf er de crick, so's to be all ready for to **shove** out en leave soon as Jack comes agin en tells me for certain you *is* dead. Lawsy, I's mighty glad to git you back again, honey."

I says:

"All right--that's mighty good; they won't find me, and they'll think I've been killed, and floated down the river--there's something up there that 'll help them think so--so don't you lose no time, Jim, but just shove off for the big water as fast as ever you can."

I never felt easy till the raft was two **mile** below there and out in the middle of the Mississippi. Then we **hung** up our **signal lantern**, and judged that we was free and safe once more. I hadn't had a **bite** to eat since yesterday, so Jim he got out some corn-dodgers and **buttermilk**, and **pork** and **cabbage** and greens--there ain't nothing in the world so good when it's **cooked** right--and whilst I eat my

Chinese Simplified

aboard：船上，在车，上.
ashore：岸上，上岸.
awful：可怕，可怕的.
bite：咬，辣，咬伤.
bless：保佑，庇佑，祝福.
bodies：身体.
buttermilk：酪乳.
cabbage：甘蓝菜，包菜.
chile：智利.
cooked：煮熟.
covering：包层，衣子.
crept：爬行.
crowded：拥挤的.
glad：高兴，高兴的.
honey：蜂蜜，蜜，蜜糖.
hung：挂.
hurry：仓促，匆忙，赶忙.
jump：跳，跳跃.
lantern：灯笼.
mighty：伟大，强势，强大的.
mile：英里.
pork：猪肉.
quick：快，玲珑，敏捷的，迅速的.
raft：筏，木排，槎，桴.
red-hot：热烈的.
shove：推.
signal：信号，手势，讯号.
souls：灵魂.
struck：敲打.
swamp：沼泽.
till：直到.
woods：树林，森林.
yell：叫喊，呐喊.

supper we **talked** and had a good time. I was **powerful glad** to get away from the feuds, and so was Jim to get away from the **swamp**. We said there warn't no home like a **raft**, after all. Other **places** do **seem** so **cramped** up and smothery, but a raft don't. You feel **mighty** free and **easy** and **comfortable** on a raft.

Chinese Simplified

comfortable: 舒服，舒服的.
cramped: 逼仄，难懂的.
easy: 容易，轻而易举，简易，安逸，便利，便当，容易的，纵横.
glad: 高兴，高兴的.
mighty: 伟大，强势，强大的.
places: 地方.
powerful: 强大，有力，强劲，强有力的.
raft: 筏，木排，槎，桴.
seem: 显得，看来，彷佛，好象.
supper: 晚饭，晚餐.
swamp: 沼泽.
talked: 谈话.

CHAPTER XIX

THE DUKE AND THE DAUPHIN COME ABOARD

Two or three days and nights went by; I **reckon** I might say they swum by, they **slid** along so **quiet** and **smooth** and **lovely**. Here is the way we put in the time. It was a **monstrous** big river down there--sometimes a **mile** and a half wide; we run nights, and **laid** up and **hid** daytimes; soon as night was most gone we **stopped** navigating and tied up--nearly always in the dead water under a towhead; and then cut young **cottonwoods** and willows, and hid the **raft** with them. Then we set out the lines. Next we slid into the river and had a **swim**, so as to freshen up and **cool** off; then we set down on the **sandy bottom** where the water was about **knee** deep, and watched the **daylight** come. Not a sound anywheres--perfectly still-- just like the whole world was **asleep**, only sometimes the bullfrogs a- **cluttering**, maybe. The first thing to see, looking away over the water, was a kind of **dull** line--that was the woods on t'other side; you couldn't make nothing else out; then a **pale** place in the **sky**; then more paleness **spreading** around; then the river softened up away off, and warn't black any more, but **gray**; you could see little dark spots drifting along ever so far away-- trading scows, and such things; and long black streaks-- **rafts**; sometimes you could hear a **sweep** screaking; or jumbled up voices, it was so still, and sounds

Chinese Simplified

asleep：睡着，睡着的．
bottom：底部，屁股，底．
cluttering：混乱．
cool：凉，镇静，镇定，凉爽，凉爽的．
daylight：日光，白天．
dull：索然，板滞，沉闷的，干燥，拙，深沉．
gray：灰色，灰．
hid：躲藏．
knee：膝盖，膝．
laid：放．
lovely：可爱，可爱的．
mile：英里．
monstrous：怪物似，似怪物的．
pale：苍白，苍白的．
quiet：安静，寂静，安定，安生，沉静，宁静的．
raft：筏，木排，槎，桴．
rafts：木排．
reckon：估计，计算．
sandy：有沙的．
sky：天空，天．
slid：滑行．
smooth：平稳，润滑，光滑，平滑，通顺．
spreading：撒，散布，传播，展开，扩展．
stopped：停止．
sweep：席卷，打扫，扫描．
swim：游泳．
woods：树林，森林．

come so far; and by and by you could see a **streak** on the water which you know by the look of the streak that there's a **snag** there in a **swift** current which **breaks** on it and makes that streak look that way; and you see the **mist curl** up off of the water, and the east reddens up, and the river, and you make out a log-cabin in the edge of the **woods**, away on the bank on t'other side of the river, being a **woodyard**, likely, and piled by them cheats so you can **throw** a dog through it anywheres; then the nice **breeze** springs up, and comes fanning you from over there, so **cool** and fresh and sweet to smell on account of the woods and the flowers; but sometimes not that way, because they've left dead fish laying around, gars and such, and they do get pretty **rank**; and next you've got the full day, and everything **smiling** in the sun, and the **song-** birds just going it!

A little smoke couldn't be noticed now, so we would take some fish off of the lines and **cook** up a hot breakfast. And afterwards we would watch the lonesomeness of the river, and kind of **lazy** along, and by and by lazy off to sleep. Wake up by and by, and look to see what done it, and maybe see a **steamboat coughing** along up-stream, so far off towards the other side you couldn't tell nothing about her only whether she was a stern-wheel or side-wheel; then for about an hour there wouldn't be nothing to hear nor nothing to see--just solid lonesomeness. Next you'd see a **raft** sliding by, away off **yonder**, and maybe a galoot on it chopping, because they're most always doing it on a raft; you'd see the **axe flash** and come down-- you don't hear nothing; you see that axe go up again, and by the time it's above the man's head then you hear the *k'chunk*!--it had took all that time to come over the water. So we would put in the day, lazying around, listening to the **stillness**. Once there was a thick **fog**, and the **rafts** and things that went by was **beating** tin pans so the steamboats wouldn't run over them. A scow or a raft went by so close we could hear them talking and cussing and laughing--heard them **plain**; but we couldn't see no sign of them; it made you feel crawly; it was like **spirits** carrying on that way in the **air**. Jim said he believed it was spirits; but I says:

"No; spirits wouldn't say, 'Dern the dern fog.'"

Chinese Simplified

air: 空气，样子，晾.
axe: 斧子，斧，削减.
beating: 脉.
breaks: 中断.
breeze: 和风.
cook: 厨子，厨司，厨师，炊事员，烹调，煮，烹煮.
cool: 凉，镇静，镇定，凉爽，凉爽的.
coughing: 咳嗽.
curl: 卷曲，卷发.
flash: 闪光，晃.
fog: 雾.
lazy: 懒惰，懒惰的.
mist: 雾，薄雾.
plain: 平原.
raft: 筏，木排，槎，桴.
rafts: 木排.
rank: 评价分类，身分，级别，等级，地位，排.
smiling: 微笑的.
snag: 故障，钉子，残干，根株.
song: 歌，歌曲，歌儿.
spirits: 精神.
steamboat: 汽船，轮船.
stillness: 静止，寂静.
streak: 斑纹，线条.
swift: 迅速的.
throw: 扔，丢掉，丢，投.
tin: 锡，罐头.
woods: 树林，森林.
woodyard: 堆木场.
yonder: 那边.

Soon as it was night out we shoved; when we got her out to about the middle we let her alone, and let her **float wherever** the current wanted her to; then we **lit** the pipes, and dangled our legs in the water, and talked about all kinds of things--we was always **naked**, day and night, whenever the mosquitoes would let us--the new clothes Buck's folks made for me was too good to be comfortable, and **besides** I didn't go much on clothes, nohow.

Sometimes we'd have that whole river all to ourselves for the **longest** time. **Yonder** was the banks and the islands, across the water; and maybe a **spark**--which was a **candle** in a **cabin** window; and sometimes on the water you could see a spark or two--on a **raft** or a scow, you know; and maybe you could hear a **fiddle** or a song coming over from one of them **crafts**. It's lovely to live on a raft. We had the sky up there, all speckled with stars, and we used to lay on our **backs** and look up at them, and **discuss** about whether they was made or only just happened. Jim he allowed they was made, but I allowed they happened; I judged it would have took too long to *make* so many. Jim said the **moon** could a *laid* them; well, that looked kind of reasonable, so I didn't say nothing against it, because I've seen a **frog** lay most as many, so of course it could be done. We used to watch the stars that fell, too, and see them **streak** down. Jim allowed they'd got spoiled and was hove out of the **nest**.

Once or twice of a night we would see a **steamboat** slipping along in the dark, and now and then she would **belch** a whole world of sparks up out of her chimbleys, and they would rain down in the river and look awful pretty; then she would turn a corner and her lights would **wink** out and her **powwow** shut off and leave the river still again; and by and by her waves would get to us, a long time after she was gone, and **joggle** the raft a bit, and after that you wouldn't hear nothing for you couldn't tell how long, except maybe frogs or something.

After **midnight** the people on **shore** went to bed, and then for two or three hours the **shores** was black--no more sparks in the cabin windows. These sparks was our clock--the first one that showed again meant morning was coming, so we hunted a place to **hide** and **tie** up right away.

Chinese Simplified

backs：支持.
belch：嗝、嗳气，打嗝.
besides：此外，另外，除了，并且，再说，况且.
cabin：小屋，船舱.
candle：蜡烛.
crafts：工艺.
discuss：商讨，商谈，讨论，商榷，洽谈.
fiddle：小提琴.
float：漂浮.
frog：青蛙，蛙.
hide：躲藏，暗藏，掩饰，藏，隐瞒，隐藏.
joggle：榫接.
lit：点燃.
longest：最长，最长的.
midnight：午夜，半夜.
moon：月亮，月球，月.
naked：赤裸裸，裸体的.
nest：窝巢，窝，巢.
powwow：巫师.
raft：筏，木排，槎，桴.
shore：岸，滨，岸边，海岸，海滨.
shores：岸.
spark：触发，火花.
steamboat：汽船，轮船.
streak：斑纹，线条.
tie：不分胜负，打结，束缚，轨枕，绑，领带.
wherever：无论何处，哪里.
wink：眨眼，眨眼睛.
yonder：那边.

One morning about **daybreak** I found a **canoe** and crossed over a **chute** to the main shore--it was only two hundred yards--and paddled about a mile up a crick amongst the **cypress** woods, to see if I couldn't get some **berries**. Just as I was passing a place where a kind of a cowpath crossed the crick, here comes a couple of men **tearing** up the path as tight as they could foot it. I thought I was a goner, for whenever anybody was after anybody I judged it was *me*--or maybe Jim. I was about to **dig** out from there in a **hurry**, but they was pretty close to me then, and **sung** out and **begged** me to save their lives--said they hadn't been doing nothing, and was being chased for it--said there was men and dogs a-coming. They wanted to jump right in, but I says:

"Don't you do it. I don't hear the dogs and horses yet; you've got time to crowd through the **brush** and get up the crick a **little** ways; then you take to the water and **wade** down to me and get in--that'll throw the dogs off the scent."

They done it, and soon as they was **aboard** I lit out for our towhead, and in about five or ten minutes we heard the dogs and the men away off, **shouting**. We heard them come along towards the crick, but couldn't see them; they seemed to stop and **fool** around a while; then, as we got further and further away all the time, we couldn't hardly hear them at all; by the time we had left a mile of woods behind us and struck the river, everything was quiet, and we paddled over to the towhead and **hid** in the cottonwoods and was safe.

One of these fellows was about **seventy** or **upwards**, and had a **bald** head and very **gray whiskers**. He had an old battered-up slouch hat on, and a **greasy** blue **woollen** shirt, and **ragged** old blue **jeans** britches stuffed into his boot-tops, and home-knit galluses--no, he only had one. He had an old long-tailed blue jeans coat with **slick brass** buttons flung over his arm, and both of them had big, fat, ratty-looking carpet-bags.

The other fellow was about thirty, and dressed about as **ornery**. After breakfast we all laid off and talked, and the first thing that come out was that these **chaps** didn't know one another.

"What got you into trouble?" says the **baldhead** to t'other chap.

Chinese Simplified

aboard：船上，在车，上.
bald：光秃秃，兀，秃头的.
baldhead：秃子.
begged：乞求.
berries：莓.
brass：黄铜.
brush：刷，毛刷，洗刷，刷子，拂，擦.
canoe：独木舟.
chap：家伙，皴裂.
chute：陡槽・滑道.
cypress：丝柏.
daybreak：黎明，破晓.
dig：挖掘.
fool：呆子，笨蛋，傻子，笨人，愚人.
gray：灰色，灰.
greasy：泥泞的，油性的.
hid：躲藏.
hurry：仓促，匆忙，赶忙.
jeans：牛仔裤.
lit：点燃.
ornery：低劣的.
ragged：破烂，衣著褴褛的.
seventy：七十.
shouting：呼喊.
slick：油头滑脑.
sung：唱歌.
tearing：撕裂的.
upwards：向上地，向上.
wade：在水步行，涉过，蹚.
whiskers：胡子.
woollen：羊毛制的，毛织品.

"Well, I'd been **selling** an **article** to take the **tartar** off the teeth--and it does take it off, too, and generly the **enamel** along with it--but I stayed about one night longer than I ought to, and was just in the act of sliding out when I **ran** across you on the **trail** this side of town, and you told me they were coming, and **begged** me to help you to get off. So I told you I was expecting trouble myself, and would **scatter** out *with* you. That's the whole yarn--what's yourn?

"Well, I'd ben a-running' a little **temperance revival** thar 'bout a week, and was the **pet** of the women folks, big and little, for I was makin' it **mighty** warm for the rummies, I *tell* you, and **takin'** as much as five or six dollars a night--ten cents a head, children and niggers free--and business a-growin' all the time, when somehow or another a little report got around last night that I had a way of puttin' in my time with a private **jug** on the **sly**. A nigger rousted me out this mornin', and told me the people was getherin' on the quiet with their dogs and horses, and they'd be along pretty soon and give me 'bout half an hour's start, and then run me down if they could; and if they got me they'd tar and **feather** me and **ride** me on a rail, sure. I didn't wait for no breakfast--I warn't hungry."

"Old man," said the young one, "I reckon we might double-team it together; what do you think?"

"I ain't **undisposed**. What's your line--mainly?"

"Jour **printer** by trade; do a little in **patent** medicines; theater-actor-- **tragedy**, you know; take a turn to mesmerism and **phrenology** when there's a chance; **teach** singing-geography school for a change; **sling** a **lecture** sometimes--oh, I do lots of things--most anything that comes **handy**, so it ain't work. What's your lay?"

"I've done considerble in the **doctoring** way in my time. Layin' on o' hands is my best holt--for **cancer** and **paralysis**, and sich things; and I k'n tell a fortune pretty good when I've got somebody along to find out the facts for me. Preachin's my line, too, and workin' camp-meetin's, and missionaryin' around."

Nobody never said anything for a while; then the young man hove a **sigh** and says:

Chinese Simplified

article: 文章，报导，本文.
begged: 乞求.
cancer: 癌，癌症.
doctoring: 医生.
enamel: 光漆，搪瓷.
feather: 羽毛.
handy: 灵巧，便当，顺手，方便的，简便.
jug: 细颈瓶，罐.
lecture: 报告，讲课，演讲.
mighty: 伟大，强势，强大的.
paralysis: 瘫痪.
patent: 专利.
pet: 宠物.
phrenology: 骨相学.
printer: 打印机，印刷者，印表机.
ran: 跑.
revival: 复苏，复兴.
ride: 乘，骑，跨，坐.
scatter: 分散，散播、驱散.
selling: 出售，卖的.
sigh: 叹息，叹气.
sling: 弹弓，吊绳，背带，吊索.
sly: 隐密，狡猾.
takin: 羚牛.
tar: 焦油.
tartar: 牙垢，难对付的人，鞑靼，酒石，鞑靼人.
teach: 教，教导，讲课.
temperance: 节制.
tragedy: 悲剧.
trail: 线索，痕迹，形迹.
undisposed: 未处理.

"Alas!"

"What 're you alassin' about?" says the bald-head.

"To think I should have lived to be leading such a life, and be degraded down into such company." And he **begun** to **wipe** the corner of his eye with a **rag**.

"Dern your skin, ain't the company good enough for you?" says the **baldhead**, pretty pert and **uppish**.

"Yes, it *is* good enough for me; it's as good as I **deserve**; for who fetched me so low when I was so high? I did myself. I don't **blame** *you*, **gentlemen**--far from it; I don't blame anybody. I deserve it all. Let the cold world do its **worst**; one thing I know--there's a **grave somewhere** for me. The world may go on just as it's always done, and take everything from me--loved ones, property, everything; but it can't take that. Some day I'll **lie** down in it and forget it all, and my poor **broken** heart will be at rest." He went on a-wiping.

"Drot your **pore** broken heart," says the baldhead; "what are you heaving your pore broken heart at *us* f'r? *we* hain't done nothing."

"No, I know you haven't. I ain't **blaming** you, gentlemen. I brought myself down--yes, I did it myself. It's right I should suffer--perfectly right--I don't make any moan."

"Brought you down from whar? Whar was you brought down from?"

"**Ah,** you would not believe me; the world never believes--let it pass-- 'tis no matter. The **secret** of my **birth**--"

"The secret of your birth! Do you mean to say--"

"Gentlemen," says the young man, very **solemn,** "I will **reveal** it to you, for I feel I may have confidence in you. By rights I am a duke!"

Jim's eyes bugged out when he heard that; and I **reckon** mine did, too. Then the baldhead says: "No! you can't mean it?"

"Yes. My **great**-grandfather, **eldest** son of the Duke of Bridgewater, **fled** to this country about the end of the last **century**, to **breathe** the **pure** air of freedom; married here, and died, leaving a son, his own father **dying** about the same time.

Chinese Simplified

ah: 啊，哎呀.
baldhead: 秃子.
begun: 开始.
birth: 出生，起源，诞生，出身，开始.
blame: 责备，咎，非难，责任，罪，责怪，归咎.
blaming: 责备.
breathe: 呼吸.
broken: 打破了.
century: 世纪.
deserve: 应得.
dying: 不行了，垂死，垂死的.
eldest: 最年长，伯仲叔季，最年长的.
fled: 逃离.
gentlemen: 绅士.
grave: 严重，庄重，坟墓，墓穴，深重.
great-grandfather: 太公.
lie: 谎言，谎话，躺，撒谎，说谎.
pore: 毛孔.
pure: 单纯，纯净的，纯洁，纯粹.
rag: 破布，碎布.
reckon: 估计，计算.
reveal: 表露，暴露，透露，流露，走漏.
secret: 秘密，机密.
solemn: 严肃，俨然，岸然，隆重，庄严的，庄重.
somewhere: 某处.
uppish: 傲慢的.
wipe: 拭，揩，擦掉，擦，擦去.
worst: 最坏的.

The second son of the late **duke** seized the **titles** and **estates**--the **infant** real duke was ignored. I am the **lineal descendant** of that infant--I am the **rightful** Duke of Bridgewater; and here am I, **forlorn**, **torn** from my high estate, hunted of men, despised by the **cold** world, **ragged**, **worn**, heart-broken, and degraded to the **companionship** of felons on a raft!"

Jim **pitied** him ever so much, and so did I. We tried to **comfort** him, but he said it warn't much use, he couldn't be much comforted; said if we was a mind to **acknowledge** him, that would do him more good than most anything else; so we said we would, if he would tell us how. He said we **ought** to **bow** when we **spoke** to him, and say "Your Grace," or "My Lord," or "Your Lordship"--and he wouldn't mind it if we called him **plain** "Bridgewater," which, he said, was a title anyway, and not a name; and one of us ought to **wait** on him at **dinner**, and do any little thing for him he wanted done.

Well, that was all easy, so we done it. All through dinner Jim stood around and waited on him, and says, "Will yo' Grace have some o' dis or some o' dat?" and so on, and a body could see it was **mighty pleasing** to him.

But the old man got **pretty silent** by and by--didn't have much to say, and didn't look pretty **comfortable** over all that petting that was going on around that duke. He seemed to have something on his mind. So, along in the afternoon, he says:

"Looky here, Bilgewater," he says, "I'm **nation** sorry for you, but you ain't the only person that's had **troubles** like that."

"No?"

"No you ain't. You ain't the only person that's ben snaked down wrongfully out'n a high place."

"Alas!"

"No, you ain't the only person that's had a **secret** of his birth." And, by jings, *he* **begins** to **cry**.

"Hold! What do you mean?"

Chinese Simplified

acknowledge: 认知，承认.
begins: 开始.
bow: 弓.
cold: 冷，感冒，寒冷，寒，冷淡.
comfort: 安慰.
comfortable: 舒服，舒服的.
companionship: 友谊.
cry: 喊，叫，哭，哭泣.
descendant: 后裔，後裔.
dinner: 晚餐，正餐.
duke: 公爵，公.
estate: 地产，产业，园丘，房地产.
forlorn: 绝望，绝望的.
infant: 婴儿.
lineal: 直系，正统的，直系的.
mighty: 伟大，强势，强大的.
nation: 国家.
ought: 应该，活该.
pitied: 同情.
plain: 平原.
pleasing: 愉快，愉快的，舒适的.
pretty: 漂亮，美丽的，秀丽.
ragged: 破烂，衣著襤褸的.
rightful: 正直的，合法的.
secret: 秘密，机密.
silent: 无声，沉默的.
spoke: 辐条，说了.
title: 锦标，标题，题目，称号，职称.
torn: 撕扯.
troubles: 坏处，麻烦.
wait: 等待，等，伺候.
worn: 穿.

"Bilgewater, **kin** I trust you?" says the old man, **still** sort of sobbing.

"To the **bitter** death!" He took the old man by the hand and squeezed it, and says, "That **secret** of your being: speak!"

"Bilgewater, I am the late Dauphin!"

You **bet** you, Jim and me stared this time. Then the **duke** says:

"You are what?"

"Yes, my **friend**, it is too true--your eyes is lookin' at this very moment on the **pore disappeared** Dauphin, Looy the Seventeen, son of Looy the Sixteen and Marry Antonette."

"You! At your age! No! You mean you're the late Charlemagne; you must be six or seven hundred years old, at the very least."

"Trouble has done it, Bilgewater, trouble has done it; trouble has brung these **gray** hairs and this **premature** balditude. Yes, **gentlemen**, you see before you, in blue **jeans** and **misery**, the wanderin', exiled, trampled-on, and sufferin' **rightful** King of France."

Well, he cried and took on so that me and Jim didn't know hardly what to do, we was so sorry--and so **glad** and **proud** we'd got him with us, too. So we set in, like we done before with the duke, and tried to **comfort** *him*. But he said it warn't no use, nothing but to be dead and done with it all could do him any good; though he said it often made him feel **easier** and better for a while if people treated him **according** to his rights, and got down on one **knee** to speak to him, and always called him "Your Majesty," and waited on him first at **meals**, and didn't set down in his **presence** till he asked them. So Jim and me set to majestying him, and doing this and that and t'other for him, and **standing** up till he told us we might set down. This done him heaps of good, and so he got **cheerful** and **comfortable**. But the duke kind of **soured** on him, and didn't look a bit **satisfied** with the way things was going; still, the king acted real **friendly** towards him, and said the duke's **great**-grandfather and all the other Dukes of Bilgewater was a good deal thought of by *his* father, and was allowed to come to

Chinese Simplified

according：根据．
bet：打赌，赌．
bitter：苦，苦味，沉痛．
cheerful：愉快，愉快的．
comfort：安慰．
comfortable：舒服，舒服的．
disappeared：不见了，消失．
duke：公爵，公．
easier：更容易．
friend：朋友，熟人，友人．
friendly：友好，友善，友好的，好客，友好地，和气．
gentlemen：绅士．
glad：高兴，高兴的．
gray：灰色，灰．
great-grandfather：太公．
jeans：牛仔裤．
kin：亲属，骨肉．
knee：膝盖，膝．
meals：膳食．
misery：不幸．
pore：毛孔．
premature：为时过早，过早的，早熟的．
presence：出席，面前．
proud：傲岸，骄矜，骄傲的，自豪的．
rightful：正直的，合法的．
satisfied：满意，乐意，心满意足的．
secret：秘密，机密．
soured：酸味．
standing：站立，地位．
till：直到．

the **palace considerable**; but the **duke stayed** huffy a good while, **till** by and by the king says:

"Like as not we got to be together a blamed long time on this h-yer **raft**, Bilgewater, and so what's the use o' your bein' **sour**? It 'll only make things oncomfortable. It ain't my **fault** I warn't **born** a duke, it ain't your fault you warn't born a king--so what's the use to **worry**? Make the best o' things the way you find 'em, says I--that's my **motto**. This ain't no bad thing that we've **struck** here--plenty **grub** and an **easy** life--come, give us your hand, duke, and le's all be friends."

The duke done it, and Jim and me was **pretty glad** to see it. It took away all the uncomfortableness and we felt **mighty** good over it, because it would a been a **miserable** business to have any unfriendliness on the raft; for what you want, above all things, on a raft, is for **everybody** to be **satisfied**, and feel right and kind towards the others.

It didn't take me long to make up my mind that these liars warn't no **kings nor** dukes at all, but just **low**-down humbugs and frauds. But I never said nothing, never let on; **kept** it to **myself**; it's the best way; then you don't have no **quarrels**, and don't get into no **trouble**. If they wanted us to call them kings and dukes, I hadn't no **objections**, 'long as it would keep **peace** in the family; and it warn't no use to tell Jim, so I didn't tell him. If I never learnt nothing else out of pap, I learnt that the best way to get along with his kind of people is to let them have their own way.

Chinese Simplified

born：出生，天生的．
considerable：可观，相当多的．
duke：公爵，公．
easy：容易，轻而易举，简易，安逸，便利，便当，容易的，纵横．
everybody：每个人，各位．
fault：故障，过失，缺点，毛病，断层，短处，缺陷．
glad：高兴，高兴的．
grub：蛆虫．
kept：收存．
kings：国王．
low-down：非常低的，下作．
mighty：伟大，强势，强大的．
miserable：悲惨，凄惨，困苦，凄惨的．
motto：座右铭．
myself：我自己．
nor：也不．
objections：反对．
palace：宫殿，宫，皇宫．
peace：和平．
pretty：漂亮，美丽的，秀丽．
quarrels：争吵．
raft：筏，木排，槎，桴．
satisfied：满意，乐意，心满意足的．
sour：酸，酸味．
stayed：停留．
struck：敲打．
till：直到．
trouble：麻烦，难度，难处．
worry：担心，使烦恼，缠绕，担忧，心事，担，烦恼，着急．

CHAPTER XX

WHAT ROYALTY DID TO PARKVILLE

They asked us **considerable** many questions; wanted to know what we covered up the **raft** that way for, and **laid** by in the **daytime instead** of running--was Jim a **runaway** nigger? Says I:

"Goodness sakes! would a runaway nigger run *south*?"

No, they **allowed** he wouldn't. I had to account for things some way, so I says:

"My folks was **living** in Pike County, in Missouri, where I was **born**, and they all died off but me and **pa** and my **brother** Ike. Pa, he 'lowed he'd **break** up and go down and live with Uncle Ben, who's got a little one- **horse** place on the **river**, forty-four **mile** below Orleans. Pa was **pretty** poor, and had some **debts**; so when he'd squared up there warn't nothing left but **sixteen** dollars and our nigger, Jim. That warn't enough to take us **fourteen** hundred mile, **deck passage** nor no other way. Well, when the river **rose** pa had a **streak** of **luck** one day; he ketched this **piece** of a raft; so we reckoned we'd go down to Orleans on it. Pa's luck didn't hold out; a **steamboat** run over the forrard **corner** of the raft one night, and we all went **overboard** and **dove** under the **wheel**; Jim and me come up all right, but pa was **drunk**, and Ike was only four years old, so they never

Chinese Simplified

allowed: 允许.
born: 出生，天生的.
break: 破坏，断，打破，犯，中断，破，裂.
brother: 弟兄，兄弟.
considerable: 可观，相当多的.
corner: 角落，隅，棱，角，转角.
daytime: 白天，白昼，日间.
debts: 债务.
deck: 甲板.
dove: 鸽.
drunk: 喝了，喝醉.
fourteen: 十四.
horse: 马.
instead: 代替，反而.
laid: 放.
living: 活泼的.
luck: 运气，幸运.
mile: 英里.
overboard: 向船外.
pa: 爸爸.
passage: 通道，通路，通过.
piece: 片，部分，一块，一片，块，部份，份.
pretty: 漂亮，美丽的，秀丽.
raft: 筏，木排，槎，桴.
river: 河，江，川，河流，条.
rose: 蔷薇，玫瑰，升起.
runaway: 逃亡者，跑道.
sixteen: 十六.
steamboat: 汽船，轮船.
streak: 斑纹，线条.
wheel: 轮子，轮，车轮.

come up no more. Well, for the next day or two we had considerable trouble, because people was always coming out in skiffs and trying to take Jim away from me, saying they believed he was a **runaway** nigger. We don't run **daytimes** no more now; nights they don't bother us."

The duke says:

"Leave me alone to **cipher** out a way so we can run in the daytime if we want to. I'll think the thing over--I'll **invent** a plan that'll **fix** it. We'll let it alone for to-day, because of course we don't want to go by that town **yonder** in daylight--it mightn't be healthy."

Towards night it begun to **darken** up and look like rain; the heat **lightning** was **squirting** around low down in the sky, and the leaves was beginning to shiver--it was going to be pretty **ugly**, it was easy to see that. So the duke and the king went to **overhauling** our **wigwam**, to see what the beds was like. My bed was a **straw tick** better than Jim's, which was a corn-shuck tick; there's always cobs around about in a **shuck** tick, and they **poke** into you and hurt; and when you roll over the dry shucks sound like you was **rolling** over in a pile of dead leaves; it makes such a rustling that you wake up. Well, the duke allowed he would take my bed; but the king allowed he wouldn't. He says:

"I should a reckoned the difference in rank would a sejested to you that a corn-shuck bed warn't just fitten for me to sleep on. Your Grace 'll take the shuck bed yourself."

Jim and me was in a **sweat** again for a minute, being afraid there was going to be some more trouble amongst them; so we was pretty glad when the duke says:

"'Tis my fate to be always ground into the **mire** under the iron **heel** of **oppression**. Misfortune has broken my once **haughty** spirit; I **yield**, I **submit**; 'tis my fate. I am alone in the world--let me **suffer**; can **bear** it."

We got away as soon as it was good and dark. The king told us to stand well out towards the middle of the river, and not show a light till we got a long ways below the town. We come in sight of the little **bunch** of lights by and by--that

Chinese Simplified

bear：熊，忍受，背负，忍耐，承担，担负，空头，堪.
bunch：束，串.
cipher：暗号，密码，阿拉伯数字.
darken：变暗，变黑.
daytime：白天，白昼，日间.
fix：安装，奠定，固定，修理.
haughty：傲慢，傲岸，骄矜，傲慢的.
heel：脚跟，踵，踝部.
invent：编造，发明.
lightning：闪电.
mire：泥潭.
oppression：压迫.
overhauling：大修，检查.
poke：戳，拨开，插入.
rolling：滚动，旋转的，起伏的，波动的.
runaway：逃亡者，跑道.
shuck：壳.
squirting：喷出.
straw：稻草，吸管.
submit：提交，呈交.
suffer：受苦，蒙受，遭受，受到，遭到.
sweat：汗，出汗，流汗.
tick：壁虱，滴答声，勾.
ugly：丑陋的，难看的，难看，丑恶，丑的.
wigwam：帐篷，陋棚.
yield：出产，产量.
yonder：那边.

was the town, you know--and **slid** by, about a half a **mile** out, all right. When we was three-quarters of a mile below we hoisted up our **signal lantern**; and about ten o'clock it come on to rain and **blow** and **thunder** and **lighten** like everything; so the king told us to both stay on watch till the weather got better; then him and the **duke** crawled into the **wigwam** and turned in for the night. It was my watch below till twelve, but I wouldn't a turned in anyway if I'd had a bed, because a body don't see such a **storm** as that every day in the week, not by a long sight. My **souls**, how the wind did **scream** along! And every second or two there'd come a **glare** that **lit** up the white-caps for a half a mile around, and you'd see the islands looking **dusty** through the rain, and the trees thrashing around in the wind; then comes a *h-whack*!--bum! bum! bumble-umble-um-bum-bum-bum-bum--and the thunder would go **rumbling** and grumbling away, and quit--and then ***rip*** comes another **flash** and another sockdolager. The waves most washed me off the **raft** sometimes, but I hadn't any clothes on, and didn't mind. We didn't have no trouble about snags; the **lightning** was glaring and flittering around so **constant** that we could see them plenty soon enough to **throw** her head this way or that and miss them.

I had the middle watch, you know, but I was pretty **sleepy** by that time, so Jim he said he would stand the first half of it for me; he was always **mighty** good that way, Jim was. I crawled into the wigwam, but the king and the duke had their legs sprawled around so there warn't no show for me; so I **laid** outside--I didn't mind the rain, because it was warm, and the waves warn't running so high now. About two they come up again, though, and Jim was going to call me; but he changed his mind, because he reckoned they warn't high enough yet to do any **harm**; but he was **mistaken** about that, for pretty soon all of a sudden along comes a regular ripper and washed me **overboard**. It most killed Jim a-laughing. He was the easiest nigger to **laugh** that ever was, anyway.

I took the watch, and Jim he laid down and snored away; and by and by the storm let up for good and all; and the first cabin-light that showed I rousted him out, and we slid the raft into **hiding quarters** for the day.

Chinese Simplified

blow：吹，打击.
constant：一贯，不变，不断，固定的，常量.
duke：公爵，公.
dusty：满身尘埃，沾尘的.
flash：闪光，晃.
glare：强光，眩目的光，眩目.
harm：伤害，损害，坏处，害处，祸害.
hiding：隐匿.
laid：放.
lantern：灯笼.
laugh：笑.
lighten：照亮，减轻.
lightning：闪电.
lit：点燃.
mighty：伟大，强势，强大的.
mile：英里.
mistaken：错误，弄错.
overboard：向船外.
quarters：住处，四分之一.
raft：筏，木排，槎，桴.
rip：扯裂，撕破，裂口.
rumbling：隆隆响.
scream：叫喊，呐喊，呼啸.
signal：信号，手势，讯号.
sleepy：想睡，眼睡的.
slid：滑行.
souls：灵魂.
storm：暴风雨，暴风，风暴.
throw：扔，丢掉，丢，投.
thunder：雷，雷声，打雷.
wigwam：帐篷，陋棚.

The king got out an old ratty **deck** of cards after **breakfast**, and him and the **duke** played seven-up a while, five cents a game. Then they got **tired** of it, and allowed they would "lay out a campaign," as they called it. The duke went down into his carpet-bag, and fetched up a lot of little printed bills and read them out **loud**. One bill said, "The **celebrated** Dr. Armand de Montalban, of Paris," would "lecture on the Science of Phrenology" at such and such a place, on the **blank** day of blank, at ten cents **admission**, and "furnish **charts** of **character** at twenty-five cents apiece." The duke said that was *him*. In another bill he was the "world-**renowned** Shakespearian **tragedian**, Garrick the Younger, of Drury Lane, London." In other bills he had a lot of other names and done other wonderful things, like finding water and gold with a "divining-rod," "dissipating **witch** spells," and so on. By and by he says:

"But the histrionic **muse** is the **darling**. Have you ever trod the **boards**, Royalty?"

"No," says the king.

"You **shall**, then, before you're three days older, Fallen Grandeur," says the duke. "The first good town we come to we'll **hire** a hall and do the **sword** fight in Richard III. and the **balcony scene** in Romeo and Juliet. How does that strike you?"

"I'm in, up to the **hub**, for anything that will pay, Bilgewater; but, you see, I don't know nothing about play-actin', and hain't ever seen much of it. I was too small when pap used to have 'em at the palace. Do you **reckon** you can learn me?"

"Easy!"

"All right. I'm jist a-freezn' for something fresh, anyway. Le's **commence** right away."

So the duke he told him all about who Romeo was and who Juliet was, and said he was used to being Romeo, so the king could be Juliet.

"But if Juliet's such a young **gal**, duke, my peeled head and my white **whiskers** is goin' to look oncommon **odd** on her, maybe."

Chinese Simplified

admission：进场，承认.
balcony：阳台，阳.
blank：空白，空白的，空.
boards：纸板.
breakfast：早餐，早饭，早点.
celebrated：着名，著名.
character：性格，字，文字，特征，字符，色彩，字元.
charts：图表.
commence：着手，开始.
darling：宝宝，宝贝，老公，老婆，打令.
deck：甲板.
duke：公爵，公.
gal：姑娘.
hall：厅，大厅，会堂，礼堂.
hire：雇，雇佣，雇用，招收，聘请，租，聘，聘用.
hub：中转站，集线器，中枢.
loud：高声，大声，大声的.
muse：瞑想，沉思.
odd：奇怪，莫名其妙，零头，奇异的.
reckon：估计，计算.
renowned：闻名，大明鼎鼎，著名的，享有声誉.
scene：景色，场面，现场，实况，镜头，景象，幕，情景.
sword：剑.
tired：疲倦，疲乏，疲倦的.
tragedian：悲剧演员.
whiskers：胡子.
witch：巫婆，女巫.

"No, don't you worry; these country jakes won't ever **think** of that. Besides, you know, you'll be in **costume**, and that makes all the difference in the world; Juliet's in a **balcony**, enjoying the **moonlight** before she goes to bed, and she's got on her night-gown and her ruffled **nightcap**. Here are the costumes for the **parts**."

He got out two or three curtain-calico suits, which he said was meedyevil **armor** for Richard III. and t'other **chap**, and a long white **cotton** nightshirt and a ruffled nightcap to **match**. The king was satisfied; so the duke got out his book and read the parts over in the most **splendid** spread-eagle way, prancing around and **acting** at the same time, to show how it had got to be done; then he give the book to the king and told him to get his part by heart.

There was a **little one**-horse town about three mile down the **bend**, and after dinner the duke said he had **ciphered** out his idea about how to run in **daylight** without it being dangersome for Jim; so he allowed he would go down to the town and **fix** that thing. The king allowed he would go, too, and see if he couldn't strike something. We was out of coffee, so Jim said I better go along with them in the **canoe** and get some.

When we got there there warn't nobody **stirring**; **streets** empty, and perfectly dead and still, like Sunday. We found a sick nigger sunning himself in a back yard, and he said everybody that warn't too young or too sick or too old was gone to camp-meeting, about two mile back in the woods. The king got the **directions**, and allowed he'd go and work that camp-meeting for all it was worth, and I might go, too.

The duke said what he was after was a printing-office. We found it; a little bit of a **concern**, up over a **carpenter** shop--carpenters and printers all gone to the **meeting**, and no doors locked. It was a dirty, littered-up place, and had ink marks, and **handbills** with pictures of horses and **runaway** niggers on them, all over the walls. The duke shed his coat and said he was all right now. So me and the king lit out for the camp-meeting.

We got there in about a half an hour fairly **dripping**, for it was a most awful hot day. There was as much as a thousand people there from twenty mile

Chinese Simplified

acting: 代理，临时的，代理的，行为.
armor: 盔甲.
balcony: 阳台，阳.
bend: 弯曲，弯折.
canoe: 独木舟.
carpenter: 木匠.
chap: 家伙，皴裂.
ciphered: 密码.
concern: 关照，有关.
costume: 服装，衣服.
cotton: 棉花，棉.
daylight: 日光，白天.
directions: 指导，说明，方向.
dripping: 滴下.
fix: 安装，奠定，固定，修理.
handbills: 传单.
ink: 墨水，墨水儿，篇幅.
lit: 点燃.
match: 比赛，相配，对手，火柴，比拟，进军.
meeting: 会议，集会，会晤，会见，聚会.
moonlight: 月光.
nightcap: 睡帽.
one-horse: 单马拉的.
parts: 部件.
runaway: 逃亡者，跑道.
splendid: 彪炳，卓越，辉煌，灿烂的，精彩，辉煌的.
stirring: 活跃的，激动人心的，忙碌的.
streets: 街道.

around. The woods was full of teams and wagons, **hitched** everywheres, feeding out of the wagon-troughs and stomping to keep off the flies. There was sheds made out of poles and roofed over with branches, where they had **lemonade** and **gingerbread** to sell, and **piles** of watermelons and green corn and such-like truck.

The **preaching** was going on under the same kinds of sheds, only they was bigger and held **crowds** of people. The **benches** was made out of outside slabs of logs, with holes **bored** in the round side to drive sticks into for legs. They didn't have no backs. The **preachers** had high **platforms** to stand on at one end of the sheds. The women had on sun-bonnets; and some had linsey-woolsey frocks, some **gingham** ones, and a few of the young ones had on **calico**. Some of the young men was **barefooted**, and some of the children didn't have on any clothes but just a tow-linen shirt. Some of the old women was knitting, and some of the young folks was courting on the **sly**.

The first shed we come to the preacher was **lining** out a **hymn**. He lined out two lines, everybody **sung** it, and it was kind of grand to hear it, there was so many of them and they done it in such a rousing way; then he lined out two more for them to sing--and so on. The people woke up more and more, and sung **louder** and louder; and towards the end some begun to **groan**, and some begun to shout. Then the preacher begun to preach, and begun in **earnest**, too; and went **weaving** first to one side of the platform and then the other, and then a-leaning down over the front of it, with his arms and his body going all the time, and shouting his words out with all his might; and every now and then he would hold up his Bible and spread it open, and kind of pass it around this way and that, shouting, "It's the brazen **serpent** in the **wilderness**! Look upon it and live!" And people would shout out, "Glory!--A-a-*men*!" And so he went on, and the people **groaning** and crying and saying **amen**:

"Oh, come to the mourners' bench! come, black with sin! (*Amen!*) come, sick and sore! (*Amen!*) come, **lame** and **halt** and blind! (*Amen!*) come, **pore** and **needy**, sunk in **shame**! (*A-A-men!*) come, all that's worn and soiled and suffering!--come with a broken spirit! come with a contrite heart! come in your **rags** and sin and

Chinese Simplified

amen：阿们，阿门.
barefooted：赤足，赤足的.
bench：长椅，长凳.
bored：无聊，沉闷的.
calico：白布，白棉布.
crowds：人群.
earnest：认真.
gingerbread：姜饼.
gingham：格子棉布，方格花布.
groan：呻吟，哼.
groaning：呻吟.
halt：停止.
hitched：蹒跚.
hymn：圣歌，圣诗.
lame：跛，跛足.
lemonade：柠檬水.
lining：衬里，衬，内裙.
louder：较大声的.
needy：贫穷的.
piles：痔，痔疮，堆.
platform：平台，站台，平，主席台，主席.
pore：毛孔.
preach：传教，讲道，鼓吹.
preacher：传道者.
preaching：讲道法.
rags：碎布.
serpent：蛇.
shame：羞耻.
sly：隐密，狡猾.
sung：唱歌.
weaving：编织.
wilderness：荒野，荒地.

dirt! the **waters** that **cleanse** is free, the door of **heaven** stands open--oh, **enter** in and be at rest!" (*A-A-men! Glory, Glory Hallelujah!*)

And so on. You couldn't make out what the **preacher** said any more, on account of the **shouting** and **crying**. Folks got up everywheres in the crowd, and worked their way just by main **strength** to the mourners' **bench**, with the tears running down their faces; and when all the mourners had got up there to the front benches in a crowd, they **sung** and shouted and flung themselves down on the **straw**, just **crazy** and wild.

Well, the first I knowed the king got a-going, and you could hear him over everybody; and next he went a-charging up on to the **platform**, and the preacher he **begged** him to speak to the people, and he done it. He told them he was a **pirate**--been a pirate for thirty years out in the Indian Ocean--and his **crew** was thinned out considerable last spring in a fight, and he was home now to take out some fresh men, and thanks to **goodness** he'd been robbed last night and put **ashore** off of a **steamboat** without a **cent**, and he was glad of it; it was the blessedest thing that ever happened to him, because he was a changed man now, and happy for the first time in his life; and, poor as he was, he was going to start right off and work his way back to the Indian Ocean, and put in the rest of his life trying to turn the pirates into the true path; for he could do it better than anybody else, being acquainted with all pirate crews in that **ocean**; and though it would take him a long time to get there without money, he would get there anyway, and every time he convinced a pirate he would say to him, "Don't you thank me, don't you give me no **credit**; it all belongs to them **dear** people in Pokeville camp-meeting, natural brothers and benefactors of the **race**, and that dear preacher there, the truest friend a pirate ever had!"

And then he busted into tears, and so did everybody. Then somebody **sings** out, "Take up a **collection** for him, take up a collection!" Well, a half a **dozen** made a **jump** to do it, but somebody sings out, "Let *him* pass the hat around!" Then everybody said it, the preacher too.

So the king went all through the crowd with his hat swabbing his eyes, and **blessing** the people and praising them and thanking them for being so good to

Chinese Simplified

ashore: 岸上，上岸.
begged: 乞求.
bench: 长椅，长凳.
blessing: 祝福.
cent: 一分钱，分.
cleanse: 擦拭，洁净，清洗.
collection: 珍藏，汇编，收集，专集.
crazy: 发狂，疯狂，颠倒，疯狂的.
credit: 信用，功劳.
crew: 人员，全体人员，包承组，工作人员.
crying: 叫喊的，嚎哭的，显著的.
dear: 亲爱，亲爱的，可爱的.
dirt: 污垢.
dozen: 一打，打.
enter: 进，进入，回车键，入.
goodness: 美德.
heaven: 天堂，天，天空.
jump: 跳，跳跃.
ocean: 海洋，洋.
pirate: 海盗，剽窃.
platform: 平台，站台，平，主席台，主席.
preacher: 传道者.
race: 种族，竞赛，人种.
shouting: 呼喊.
sings: 唱.
steamboat: 汽船，轮船.
straw: 稻草，吸管.
strength: 力量，力，强度，实力，力气、气力，浓度.
sung: 唱歌.
waters: 水域.

the poor pirates away off there; and every little while the prettiest kind of girls, with the tears running down their cheeks, would up and ask him would he let them **kiss** him for to remember him by; and he always done it; and some of them he hugged and kissed as many as five or six times--and he was **invited** to stay a week; and everybody wanted him to live in their houses, and said they'd think it was an **honor**; but he said as this was the last day of the camp-meeting he couldn't do no good, and **besides** he was in a **sweat** to get to the Indian Ocean right off and go to work on the pirates.

When we got back to the **raft** and he come to **count** up he found he had **collected** eighty-seven **dollars** and seventy-five cents. And then he had fetched away a three-gallon **jug** of **whisky**, too, that he found under a **wagon** when he was **starting** home through the **woods**. The king said, take it all around, it **laid** over any day he'd ever put in in the missionarying line. He said it warn't no use talking, heathens don't amount to shucks **alongside** of pirates to work a camp-meeting with.

The **duke** was thinking *he'd* been doing pretty well till the king come to show up, but after that he didn't think so so much. He had set up and **printed** off two little jobs for farmers in that printing-office--horse bills--and took the money, four dollars. And he had got in ten dollars' worth of advertisements for the paper, which he said he would put in for four dollars if they would pay in **advance**--so they done it. The price of the paper was two dollars a year, but he took in three **subscriptions** for half a dollar **apiece** on condition of them **paying** him in advance; they were going to pay in cordwood and onions as usual, but he said he had just bought the concern and knocked down the price as low as he could **afford** it, and was going to run it for cash. He set up a little piece of **poetry**, which he made, himself, out of his own head--three verses--kind of **sweet** and saddish--the name of it was, "Yes, **crush**, cold world, this breaking heart"--and he left that all set up and ready to print in the paper, and didn't **charge** nothing for it. Well, he took in nine dollars and a half, and said he'd done a pretty square day's work for it.

Chinese Simplified

advance: 进，前进，进军，进步.
afford: 力足以做，负担得起.
alongside: 并肩，在旁边.
apiece: 各自，各自地.
besides: 此外，另外，除了，并且，再说，况且.
charge: 收费，控告，记帐，冲锋，指责，负荷.
collected: 收集成的，镇定的.
count: 计数，伯爵，计算，有价值，认为.
crush: 压碎，粉碎.
dollar: 元.
duke: 公爵，公.
honor: 荣誉，荣耀，尊严，面子，尊敬.
invited: 约了.
jug: 细颈瓶，罐.
kiss: 吻，接吻，轻抚，轻触.
laid: 放.
paying: 有利的，合算的，支付的.
poetry: 诗，诗歌.
print: 印刷，印，版画，打印.
raft: 筏，木排，槎，桴.
starting: 起步.
subscriptions: 订阅.
sweat: 汗，出汗，流汗.
sweet: 甜，甜食，糖果.
wagon: 列车厢.
whisky: 威士忌酒.
woods: 树林，森林.

Then he showed us another little job he'd printed and hadn't charged for, because it was for us. It had a picture of a **runaway** nigger with a **bundle** on a stick over his shoulder, and "$200 **reward**" under it. The reading was all about Jim, and just described him to a **dot**. It said he run away from St. Jacques' **plantation**, forty mile below New Orleans, last winter, and likely went north, and **whoever** would catch him and send him back he could have the reward and expenses.

"Now," says the duke, "after to-night we can run in the **daytime** if we want to. Whenever we see anybody coming we can **tie** Jim hand and foot with a **rope**, and lay him in the **wigwam** and show this **handbill** and say we captured him up the river, and were too poor to travel on a **steamboat**, so we got this little **raft** on credit from our friends and are going down to get the reward. Handcuffs and **chains** would look still better on Jim, but it wouldn't go well with the story of us being so poor. Too much like **jewelry**. Ropes are the correct thing--we must **preserve** the **unities**, as we say on the boards."

We all said the duke was pretty **smart**, and there couldn't be no trouble about running daytimes. We judged we could make miles enough that night to get out of the reach of the **powwow** we **reckoned** the duke's work in the **printing** office was going to make in that little town; then we could **boom** right along if we wanted to.

We laid low and kept still, and never shoved out till nearly ten o'clock; then we **slid** by, pretty wide away from the town, and didn't **hoist** our **lantern** till we was clear out of sight of it.

When Jim called me to take the watch at four in the morning, he says:

"Huck, does you reck'n we gwyne to run acrost any mo' **kings** on dis trip?"

"No," I says, "I reckon not."

"Well," says he, "dat's all right, **den**. I doan' mine one er two kings, but dat's enough. Dis one's powerful **drunk**, en de duke ain' much better."

Chinese Simplified

boom：景气，繁荣，吊杆，盛旺.
bundle：捆，包裹，包，包扎，束，把.
chains：连锁.
daytime：白天，白昼，日间.
den：窝.
dot：点，点缀，点子，圆点，嫁妆.
drunk：喝了，喝醉.
handbill：传单.
hoist：升起，吊车，举起.
jewelry：首饰.
kings：国王.
lantern：灯笼.
plantation：农园，种植园.
powwow：巫师.
preserve：保藏，保全，保留，维修.
printing：印花，印刷，印数，印刷术.
raft：筏，木排，槎，桴.
reckon：估计，计算.
reward：报酬，酬劳，酬金，奖励，奖赏.
rope：绳索，绳子.
runaway：逃亡者，跑道.
slid：滑行.
smart：高明，时髦的.
steamboat：汽船，轮船.
tie：不分胜负，打结，束缚，轨枕，绑，领带.
unities：统一.
whoever：无论何人.
wigwam：帐篷，陋棚.

I found Jim had been **trying** to get him to **talk** French, so he could **hear** what it was like; but he said he had been in this country so long, and had so much **trouble**, he'd **forgot** it.

Chinese Simplified

forgot: 忘记.
hear: 听见, 听取, 听.
talk: 谈话, 报告, 言语, 谈.
trouble: 麻烦, 难度, 难处.
trying: 难捱, 设法.

CHAPTER XXI

AN ARKSANSAW DIFFICULTY

It was after sun-up now, but we went right on and didn't **tie** up. The king and the **duke** turned out by and by looking **pretty rusty**; but after they'd **jumped overboard** and took a **swim** it chippered them up a good deal. After **breakfast** the king he took a seat on the corner of the **raft**, and pulled off his **boots** and **rolled** up his britches, and let his legs **dangle** in the water, so as to be **comfortable**, and **lit** his **pipe**, and went to getting his Romeo and Juliet by heart. When he had got it pretty good him and the duke **begun** to **practice** it together. The duke had to learn him over and over again how to say every speech; and he made him **sigh**, and put his hand on his heart, and after a while he said he done it pretty well; "only," he says, "you mustn't **bellow** out *Romeo*! that way, like a bull--you must say it **soft** and **sick** and languishy, so--R-o-o-meo! that is the idea; for Juliet's a dear **sweet mere** child of a girl, you know, and she doesn't **bray** like a jackass."

Well, next they got out a couple of long **swords** that the duke made out of **oak** laths, and begun to practice the sword fight--the duke called himself Richard III.; and the way they **laid** on and pranced around the raft was **grand** to see. But by and by the king **tripped** and fell overboard, and after that they took a rest,

Chinese Simplified

begun: 开始.
bellow: 怒吼.
boots: 靴子.
bray: 驴叫声.
breakfast: 早餐, 早饭, 早点.
comfortable: 舒服, 舒服的.
dangle: 吊着, 摇晃.
duke: 公爵, 公.
grand: 堂皇, 隆重, 雄伟, 盛大, 宏大, 大型的, 宏伟.
jumped: 跳跃.
laid: 放.
lit: 点燃.
mere: 只有.
oak: 橡树, 橡.
overboard: 向船外.
pipe: 管, 管子, 筒, 喉管.
practice: 演习, 实际, 操练, 作法, 练习, 实践, 实习.
pretty: 漂亮, 美丽的, 秀丽.
raft: 筏, 木排, 槎, 桴.
rolled: 卷.
rusty: 腐蚀, 生锈的.
sick: 生病.
sigh: 叹息, 叹气.
soft: 柔软, 柔和, 柔软的.
sweet: 甜, 甜食, 糖果.
swim: 游泳.
sword: 剑.
swords: 剑.
tie: 不分胜负, 打结, 束缚, 轨枕, 绑, 领带.
tripped: 旅行.

and had a talk about all kinds of adventures they'd had in other times along the river.

After dinner the duke says:

"Well, Capet, we'll want to make this a **first**-class show, you know, so I guess we'll **add** a little more to it. We want a little something to answer encores with, anyway."

"What's onkores, Bilgewater?"

The duke told him, and then says:

"I'll answer by doing the Highland **fling** or the sailor's **hornpipe**; and you--well, let me see--oh, I've got it--you can do Hamlet's **soliloquy**."

"Hamlet's which?"

"Hamlet's soliloquy, you know; the most celebrated thing in Shakespeare. Ah, it's **sublime**, sublime! Always fetches the house. I haven't got it in the book--I've only got one volume--but I reckon I can piece it out from **memory**. I'll just walk up and down a minute, and see if I can call it back from recollection's vaults."

So he went to **marching** up and down, thinking, and **frowning horrible** every now and then; then he would **hoist** up his eyebrows; next he would squeeze his hand on his forehead and **stagger** back and kind of **moan**; next he would sigh, and next he'd let on to drop a tear. It was beautiful to see him. By and by he got it. He told us to give **attention**. Then he **strikes** a most **noble attitude**, with one leg shoved forwards, and his arms stretched away up, and his head **tilted** back, looking up at the sky; and then he begins to **rip** and **rave** and **grit** his teeth; and after that, all through his speech, he howled, and spread around, and **swelled** up his chest, and just knocked the spots out of any acting ever I see before. This is the speech--I **learned** it, easy enough, while he was learning it to the king:

To be, or not to be; that is the **bare bodkin** That makes **calamity** of so long life; For who would fardels bear, till Birnam Wood do come to Dunsinane, But that the **fear** of something after death Murders the innocent sleep, Great nature's second course, And makes us rather **sling** the **arrows** of **outrageous** fortune Than

Chinese Simplified

add：加，增加，增添.
arrows：箭.
attention：注意，注意力.
attitude：态度，姿态，架势.
bare：赤裸裸，赤裸的.
bodkin：锥子.
calamity：危难，灾难，灾祸.
fear：恐惧，忌惮，畏惧，生怕，害怕.
first-class：第一流，第一流的.
fling：扔丢.
frowning：皱眉.
grit：粗砂，砂砾，沙子.
hoist：升起，吊车，举起.
hornpipe：号笛.
horrible：可怕，恐怖的.
learned：有学问，博学，博雅，饱学.
marching：游行.
memory：记忆、存储器，存储，记忆体，回忆.
moan：悲叹.
noble：高贵，高贵的，贵族.
outrageous：不像话，残暴的，岂有此理.
rave：怒吼，谵，咆哮.
rip：扯裂，撕破，裂口.
sling：弹弓，吊绳，背带，吊索.
soliloquy：独白，自言自语.
stagger：蹒跚，脚步蹒跚.
strikes：打击.
sublime：崇高，崇高的.
swelled：膨胀.
tilted：倾斜的.

fly to others that we know not of. There's the **respect** must give us **pause**: Wake Duncan with thy knocking! I would thou couldst; For who would bear the whips and scorns of time, The oppressor's wrong, the proud man's contumely, The law's **delay**, and the **quietus** which his pangs might take, In the dead **waste** and middle of the night, when churchyards **yawn** In **customary** suits of **solemn** black, But that the **undiscovered** country from **whose** bourne no **traveler** **returns**, Breathes forth contagion on the world, And thus the **native** **hue** of **resolution**, like the poor cat i' the **adage**, Is sicklied o'er with care, And all the clouds that lowered o'er our housetops, With this **regard** their currents turn **awry**, And lose the name of action. 'Tis a consummation devoutly to be wished. But soft you, the fair Ophelia: Ope not thy **ponderous** and **marble** **jaws**, But get **thee** to a nunnery--go!

Well, the old man he liked that speech, and he mighty soon got it so he could do it first-rate. It seemed like he was just born for it; and when he had his hand in and was excited, it was perfectly lovely the way he would **rip** and tear and rair up behind when he was getting it off.

The first chance we got the duke he had some showbills printed; and after that, for two or three days as we floated along, the **raft** was a most uncommon lively place, for there warn't nothing but sword **fighting** and rehearsing--as the duke called it--going on all the time. One morning, when we was pretty well down the State of Arkansaw, we come in sight of a little **one**-horse town in a big bend; so we tied up about three-quarters of a mile above it, in the mouth of a crick which was shut in like a **tunnel** by the **cypress** trees, and all of us but Jim took the **canoe** and went down there to see if there was any chance in that place for our show.

We struck it mighty lucky; there was going to be a **circus** there that afternoon, and the country people was already beginning to come in, in all kinds of old shackly wagons, and on horses. The circus would leave before night, so our show would have a pretty good chance. The duke he hired the courthouse, and we went around and stuck up our bills. They read like this:

Chinese Simplified

adage：格言.
awry：歪.
canoe：独木舟.
circus：马戏团，杂技团，马戏.
customary：习惯性，习惯性的.
cypress：丝柏.
delay：延迟，延期，耽搁，耽误，耽.
fighting：兵戈，战事，殴斗，战斗.
hue：色调，色.
jaws：咽喉，颌.
marble：大理石.
native：土着，土生的，土著.
one-horse：单马拉的.
pause：暂停，停顿.
ponderous：笨重的.
quietus：平息.
raft：筏，木排，槎，桴.
regard：看待，关系，认为，留意，注意，心意.
resolution：决议，决心，决议案，分解.
respect：尊敬，方面，遵守，尊重.
returns：返回.
rip：扯裂，撕破，裂口.
solemn：严肃，俨然，岸然，隆重，庄严的，庄重.
thee：你.
traveler：旅客，旅游者，游客.
tunnel：隧道，地道.
undiscovered：未被发现，未知的.
waste：荒芜，白费，浪费，糟蹋.
whose：谁的.
yawn：哈欠，打呵欠，呵欠.

Shaksperean Revival!!!
Wonderful Attraction!
For One Night Only!

The world **renowned** tragedians, David Garrick the Younger, of Drury Lane Theatre London, and Edmund Kean the **elder**, of the Royal Haymarket Theatre, Whitechapel, Pudding Lane, Piccadilly, London, and the Royal Continental Theatres, in their **sublime** Shaksperean Spectacle entitled:

The Balcony Scene in Romeo and Juliet!!!
Romeo...................Mr. Garrick
Juliet..................Mr. Kean
Assisted by the whole **strength** of the company!
New costumes, new scenes, new **appointments**!

Also:
The **thrilling**, **masterly**, and blood-curdling
Broad-sword **conflict**
In Richard III!!!

Richard III.............Mr. Garrick
Richmond................Mr. Kean

Also:
(by special **request**)
Hamlet's Immortal Soliloquy!!
By The Illustrious Kean!
Done by him 300 **consecutive** nights in Paris!
For One Night Only,
On **account** of **imperative** European **engagements**!
Admission 25 cents; children and servants, 10 cents.

Chinese Simplified

account: 帐户，账，帐，户口，重要性.
admission: 进场，承认.
appointments: 约会.
conflict: 冲突、争端，战争.
consecutive: 连续的.
elder: 长老，较长.
engagements: 约会.
imperative: 必要的.
masterly: 巧妙地、巧妙的.
renowned: 闻名，大明鼎鼎，著名的，享有声誉.
request: 要求，请求.
strength: 力量，力，强度，实力，力气，气力，浓度.
sublime: 崇高，崇高的.
thrilling: 毛骨悚然的.
wonderful: 奇妙，奇妙的.

Then we went loafing around town. The **stores** and houses was most all old, shackly, **dried** up frame concerns that hadn't ever been painted; they was set up three or four foot above ground on **stilts**, so as to be out of reach of the water when the river was over-flowed. The houses had little **gardens** around them, but they didn't seem to raise hardly anything in them but jimpson-weeds, and sunflowers, and **ash piles**, and old curled-up **boots** and shoes, and pieces of bottles, and **rags**, and played-out tinware. The **fences** was made of different kinds of **boards**, nailed on at different times; and they **leaned** every which way, and had **gates** that didn't generly have but one hinge--a **leather** one. Some of the fences had been white- washed some time or another, but the duke said it was in Clumbus' time, like enough. There was generly hogs in the garden, and people driving them out.

All the stores was along one **street**. They had white **domestic** awnings in front, and the country people **hitched** their horses to the awning-posts. There was empty drygoods boxes under the awnings, and **loafers** roosting on them all day long, whittling them with their Barlow knives; and chawing **tobacco**, and **gaping** and **yawning** and stretching--a **mighty ornery** lot. They generly had on **yellow straw** hats most as wide as an **umbrella**, but didn't **wear** no **coats** nor waistcoats, they called one another Bill, and Buck, and Hank, and Joe, and Andy, and talked **lazy** and drawly, and used considerable many cuss words. There was as many as one loafer leaning up against every awning-post, and he most always had his hands in his britches-pockets, except when he fetched them out to **lend** a chaw of tobacco or **scratch**. What a body was **hearing** amongst them all the time was:

"Gimme a chaw 'v tobacker, Hank."

"Cain't; I hain't got but one chaw left. Ask Bill."

Maybe Bill he gives him a chaw; maybe he lies and says he ain't got none. Some of them kinds of loafers never has a **cent** in the world, nor a chaw of tobacco of their own. They get all their chawing by **borrowing**; they say to a fellow, "I wisht you'd len' me a chaw, Jack, I jist this minute give Ben Thompson

Chinese Simplified

ash：灰，灰烬.
boards：纸板.
boots：靴子.
borrowing：借.
cent：一分钱，分.
coats：上衣.
domestic：国内，家里的.
dried：干燥的.
fences：栅栏.
gaping：目瞪口呆.
gardens：园林，花园.
gates：盖茨.
hearing：听力，听见.
hitched：蹒跚.
lazy：懒惰，懒惰的.
leaned：倾斜.
leather：皮革，皮.
lend：借出，借.
loafer：浪子，游荡.
mighty：伟大，强势，强大的.
ornery：低劣的.
piles：痔，痔疮，堆.
rags：碎布.
scratch：抓伤，抓，搔刮.
stilts：高跷.
stores：商店，备用品.
straw：稻草，吸管.
street：街道，街，马路，大街，街头.
tobacco：烟草.
umbrella：雨伞，伞.
wear：穿带，穿.
yawning：打呵欠.
yellow：黄，黄色.

the last chaw I had"--which is a lie pretty much everytime; it don't **fool** nobody but a **stranger**; but Jack ain't no stranger, so he says:

"*You* give him a chaw, did you? So did your sister's cat's **grandmother**. You pay me back the chaws you've awready borry'd off'n me, Lafe Buckner, then I'll **loan** you one or two **ton** of it, and won't charge you no back intrust, nuther."

"Well, I *did* pay you back some of it wunst."

"Yes, you did--'bout six chaws. You borry'd store tobacker and paid back nigger-head."

Store **tobacco** is flat black **plug**, but these fellows mostly chaws the natural **leaf** twisted. When they **borrow** a chaw they don't generly cut it off with a knife, but set the plug in between their teeth, and **gnaw** with their teeth and **tug** at the plug with their hands till they get it in two; then sometimes the one that owns the tobacco looks **mournful** at it when it's handed back, and says, **sarcastic**:

"Here, gimme the *chaw*, and you take the *plug*."

All the streets and lanes was just **mud**; they warn't nothing else *but* mud -- mud as black as **tar** and nigh about a foot deep in some places, and two or three inches deep in *all* the places. The hogs loafed and grunted around everywheres. You'd see a **muddy sow** and a **litter** of **pigs** come lazying along the street and whollop herself right down in the way, where folks had to walk around her, and she'd stretch out and shut her eyes and **wave** her ears whilst the pigs was **milking** her, and look as happy as if she was on **salary**. And pretty soon you'd hear a **loafer** sing out, "Hi! *So* boy! sick him, Tige!" and away the sow would go, **squealing** most **horrible**, with a dog or two swinging to each ear, and three or four dozen more a- coming; and then you would see all the loafers get up and watch the thing out of sight, and laugh at the fun and look **grateful** for the noise. Then they'd settle back again till there was a dog fight. There couldn't anything wake them up all over, and make them happy all over, like a dog fight--unless it might be **putting turpentine** on a **stray** dog and setting fire to him, or tying a tin **pan** to his **tail** and see him run himself to death.

Chinese Simplified

borrow：借.
fool：呆子，笨蛋，傻子，笨人，愚人.
gnaw：啃.
grandmother：祖母，婆婆.
grateful：感谢，感激的.
horrible：可怕，恐怖的.
leaf：叶子，箔.
litter：残馀物，丢垃圾.
loafer：浪子，游荡.
loan：贷款，借款，贷.
milking：挤奶.
mournful：悲切，悲恸，悲恸的.
mud：泥，泥浆.
muddy：泥泞的，混浊.
pan：平锅.
pigs：猪.
plug：插头，板烟，插.
salary：薪水，薪金，工钱，待遇.
sarcastic：讽刺的.
sow：播种，播.
squealing：啸声，振鸣声.
stranger：陌生人，异乡人，生人.
stray：游荡，迷路.
tail：尾巴，跟踪.
tar：焦油.
tin：锡，罐头.
tobacco：烟草.
ton：吨，公吨.
tug：强拉，拖.
turpentine：松节油.
wave：波浪，波，浪，浪头，浪潮，飘扬，摇，挥动.

On the river front some of the houses was sticking out over the bank, and they was **bowed** and **bent**, and about ready to **tumble** in, The people had moved out of them. The bank was **caved** away under one corner of some others, and that corner was hanging over. People lived in them yet, but it was dangersome, because sometimes a **strip** of land as wide as a house caves in at a time. Sometimes a **belt** of land a quarter of a **mile** deep will start in and cave along and cave along **till** it all caves into the river in one summer. Such a town as that has to be always moving back, and back, and back, because the river's always **gnawing** at it.

The nearer it got to **noon** that day the **thicker** and thicker was the wagons and horses in the **streets**, and more coming all the time. Families fetched their dinners with them from the country, and eat them in the wagons. There was considerable **whisky drinking** going on, and I seen three **fights**. By and by somebody **sings** out:

"Here comes old Boggs!--in from the country for his little old **monthly drunk**; here he comes, boys!"

All the loafers looked **glad**; I reckoned they was used to having **fun** out of Boggs. One of them says:

"Wonder who he's a-gwyne to chaw up this time. If he'd a-chawed up all the men he's ben a-gwyne to chaw up in the last twenty year he'd have considerable ruputation now."

Another one says, "I wisht old Boggs 'd **threaten** me, 'cuz then I'd know I warn't gwyne to **die** for a thousan' year."

Boggs comes a-tearing along on his horse, whooping and **yelling** like an Injun, and **singing** out:

"Cler the **track**, thar. I'm on the waw-path, and the **price** uv **coffins** is a-gwyne to raise."

He was drunk, and **weaving** about in his **saddle**; he was over fifty year old, and had a very red face. Everybody **yelled** at him and **laughed** at him and sassed him, and he sassed back, and said he'd **attend** to them and lay them out in

Chinese Simplified

attend：出席，参加.
belt：带，带子，地带，带儿.
bent：曲，弯，弯曲，弯折.
bowed：有弓的.
cave：洞穴，洞，穴.
coffins：棺材.
die：逝世，不讳，死.
drinking：喝.
drunk：喝了，喝醉.
fights：战斗.
fun：娱乐.
glad：高兴，高兴的.
gnawing：不断的苦痛，咬的.
laughed：笑.
mile：英里.
monthly：每月，单月.
noon：中午，正午，晌午.
price：价钱，价格，代价，价目.
saddle：鞍，鞍状物，马鞍.
singing：歌咏，歌唱.
sings：唱.
streets：街道.
strip：长条，剥夺，剥，简易机场.
thicker：厚.
threaten：威胁.
till：直到.
track：跑道，迳赛，迳迹，轨道，行踪，履带，踪迹.
tumble：跌倒，下跌，滚落，滚动.
weaving：编织.
whisky：威士忌酒.
yelled：叫喊.
yelling：叫声，叫喊.

their regular turns, but he couldn't wait now because he'd come to town to kill old Colonel Sherburn, and his **motto** was, "Meat first, and **spoon** vittles to top off on."

He see me, and **rode** up and says:

"Whar'd you come f'm, boy? You prepared to die?"

Then he rode on. I was scared, but a man says:

"He don't mean nothing; he's always a-carryin' on like **that** when he's **drunk**. He's the best naturedest old **fool** in Arkansaw--never **hurt** nobody, drunk nor **sober**."

Boggs rode up before the **biggest store** in town, and **bent** his head down so he could see under the **curtain** of the **awning** and **yells**:

"Come out here, Sherburn! Come out and meet the man you've swindled. You're the houn' I'm after, and I'm a-gwyne to have you, too!"

And so he went on, calling Sherburn everything he could lay his **tongue** to, and the whole street **packed** with people **listening** and **laughing** and going on. By and by a proud-looking man about fifty-five--and he was a **heap** the best dressed man in that town, too--steps out of the store, and the crowd drops back on each side to let him come. He says to Boggs, **mighty** ca'm and slow--he says:

"I'm **tired** of this, but I'll **endure** it **till** one o'clock. Till one o'clock, mind--no longer. If you open your mouth against me only once after that time you can't **travel** so far but I will find you."

Then he turns and goes in. The crowd looked mighty sober; nobody stirred, and there warn't no more laughing. Boggs rode off blackguarding Sherburn as **loud** as he could yell, all down the street; and pretty soon back he comes and **stops** before the store, still keeping it up. Some men **crowded** around him and tried to get him to **shut** up, but he wouldn't; they told him it would be one o'clock in about fifteen minutes, and so he *must* go home--he must go right away. But it didn't do no good. He cussed away with all his might, and throwed his hat down in the **mud** and rode over it, and pretty soon away he went a-raging down the street again, with his **gray** hair a-flying. Everybody that could get a chance at

Chinese Simplified

awning：雨篷．
bent：曲，弯，弯曲，弯折．
biggest：最大．
crowded：拥挤的．
curtain：布帘．
drunk：喝了，喝醉．
endure：持久，忍受，忍耐．
fool：呆子，笨蛋，傻子，笨人，愚人．
gray：灰色，灰．
hat：帽子．
heap：堆，堆积．
hurt：伤害，使受伤．
laughing：可笑的，笑．
listening：听．
loud：高声，大声，大声的．
mighty：伟大，强势，强大的．
motto：座右铭．
mud：泥，泥浆．
packed：挤得满满的．
rode：骑．
shut：关闭．
sober：清醒，清醒的．
spoon：匙，调羹．
stops：停止．
store：商店，储藏，商号，贮藏，店铺．
till：直到．
tired：疲倦，疲乏，疲倦的．
tongue：舌头，舌．
travel：旅行，遨游，旅游，游历．
yell：叫喊，呐喊．

him tried their best to **coax** him off of his horse so they could **lock** him up and get him **sober**; but it warn't no use--up the street he would **tear** again, and give Sherburn another cussing. By and by somebody says:

"Go for his **daughter**!--quick, go for his daughter; sometimes he'll listen to her. If **anybody** can **persuade** him, she can."

So somebody started on a run. I walked down street a ways and stopped. In about five or ten minutes here comes Boggs again, but not on his horse. He was a-reeling across the street towards me, bare-headed, with a friend on both sides of him a-holt of his arms and hurrying him along. He was quiet, and looked **uneasy**; and he warn't hanging back any, but was doing some of the hurrying himself. Somebody **sings** out:

"Boggs!"

I looked over there to see who said it, and it was that **Colonel** Sherburn. He was standing **perfectly** still in the street, and had a **pistol** raised in his right hand--not **aiming** it, but holding it out with the **barrel tilted** up towards the **sky**. The same second I see a young girl coming on the run, and two men with her. Boggs and the men turned round to see who called him, and when they see the pistol the men **jumped** to one side, and the pistol-barrel come down **slow** and **steady** to a level--both **barrels** cocked. Boggs throws up both of his hands and says, "O Lord, don't shoot!" Bang! goes the first shot, and he staggers back, clawing at the air--bang! goes the second one, and he **tumbles backwards** on to the ground, heavy and **solid**, with his arms **spread** out. That young girl screamed out and comes rushing, and down she throws herself on her father, **crying**, and saying, "Oh, he's killed him, he's killed him!" The **crowd** closed up around them, and shouldered and **jammed** one another, with their necks **stretched**, trying to see, and people on the inside trying to **shove** them back and **shouting**, "Back, back! give him air, give him air!"

Colonel Sherburn he tossed his pistol on to the ground, and turned around on his heels and walked off.

Chinese Simplified

aiming: 照准.
anybody: 任何人.
backwards: 逆，逆向，向后.
barrel: 桶，大桶.
barrels: 桶.
coax: 哄.
colonel: 陆军上校.
crowd: 人群.
crying: 叫喊的，嚎哭的，显著的.
daughter: 女儿，女孩儿，闺女.
jammed: 挤满.
jumped: 跳跃.
lock: 锁，撞锁.
perfectly: 完美，完美地.
persuade: 劝说，说服.
pistol: 手枪.
shouting: 呼喊.
shove: 推.
sings: 唱.
sky: 天空，天.
slow: 慢，缓慢，迟慢，迟钝，迟迟，迟缓.
sober: 清醒，清醒的.
solid: 固体，立体，固体的，坚硬，扎实，实心的，坚固的，坚实.
spread: 扩散，流传，传播，散播，敷，撒.
steady: 稳定，坚定，平稳，平稳的.
stretched: 伸展.
tear: 眼泪，撕破，撕.
tilted: 倾斜的.
tumbles: 跌倒.
uneasy: 不安，担心，不安的.

They took Boggs to a little **drug store**, the crowd **pressing** around just the same, and the whole town following, and I rushed and got a good place at the window, where I was close to him and could see in. They **laid** him on the floor and put one large Bible under his head, and opened another one and spread it on his **breast**; but they tore open his **shirt** first, and I seen where one of the **bullets** went in. He made about a **dozen** long gasps, his breast lifting the Bible up when he drawed in his breath, and letting it down again when he breathed it out--and after **that** he laid still; he was dead. Then they pulled his daughter away from him, screaming and **crying**, and took her off. She was about **sixteen**, and very **sweet** and **gentle** looking, but **awful** pale and scared.

Well, pretty soon the whole town was there, **squirming** and scrouging and pushing and shoving to get at the window and have a look, but people that had the places wouldn't give them up, and folks behind them was saying all the time, "Say, now, you've looked enough, you fellows; 'tain't right and 'tain't fair for you to stay thar all the time, and never give nobody a chance; other folks has their rights as well as you."

There was considerable jawing back, so I **slid** out, thinking maybe there was going to be trouble. The streets was full, and everybody was **excited**. Everybody that seen the **shooting** was telling how it happened, and there was a big crowd **packed** around each one of these fellows, **stretching** their necks and listening. One long, **lanky** man, with long hair and a big white **fur** stovepipe hat on the back of his head, and a crooked-handled **cane**, marked out the places on the ground where Boggs stood and where Sherburn stood, and the people following him around from one place to t'other and watching everything he done, and bobbing their heads to show they understood, and **stooping** a little and **resting** their hands on their **thighs** to watch him mark the places on the ground with his cane; and then he stood up straight and **stiff** where Sherburn had stood, **frowning** and having his hat-brim down over his eyes, and **sung** out, "Boggs!" and then fetched his cane down slow to a level, and says "Bang!" **staggered backwards**, says "Bang!" again, and fell down flat on his back. The people that had seen the thing said he done it perfect; said it was just exactly the way it all

Chinese Simplified

awful: 可怕，可怕的.
backwards: 逆，逆向，向后.
breast: 奶子，乳房，胸，胸部.
bullets: 子弹.
cane: 手杖，甘蔗，杖，鞭打.
crying: 叫喊的，嚎哭的，显著的.
dozen: 一打，打.
drug: 药品，药物，药.
excited: 兴奋，兴奋的，兴高采烈，激昂的.
frowning: 皱眉.
fur: 毛，软毛.
gentle: 轻松，文雅的，斯文，柔和.
hat: 帽子.
laid: 放.
lanky: 过分瘦长.
packed: 挤得满满的.
pressing: 紧迫，逼人，迫切，紧迫的.
resting: 静止的.
shirt: 衬衫，衬衣.
shooting: 射击，猎场.
sixteen: 十六.
slid: 滑行.
squirming: 蠕蠕，蠕动.
staggered: 交错.
stiff: 僵硬，板滞，僵硬的.
stooping: 弯腰.
stretching: 伸展.
sung: 唱歌.
sweet: 甜，甜食，糖果.
thighs: 大腿.
tore: 撕扯.

happened. Then as much as a **dozen** people got out their bottles and treated him.

Well, by and by **somebody** said Sherburn **ought** to be lynched. In about a **minute everybody** was **saying** it; so away they went, **mad** and **yelling**, and snatching down every clothes-line they come to to do the hanging with.

Chinese Simplified

dozen: 一打，打.
everybody: 每个人，各位.
happened: 发生.
mad: 狂，发怒，发狂，生气，疯狂的.
minute: 分钟，详细，分，微小的，渺小.
ought: 应该，活该.
saying: 名言，说.
somebody: 某人，有人.
yelling: 叫声，叫喊.

CHAPTER XXII

WHY THE LYNCHING BEE FAILED

They **swarmed** up towards Sherburn's house, a-whooping and **raging** like Injuns, and everything had to clear the way or get run over and tromped to mush, and it was **awful** to see. Children was heeling it **ahead** of the **mob**, screaming and trying to get out of the way; and every window along the road was full of women's **heads**, and there was nigger **boys** in every **tree**, and bucks and wenches looking over every **fence**; and as soon as the mob would get nearly to them they would break and skaddle back out of **reach**. Lots of the women and girls was **crying** and taking on, scared most to death.

They swarmed up in front of Sherburn's palings as **thick** as they could **jam** together, and you couldn't hear yourself think for the noise. It was a little twenty-foot **yard**. Some **sung** out "Tear down the fence! **tear** down the fence!" Then there was a **racket** of ripping and **tearing** and smashing, and down she goes, and the front wall of the **crowd begins** to **roll** in like a **wave**.

Just then Sherburn **steps** out on to the **roof** of his little front **porch**, with a double-barrel **gun** in his hand, and takes his **stand**, **perfectly** ca'm and **deliberate**, not saying a word. The racket **stopped**, and the wave sucked back.

Chinese Simplified

ahead: 前头，前方，前面的.
awful: 可怕，可怕的.
begins: 开始.
boys: 哥儿，男孩.
crowd: 人群.
crying: 叫喊的，嚎哭的，显著的.
deliberate: 商讨，故意的，成心.
fence: 篱笆，栅栏，栏位，栏.
gun: 枪，炮，长枪.
heads: 头.
jam: 果酱，干扰.
mob: 乌合之众，暴民.
perfectly: 完美，完美地.
porch: 阳台，门廊.
racket: 球拍，拍子.
raging: 熊熊，狂怒，猛烈的，狂暴的，愤怒的.
reach: 抵达，到达，抵，到.
roll: 滚动，簸荡，卷.
roof: 屋顶，顶部，顶板.
stand: 站住，主张，架子，站立，耐，站，架.
steps: 步骤.
stopped: 停止.
sung: 唱歌.
swarmed: 蜂涌.
tear: 眼泪，撕破，撕.
tearing: 撕裂的.
thick: 厚，密，浓厚.
tree: 树.
wave: 波浪，波，浪，浪头，浪潮，飘扬，摇，挥动.
yard: 码，厂，厂子，场地.

Sherburn never said a word--just stood there, looking down. The **stillness** was **awful creepy** and **uncomfortable**. Sherburn run his eye slow along the crowd; and **wherever** it **struck** the people tried a little to out- **gaze** him, but they couldn't; they dropped their eyes and looked sneaky. Then pretty soon Sherburn sort of laughed; not the **pleasant** kind, but the kind that makes you feel like when you are **eating** bread that's got **sand** in it.

Then he says, slow and **scornful**:

"The idea of *you* lynching anybody! It's **amusing**. The idea of you thinking you had **pluck** enough to lynch a *man*! Because you're **brave** enough to **tar** and **feather** poor **friendless** cast-out women that come along here, did that make you think you had **grit** enough to lay your hands on a *man*? Why, a *man's* safe in the hands of ten thousand of your kind--as long as it's **daytime** and you're not behind him.

"Do I know you? I know you clear through was born and raised in the South, and I've lived in the North; so I know the **average** all around. The average man's a **coward**. In the North he **lets** anybody walk over him that wants to, and goes home and prays for a **humble** spirit to bear it. In the South one man all by himself, has stopped a **stage** full of men in the daytime, and robbed the lot. Your newspapers call you a brave people so much that you think you are braver than any other people--whereas you're just *as* brave, and no braver. Why don't your **juries** hang murderers? Because they're afraid the man's friends will **shoot** them in the back, in the dark--and it's just what they *would* do.

"So they always **acquit**; and then a *man* goes in the night, with a hundred **masked** cowards at his back and lynches the **rascal**. Your mistake is, that you didn't bring a man with you; that's one mistake, and the other is that you didn't come in the dark and **fetch** your masks. You brought *part* of a man--Buck Harkness, there--and if you hadn't had him to start you, you'd a taken it out in **blowing**.

"You didn't want to come. The average man don't like trouble and **danger**. *You* don't like trouble and danger. But if only *half* a man--like Buck Harkness, there--shouts 'Lynch him! lynch him!' you're afraid to back down--afraid you'll

Chinese Simplified

acquit: 宣判无罪.
amusing: 有趣, 有趣的.
average: 平均, 普通, 平均的, 通俗.
awful: 可怕, 可怕的.
blowing: 吹.
brave: 勇敢, 勇敢的, 勇士.
coward: 懦夫, 胆小鬼.
creepy: 毛骨悚然的.
danger: 危险.
daytime: 白天, 白昼, 日间.
eating: 吃.
feather: 羽毛.
fetch: 拿, 取, 带来.
friendless: 没有朋友的, 无依无靠的.
gaze: 凝视.
grit: 粗砂, 砂砾, 沙子.
humble: 谦逊, 谦恭的.
juries: 陪审团.
lets: 让我们, 让.
masked: 戴面具.
pleasant: 愉快, 愉快的, 舒适的.
pluck: 采摘, 摘, 勇气, 采.
rascal: 小淘气, 流氓.
sand: 沙, 沙子.
scornful: 轻视, 轻视的.
shoot: 射击, 芽, 射门.
stage: 舞台, 阶段, 层次, 发动, 段.
stillness: 静止, 寂静.
struck: 敲打.
tar: 焦油.
uncomfortable: 不舒适, 不舒适的, 拘束, 别扭.
wherever: 无论何处, 哪里.

be found out to be what you are--*cowards*--and so you raise a **yell**, and hang **yourselves** on to that half-a-man's coat-tail, and come **raging** up here, swearing what big things you're going to do. The pitifulest thing out is a mob; that's what an **army** is--a mob; they don't fight with **courage** that's born in them, but with courage that's borrowed from their **mass**, and from their **officers**. But a mob without any *man* at the head of it is ***beneath*** pitifulness. Now the thing for *you* to do is to **droop** your **tails** and go home and **crawl** in a hole. If any real lynching's going to be done it will be done in the dark, Southern **fashion**; and when they come they'll bring their masks, and fetch a *man* along. Now *leave*--and take your half-a-man with you"--tossing his gun up across his left arm and cocking it when he says this.

The crowd washed back sudden, and then broke all apart, and went **tearing** off every which way, and Buck Harkness he **heeled** it after them, looking **tolerable cheap**. I could a stayed if I wanted to, but I didn't want to.

I went to the circus and loafed around the back side till the **watchman** went by, and then **dived** in under the tent. I had my twenty-dollar gold piece and some other money, but I reckoned I better save it, because there ain't no telling how soon you are going to need it, away from home and amongst strangers that way. You can't be too careful. I ain't **opposed** to spending money on circuses when there ain't no other way, but there ain't no use in *wasting* it on them.

It was a real **bully** circus. It was the splendidest sight that ever was when they all come riding in, two and two, a gentleman and lady, side by side, the men just in their **drawers** and undershirts, and no shoes nor stirrups, and resting their hands on their thighs easy and comfortable-- there must a been twenty of them--and every lady with a lovely **complexion**, and perfectly beautiful, and looking just like a gang of real sure-enough **queens**, and dressed in clothes that **cost millions** of dollars, and just littered with **diamonds**. It was a powerful fine sight; I never see anything so lovely. And then one by one they got up and stood, and went a-weaving around the ring so gentle and wavy and **graceful**, the men looking ever so tall and **airy** and straight, with their heads bobbing and **skimming** along, away up there under the tent-roof, and every lady's rose- leafy

Chinese Simplified

airy: 通风，通风的.
army: 陆军，兵团，陆海空三军，部队，军，军队.
beneath: 在下方，之下，下面.
bully: 欺负.
cheap: 低廉，便宜的，便宜.
complexion: 气色，脸色，肤色.
cost: 费用，花费，代价，价款，价钱是.
courage: 勇气，胆子，胆量，精神.
crawl: 爬，爬行.
diamonds: 钻石.
dived: 跳水.
drawers: 抽屉.
droop: 垂下.
fashion: 时尚，方式，时装.
graceful: 优雅，优美，优雅的，优美的.
heeled: 有鞋后跟的.
mass: 群众.
millions: 百万.
officers: 官员.
opposed: 反对的，对抗的，敌对的.
queens: 女王.
raging: 熊熊，狂怒，猛烈的，狂暴的，愤怒的.
skimming: 撇沫.
tails: 尾巴.
tearing: 撕裂的.
tolerable: 可容忍，可容忍的.
watchman: 看守者，更夫.
yell: 叫喊，呐喊.
yourselves: 你们自己.

dress **flapping** soft and **silky** around her hips, and she looking like the most loveliest parasol.

And then **faster** and faster they went, all of them **dancing**, first one foot out in the air and then the other, the horses **leaning** more and more, and the ringmaster going round and round the center-pole, cracking his **whip** and **shouting** "Hi!--hi!" and the **clown** cracking **jokes** behind him; and by and by all hands dropped the **reins**, and every lady put her **knuckles** on her hips and every gentleman folded his arms, and then how the horses did lean over and **hump** themselves! And so one after the other they all skipped off into the ring, and **made** the sweetest **bow** I ever see, and then scampered out, and everybody clapped their hands and went just about wild.

Well, all through the **circus** they done the most **astonishing** things; and all the time that clown carried on so it most killed the people. The ringmaster couldn't ever say a word to him but he was back at him quick as a **wink** with the **funniest** things a body ever said; and how he ever *could* think of so many of them, and so sudden and so **pat**, was what I couldn't noway understand. Why, I couldn't a thought of them in a year. And by and by a **drunk** man tried to get into the ring--said he wanted to **ride**; said he could ride as well as anybody that ever was. They argued and tried to keep him out, but he wouldn't listen, and the whole show come to a **standstill**. Then the people begun to holler at him and make fun of him, and that made him mad, and he begun to **rip** and **tear**; so that stirred up the people, and a lot of men begun to **pile** down off of the benches and **swarm** towards the ring, saying, "Knock him down! throw him out!" and one or two women begun to **scream**. So, then, the ringmaster he made a little speech, and said he hoped there wouldn't be no **disturbance**, and if the man would promise he wouldn't make no more trouble he would let him ride if he thought he could stay on the horse. So everybody laughed and said all right, and the man got on. The minute he was on, the horse begun to rip and tear and **jump** and cavort around, with two circus men hanging on to his **bridle** trying to hold him, and the drunk man hanging on to his neck, and his heels **flying** in the air every jump, and the whole crowd of people standing up shouting and laughing

Chinese Simplified

astonishing: 可惊，惊人，惊人的.
bow: 弓.
bridle: 勒马缰绳.
circus: 马戏团，杂技团，马戏.
clown: 小丑.
dancing: 跳舞.
disturbance: 风波，骚动，干扰，骚乱.
drunk: 喝了，喝醉.
faster: 快些.
flapping: 拍打.
flying: 飞行，飞.
fun: 娱乐.
hump: 驼背.
jokes: 笑林，笑话.
jump: 跳，跳跃.
knuckles: 关节.
lean: 倾斜.
mad: 狂，发怒，发狂，生气，疯狂的.
pat: 轻拍，拍，恰好的，人为的.
pile: 一堆，桩，堆.
reins: 缰.
ride: 乘，骑，跨，坐.
rip: 扯裂，撕破，裂口.
scream: 叫喊，呐喊，呼啸.
shouting: 呼喊.
silky: 柔软光滑.
standstill: 瘫痪.
swarm: 蜂群，一群.
tear: 眼泪，撕破，撕.
whip: 鞭打，鞭子，鞭.
wink: 眨眼，眨眼睛.

till tears **rolled** down. And at last, sure enough, all the **circus** men could do, the horse broke **loose**, and away he went like the very nation, round and round the ring, with that sot laying down on him and hanging to his neck, with first one leg hanging most to the ground on one side, and then t'other one on t'other side, and the people just **crazy**. It warn't funny to me, though; I was all of a **tremble** to see his danger. But pretty soon he struggled up astraddle and grabbed the **bridle**, a-reeling this way and that; and the next minute he **sprung** up and dropped the bridle and stood! and the horse a-going like a house **afire** too. He just stood up there, a- **sailing** around as easy and comfortable as if he warn't ever **drunk** in his life--and then he begun to pull off his clothes and **sling** them. He **shed** them so thick they kind of clogged up the air, and **altogether** he shed **seventeen** suits. And, then, there he was, **slim** and **handsome**, and dressed the gaudiest and prettiest you ever saw, and he **lit** into that horse with his **whip** and made him fairly hum--and **finally** skipped off, and made his **bow** and danced off to the dressing-room, and everybody just a-howling with pleasure and astonishment.

Then the ringmaster he see how he had been fooled, and he *was* the sickest ringmaster you ever see, I **reckon**. Why, it was one of his own men! He had got up that **joke** all out of his own head, and never let on to nobody. Well, I felt sheepish enough to be took in so, but I wouldn't a been in that ringmaster's place, not for a thousand dollars. I don't know; there may be bullier circuses than what that one was, but I never struck them yet. Anyways, it was plenty good enough for *me*; and **wherever** I run across it, it can have all of *my* **custom** every time.

Well, that night we had *our* show; but there warn't only about twelve people there--just enough to pay **expenses**. And they laughed all the time, and that made the duke mad; and everybody left, anyway, before the show was over, but one boy which was **asleep**. So the duke said these Arkansaw lunkheads couldn't come up to Shakespeare; what they wanted was low **comedy**--and maybe something ruther worse than low comedy, he reckoned. He said he could size their style. So next morning he got some big **sheets** of **wrapping** paper and some black **paint**, and drawed off some **handbills**, and **stuck** them up all over the village. The bills said:

Chinese Simplified

afire: 大为激动.
altogether: 总共，一共.
asleep: 睡着，睡着的.
bow: 弓.
bridle: 勒马缰绳.
circus: 马戏团，杂技团，马戏.
comedy: 喜剧.
crazy: 发狂，疯狂，颠倒，疯狂的.
custom: 风俗，习惯，规矩，习俗.
drunk: 喝了，喝醉.
expenses: 开支.
finally: 最后，到底，终于，最後，总算.
handbills: 传单.
handsome: 英俊，慷慨的，英俊的.
joke: 笑话，玩笑，开玩笑.
lit: 点燃.
loose: 松开，松弛的.
paint: 颜料，油漆，涂料，绘画.
reckon: 估计，计算.
rolled: 卷.
sailing: 航海术，航海，航行.
seventeen: 十七.
shed: 散出，棚子，流出，脱落.
sheets: 纸张.
slim: 瘦长，纤细，苗条的.
sling: 弹弓，吊绳，背带，吊索.
sprung: 弹跳.
stuck: 黏贴.
tremble: 发抖，哆嗦.
wherever: 无论何处，哪里.
whip: 鞭打，鞭子，鞭.
wrapping: 包皮.

AT THE COURT HOUSE!
FOR 3 NIGHTS ONLY!
The World-Renowned Tragedians
DAVID GARRICK THE YOUNGER!
AND
EDMUND KEAN THE ELDER!
Of the London and Continental Theatres,
In their Thrilling Tragedy of:

THE KING'S CAMELEOPARD, OR
THE ROYAL NONESUCH!!!
***Admission** 50 cents.*

Then at the **bottom** was the **biggest** line of all, which said:

LADIES AND CHILDREN NOT ADMITTED.

"There," says he, "if that line don't **fetch** them, I don't know Arkansaw!"

Chinese Simplified

admission: 进场, 承认.
biggest: 最大.
bottom: 底部, 屁股, 底.
fetch: 拿, 取, 带来.

CHAPTER XXIII

THE ORNERINESS OF KINGS

Well, all day him and the king was hard at it, **rigging** up a stage and a **curtain** and a **row** of **candles** for footlights; and that night the house was **jam** full of men in no time. When the place couldn't hold no more, the **duke** he **quit** tending door and went around the back way and come on to the stage and stood up before the curtain and made a little speech, and praised up this **tragedy**, and said it was the most thrillingest one that ever was; and so he went on a-bragging about the tragedy, and about Edmund Kean the Elder, which was to play the main **principal** part in it; and at last when he'd got everybody's expectations up high enough, he **rolled** up the curtain, and the next **minute** the king come a-prancing out on all fours, **naked**; and he was painted all over, ring-streaked-and-**striped**, all **sorts** of **colors**, as **splendid** as a **rainbow**. And--but never mind the rest of his **outfit**; it was just **wild**, but it was **awful funny**. The people most killed themselves **laughing**; and when the king got done capering and capered off behind the scenes, they roared and clapped and stormed and haw-hawed **till** he come back and done it over again, and after that they made him do it another time. Well, it would make a **cow** laugh to see the **shines** that old **idiot** cut.

Then the duke he **lets** the curtain down, and **bows** to the people, and says the great tragedy will be performed only two nights more, on **accounts** of pressing

Chinese Simplified

accounts: 据闻.
awful: 可怕, 可怕的.
bows: 弓.
candles: 蜡烛.
colors: 颜色.
cow: 母牛, 牛.
curtain: 布帘.
duke: 公爵, 公.
funny: 有趣的.
idiot: 白痴, 笨蛋, 傻子.
jam: 果酱, 干扰.
laugh: 笑.
laughing: 可笑的, 笑.
lets: 让我们, 让.
minute: 分钟, 详细, 分, 微小的, 渺小.
naked: 赤裸裸, 裸体的.
outfit: 旅行装备, 装备.
principal: 本金, 主要, 校长, 首长.
quit: 退出, 退离.
rainbow: 虹.
rigging: 索具, 帆具.
rolled: 卷.
row: 一排, 划, 行.
shines: 发光.
sorts: 种类.
splendid: 彪炳, 卓越, 辉煌, 灿烂的, 精彩, 辉煌的.
striped: 有条纹, 有条纹的.
till: 直到.
tragedy: 悲剧.
wild: 野, 猖披, 猖獗, 野生, 野性的.

London **engagements**, where the **seats** is all sold already for it in Drury Lane; and then he makes them another **bow**, and says if he has succeeded in **pleasing** them and instructing them, he will be **deeply** obleeged if they will **mention** it to their friends and get them to come and see it.

Twenty people **sings** out:

"What, is it over? Is that *all*?"

The **duke** says yes. Then there was a fine time. Everybody sings out, "Sold!" and rose up mad, and was a-going for that stage and them tragedians. But a big, fine looking man **jumps** up on a **bench** and **shouts**:

"Hold on! Just a word, gentlemen." They stopped to listen. "We are sold--mighty **badly** sold. But we don't want to be the **laughing** stock of this whole town, I **reckon**, and never hear the last of this thing as long as we live. *No*. What we want is to go out of here quiet, and talk this show up, and sell the *rest* of the town! Then we'll all be in the same boat. Ain't that sensible?" ("You **bet** it is!--the jedge is right!" everybody sings out.) "All right, then--not a word about any sell. Go along home, and **advise** everybody to come and see the tragedy."

Next day you couldn't hear nothing around that town but how **splendid** that show was. House was **jammed** again that night, and we sold this crowd the same way. When me and the king and the duke got home to the **raft** we all had a **supper**; and by and by, about **midnight**, they made Jim and me back her out and **float** her down the middle of the river, and **fetch** her in and **hide** her about two mile below town.

The third night the house was crammed again--and they warn't new-comers this time, but people that was at the show the other two nights. I stood by the duke at the door, and I see that every man that went in had his pockets **bulging**, or something muffled up under his coat--and I see it warn't no **perfumery**, neither, not by a long sight. I **smelt** sickly **eggs** by the **barrel**, and **rotten** cabbages, and such things; and if I know the signs of a dead cat being around, and I bet I do, there was sixty-four of them went in. I shoved in there for a minute, but it was too **various** for me; I couldn't stand it. Well, when the place

Chinese Simplified

advise: 忠告，劝告，劝导，劝说.
badly: 非常的.
barrel: 桶，大桶.
bench: 长椅，长凳.
bet: 打赌，赌.
bow: 弓.
bulging: 膨胀.
deeply: 在深处，深深地.
duke: 公爵，公.
eggs: 蛋.
engagements: 约会.
fetch: 拿，取，带来.
float: 漂浮.
hide: 躲藏，暗藏，掩饰，藏，隐瞒，隐藏.
jammed: 挤满.
jumps: 跳跃.
laughing: 可笑的，笑.
mention: 提到，提及.
midnight: 午夜，半夜.
perfumery: 香料店.
pleasing: 愉快，愉快的，舒适的.
raft: 筏，木排，槎，桴.
reckon: 估计，计算.
rotten: 腐败的，腐朽.
seats: 座位.
shouts: 呼喊.
sings: 唱.
smelt: 熔炼，溶解.
splendid: 彪炳，卓越，辉煌，灿烂的，精彩，辉煌的.
supper: 晚饭，晚餐.
various: 各个，各式各样，数.

couldn't hold no more people the **duke** he give a **fellow** a quarter and told him to **tend** door for him a minute, and then he started around for the stage door, I after him; but the minute we turned the corner and was in the dark he says:

"Walk **fast** now **till** you get away from the houses, and then **shin** for the **raft** like the dickens was after you!"

I done it, and he done the same. We **struck** the raft at the same time, and in less than two **seconds** we was **gliding** down **stream**, all dark and still, and **edging** towards the middle of the river, nobody saying a word. I **reckoned** the poor king was in for a **gaudy** time of it with the **audience**, but nothing of the sort; **pretty** soon he **crawls** out from under the **wigwam**, and says:

"Well, how'd the old thing **pan** out this time, duke?" He hadn't been up-town at all.

We never showed a light till we was about ten **mile** below the village. Then we **lit** up and had a **supper**, and the king and the duke fairly **laughed** their bones **loose** over the way they'd served them people. The duke says:

"Greenhorns, flatheads! I knew the first house would keep mum and let the rest of the town get roped in; and I knew they'd lay for us the third night, and **consider** it was *their* turn now. Well, it *is* their turn, and I'd give something to know how much they'd take for it. I *would* just like to know how they're putting in their **opportunity**. They can turn it into a **picnic** if they want to--they brought **plenty** provisions."

Them rapscallions took in four hundred and **sixty**-five dollars in that three nights. I never see money hauled in by the wagon-load like that before. By and by, when they was **asleep** and **snoring**, Jim says:

"Don't it s'prise you de way dem **kings** carries on, Huck?"

"No," I says, "it don't."

"Why don't it, Huck?"

"Well, it don't, because it's in the **breed**. I reckon they're all alike,"

Chinese Simplified

asleep: 睡着，睡着的.
audience: 听众.
breed: 品种，繁殖，饲养.
consider: 以为，考虑，考量.
crawls: 爬行.
duke: 公爵，公.
edging: 边缘.
fast: 快，禁食，快速，迅速，速.
fellow: 同伴，伙伴.
gaudy: 花哨，花里胡哨.
gliding: 滑行的，下滑.
kings: 国王.
laughed: 笑.
lit: 点燃.
loose: 松开，松弛的.
mile: 英里.
opportunity: 机会，时机，机遇.
pan: 平锅.
picnic: 野餐.
plenty: 丰富，许多.
pretty: 漂亮，美丽的，秀丽.
raft: 筏，木排，槎，桴.
reckon: 估计，计算.
seconds: 秒.
shin: 外小腿，胫.
sixty-five: 六十五.
snoring: 打鼾.
stream: 溪流，河流，流，小溪，川.
struck: 敲打.
supper: 晚饭，晚餐.
tend: 照料，倾向.
till: 直到.
wigwam: 帐篷，陋棚.

"But, Huck, dese **kings** o' ourn is reglar rapscallions; dat's jist what dey is; dey's reglar rapscallions."

"Well, that's what I'm a-saying; all kings is **mostly** rapscallions, as **fur** as I can make out."

"Is dat so?"

"You read about them once--you'll see. Look at Henry the Eight; this 'n 's a Sunday-school Superintendent to *him*. And look at Charles Second, and Louis Fourteen, and Louis Fifteen, and James Second, and Edward Second, and Richard Third, and forty more; **besides** all them Saxon heptarchies that used to **rip** around so in old times and raise Cain. My, you ought to seen old Henry the Eight when he was in **bloom**. He *was* a **blossom**. He used to **marry** a new wife every day, and **chop** off her head next morning. And he would do it just as **indifferent** as if he was **ordering** up **eggs**. 'Fetch up Nell Gwynn,' he says. They **fetch** her up. Next morning, 'Chop off her head!' And they chop it off. 'Fetch up Jane Shore,' he says; and up she comes, Next morning, 'Chop off her head'--and they chop it off. 'Ring up Fair Rosamun.' Fair Rosamun **answers** the **bell**. Next morning, 'Chop off her head.' And he made every one of them tell him a **tale** every night; and he kept that up till he had hogged a thousand and one **tales** that way, and then he put them all in a book, and called it Domesday Book--which was a good name and **stated** the case. You don't know kings, Jim, but I know them; and this old rip of ourn is one of the cleanest I've **struck** in **history**. Well, Henry he takes a **notion** he wants to get up some trouble with this country. How does he go at it-- give notice?--give the country a show? No. All of a **sudden** he heaves all the **tea** in Boston Harbor **overboard**, and whacks out a **declaration** of **independence**, and dares them to come on. That was *his* style--he never give anybody a chance. He had **suspicions** of his father, the Duke of Wellington. Well, what did he do? Ask him to show up? No--drownded him in a **butt** of mamsey, like a **cat**. S'pose people left money laying around where he was--what did he do? He collared it. S'pose he **contracted** to do a thing, and you paid him, and didn't set down there and see that he done it--what did he do? He always done the other thing. S'pose he opened his mouth--what then? If he didn't shut it

Chinese Simplified

answers：回答.
bell：钟，铃.
besides：此外，另外，除了，并且，再说，况且.
bloom：花开，开花.
blossom：群花，花，开花.
butt：臀部，屁股，枪托.
cat：猫.
chop：劈，剁，砍，伐.
contracted：收缩了的.
declaration：声明，宣言.
eggs：蛋.
fetch：拿，取，带来.
fur：毛，软毛.
history：历史，来历，过去的事，历史学.
independence：独立.
indifferent：冷淡，无关紧要，漠不关心的.
kings：国王.
marry：结婚.
mostly：大多，多半，大部份.
notion：观念.
ordering：排序，命令.
overboard：向船外.
rip：扯裂，撕破，裂口.
stated：志明.
struck：敲打.
sudden：突然，急剧，突然的.
suspicions：怀疑.
tale：故事.
tales：候补陪审员召集令.
tea：茶，茶叶.

up powerful **quick** he'd **lose** a **lie** every time. That's the **kind** of a **bug** Henry was; and if we'd a had him along 'stead of our **kings** he'd a fooled that town a **heap** worse than ourn done. I don't say that ourn is **lambs**, because they ain't, when you come right down to the cold **facts**; but they ain't nothing to *that* old **ram**, anyway. All I say is, kings is kings, and you got to make allowances. Take them all around, they're a **mighty ornery** lot. It's the way they're raised."

"But dis one do *smell* so like de **nation**, Huck."

"Well, they all do, Jim. We can't help the way a king **smells**; history don't tell no way."

"Now de **duke**, he's a tolerble likely man in some ways."

"Yes, a duke's different. But not very different. This one's a **middling** hard lot for a duke. When he's **drunk** there ain't no **near**-sighted man could tell him from a king."

"Well, anyways, I doan' **hanker** for no mo' un um, Huck. Dese is all I kin stan'."

"It's the way I feel, too, Jim. But we've got them on our hands, and we got to remember what they are, and make allowances. Sometimes I wish we could hear of a country that's out of kings."

What was the use to tell Jim these warn't real kings and dukes? It wouldn't a done no good; and, **besides**, it was just as I said: you couldn't tell them from the real kind.

I went to **sleep**, and Jim didn't call me when it was my turn. He often done that. When I waked up just at **daybreak** he was **sitting** there with his head down **betwixt** his **knees**, moaning and **mourning** to himself. I didn't take notice nor let on. I knowed what it was about. He was thinking about his wife and his children, away up **yonder**, and he was low and **homesick**; because he hadn't ever been away from home before in his life; and I do believe he cared just as much for his people as white folks does for their'n. It don't seem natural, but I **reckon** it's so. He was often moaning and mourning that way nights, when he judged I was **asleep**, and saying, "Po' little 'Lizabeth! po' little Johnny! it's mighty

Chinese Simplified

asleep: 睡着，睡着的.
besides: 此外，另外，除了，并且，再说，况且.
betwixt: 中间，在…之间.
bug: 飞虫，错误，臭虫.
daybreak: 黎明，破晓.
drunk: 喝了，喝醉.
duke: 公爵，公.
facts: 事实.
hanker: 渴望.
heap: 堆，堆积.
homesick: 想家.
kin: 亲属，骨肉.
kings: 国王.
knees: 膝盖.
lambs: 小羊.
lie: 谎言，谎话，躺，撒谎，说谎.
lose: 丢失，丧失，失掉，遗失.
middling: 中级品.
mighty: 伟大，强势，强大的.
mourning: 追悼，丧.
nation: 国家.
near-**sighted**: 近视的.
ornery: 低劣的.
quick: 快，玲珑，敏捷的，迅速的.
ram: 公羊，随机存取存储器，灌输，撞.
reckon: 估计，计算.
sitting: 坐，开庭期间.
sleep: 梦寐，睡觉，睡眠，睡.
smell: 嗅，臭，香味.
smells: 臭.
yonder: 那边.

hard; I spec' I ain't ever gwyne to see you no mo', no mo'!" He was a **mighty** good nigger, Jim was.

But this time I **somehow** got to talking to him about his wife and young ones; and by and by he says:

"What makes me feel so bad dis time 'uz bekase I hear sumpn over **yonder** on de bank like a **whack**, er a **slam**, while ago, en it **mine** me er de time I **treat** my little 'Lizabeth so **ornery**. She warn't on'y 'bout fo' year ole, en she **tuck** de sk'yarlet **fever**, en had a powful **rough spell**; but she got well, en one day she was a-stannin' aroun', en I says to her, I says:

"'Shet de do'.'

"She never done it; **jis'** stood dah, kiner smilin' up at me. It make me **mad**; en I says agin, mighty **loud**, I says:

"'Doan' you hear me? Shet de do'!'

"She jis stood de same way, kiner smilin' up. I was a-bilin'! I says:

"'I lay I *make* you mine!'

"En wid dat I **fetch'** her a **slap** side de head dat sont her a-sprawlin'. **Den** I went into de yuther room, en 'uz gone 'bout ten minutes; en when I come back dah was dat do' a-stannin' open *yit*, en dat **chile** stannin' mos' right in it, a-lookin' down and mournin', en de **tears** runnin' down. My, but I *wuz* mad! I was a-gwyne for de chile, but jis' den--it was a do' dat open innerds--jis' den, 'long come de **wind** en slam it to, behine de chile, ker-*blam*!--en my lan', de chile never move'! My breff mos' **hop outer** me; en I feel so--so--I doan' know *how* I feel. I crope out, all a- tremblin', en crope aroun' en open de do' easy en **slow**, en **poke** my head in behine de chile, sof' en still, en all uv a **sudden** I says *pow*! jis' as loud as I could **yell**. *She never **budge***! Oh, Huck, I **bust** out a-cryin' en **grab** her up in my arms, en say, 'Oh, de po' little thing! De Lord God Amighty fogive po' ole Jim, kaze he never gwyne to fogive hisself as long's he live!' Oh, she was plumb deef en **dumb**, Huck, plumb deef en dumb--en I'd ben a-treat'n her so!"

Chinese Simplified

budge：微微一动，改变态度，羔皮．
bust：半身像，逮捕，破产．
chile：智利．
den：窝．
dumb：哑．
fetch：拿，取，带来．
fever：发烧，发热．
grab：抓住，攫取，抓斗．
hop：跳跃，三级跳远．
jis：日本工业标准．
loud：高声，大声，大声的．
mad：狂，发怒，发狂，生气，疯狂的．
mighty：伟大，强势，强大的．
mine：矿，我的，矿山，矿井．
ornery：低劣的．
outer：在外，帮子，外部的．
poke：戳，拨开，插入．
rough：粗暴，大概，粗糙，粗鲁．
slam：猛撞，猛力关．
slap：掌击，拍．
slow：慢，缓慢，迟慢，迟钝，迟迟，迟缓．
somehow：不知何故．
spell：拼写，咒语，符咒．
sudden：突然，急剧，突然的．
tears：泪，泪水，眼泪．
treat：对待．
tuck：挤进，塞进．
whack：重打．
wind：风，弯曲，上弦，缠绕．
yell：叫喊，呐喊．
yonder：那边．

CHAPTER XXIV

THE KING TURNS PARSON

Next day, towards night, we **laid** up under a little **willow** towhead out in the middle, where there was a village on each side of the **river**, and the **duke** and the king **begun** to lay out a plan for working them towns. Jim he **spoke** to the duke, and said he **hoped** it wouldn't take but a few hours, because it got **mighty heavy** and **tiresome** to him when he had to lay all day in the **wigwam tied** with the **rope**. You see, when we left him all **alone** we had to tie him, because if **anybody** happened on to him all by himself and not tied it wouldn't look much like he was a **runaway** nigger, you know. So the duke said it *was* kind of hard to have to lay roped all day, and he'd **cipher** out some way to get around it.

He was **uncommon** bright, the duke was, and he soon **struck** it. He dressed Jim up in King Lear's outfit--it was a long curtain-calico **gown**, and a white horse-hair wig and **whiskers**; and then he took his **theater paint** and painted Jim's face and hands and **ears** and **neck** all over a dead, **dull**, solid **blue**, like a man that's been drownded nine days. Blamed if he warn't the horriblest looking **outrage** I ever see. Then the duke took and wrote out a sign on a **shingle** so:

Sick Arab--but **harmless** when not out of his head.

Chinese Simplified

alone：独自，单独，单纯，单独地.
anybody：任何人.
begun：开始.
blue：蓝，蓝色，青.
cipher：暗号，密码，阿拉伯数字.
duke：公爵，公.
dull：索然，板滞，沉闷的，干燥，拙，深沉.
ears：耳朵.
gown：长袍，女装长袍.
harmless：无害，无害的.
heavy：重，沉重，笨重，沈重，沉闷.
hop：跳跃，三级跳远.
laid：放.
mighty：伟大，强势，强大的.
neck：颈项，脖子，颈.
outrage：暴行，使愤慨.
paint：颜料，油漆，涂料，绘画.
river：河，江，川，河流，条.
rope：绳索，绳子.
runaway：逃亡者，跑道.
shingle：木瓦，屋顶板.
spoke：辐条，说了.
struck：敲打.
theater：剧场，戏剧，戏院，剧院.
tie：不分胜负，打结，束缚，轨枕，绑，领带.
tiresome：使人疲惫的.
uncommon：稀有，稀有的.
whiskers：胡子.
wig：假发.
wigwam：帐篷，陋棚.
willow：柳树.

And he nailed that **shingle** to a **lath**, and stood the lath up four or five foot in front of the **wigwam**. Jim was **satisfied**. He said it was a sight better than **lying** tied a couple of years every day, and **trembling** all over every time there was a sound. The duke told him to make himself free and easy, and if anybody ever come meddling around, he must **hop** out of the wigwam, and carry on a little, and **fetch** a **howl** or two like a wild **beast**, and he **reckoned** they would light out and leave him alone. Which was sound enough judgment; but you take the average man, and he wouldn't wait for him to howl. Why, he didn't only look like he was dead, he looked considerable more than that.

These rapscallions wanted to try the Nonesuch again, because there was so much money in it, but they judged it wouldn't be safe, because maybe the news might a worked along down by this time. They couldn't hit no **project** that **suited** exactly; so at last the duke said he reckoned he'd lay off and work his **brains** an hour or two and see if he couldn't put up something on the Arkansaw village; and the king he allowed he would drop over to t'other village without any plan, but just trust in Providence to lead him the **profitable** way--meaning the **devil**, I reckon. We had all bought store clothes where we stopped last; and now the king put his'n on, and he told me to put mine on. I done it, of course. The king's duds was all black, and he did look real **swell** and **starchy**. I never knowed how clothes could change a body before. Why, before, he looked like the orneriest old **rip** that ever was; but now, when he'd take off his new white **beaver** and make a **bow** and do a **smile**, he looked that grand and good and **pious** that you'd say he had walked right out of the **ark**, and maybe was old Leviticus himself. Jim cleaned up the **canoe**, and I got my **paddle** ready. There was a big **steamboat** laying at the **shore** away up under the point, about three mile above the town--been there a couple of hours, taking on **freight**. Says the king:

"Seein' how I'm dressed, I reckon maybe I better **arrive** down from St. **Louis** or Cincinnati, or some other big place. Go for the steamboat, Huckleberry; we'll come down to the village on her."

Chinese Simplified

ark：方舟.
arrive：抵达，到达，到.
beast：野兽，动物.
beaver：海狸，河狸.
bow：弓.
brains：头脑，脑子，脑筋，脑袋，脑髓.
canoe：独木舟.
devil：魔鬼，妖怪，鬼.
fetch：拿，取，带来.
freight：货物运输.
hop：跳跃，三级跳远.
howl：狂吠，号叫.
lath：板条.
louis：路易斯.
lying：撒谎的.
paddle：桨.
pious：虔诚的.
profitable：有利可图，有利可图的.
project：计划，项目，工程，规划，方案，专案，设计，投影.
reckon：估计，计算.
rip：扯裂，撕破，裂口.
satisfied：满意，乐意，心满意足的.
shingle：木瓦，屋顶板.
shore：岸，滨，岸边，海岸，海滨.
smile：微笑，笑容.
starchy：含淀粉，古板的.
steamboat：汽船，轮船.
suited：适宜于.
swell：涨满，膨胀.
trembling：发抖，发抖的.
wigwam：帐篷，陋棚.

I didn't have to be ordered **twice** to go and take a **steamboat ride**. I fetched the **shore** a half a **mile** above the village, and then went scooting along the **bluff** bank in the easy water. Pretty soon we come to a nice innocent-looking young country jake **setting** on a **log** swabbing the **sweat** off of his face, for it was powerful **warm weather**; and he had a couple of big carpet-bags by him.

"Run her **nose** in shore," says the king. I done it. "Wher' you **bound** for, young man?"

"For the steamboat; going to Orleans."

"Git aboard," says the king. "Hold on a **minute**, my **servant** 'll he'p you with them bags. Jump out and he'p the **gentleman**, Adolphus"--meaning me, I see.

I done so, and then we all three started on again. The young **chap** was **mighty thankful**; said it was **tough** work toting his **baggage** such weather. He asked the king where he was going, and the king told him he'd come down the river and **landed** at the other village this morning, and now he was going up a few mile to see an old friend on a **farm** up there. The young **fellow** says:

"When I first see you I says to myself, 'It's Mr. Wilks, sure, and he come mighty near getting here in time.' But then I says again, 'No, I **reckon** it ain't him, or else he wouldn't be paddling up the river.' You *ain't* him, are you?"

"No, my name's Blodgett--Elexander Blodgett--*Reverend* Elexander Blodgett, I s'pose I must say, as I'm one o' the Lord's poor servants. But still I'm jist as able to be sorry for Mr. Wilks for not **arriving** in time, all the same, if he's missed anything by it--which I hope he hasn't."

"Well, he don't miss any property by it, because he'll get that all right; but he's missed **seeing** his brother Peter die--which he mayn't mind, **nobody** can tell as to that--but his brother would a give anything in this world to see *him* before he died; never **talked** about nothing else all these three weeks; hadn't seen him since they was boys together--and hadn't ever seen his brother William at all--that's the deef and **dumb** one--William ain't more than thirty or thirty-five. Peter and George were the only ones that come out here; George was the married brother;

Chinese Simplified

arriving: 到达.
baggage: 行李.
bluff: 虚张声势, 吹牛.
bound: 限, 边际, 弹回, 范围.
chap: 家伙, 皴裂.
dumb: 哑.
farm: 农场, 田间.
fellow: 同伴, 伙伴.
gentleman: 绅士.
landed: 着陆.
log: 圆形木材, 圆木, 木头.
mighty: 伟大, 强势, 强大的.
mile: 英里.
minute: 分钟, 详细, 分, 微小的, 渺小.
nobody: 没有人, 没人.
nose: 鼻子.
reckon: 估计, 计算.
ride: 乘, 骑, 跨, 坐.
seeing: 有鉴于.
servant: 仆人, 佣人, 用人.
setting: 排字, 设定.
shore: 岸, 滨, 岸边, 海岸, 海滨.
steamboat: 汽船, 轮船.
sweat: 汗, 出汗, 流汗.
talked: 谈话.
thankful: 感谢, 感谢的.
tough: 强硬, 坚韧的.
twice: 两次.
warm: 暖, 暖和, 温暖, 热烈, 温暖的.
weather: 天气.

him and his wife both died last year. Harvey and William's the only ones that's left now; and, as I was saying, they haven't got here in time."

"Did **anybody send** 'em word?"

"Oh, yes; a month or two ago, when Peter was first took; because Peter said then that he **sorter** felt like he warn't going to get well this time. You see, he was **pretty** old, and George's g'yirls was too young to be much company for him, **except Mary** Jane, the red-headed one; and so he was kinder **lonesome** after George and his wife died, and didn't seem to care much to live. He most desperately wanted to see Harvey--and William, too, for that matter--because he was one of them kind that can't **bear** to make a will. He left a letter behind for Harvey, and said he'd told in it where his money was **hid**, and how he wanted the rest of the property divided up so George's g'yirls would be all right--for George didn't leave nothing. And that letter was all they could get him to put a **pen** to."

"Why do you **reckon** Harvey don't come? Wher' does he live?"

"Oh, he lives in England--Sheffield--preaches there--hasn't ever been in this country. He hasn't had any too much time--and **besides** he mightn't a got the letter at all, you know."

"Too bad, too bad he couldn't a lived to see his **brothers**, poor **soul**. You going to Orleans, you say?"

"Yes, but that ain't only a part of it. I'm going in a **ship**, next Wednesday, for Ryo Janeero, where my **uncle** lives."

"It's a pretty long **journey**. But it'll be **lovely**; wisht I was a-going. Is Mary Jane the **oldest**? How old is the others?"

"Mary Jane's **nineteen**, Susan's **fifteen**, and Joanna's about fourteen-- that's the one that gives herself to good works and has a hare-lip."

"Poor things! to be left **alone** in the **cold** world so."

"Well, they could be **worse** off. Old Peter had friends, and they ain't going to let them come to no **harm**. There's Hobson, the Babtis' **preacher**; and Deacon Lot

Chinese Simplified

alone：独自，单独，单纯，单独地．
anybody：任何人．
bear：熊，忍受，背负，忍耐，承担，担负，空头，堪．
besides：此外，另外，除了，并且，再说，况且．
brothers：兄弟，哥儿．
cold：冷，感冒，寒冷，寒，冷淡．
except：除了，除了之外．
fifteen：十五．
harm：伤害，损害，坏处，害处，祸害．
hid：躲藏．
journey：旅程，旅途，旅游，旅行．
lonesome：寂寞，寂寞的．
lovely：可爱，可爱的．
mary：玛莉．
nineteen：十九．
oldest：最年长的．
pen：笔，栏圈，笔杆，笔杆子，栏位，栏，钢笔．
preacher：传道者．
pretty：漂亮，美丽的，秀丽．
reckon：估计，计算．
send：派遣，派出，送，发送，寄，投，派．
ship：船．
sorter：分类者．
soul：灵魂．
uncle：叔叔，伯伯，叔父，大爷，老大爷，姑夫．
worse：更坏，更糟．

Hovey, and Ben Rucker, and Abner Shackleford, and Levi Bell, the **lawyer**; and Dr. **Robinson**, and their wives, and the **widow** Bartley, and--well, there's a lot of them; but these are the ones that Peter was thickest with, and used to write about sometimes, when he wrote home; so Harvey 'll know where to look for friends when he gets here."

Well, the old man went on asking questions **till** he just **fairly emptied** that young **fellow**. Blamed if he didn't **inquire** about **everybody** and everything in that **blessed** town, and all about the Wilkses; and about Peter's business--which was a **tanner**; and about George's--which was a **carpenter**; and about Harvey's--which was a dissentering minister; and so on, and so on. Then he says:

"What did you want to walk all the way up to the **steamboat** for?"

"Because she's a big Orleans boat, and I was afeard she mightn't stop there. When they're deep they won't stop for a **hail**. A Cincinnati boat will, but this is a St. **Louis** one."

"Was Peter Wilks well off?"

"Oh, yes, **pretty** well off. He had houses and land, and it's reckoned he left three or four thousand in cash **hid** up som'ers."

"When did you say he died?"

"I didn't say, but it was last night."

"**Funeral** to-morrow, likely?"

"Yes, 'bout the middle of the day."

"Well, it's all **terrible sad**; but we've all got to go, one time or another. So what we want to do is to be **prepared**; then we're all right."

"Yes, sir, it's the best way. Ma used to always say that."

When we **struck** the boat she was about done **loading**, and pretty soon she got off. The king never said nothing about going **aboard**, so I lost my **ride**, after all. When the boat was gone the king made me **paddle** up another **mile** to a **lonesome** place, and then he got **ashore** and says:

Chinese Simplified

aboard：船上，在车，上.
ashore：岸上，上岸.
blessed：幸福，幸福的.
boat：小船，船，帆船，乘务员.
carpenter：木匠.
emptied：空.
everybody：每个人，各位.
fairly：相当，比较，公平地.
fellow：同伴，伙伴.
funeral：葬礼.
hail：冰雹，雹，雹子，欢呼.
hid：躲藏.
inquire：查调，质问，询问.
lawyer：律师，法人.
loading：荷重.
lonesome：寂寞，寂寞的.
louis：路易斯.
mile：英里.
paddle：桨.
prepared：有准备的，准备好的，精制的.
pretty：漂亮，美丽的，秀丽.
ride：乘，骑，跨，坐.
robinson：鲁滨逊.
sad：悲伤，哀愁，不幸，哀伤，哀怨，悲伤的，悲哀的.
steamboat：汽船，轮船.
struck：敲打.
tanner：唐纳.
terrible：可怕，糟糕，可怕的.
till：直到.
widow：寡妇.

"Now hustle back, right off, and **fetch** the **duke** up here, and the new carpet-bags. And if he's gone over to t'other side, go over there and git him. And tell him to git himself up **regardless**. Shove along, now."

I see what *he* was up to; but I never said nothing, of course. When I got back with the duke we **hid** the **canoe**, and then they set down on a **log**, and the **king** told him everything, just like the young **fellow** had said it-- every last word of it. And all the time he was a-doing it he tried to talk like an Englishman; and he done it **pretty** well, too, for a slouch. I can't **imitate** him, and so I ain't a-going to try to; but he really done it pretty good. Then he says:

"How are you on the deef and **dumb**, Bilgewater?"

The duke said, leave him **alone** for that; said he had played a deef and dumb person on the histronic **boards**. So then they waited for a **steamboat**.

About the middle of the **afternoon** a couple of little **boats** come along, but they didn't come from high enough up the river; but at last there was a big one, and they hailed her. She sent out her **yawl**, and we went **aboard**, and she was from Cincinnati; and when they found we only wanted to go four or five **mile** they was **booming mad**, and gave us a cussing, and said they wouldn't land us. But the king was ca'm. He says:

"If **gentlemen** kin **afford** to pay a **dollar** a mile **apiece** to be took on and put off in a yawl, a steamboat kin afford to carry 'em, can't it?"

So they **softened** down and said it was all right; and when we got to the village they yawled us **ashore**. About two **dozen** men flocked down when they see the yawl a-coming, and when the king says:

"Kin any of you gentlemen tell me wher' Mr. Peter Wilks lives?" they give a **glance** at one another, and nodded their **heads**, as much as to say, "What d' I tell you?" Then one of them says, kind of soft and gentle:

"I'm sorry sir, but the best we can do is to tell you where he *did* live yesterday evening."

Chinese Simplified

aboard: 船上，在车，上.
afford: 力足以做，负担得起.
afternoon: 下午，午后.
alone: 独自，单独，单纯，单独地.
apiece: 各自，各自地.
ashore: 岸上，上岸.
boards: 纸板.
boats: 船舶.
booming: 繁荣.
canoe: 独木舟.
dollar: 元.
dozen: 一打，打.
duke: 公爵，公.
dumb: 哑.
fellow: 同伴，伙伴.
fetch: 拿，取，带来.
gentle: 轻松，文雅的，斯文，柔和.
gentlemen: 绅士.
glance: 一瞥，匆匆一看.
heads: 头.
hid: 躲藏.
imitate: 模仿.
kin: 亲属，骨肉.
log: 圆形木材，圆木，木头.
mad: 狂，发怒，发狂，生气，疯狂的.
mile: 英里.
pretty: 漂亮，美丽的，秀丽.
regardless: 不管.
soft: 柔软，柔和，柔软的.
steamboat: 汽船，轮船.
yawl: 双桅帆船，舰载杂用船，船载小艇.

Sudden as **winking** the **ornery** old cretur went an to **smash**, and **fell** up against the man, and put his **chin** on his **shoulder**, and cried down his back, and says:

"Alas, **alas**, our **poor** brother--gone, and we never got to see him; oh, it's too, too hard!"

Then he turns around, blubbering, and makes a **lot** of **idiotic** signs to the **duke** on his **hands**, and blamed if he didn't **drop** a carpet-bag and **bust** out a-crying. If they warn't the beatenest lot, them two frauds, that ever I **struck**.

Well, the men gathered around and sympathized with them, and said all **sorts** of kind things to them, and carried their carpet-bags up the **hill** for them, and let them **lean** on them and **cry**, and told the king all about his brother's last moments, and the king he told it all over again on his hands to the duke, and both of them took on about that **dead tanner** like they'd **lost** the **twelve disciples**. Well, if ever I struck anything like it, I'm a nigger. It was enough to make a body **ashamed** of the **human race**.

Chinese Simplified

alas：呜呼．
ashamed：惭愧，羞愧，惭愧的．
bust：半身像，逮捕，破产．
chin：下巴，颏．
cry：喊，叫，哭，哭泣．
dead：死．
disciples：门徒．
drop：落，水滴，衰退，掉落，降，点子．
duke：公爵，公．
fell：采伐，伐，跌落．
hands：手．
hill：小丘，山坡，山岗，陵．
human：人性，人类，人的．
idiotic：白痴般，愚蠢的．
king：国王，王．
lean：倾斜．
lost：遗失．
lot：地皮，批量，地段．
ornery：低劣的．
poor：差，贫穷，穷，差劲，贫瘠，贫穷的，贫苦，困苦．
race：种族，竞赛，人种．
shoulder：肩，肩膀，担负．
smash：捣碎，粉碎，破碎．
sorts：种类．
struck：敲打．
tanner：唐纳．
twelve：十二．
winking：眨眼．

CHAPTER XXV

ALL FULL OF TEARS AND FLAPDOODLE

The news was all over town in two minutes, and you could see the people **tearing** down on the run from every which way, some of them putting on their **coats** as they come. Pretty soon we was in the middle of a **crowd**, and the **noise** of the **tramping** was like a **soldier** march. The **windows** and dooryards was full; and every minute **somebody** would say, over a **fence**:

"Is it *them*?"

And somebody trotting along with the **gang** would answer back and say:

"You **bet** it is."

When we got to the house the street in **front** of it was **packed**, and the three girls was **standing** in the door. Mary Jane *was* red-headed, but that don't make no difference, she was most **awful beautiful**, and her face and her eyes was all **lit** up like **glory**, she was so **glad** her uncles was come. The king he **spread** his **arms**, and Marsy Jane she **jumped** for them, and the hare-lip jumped for the **duke**, and there they *had* it! Everybody most, leastways women, cried for **joy** to see them meet again at last and have such good times.

Then the king he **hunched** the duke private--I see him do it--and then he looked around and see the **coffin**, over in the **corner** on two **chairs**; so then him

Chinese Simplified

arms：武器，武装，军备，兵戈，兵器，军火，兵戎.
awful：可怕，可怕的.
beautiful：漂亮，美，美丽，菲菲，锦绣，美丽的，秀丽，美观.
bet：打赌，赌.
chairs：椅子.
coats：上衣.
coffin：棺材，寿材.
corner：角落，隅，棱，角，转角.
crowd：人群.
duke：公爵，公.
fence：篱笆，栅栏，栏位，栏.
front：前面，正面，跟前，战线，阵地.
gang：一群，帮.
glad：高兴，高兴的.
glory：荣耀，光荣，辉煌.
hunched：肉峰.
joy：乐趣，快乐，高兴，喜悦.
jumped：跳跃.
lit：点燃.
noise：噪音，噪声，响声，吵闹声，吵声.
packed：挤得满满的.
pin：别针，个人鉴别码.
soldier：士兵，战士，军人，兵家.
somebody：某人，有人.
spread：扩散，流传，传播，散播，敷，撒.
standing：站立，地位.
tearing：撕裂的.
windows：视窗.

and the **duke**, with a hand across each other's shoulder, and t'other hand to their eyes, walked slow and **solemn** over there, everybody **dropping** back to give them room, and all the talk and noise **stopping**, people saying "Sh!" and all the men taking their hats off and drooping their heads, so you could a heard a pin fall. And when they got there they **bent** over and looked in the **coffin**, and took one sight, and then they **bust** out a-crying so you could a heard them to Orleans, most; and then they put their arms around each other's necks, and **hung** their chins over each other's shoulders; and then for three minutes, or maybe four, I never see two men **leak** the way they done. And, mind you, everybody was doing the same; and the place was that **damp** I never see anything like it. Then one of them got on one side of the coffin, and t'other on t'other side, and they kneeled down and rested their **foreheads** on the coffin, and let on to **pray** all to themselves. Well, when it come to that it worked the crowd like you never see anything like it, and everybody broke down and went to sobbing right out loud--the poor girls, too; and every woman, nearly, went up to the girls, without saying a word, and kissed them, solemn, on the forehead, and then put their hand on their head, and looked up towards the sky, with the tears running down, and then busted out and went off sobbing and swabbing, and give the next woman a show. I never see anything so **disgusting**.

Well, by and by the king he gets up and comes forward a little, and works himself up and **slobbers** out a speech, all full of tears and flapdoodle about its being a **sore** trial for him and his poor **brother** to lose the **diseased**, and to miss seeing diseased alive after the long journey of four thousand **mile**, but it's a trial that's sweetened and sanctified to us by this dear **sympathy** and these **holy** tears, and so he thanks them out of his heart and out of his brother's heart, because out of their **mouths** they can't, words being too **weak** and cold, and all that kind of rot and **slush**, **till** it was just sickening; and then he blubbers out a **pious** goody-goody Amen, and turns himself **loose** and goes to **crying** fit to bust.

And the minute the words were out of his mouth somebody over in the crowd **struck** up the doxolojer, and everybody joined in with all their might, and it just warmed you up and made you feel as good as church letting out. **Music** is

Chinese Simplified

bent: 曲，弯，弯曲，弯折.
bust: 半身像，逮捕，破产.
coffin: 棺材，寿材.
crying: 叫喊的，嚎哭的，显著的.
damp: 潮湿，潮湿的.
diseased: 有病.
disgusting: 讨厌，令人恶心的，令人作呕的.
dropping: 点滴，落下.
duke: 公爵，公.
forehead: 前额，额，额头.
holy: 神圣，神圣的，神圣的东西.
hung: 挂.
leak: 漏洞，会漏，泄露，漏.
loose: 松开，松弛的.
mile: 英里.
mouths: 口.
music: 音乐，民乐，曲子.
pin: 别针，个人鉴别码.
pious: 虔诚的.
pray: 祈祷.
rot: 腐坏，腐烂，腐化.
slobbers: 口水.
slush: 雪水，烂泥.
solemn: 严肃，俨然，岸然，隆重，庄严的，庄重.
sore: 疼痛，疮，疼痛的.
stopping: 停止.
struck: 敲打.
sympathy: 同情.
till: 直到.
weak: 衰弱，瘫软，脆弱，薄弱，虚弱，虚弱的，软弱，微弱.

a good thing; and after all that soul-butter and **hogwash** I never see it freshen up things so, and sound so **honest** and bully.

Then the king **begins** to work his **jaw** again, and says how him and his nieces would be **glad** if a few of the main **principal** friends of the family would take **supper** here **with** them this evening, and help set up with the **ashes** of the **diseased**; and says if his poor brother laying **yonder** could speak he knows who he would name, for they was names that was very dear to him, and mentioned often in his **letters**; and so he will name the same, to wit, as follows, vizz.:--Rev. Mr. Hobson, and Deacon Lot Hovey, and Mr. Ben Rucker, and Abner Shackleford, and Levi Bell, and Dr. **Robinson**, and their wives, and the **widow** Bartley.

Rev. Hobson and Dr. Robinson was down to the end of the town a-hunting together--that is, I mean the doctor was **shipping** a **sick** man to t'other world, and the **preacher** was pinting him right. Lawyer Bell was away up to Louisville on business. But the rest was on hand, and so they all come and **shook** hands with the king and thanked him and **talked** to him; and then they shook hands with the **duke** and didn't say nothing, but just kept a-smiling and bobbing their **heads** like a passel of sapheads whilst he made all **sorts** of signs with his hands and said "Goo-goo--goo-goo-goo" all the time, like a baby that can't talk.

So the king he blattered along, and managed to **inquire** about pretty much everybody and dog in town, by his name, and mentioned all sorts of little things that happened one time or another in the town, or to George's family, or to Peter. And he always let on that Peter wrote him the things; but that was a **lie**: he got every **blessed** one of them out of that young flathead that we canoed up to the **steamboat**.

Then Mary Jane she fetched the letter her father left behind, and the king he read it out **loud** and cried over it. It give the dwelling-house and three thousand dollars, **gold**, to the girls; and it give the tanyard (which was doing a good business), along with some other houses and land (worth about seven thousand), and three thousand dollars in gold to Harvey and William, and told where the six thousand cash was **hid** down **cellar**. So these two frauds said they'd go and

Chinese Simplified

ashes: 灰烬.
begins: 开始.
blessed: 幸福, 幸福的.
cellar: 地下室, 地窖.
diseased: 有病.
duke: 公爵, 公.
glad: 高兴, 高兴的.
gold: 金, 黄金.
heads: 头.
hid: 躲藏.
hogwash: 猪食, 废话, 空洞的作品.
honest: 诚实, 正直, 清廉, 刚正, 坦白, 正值, 诚实的, 体面, 廉洁, 深切.
inquire: 查调, 质问, 询问.
jaw: 颚, 颌.
letters: 信件, 函件.
lie: 谎言, 谎话, 躺, 撒谎, 说谎.
loud: 高声, 大声, 大声的.
preacher: 传道者.
principal: 本金, 主要, 校长, 首长.
robinson: 鲁滨逊.
shipping: 航运, 装货, 装运, 海运, 船舶.
shook: 摇动.
sick: 生病.
sorts: 种类.
steamboat: 汽船, 轮船.
supper: 晚饭, 晚餐.
talked: 谈话.
widow: 寡妇.
wit: 风趣, 机智, 智慧.
yonder: 那边.

fetch it up, and have everything **square** and above-board; and told me to come with a **candle**. We **shut** the **cellar** door behind us, and when they found the **bag** they spilt it out on the floor, and it was a lovely sight, all them yaller-boys. My, the way the king's eyes did **shine**! He slaps the **duke** on the **shoulder** and says:

"Oh, *this* ain't **bully** nor noth'n! Oh, no, I **reckon** not! Why, Biljy, it **beats** the Nonesuch, *don't* it?"

The duke allowed it did. They pawed the yaller-boys, and sifted them through their fingers and let them **jingle** down on the floor; and the king says:

"It ain't no use talkin'; bein' **brothers** to a rich dead man and representatives of furrin **heirs** that's got left is the line for you and me, Bilge. Thish yer comes of trust'n to Providence. It's the best way, in the long run. I've tried 'em all, and ther' ain't no better way."

Most everybody would a been **satisfied** with the **pile**, and took it on trust; but no, they must **count** it. So they counts it, and it comes out four hundred and **fifteen** dollars short. Says the king:

"Dern him, I **wonder** what he done with that four hundred and fifteen dollars?"

They **worried** over that **awhile**, and ransacked all around for it. Then the duke says:

"Well, he was a **pretty sick** man, and likely he made a mistake--I reckon that's the way of it. The best way's to let it go, and keep still about it. We can **spare** it."

"Oh, shucks, yes, we can *spare* it. I don't k'yer noth'n 'bout that--it's the *count* I'm thinkin' about. We want to be **awful** square and open and above-board here, you know. We want to **lug** this h-yer money up **stairs** and count it before everybody--then ther' ain't noth'n **suspicious**. But when the dead man says ther's six thous'n dollars, you know, we don't want to--"

"Hold on," says the duke. "Le's make up the deffisit," and he **begun** to **haul** out yaller-boys out of his **pocket**.

Chinese Simplified

awful: 可怕，可怕的.
awhile: 一会儿.
bag: 袋子，袋，手提包，提包，囊.
beats: 节奏.
begun: 开始.
brothers: 兄弟，哥儿.
bully: 欺负.
candle: 蜡烛.
cellar: 地下室，地窖.
count: 计数，伯爵，计算，有价値，认为.
duke: 公爵，公.
fetch: 拿，取，带来.
fifteen: 十五.
haul: 拖拉，曳.
heirs: 继承人.
jingle: 叮铃.
lug: 拖拉.
pile: 一堆，桩，堆.
pocket: 口袋，衣袋，兜儿，窟窿.
pretty: 漂亮，美丽的，秀丽.
reckon: 估计，计算.
satisfied: 满意，乐意，心满意足的.
shine: 发光，发亮，照射，照耀，光.
shoulder: 肩，肩膀，担负.
shut: 关闭.
sick: 生病.
spare: 备用，饶恕.
square: 正方形，平方，四方形.
stairs: 楼梯.
suspicious: 可疑，可疑的.
wonder: 奇迹，惊奇.
worried: 担心，不安，忧虑.

"It's a most amaz'n' good idea, **duke**--you *have* got a rattlin' **clever** head on you," says the king. "Blest if the old Nonesuch ain't a heppin' us out agin," and *he* begun to **haul** out yaller-jackets and **stack** them up.

It most busted them, but they made up the six thousand clean and clear.

"Say," says the duke, "I got another idea. Le's go up stairs and count this money, and then take and *give it to the girls*."

"Good land, duke, lemme **hug** you! It's the most **dazzling** idea 'at ever a man **struck**. You have cert'nly got the most astonishin' head I ever see. Oh, this is the **boss dodge**, ther' ain't no mistake 'bout it. Let 'em **fetch** along their **suspicions** now if they want to--this 'll lay 'em out."

When we got up-stairs everybody gethered around the table, and the king he counted it and stacked it up, three hundred dollars in a pile--twenty **elegant** little **piles**. Everybody looked **hungry** at it, and licked their chops. Then they raked it into the bag again, and I see the king begin to **swell** himself up for another speech. He says:

"Friends all, my poor brother that lays **yonder** has done **generous** by them that's left behind in the **vale** of sorrers. He has done generous by these yer poor little **lambs** that he loved and sheltered, and that's left fatherless and motherless. Yes, and we that knowed him knows that he would a done *more* generous by 'em if he hadn't ben afeard o' woundin' his dear William and me. Now, *wouldn't* he? Ther' ain't no question 'bout it in *my* mind. Well, then, what kind o' brothers would it be that 'd stand in his way at sech a time? And what kind o' uncles would it be that 'd rob--yes, *Rob*--sech poor sweet lambs as these 'at he loved so at sech a time? If I know William--and I *think* I do--he--well, I'll **jest** ask him." He turns around and begins to make a lot of signs to the duke with his hands, and the duke he looks at him **stupid** and leather-headed a while; then all of a sudden he seems to catch his meaning, and **jumps** for the king, goo-gooing with all his might for **joy**, and **hugs** him about fifteen times before he **lets** up. Then the king says, "I knowed it; I **reckon** *that* 'll **convince** anybody the way *he* **feels** about it. Here, Mary Jane, Susan, Joanner, take the money--take it *all*. It's the **gift** of him that lays yonder, cold but joyful."

Chinese Simplified

boss：老板，上司，头子，浮雕．
clever：高明，聪明的，伶俐，玲珑，机灵，巧妙，聪明．
convince：说服．
dazzling：耀眼的，有声有色．
dodge：躲闪，躲避．
duke：公爵，公．
elegant：高雅，文雅，优美，讲究的，优雅的．
feels：感觉．
fetch：拿，取，带来．
generous：大方，雍容大度，慷慨，慷慨的．
gift：礼物，天赋，天才，禀赋，礼品．
haul：拖拉，曳．
hug：紧抱，拥抱．
hugs：拥抱．
hungry：饥饿，饿，饥饿的．
jest：玩笑，笑话，戏弄，戏谑．
joy：乐趣，快乐，高兴，喜悦．
jumps：跳跃．
lambs：小羊．
lets：让我们，让．
piles：痔，痔疮，堆．
reckon：估计，计算．
stack：堆，栈，垛，堆叠，堆积，堆置．
struck：敲打．
stupid：愚笨，笨拙，愚笨的．
suspicions：怀疑．
swell：涨满，膨胀．
vale：再会．
yonder：那边．

Mary Jane she went for him, Susan and the hare-lip went for the **duke**, and then such another **hugging** and kissing I never see yet. And everybody **crowded** up with the tears in their eyes, and most shook the hands off of them frauds, saying all the time:

"You *dear* good souls!--how *lovely*!--how *could* you!"

Well, then, pretty soon all hands got to talking about the **diseased** again, and how good he was, and what a **loss** he was, and all that; and before long a big iron-jawed man worked himself in there from outside, and stood a-listening and looking, and not saying anything; and nobody saying anything to him either, because the king was talking and they was all **busy listening**. The king was saying--in the middle of something he'd started in on--

"--they bein' partickler friends o' the diseased. That's why they're **invited** here this evenin'; but **tomorrow** we want *all* to come--everybody; for he respected everybody, he liked everybody, and so it's fitten that his **funeral** orgies sh'd be public."

And so he went a-mooning on and on, **liking** to hear himself talk, and every little while he fetched in his funeral orgies again, **till** the duke he couldn't stand it no more; so he **writes** on a little **scrap** of paper, "***obsequies***, you old fool," and folds it up, and goes to goo-gooing and **reaching** it over people's heads to him. The king he **reads** it and **puts** it in his **pocket**, and says:

"Poor William, **afflicted** as he is, his *heart's* aluz right. Asks me to invite everybody to come to the funeral--wants me to make 'em all **welcome**. But he needn't a worried--it was **jest** what I was at."

Then he **weaves** along again, perfectly ca'm, and goes to **dropping** in his funeral orgies again every now and then, just like he done before. And when he done it the third time he says:

"I say orgies, not because it's the **common term**, because it ain't-- obsequies bein' the common term--but because orgies is the right term. Obsequies ain't used in England no more now--it's gone out. We say orgies now in England. Orgies is better, because it means the thing you're after more **exact**. It's a word that's made

Chinese Simplified

afflicted: 使苦恼.
busy: 忙、繁忙、忙碌、占线、忙碌的.
common: 通用、共同、公共、寻常、常规、平常、普通、一般、普通的、通俗.
crowded: 拥挤的.
diseased: 有病.
dropping: 点滴、落下.
duke: 公爵、公.
exact: 确切、精密、准确、正确的.
funeral: 葬礼.
hugging: 拥抱.
invite: 邀请.
invited: 约了.
jest: 玩笑、笑话、戏弄、戏谑.
liking: 爱好.
listening: 听.
loss: 亏损、损失.
obsequies: 丧礼.
pocket: 口袋、衣袋、兜儿、窟窿.
puts: 放.
reaching: 到达.
reads: 阅读.
scrap: 零头、剪报、报废、碎屑、废品.
term: 术语、学期、期限、项.
till: 直到.
tomorrow: 明天、未来、明日.
weaves: 编织.
welcome: 欢迎、受欢迎、欢迎光临、受欢迎的、款待.
writes: 写.

up out'n the Greek *orgo*, outside, open, **abroad**; and the Hebrew *jeesum*, to **plant**, cover up; **hence** in*ter*. So, you see, funeral orgies is an open er public funeral."

He was the *worst* I ever struck. Well, the iron-jawed man he laughed right in his face. Everybody was shocked. Everybody says, "Why, *doctor*!" and Abner Shackleford says:

"Why, Robinson, hain't you heard the news? This is Harvey Wilks."

The king he smiled **eager**, and shoved out his flapper, and says:

"Is it my poor brother's dear good friend and **physician**? I--"

"Keep your hands off of me!" says the doctor. "*You* talk like an Englishman, *don't* you? It's the worst **imitation** I ever heard. *you* Peter Wilks's brother! You're a **fraud**, that's what you are!"

Well, how they all took on! They **crowded** around the doctor and tried to quiet him down, and tried to **explain** to him and tell him how Harvey 'd showed in forty ways that he *was* Harvey, and knowed everybody by name, and the names of the very dogs, and **begged** and *begged* him not to hurt Harvey's **feelings** and the poor girl's feelings, and all that. But it **warn't** no use; he stormed right along, and said any man that pretended to be an Englishman and couldn't **imitate** the lingo no better than what he did was a fraud and a **liar**. The poor girls was hanging to the king and **crying**; and all of a sudden the doctor **ups** and turns on *them*. He says:

"I was your father's friend, and I'm your friend; and I warn you as a friend, and an honest one that wants to **protect** you and keep you out of harm and trouble, to turn your **backs** on that **scoundrel** and have nothing to do with him, the **ignorant tramp**, with his **idiotic** Greek and Hebrew, as he calls it. He is the thinnest kind of an impostor--has come here with a lot of empty names and facts which he **picked** up somewheres, and you take them for *proofs*, and are helped to **fool yourselves** by these **foolish** friends here, who ought to know better. Mary Jane Wilks, you know me for your friend, and for your unselfish friend, too. Now listen to me; turn this **pitiful rascal** out--I *beg* you to do it. Will you?"

Mary Jane straightened herself up, and my, but she was **handsome**! She says:

Chinese Simplified

abroad: 海外，国外，在国外，到国外，到处.
backs: 支持.
beg: 恳求，乞求，要求.
begged: 乞求.
crowded: 拥挤的.
crying: 叫喊的，嚎哭的，显著的.
eager: 切望，踊跃，急切，渴望的.
explain: 辩解，解释，申述，交代，澄清.
feelings: 感情，面子.
fool: 呆子，笨蛋，傻子，笨人，愚人.
foolish: 愚蠢的.
fraud: 舞弊，骗局，作弊，欺骗.
handsome: 英俊，慷慨的，英俊的.
hence: 因此，於是.
idiotic: 白痴般，愚蠢的.
ignorant: 愚昧，无知的，茫然.
imitate: 模仿.
imitation: 模拟，冒牌，模仿.
liar: 说谎者，撒谎者.
physician: 医生.
picked: 精选的.
pitiful: 可怜，可怜的.
plant: 植物，安插，事业，种植，插.
protect: 防守，保佑，保护，维护.
rascal: 小淘气，流氓.
scoundrel: 无籁，坏蛋，无赖.
tramp: 沉重脚步.
ups: 电供衡常器.
warn: 告诫，警告.
yourselves: 你们自己.

"*Here* is my answer." She hove up the **bag** of money and put it in the **king's hands**, and says, "Take this six **thousand** dollars, and **invest** for me and my **sisters** any way you want to, and don't give us no **receipt** for it."

Then she put her **arm** around the king on one side, and Susan and the **hare-lip** done the same on the other. Everybody clapped their hands and stomped on the **floor** like a **perfect storm**, whilst the king **held** up his head and smiled **proud**. The **doctor** says:

"All right; I **wash** *my* hands of the **matter**. But I **warn** you all that a time 's **coming** when you're going to feel **sick whenever** you think of this day." And away he went.

"All right, doctor," says the king, kinder **mocking** him; "we'll try and get 'em to **send** for you;" which made them all **laugh**, and they said it was a **prime** good **hit**.

Chinese Simplified

arm: 手臂，膀子，臂膀，臂，膀臂，胳膊，肩膀，武器.
bag: 袋子，袋，手提包，提包，囊.
coming: 未来，到来.
doctor: 医生，大夫，医师，博士.
floor: 地板，地面.
hands: 手.
hare: 野兔，兔子.
held: 握住.
hit: 袭击，命中，击中，打.
invest: 投资，投产.
king: 国王，王.
laugh: 笑.
lip: 唇，嘴唇，口头上的.
matter: 事情，事，物质，事项.
mocking: 嘲讽，嘲弄.
perfect: 完美，完善，完美的，无话可说，完备.
prime: 首要的.
proud: 傲岸，骄矜，骄傲的，自豪的.
receipt: 收据，收条.
send: 派遣，派出，送，发送，寄，投，派.
sick: 生病.
sisters: 姊妹，姐妹.
storm: 暴风雨，暴风，风暴.
thousand: 千.
warn: 告诫，警告.
wash: 洗涤，洗刷，洗.
whenever: 无论何时，每当.

CHAPTER XXVI

I STEAL THE KING'S PLUNDER

Well, when they was all **gone** the **king** he **asks** Mary Jane how they was off for **spare rooms**, and she said she had one spare room, which would do for Uncle William, and she'd give her own room to Uncle Harvey, which was a little **bigger**, and she would **turn** into the room with her **sisters** and **sleep** on a cot; and up **garret** was a little cubby, with a **pallet** in it. The king said the cubby would do for his valley--meaning me.

So Mary Jane took us up, and she **showed** them their rooms, which was **plain** but **nice**. She said she'd have her frocks and a **lot** of other traps took out of her room if they was in Uncle Harvey's way, but he said they warn't. The frocks was **hung along** the **wall**, and before them was a **curtain** made out of **calico** that hung down to the **floor**. There was an old **hair trunk** in one **corner**, and a guitar-box in another, and all **sorts** of little knickknacks and jimcracks around, like girls brisken up a room with. The king said it was all the more **homely** and more pleasanter for these fixings, and so don't **disturb** them. The duke's room was **pretty** small, but **plenty** good enough, and so was my cubby.

That night they had a big **supper**, and all them men and women was there, and I **stood** behind the king and the duke's **chairs** and waited on them, and the niggers waited on the **rest**. Mary Jane she set at the head of the table, with Susan

Chinese Simplified

along: 沿着，沿，一同.
asks: 问.
bigger: 更大，较大.
calico: 白布，白棉布.
chairs: 椅子.
corner: 角落，隅，棱，角，转角.
curtain: 布帘.
disturb: 打扰，惊动，扰乱，干扰.
floor: 地板，地面.
garret: 阁楼，顶楼.
gone: 去.
hair: 头发.
homely: 家常的.
hung: 挂.
king: 国王，王.
lot: 地皮，批量，地段.
nice: 和蔼，可亲，好，尼斯.
pallet: 草荐，棘爪.
plain: 平原.
plenty: 丰富，许多.
pretty: 漂亮，美丽的，秀丽.
rest: 休息，安息，其余.
rooms: 房间.
showed: 展示.
sisters: 姊妹，姐妹.
sleep: 梦寐，睡觉，睡眠，睡.
sorts: 种类.
spare: 备用，饶恕.
stood: 站了.
supper: 晚饭，晚餐.
trunk: 躯干，主干，树干.
turn: 转动，转弯.
wall: 墙壁，墙.

alongside of her, and said how bad the **biscuits** was, and how mean the preserves was, and how **ornery** and **tough** the **fried chickens** was--and all that kind of **rot**, the way women always do for to **force** out **compliments**; and the people all knowed **everything** was **tiptop**, and said so--said "How *do* you get biscuits to **brown** so **nice**?" and "Where, for the land's **sake**, *did* you get these amaz'n **pickles**? and all that kind of **humbug** talky-talk, just the way people always does at a **supper**, you know.

And when it was all done me and the hare-lip had supper in the kitchen off of the **leavings**, whilst the others was **helping** the niggers **clean** up the things. The hare-lip she got to pumping me about England, and blest if I didn't think the ice was getting **mighty** thin sometimes. She says:

"Did you ever see the king?"

"Who? William Fourth? Well, I **bet** I have--he goes to our church." I knowed he was dead years ago, but I never let on. So when I says he goes to our church, she says:

"What--regular?"

"Yes--regular. His pew's right over **opposite** ourn--on t'other side the pulpit."

"I thought he lived in London?"

"Well, he does. Where *would* he live?"

"But I thought *you* lived in Sheffield?"

I see I was up a **stump**. I had to let on to get choked with a chicken **bone**, so as to get time to think how to get down again. Then I says:

"I mean he goes to our church **regular** when he's in Sheffield. That's only in the summer time, when he comes there to take the **sea** baths."

"Why, how you talk--Sheffield ain't on the sea."

"Well, who said it was?"

"Why, you did."

"I *didn't* nuther."

Chinese Simplified

alongside：并肩，在旁边.
bet：打赌，赌.
biscuits：饼干.
bone：骨头，骨，骨法.
brown：褐色，棕色，布朗.
chicken：鸡，小鸡.
chickens：小鸡.
clean：清洁，擦拭，乾净，刷，清洗，干净.
compliments：敬意.
force：力，部队，力量，暴力，强迫，迫使，逼迫，动力.
fried：炸.
helping：帮助人的，辅助的，帮助.
humbug：骗子.
ice：冰.
leavings：剩余物.
mighty：伟大，强势，强大的.
opposite：相反，相对，对面，对立面，相反的.
ornery：低劣的.
pickles：泡菜.
regular：固定，正常，通常，端正，正规的，常例的，定期的，整齐的，有秩序的，正规，经常.
rot：腐坏，腐烂，腐化.
sake：缘故.
sea：海.
stump：树桩，残肢.
supper：晚饭，晚餐.
thin：薄，疏，细，淡.
tiptop：拔尖儿，极好的，绝佳.
tough：强硬，坚韧的.

"You did!"

"I didn't."

"You did."

"I never said nothing of the kind."

"Well, what *did* you say, then?"

"Said he come to take the **sea** ***baths***--that's what I said."

"Well, then, how's he going to take the sea baths if it ain't on the sea?"

"Looky here," I says; "did you ever see any Congress-water?"

"Yes."

"Well, did you have to go to Congress to get it?"

"Why, no."

"Well, **neither** does William Fourth have to go to the sea to get a sea bath."

"How does he get it, then?"

"Gets it the way people down here gets Congress-water--in **barrels**. There in the **palace** at Sheffield they've got **furnaces**, and he wants his water **hot**. They can't **bile** that **amount** of water away off there at the sea. They haven't got no conveniences for it."

"Oh, I see, now. You might a said that in the first place and saved time."

When she said that I see I was out of the **woods** again, and so I was **comfortable** and **glad**. Next, she says:

"Do you go to church, too?"

"Yes--regular."

"Where do you set?"

"Why, in our pew."

"***Whose*** pew?"

"Why, *ourn*--your Uncle Harvey's."

"His'n? What does *he* want with a pew?"

Chinese Simplified

amount：数量，量，数字，数目，数额．
barrels：桶．
baths：洗澡．
bile：胆汁．
comfortable：舒服，舒服的．
furnaces：炉子．
glad：高兴，高兴的．
hot：热．
neither：也不，二者，两者都不是．
palace：宫殿，宫，皇宫．
sea：海．
whose：谁的．
woods：树林，森林．

"Wants it to set in. What did you ***reckon*** he wanted with it?"

"Why, I thought he'd be in the pulpit."

Rot him, I **forgot** he was a **preacher**. I see I was up a **stump** again, so I played another **chicken bone** and got another think. Then I says:

"Blame it, do you **suppose** there ain't but one preacher to a church?"

"Why, what do they want with more?"

"What!--to preach before a **king**? I never did see such a **girl** as you. They don't have no less than seventeen."

"**Seventeen**! My **land**! Why, I wouldn't set out such a **string** as that, not if I *never* got to **glory**. It must take 'em a week."

"Shucks, they don't *all* of 'em preach the same day--only *one* of 'em."

"Well, then, what does the **rest** of 'em do?"

"Oh, nothing much. Loll around, **pass** the plate--and one thing or another. But **mainly** they don't do nothing."

"Well, then, what are they *for*?"

"Why, they're for ***style***. Don't you know nothing?"

"Well, I don't *want* to know no such **foolishness** as that. How is **servants treated** in England? Do they treat 'em better 'n we treat our niggers?"

"*No!* A servant ain't **nobody** there. They treat them **worse** than dogs."

"Don't they give 'em **holidays**, the way we do, Christmas and New Year's week, and Fourth of July?"

"Oh, just **listen**! A body could tell *you* hain't ever been to England by that. Why, Hare-l--why, Joanna, they never see a holiday from year's end to year's end; never go to the **circus, nor theater**, nor nigger **shows**, nor nowheres."

"Nor church?"

"Nor church."

"But *you* always went to church."

Chinese Simplified

bone：骨头，骨，骨法．
chicken：鸡，小鸡．
circus：马戏团，杂技团，马戏．
foolishness：愚蠢．
forgot：忘记．
girl：女孩，姑娘，女孩子．
glory：荣耀，光荣，辉煌．
holiday：假日，节日，假期．
holidays：每逢假日．
king：国王，王．
land：土地，着陆，陆地．
listen：听，倾听．
mainly：主要地．
nobody：没有人，没人．
nor：也不．
pass：隘口，及格，传递，度过，要隘．
preach：传教，讲道，鼓吹．
preacher：传道者．
reckon：估计，计算．
rest：休息，安息，其余．
rot：腐坏，腐烂，腐化．
servant：仆人，佣人，用人．
seventeen：十七．
shows：显示．
string：绳子，串，线，细线，弦．
stump：树桩，残肢．
style：方式，风格，式样，样式，试样，笔调，模样，作风．
suppose：假使，猜想，假定．
theater：剧场，戏剧，戏院，剧院．
treat：对待．
worse：更坏，更糟．

Well, I was gone up again. I **forgot** I was the old man's **servant**. But next **minute** I whirled in on a kind of an **explanation** how a **valley** was different from a common servant and *had* to go to church whether he wanted to or not, and set with the family, on account of its being the law. But I didn't do it **pretty** good, and when I got done I see she warn't **satisfied**. She says:

"**Honest** injun, now, hain't you been telling me a lot of **lies**?"

"Honest injun," says I.

"**None** of it at all?"

"None of it at all. Not a lie in it," says I.

"**Lay** your hand on this book and say it."

I see it warn't nothing but a **dictionary**, so I **laid** my hand on it and said it. So then she looked a little better satisfied, and says:

"Well, then, I'll believe some of it; but I hope to **gracious** if I'll believe the rest."

"What is it you won't believe, Joe?" says Mary Jane, stepping in with Susan behind her. "It ain't right **nor** kind for you to talk so to him, and him a **stranger** and so far from his people. How would you like to be **treated** so?"

"That's always your way, Maim--always **sailing** in to help **somebody** before they're **hurt**. I hain't done nothing to him. He's told some **stretchers**, I **reckon**, and I said I wouldn't **swallow** it all; and that's every **bit** and **grain** I *did* say. I reckon he can **stand** a little thing like that, can't he?"

"I don't care whether 'twas little or whether 'twas big; he's here in our house and a stranger, and it wasn't good of you to say it. If you was in his place it would make you feel **ashamed**; and so you oughtn't to say a thing to another person that will make *them* feel ashamed."

"Why, Maim, he said--"

"It don't make no **difference** what he *said*--that ain't the thing. The thing is for you to treat him *kind*, and not be saying things to make him remember he ain't in his own country and amongst his own folks."

Chinese Simplified

ashamed: 惭愧，羞愧，惭愧的.
bit: 位元，咬.
dictionary: 字典，词典.
difference: 差异，差，差别，区别，分歧，分别，误差.
explanation: 说明，解释，解答.
forgot: 忘记.
gracious: 亲切，亲切的，有礼貌的.
grain: 谷类.
honest: 诚实，正直，清廉，刚正，坦白，正値，诚实的，体面，廉洁，深切.
hurt: 伤害，使受伤.
laid: 放.
lay: 产卵，安放，放，凡俗.
lie: 谎言，谎话，躺，撒谎，说谎.
minute: 分钟，详细，分，微小的，渺小.
none: 无，没有.
nor: 也不.
pretty: 漂亮，美丽的，秀丽.
reckon: 估计，计算.
sailing: 航海术，航海，航行.
satisfied: 满意，乐意，心满意足的.
servant: 仆人，佣人，用人.
somebody: 某人，有人.
stand: 站住，主张，架子，站立，耐，站，架.
stranger: 陌生人，异乡人，生人.
stretchers: 担架.
swallow: 燕子，吞，咽.
treat: 对待.
valley: 山谷，峪，谷，流域，山沟.

I says to myself, *this* is a girl that I'm letting that old reptle **rob** her of her money!

Then Susan *she* waltzed in; and if you'll believe me, she did give Hare- **lip** **hark** from the **tomb**!

Says I to myself, and this is *another* one that I'm letting him rob her of her money!

Then Mary Jane she took another **inning**, and went in **sweet** and **lovely** again--which was her way; but when she got done there warn't hardly anything left o' poor Hare-lip. So she hollered.

"All right, then," says the other girls; "you just ask his pardon."

She done it, too; and she done it beautiful. She done it so beautiful it was good to hear; and I wished I could tell her a thousand **lies**, so she could do it again.

I says to myself, this is *another* one that I'm letting him rob her of her money. And when she got through they all **jest laid** theirselves out to make me feel at home and know I was amongst friends. I felt so **ornery** and low down and mean that I says to myself, my mind's made up; I'll **hive** that money for them or **bust**.

So then I **lit** out--for bed, I said, **meaning** some time or another. When I got by myself I went to thinking the thing over. I says to myself, shall I go to that doctor, private, and **blow** on these frauds? No--that won't do. He might tell who told him; then the king and the **duke** would make it warm for me. Shall I go, private, and tell Mary Jane? No--I dasn't do it. Her face would give them a **hint**, sure; they've got the money, and they'd **slide** right out and get away with it. If she was to **fetch** in help I'd get **mixed** up in the business before it was done with, I **judge**. No; there ain't no good way but one. I got to **steal** that money, **somehow**; and I got to steal it some way that they won't **suspicion** that I done it. They've got a good thing here, and they ain't a-going to leave **till** they've played this family and this town for all they're worth, so I'll find a chance time enough. I'll steal it and **hide** it; and by and by, when I'm away down the river, I'll write a letter and tell Mary Jane where it's hid. But I better hive it **tonight** if I can,

Chinese Simplified

blow: 吹，打击.
bust: 半身像，逮捕，破产.
duke: 公爵，公.
fetch: 拿，取，带来.
hark: 倾听.
hid: 躲藏.
hide: 躲藏，暗藏，掩饰，藏，隐瞒，隐藏.
hint: 暗示.
hive: 蜂房，蜂巢，蜂箱.
inning: 一局，轮到击球.
jest: 玩笑，笑话，戏弄，戏谑.
judge: 法官，裁判，判定，判断，审判员.
laid: 放.
lies: 谎言.
lip: 唇，嘴唇，口头上的.
lit: 点燃.
lovely: 可爱，可爱的.
meaning: 意义，意思，含义，含意，意味着.
mixed: 混合，混合的，错杂.
ornery: 低劣的.
rob: 抢劫.
slide: 滑落，滑行，滑.
somehow: 不知何故.
steal: 偷窃，盗窃，偷，窃取.
suspicion: 疑心，怀疑，嫌疑.
sweet: 甜，甜食，糖果.
till: 直到.
tomb: 陵墓，坟墓.
tonight: 今晚，今夜.

because the doctor maybe hasn't let up as much as he **lets** on he has; he might **scare** them out of here yet.

So, **thinks** I, I'll go and **search** them rooms. Upstairs the hall was dark, but I found the **duke's** room, and started to **paw** around it with my hands; but I recollected it wouldn't be much like the king to let **anybody** else take care of that money but his own **self**; so then I went to his room and **begun** to paw around there. But I see I couldn't do nothing without a **candle**, and I dasn't light one, of course. So I judged I'd got to do the other thing--lay for them and **eavesdrop**. About that time I hears their **footsteps** coming, and was going to **skip** under the bed; I reached for it, but it wasn't where I thought it would be; but I touched the **curtain** that **hid** Mary Jane's frocks, so I **jumped** in behind that and **snuggled** in amongst the **gowns**, and stood there **perfectly** still.

They come in and **shut** the door; and the first thing the duke done was to get down and look under the bed. Then I was **glad** I hadn't found the bed when I wanted it. And yet, you know, it's kind of natural to **hide** under the bed when you are up to anything private. They **sets** down then, and the king says:

"Well, what is it? And cut it middlin' short, because it's better for us to be down there a-whoopin' up the mournin' than up here givin' 'em a chance to talk us over."

"Well, this is it, Capet. I ain't easy; I ain't **comfortable**. That doctor lays on my mind. I wanted to know your plans. I've got a **notion**, and I think it's a sound one."

"What is it, duke?"

"That we better **glide** out of this before three in the morning, and **clip** it down the river with what we've got. Specially, seeing we got it so easy--*given* back to us, flung at our heads, as you may say, when of course we allowed to have to **steal** it back. I'm for knocking off and **lighting** out."

That made me feel pretty bad. About an hour or two ago it would a been a little different, but now it made me feel bad and **disappointed**, The king **rips** out and says:

Chinese Simplified

anybody: 任何人.
begun: 开始.
candle: 蜡烛.
clip: 夹子, 回形针.
comfortable: 舒服, 舒服的.
curtain: 布帘.
disappointed: 败兴, 失望的, 惆.
duke: 公爵, 公.
eavesdrop: 窃听.
footsteps: 脚步.
glad: 高兴, 高兴的.
glide: 滑翔, 滑行.
gowns: 长袍.
hid: 躲藏.
hide: 躲藏, 暗藏, 掩饰, 藏, 隐瞒, 隐藏.
jumped: 跳跃.
lets: 让我们, 让.
lighting: 灯光, 采光, 照明.
notion: 观念.
paw: 爪子.
perfectly: 完美, 完美地.
rips: 裂口.
scare: 恐慌.
search: 搜索, 搜查, 寻见, 寻找, 找.
self: 自己, 自, 自我, 我.
sets: 装置.
shut: 关闭.
skip: 跳跃, 跳过.
snuggled: 偎依.
steal: 偷窃, 盗窃, 偷, 窃取.
thinks: 想.

"What! And not **sell** out the rest o' the property? March off like a passel of fools and leave eight or nine thous'n' dollars' worth o' property layin' around **jest sufferin'** to be scooped in?--and all good, **salable stuff**, too."

The **duke** he grumbled; said the **bag** of **gold** was enough, and he didn't want to go no deeper--didn't want to **rob** a lot of orphans of *everything* they had.

"Why, how you talk!" says the king. "We sha'n't rob 'em of nothing at all but jest this money. The people that ***buys*** the property is the suff'rers; because as soon 's it's found out 'at we didn't own it--which won't be long after we've slid--the **sale** won't be **valid**, and it 'll all go back to the **estate**. These yer orphans 'll git their house back agin, and that's enough for *them*; they're young and **spry**, and k'n easy **earn** a livin'. *they* ain't a-goin to suffer. Why, jest think--there's thous'n's and thous'n's that ain't nigh so well off. Bless you, *they* ain't got noth'n' to **complain** of."

Well, the king he **talked** him **blind**; so at last he give in, and said all right, but said he believed it was blamed **foolishness** to stay, and that doctor hanging over them. But the king says:

"Cuss the doctor! What do we k'yer for *him*? Hain't we got all the fools in town on our side? And ain't that a big enough **majority** in any town?"

So they got ready to go down **stairs** again. The duke says:

"I don't think we put that money in a good place."

That cheered me up. I'd **begun** to think I warn't going to get a **hint** of no kind to help me. The king says:

"Why?"

"Because Mary Jane 'll be in **mourning** from this out; and first you know the nigger that does up the **rooms** will get an order to **box** these duds up and put 'em away; and do you **reckon** a nigger can run across money and not **borrow** some of it?"

"Your head's level agin, duke," says the king; and he comes a-fumbling under the **curtain** two or three foot from where I was. I **stuck tight** to the wall and kept

Chinese Simplified

bag：袋子，袋，手提包，提包，囊．
begun：开始．
blind：瞎，盲，百叶窗，盲目，盲的．
borrow：借．
box：箱，匣，包厢，拳击，拳打．
buys：购买．
complain：抱怨，投诉，埋怨．
curtain：布帘．
duke：公爵，公．
earn：赚得，挣得．
estate：地产，产业，园丘，房地产．
foolishness：愚蠢．
gold：金，黄金．
hint：暗示．
jest：玩笑，笑话，戏弄，戏谑．
majority：多数，大多数．
mourning：追悼，丧．
reckon：估计，计算．
rob：抢劫．
rooms：房间．
salable：有销路的．
sale：销路，销售．
sell：销售，游说，贩卖，出售．
spry：轻快．
stairs：楼梯．
stuck：黏贴．
stuff：材料，填塞，职员．
suffer：受苦，蒙受，遭受，受到，遭到．
talked：谈话．
tight：严格，严密，紧，紧的，严竣，狭隘．
valid：有效，有效的．

mighty still, though quivery; and I wondered what them fellows would say to me if they **catched** me; and I tried to think what I'd better do if they did catch me. But the king he got the **bag** before I could think more than about a half a thought, and he never suspicioned I was around. They took and shoved the bag through a **rip** in the **straw tick** that was under the feather-bed, and crammed it in a **foot** or two amongst the straw and said it was all right now, because a nigger only makes up the feather-bed, and don't turn over the straw tick only about **twice** a year, and so it warn't in no **danger** of getting **stole** now.

But I knowed better. I had it out of there before they was **half**-way down **stairs**. I groped along up to my cubby, and **hid** it there till I could get a **chance** to do better. I judged I better **hide** it outside of the house somewheres, because if they missed it they would give the house a good ransacking: I knowed that very well. Then I turned in, with my **clothes** all on; but I couldn't a gone to **sleep** if I'd a wanted to, I was in such a **sweat** to get through with the business. By and by I heard the king and the **duke** come up; so I **rolled** off my **pallet** and **laid** with my **chin** at the top of my **ladder**, and waited to see if anything was going to **happen**. But nothing did.

So I held on till all the **late sounds** had **quit** and the early ones hadn't **begun** yet; and then I **slipped** down the ladder.

Chinese Simplified

bag：袋子，袋，手提包，提包，囊.
begun：开始.
catch：捕捉，捕捞，捕拿，捉.
chance：机会.
chin：下巴，颏.
clothes：衣服，服装，西装，件，衣裳.
danger：危险.
duke：公爵，公.
foot：脚，足，步兵，英尺，呎.
half-way：半途.
happen：发生.
hid：躲藏.
hide：躲藏，暗藏，掩饰，藏，隐瞒，隐藏.
ladder：阶梯，梯子.
laid：放.
late：晚，迟，迟慢，迟了，迟迟.
mighty：伟大，强势，强大的.
pallet：草荐，棘爪.
quit：退出，退离.
rip：扯裂，撕破，裂口.
rolled：卷.
sleep：梦寐，睡觉，睡眠，睡.
slipped：滑落.
sounds：声音.
stairs：楼梯.
stole：偷了.
straw：稻草，吸管.
sweat：汗，出汗，流汗.
tick：壁虱，滴答声，勾.
till：直到.
twice：两次.

CHAPTER XXVII

DEAD PETER HAS HIS GOLD

I crept to their **doors** and **listened**; they was **snoring**. So I tiptoed along, and got down **stairs** all right. There warn't a sound anywheres. I peeped through a **crack** of the dining-room door, and see the men that was watching the **corpse** all sound **asleep** on their **chairs**. The door was open into the **parlor**, where the corpse was laying, and there was a **candle** in both **rooms**. I passed along, and the parlor door was open; but I see there warn't **nobody** in there but the remainders of Peter; so I shoved on by; but the front door was locked, and the **key** wasn't there. Just then I heard **somebody** coming down the stairs, back behind me. I run in the parlor and took a **swift** look around, and the only place I see to **hide** the **bag** was in the **coffin**. The **lid** was shoved along about a **foot**, showing the dead man's face down in there, with a **wet cloth** over it, and his **shroud** on. I tucked the money-bag in under the lid, just down **beyond** where his hands was crossed, which made me **creep**, they was so **cold**, and then I run back across the room and in behind the door.

The person coming was Mary Jane. She went to the coffin, very **soft**, and kneeled down and looked in; then she put up her **handkerchief**, and I see she **begun** to **cry**, though I couldn't hear her, and her back was to me. I **slid** out, and as I passed the dining-room I thought I'd make sure them watchers hadn't seen

Chinese Simplified

asleep: 睡着，睡着的.
bag: 袋子，袋，手提包，提包，囊.
begun: 开始.
beyond: 超越.
candle: 蜡烛.
chairs: 椅子.
cloth: 布，布帛菽粟，布料.
coffin: 棺材，寿材.
cold: 冷，感冒，寒冷，寒，冷淡.
corpse: 尸体.
crack: 裂缝，精干，崩裂，爆裂，裂开，空隙.
creep: 爬行.
cry: 喊，叫，哭，哭泣.
doors: 门.
foot: 脚，足，步兵，英尺，呎.
handkerchief: 手帕，手绢.
hide: 躲藏，暗藏，掩饰，藏，隐瞒，隐藏.
key: 钥匙，关键，题解，键，主要的.
lid: 盖子.
listened: 听.
nobody: 没有人，没人.
parlor: 会客室.
rooms: 房间.
shroud: 笼罩.
slid: 滑行.
snoring: 打鼾.
soft: 柔软，柔和，柔软的.
somebody: 某人，有人.
stairs: 楼梯.
swift: 迅速的.
wet: 湿.

me; so I looked through the **crack**, and everything was all right. They hadn't **stirred**.

I **slipped** up to bed, feeling ruther blue, on accounts of the thing playing out that way after I had took so much trouble and run so much resk about it. Says I, if it could stay where it is, all right; because when we get down the river a hundred **mile** or two I could write back to Mary Jane, and she could **dig** him up again and get it; but that ain't the thing that's going to happen; the thing that's going to happen is, the money 'll be found when they come to **screw** on the **lid**. Then the king 'll get it again, and it 'll be a long day before he gives anybody another chance to smouch it from him. Of course I *wanted* to **slide** down and get it out of there, but I dasn't try it. Every minute it was getting **earlier** now, and pretty soon some of them watchers would begin to stir, and I might get catched--catched with six thousand dollars in my hands that nobody hadn't hired me to take care of. I don't wish to be **mixed** up in no such business as that, I says to myself.

When I got down **stairs** in the morning the **parlor** was **shut** up, and the watchers was gone. There warn't nobody around but the family and the **widow** Bartley and our **tribe**. I watched their faces to see if anything had been **happening**, but I couldn't tell.

Towards the middle of the day the **undertaker** come with his man, and they set the **coffin** in the middle of the room on a couple of **chairs**, and then set all our chairs in rows, and borrowed more from the neighbors **till** the hall and the parlor and the dining-room was full. I see the coffin lid was the way it was before, but I dasn't go to look in under it, with folks around.

Then the people **begun** to **flock** in, and the **beats** and the girls took **seats** in the front row at the head of the coffin, and for a half an hour the people filed around slow, in single **rank**, and looked down at the dead man's face a minute, and some **dropped** in a **tear**, and it was all very still and **solemn**, only the girls and the beats holding handkerchiefs to their eyes and keeping their heads **bent**, and sobbing a little. There warn't no other sound but the scraping of the feet on

Chinese Simplified

beats：节奏．
begun：开始．
bent：曲，弯，弯曲，弯折．
chairs：椅子．
coffin：棺材，寿材．
crack：裂缝，精干，崩裂，爆裂，裂开，空隙．
dig：挖掘．
dropped：落下．
earlier：一向，早些，早，先，较早时．
flock：一群．
happening：事件，发生．
lid：盖子．
mile：英里．
mixed：混合，混合的，错杂．
parlor：会客室．
rank：评价分类，身分，级别，等级，地位，排．
screw：螺丝钉，螺钉．
seats：座位．
shut：关闭．
slide：滑落，滑行，滑．
slipped：滑落．
solemn：严肃，俨然，岸然，隆重，庄严的，庄重．
stairs：楼梯．
stir：轰动，搅拌，鼓动．
tear：眼泪，撕破，撕．
till：直到．
tribe：部落，部族．
undertaker：承担人，殡仪馆．
widow：寡妇．

the floor and **blowing** noses--because people always **blows** them more at a funeral than they do at other places except church.

When the place was packed full the **undertaker** he **slid** around in his black **gloves** with his softy soothering ways, putting on the last **touches**, and getting people and things all ship-shape and comfortable, and making no more sound than a cat. He never spoke; he moved people around, he squeezed in late ones, he opened up passageways, and done it with **nods**, and signs with his hands. Then he took his place over against the wall. He was the softest, **glidingest**, stealthiest man I ever see; and there warn't no more smile to him than there is to a **ham**.

They had borrowed a melodeum--a sick one; and when everything was ready a young woman set down and worked it, and it was pretty skreeky and colicky, and everybody joined in and **sung**, and Peter was the only one that had a good thing, **according** to my notion. Then the Reverend Hobson opened up, slow and **solemn**, and begun to talk; and straight off the most **outrageous** row busted out in the **cellar** a body ever heard; it was only one dog, but he made a most powerful **racket**, and he kept it up right along; the **parson** he had to stand there, over the **coffin**, and wait--you couldn't hear yourself think. It was right down **awkward**, and nobody didn't seem to know what to do. But pretty soon they see that long- legged undertaker make a sign to the **preacher** as much as to say, "Don't you worry--just **depend** on me." Then he **stooped** down and begun to **glide** along the wall, just his shoulders showing over the people's heads. So he glided along, and the **powwow** and racket getting more and more outrageous all the time; and at last, when he had gone around two sides of the room, he **disappears** down cellar. Then in about two seconds we heard a **whack**, and the dog he **finished** up with a most **amazing howl** or two, and then everything was dead still, and the parson begun his solemn talk where he left off. In a minute or two here comes this undertaker's back and shoulders gliding along the wall again; and so he glided and glided around three sides of the room, and then rose up, and shaded his mouth with his hands, and stretched his neck out towards the preacher, over the people's heads, and says, in a kind of a **coarse whisper**, "*He*

Chinese Simplified

according: 根据.
amazing: 了不起，迷人的.
awkward: 笨拙，尴尬，不得劲，拙，迟钝的.
blowing: 吹.
blows: 打击.
cellar: 地下室，地窖.
coarse: 粗劣，粗糙的，淫秽，粗鲁.
coffin: 棺材，寿材.
depend: 依赖，取决.
disappears: 消失.
finished: 完结了的，完蛋了的.
glide: 滑翔，滑行.
gliding: 滑行的，下滑.
gloves: 手套.
ham: 火腿.
howl: 狂吠，号叫.
nods: 点头.
outrageous: 不像话，残暴的，岂有此理.
parson: 牧师.
powwow: 巫师.
preacher: 传道者.
racket: 球拍，拍子.
slid: 滑行.
solemn: 严肃，俨然，岸然，隆重，庄严的，庄重.
stooped: 弯腰.
sung: 唱歌.
touches: 接触.
undertaker: 承担人，殡仪馆.
whack: 重打.
whisper: 耳语，低语.

had a rat!" Then he drooped down and **glided** along the wall again to his place. You could see it was a great **satisfaction** to the people, because naturally they wanted to know. A little thing like that don't cost nothing, and it's just the little things that makes a man to be looked up to and liked. There warn't no more **popular** man in town than what that **undertaker** was.

Well, the **funeral sermon** was very good, but pison long and **tiresome**; and then the king he shoved in and got off some of his usual rubbage, and at last the job was through, and the undertaker begun to **sneak** up on the **coffin** with his screw-driver. I was in a **sweat** then, and watched him pretty **keen**. But he never meddled at all; just **slid** the lid along as soft as mush, and screwed it down **tight** and fast. So there I was! I didn't know whether the money was in there or not. So, says I, s'pose somebody has hogged that bag on the sly?--now how do I know whether to write to Mary Jane or not? S'pose she **dug** him up and didn't find nothing, what would she think of me? **Blame** it, I says, I might get hunted up and jailed; I'd better lay low and keep dark, and not write at all; the thing's **awful mixed** now; trying to better it, I've **worsened** it a hundred times, and I wish to **goodness** I'd just let it alone, dad **fetch** the whole business!

They **buried** him, and we come back home, and I went to watching faces again--I couldn't help it, and I couldn't rest easy. But nothing come of it; the faces didn't tell me nothing.

The king he visited around in the evening, and sweetened everybody up, and made himself ever so **friendly**; and he give out the idea that his **congregation** over in England would be in a sweat about him, so he must **hurry** and **settle** up the estate right away and leave for home. He was very sorry he was so pushed, and so was everybody; they wished he could stay longer, but they said they could see it couldn't be done. And he said of course him and William would take the girls home with them; and that **pleased** everybody too, because then the girls would be well fixed and amongst their own relations; and it pleased the girls, too--tickled them so they clean **forgot** they ever had a trouble in the world; and told him to sell out as quick as he wanted to, they would be ready. Them poor things was that **glad** and happy it made my heart **ache** to see them getting fooled

Chinese Simplified

ache：疼痛，酸痛，痛．
awful：可怕，可怕的．
blame：责备，咎，非难，责任，罪，责怪，归咎．
buried：埋下．
coffin：棺材，寿材．
congregation：集合．
dug：挖掘．
fetch：拿，取，带来．
forgot：忘记．
friendly：友好，友善，友好的，好客，友好地，和气．
funeral：葬礼．
glad：高兴，高兴的．
goodness：美德．
hurry：仓促，匆忙，赶忙．
keen：敏锐，渴望．
lid：盖子．
mixed：混合，混合的，错杂．
pleased：满意，高兴的．
popular：流行，普及，受欢迎，民间，流行的．
satisfaction：满意．
sermon：传教．
settle：奠定，安家落户，澄清，解决．
slid：滑行．
sneak：潜行，潜入．
sweat：汗，出汗，流汗．
tight：严格，严密，紧，紧的，严峻，狭隘．
tiresome：使人疲惫的．
undertaker：承担人，殡仪馆．
worsened：恶化．

and lied to so, but I didn't see no safe way for me to **chip** in and change the general tune.

Well, blamed if the king didn't bill the house and the niggers and all the property for **auction** straight off--sale two days after the **funeral**; but **anybody** could buy private **beforehand** if they wanted to.

So the next day after the funeral, along about noon-time, the girls' **joy** got the first **jolt**. A couple of nigger traders come along, and the king sold them the niggers reasonable, for three-day **drafts** as they called it, and away they went, the two **sons** up the river to Memphis, and their mother down the river to Orleans. I thought them poor girls and them niggers would break their **hearts** for **grief**; they cried around each other, and took on so it most made me down **sick** to see it. The girls said they hadn't ever dreamed of seeing the family **separated** or sold away from the town. I can't ever get it out of my memory, the sight of them poor **miserable** girls and niggers hanging around each other's necks and **crying**; and I **reckon** I couldn't a stood it all, but would a had to **bust** out and tell on our **gang** if I hadn't knowed the sale warn't no account and the niggers would be back home in a week or two.

The thing made a big **stir** in the town, too, and a good many come out flatfooted and said it was **scandalous** to separate the mother and the children that way. It **injured** the frauds some; but the old **fool** he bulled right along, **spite** of all the **duke** could say or do, and I tell you the duke was powerful **uneasy**.

Next day was auction day. About **broad** day in the morning the king and the duke come up in the **garret** and **woke** me up, and I see by their look that there was trouble. The king says:

"Was you in my room night before last?"

"No, your majesty"--which was the way I always called him when nobody but our gang warn't around.

"Was you in there yisterday er last night?"

"No, your majesty."

"**Honor** bright, now--no lies."

Chinese Simplified

anybody: 任何人.
auction: 拍卖.
beforehand: 预先，较早.
broad: 宽，宽广.
bust: 半身像，逮捕，破产.
chip: 碎片，芯片，晶片.
crying: 叫喊的，嚎哭的，显著的.
drafts: 草案.
duke: 公爵，公.
fool: 呆子，笨蛋，傻子，笨人，愚人.
funeral: 葬礼.
gang: 一群，帮.
garret: 阁楼，顶楼.
grief: 哀思，哀痛，悲伤，忧伤.
hearts: 心.
honor: 荣誉，荣耀，尊严，面子，尊敬.
injured: 受伤，受伤的，受损害的.
jolt: 颠簸，摇晃.
joy: 乐趣，快乐，高兴，喜悦.
miserable: 悲惨，凄惨，困苦，凄惨的.
reckon: 估计，计算.
scandalous: 恶意中伤.
separated: 分开.
sick: 生病.
sons: 儿子.
spite: 恶意.
stir: 轰动，搅拌，鼓动.
uneasy: 不安，担心，不安的.
woke: 醒觉.

"Honor **bright**, your **majesty**, I'm telling you the truth. I hain't been a- near your room since Miss Mary Jane took you and the **duke** and showed it to you."

The duke says:

"Have you seen **anybody** else go in there?"

"No, your **grace**, not as I remember, I believe."

"Stop and think."

I studied **awhile** and see my chance; then I says:

"Well, I see the niggers go in there several times."

Both of them gave a little **jump**, and looked like they hadn't ever expected it, and then like they *had*. Then the duke says:

"What, all of them?"

"No--leastways, not all at once--that is, I don't think I ever see them all come *out* at once but just one time."

"**Hello**! When was that?"

"It was the day we had the **funeral**. In the morning. It warn't early, because I overslept. I was just starting down the **ladder**, and I see them."

"Well, go on, *go* on! What did they do? How'd they act?"

"They didn't do nothing. And they didn't act anyway much, as **fur** as I see. They tiptoed away; so I seen, easy enough, that they'd shoved in there to do up your majesty's room, or something, s'posing you was up; and found you *warn't* up, and so they was **hoping** to **slide** out of the way of trouble without **waking** you up, if they hadn't already waked you up."

"Great **guns**, *this* is a go!" says the king; and both of them looked **pretty sick** and **tolerable silly**. They stood there a-thinking and **scratching** their **heads** a minute, and the duke he **bust** into a kind of a little **raspy chuckle**, and says:

"It does **beat** all how **neat** the niggers played their hand. They let on to be *sorry* they was going out of this **region**! And I believed they *was* sorry, and so did you, and so did everybody. Don't ever tell *me* any more that a nigger ain't

Chinese Simplified

anybody: 任何人.
awhile: 一会儿.
beat: 打, 击败, 拍击, 敲打, 拍子, 敲.
bright: 聪明, 光明, 光亮, 光明的, 鲜明.
bust: 半身像, 逮捕, 破产.
chuckle: 咯咯笑, 暗笑.
duke: 公爵, 公.
funeral: 葬礼.
fur: 毛, 软毛.
grace: 优雅, 恩典, 天恩, 魅力, 宽限.
guns: 枪支.
heads: 头.
hello: 你好, 哈罗.
hoping: 希望.
jump: 跳, 跳跃.
ladder: 阶梯, 梯子.
majesty: 威严.
neat: 整齐, 乾净, 干净, 平整, 整洁的.
pretty: 漂亮, 美丽的, 秀丽.
raspy: 易怒的.
region: 区域, 地区, 地域, 一带, 区, 境.
scratching: 刮痕, 抓.
sick: 生病.
silly: 愚蠢, 糊涂, 愚蠢的, 傻的, 傻.
slide: 滑落, 滑行, 滑.
tolerable: 可容忍, 可容忍的.
waking: 醒来, 醒着的.

got any histrionic **talent**. Why, the way they played that thing it would **fool** ***anybody***. In my **opinion**, there's a **fortune** in 'em. If I had **capital** and a **theater**, I wouldn't want a better lay-out than that--and here we've gone and **sold** 'em for a **song**. Yes, and ain't **privileged** to **sing** the song yet. Say, where *is* that song--that draft?"

"In the bank for to be **collected**. Where *would* it be?"

"Well, *that's* all right then, thank goodness."

Says I, kind of timid-like:

"Is something gone wrong?"

The king **whirls** on me and **rips** out:

"None o' your business! You keep your head shet, and mind y'r own affairs--if you got any. Long as you're in this town don't you forgit *that*--you hear?" Then he says to the **duke**, "We got to **jest** swaller it and say noth'n': mum's the word for *us*."

As they was **starting** down the **ladder** the duke he chuckles again, and says:

"Quick **sales** *and* small **profits**! It's a good business--yes."

The king **snarls** around on him and says:

"I was trying to do for the best in sellin' 'em out so **quick**. If the profits has turned out to be none, lackin' considable, and none to carry, is it my **fault** any more'n it's yourn?"

"Well, *they'd* be in this house yet and we *wouldn't* if I could a got my **advice** **listened** to."

The king sassed back as much as was **safe** for him, and then swapped around and **lit** into *me* again. He give me down the banks for not coming and *telling* him I see the niggers come out of his room **acting** that way--said any fool would a *knowed* something was up. And then waltzed in and cussed *himself* **awhile**, and said it all come of him not laying late and taking his natural rest that morning, and he'd be blamed if he'd ever do it again. So they went off a-jawing; and I felt

Chinese Simplified

acting：代理，临时的，代理的，行为.
advice：忠告，劝告，建议.
anybody：任何人.
awhile：一会儿.
capital：首都，本钱，资本，本金.
collected：收集成的，镇定的.
duke：公爵，公.
fault：故障，过失，缺点，毛病，断层，短处，缺陷.
fool：呆子，笨蛋，傻子，笨人，愚人.
fortune：幸运，命运，运气.
jest：玩笑，笑话，戏弄，戏谑.
ladder：阶梯，梯子.
listened：听.
lit：点燃.
opinion：意见，看法，意思，见解.
privileged：特权，有特权的.
profits：利润.
quick：快，玲珑，敏捷的，迅速的.
rips：裂口.
safe：安全，保险，安全的，稳妥，保险箱.
sales：销售，销售额，营收.
sing：唱，歌唱，唱歌.
snarls：缠结.
sold：卖了.
song：歌，歌曲，歌儿.
starting：起步.
talent：才能，天才，天资，才华.
theater：剧场，戏剧，戏院，剧院.
whirls：旋转.

dreadful glad I'd worked it all off on to the niggers, and yet hadn't done the niggers no **harm** by it.

Chinese Simplified

dreadful：可怕，恐怖的.
glad：高兴，高兴的.
harm：伤害，损害，坏处，害处，祸害.

CHAPTER XXVIII

OVERREACHING DON'T PAY

By and by it was getting-up time. So I come down the **ladder** and **started** for down-stairs; but as I come to the girls' room the door was open, and I see Mary Jane **setting** by her old **hair trunk**, which was open and she'd been **packing** things in it--getting **ready** to go to England. But she had **stopped** now with a folded **gown** in her **lap**, and had her face in her **hands**, **crying**. I felt **awful bad** to see it; of course **anybody** would. I went in there and says:

"Miss Mary Jane, you can't a-bear to see people in **trouble**, and I can't-- most always. Tell me about it."

So she done it. And it was the niggers--I just **expected** it. She said the beautiful **trip** to England was most about spoiled for her; she didn't know *how* she was ever going to be happy there, **knowing** the mother and the children warn't ever going to see each other no more--and then busted out bitterer than ever, and flung up her hands, and says:

"Oh, **dear**, dear, to think they ain't *ever* going to see each other any more!"

"But they *will*--and inside of two weeks--and I *know* it!" says I.

Laws, it was out before I could think! And before I could **budge** she throws her arms around my **neck** and told me to say it *again*, say it *again*, say it *again*!

Chinese Simplified

anybody: 任何人.
awful: 可怕, 可怕的.
bad: 坏, 糟糕, 不良, 不善, 淘气, 坏的.
budge: 微微一动, 改变态度, 羔皮.
crying: 叫喊的, 嚎哭的, 显著的.
dear: 亲爱, 亲爱的, 可爱的.
expected: 预期.
gown: 长袍, 女装长袍.
hair: 头发.
hands: 手.
knowing: 博学的, 知道.
ladder: 阶梯, 梯子.
lap: 一段行程, 大腿, 山坳, 被包住.
neck: 颈项, 脖子, 颈.
packing: 包装.
ready: 就绪, 愿意, 准备, 妥当.
setting: 排字, 设定.
started: 开始.
stopped: 停止.
trip: 旅程, 旅游, 旅行, 跟头, 旅途.
trouble: 麻烦, 难度, 难处.
trunk: 躯干, 主干, 树干.

I see I had **spoke** too **sudden** and said too much, and was in a close place. I asked her to let me think a **minute**; and she set there, very **impatient** and **excited** and **handsome**, but looking kind of happy and eased-up, like a person that's had a **tooth** pulled out. So I went to **studying** it out. I says to myself, I **reckon** a body that **ups** and tells the truth when he is in a **tight** place is taking considerable many resks, though I ain't had no experience, and can't say for certain; but it looks so to me, anyway; and yet here's a case where I'm blest if it don't look to me like the truth is better and actuly *safer* than a **lie**. I must lay it by in my mind, and think it over some time or other, it's so kind of **strange** and unregular. I never see nothing like it. Well, I says to myself at last, I'm a-going to chance it; I'll up and tell the truth this time, though it does seem most like **setting** down on a kag of **powder** and **touching** it off just to see where you'll go to. Then I says:

"Miss Mary Jane, is there any place out of town a little ways where you could go and stay three or four days?"

"Yes; Mr. Lothrop's. Why?"

"Never mind why yet. If I'll tell you how I know the niggers will see each other again inside of two weeks--here in this house--and *prove* how I know it--will you go to Mr. Lothrop's and stay four days?"

"Four days!" she says; "I'll stay a year!"

"All right," I says, "I don't want nothing more out of *you* than just your word--I druther have it than another man's kiss-the-Bible." She smiled and **reddened** up very **sweet**, and I says, "If you don't mind it, I'll **shut** the door--and **bolt** it."

Then I come back and set down again, and says:

"Don't you holler. Just set still and take it like a man. I got to tell the truth, and you want to **brace** up, Miss Mary, because it's a bad kind, and going to be hard to take, but there ain't no help for it. These uncles of yourn ain't no uncles at all; they're a couple of frauds-- regular dead-beats. There, now we're over the **worst** of it, you can stand the rest **middling** easy."

It **jolted** her up like everything, of course; but I was over the **shoal** water now, so I went right along, her eyes a-blazing higher and higher all the time, and

Chinese Simplified

bolt：门栓，螺栓，枪栓．
brace：支柱．
excited：兴奋，兴奋的，兴高采烈，激昂的．
handsome：英俊，慷慨的，英俊的．
impatient：不耐烦，无耐心的．
jolted：摇晃．
lie：谎言，谎话，躺，撒谎，说谎．
middling：中级品．
minute：分钟，详细，分，微小的，渺小．
powder：粉，细粉．
prove：证明．
reckon：估计，计算．
reddened：变红．
safer：安全．
setting：排字，设定．
shoal：浅滩．
shut：关闭．
spoke：辐条，说了．
strange：奇怪，奇特，陌生，奇异的，生疏．
studying：学习．
sudden：突然，急剧，突然的．
sweet：甜，甜食，糖果．
tight：严格，严密，紧，紧的，严竣，狭隘．
tooth：牙齿．
touching：动人．
ups：电供衡常器．
worst：最坏的．

told her every **blame** thing, from where we first **struck** that young **fool** going up to the **steamboat**, clear **through** to where she flung herself on to the king's **breast** at the front door and he kissed her **sixteen** or **seventeen** times--and then up she **jumps**, with her face **afire** like **sunset**, and says:

"The **brute**! Come, don't **waste** a minute--not a *second*--we'll have them tarred and **feathered**, and flung in the river!"

Says I:

"Cert'nly. But do you mean *before* you go to Mr. Lothrop's, or--"

"Oh," she says, "what am I *thinking* about!" she says, and set right down again. "Don't mind what I said--please don't--you *won't*, now, *will* you?" Laying her **silky** hand on mine in that kind of a way that I said I would **die** first. "I never thought, I was so stirred up," she says; "now go on, and I won't do so any more. You tell me what to do, and whatever you say I'll do it."

"Well," I says, "it's a rough **gang**, them two frauds, and I'm **fixed** so I got to **travel** with them a while longer, whether I want to or not--I druther not tell you why; and if you was to **blow** on them this town would get me out of their claws, and I'd be all right; but there'd be another person that you don't know about who'd be in big trouble. Well, we got to save *him*, hain't we? Of course. Well, then, we won't blow on them."

Saying them words put a good idea in my head. I see how maybe I could get me and Jim **rid** of the frauds; get them jailed here, and then leave. But I didn't want to run the **raft** in the **daytime** without **anybody aboard** to answer questions but me; so I didn't want the plan to begin working **till pretty** late to-night. I says:

"Miss Mary Jane, I'll tell you what we'll do, and you won't have to stay at Mr. Lothrop's so long, nuther. How **fur** is it?"

"A little short of four miles--right out in the country, back here."

"Well, that 'll answer. Now you go along out there, and lay low till nine or half-past to-night, and then get them to **fetch** you home again-- tell them you've thought of something. If you get here before **eleven** put a **candle** in this window, and if I don't turn up wait *till* eleven, and *then* if I don't turn up it means I'm

Chinese Simplified

aboard: 船上，在车，上.
afire: 大为激动.
anybody: 任何人.
blame: 责备，咎，非难，责任，罪，责怪，归咎.
blow: 吹，打击.
breast: 奶子，乳房，胸，胸部.
brute: 畜，畜生.
candle: 蜡烛.
daytime: 白天，白昼，日间.
die: 逝世，不讳，死.
eleven: 十一.
feathered: 有羽毛的.
fetch: 拿，取，带来.
fixed: 固定，确定，一定，固定的.
fool: 呆子，笨蛋，傻子，笨人，愚人.
fur: 毛，软毛.
gang: 一群，帮.
jumps: 跳跃.
pretty: 漂亮，美丽的，秀丽.
raft: 筏，木排，槎，桴.
rid: 摆脱.
rough: 粗暴，大概，粗糙，粗鲁.
seventeen: 十七.
silky: 柔软光滑.
sixteen: 十六.
steamboat: 汽船，轮船.
struck: 敲打.
sunset: 日落，傍晚.
till: 直到.
travel: 旅行，遨游，旅游，游历.
waste: 荒芜，白费，浪费，糟蹋.

gone, and out of the way, and **safe**. Then you come out and **spread** the news around, and get these **beats** jailed."

"Good," she says, "I'll do it."

"And if it just **happens** so that I don't get away, but get took up along with them, you must up and say I told you the whole thing **beforehand**, and you must stand by me all you can."

"Stand by you! indeed I will. They sha'n't touch a hair of your head!" she says, and I see her nostrils spread and her eyes **snap** when she said it, too.

"If I get away I sha'n't be here," I says, "to **prove** these rapscallions ain't your uncles, and I couldn't do it if I *was* here. I could **swear** they was beats and bummers, that's all, though that's worth something. Well, there's others can do that better than what I can, and they're people that ain't going to be doubted as **quick** as I'd be. I'll tell you how to find them. Gimme a **pencil** and a piece of paper. There--'Royal Nonesuch, Bricksville.' Put it away, and don't lose it. When the court wants to find out something about these two, let them send up to Bricksville and say they've got the men that played the Royal Nonesuch, and ask for some witnesses--why, you'll have that **entire** town down here before you can hardly **wink**, Miss Mary. And they'll come a-biling, too."

I judged we had got everything **fixed** about right now. So I says:

"Just let the **auction** go right along, and don't **worry**. Nobody don't have to pay for the things they buy **till** a whole day after the auction on **accounts** of the short notice, and they ain't going out of this till they get that money; and the way we've fixed it the sale ain't going to count, and they ain't going to get no money. It's just like the way it was with the niggers--it warn't no sale, and the niggers will be back before long. Why, they can't **collect** the money for the *niggers* yet--they're in the **worst** kind of a fix, Miss Mary."

"Well," she says, "I'll run down to **breakfast** now, and then I'll start straight for Mr. Lothrop's."

"'Deed, *that* ain't the **ticket**, Miss Mary Jane," I says, "by no **manner** of means; go *before* breakfast."

Chinese Simplified

accounts：据闻.
auction：拍卖.
beats：节奏.
beforehand：预先，较早.
breakfast：早餐，早饭，早点.
collect：收藏，珍藏，收集，采集，捡，搜集.
count：计数，伯爵，计算，有价值，认为.
entire：整个，全部，全球，通通，总体，全体，全部的，完整的.
fix：安装，奠定，固定，修理.
fixed：固定，确定，一定，固定的.
happens：发生.
manner：方式，样子，态度，礼貌，神态，神气.
pencil：铅笔，笔套，笔帽.
prove：证明.
quick：快，玲珑，敏捷的，迅速的.
safe：安全，保险，安全的，稳妥，保险箱.
snap：折断，抢夺，猛咬.
spread：扩散，流传，传播，散播，敷，撒.
swear：立誓，发誓.
ticket：票.
till：直到.
wink：眨眼，眨眼睛.
worry：担心，使烦恼，缠绕，担忧，心事，担，烦恼，着急.
worst：最坏的.

"Why?"

"What did you **reckon** I wanted you to go at all for, Miss Mary?"

"Well, I never thought--and come to think, I don't know. What was it?"

"Why, it's because you ain't one of these leather-face people. I don't want no better book than what your face is. A body can set down and read it off like **coarse print**. Do you reckon you can go and face your uncles when they come to **kiss** you good-morning, and never--"

"There, there, don't! Yes, I'll go before breakfast--I'll be **glad** to. And leave my **sisters** with them?"

"Yes; never mind about them. They've got to **stand** it yet a while. They might **suspicion** something if all of you was to go. I don't want you to see them, **nor** your sisters, nor **nobody** in this **town**; if a **neighbor** was to ask how is your uncles this morning your face would tell something. No, you go right **along**, Miss Mary Jane, and I'll **fix** it with all of them. I'll tell Miss Susan to give your love to your uncles and say you've went away for a few hours for to get a little **rest** and change, or to see a **friend**, and you'll be back to-night or early in the morning."

"Gone to see a friend is all right, but I won't have my love given to them."

"Well, then, it sha'n't be." It was well enough to tell *her* so--no **harm** in it. It was only a little thing to do, and no **trouble**; and it's the little things that smooths people's **roads** the most, down here **below**; it would make Mary Jane **comfortable**, and it wouldn't cost nothing. Then I says: "There's one more thing--that **bag** of money."

"Well, they've got that; and it makes me feel **pretty silly** to think *how* they got it."

"No, you're out, there. They hain't got it."

"Why, who's got it?"

"I **wish** I knowed, but I don't. I *had* it, because I **stole** it from them; and I stole it to give to you; and I know where I **hid** it, but I'm **afraid** it ain't there no more.

Chinese Simplified

afraid: 危惧，恐怕，害怕.
along: 沿着，沿，一同.
bag: 袋子，袋，手提包，提包，囊.
below: 下面，以下.
coarse: 粗劣，粗糙的，淫秽，粗鲁.
comfortable: 舒服，舒服的.
fix: 安装，奠定，固定，修理.
friend: 朋友，熟人，友人.
glad: 高兴，高兴的.
harm: 伤害，损害，坏处，害处，祸害.
hid: 躲藏.
kiss: 吻，接吻，轻抚，轻触.
neighbor: 邻居，比邻.
nobody: 没有人，没人.
nor: 也不.
pretty: 漂亮，美丽的，秀丽.
print: 印刷，印，版画，打印.
reckon: 估计，计算.
rest: 休息，安息，其余.
roads: 道路.
silly: 愚蠢，糊涂，愚蠢的，傻的，傻.
sisters: 姊妹，姐妹.
stand: 站住，主张，架子，站立，耐，站，架.
stole: 偷了.
suspicion: 疑心，怀疑，嫌疑.
town: 城镇，城市，市镇.
trouble: 麻烦，难度，难处.
wish: 愿望，希望，意愿，祝，祝愿，志愿.

I'm awful sorry, Miss Mary Jane, I'm just as sorry as I can be; but I done the best I could; I did **honest**. I come nigh getting **caught**, and I had to **shove** it into the first place I come to, and run--and it warn't a good place."

"Oh, stop **blaming** yourself--it's too bad to do it, and I won't allow it-- you couldn't help it; it wasn't your **fault**. Where did you **hide** it?"

I didn't want to set her to thinking about her **troubles** again; and I couldn't seem to get my mouth to tell her what would make her see that **corpse** laying in the **coffin** with that **bag** of money on his **stomach**. So for a minute I didn't say nothing; then I says:

"I'd ruther not *tell* you where I put it, Miss Mary Jane, if you don't mind letting me off; but I'll write it for you on a piece of paper, and you can read it along the road to Mr. Lothrop's, if you want to. Do you **reckon** that 'll do?"

"Oh, yes."

So I wrote: "I put it in the coffin. It was in there when you was **crying** there, away in the night. I was behind the door, and I was **mighty** sorry for you, Miss Mary Jane."

It made my eyes water a little to remember her crying there all by herself in the night, and them devils laying there right under her own **roof**, shaming her and **robbing** her; and when I folded it up and give it to her I see the water come into her eyes, too; and she **shook** me by the hand, hard, and says:

"*Good*-bye. I'm going to do everything just as you've told me; and if I don't ever see you again, I sha'n't ever **forget** you and I'll think of you a many and a many a time, and I'll ***pray*** for you, too!"--and she was gone.

Pray for me! I reckoned if she knowed me she'd take a job that was more nearer her size. But I **bet** she done it, just the same--she was just that kind. She had the **grit** to pray for Judus if she took the notion--there warn't no back-down to her, I **judge**. You may say what you want to, but in my opinion she had more **sand** in her than any girl I ever see; in my opinion she was just full of sand. It **sounds** like **flattery**, but it ain't no flattery. And when it comes to beauty--and **goodness**, too--she lays over them all. I hain't ever seen her since that time that I

Chinese Simplified

bag: 袋子，袋，手提包，提包，囊.
bet: 打赌，赌.
blaming: 责备.
caught: 捉了.
coffin: 棺材，寿材.
corpse: 尸体.
crying: 叫喊的，嚎哭的，显著的.
fault: 故障，过失，缺点，毛病，断层，短处，缺陷.
flattery: 媚词.
forget: 忘记，忘，忘却.
goodness: 美德.
grit: 粗砂，砂砾，沙子.
hide: 躲藏，暗藏，掩饰，藏，隐瞒，隐藏.
honest: 诚实，正直，清廉，刚正，坦白，正值，诚实的，体面，廉洁，深切.
judge: 法官，裁判，判定，判断，审判员.
mighty: 伟大，强势，强大的.
pray: 祈祷.
reckon: 估计，计算.
robbing: 抢劫.
roof: 屋顶，顶部，顶板.
sand: 沙，沙子.
shook: 摇动.
shove: 推.
sounds: 声音.
stomach: 胃，肚子.
troubles: 坏处，麻烦.

see her go out of that door; no, I hain't ever seen her since, but I **reckon** I've thought of her a many and a many a million times, and of her **saying** she would **pray** for me; and if ever I'd a thought it would do any good for me to pray for *her*, blamed if I wouldn't a done it or bust.

Well, Mary Jane she **lit** out the back way, I reckon; because **nobody** see her go. When I **struck** Susan and the hare-lip, I says:

"What's the name of them people over on t'other side of the **river** that you all **goes** to see sometimes?"

They says:

"There's several; but it's the Proctors, mainly."

"That's the name," I says; "I most **forgot** it. Well, Miss Mary Jane she told me to tell you she's **gone** over there in a **dreadful** hurry--one of them's sick."

"Which one?"

"I don't know; leastways, I kinder **forget**; but I **thinks** it's--"

"Sakes **alive**, I **hope** it ain't *Hanner*?"

"I'm **sorry** to say it," I says, "but Hanner's the very one."

"My **goodness**, and she so well only last week! Is she took bad?"

"It ain't no name for it. They set up with her all night, Miss Mary Jane said, and they don't think she'll last many hours."

"Only think of that, now! What's the **matter** with her?"

I couldn't think of anything **reasonable**, right off that way, so I says:

"**Mumps**."

"Mumps your **granny**! They don't set up with people that's got the mumps."

"They don't, don't they? You **better** bet they do with *these* mumps. These mumps is different. It's a new kind, Miss Mary Jane said."

"How's it a new kind?"

"Because it's **mixed** up with other things."

Chinese Simplified

alive: 活着，活，活泼的，活着的.
bet: 打赌，赌.
dreadful: 可怕，恐怖的.
forget: 忘记，忘，忘却.
forgot: 忘记.
goes: 去.
gone: 去.
goodness: 美德.
granny: 婆婆，老大娘.
hope: 期望，希望，指望.
lit: 点燃.
matter: 事情，事，物质，事项.
mixed: 混合，混合的，错杂.
mumps: 流行性腮腺炎.
nobody: 没有人，没人.
pray: 祈祷.
reasonable: 合理，合理的.
reckon: 估计，计算.
river: 河，江，川，河流，条.
saying: 名言，说.
sorry: 遗憾，对不起.
struck: 敲打.
thinks: 想.

"What other things?"

"Well, **measles**, and whooping-cough, and erysiplas, and **consumption**, and yaller janders, and brain-fever, and I don't know what all."

"My land! And they call it the ***mumps***?"

"That's what Miss Mary Jane said."

"Well, what in the **nation** do they call it the *mumps* for?"

"Why, because it *is* the mumps. That's what it **starts** with."

"Well, ther' ain't no sense in it. A body might **stump** his **toe**, and take pison, and fall down the well, and break his neck, and **bust** his **brains** out, and somebody come along and ask what killed him, and some numskull up and say, 'Why, he stumped his *toe*.' Would ther' be any sense in that? *no*. And ther' ain't no sense in *this*, nuther. Is it ketching?"

"Is it *ketching*? Why, how you talk. Is a ***harrow*** catching--in the dark? If you don't **hitch** on to one **tooth**, you're **bound** to on another, ain't you? And you can't get away with that tooth without **fetching** the whole harrow along, can you? Well, these kind of mumps is a kind of a harrow, as you may say--and it ain't no slouch of a harrow, nuther, you come to get it **hitched** on good."

"Well, it's **awful,** I think," says the hare-lip. "I'll go to Uncle Harvey and--"

"Oh, yes," I says, "I *would*. Of *course* I would. I wouldn't lose no time."

"Well, why wouldn't you?"

"Just look at it a minute, and maybe you can see. Hain't your **uncles** obleegd to get along home to England as fast as they can? And do you **reckon** they'd be mean enough to go off and leave you to go all that **journey** by **yourselves**? *You* know they'll wait for you. So **fur**, so good. Your uncle Harvey's a **preacher**, ain't he? Very well, then; is a *preacher* going to **deceive** a **steamboat clerk**? is he going to deceive a ***ship clerk***? --so as to get them to let Miss Mary Jane go **aboard**? Now *you* know he ain't. What *will* he do, then? Why, he'll say, 'It's a great **pity**, but my church matters has got to get along the best way they can; for my **niece** has been **exposed** to the **dreadful** pluribus-unum mumps, and so it's my bounden

Chinese Simplified

aboard: 船上，在车，上.
awful: 可怕，可怕的.
bound: 限，边际，弹回，范围.
brains: 头脑，脑子，脑筋，脑袋，脑髓.
bust: 半身像，逮捕，破产.
clerk: 书记，营业员，办事员，职员.
consumption: 消耗量.
deceive: 欺骗，欺.
dreadful: 可怕，恐怖的.
exposed: 暴露的，无掩蔽的.
fetching: 迷人的.
fur: 毛，软毛.
harrow: 耙.
hitch: 拴住，蹒跚.
hitched: 蹒跚.
journey: 旅程，旅途，旅游，旅行.
measles: 麻疹.
mumps: 流行性腮腺炎.
nation: 国家.
niece: 侄女，甥女.
pity: 怜悯，遗憾，哀怜，同情.
preacher: 传道者.
reckon: 估计，计算.
ship: 船.
starts: 开始.
steamboat: 汽船，轮船.
stump: 树桩，残肢.
toe: 脚趾.
tooth: 牙齿.
uncle: 叔叔，伯伯，叔父，大爷，老大爷，姑夫.
yourselves: 你们自己.

duty to set down here and **wait** the three months it takes to show on her if she's got it.' But never mind, if you think it's best to tell your **uncle** Harvey--"

"Shucks, and stay fooling around here when we could all be having good times in England whilst we was **waiting** to find out whether Mary Jane's got it or not? Why, you talk like a muggins."

"Well, anyway, maybe you'd better tell some of the neighbors."

"**Listen** at that, now. You do **beat** all for natural stupidness. Can't you *see* that *they'd* go and tell? Ther' ain't no way but just to not tell **anybody** at *all*."

"Well, maybe you're right--yes, I **judge** you *are* right."

"But I **reckon** we **ought** to tell Uncle Harvey she's gone out a while, anyway, so he won't be **uneasy** about her?"

"Yes, Miss Mary Jane she wanted you to do that. She says, 'Tell them to give Uncle Harvey and William my love and a **kiss**, and say I've run over the **river** to see Mr.'--Mr.--what *is* the name of that **rich** family your uncle Peter used to think so much of?--I mean the one that--"

"Why, you must mean the Apthorps, ain't it?"

"Of course; **bother** them kind of names, a body can't ever seem to remember them, half the time, **somehow**. Yes, she said, say she has run over for to ask the Apthorps to be sure and come to the **auction** and buy this house, because she **allowed** her uncle Peter would ruther they had it than anybody else; and she's going to **stick** to them **till** they say they'll come, and then, if she ain't too **tired**, she's coming home; and if she is, she'll be home in the morning anyway. She said, don't say nothing about the Proctors, but only about the Apthorps--which 'll be **perfectly** true, because she is going there to **speak** about their **buying** the house; I know it, because she told me so herself."

"All right," they said, and cleared out to **lay** for their uncles, and give them the love and the **kisses**, and tell them the **message**.

Everything was all right now. The girls wouldn't say nothing because they wanted to go to England; and the king and the **duke** would ruther Mary Jane

Chinese Simplified

allowed: 允许.
anybody: 任何人.
auction: 拍卖.
beat: 打, 击败, 拍击, 敲打, 拍子, 敲.
bother: 烦扰, 打扰, 理会.
buying: 购买.
duke: 公爵, 公.
duty: 任务, 义务, 责任, 关税, 职责.
judge: 法官, 裁判, 判定, 判断, 审判员.
kiss: 吻, 接吻, 轻抚, 轻触.
kisses: 吻.
lay: 产卵, 安放, 放, 凡俗.
listen: 听, 倾听.
message: 信息, 讯息, 音信, 消息.
ought: 应该, 活该.
perfectly: 完美, 完美地.
reckon: 估计, 计算.
rich: 富有, 丰富, 富有的, 充实.
river: 河, 江, 川, 河流, 条.
somehow: 不知何故.
speak: 说, 讲.
stick: 棍, 棒子, 棍子, 插入, 棒, 黏贴, 手杖.
till: 直到.
tired: 疲倦, 疲乏, 疲倦的.
uncle: 叔叔, 伯伯, 叔父, 大爷, 老大爷, 姑夫.
uneasy: 不安, 担心, 不安的.
wait: 等待, 等, 伺候.
waiting: 等候, 等待.

was off **working** for the **auction** than around in **reach** of Doctor Robinson. I felt very good; I judged I had done it **pretty** neat--I reckoned Tom Sawyer couldn't a done it no neater himself. Of course he would a throwed more **style** into it, but I can't do that very **handy**, not being brung up to it.

Well, they held the auction in the public **square**, **along** towards the end of the **afternoon**, and it strung along, and strung along, and the old man he was on hand and looking his level pisonest, up there longside of the **auctioneer**, and chipping in a little Scripture now and then, or a little goody-goody saying of some kind, and the **duke** he was around goo-gooing for **sympathy** all he knowed how, and just **spreading** himself generly.

But by and by the thing **dragged** through, and everything was sold--everything but a little old **trifling** lot in the **graveyard**. So they'd got to work that off--I never see such a girafft as the king was for **wanting** to **swallow** *everything*. Well, whilst they was at it a **steamboat landed**, and in about two minutes up comes a **crowd** a-whooping and **yelling** and **laughing** and **carrying** on, and **singing** out:

"*Here's* your **opposition** line! here's your two **sets** o' **heirs** to old Peter Wilks--and you **pays** your money and you **takes** your choice!"

Chinese Simplified

afternoon：下午，午后．
along：沿着，沿，一同．
auction：拍卖．
auctioneer：拍卖人．
carrying：运送的，运输的．
crowd：人群．
dragged：拖拉，拖曳．
duke：公爵，公．
graveyard：坟地，墓地．
handy：灵巧，便当，顺手，方便的，简便．
heirs：继承人．
king：国王，王．
landed：着陆．
laughing：可笑的，笑．
opposition：反对．
pays：支付．
pretty：漂亮，美丽的，秀丽．
reach：抵达，到达，抵，到．
sets：装置．
singing：歌咏，歌唱．
spreading：撒，散布，传播，展开，扩展．
square：正方形，平方，四方形．
steamboat：汽船，轮船．
style：方式，风格，式样，样式，试样，笔调，模样，作风．
swallow：燕子，吞，咽．
sympathy：同情．
takes：拿，取走．
trifling：些许，不重要的．
wanting：缺少的，不足的．
yelling：叫声，叫喊．

CHAPTER XXIX

I LIGHT OUT IN THE STORM

They was **fetching** a very **nice**-looking old **gentleman** along, and a nice-looking **younger** one, with his right arm in a **sling**. And, my **souls**, how the people **yelled** and **laughed**, and kept it up. But I didn't see no **jokc** about it, and I judged it would **strain** the **duke** and the king some to see any. I reckoned they'd turn **pale**. But no, nary a pale did *they* turn. The duke he never let on he suspicioned what was up, but just went a goo- gooing around, happy and **satisfied**, like a **jug** that's googling out **buttermilk**; and as for the king, he just gazed and gazed down **sorrowful** on them new-comers like it give him the **stomach**-ache in his very heart to think there could be such frauds and rascals in the world. Oh, he done it **admirable**. Lots of the **principal** people gethered around the king, to let him see they was on his side. That old gentleman that had just come looked all **puzzled** to death. Pretty soon he **begun** to speak, and I see straight off he **pronounced** *like* an Englishman--not the king's way, though the king's *was* pretty good for an **imitation**. I can't give the old gent's words, nor I can't **imitate** him; but he turned around to the **crowd**, and says, about like this:

"This is a surprise to me which I wasn't looking for; and I'll **acknowledge**, **candid** and **frank**, I ain't very well **fixed** to meet it and answer it; for my brother and me has had misfortunes; he's **broke** his arm, and our **baggage** got put off at a

Chinese Simplified

acknowledge: 认知，承认.
admirable: 令人钦佩，令人钦佩的.
baggage: 行李.
begun: 开始.
broke: 打破.
buttermilk: 酪乳.
candid: 公正地.
crowd: 人群.
duke: 公爵，公.
fetching: 迷人的.
fixed: 固定，确定，一定，固定的.
frank: 坦率，率直，坦白的.
gentleman: 绅士.
imitate: 模仿.
imitation: 模拟，冒牌，模仿.
joke: 笑话、玩笑，开玩笑.
jug: 细颈瓶，罐.
laughed: 笑.
nice-looking: 好看.
pale: 苍白，苍白的.
principal: 本金，主要，校长，首长.
pronounced: 明言.
puzzled: 惑.
satisfied: 满意，乐意，心满意足的.
sling: 弹弓，吊绳，背带，吊索.
sorrowful: 悲痛，悲哀，哀愁，悲伤，悲伤的.
souls: 灵魂.
stomach-ache: 肚痛.
strain: 拉紧，种，系，紧张，菌株，品系.
yelled: 叫喊.
younger: 较年轻的.

town above here last night in the night by a **mistake**. I am Peter Wilks' **brother** Harvey, and this is his brother William, which can't hear nor speak--and can't even make signs to amount to much, now't he's only got one hand to work them with. We are who we say we are; and in a day or two, when I get the **baggage**, I can **prove** it. But up **till** then I won't say nothing more, but go to the **hotel** and wait."

So him and the new **dummy started** off; and the king he **laughs**, and blethers out:

"Broke his arm--*very* likely, *ain't* it?--and very **convenient**, too, for a **fraud** that's got to make signs, and ain't learnt how. Lost their baggage! That's *mighty* good!--and mighty ingenious--under the *circumstances*!"

So he **laughed** again; and so did **everybody** else, **except** three or four, or **maybe** half a **dozen**. One of these was that **doctor**; another one was a sharp-looking **gentleman**, with a carpet-bag of the **old**-fashioned kind made out of carpet-stuff, that had just come off of the **steamboat** and was talking to him in a **low** voice, and **glancing** towards the king now and then and **nodding** their heads--it was Levi Bell, the **lawyer** that was gone up to Louisville; and another one was a big **rough husky** that come along and **listened** to all the old gentleman said, and was **listening** to the king now. And when the king got done this husky up and says:

"Say, looky here; if you are Harvey Wilks, when'd you come to this town?"

"The day before the **funeral**, friend," says the king.

"But what time o' day?"

"In the evenin'--'bout an **hour** er two before sundown."

"*How'd* you come?"

"I come down on the Susan Powell from Cincinnati."

"Well, then, how'd you come to be up at the Pint in the *mornin'*--in a canoe?"

"I warn't up at the Pint in the mornin'."

"It's a lie."

Chinese Simplified

baggage: 行李.
brother: 弟兄, 兄弟.
convenient: 方便, 便利, 便当, 手, 方便的.
doctor: 医生, 大夫, 医师, 博士.
dozen: 一打, 打.
dummy: 假的, 傀儡.
everybody: 每个人, 各位.
except: 除了, 除了之外.
fraud: 舞弊, 骗局, 作弊, 欺骗.
funeral: 葬礼.
gentleman: 绅士.
glancing: 粗略的.
hotel: 旅馆, 酒店.
hour: 小时, 钟头, 钟点, 现在.
husky: 壳的.
laughed: 笑.
laughs: 笑.
lawyer: 律师, 法人.
listened: 听.
listening: 听.
low: 低, 卑下, 低廉, 浅的, 低的.
maybe: 或许, 也许, 或者, 说不定, 可能, 不一定.
mighty: 伟大, 强势, 强大的.
mistake: 错误, 差错.
nodding: 点头.
old-fashioned: 过时, 旧式的.
prove: 证明.
rough: 粗暴, 大概, 粗糙, 粗鲁.
started: 开始.
steamboat: 汽船, 轮船.
till: 直到.

Several of them **jumped** for him and **begged** him not to talk that way to an old man and a preacher.

"Preacher be hanged, he's a **fraud** and a **liar**. He was up at the Pint that mornin'. I live up there, don't I? Well, I was up there, and he was up there. I see him there. He come in a **canoe**, along with Tim Collins and a boy."

The doctor he up and says:

"Would you know the boy again if you was to see him, Hines?"

"I **reckon** I would, but I don't know. Why, **yonder** he is, now. I know him **perfectly** easy."

It was me he **pointed** at. The doctor says:

"Neighbors, I don't know whether the new couple is frauds or not; but if *these* two ain't frauds, I am an **idiot**, that's all. I think it's our duty to see that they don't get away from here **till** we've looked into this thing. Come along, Hines; come along, the rest of you. We'll take these fellows to the **tavern** and **affront** them with t'other couple, and I reckon we'll find out *something* before we get through."

It was **nuts** for the **crowd**, though maybe not for the king's friends; so we all started. It was about **sundown**. The doctor he **led** me along by the hand, and was **plenty** kind enough, but he never let go my hand.

We all got in a big room in the hotel, and **lit** up some **candles**, and fetched in the new couple. First, the doctor says:

"I don't wish to be too hard on these two men, but I think they're frauds, and they may have complices that we don't know nothing about. If they have, won't the complices get away with that **bag** of **gold** Peter Wilks left? It ain't **unlikely**. If these men ain't frauds, they won't **object** to **sending** for that money and letting us keep it till they **prove** they're all right--ain't that so?"

Everybody agreed to that. So I judged they had our **gang** in a **pretty tight** place right at the outstart. But the king he only looked **sorrowful**, and says:

Chinese Simplified

affront：泰然面对，冒犯，侮辱.
bag：袋子，袋，手提包，提包，囊.
begged：乞求.
candles：蜡烛.
canoe：独木舟.
crowd：人群.
fraud：舞弊，骗局，作弊，欺骗.
gang：一群，帮.
gold：金，黄金.
idiot：白痴，笨蛋，傻子.
jumped：跳跃.
led：光二极管，领导.
liar：说谎者，撒谎者.
lit：点燃.
nuts：螺母.
object：对象，物件，宾语，物体，物，事物.
perfectly：完美，完美地.
plenty：丰富，许多.
pointed：尖锐.
pretty：漂亮，美丽的，秀丽.
prove：证明.
reckon：估计，计算.
sending：发送.
sorrowful：悲痛，悲哀，哀愁，悲伤，悲伤的.
sundown：日落.
tavern：客栈，酒馆.
tight：严格，严密，紧，紧的，严竣，狭隘.
till：直到.
unlikely：不会，不可能.
yonder：那边.

"Gentlemen, I wish the money was there, for I ain't got no **disposition** to **throw** anything in the way of a fair, open, **out**-and-out **investigation** o' this misable business; but, **alas**, the money ain't there; you k'n send and see, if you want to."

"Where is it, then?"

"Well, when my **niece** give it to me to keep for her I took and **hid** it inside o' the **straw tick** o' my bed, not wishin' to bank it for the few days we'd be here, and considerin' the bed a safe place, we not bein' used to niggers, and suppos'n' 'em **honest**, like **servants** in England. The niggers **stole** it the very next mornin' after I had went down **stairs**; and when I sold 'em I hadn't missed the money yit, so they got clean away with it. My servant here k'n tell you 'bout it, gentlemen."

The doctor and several said "Shucks!" and I see nobody didn't **altogether** believe him. One man asked me if I see the niggers **steal** it. I said no, but I see them **sneaking** out of the room and hustling away, and I never thought nothing, only I reckoned they was afraid they had waked up my master and was trying to get away before he made trouble with them. That was all they asked me. Then the doctor **whirls** on me and says:

"Are *you* English, too?"

I says yes; and him and some others **laughed**, and said, "Stuff!"

Well, then they sailed in on the general investigation, and there we had it, up and down, hour in, hour out, and nobody never said a word about **supper**, nor ever seemed to think about it--and so they kept it up, and kept it up; and it *was* the **worst** mixed-up thing you ever see. They made the king tell his **yarn**, and they made the old gentleman tell his'n; and **anybody** but a lot of prejudiced chuckleheads would a *seen* that the old gentleman was **spinning** truth and t'other one **lies**. And by and by they had me up to tell what I knowed. The king he give me a **left**-handed look out of the corner of his eye, and so I knowed enough to talk on the right side. I **begun** to tell about Sheffield, and how we lived there, and all about the English Wilkses, and so on; but I didn't get pretty **fur till** the doctor begun to laugh; and Levi Bell, the **lawyer**, says:

Chinese Simplified

alas：呜呼.
altogether：总共，一共.
anybody：任何人.
begun：开始.
disposition：意向，性格，脾气，安排，部署.
fur：毛，软毛.
hid：躲藏.
honest：诚实，正直，清廉，刚正，坦白，正値，诚实的，体面，廉洁，深切.
investigation：调查.
laugh：笑.
laughed：笑.
lawyer：律师，法人.
left-handed：左撇子.
lies：谎言.
niece：侄女，甥女.
out-and-out：不折不扣.
servant：仆人，佣人，用人.
sneaking：鬼鬼祟祟的.
spinning：纺织，旋转.
stairs：楼梯.
steal：偷窃，盗窃，偷，窃取.
stole：偷了.
straw：稻草，吸管.
supper：晚饭，晚餐.
throw：扔，丢掉，丢，投.
tick：壁虱，滴答声，勾.
till：直到.
whirls：旋转.
worst：最坏的.
yarn：毛线.

"Set down, my boy; I wouldn't **strain** myself if I was you. I **reckon** you ain't used to **lying**, it don't seem to come **handy**; what you want is practice. You do it **pretty** awkward."

I didn't care nothing for the **compliment**, but I was **glad** to be let off, anyway.

The doctor he started to say something, and turns and says:

"If you'd been in town at first, Levi Bell--" The king **broke** in and reached out his hand, and says:

"Why, is this my poor dead brother's old friend that he's wrote so often about?"

The **lawyer** and him **shook** hands, and the lawyer smiled and looked **pleased**, and they **talked** right along **awhile**, and then got to one side and talked low; and at last the lawyer speaks up and says:

"That 'll **fix** it. I'll take the order and send it, along with your brother's, and then they'll know it's all right."

So they got some paper and a **pen**, and the king he set down and twisted his head to one side, and chawed his **tongue**, and scrawled off something; and then they give the pen to the **duke**--and then for the first time the duke looked **sick**. But he took the pen and wrote. So then the lawyer turns to the new old **gentleman** and says:

"You and your brother please write a line or two and sign your names."

The old gentleman wrote, but **nobody** couldn't read it. The lawyer looked **powerful astonished**, and says:

"Well, it **beats** *me*"--and snaked a lot of old letters out of his **pocket**, and examined them, and then examined the old man's writing, and then *them* again; and then says: "These old letters is from Harvey Wilks; and here's *these* two **handwritings**, and **anybody** can see they didn't write them" (the king and the duke looked **sold** and **foolish**, I tell you, to see how the lawyer had took them in), "and here's *this* old gentleman's hand writing, and anybody can tell, easy

Chinese Simplified

anybody：任何人．
astonished：诧异．
awhile：一会儿．
beats：节奏．
broke：打破．
compliment：道贺，祝贺，敬意．
duke：公爵，公．
fix：安装，奠定，固定，修理．
foolish：愚蠢的．
gentleman：绅士．
glad：高兴，高兴的．
handwritings：笔迹．
handy：灵巧，便当，顺手，方便的，简便．
lawyer：律师，法人．
lying：撒谎的．
nobody：没有人，没人．
pen：笔，栏圈，笔杆，笔杆子，栏位，栏，钢笔．
pleased：满意，高兴的．
pocket：口袋，衣袋，兜儿，窟窿．
powerful：强大，有力，强劲，强有力的．
pretty：漂亮，美丽的，秀丽．
reckon：估计，计算．
shook：摇动．
sick：生病．
sold：卖了．
strain：拉紧，种，系，紧张，菌株，品系．
talked：谈话．
tongue：舌头，舌．

enough, *he* didn't write them--fact is, the **scratches** he makes ain't **properly** *writing* at all. Now, here's some letters from--"

The new old **gentleman** says:

"If you please, let me explain. Nobody can read my hand but my brother there--so he **copies** for me. It's *his* hand you've got there, not mine."

"*Well!*" says the **lawyer**, "this *is* a state of things. I've got some of William's letters, too; so if you'll get him to write a line or so we can com--"

"He *can't* write with his left hand," says the old gentleman. "If he could use his right hand, you would see that he wrote his own letters and mine too. Look at both, please--they're by the same hand."

The lawyer done it, and says:

"I believe it's so--and if it ain't so, there's a **heap stronger resemblance** than I'd noticed before, anyway. Well, well, well! I thought we was right on the **track** of a slution, but it's gone to **grass**, **partly**. But anyway, one thing is proved--*these* two ain't either of 'em Wilkses"--and he wagged his head towards the king and the **duke**.

Well, what do you think? That muleheaded old **fool** wouldn't give in *then*! **Indeed** he wouldn't. Said it warn't no **fair test**. Said his brother William was the cussedest **joker** in the world, and hadn't tried to write-- *he* see William was going to play one of his **jokes** the minute he put the **pen** to paper. And so he warmed up and went warbling right along **till** he was actuly beginning to believe what he was saying *himself*; but **pretty** soon the new gentleman **broke** in, and says:

"I've thought of something. Is there **anybody** here that helped to lay out my br--helped to lay out the late Peter Wilks for burying?"

"Yes," says somebody, "me and Ab Turner done it. We're both here."

Then the old man turns towards the king, and says:

"Peraps this gentleman can tell me what was tattooed on his breast?"

Blamed if the king didn't have to **brace** up **mighty quick**, or he'd a squshed down like a **bluff** bank that the river has cut under, it took him so **sudden**; and,

Chinese Simplified

anybody: 任何人.
bluff: 虚张声势, 吹牛.
brace: 支柱.
broke: 打破.
copies: 拷贝.
duke: 公爵, 公.
fair: 公平, 博览会, 清澈, 公正, 公道, 展, 直.
fool: 呆子, 笨蛋, 傻子, 笨人, 愚人.
gentleman: 绅士.
grass: 草, 青草.
heap: 堆, 堆积.
indeed: 的确, 确实, 果真.
joker: 家伙, 爱开玩笑的人, 诙谐者.
jokes: 笑林, 笑话.
lawyer: 律师, 法人.
mighty: 伟大, 强势, 强大的.
partly: 部分地.
pen: 笔, 栏圈, 笔杆, 笔杆子, 栏位, 栏, 钢笔.
pretty: 漂亮, 美丽的, 秀丽.
properly: 好好儿地, 适当地.
quick: 快, 玲珑, 敏捷的, 迅速的.
resemblance: 相似, 类似点, 相似点, 相似性, 像.
scratches: 抓.
stronger: 较强.
sudden: 突然, 急剧, 突然的.
test: 试验, 測验, 考验, 检验.
till: 直到.
track: 跑道, 迳赛, 迳迹, 轨道, 行踪, 履带, 踪迹.

mind you, it was a **thing** that was calculated to make most ***anybody*** sqush to get fetched such a **solid** one as that without any notice, because how was *he* going to know what was tattooed on the man? He whitened a little; he couldn't help it; and it was **mighty still** in there, and everybody bending a little forwards and **gazing** at him. Says I to myself, *now* he'll **throw** up the sponge--there ain't no more use. Well, did he? A body can't hardly believe it, but he didn't. I **reckon** he thought he'd keep the thing up till he **tired** them people out, so they'd thin out, and him and the **duke** could break **loose** and get away. Anyway, he set there, and **pretty** soon he **begun** to smile, and says:

"Mf! It's a *very* **tough** question, *ain't* it! *Yes*, sir, I k'n tell you what's tattooed on his **breast**. It's **jest** a small, thin, blue arrow-- that's what it is; and if you don't look clost, you can't see it. *Now* what do you say--hey?"

Well, I never see anything like that old **blister** for clean **out**-and-out cheek.

The new old **gentleman** turns **brisk** towards Ab Turner and his pard, and his eye **lights** up like he judged he'd got the king *this* time, and says:

"There--you've heard what he said! Was there any such mark on Peter Wilks' breast?"

Both of them spoke up and says:

"We didn't see no such mark."

"Good!" says the old gentleman. "Now, what you *did* see on his breast was a small **dim** P, and a B (which is an **initial** he **dropped** when he was young), and a W, with dashes between them, so: P--B--W"--and he marked them that way on a piece of paper. "Come, ain't that what you saw?"

Both of them spoke up again, and says:

"No, we *didn't*. We never seen any marks at all."

Well, everybody *was* in a state of mind now, and they **sings** out:

"The whole *bilin'* of 'm 's frauds! Le's **duck** 'em! le's **drown** 'em! le's **ride** 'em on a rail!" and everybody was whooping at once, and there was a rattling **powwow**. But the **lawyer** he **jumps** on the table and yells, and says:

Chinese Simplified

anybody: 任何人.
begun: 开始.
blister: 水泡.
breast: 奶子，乳房，胸，胸部.
brisk: 活泼，活泼的.
dim: 阴暗，暗淡，暗淡的.
dropped: 落下.
drown: 使溺死，淹死，溺死.
duck: 鸭，鸭子.
duke: 公爵，公.
gazing: 凝视.
gentleman: 绅士.
initial: 开始，初步，最初，最初的.
jest: 玩笑，笑话，戏弄，戏谑.
jumps: 跳跃.
lawyer: 律师，法人.
lights: 灯火.
loose: 松开，松弛的.
mighty: 伟大，强势，强大的.
out-and-out: 不折不扣.
powwow: 巫师.
pretty: 漂亮，美丽的，秀丽.
reckon: 估计，计算.
ride: 乘，骑，跨，坐.
sings: 唱.
solid: 固体，立体，固体的，坚硬，扎实，实心的，坚固的，坚实.
thin: 薄，疏，细，淡.
throw: 扔，丢掉，丢，投.
till: 直到.
tired: 疲倦，疲乏，疲倦的.
tough: 强硬，坚韧的.

"Gentlemen--gentle*men*! Hear me just a word--just a *single* word--if you *please*! There's one way yet--let's go and **dig** up the **corpse** and look."

That took them.

"Hooray!" they all shouted, and was starting right off; but the **lawyer** and the doctor **sung** out:

"Hold on, hold on! Collar all these four men and the boy, and **fetch** *them* along, too!"

"We'll do it!" they all shouted; "and if we don't find them marks we'll lynch the whole gang!"

I *was* scared, now, I tell you. But there warn't no getting away, you know. They gripped us all, and **marched** us right along, straight for the **graveyard**, which was a **mile** and a half down the river, and the whole town at our heels, for we made **noise** enough, and it was only nine in the evening.

As we went by our house I wished I hadn't sent Mary Jane out of town; because now if I could **tip** her the **wink** she'd light out and save me, and **blow** on our dead-beats.

Well, we **swarmed** along down the river road, just carrying on like wildcats; and to make it more **scary** the **sky** was darking up, and the **lightning** beginning to wink and **flitter**, and the wind to **shiver** amongst the leaves. This was the most **awful** trouble and most dangersome I ever was in; and I was kinder **stunned**; everything was going so different from what I had allowed for; stead of being **fixed** so I could take my own time if I wanted to, and see all the **fun**, and have Mary Jane at my back to save me and set me free when the close-fit come, here was nothing in the world **betwixt** me and **sudden** death but just them tattoo-marks. If they didn't find them--

I couldn't bear to think about it; and yet, **somehow**, I couldn't think about nothing else. It got darker and darker, and it was a beautiful time to give the **crowd** the **slip**; but that big **husky** had me by the wrist-- Hines--and a body might as well try to give Goliar the slip. He **dragged** me right along, he was so **excited**, and I had to run to keep up.

Chinese Simplified

awful：可怕，可怕的.
betwixt：中间，在…之间.
blow：吹，打击.
corpse：尸体.
crowd：人群.
dig：挖掘.
dragged：拖拉，拖曳.
excited：兴奋，兴奋的，兴高采烈，激昂的.
fetch：拿，取，带来.
fixed：固定，确定，一定，固定的.
flitter：飞来飞去.
fun：娱乐.
graveyard：坟地，墓地.
husky：壳的.
lawyer：律师，法人.
lightning：闪电.
marched：游行.
mile：英里.
noise：噪音，噪声，响声，吵闹声，吵声.
scary：引起惊慌.
shiver：发抖，颤抖，哆嗦.
sky：天空，天.
slip：滑倒，溜走，溜.
somehow：不知何故.
stunned：愕然.
sudden：突然，急剧，突然的.
sung：唱歌.
swarmed：蜂涌.
tip：小费，尖端，尾端.
wink：眨眼，眨眼睛.

When they got there they **swarmed** into the **graveyard** and washed over it like an **overflow**. And when they got to the grave they found they had about a hundred times as many **shovels** as they wanted, but nobody hadn't thought to **fetch** a **lantern**. But they sailed into **digging** anyway by the **flicker** of the **lightning**, and sent a man to the nearest house, a half a mile off, to borrow one.

So they **dug** and dug like everything; and it got awful dark, and the rain started, and the wind swished and swushed along, and the lightning come brisker and brisker, and the **thunder boomed**; but them people never took no notice of it, they was so full of this business; and one minute you could see everything and every face in that big crowd, and the shovelfuls of **dirt sailing** up out of the grave, and the next second the dark wiped it all out, and you couldn't see nothing at all.

At last they got out the **coffin** and begun to unscrew the **lid**, and then such another **crowding** and shouldering and shoving as there was, to scrouge in and get a sight, you never see; and in the dark, that way, it was awful. Hines he hurt my **wrist** dreadful pulling and tugging so, and I reckon he clean forgot I was in the world, he was so **excited** and **panting**.

All of a sudden the lightning let go a perfect **sluice** of white **glare**, and somebody **sings** out:

"By the living **jingo**, here's the bag of gold on his breast!"

Hines let out a **whoop**, like everybody else, and dropped my wrist and give a big **surge** to **bust** his way in and get a look, and the way I lit out and shinned for the road in the dark there ain't nobody can tell.

I had the road all to myself, and I fairly flew--leastways, I had it all to myself except the solid dark, and the now-and-then **glares**, and the buzzing of the rain, and the thrashing of the wind, and the **splitting** of the thunder; and sure as you are born I did **clip** it along!

When I struck the town I see there warn't nobody out in the storm, so I never hunted for no back streets, but humped it straight through the main one; and when I begun to get towards our house I aimed my eye and set it. No light there;

Chinese Simplified

boomed: 繁荣.
bust: 半身像，逮捕，破产.
clip: 夹子，回形针.
coffin: 棺材，寿材.
crowding: 人群，拥挤.
digging: 挖掘.
dirt: 污垢.
dug: 挖掘.
excited: 兴奋，兴奋的，兴高采烈，激昂的.
fetch: 拿，取，带来.
flicker: 闪烁.
glare: 强光，眩目的光，眩目.
glares: 眩目的光.
graveyard: 坟地，墓地.
jingo: 侵略主义，沙文主义.
lantern: 灯笼.
lid: 盖子.
lightning: 闪电.
overflow: 溢出，泛滥，溢流.
panting: 气吁吁.
sailing: 航海术，航海，航行.
shovels: 铁锹.
sings: 唱.
sluice: 水闸.
splitting: 极快的.
surge: 浪涌，大浪，波荡，波涛.
swarmed: 蜂涌.
thunder: 雷，雷声，打雷.
whoop: 呼叫声.
wrist: 腕，腕部.

the house all dark--which made me feel sorry and **disappointed**, I didn't know why. But at last, just as I was **sailing** by, ***flash*** comes the light in Mary Jane's window! and my heart **swelled** up sudden, like to **bust**; and the same second the house and all was behind me in the dark, and wasn't ever going to be before me no more in this world. She *was* the best girl I ever see, and had the most sand.

The minute I was far enough above the town to see I could make the towhead, I begun to look sharp for a boat to **borrow**, and the first time the **lightning** showed me one that wasn't chained I snatched it and shoved. It was a **canoe**, and warn't fastened with nothing but a **rope**. The towhead was a rattling big distance off, away out there in the middle of the river, but I didn't lose no time; and when I **struck** the **raft** at last I was so **fagged** I would a just laid down to blow and **gasp** if I could afforded it. But I didn't. As I **sprung aboard** I **sung** out:

"Out with you, Jim, and set her **loose**! Glory be to **goodness**, we're shut of them!"

Jim **lit** out, and was a-coming for me with both arms spread, he was so full of joy; but when I glimpsed him in the lightning my heart shot up in my mouth and I went **overboard backwards**; for I **forgot** he was old King Lear and a drownded A-rab all in one, and it most scared the livers and lights out of me. But Jim fished me out, and was going to **hug** me and **bless** me, and so on, he was so glad I was back and we was shut of the king and the duke, but I says:

"Not now; have it for breakfast, have it for breakfast! Cut loose and let her slide!"

So in two seconds away we went a-sliding down the river, and it *did* seem so good to be free again and all by ourselves on the big river, and nobody to **bother** us. I had to **skip** around a bit, and **jump** up and **crack** my heels a few times--I couldn't help it; but about the third crack I noticed a sound that I knowed **mighty** well, and held my breath and **listened** and waited; and sure enough, when the next flash busted out over the water, here they come!--and just a-laying to their oars and making their **skiff hum**! It was the king and the duke.

Chinese Simplified

aboard：船上，在车，上．
backwards：逆，逆向，向后．
bless：保佑，庇佑，祝福．
borrow：借．
bother：烦扰，打扰，理会．
bust：半身像，逮捕，破产．
canoe：独木舟．
crack：裂缝，精干，崩裂，爆裂，裂开，空隙．
disappointed：败兴，失望的，惆．
fagged：累坏了的．
flash：闪光，晃．
forgot：忘记．
gasp：喘气，喘．
goodness：美德．
hug：紧抱，拥抱．
hum：哼，哼声，嗡嗡声，嗡嗡．
jump：跳，跳跃．
lightning：闪电．
listened：听．
lit：点燃．
loose：松开，松弛的．
mighty：伟大，强势，强大的．
overboard：向船外．
raft：筏，木排，槎，桴．
rope：绳索，绳子．
sailing：航海术，航海，航行．
skiff：小船，小艇．
skip：跳跃，跳过．
sprung：弹跳．
struck：敲打．
sung：唱歌．
swelled：膨胀．

So I wilted right down on to the planks then, and give up; and it was all I could do to keep from crying.

CHAPTER XXX

THE **GOLD** SAVES THE THIEVES

When they got **aboard** the king went for me, and **shook** me by the **collar**, and says:

"Tryin' to give us the **slip**, was **ye**, you **pup**! Tired of our company, hey?"

I says:

"No, your **majesty**, we warn't--*please* don't, your majesty!"

"**Quick**, then, and tell us what *was* your idea, or I'll **shake** the **insides** out o' you!"

"**Honest**, I'll tell you everything just as it happened, your majesty. The man that had a-holt of me was very good to me, and **kept** saying he had a boy about as big as me that died last year, and he was sorry to see a boy in such a **dangerous fix**; and when they was all took by **surprise** by **finding** the gold, and made a **rush** for the **coffin**, he **lets** go of me and **whispers**, 'Heel it now, or they'll **hang** ye, sure!' and I **lit** out. It didn't seem no good for *me* to stay--I couldn't do nothing, and I didn't want to be **hung** if I could get away. So I never **stopped running till** I found the **canoe**; and when I got here I told Jim to **hurry**, or they'd **catch** me and hang me yet, and said I was afeard you and the **duke** wasn't alive

Chinese Simplified

aboard：船上，在车，上．
canoe：独木舟．
catch：捕捉，捕捞，捕拿，捉．
coffin：棺材，寿材．
collar：硬领，衣领．
dangerous：危险，危险的．
duke：公爵，公．
finding：发现物，发现．
fix：安装，奠定，固定，修理．
gold：金，黄金．
hang：挂，悬挂．
honest：诚实，正直，清廉，刚正，坦白，正値，诚实的，体面，廉洁，深切．
hung：挂．
hurry：仓促，匆忙，赶忙．
insides：内部．
kept：收存．
lets：让我们，让．
lit：点燃．
majesty：威严．
pup：小狗．
quick：快，玲珑，敏捷的，迅速的．
running：一连．
rush：速行，匆匆．
shake：摇动，震动，摇，震荡，颠簸．
shook：摇动．
slip：滑倒，溜走，溜．
stopped：停止．
surprise：使吃惊，惊奇，惊骇．
till：直到．
whispers：耳语．
ye：你们．

now, and I was **awful** sorry, and so was Jim, and was awful **glad** when we see you coming; you may ask Jim if I didn't."

Jim said it was so; and the king told him to **shut** up, and said, "Oh, yes, it's *mighty* likely!" and shook me up again, and said he reckoned he'd drownd me. But the **duke** says:

"Leggo the boy, you old **idiot**! Would *you* a done any different? Did you **inquire** around for *him* when you got **loose**? I don't remember it."

So the king let go of me, and begun to cuss that town and everybody in it. But the duke says:

"You **better** a **blame'** sight give *yourself* a good cussing, for you're the one that's entitled to it most. You hain't done a thing from the start that had any sense in it, except coming out so **cool** and **cheeky** with that **imaginary** blue-arrow mark. That *was* bright--it was right down **bully**; and it was the thing that saved us. For if it hadn't been for that they'd a jailed us **till** them Englishmen's **baggage** come--and then--the penitentiary, you bet! But that **trick** took 'em to the **graveyard**, and the gold done us a still **bigger kindness**; for if the **excited** fools hadn't let go all holts and made that **rush** to get a look we'd a **slept** in our cravats to-night--cravats warranted to *wear*, too--longer than *we'd* need 'em."

They was still a minute--thinking; then the king says, kind of **absent**- minded like:

"Mf! And we reckoned the *niggers* **stole** it!"

That made me **squirm**!

"Yes," says the duke, kinder slow and **deliberate** and **sarcastic**, "*we* did."

After about a half a minute the king drawls out:

"Leastways, I did."

The duke says, the same way:

"On the **contrary**, I did."

The king kind of ruffles up, and says:

"Looky here, Bilgewater, what'r you referrin' to?"

Chinese Simplified

absent：缺席，缺席的．
awful：可怕，可怕的．
baggage：行李．
bet：打赌，赌．
bigger：更大，较大．
blame：责备，咎，非难，责任，罪，责怪，归咎．
bully：欺负．
cheeky：不要脸的．
contrary：相反，反而，相反的．
cool：凉，镇静，镇定，凉爽，凉爽的．
deliberate：商讨，故意的，成心．
duke：公爵，公．
excited：兴奋，兴奋的，兴高采烈，激昂的．
glad：高兴，高兴的．
graveyard：坟地，墓地．
idiot：白痴，笨蛋，傻子．
imaginary：虚构，虚构的．
inquire：查调，质问，询问．
kindness：仁慈，好意．
loose：松开，松弛的．
mighty：伟大，强势，强大的．
rush：速行，匆匆．
sarcastic：讽刺的．
shut：关闭．
slept：睡了．
squirm：蠕动．
stole：偷了．
till：直到．
trick：手法，骗术，秘诀，欺骗，玩意儿，花样．

The **duke** says, **pretty brisk**:

"When it comes to that, maybe you'll let me ask, what was *you* **referring** to?"

"Shucks!" says the king, very **sarcastic**; "but I don't know--maybe you was **asleep**, and didn't know what you was about."

The duke bristles up now, and says:

"Oh, let *up* on this cussed **nonsense**; do you take me for a **blame' fool**? Don't you **reckon** I know who **hid** that money in that coffin?"

"*Yes*, sir! I know you *do* know, because you done it yourself!"

"It's a **lie**!"--and the duke went for him. The king **sings** out:

"Take y'r hands off!--leggo my throat!--I take it all back!"

The duke says:

"Well, you just own up, first, that you *did* **hide** that money there, intending to give me the **slip** one of these days, and come back and **dig** it up, and have it all to yourself."

"Wait **jest** a minute, duke--answer me this one question, **honest** and **fair**; if you didn't put the money there, say it, and I'll b'lieve you, and take back everything I said."

"You old **scoundrel**, I didn't, and you know I didn't. There, now!"

"Well, then, I b'lieve you. But answer me only jest this one more--now *don't* git **mad**; didn't you have it in your mind to **hook** the money and hide it?"

The duke never said nothing for a little bit; then he says:

"Well, I don't care if I *did*, I didn't *do* it, anyway. But you not only had it in mind to do it, but you *done* it."

"I wisht I never **die** if I done it, duke, and that's honest. I won't say I warn't goin' to do it, because I *was*; but you--I mean somebody--got in **ahead** o' me."

"It's a lie! You done it, and you got to *say* you done it, or--"

The king began to **gurgle**, and then he gasps out:

"'Nough!--I *own up*!"

Chinese Simplified

ahead：前头，前方，前面的.
asleep：睡着，睡着的.
blame：责备，咎，非难，责任，罪，责怪，归咎.
brisk：活泼，活泼的.
die：逝世，不讳，死.
dig：挖掘.
duke：公爵，公.
fair：公平，博览会，清澈，公正，公道，展，直.
fool：呆子，笨蛋，傻子，笨人，愚人.
gurgle：汩汩声，汩汩.
hid：躲藏.
hide：躲藏，暗藏，掩饰，藏，隐瞒，隐藏.
honest：诚实，正直，清廉，刚正，坦白，正值，诚实的，体面，廉洁，深切.
hook：钩，钩子.
jest：玩笑，笑话，戏弄，戏谑.
lie：谎言，谎话，躺，撒谎，说谎.
mad：狂，发怒，发狂，生气，疯狂的.
nonsense：无聊，废话，屁话.
pretty：漂亮，美丽的，秀丽.
reckon：估计，计算.
referring：参考.
sarcastic：讽刺的.
scoundrel：无籁，坏蛋，无赖.
sings：唱.
slip：滑倒，溜走，溜.

I was very **glad** to hear him say that; it made me feel much more **easier** than what I was feeling before. So the **duke** took his hands off and says:

"If you ever **deny** it again I'll **drown** you. It's *well* for you to set there and **blubber** like a baby--it's fitten for you, after the way you've acted. I never see such an old **ostrich** for **wanting** to **gobble** everything-- and I a-trusting you all the time, like you was my own father. You **ought** to been **ashamed** of yourself to stand by and hear it saddled on to a lot of poor niggers, and you never say a word for 'em. It makes me feel **ridiculous** to think I was **soft** enough to *believe* that rubbage. Cuss you, I can see now why you was so **anxious** to make up the deffisit--you wanted to get what money I'd got out of the Nonesuch and one thing or another, and **scoop** it *all*!"

The king says, **timid**, and still a-snuffling:

"Why, duke, it was you that said make up the deffisit; it warn't me."

"**Dry** up! I don't want to hear no more out of you!" says the duke. "And *now* you see what you *got* by it. They've got all their own money back, and all of *ourn* but a shekel or two ***besides***. G'long to bed, and don't you deffersit *me* no more deffersits, long 's *you* live!"

So the king sneaked into the **wigwam** and took to his **bottle** for **comfort**, and before long the duke tackled *his* bottle; and so in about a half an hour they was as **thick** as thieves again, and the tighter they got the lovinger they got, and went off a-snoring in each other's arms. They both got **powerful mellow**, but I noticed the king didn't get mellow enough to **forget** to remember to not deny about **hiding** the money-bag again. That made me feel easy and **satisfied**. Of course when they got to **snoring** we had a long **gabble**, and I told Jim everything.

Chinese Simplified

anxious: 焦急，巴不得，担心，焦虑的.
ashamed: 惭愧，羞愧，惭愧的.
besides: 此外，另外，除了，并且，再说，况且.
blubber: 鲸脂.
bottle: 瓶，瓶子.
comfort: 安慰.
deny: 驳斥，否认.
drown: 使溺死，淹死，溺死.
dry: 索然，干燥，乾，干旱，乾燥.
duke: 公爵，公.
easier: 更容易.
forget: 忘记，忘，忘却.
gabble: 叽里咕噜.
glad: 高兴，高兴的.
gobble: 大吃，狼吞虎咽.
hiding: 隐匿.
mellow: 甜美多汁的.
ostrich: 鸵鸟.
ought: 应该，活该.
powerful: 强大，有力，强劲，强有力的.
ridiculous: 荒谬，荒谬的，岂有此理，可笑的.
satisfied: 满意，乐意，心满意足的.
scoop: 杓子，勺子，勺.
snoring: 打鼾.
soft: 柔软，柔和，柔软的.
thick: 厚，密，浓厚.
timid: 胆小，胆怯，胆怯的.
wanting: 缺少的，不足的.
wigwam: 帐篷，陋棚.

CHAPTER XXXI

YOU CAN'T PRAY A LIE

We dasn't stop again at any town for days and days; kept right along down the river. We was down south in the **warm weather** now, and a **mighty** long ways from home. We **begun** to come to **trees** with Spanish **moss** on them, hanging down from the limbs like long, **gray** beards. It was the first I ever see it growing, and it made the **woods** look **solemn** and **dismal**. So now the frauds reckoned they was out of **danger**, and they begun to work the **villages** again.

First they done a **lecture** on **temperance**; but they didn't make enough for them both to get **drunk** on. Then in another village they started a dancing-school; but they didn't know no more how to **dance** than a **kangaroo** does; so the first prance they made the general public **jumped** in and pranced them out of town. Another time they tried to go at yellocution; but they didn't yellocute long **till** the **audience** got up and give them a **solid** good cussing, and made them **skip** out. They tackled missionarying, and mesmerizing, and **doctoring**, and telling **fortunes**, and a little of everything; but they couldn't seem to have no **luck**. So at last they got just about dead **broke**, and **laid** around the **raft** as she floated along, thinking and thinking, and never saying nothing, by the half a day at a time, and **dreadful** blue and **desperate**.

Chinese Simplified

audience：听众．
begun：开始．
broke：打破．
dance：舞蹈，舞会，跳舞，舞．
danger：危险．
desperate：危急，非常的．
dismal：暗淡，忧郁的．
doctoring：医生．
dreadful：可怕，恐怖的．
drunk：喝了，喝醉．
fortunes：命运．
gray：灰色，灰．
jumped：跳跃．
kangaroo：袋鼠．
laid：放．
lecture：报告，讲课，演讲．
luck：运气，幸运．
mighty：伟大，强势，强大的．
moss：苔藓，苔．
raft：筏，木排，槎，桴．
skip：跳跃，跳过．
solemn：严肃，俨然，岸然，隆重，庄严的，庄重．
solid：固体，立体，固体的，坚硬，扎实，实心的，坚固的，坚实．
temperance：节制．
till：直到．
trees：树木．
villages：村庄．
warm：暖，暖和，温暖，热烈，温暖的．
weather：天气．
woods：树林，森林．

And at last they took a change and begun to lay their heads together in the **wigwam** and talk low and **confidential** two or three hours at a time. Jim and me got **uneasy**. We didn't like the look of it. We judged they was **studying** up some kind of worse deviltry than ever. We turned it over and over, and at last we made up our minds they was going to break into somebody's house or store, or was going into the counterfeit-money business, or something. So then we was pretty scared, and made up an **agreement** that we wouldn't have nothing in the world to do with such **actions**, and if we ever got the least show we would give them the cold **shake** and clear out and leave them **behind**. Well, early one morning we **hid** the **raft** in a good, safe place about two mile below a **little** bit of a **shabby** village named Pikesville, and the king he went **ashore** and told us all to stay hid whilst he went up to town and **smelt** around to see if anybody had got any wind of the Royal Nonesuch there yet. ("House to **rob**, you *mean*," says I to myself; "and when you get through **robbing** it you'll come back here and wonder what has become of me and Jim and the raft--and you'll have to take it out in wondering.") And he said if he warn't back by **midday** the **duke** and me would know it was all right, and we was to come along.

So we stayed where we was. The duke he fretted and **sweated** around, and was in a **mighty sour** way. He scolded us for everything, and we couldn't seem to do nothing right; he found fault with every little thing. Something was a-brewing, sure. I was good and glad when midday come and no king; we could have a change, anyway--and maybe a chance for *the* chance on top of it. So me and the duke went up to the village, and hunted around there for the king, and by and by we found him in the back room of a little low doggery, very **tight**, and a lot of loafers bullyragging him for sport, and he a-cussing and a-threatening with all his might, and so tight he couldn't walk, and couldn't do nothing to them. The duke he begun to **abuse** him for an old **fool**, and the king begun to **sass** back, and the minute they was fairly at it I lit out and shook the reefs out of my hind legs, and **spun** down the river road like a **deer**, for I see our chance; and I made up my mind that it would be a long day before they ever see me and Jim again. I got down there all out of breath but **loaded** up with **joy**, and **sung** out:

Chinese Simplified

abuse: 滥用，弊端，骂，虐待.
actions: 作用，行动.
agreement: 协定，协议，契约，合约，同意.
ashore: 岸上，上岸.
confidential: 机密的.
deer: 鹿.
duke: 公爵，公.
fool: 呆子，笨蛋，傻子，笨人，愚人.
hid: 躲藏.
hind: 后面的.
joy: 乐趣，快乐，高兴，喜悦.
lit: 点燃.
loaded: 载入.
midday: 正午，中午.
mighty: 伟大，强势，强大的.
raft: 筏，木排，槎，桴.
rob: 抢劫.
robbing: 抢劫.
sass: 顶嘴.
shabby: 破旧，破旧的.
shake: 摇动，震动，摇，震荡，颠簸.
smelt: 熔炼，溶解.
sour: 酸，酸味.
spun: 旋转.
studying: 学习.
sung: 唱歌.
sweated: 出汗.
tight: 严格，严密，紧，紧的，严竣，狭隘.
uneasy: 不安，担心，不安的.
wigwam: 帐篷，陋棚.

"Set her **loose**, Jim! we're all right now!"

But there warn't no **answer**, and **nobody** come out of the **wigwam**. Jim was gone! I set up a shout--and then another--and then another one; and run this way and that in the **woods**, whooping and screeching; but it warn't no use--old Jim was gone. Then I set down and cried; I couldn't help it. But I couldn't set still long. Pretty soon I went out on the road, trying to think what I **better** do, and I run across a **boy walking**, and asked him if he'd seen a **strange** nigger dressed so and so, and he says:

"Yes."

"Whereabouts?" says I.

"Down to Silas Phelps' place, two **mile below** here. He's a **runaway** nigger, and they've got him. Was you looking for him?"

"You bet I ain't! I run across him in the woods about an **hour** or two ago, and he said if I hollered he'd cut my livers out--and told me to **lay** down and **stay** where I was; and I done it. Been there ever since; afeard to come out."

"Well," he says, "you needn't be afeard no more, becuz they've got him. He run off f'm down South, som'ers."

"It's a good job they got him."

"Well, I *reckon*! There's two hunderd dollars **reward** on him. It's like **picking** up money out'n the road."

"Yes, it is--and I could a had it if I'd been big enough; I see him *first*. Who nailed him?"

"It was an old fellow--a stranger--and he **sold** out his **chance** in him for **forty** dollars, becuz he's got to go up the **river** and can't **wait**. Think o' that, now! You bet *I'd* wait, if it was seven year."

"That's me, every time," says I. "But **maybe** his chance ain't **worth** no more than that, if he'll **sell** it so **cheap**. Maybe there's something ain't **straight** about it."

Chinese Simplified

answer：回答，解答，答案，答复，答，响应，适合，负责，符合.
below：下面，以下.
bet：打赌，赌.
boy：男孩，男孩子，男孩儿，小子.
chance：机会.
cheap：低廉，便宜的，便宜.
forty：四十.
hour：小时，钟头，钟点，现在.
lay：产卵，安放，放，凡俗.
loose：松开，松弛的.
maybe：或许，也许，或者，说不定，可能，不一定.
mile：英里.
nobody：没有人，没人.
picking：选择，投纬.
reckon：估计，计算.
reward：报酬，酬劳，酬金，奖励，奖赏.
river：河，江，川，河流，条.
runaway：逃亡者，跑道.
sell：销售，游说，贩卖，出售.
sold：卖了.
stay：延缓，逗留，停留.
straight：直，海峡，径直，直接，笔直，一直.
strange：奇怪，奇特，陌生，奇异的，生疏.
wait：等待，等，伺候.
walking：步态，步行.
wigwam：帐篷，陋棚.
woods：树林，森林.
worth：价值，值，值得.

"But it *is*, though--straight as a string. I see the **handbill** myself. It tells all about him, to a dot--paints him like a picture, and tells the **plantation** he's frum, below Newr*leans*. No-sirree-*Bob*, they ain't no trouble 'bout *that* **speculation**, you bet you. Say, gimme a chaw tobacker, won't ye?"

I didn't have none, so he left. I went to the **raft**, and set down in the **wigwam** to think. But I couldn't come to nothing. I thought till I wore my head **sore**, but I couldn't see no way out of the trouble. After all this long journey, and after all we'd done for them scoundrels, here it was all come to nothing, everything all busted up and **ruined**, because they could have the heart to **serve** Jim such a **trick** as that, and make him a **slave** again all his life, and amongst **strangers**, too, for forty dirty dollars.

Once I said to myself it would be a thousand times better for Jim to be a slave at home where his family was, as long as he'd *got* to be a slave, and so I'd better write a letter to Tom Sawyer and tell him to tell Miss Watson where he was. But I soon give up that notion for two things: she'd be mad and **disgusted** at his rascality and **ungratefulness** for leaving her, and so she'd sell him straight down the river again; and if she didn't, everybody naturally despises an ungrateful nigger, and they'd make Jim feel it all the time, and so he'd feel **ornery** and **disgraced**. And then think of *me*! It would get all around that Huck Finn helped a nigger to get his freedom; and if I was ever to see anybody from that town again I'd be ready to get down and **lick** his boots for **shame**. That's just the way: a person does a **low**-down thing, and then he don't want to take no **consequences** of it. Thinks as long as he can hide, it ain't no disgrace. That was my **fix** exactly. The more I studied about this the more my **conscience** went to **grinding** me, and the more **wicked** and low-down and ornery I got to feeling. And at last, when it hit me all of a sudden that here was the **plain** hand of Providence slapping me in the face and letting me know my wickedness was being watched all the time from up there in **heaven**, whilst I was **stealing** a poor old woman's nigger that hadn't ever done me no harm, and now was showing me there's One that's always on the **lookout**, and ain't a-going to **allow** no such **miserable doings** to go only just so **fur** and no further, I most dropped in my

Chinese Simplified

allow: 容许，允许，任.
conscience: 良心.
consequences: 后果，後果.
disgrace: 耻辱.
disgusted: 厌恶.
doings: 做.
fix: 安装，奠定，固定，修理.
fur: 毛，软毛.
grinding: 磨的，磨削.
handbill: 传单.
heaven: 天堂，天，天空.
lick: 舔，舐.
lookout: 眺望，伸出窗口观看.
low-down: 非常低的，下作.
miserable: 悲惨，凄惨，困苦，凄惨的.
ornery: 低劣的.
plain: 平原.
plantation: 农园，种植园.
raft: 筏，木排，槎，桴.
ruined: 破败，毁坏.
serve: 侍候，伺候，待候.
shame: 羞耻.
slave: 奴隶.
sore: 疼痛，疮，疼痛的.
speculation: 推测，思索.
stealing: 偷垒，偷窃.
strangers: 陌生人.
trick: 手法，骗术，秘诀，欺骗，玩意儿，花样.
ungrateful: 忘恩负义，忘恩负义的.
wicked: 邪恶，邪恶的，恶性.
wigwam: 帐篷，陋棚.

tracks I was so scared. Well, I tried the best I could to kinder **soften** it up **somehow** for myself by saying I was brung up **wicked**, and so I warn't so much to **blame**; but something inside of me kept saying, "There was the Sunday-school, you could a gone to it; and if you'd a done it they'd a learnt you there that people that **acts** as I'd been **acting** about that nigger goes to **everlasting** fire."

It made me **shiver**. And I about made up my mind to **pray**, and see if I couldn't try to **quit** being the kind of a boy I was and be better. So I kneeled down. But the words wouldn't come. Why wouldn't they? It warn't no use to try and **hide** it from Him. Nor from *me*, neither. I knowed very well why they wouldn't come. It was because my heart warn't right; it was because I warn't square; it was because I was playing double. I was letting *on* to give up **sin**, but away inside of me I was holding on to the **biggest** one of all. I was trying to make my mouth *say* I would do the right thing and the clean thing, and go and write to that nigger's owner and tell where he was; but deep down in me I knowed it was a **lie**, and He knowed it. You can't pray a lie--I found that out.

So I was full of trouble, full as I could be; and didn't know what to do. At last I had an idea; and I says, I'll go and write the letter--and then see if I can pray. Why, it was **astonishing**, the way I felt as light as a **feather** right straight off, and my **troubles** all gone. So I got a piece of paper and a **pencil**, all **glad** and **excited**, and set down and wrote:

> Miss Watson, your **runaway** nigger Jim is down here two **mile** below Pikesville, and Mr. Phelps has got him and he will give him up for the **reward** if you send.
>
> HUCK FINN.

I felt good and all washed clean of sin for the first time I had ever felt so in my life, and I knowed I could pray now. But I didn't do it straight off, but **laid** the paper down and set there thinking--thinking how good it was all this happened so, and how near I come to being lost and going to hell. And went on thinking. And got to thinking over our **trip** down the river; and I see Jim before

Chinese Simplified

acting: 代理，临时的，代理的，行为．
acts: 作用，法案．
astonishing: 可惊，惊人，惊人的．
biggest: 最大．
blame: 责备，咎，非难，责任，罪，责怪，归咎．
everlasting: 永久，永久的，永恒的．
excited: 兴奋，兴奋的，兴高采烈，激昂的．
feather: 羽毛．
glad: 高兴，高兴的．
hide: 躲藏，暗藏，掩饰，藏，隐瞒，隐藏．
laid: 放．
lie: 谎言，谎话，躺，撒谎，说谎．
mile: 英里．
pencil: 铅笔，笔套，笔帽．
pray: 祈祷．
quit: 退出，退离．
reward: 报酬，酬劳，酬金，奖励，奖赏．
runaway: 逃亡者，跑道．
shiver: 发抖，颤抖，哆嗦．
sin: 罪恶，罪行．
soften: 变软，软化．
somehow: 不知何故．
tracks: 轨道．
trip: 旅程，旅游，旅行，跟头，旅途．
troubles: 坏处，麻烦．
wicked: 邪恶，邪恶的，恶性．

me all the time: in the day and in the night-time, sometimes **moonlight**, sometimes **storms**, and we a- **floating** along, talking and singing and laughing. But somehow I couldn't seem to strike no places to **harden** me against him, but only the other kind. I'd see him standing my watch on top of his'n, 'stead of calling me, so I could go on **sleeping**; and see him how glad he was when I come back out of the **fog**; and when I come to him again in the **swamp**, up there where the **feud** was; and such-like times; and would always call me **honey**, and **pet** me and do everything he could think of for me, and how good he always was; and at last I struck the time I saved him by telling the men we had small-pox **aboard**, and he was so grateful, and said I was the best friend old Jim ever had in the world, and the *only* one he's got now; and then I happened to look around and see that paper.

It was a close place. I took it up, and held it in my hand. I was a- **trembling**, because I'd got to **decide**, forever, **betwixt** two things, and I knowed it. I studied a minute, sort of holding my breath, and then says to myself:

"All right, then, I'll *go* to hell"--and **tore** it up.

It was awful **thoughts** and awful words, but they was said. And I let them stay said; and never thought no more about **reforming**. I shoved the whole thing out of my head, and said I would take up wickedness again, which was in my line, being brung up to it, and the other warn't. And for a **starter** I would go to work and **steal** Jim out of **slavery** again; and if I could think up anything worse, I would do that, too; because as long as I was in, and in for good, I might as well go the whole **hog**.

Then I set to thinking over how to get at it, and turned over some considerable many ways in my mind; and at last fixed up a plan that **suited** me. So then I took the **bearings** of a **woody** island that was down the river a piece, and as soon as it was fairly dark I **crept** out with my **raft** and went for it, and **hid** it there, and then turned in. I **slept** the night through, and got up before it was light, and had my breakfast, and put on my store clothes, and tied up some others and one thing or another in a **bundle**, and took the **canoe** and cleared for **shore**. I landed below where I judged was Phelps's place, and hid my bundle in

Chinese Simplified

aboard: 船上，在车，上.
bearings: 轴承.
betwixt: 中间，在…之间.
bundle: 捆，包裹，包，包扎，束，把.
canoe: 独木舟.
crept: 爬行.
decide: 判定，决定，作主.
feud: 世仇.
floating: 漂浮的，移动的，浮动的，飘浮.
fog: 雾.
harden: 板结，使硬化，硬化.
hid: 躲藏.
hog: 猪.
honey: 蜂蜜，蜜，蜜糖.
moonlight: 月光.
pet: 宠物.
raft: 筏，木排，槎，桴.
reforming: 改革.
shore: 岸，滨，岸边，海岸，海滨.
slavery: 奴隶制度，奴隶制.
sleeping: 睡眠，睡着.
slept: 睡了.
starter: 启动器，起动装置.
steal: 偷窃，盗窃，偷，窃取.
storms: 暴风雨.
suited: 适宜于.
swamp: 沼泽.
thoughts: 心头，感想.
tore: 撕扯.
trembling: 发抖，发抖的.
woody: 木制的，木质的.

the **woods**, and then filled up the **canoe** with water, and **loaded rocks** into her and **sunk** her where I could find her again when I wanted her, about a quarter of a **mile** below a little **steam sawmill** that was on the bank.

Then I **struck** up the road, and when I passed the mill I see a sign on it, "Phelps's Sawmill," and when I come to the farm-houses, two or three hundred **yards** further along, I kept my eyes peeled, but didn't see nobody around, though it was good **daylight** now. But I didn't mind, because I didn't want to see nobody just yet--I only wanted to get the lay of the land. **According** to my plan, I was going to turn up there from the village, not from below. So I just took a look, and **shoved** along, straight for town. Well, the very first man I see when I got there was the **duke**. He was sticking up a bill for the Royal Nonesuch--three-night performance--like that other time. They had the **cheek**, them frauds! I was right on him before I could **shirk**. He looked **astonished**, and says:

"Hel-*lo*! Where'd *you* come from?" Then he says, kind of **glad** and **eager**, "Where's the **raft**?--got her in a good place?"

I says:

"Why, that's just what I was going to ask your grace."

Then he didn't look so **joyful**, and says:

"What was your idea for asking *me*?" he says.

"Well," I says, "when I see the king in that doggery yesterday I says to myself, we can't get him home for hours, **till** he's soberer; so I went a- loafing around town to put in the time and wait. A man up and offered me ten cents to help him **pull** a **skiff** over the river and back to **fetch** a **sheep**, and so I went along; but when we was **dragging** him to the **boat**, and the man left me a-holt of the **rope** and went behind him to shove him along, he was too strong for me and jerked **loose** and run, and we after him. We didn't have no dog, and so we had to **chase** him all over the country till we **tired** him out. We never got him till dark; then we fetched him over, and I started down for the raft. When I got there and see it was gone, I says to myself, 'They've got into trouble and had to leave; and they've took my nigger, which is the only nigger I've got in the world, and now

Chinese Simplified

according: 根据.
astonished: 诧异.
boat: 小船，船，帆船，乘务员.
canoe: 独木舟.
chase: 追逐，驱赶.
cheek: 脸颊.
daylight: 日光，白天.
dragging: 拖，拖动，拖曳.
duke: 公爵，公.
eager: 切望，踊跃，急切，渴望的.
fetch: 拿，取，带来.
glad: 高兴，高兴的.
joyful: 欢喜，快乐的，欢喜的.
loaded: 载入.
loose: 松开，松弛的.
mile: 英里.
mill: 磨子，磨坊.
pull: 拉，牵引.
raft: 筏，木排，槎，桴.
rocks: 岩石.
rope: 绳索，绳子.
sawmill: 锯木厂.
sheep: 羊，绵羊.
shirk: 逃避，推卸.
shove: 推.
skiff: 小船，小艇.
steam: 蒸汽，热气，废气，蒸.
struck: 敲打.
sunk: 沉没.
till: 直到.
tired: 疲倦，疲乏，疲倦的.
woods: 树林，森林.
yards: 场地.

I'm in a **strange** country, and ain't got no property no more, nor nothing, and no way to make my living;' so I set down and cried. I **slept** in the **woods** all night. But what *did* become of the **raft**, then?--and Jim--poor Jim!"

"Blamed if I know--that is, what's become of the raft. That old **fool** had made a trade and got **forty** dollars, and when we found him in the doggery the loafers had matched half-dollars with him and got every **cent** but what he'd **spent** for **whisky**; and when I got him home late last night and found the raft gone, we said, 'That little **rascal** has **stole** our raft and **shook** us, and run off down the river.'"

"I wouldn't **shake** my *nigger*, would I?--the only nigger I had in the world, and the only property."

"We never thought of that. Fact is, I **reckon** we'd come to consider him *our* nigger; yes, we did consider him so--goodness **knows** we had trouble enough for him. So when we see the raft was gone and we **flat broke**, there warn't anything for it but to try the Royal Nonesuch another shake. And I've pegged along ever since, **dry** as a powder-horn. Where's that ten cents? Give it here."

I had considerable money, so I give him ten cents, but **begged** him to **spend** it for something to **eat**, and give me some, because it was all the money I had, and I hadn't had nothing to eat since yesterday. He never said nothing. The next **minute** he **whirls** on me and says:

"Do you reckon that nigger would **blow** on us? We'd **skin** him if he done that!"

"How can he blow? Hain't he run off?"

"No! That old fool **sold** him, and never divided with me, and the money's gone."

"*Sold* him?" I says, and **begun** to **cry**; "why, he was *My* nigger, and that was my money. Where is he?--I want my nigger."

"Well, you can't *get* your nigger, that's all--so dry up your blubbering. Looky here--do you think *You'd* **venture** to blow on us? Blamed if I think I'd trust you. Why, if you *was* to blow on us--"

Chinese Simplified

begged: 乞求.
begun: 开始.
blow: 吹, 打击.
broke: 打破.
cent: 一分钱, 分.
cry: 喊, 叫, 哭, 哭泣.
dry: 索然, 干燥, 乾, 干旱, 乾燥.
eat: 吃.
flat: 平坦, 平板, 平坦的, 平的, 居室.
fool: 呆子, 笨蛋, 傻子, 笨人, 愚人.
forty: 四十.
knows: 知道.
minute: 分钟, 详细, 分, 微小的, 渺小.
raft: 筏, 木排, 槎, 桴.
rascal: 小淘气, 流氓.
reckon: 估计, 计算.
shake: 摇动, 震动, 摇, 震荡, 颠簸.
shook: 摇动.
skin: 皮肤, 剥皮.
slept: 睡了.
sold: 卖了.
spend: 度过, 花费, 支出, 耗费.
spent: 耗费了.
stole: 偷了.
strange: 奇怪, 奇特, 陌生, 奇异的, 生疏.
venture: 冒险, 敢.
whirls: 旋转.
whisky: 威士忌酒.
woods: 树林, 森林.

He **stopped**, but I never see the **duke** look so **ugly** out of his eyes before. I went on a-whimpering, and says:

"I don't want to **blow** on **nobody**; and I ain't got no time to blow, nohow. I got to turn out and find my nigger."

He looked kinder bothered, and stood there with his bills **fluttering** on his arm, thinking, and wrinkling up his **forehead**. At last he says:

"I'll tell you something. We got to be here three days. If you'll **promise** you won't blow, and won't let the nigger blow, I'll tell you where to find him."

So I promised, and he says:

"A **farmer** by the name of Silas Ph--" and then he stopped. You see, he started to tell me the **truth**; but when he stopped that way, and **begun** to study and think again, I reckoned he was **changing** his mind. And so he was. He wouldn't trust me; he wanted to make sure of having me out of the way the whole three days. So **pretty** soon he says:

"The man that **bought** him is named Abram **Foster**--Abram G. Foster--and he lives **forty mile** back here in the country, on the road to Lafayette."

"All right," I says, "I can walk it in three days. And I'll start this very afternoon."

"No you **wont**, you'll start *now*; and don't you **lose** any time about it, **neither**, nor do any gabbling by the way. Just keep a **tight tongue** in your head and move right along, and then you won't get into **trouble** with *us*, d'ye hear?"

That was the order I wanted, and that was the one I played for. I wanted to be left free to work my plans.

"So clear out," he says; "and you can tell Mr. Foster whatever you want to. Maybe you can get him to believe that Jim *is* your nigger--some **idiots** don't **require** documents--leastways I've heard there's such down South here. And when you tell him the **handbill** and the reward's **bogus**, maybe he'll believe you when you **explain** to him what the idea was for getting 'em out. Go 'long now,

Chinese Simplified

begun: 开始.
blow: 吹，打击.
bogus: 假的.
bought: 买了.
changing: 变化.
duke: 公爵，公.
explain: 辩解，解释，申述，交代，澄清.
farmer: 农人，农夫.
fluttering: 颤动.
forehead: 前额，额，额头.
forty: 四十.
foster: 养育，扶植，哺育，助长，养母，养父.
handbill: 传单.
idiots: 白痴.
lose: 丢失，丧失，失掉，遗失.
mile: 英里.
neither: 也不，二者，两者都不是.
nobody: 没有人，没人.
pretty: 漂亮，美丽的，秀丽.
promise: 答应，约定，承诺，誓言，诺言，允诺.
require: 要求，要有，需要.
stopped: 停止.
tight: 严格，严密，紧，紧的，严竣，狭隘.
tongue: 舌头，舌.
trouble: 麻烦，难度，难处.
truth: 真理，实话.
ugly: 丑陋的，难看的，难看，丑恶，丑的.
wont: 习惯.

and tell him anything you want to; but mind you don't work your **jaw** any *between* here and there."

So I left, and **struck** for the back country. I didn't look around, but I kinder felt like he was watching me. But I knowed I could **tire** him out at that. I went **straight** out in the country as much as a **mile** before I **stopped**; then I **doubled** back through the **woods** towards Phelps'. I reckoned I better start in on my **plan** straight off without fooling around, because I wanted to stop Jim's **mouth till** these fellows could get away. I didn't want no **trouble** with their kind. I'd seen all I wanted to of them, and wanted to get **entirely shut** of them.

Chinese Simplified

doubled：双，加倍努力.
entirely：完全，全部地.
jaw：颚，颌.
mile：英里.
mouth：口，嘴巴，嘴，吻.
plan：计划，方案，规划，设计，主意，计画，擘画，打算，设计图.
shut：关闭.
stop：停止，终止，截止，站.
stopped：停止.
straight：直，海峡，迳直，直接，笔直，一直.
struck：敲打.
till：直到.
tire：疲倦.
trouble：麻烦，难度，难处.
woods：树林，森林.

CHAPTER XXXII

I HAVE A NEW NAME

When I got there it was all still and Sunday-like, and hot and **sunshiny**; the hands was gone to the fields; and there was them kind of **faint** dronings of bugs and flies in the air **that** makes it seem so **lonesome** and like everybody's dead and gone; and if a **breeze** fans along and quivers the **leaves** it makes you feel **mournful**, because you feel like it's **spirits** whispering--spirits that's been dead ever so many years--and you always think they're talking about *you*. As a general thing it makes a body wish *he* was dead, too, and done with it all.

Phelps' was one of these little **one**-horse **cotton plantations**, and they all look **alike**. A **rail fence** round a two-acre **yard**; a stile made out of **logs sawed** off and up-ended in steps, like **barrels** of a different length, to **climb** over the fence with, and for the women to stand on when they are going to **jump** on to a horse; some sickly grass-patches in the big yard, but **mostly** it was **bare** and **smooth**, like an old hat with the **nap rubbed** off; big **double** log-house for the white folks--hewed logs, with the chinks stopped up with **mud** or **mortar**, and these mud-stripes been whitewashed some time or another; round-log kitchen, with a big **broad**, open but roofed **passage** joining it to the house; log smoke-house back of the kitchen; three little log nigger-cabins in a **row** t'other side the smoke-house; one little **hut** all by itself away down against the back fence, and some outbuildings

Chinese Simplified

alike：相同.
bare：赤裸裸，赤裸的.
barrels：桶.
breeze：和风.
broad：宽，宽广.
climb：爬，攀登.
cotton：棉花，棉.
double：双重，双，加倍.
faint：暗淡，隐约，昏厥，微弱.
fence：篱笆，栅栏，栏位，栏.
hat：帽子.
hut：茅舍，棚屋.
jump：跳，跳跃.
leaves：离开.
log：圆形木材，圆木，木头.
lonesome：寂寞，寂寞的.
mortar：臼，迫击炮.
mostly：大多，多半，大部份.
mournful：悲切，悲恸，悲恸的.
mud：泥，泥浆.
nap：瞌睡.
one-horse：单马拉的.
passage：通道，通路，通过.
plantations：种植园.
rail：铁路，轨道.
row：一排，划，行.
rubbed：摩擦.
sawed：锯.
smooth：平稳，润滑，光滑，平滑，通顺.
spirits：精神.
sunshiny：阳光照耀的.
yard：码，厂，厂子，场地.

down a piece the other side; ash-hopper and big **kettle** to **bile soap** in by the little **hut**; **bench** by the kitchen door, with **bucket** of water and a **gourd**; **hound** asleep there in the sun; more hounds asleep round about; about three **shade** trees away off in a corner; some currant **bushes** and **gooseberry** bushes in one place by the **fence**; outside of the fence a garden and a **watermelon patch**; then the cotton fields begins, and after the fields the woods.

I went around and clumb over the back stile by the ash-hopper, and started for the kitchen. When I got a little ways I heard the **dim hum** of a spinning-wheel wailing along up and **sinking** along down again; and then I knowed for certain I wished I was dead--for that *is* the lonesomest sound in the whole world.

I went right along, not **fixing** up any particular plan, but just trusting to Providence to put the right words in my mouth when the time come; for I'd noticed that Providence always did put the right words in my mouth if I left it alone.

When I got **half**-way, first one hound and then another got up and went for me, and of course I stopped and faced them, and kept still. And such another **powwow** as they made! In a quarter of a minute I was a kind of a **hub** of a wheel, as you may say--spokes made out of dogs--circle of fifteen of them **packed** together around me, with their necks and noses **stretched** up towards me, a-barking and **howling**; and more a-coming; you could see them **sailing** over **fences** and around corners from everywheres.

A nigger woman come **tearing** out of the kitchen with a rolling-pin in her hand, singing out, "Begone *you* Tige! you Spot! begone sah!" and she fetched first one and then another of them a **clip** and sent them howling, and then the rest followed; and the next second half of them come back, wagging their **tails** around me, and making friends with me. There ain't no harm in a hound, nohow.

And behind the woman comes a little nigger girl and two little nigger boys without anything on but tow-linen shirts, and they **hung** on to their mother's **gown**, and peeped out from behind her at me, **bashful**, the way they always do. And here comes the white woman running from the house, about **forty**-five or

Chinese Simplified

bashful: 怕羞，怕羞的.
bench: 长椅，长凳.
bile: 胆汁.
bucket: 水桶，桶.
bushes: 灌木.
clip: 夹子，回形针.
dim: 阴暗，暗淡，暗淡的.
fence: 篱笆，栅栏，栏位，栏.
fences: 栅栏.
fixing: 定影，固定.
forty-five: 四十五，四十五个.
gooseberry: 醋栗，醋栗酒.
gourd: 葫芦.
gown: 长袍，女装长袍.
half-way: 半途.
hound: 猎犬.
howling: 咆哮的，啸声.
hub: 中转站，集线器，中枢.
hum: 哼，哼声，嗡嗡声，嗡嗡.
hung: 挂.
hut: 茅舍，棚屋.
kettle: 水壶.
packed: 挤得满满的.
patch: 补缀，补丁，补.
powwow: 巫师.
sailing: 航海术，航海，航行.
shade: 荫，荫凉，阴影，树阴.
sinking: 沉没.
soap: 肥皂.
stretched: 伸展.
tails: 尾巴.
tearing: 撕裂的.
watermelon: 西瓜.

fifty year old, **bareheaded**, and her spinning-stick in her hand; and behind her comes her little white children, **acting** the same way the little niggers was going. She was **smiling** all over so she could **hardly** stand--and says:

"It's *you*, at last!--*ain't* it?"

I out with a "Yes'm" before I thought.

She grabbed me and **hugged** me **tight**; and then gripped me by both hands and **shook** and shook; and the **tears** come in her eyes, and run down over; and she couldn't seem to hug and **shake** enough, and kept saying, "You don't look as much like your mother as I reckoned you would; but law sakes, I don't care for that, I'm so **glad** to see you! Dear, **dear**, it does seem like I could **eat** you up! Children, it's your **cousin** Tom!--tell him howdy."

But they **ducked** their **heads**, and put their fingers in their **mouths**, and **hid** behind her. So she run on:

"Lize, **hurry** up and get him a **hot breakfast** right away--or did you get your breakfast on the **boat**?"

I said I had got it on the boat. So then she started for the house, **leading** me by the hand, and the children **tagging** after. When we got there she set me down in a split-bottomed **chair**, and set herself down on a little low **stool** in front of me, holding both of my hands, and says:

"Now I can have a *good* look at you; and, laws-a-me, I've been **hungry** for it a many and a many a time, all these long years, and it's come at last! We been expecting you a couple of days and more. What kep' you?--boat get aground?"

"Yes'm--she--"

"Don't say yes'm--say Aunt Sally. Where'd she get aground?"

I didn't **rightly** know what to say, because I didn't know whether the boat would be coming up the **river** or down. But I go a good deal on **instinct**; and my instinct said she would be coming up--from down towards Orleans. That didn't help me much, though; for I didn't know the names of bars down that way. I see

Chinese Simplified

acting: 代理，临时的，代理的，行为.
bareheaded: 光头.
boat: 小船，船，帆船，乘务员.
breakfast: 早餐，早饭，早点.
chair: 椅子.
cousin: 表亲，表哥，堂表.
dear: 亲爱，亲爱的，可爱的.
ducked: 鸭.
eat: 吃.
fifty: 五十，半白.
glad: 高兴，高兴的.
hardly: 几乎不，毫不，辛苦地.
heads: 头.
hid: 躲藏.
hot: 热.
hug: 紧抱，拥抱.
hungry: 饥饿，饿，饥饿的.
hurry: 仓促，匆忙，赶忙.
instinct: 本能.
leading: 领导.
mouths: 口.
rightly: 正确地.
river: 河，江，川，河流，条.
shake: 摇动，震动，摇，震荡，颠簸.
shook: 摇动.
smiling: 微笑的.
stool: 凳，凳子.
tagging: 加标签.
tears: 泪，泪水，眼泪.
tight: 严格，严密，紧，紧的，严竣，狭隘.

I'd got to **invent** a bar, or **forget** the name of the one we got **aground** on--or-- Now I **struck** an idea, and **fetched** it out:

"It warn't the grounding--that didn't keep us back but a little. We blowed out a cylinder-head."

"Good **gracious**! **anybody hurt**?"

"No'm. Killed a nigger."

"Well, it's **lucky**; because sometimes people do get hurt. Two years ago last Christmas your **uncle** Silas was coming up from Newrleans on the old Lally Rook, and she blowed out a cylinder-head and **crippled** a man. And I **think** he **died afterwards**. He was a Baptist. Your uncle Silas knowed a family in Baton Rouge that knowed his people very well. Yes, I remember now, he *did* die. Mortification set in, and they had to amputate him. But it didn't save him. Yes, it was mortification--that was it. He turned blue all over, and died in the hope of a **glorious resurrection**. They say he was a **sight** to look at. Your uncle's been up to the town every day to fetch you. And he's gone again, not more'n an hour ago; he'll be back any **minute** now. You must a met him on the road, didn't you?-- oldish man, with a--"

"No, I didn't see **nobody**, Aunt Sally. The **boat landed** just at **daylight**, and I left my **baggage** on the wharf-boat and went looking around the town and out a piece in the country, to put in the time and not get here too soon; and so I come down the back way."

"Who'd you give the baggage to?"

"Nobody."

"Why, child, it 'll be stole!"

"Not where I **hid** it I **reckon** it won't," I says.

"How'd you get your **breakfast** so early on the boat?"

It was kinder thin **ice**, but I says:

Chinese Simplified

afterwards: 后来，然后，以后，此后，後，然後，后，过后，底下，此後，後来.
aground: 在地上.
anybody: 任何人.
baggage: 行李.
boat: 小船，船，帆船，乘务员.
breakfast: 早餐，早饭，早点.
crippled: 瘫痪.
daylight: 日光，白天.
die: 逝世，不讳，死.
fetch: 拿，取，带来.
forget: 忘记，忘，忘却.
glorious: 壮丽，辉煌，光荣的.
gracious: 亲切，亲切的，有礼貌的.
hid: 躲藏.
hurt: 伤害，使受伤.
ice: 冰.
invent: 编造，发明.
landed: 着陆.
lucky: 幸运，幸运的，吉祥.
minute: 分钟，详细，分，微小的，渺小.
nobody: 没有人，没人.
reckon: 估计，计算.
resurrection: 复活.
sight: 视觉，景象，情景，目光，视力，视线.
struck: 敲打.
thin: 薄，疏，细，淡.
uncle: 叔叔，伯伯，叔父，大爷，老大爷，姑夫.

"The captain see me **standing** around, and told me I better have something to **eat** before I went **ashore**; so he took me in the **texas** to the **officers' lunch**, and give me all I wanted."

I was getting so **uneasy** I couldn't **listen** good. I had my mind on the children all the time; I wanted to get them out to one side and **pump** them a little, and find out who I was. But I couldn't get no show, Mrs. Phelps kept it up and run on so. Pretty soon she made the **cold chills streak** all down my back, because she says:

"But here we're a-running on this way, and you hain't told me a word about Sis, nor any of them. Now I'll rest my works a little, and you start up yourn; just tell me *everything*--tell me all about 'm all every one of 'm; and how they are, and what they're doing, and what they told you to tell me; and every last thing you can think of."

Well, I see I was up a stump--and up it good. Providence had stood by me this **fur** all right, but I was hard and **tight aground** now. I see it warn't a bit of use to try to go ahead--I'd got to **throw** up my hand. So I says to myself, here's another place where I got to resk the **truth**. I **opened** my **mouth** to **begin**; but she grabbed me and hustled me in behind the bed, and says:

"Here he comes! Stick your head down lower--there, that'll do; you can't be seen now. Don't you let on you're here. I'll play a **joke** on him. Children, don't you say a word."

I see I was in a **fix** now. But it warn't no use to **worry**; there warn't nothing to do but just hold still, and try and be **ready** to stand from under when the **lightning struck**.

I had just one little **glimpse** of the old **gentleman** when he come in; then the bed **hid** him. Mrs. Phelps she **jumps** for him, and says:

"Has he come?"

"No," says her husband.

"Good-*ness* gracious!" she says, "what in the warld can have become of him?"

Chinese Simplified

aground：在地上.
ashore：岸上，上岸.
begin：开始，开创，发起，掀起，兴办.
chills：寒冷.
cold：冷，感冒，寒冷，寒，冷淡.
eat：吃.
fix：安装，奠定，固定，修理.
fur：毛，软毛.
gentleman：绅士.
glimpse：一瞥，瞥见.
hid：躲藏.
joke：笑话，玩笑，开玩笑.
jumps：跳跃.
lightning：闪电.
listen：听，倾听.
lunch：午餐，午饭.
mouth：口，嘴巴，嘴，吻.
officers：官员.
opened：打开.
pump：唧筒，泵.
ready：就绪，愿意，准备，妥当.
standing：站立，地位.
streak：斑纹，线条.
struck：敲打.
texas：德克萨斯，得克萨斯.
throw：扔，丢掉，丢，投.
tight：严格，严密，紧，紧的，严竣，狭隘.
truth：真理，实话.
uneasy：不安，担心，不安的.
worry：担心，使烦恼，缠绕，担忧，心事，担，烦恼，着急.

"I can't imagine," says the old **gentleman**; "and I must say it makes me **dreadful** uneasy."

"Uneasy!" she says; "I'm **ready** to go **distracted**! He *must* a come; and you've missed him along the road. I *know* it's so--something tells me so."

"Why, Sally, I *couldn't* miss him along the road--*you* know that."

"But oh, **dear**, dear, what *will* Sis say! He must a come! You must a missed him. He--"

"Oh, don't **distress** me any more'n I'm already **distressed**. I don't know what in the world to make of it. I'm at my wit's end, and I don't mind **acknowledging** 't I'm right down scared. But there's no hope that he's come; for he *couldn't* come and me miss him. Sally, it's terrible--just terrible--something's happened to the **boat**, sure!"

"Why, Silas! Look yonder!--up the road!--ain't that **somebody** coming?"

He **sprung** to the **window** at the head of the bed, and that give Mrs. Phelps the chance she wanted. She **stooped** down **quick** at the **foot** of the bed and give me a **pull**, and out I come; and when he turned back from the window there she stood, a-beaming and a-smiling like a house **afire**, and I **standing pretty meek** and sweaty **alongside**. The old gentleman stared, and says:

"Why, who's that?"

"Who do you **reckon** 't is?"

"I hain't no idea. Who *is* it?"

"It's *Tom Sawyer*!"

By jings, I most slumped through the floor! But there warn't no time to **swap** knives; the old man grabbed me by the hand and **shook**, and **kept** on **shaking**; and all the time how the woman did **dance** around and **laugh** and **cry**; and then how they both did fire off questions about Sid, and Mary, and the rest of the **tribe**.

But if they was **joyful**, it warn't nothing to what I was; for it was like being **born** again, I was so **glad** to find out who I was. Well, they froze to me for two

Chinese Simplified

acknowledging: 承认.
afire: 大为激动.
alongside: 并肩, 在旁边.
boat: 小船, 船, 帆船, 乘务员.
born: 出生, 天生的.
cry: 喊, 叫, 哭, 哭泣.
dance: 舞蹈, 舞会, 跳舞, 舞.
dear: 亲爱, 亲爱的, 可爱的.
distracted: 怅惘, 心烦意乱的.
distress: 苦恼, 悲痛.
distressed: 苦恼, 哀伤.
dreadful: 可怕, 恐怖的.
foot: 脚, 足, 步兵, 英尺, 呎.
gentleman: 绅士.
glad: 高兴, 高兴的.
joyful: 欢喜, 快乐的, 欢喜的.
kept: 收存.
laugh: 笑.
meek: 谦顺的.
pretty: 漂亮, 美丽的, 秀丽.
pull: 拉, 牵引.
quick: 快, 玲珑, 敏捷的, 迅速的.
ready: 就绪, 愿意, 准备, 妥当.
reckon: 估计, 计算.
shaking: 摇动.
shook: 摇动.
somebody: 某人, 有人.
sprung: 弹跳.
standing: 站立, 地位.
stooped: 弯腰.
swap: 交换.
tribe: 部落, 部族.
window: 窗口, 窗户, 窗, 窗子.

hours; and at last, when my **chin** was so **tired** it couldn't **hardly** go any more, I had told them more about my family--I mean the Sawyer family--than ever happened to any six Sawyer **families**. And I explained all about how we blowed out a cylinder-head at the **mouth** of White River, and it took us three days to **fix** it. Which was all right, and worked first-rate; because *they* didn't know but what it would take three days to fix it. If I'd a called it a bolthead it would a done just as well.

Now I was **feeling pretty comfortable** all down one side, and pretty **uncomfortable** all up the other. Being Tom Sawyer was easy and comfortable, and it **stayed** easy and comfortable **till** by and by I hear a **steamboat coughing** along down the **river**. Then I says to myself, s'pose Tom Sawyer comes down on that boat? And s'pose he **steps** in here any **minute**, and **sings** out my name before I can **throw** him a **wink** to keep **quiet**?

Well, I couldn't *have* it that way; it wouldn't do at all. I must go up the road and waylay him. So I told the folks I reckoned I would go up to the town and **fetch** down my **baggage**. The old **gentleman** was for going along with me, but I said no, I could **drive** the **horse** myself, and I druther he wouldn't take no **trouble** about me.

Chinese Simplified

baggage: 行李.
boat: 小船, 船, 帆船, 乘务员.
chin: 下巴, 颏.
comfortable: 舒服, 舒服的.
coughing: 咳嗽.
drive: 驱动器, 精神, 驾车, 驾驶, 志气, 驾.
families: 家庭.
feeling: 感觉, 情绪, 感情, 情感, 思绪.
fetch: 拿, 取, 带来.
fix: 安装, 奠定, 固定, 修理.
gentleman: 绅士.
hardly: 几乎不, 毫不, 辛苦地.
horse: 马.
minute: 分钟, 详细, 分, 微小的, 渺小.
mouth: 口, 嘴巴, 嘴, 吻.
pretty: 漂亮, 美丽的, 秀丽.
quiet: 安静, 寂静, 安定, 安生, 沉静, 宁静的.
river: 河, 江, 川, 河流, 条.
sings: 唱.
stayed: 停留.
steamboat: 汽船, 轮船.
steps: 步骤.
throw: 扔, 丢掉, 丢, 投.
till: 直到.
tired: 疲倦, 疲乏, 疲倦的.
trouble: 麻烦, 难度, 难处.
uncomfortable: 不舒适, 不舒适的, 拘束, 别扭.
wink: 眨眼, 眨眼睛.

CHAPTER XXXIII

THE PITIFUL ENDING OF ROYALTY

So I **started** for **town** in the **wagon**, and when I was **half**-way I see a wagon **coming**, and **sure** enough it was Tom Sawyer, and I **stopped** and waited **till** he come **along**. I says "Hold on!" and it stopped **alongside**, and his **mouth opened** up like a **trunk**, and **stayed** so; and he swallowed two or three times like a person that's got a **dry throat**, and then says:

"I hain't ever done you no **harm**. You know that. So, then, what you want to come back and ha'nt *me* for?"

I says:

"I hain't come back--I hain't been *gone*."

When he **heard** my voice it righted him up some, but he warn't quite **satisfied** yet. He says:

"Don't you **play** nothing on me, because I wouldn't on you. **Honest** injun, you ain't a ghost?"

"Honest injun, I ain't," I says.

"Well--I--I--well, that **ought** to **settle** it, of **course**; but I can't **somehow seem** to **understand** it no way. Looky here, warn't you ever murdered *at all*?"

Chinese Simplified

along: 沿着，沿，一同.
alongside: 并肩，在旁边.
coming: 未来，到来.
course: 课程，经过，进程，路程，路线，学科，过程.
dry: 索然，干燥，乾，干旱，乾燥.
half-way: 半途.
harm: 伤害，损害，坏处，害处，祸害.
heard: 听见.
honest: 诚实，正直，清廉，刚正，坦白，正値，诚实的，体面，廉洁，深切.
mouth: 口，嘴巴，嘴，吻.
opened: 打开.
ought: 应该，活该.
play: 表演，戏剧，游戏，玩，演出，戏，剧本，扮演，悬念，弹奏，奏.
satisfied: 满意，乐意，心满意足的.
seem: 显得，看来，彷佛，好象.
settle: 奠定，安家落户，澄清，解决.
somehow: 不知何故.
started: 开始.
stayed: 停留.
stopped: 停止.
sure: 肯定.
throat: 嗓子，喉咙，喉头，咽喉.
till: 直到.
town: 城镇，城市，市镇.
trunk: 躯干，主干，树干.
understand: 了解，明白，理解，领会.
wagon: 列车厢.

"No. I warn't ever murdered at all--I played it on them. You come in here and feel of me if you don't believe me."

So he done it; and it **satisfied** him; and he was that **glad** to see me again he didn't know what to do. And he wanted to know all about it right off, because it was a **grand adventure**, and **mysterious**, and so it hit him where he lived. But I said, leave it **alone till** by and by; and told his **driver** to wait, and we **drove** off a **little** piece, and I told him the kind of a **fix** I was in, and what did he **reckon** we better do? He said, let him alone a minute, and don't **disturb** him. So he **thought** and thought, and **pretty** soon he says:

"It's all right; I've got it. Take my **trunk** in your **wagon**, and let on it's your'n; and you turn back and **fool** along **slow**, so as to get to the house about the time you ought to; and I'll go towards town a piece, and take a fresh start, and get there a quarter or a half an hour after you; and you needn't let on to know me at first."

I says:

"All right; but wait a minute. There's one more thing--a thing that ***nobody*** don't know but me. And that is, there's a nigger here that I'm a- trying to **steal** out of **slavery**, and his name is *Jim*--old Miss Watson's Jim."

He says:

"What! Why, Jim is--"

He stopped and went to **studying**. I says:

"I know what you'll say. You'll say it's **dirty**, **low**-down business; but what if it is? I'm low down; and I'm a-going to steal him, and I want you keep mum and not let on. Will you?"

His eye lit up, and he says:

"I'll *help* you steal him!"

Well, I let go all holts then, like I was shot. It was the most **astonishing** speech I ever heard--and I'm **bound** to say Tom Sawyer fell considerable in my **estimation**. Only I couldn't believe it. Tom Sawyer a *nigger-stealer*!

Chinese Simplified

adventure：冒险，探险.
alone：独自，单独，单纯，单独地.
astonishing：可惊，惊人，惊人的.
bound：限，边际，弹回，范围.
dirty：肮脏，脏脏，肮脏的，混浊.
disturb：打扰，惊动，扰乱，干扰.
driver：司机，开车人.
drove：驾.
estimation：估计.
fix：安装，奠定，固定，修理.
fool：呆子，笨蛋，傻子，笨人，愚人.
glad：高兴，高兴的.
grand：堂皇，隆重，雄伟，盛大，宏大，大型的，宏伟.
lit：点燃.
low-down：非常低的，下作.
mysterious：神秘，莫名其妙，神秘的.
nobody：没有人，没人.
ought：应该，活该.
pretty：漂亮，美丽的，秀丽.
reckon：估计，计算.
satisfied：满意，乐意，心满意足的.
slavery：奴隶制度，奴隶制.
slow：慢，缓慢，迟慢，迟钝，迟迟，迟缓.
steal：偷窃，盗窃，偷，窃取.
studying：学习.
till：直到.
trunk：躯干，主干，树干.
wagon：列车厢.

"Oh, shucks!" I says; "you're **joking**."

"I ain't joking, either."

"Well, then," I says, "joking or no joking, if you hear anything said about a **runaway** nigger, don't forget to remember that *you* don't know nothing about him, and I don't know nothing about him."

Then we took the **trunk** and put it in my **wagon**, and he **drove** off his way and I drove mine. But of course I **forgot** all about driving slow on accounts of being **glad** and full of thinking; so I got home a **heap** too quick for that length of a **trip**. The old gentleman was at the door, and he says:

"Why, this is wonderful! Whoever would a thought it was in that **mare** to do it? I wish we'd a timed her. And she hain't **sweated** a hair--not a hair. It's wonderful. Why, I wouldn't take a hundred dollars for that horse now--I wouldn't, **honest**; and yet I'd a sold her for fifteen before, and thought 'twas all she was worth."

That's all he said. He was the innocentest, best old **soul** I ever see. But it warn't **surprising**; because he warn't only just a **farmer**, he was a **preacher**, too, and had a little **one**-horse **log** church down back of the **plantation**, which he built it himself at his own **expense**, for a church and **schoolhouse**, and never charged nothing for his **preaching**, and it was worth it, too. There was plenty other farmer-preachers like that, and done the same way, down South.

In about half an hour Tom's wagon drove up to the front stile, and Aunt Sally she see it through the window, because it was only about fifty **yards**, and says:

"Why, there's somebody come! I wonder who 'tis? Why, I do believe it's a **stranger**. Jimmy" (that's one of the children) "run and tell Lize to put on another **plate** for dinner."

Everybody made a **rush** for the front door, because, of course, a stranger don't come *every* year, and so he lays over the yaller-fever, for interest, when he does come. Tom was over the stile and starting for the house; the wagon was **spinning** up the road for the village, and we was all bunched in the front door. Tom had his **store** clothes on, and an audience--and that was always **nuts** for

Chinese Simplified

drove: 驾.
expense: 花费, 费用, 支出.
farmer: 农人, 农夫.
forgot: 忘记.
glad: 高兴, 高兴的.
heap: 堆, 堆积.
honest: 诚实, 正直, 清廉, 刚正, 坦白, 正値, 诚实的, 体面, 廉洁, 深切.
joking: 开玩笑的.
log: 圆形木材, 圆木, 木头.
mare: 母马, 牝马.
nuts: 螺母.
one-horse: 单马拉的.
plantation: 农园, 种植园.
plate: 碟, 盘子.
preacher: 传道者.
preaching: 讲道法.
runaway: 逃亡者, 跑道.
rush: 速行, 匆匆.
schoolhouse: 校舍.
soul: 灵魂.
spinning: 纺织, 旋转.
store: 商店, 储藏, 商号, 贮藏, 店铺.
stranger: 陌生人, 异乡人, 生人.
surprising: 可惊.
sweated: 出汗.
trip: 旅程, 旅游, 旅行, 跟头, 旅途.
trunk: 躯干, 主干, 树干.
wagon: 列车厢.
yards: 场地.

Tom Sawyer. In them **circumstances** it warn't no trouble to him to **throw** in an amount of style **that** was **suitable**. He warn't a boy to meeky along up that **yard** like a **sheep**; no, he come ca'm and important, like the **ram**. When he got a-front of us he lifts his hat ever so **gracious** and **dainty**, like it was the **lid** of a box that had **butterflies asleep** in it and he didn't want to **disturb** them, and says:

"Mr. Archibald Nichols, I presume?"

"No, my boy," says the old **gentleman**, "I'm sorry to say 't your driver has deceived you; Nichols's place is down a matter of three **mile** more. Come in, come in."

Tom he took a look back over his **shoulder**, and says, "Too late--he's out of sight."

"Yes, he's gone, my son, and you must come in and eat your dinner with us; and then we'll **hitch** up and take you down to Nichols's."

"Oh, I *can't* make you so much trouble; I couldn't think of it. I'll walk --I don't mind the distance."

"But we won't *let* you walk--it wouldn't be Southern **hospitality** to do it. Come right in."

"Oh, *do*," says Aunt Sally; "it ain't a bit of trouble to us, not a bit in the world. You must stay. It's a long, **dusty** three mile, and we can't let you walk. And, **besides**, I've already told 'em to put on another **plate** when I see you coming; so you mustn't **disappoint** us. Come right in and make yourself at home."

So Tom he thanked them very **hearty** and **handsome**, and let himself be persuaded, and come in; and when he was in he said he was a **stranger** from Hicksville, Ohio, and his name was William Thompson--and he made another **bow**.

Well, he run on, and on, and on, making up stuff about Hicksville and everybody in it he could **invent**, and I getting a little nervious, and wondering how this was going to help me out of my **scrape**; and at last, still talking along, he reached over and kissed Aunt Sally right on the mouth, and then **settled** back

Chinese Simplified

asleep: 睡着，睡着的.
besides: 此外，另外，除了，并且，再说，况且.
bow: 弓.
butterflies: 蝴蝶.
circumstances: 环境，情况，情形，境况，境地，形势，情景.
dainty: 纤巧，高雅，精致的.
disappoint: 使失望，辜负.
disturb: 打扰，惊动，扰乱，干扰.
dusty: 满身尘埃，沾尘的.
gentleman: 绅士.
gracious: 亲切，亲切的，有礼貌的.
handsome: 英俊，慷慨的，英俊的.
hat: 帽子.
hearty: 诚恳，热诚的.
hitch: 拴住，蹒跚.
hospitality: 亲切，殷勤招待.
invent: 编造，发明.
lid: 盖子.
mile: 英里.
plate: 碟，盘子.
ram: 公羊，随机存取存储器，灌输，撞.
scrape: 刮掉，削刮.
settled: 安定.
sheep: 羊，绵羊.
shoulder: 肩，肩膀，担负.
stranger: 陌生人，异乡人，生人.
suitable: 得宜，适宜，适当，允当，合适，恰当，适当的，适.
throw: 扔，丢掉，丢，投.
yard: 码，厂，厂子，场地.

again in his **chair comfortable**, and was going on talking; but she **jumped** up and wiped it off with the back of her hand, and says:

"You owdacious puppy!"

He looked kind of **hurt**, and says:

"I'm **surprised** at you, m'am."

"You're s'rp--Why, **what** do you **reckon** I am? I've a good **notion** to take and--Say, what do you mean by **kissing** me?"

He looked kind of **humble**, and says:

"I didn't mean nothing, m'am. I didn't mean no **harm**. I--I--thought you'd like it."

"Why, you **born** fool!" She took up the **spinning stick**, and it looked like it was all she could do to keep from giving him a **crack** with it. "What made you think I'd like it?"

"Well, I don't know. Only, they--they--told me you would."

"*They* told you I would. Whoever told you's *another* **lunatic**. I never heard the **beat** of it. Who's *they*?"

"Why, **everybody**. They all said so, m'am."

It was all she could do to hold in; and her eyes **snapped**, and her fingers worked like she wanted to **scratch** him; and she says:

"Who's 'everybody'? Out with their names, or ther'll be an **idiot** short."

He got up and looked **distressed**, and fumbled his hat, and says:

"I'm **sorry**, and I warn't expecting it. They told me to. They all told me to. They all said, kiss her; and said she'd like it. They all said it--every one of them. But I'm sorry, m'am, and I won't do it no more --I won't, **honest**."

"You won't, won't you? Well, I sh'd *reckon* you won't!"

"No'm, I'm honest about it; I won't ever do it again--till you ask me."

"**Till** I *ask* you! Well, I never see the beat of it in my born days! I **lay** you'll be the Methusalem-numskull of **creation** before ever I ask you-- or the likes of you."

Chinese Simplified

beat: 打，击败，拍击，敲打，拍子，敲.
born: 出生，天生的.
chair: 椅子.
comfortable: 舒服，舒服的.
crack: 裂缝，精干，崩裂，爆裂，裂开，空隙.
creation: 创作，建立，创造.
distressed: 苦恼，哀伤.
everybody: 每个人，各位.
harm: 伤害，损害，坏处，害处，祸害.
hat: 帽子.
honest: 诚实，正直，清廉，刚正，坦白，正値，诚实的，体面，廉洁，深切.
humble: 谦逊，谦恭的.
hurt: 伤害，使受伤.
idiot: 白痴，笨蛋，傻子.
jumped: 跳跃.
kiss: 吻，接吻，轻抚，轻触.
lay: 产卵，安放，放，凡俗.
lunatic: 丧心病狂，疯子.
notion: 观念.
reckon: 估计，计算.
scratch: 抓伤，抓，搔刮.
snapped: 猛咬.
sorry: 遗憾，对不起.
spinning: 纺织，旋转.
stick: 棍，棒子，棍子，插入，棒，黏贴，手杖.
surprised: 惊讶.
till: 直到.

"Well," he says, "it does **surprise** me so. I can't make it out, **somehow**. They said you would, and I **thought** you would. But--" He stopped and looked around **slow**, like he wished he could run across a **friendly** eye somewheres, and fetched up on the old gentleman's, and says, "Didn't *you* think she'd like me to **kiss** her, sir?"

"Why, no; I--I--well, no, I b'lieve I didn't."

Then he looks on around the same way to me, and says:

"Tom, didn't *you* think Aunt Sally 'd open out her arms and say, 'Sid Sawyer--'"

"My land!" she says, breaking in and jumping for him, "you **impudent** young **rascal**, to **fool** a body so--" and was going to **hug** him, but he fended her off, and says:

"No, not **till** you've asked me first."

So she didn't lose no time, but asked him; and hugged him and kissed him over and over again, and then turned him over to the old man, and he took what was left. And after they got a little **quiet** again she says:

"Why, dear me, I never see such a surprise. We warn't looking for *you* at all, but only Tom. Sis never wrote to me about **anybody** coming but him."

"It's because it warn't *intended* for any of us to come but Tom," he says; "but I **begged** and begged, and at the last **minute** she let me come, too; so, coming down the river, me and Tom thought it would be a first-rate surprise for him to come here to the house first, and for me to by and by **tag** along and **drop** in, and let on to be a **stranger**. But it was a **mistake**, Aunt Sally. This ain't no **healthy** place for a stranger to come."

"No--not impudent whelps, Sid. You ought to had your **jaws** boxed; I hain't been so put out since I don't know when. But I don't care, I don't mind the terms--I'd be **willing** to stand a thousand such **jokes** to have you here. Well, to think of that **performance**! I don't **deny** it, I was most putrified with **astonishment** when you give me that smack."

Chinese Simplified

anybody: 任何人.
astonishment: 惊愕, 惊讶.
begged: 乞求.
deny: 驳斥, 否认.
drop: 落, 水滴, 衰退, 掉落, 降, 点子.
fool: 呆子, 笨蛋, 傻子, 笨人, 愚人.
friendly: 友好, 友善, 友好的, 好客, 友好地, 和气.
healthy: 健康的, 健壮.
hug: 紧抱, 拥抱.
impudent: 厚颜无耻.
jaws: 咽喉, 颌.
jokes: 笑林, 笑话.
kiss: 吻, 接吻, 轻抚, 轻触.
minute: 分钟, 详细, 分, 微小的, 渺小.
mistake: 错误, 差错.
ought: 应该, 活该.
performance: 性能, 成绩, 表演, 表现, 演出, 完成, 执行.
quiet: 安静, 寂静, 安定, 安生, 沉静, 宁静的.
rascal: 小淘气, 流氓.
slow: 慢, 缓慢, 迟慢, 迟钝, 迟迟, 迟缓.
somehow: 不知何故.
stranger: 陌生人, 异乡人, 生人.
surprise: 使吃惊, 惊奇, 惊骇.
tag: 标签, 标记.
till: 直到.
willing: 愿意, 高兴, 情愿的.

We had dinner out in that broad open passage **betwixt** the house and the kitchen; and there was things enough on that table for seven families-- and all hot, too; none of your **flabby**, tough meat that's laid in a **cupboard** in a **damp cellar** all night and tastes like a hunk of old cold **cannibal** in the morning. Uncle Silas he asked a pretty long **blessing** over it, but it was worth it; and it didn't **cool** it a bit, neither, the way I've seen them kind of interruptions do lots of times. There was a considerable good deal of talk all the afternoon, and me and Tom was on the **lookout** all the time; but it warn't no use, they didn't happen to say nothing about any **runaway** nigger, and we was afraid to try to work up to it. But at **supper**, at night, one of the little boys says:

"Pa, mayn't Tom and Sid and me go to the show?"

"No," says the old man, "I **reckon** there ain't going to be any; and you couldn't go if there was; because the runaway nigger told Burton and me all about that **scandalous** show, and Burton said he would tell the people; so I reckon they've drove the owdacious loafers out of town before this time."

So there it was!--but I couldn't help it. Tom and me was to sleep in the same room and bed; so, being tired, we **bid** good-night and went up to bed right after supper, and clumb out of the window and down the **lightning- rod**, and shoved for the town; for I didn't believe anybody was going to give the king and the duke a **hint**, and so if I didn't **hurry** up and give them one they'd get into trouble sure.

On the road Tom he told me all about how it was reckoned I was murdered, and how pap **disappeared** pretty soon, and didn't come back no more, and what a **stir** there was when Jim run away; and I told Tom all about our Royal Nonesuch rapscallions, and as much of the **raft voyage** as I had time to; and as we **struck** into the town and up through the--here comes a **raging rush** of people with torches, and an awful whooping and **yelling**, and banging **tin** pans and **blowing** horns; and we **jumped** to one side to let them go by; and as they went by I see they had the king and the duke astraddle of a rail--that is, I knowed it *was* the king and the duke, though they was all over **tar** and **feathers**, and didn't look like nothing in the world that was human--just looked like a couple of

Chinese Simplified

betwixt: 中间，在…之间.
bid: 出价，企图，标，投标.
blessing: 祝福.
blowing: 吹.
cannibal: 吃同类的动物，食人者.
cellar: 地下室，地窖.
cool: 凉，镇静，镇定，凉爽，凉爽的.
cupboard: 碗柜，柜子，橱.
damp: 潮湿，潮湿的.
disappeared: 不见了，消失.
feathers: 翎毛，羽毛.
flabby: 松弛的，软弱，软弱的.
hint: 暗示.
hurry: 仓促，匆忙，赶忙.
jumped: 跳跃.
lightning: 闪电.
lookout: 眺望，伸出窗口观看.
raft: 筏，木排，槎，桴.
raging: 熊熊，狂怒，猛烈的，狂暴的，愤怒的.
reckon: 估计，计算.
rod: 棍子，棍.
runaway: 逃亡者，跑道.
rush: 速行，匆匆.
scandalous: 恶意中伤.
stir: 轰动，搅拌，鼓动.
struck: 敲打.
supper: 晚饭，晚餐.
tar: 焦油.
tin: 锡，罐头.
voyage: 航行.
yelling: 叫声，叫喊.

monstrous big soldier-plumes. Well, it made me **sick** to see it; and I was **sorry** for them poor **pitiful** rascals, it seemed like I couldn't ever feel any **hardness** against them any more in the world. It was a **dreadful** thing to see. Human beings *can* be **awful cruel** to one another.

We see we was too late--couldn't do no good. We asked some stragglers about it, and they said **everybody** went to the show looking very **innocent**; and **laid** low and **kept dark till** the poor old king was in the **middle** of his cavortings on the stage; then **somebody** give a **signal**, and the house **rose** up and went for them.

So we poked along back home, and I warn't **feeling** so **brash** as I was before, but kind of **ornery**, and **humble**, and to **blame**, somehow--though I hadn't done nothing. But that's always the way; it don't make no **difference** whether you do right or wrong, a person's **conscience** ain't got no sense, and just goes for him **anyway**. If I had a yaller **dog** that didn't know no more than a person's conscience does I would pison him. It **takes** up more room than all the rest of a person's **insides**, and yet ain't no good, nohow. Tom Sawyer he says the same.

Chinese Simplified

anyway: 无论如何，反正.
awful: 可怕，可怕的.
blame: 责备，咎，非难，责任，罪，责怪，归咎.
brash: 胃灼热，无礼的，傲慢的.
conscience: 良心.
cruel: 粗暴，残酷，残酷的，狠毒.
dark: 暗，黑暗，夜.
difference: 差异，差，差别，区别，分歧，分别，误差.
dog: 狗，犬.
dreadful: 可怕，恐怖的.
everybody: 每个人，各位.
feeling: 感觉，情绪，感情，情感，思绪.
hardness: 硬度.
humble: 谦逊，谦恭的.
innocent: 无辜，无罪的，天真.
insides: 内部.
kept: 收存.
laid: 放.
middle: 中央，中间，半中腰，中间的，中部，中央的.
monstrous: 怪物似，似怪物的.
ornery: 低劣的.
pitiful: 可怜，可怜的.
rose: 蔷薇，玫瑰，升起.
sick: 生病.
signal: 信号，手势，讯号.
somebody: 某人，有人.
sorry: 遗憾，对不起.
takes: 拿，取走.
till: 直到.

CHAPTER XXXIV

WE CHEER UP JIM

We stopped talking, and got to **thinking**. By and by Tom says:

"Looky here, Huck, what fools we are to not think of it before! I **bet** I know where Jim is."

"No! Where?"

"In that **hut** down by the ash-hopper. Why, looky here. When we was at **dinner**, didn't you see a nigger man go in there with some vittles?"

"Yes."

"What did you think the vittles was for?"

"For a **dog**."

"So 'd I. Well, it wasn't for a dog."

"Why?"

"Because part of it was **watermelon**."

"So it was--I noticed it. Well, it does **beat** all that I never thought about a dog not **eating** watermelon. It **shows** how a body can see and don't see at the same time."

Chinese Simplified

beat: 打，击败，拍击，敲打，拍子，敲.
bet: 打赌，赌.
dinner: 晚餐，正餐.
dog: 狗，犬.
eating: 吃.
hut: 茅舍，棚屋.
shows: 显示.
thinking: 思想，思维.
watermelon: 西瓜.

"Well, the nigger **unlocked** the **padlock** when he went in, and he locked it again when he came out. He **fetched uncle** a **key** about the time we got up from table--same key, I **bet**. Watermelon shows man, lock shows **prisoner**; and it ain't likely there's two **prisoners** on such a little **plantation**, and where the people's all so kind and good. Jim's the prisoner. All right--I'm **glad** we found it out **detective fashion**; I wouldn't give shucks for any other way. Now you work your mind, and study out a plan to **steal** Jim, and I will study out one, too; and we'll take the one we like the best."

What a head for just a boy to have! If I had Tom Sawyer's head I wouldn't trade it off to be a **duke**, nor **mate** of a **steamboat**, nor **clown** in a **circus**, nor nothing I can think of. I went to thinking out a plan, but only just to be doing something; I knowed very well where the right plan was going to come from. Pretty soon Tom says:

"Ready?"

"Yes," I says.

"All right--bring it out."

"My plan is this," I says. "We can easy find out if it's Jim in there. Then get up my **canoe** to-morrow night, and fetch my **raft** over from the **island**. Then the first dark night that comes steal the key out of the old man's britches after he goes to bed, and **shove** off down the river on the raft with Jim, **hiding** daytimes and running nights, the way me and Jim used to do before. Wouldn't that plan work?"

"*Work*? Why, cert'nly it would work, like rats a-fighting. But it's too **blame' simple**; there ain't nothing *to* it. What's the good of a plan that ain't no more trouble than that? It's as **mild** as goose-milk. Why, Huck, it wouldn't make no more talk than breaking into a **soap** factory."

I never said nothing, because I warn't expecting nothing different; but I knowed **mighty** well that **whenever** he got *his* plan ready it wouldn't have none of them **objections** to it.

Chinese Simplified

bet：打赌，赌.
blame：责备，咎，非难，责任，罪，责怪，归咎.
canoe：独木舟.
circus：马戏团，杂技团，马戏.
clown：小丑.
detective：侦探，暗探.
duke：公爵，公.
fashion：时尚，方式，时装.
fetch：拿，取，带来.
glad：高兴，高兴的.
hiding：隐匿.
island：岛.
key：钥匙，关键，题解，键，主要的.
lock：锁，撞锁.
mate：伴侣，配偶，伙伴.
mighty：伟大，强势，强大的.
mild：温和的.
objections：反对.
padlock：挂锁.
plantation：农园，种植园.
prisoner：犯人，罪犯，囚犯.
prisoners：囚犯.
raft：筏，木排，槎，桴.
shove：推.
simple：简单，简易，简略，简单的，单纯.
soap：肥皂.
steal：偷窃，盗窃，偷，窃取.
steamboat：汽船，轮船.
uncle：叔叔，伯伯，叔父，大爷，老大爷，姑夫.
whenever：无论何时，每当.

And it didn't. He told me what it was, and I see in a minute it was worth **fifteen** of mine for style, and would make Jim just as free a man as mine would, and maybe get us all killed **besides**. So I was **satisfied**, and said we would **waltz** in on it. I needn't tell what it was here, because I knowed it wouldn't stay the way, it was. I knowed he would be **changing** it around every which way as we went along, and heaving in new bullinesses **wherever** he got a chance. And that is what he done.

Well, one thing was dead sure, and that was that Tom Sawyer was in **earnest**, and was actuly going to help **steal** that nigger out of **slavery**. That was the thing that was too many for me. Here was a boy that was **respectable** and well brung up; and had a character to lose; and folks at home that had **characters**; and he was **bright** and not leather-headed; and **knowing** and not **ignorant**; and not mean, but kind; and yet here he was, without any more **pride**, or rightness, or feeling, than to **stoop** to this business, and make himself a **shame**, and his family a shame, before **everybody**. I *couldn't* understand it no way at all. It was **outrageous**, and I knowed I **ought** to just up and tell him so; and so be his true friend, and let him **quit** the thing right where he was and save himself. And I *did* start to tell him; but he **shut** me up, and says:

"Don't you **reckon** I know what I'm about? Don't I generly know what I'm about?"

"Yes."

"Didn't I *say* I was going to help steal the nigger?"

"Yes."

"*Well*, then."

That's all he said, and that's all I said. It warn't no use to say any more; because when he said he'd do a thing, he always done it. But I couldn't make out how he was **willing** to go into this thing; so I just let it go, and never bothered no more about it. If he was **bound** to have it so, I couldn't help it.

When we got home the house was all dark and still; so we went on down to the hut by the ash-hopper for to **examine** it. We went through the **yard** so as to

Chinese Simplified

besides: 此外，另外，除了，并且，再说，况且.
bound: 限，边际，弹回，范围.
bright: 聪明，光明，光亮，光明的，鲜明.
changing: 变化.
characters: 人物，字符.
earnest: 认真.
everybody: 每个人，各位.
examine: 检查，核查，检验，考核，视察.
fifteen: 十五.
hut: 茅舍，棚屋.
ignorant: 愚昧，无知的，茫然.
knowing: 博学的，知道.
ought: 应该，活该.
outrageous: 不像话，残暴的，岂有此理.
pride: 自豪，骄傲.
quit: 退出，退离.
reckon: 估计，计算.
respectable: 可尊敬，可尊敬的.
satisfied: 满意，乐意，心满意足的.
shame: 羞耻.
shut: 关闭.
slavery: 奴隶制度，奴隶制.
steal: 偷窃，盗窃，偷，窃取.
stoop: 弯腰，门廊.
waltz: 华尔滋舞.
wherever: 无论何处，哪里.
willing: 愿意，高兴，情愿的.
yard: 码，厂，厂子，场地.

see what the hounds would do. They knowed us, and didn't make no more noise than country dogs is always doing when anything comes by in the night. When we got to the **cabin** we took a look at the front and the two sides; and on the side I warn't acquainted with--which was the north side--we found a square window-hole, up **tolerable** high, with just one **stout** board nailed across it. I says:

"Here's the **ticket**. This hole's big enough for Jim to get through if we **wrench** off the board."

Tom says:

"It's as simple as tit-tat-toe, three-in-a-row, and as easy as playing **hooky**. I should *hope* we can find a way that's a little more **complicated** than *that*, Huck Finn."

"Well, then," I says, "how 'll it do to saw him out, the way I done before I was murdered that time?"

"That's more *like*," he says. "It's real **mysterious**, and **troublesome**, and good," he says; "but I **bet** we can find a way that's twice as long. There ain't no **hurry**; le's keep on looking around."

Betwixt the **hut** and the **fence**, on the back side, was a lean-to that joined the hut at the **eaves**, and was made out of **plank**. It was as long as the hut, but narrow--only about six foot wide. The door to it was at the south end, and was padlocked. Tom he went to the soap-kettle and searched around, and fetched back the iron thing they **lift** the **lid** with; so he took it and prized out one of the **staples**. The chain fell down, and we opened the door and went in, and shut it, and **struck** a match, and see the **shed** was only built against a cabin and hadn't no **connection** with it; and there warn't no floor to the shed, nor nothing in it but some old **rusty** played-out hoes and spades and **picks** and a **crippled** **plow**. The match went out, and so did we, and shoved in the staple again, and the door was locked as good as ever. Tom was **joyful**. He says;

"Now we're all right. We'll *dig* him out. It 'll take about a week!"

Chinese Simplified

bet：打赌，赌．
betwixt：中间，在…之间．
cabin：小屋，船舱．
complicated：复杂，繁复，曲折，复杂的，疑难．
connection：连接，相连，联系，联通，环节．
crippled：瘫痪．
dig：挖掘．
eaves：屋檐．
fence：篱笆，栅栏，栏位，栏．
hooky：钩状．
hurry：仓促，匆忙，赶忙．
hut：茅舍，棚屋．
joyful：欢喜，快乐的，欢喜的．
lid：盖子．
lift：举起，开放，掀起，电梯，抬起．
mysterious：神秘，莫名其妙，神秘的．
picks：选择．
plank：板，木板，木版，板子．
plow：犁，耕．
rusty：腐蚀，生锈的．
shed：散出，棚子，流出，脱落．
staple：钉书针，名产，主要成分．
staples：主要成分．
stout：肥硕，强壮的．
struck：敲打．
ticket：票．
tolerable：可容忍，可容忍的．
troublesome：淘神，讨厌，麻烦，麻烦的，伤脑筋．
wrench：螺旋钳，扳子，扳手，扳钳．

Then we started for the house, and I went in the back door--you only have to **pull** a buckskin latch-string, they don't **fasten** the doors--but that warn't romantical enough for Tom Sawyer; no way would do him but he must **climb** up the lightning-rod. But after he got up half way about three times, and missed fire and fell every time, and the last time most busted his **brains** out, he thought he'd got to give it up; but after he was rested he allowed he would give her one more turn for **luck**, and this time he made the trip.

In the morning we was up at break of day, and down to the nigger cabins to **pet** the **dogs** and make friends with the nigger that fed Jim--if it *was* Jim that was being fed. The niggers was just **getting** through **breakfast** and **starting** for the fields; and Jim's nigger was **piling** up a tin **pan** with **bread** and **meat** and things; and whilst the others was leaving, the **key** come from the house.

This nigger had a **good**-natured, chuckle-headed face, and his **wool** was all tied up in little bunches with **thread**. That was to keep witches off. He said the witches was pestering him **awful** these nights, and making him see all kinds of **strange** things, and hear all kinds of strange words and noises, and he didn't believe he was ever witched so long before in his life. He got so worked up, and got to running on so about his **troubles**, he **forgot** all about what he'd been a-going to do. So Tom says:

"What's the vittles for? Going to **feed** the dogs?"

The nigger kind of smiled around graduly over his face, like when you **heave** a brickbat in a mud-puddle, and he says:

"Yes, Mars Sid, A dog. Cur'us dog, too. Does you want to go en look at 'im?"

"Yes."

I **hunched** Tom, and **whispers**:

"You going, right here in the **daybreak**? *That* warn't the plan."

"No, it warn't; but it's the plan *now*."

Chinese Simplified

awful: 可怕，可怕的.
brains: 头脑，脑子，脑筋，脑袋，脑髓.
bread: 面包.
breakfast: 早餐，早饭，早点.
climb: 爬，攀登.
daybreak: 黎明，破晓.
dog: 狗，犬.
dogs: 狗.
fasten: 绑住.
feed: 饲料，哺养，哺育，喂养，饲养.
forgot: 忘记.
good-natured: 和善，心眼好，性格好.
heave: 举起，波荡，喘气.
hunched: 肉峰.
key: 钥匙，关键，题解，键，主要的.
luck: 运气，幸运.
meat: 肉.
pan: 平锅.
pet: 宠物.
piling: 打桩，打桩工程，桩材.
pull: 拉，牵引.
starting: 起步.
strange: 奇怪，奇特，陌生，奇异的，生疏.
thread: 线，线索，细线，运作.
tin: 锡，罐头.
troubles: 坏处，麻烦.
whispers: 耳语.
wool: 羊毛.

So, drat him, we went **along**, but I didn't like it much. When we got in we couldn't **hardly** see anything, it was so **dark**; but Jim was there, **sure** enough, and could see us; and he **sings** out:

"Why, *Huck*! En good *lan*'! ain' dat Misto Tom?"

I just knowed how it would be; I just **expected** it. I didn't know nothing to do; and if I had I couldn't a done it, because that nigger busted in and says:

"Why, **de gracious** sakes! do he know you genlmen?"

We could see **pretty** well now. Tom he looked at the nigger, **steady** and kind of wondering, and says:

"Does *who* know us?"

"Why, dis-yer **runaway** nigger."

"I don't **reckon** he does; but what put that into your head?"

"What *put* it dar? Didn' he **jis'** dis **minute** sing out like he knowed you?"

Tom says, in a puzzled-up kind of way:

"Well, that's **mighty curious**. *Who* **sung** out? *When* did he sing out? *What* did he sing out?" And turns to me, **perfectly** ca'm, and says, "Did *you* **hear anybody** sing out?"

Of **course** there warn't nothing to be said but the one thing; so I says:

"No; I ain't **heard nobody** say nothing."

Then he turns to Jim, and **looks** him over like he never see him before, and says:

"Did you sing out?"

"No, sah," says Jim; "I hain't said nothing, sah."

"Not a word?"

"No, sah, I hain't said a word."

"Did you ever see us before?"

"No, sah; not as I **knows** on."

Chinese Simplified

along: 沿着，沿，一同.
anybody: 任何人.
course: 课程，经过，进程，路程，路线，学科，过程.
curious: 有好奇心，好奇，好奇的.
dark: 暗，黑暗，夜.
de: 可选择丢弃.
expected: 预期.
gracious: 亲切，亲切的，有礼貌的.
hardly: 几乎不，毫不，辛苦地.
hear: 听见，听取，听.
heard: 听见.
jis: 日本工业标准.
knows: 知道.
looks: 样子，姿容，神态，看.
mighty: 伟大，强势，强大的.
minute: 分钟，详细，分，微小的，渺小.
nobody: 没有人，没人.
perfectly: 完美，完美地.
pretty: 漂亮，美丽的，秀丽.
reckon: 估计，计算.
runaway: 逃亡者，跑道.
sing: 唱，歌唱，唱歌.
sings: 唱.
steady: 稳定，坚定，平稳，平稳的.
sung: 唱歌.
sure: 肯定.

So Tom turns to the nigger, which was looking **wild** and **distressed**, and says, kind of **severe**:

"What do you reckon's the matter with you, anyway? What made you think **somebody sung** out?"

"Oh, it's de dad-blame' witches, sah, en I **wisht** I was dead, I do. Dey's awluz at it, sah, en dey do mos' **kill** me, dey sk'yers me so. Please to don't tell **nobody** 'bout it sah, er ole Mars Silas he'll scole me; 'kase he say dey *ain't* no witches. I **jis'** wish to **goodness** he was heah now-- ***den*** what would he say! I jis' **bet** he couldn' fine no way to git aroun' it *dis* time. But it's awluz jis' so; people dat's *sot*, **stays** sot; dey won't look into noth'n'en fine it out f'r deyselves, en when *you* fine it out en tell um 'bout it, dey doan' b'lieve you."

Tom give him a **dime**, and said we wouldn't tell nobody; and told him to buy some more **thread** to **tie** up his **wool** with; and then **looks** at Jim, and says:

"I **wonder** if Uncle Silas is going to **hang** this nigger. If I was to **catch** a nigger that was **ungrateful** enough to run away, I wouldn't give him up, I'd hang him." And whilst the nigger stepped to the door to look at the dime and **bite** it to see if it was good, he **whispers** to Jim and says:

"Don't ever let on to know us. And if you hear any **digging** going on nights, it's us; we're going to set you free."

Jim only had time to **grab** us by the hand and **squeeze** it; then the nigger come back, and we said we'd come again some time if the nigger wanted us to; and he said he would, more particular if it was **dark**, because the witches went for him **mostly** in the dark, and it was good to have folks around then.

Chinese Simplified

bet：打赌，赌.
bite：咬，辣，咬伤.
catch：捕捉，捕捞，捕拿，捉.
dark：暗，黑暗，夜.
den：窝.
digging：挖掘.
dime：一角银币，一角硬币.
distressed：苦恼，哀伤.
goodness：美德.
grab：抓住，攫取，抓斗.
hang：挂，悬挂.
jis：日本工业标准.
kill：打死，杀害，杀死.
looks：样子，姿容，神态，看.
mostly：大多，多半，大部份.
nobody：没有人，没人.
severe：严重，严竣，严厉，严峻，剧烈，严肃的.
somebody：某人，有人.
squeeze：压扁，压挤，榨.
stays：停留.
sung：唱歌.
thread：线，线索，细线，运作.
tie：不分胜负，打结，束缚，轨枕，绑，领带.
ungrateful：忘恩负义，忘恩负义的.
whispers：耳语.
wild：野，猖披，猖獗，野生，野性的.
wish：愿望，希望，意愿，祝，祝愿，志愿.
wonder：奇迹，惊奇.
wool：羊毛.

CHAPTER XXXV

DARK, DEEP-LAID PLANS

It would be most an hour yet **till breakfast**, so we left and **struck** down into the **woods**; because Tom said we got to have *some* light to see how to **dig** by, and a **lantern** makes too much, and might get us into trouble; what we must have was a lot of them **rotten** chunks that's called fox-fire, and just makes a **soft** kind of a **glow** when you lay them in a dark place. We fetched an armful and **hid** it in the weeds, and set down to rest, and Tom says, kind of **dissatisfied**:

"Blame it, this whole thing is just as easy and **awkward** as it can be. And so it makes it so rotten difficult to get up a difficult plan. There ain't no **watchman** to be drugged--now there ***ought*** to be a watchman. There ain't even a dog to give a sleeping-mixture to. And there's Jim **chained** by one **leg**, with a ten-foot chain, to the leg of his bed: why, all you got to do is to **lift** up the **bedstead** and **slip** off the chain. And Uncle Silas he **trusts everybody**; sends the **key** to the punkin-headed nigger, and don't send **nobody** to watch the nigger. Jim could a got out of that window-hole before this, only there wouldn't be no use trying to **travel** with a ten-foot chain on his leg. Why, drat it, Huck, it's the stupidest **arrangement** I ever see. You got to **invent** *all* the **difficulties**. Well, we can't help it; we got to do the best we can with the **materials** we've got. **Anyhow**, there's one thing--there's more **honor** in getting him out through a lot of difficulties and

Chinese Simplified

anyhow: 无论如何，反正.
arrangement: 安排，布局，条理.
awkward: 笨拙，尴尬，不得劲，拙，迟钝的.
bedstead: 床架.
breakfast: 早餐，早饭，早点.
chain: 链，链子，连锁.
difficulties: 困难.
dig: 挖掘.
dissatisfied: 不满，不满意的.
everybody: 每个人，各位.
glow: 炽热，发光.
hid: 躲藏.
honor: 荣誉，荣耀，尊严，面子，尊敬.
invent: 编造，发明.
key: 钥匙，关键，题解，键，主要的.
lantern: 灯笼.
leg: 腿，脚.
lift: 举起，开放，掀起，电梯，抬起.
materials: 物品，材料.
nobody: 没有人，没人.
ought: 应该，活该.
rotten: 腐败的，腐朽.
slip: 滑倒，溜走，溜.
soft: 柔软，柔和，柔软的.
struck: 敲打.
till: 直到.
travel: 旅行，遨游，旅游，游历.
trusts: 信任.
watchman: 看守者，更夫.
woods: 树林，森林.

dangers, where there warn't one of them **furnished** to you by the people who it was their duty to furnish them, and you had to **contrive** them all out of your own head. Now look at just that one thing of the **lantern**. When you come down to the cold facts, we **simply** got to *let on* that a lantern's resky. Why, we could work with a **torchlight procession** if we wanted to, I believe. Now, whilst I think of it, we got to hunt up something to make a saw out of the first chance we get."

"What do we want of a saw?"

"What do we *want* of a saw? Hain't we got to saw the leg of Jim's bed off, so as to get the chain loose?"

"Why, you just said a body could lift up the **bedstead** and slip the chain off."

"Well, if that ain't just like you, Huck Finn. You *can* get up the infant-schooliest ways of going at a thing. Why, hain't you ever read any books at all?--Baron Trenck, nor Casanova, nor Benvenuto Chelleeny, nor Henri IV., nor none of them **heroes**? Who ever heard of getting a prisoner loose in such an old-maidy way as that? No; the way all the best authorities does is to saw the bed-leg in two, and leave it just so, and **swallow** the **sawdust**, so it can't be found, and put some **dirt** and **grease** around the **sawed** place so the very keenest seneskal can't see no sign of it's being sawed, and thinks the bed-leg is perfectly sound. Then, the night you're ready, **fetch** the leg a kick, down she goes; slip off your chain, and there you are. Nothing to do but **hitch** your **rope ladder** to the **battlements**, **shin** down it, break your leg in the **moat**-- because a rope ladder is nineteen foot too short, you know--and there's your horses and your **trusty** vassles, and they **scoop** you up and **fling** you across a **saddle**, and away you go to your native Langudoc, or Navarre, or wherever it is. It's **gaudy**, Huck. I wish there was a moat to this **cabin**. If we get time, the night of the **escape**, we'll **dig** one."

I says:

"What do we want of a moat when we're going to **snake** him out from under the cabin?"

Chinese Simplified

battlements：堞.
bedstead：床架.
cabin：小屋，船舱.
contrive：设计.
dangers：危险.
dig：挖掘.
dirt：污垢.
escape：逃走，逃之夭夭，逃跑，逃避，逃脱，逃离，逃亡.
fetch：拿，取，带来.
fling：扔丢.
furnish：供给，提供.
furnished：供给.
gaudy：花哨，花里胡哨.
grease：油脂.
heroes：英雄.
hitch：拴住，蹒跚.
ladder：阶梯，梯子.
lantern：灯笼.
moat：护城河.
procession：行列，游行.
rope：绳索，绳子.
saddle：鞍，鞍状物，马鞍.
sawdust：木屑.
sawed：锯.
scoop：杓子，勺子，勺.
shin：外小腿，胫.
simply：简直，只是，根本，简单地，高低，只管，只需，只顾.
snake：蛇.
swallow：燕子，吞，咽.
torchlight：手电筒.
trusty：可信任，可信任的.

But he never heard me. He had **forgot** me and everything else. He had his **chin** in his hand, **thinking**. Pretty soon he **sighs** and **shakes** his head; then sighs again, and says:

"No, it wouldn't do--there ain't **necessity** enough for it."

"For what?" I says.

"Why, to saw Jim's **leg** off," he says.

"Good land!" I says; "why, there ain't *no* necessity for it. And what would you want to saw his leg off for, anyway?"

"Well, some of the best authorities has done it. They couldn't get the **chain** off, so they just cut their hand off and shoved. And a leg would be better still. But we got to let that go. There ain't necessity enough in this case; and, **besides**, Jim's a nigger, and wouldn't understand the reasons for it, and how it's the **custom** in **Europe**; so we'll let it go. But there's one thing--he can have a rope **ladder**; we can **tear** up our **sheets** and make him a rope ladder easy enough. And we can **send** it to him in a **pie**; it's **mostly** done that way. And I've et **worse** pies."

"Why, Tom Sawyer, how you talk," I says; "Jim ain't got no use for a rope ladder."

"He *has* got use for it. How *you* talk, you better say; you don't know nothing about it. He's *got* to have a rope ladder; they all do."

"What in the **nation** can he *do* with it?"

"*Do* with it? He can **hide** it in his bed, can't he?" That's what they all do; and *he's* got to, too. Huck, you don't ever seem to want to do anything that's **regular**; you want to be **starting** something **fresh** all the time. S'pose he *don't* do nothing with it? ain't it there in his bed, for a clew, after he's gone? and don't you **reckon** they'll want clews? Of course they will. And you wouldn't leave them any? That would be a ***pretty*** howdy-do, *wouldn't* it! I never heard of such a thing."

"Well," I says, "if it's in the **regulations**, and he's got to have it, all right, let him have it; because I don't wish to go back on no regulations; but there's one

Chinese Simplified

besides: 此外，另外，除了，并且，再说，况且．
chain: 链，链子，连锁．
chin: 下巴，颏．
custom: 风俗，习惯，规矩，习俗．
forgot: 忘记．
fresh: 新鲜，新鲜的，新．
hide: 躲藏，暗藏，掩饰，藏，隐瞒，隐藏．
ladder: 阶梯，梯子．
leg: 腿，脚．
mostly: 大多，多半，大部份．
nation: 国家．
necessity: 必要性，必然，必需品，必需．
pie: 馅饼．
pretty: 漂亮，美丽的，秀丽．
reckon: 估计，计算．
regular: 固定，正常，通常，端正，正规的，常例的，定期的，整齐的，有秩序的，正规，经常．
regulations: 条例，规程，章程，规章．
rope: 绳索，绳子．
send: 派遣，派出，送，发送，寄，投，派．
shakes: 摇动．
sheets: 纸张．
sighs: 叹息．
starting: 起步．
tear: 眼泪，撕破，撕．
thinking: 思想，思维．
worse: 更坏，更糟．

thing, Tom Sawyer--if we go to **tearing** up our **sheets** to make Jim a **rope ladder**, we're going to get into trouble with Aunt Sally, just as sure as you're born. Now, the way I look at it, a hickry-bark ladder don't cost nothing, and don't waste nothing, and is just as good to **load** up a **pie** with, and **hide** in a **straw tick**, as any **rag** ladder you can start; and as for Jim, he ain't had no experience, and so he don't care what kind of a--"

"Oh, shucks, Huck Finn, if I was as **ignorant** as you I'd keep still-- that's what *I'd* do. Who ever heard of a state **prisoner** escaping by a hickry-bark ladder? Why, it's perfectly ridiculous."

"Well, all right, Tom, **fix** it your own way; but if you'll take my advice, you'll let me **borrow** a sheet off of the clothesline."

He said that would do. And that gave him another idea, and he says:

"Borrow a **shirt**, too."

"What do we want of a shirt, Tom?"

"Want it for Jim to keep a **journal** on."

"Journal your granny--*Jim* can't write."

"S'pose he *can't* write--he can make marks on the shirt, can't he, if we make him a **pen** out of an old pewter **spoon** or a piece of an old iron barrel-hoop?"

"Why, Tom, we can pull a **feather** out of a **goose** and make him a better one; and quicker, too."

"*Prisoners* don't have **geese** running around the donjon-keep to pull pens out of, you **muggins**. They *always* make their pens out of the hardest, toughest, troublesomest piece of old **brass candlestick** or something like that they can get their hands on; and it takes them weeks and weeks and months and months to **file** it out, too, because they've got to do it by **rubbing** it on the wall. *they* wouldn't use a goose-quill if they had it. It ain't regular."

"Well, then, what'll we make him the **ink** out of?"

"Many makes it out of iron-rust and **tears**; but that's the common sort and women; the best authorities uses their own blood. Jim can do that; and when he

Chinese Simplified

borrow: 借.
brass: 黄铜.
candlestick: 烛台, 蜡台.
feather: 羽毛.
file: 文件, 档案, 文档.
fix: 安装, 奠定, 固定, 修理.
geese: 鹅.
goose: 鹅.
hide: 躲藏, 暗藏, 掩饰, 藏, 隐瞒, 隐藏.
ignorant: 愚昧, 无知的, 茫然.
ink: 墨水, 墨水儿, 篇幅.
journal: 日志, 通报.
ladder: 阶梯, 梯子.
load: 包袱, 负载, 装满, 担子, 装载, 负荷, 载重.
muggins: 蠢人.
pen: 笔, 栏圈, 笔杆, 笔杆子, 栏位, 栏, 钢笔.
pie: 馅饼.
prisoner: 犯人, 罪犯, 囚犯.
prisoners: 囚犯.
rag: 破布, 碎布.
rope: 绳索, 绳子.
rubbing: 研磨, 拓片, 摩擦.
sheet: 片, 一张, 床单, 纸张.
sheets: 纸张.
shirt: 衬衫, 衬衣.
spoon: 匙, 调羹.
straw: 稻草, 吸管.
tearing: 撕裂的.
tears: 泪, 泪水, 眼泪.
tick: 壁虱, 滴答声, 勾.

wants to send any little common **ordinary mysterious** message to let the world know where he's **captivated**, he can write it on the bottom of a **tin** plate with a **fork** and throw it out of the window. The Iron Mask always done that, and it's a **blame'** good way, too."

"Jim ain't got no tin **plates**. They **feed** him in a pan."

"That ain't nothing; we can get him some."

"Can't nobody *read* his plates."

"That ain't got anything to *do* with it, Huck Finn. All *he's* got to do is to write on the plate and throw it out. You don't *have* to be able to read it. Why, half the time you can't read anything a **prisoner writes** on a tin plate, or anywhere else."

"Well, then, what's the sense in **wasting** the plates?"

"Why, blame it all, it ain't the *prisoner's* plates."

"But it's *somebody's* plates, ain't it?"

"Well, spos'n it is? What does the *prisoner* care whose--"

He broke off there, because we heard the breakfast-horn **blowing**. So we cleared out for the house.

Along during the morning I borrowed a sheet and a white **shirt** off of the clothes-line; and I found an old **sack** and put them in it, and we went down and got the fox-fire, and put that in too. I called it **borrowing**, because that was what pap always called it; but Tom said it warn't borrowing, it was **stealing**. He said we was **representing prisoners**; and prisoners don't care how they get a thing so they get it, and nobody don't blame them for it, either. It ain't no **crime** in a prisoner to steal the thing he **needs** to get away with, Tom said; it's his right; and so, as long as we was representing a prisoner, we had a perfect right to steal anything on this place we had the least use for to get ourselves out of prison with. He said if we warn't prisoners it would be a very different thing, and nobody but a mean, **ornery** person would steal when he warn't a prisoner. So we allowed we would steal everything there was that come **handy**. And yet he made a **mighty fuss**, one day, after that, when I **stole** a **watermelon** out of the

Chinese Simplified

blame: 责备，咎，非难，责任，罪，责怪，归咎.
blowing: 吹.
borrowing: 借.
captivated: 如醉如痴.
crime: 罪行，犯罪.
feed: 饲料，哺养，哺育，喂养，饲养.
fork: 叉，叉子.
fuss: 大惊小怪.
handy: 灵巧，便当，顺手，方便的，简便.
mighty: 伟大，强势，强大的.
mysterious: 神秘，莫名其妙，神秘的.
needs: 需要.
ordinary: 通常，普通，平常，寻常，一般，正常，普通的，正常的.
ornery: 低劣的.
plates: 盘子.
prison: 监狱.
prisoner: 犯人，罪犯，囚犯.
prisoners: 囚犯.
representing: 代表.
sack: 大袋子，开除.
shirt: 衬衫，衬衣.
steal: 偷窃，盗窃，偷，窃取.
stealing: 偷垒，偷窃.
stole: 偷了.
tin: 锡，罐头.
wasting: 消耗.
watermelon: 西瓜.
writes: 写.

nigger-patch and eat it; and he made me go and give the niggers a **dime** without telling them what it was for. Tom said that what he meant was, we could **steal** anything we ***needed***. Well, I says, I needed the **watermelon**. But he said I didn't need it to get out of prison with; there's where the difference was. He said if I'd a wanted it to **hide** a **knife** in, and **smuggle** it to Jim to **kill** the seneskal with, it would a been all right. So I let it go at that, though I couldn't see no advantage in my **representing** a **prisoner** if I got to set down and chaw over a lot of gold-leaf distinctions like that every time I see a chance to **hog** a watermelon.

Well, as I was saying, we waited that morning **till** everybody was **settled** down to business, and nobody in sight around the **yard**; then Tom he carried the **sack** into the lean-to whilst I stood off a piece to keep watch. By and by he come out, and we went and set down on the **woodpile** to talk. He says:

"Everything's all right now except **tools**; and that's easy fixed."

"Tools?" I says.

"Yes."

"Tools for what?"

"Why, to **dig** with. We ain't a-going to *gnaw* him out, are we?"

"Ain't them old **crippled picks** and things in there good enough to dig a nigger out with?" I says.

He turns on me, looking **pitying** enough to make a body **cry**, and says:

"Huck Finn, did you *ever* hear of a prisoner having picks and **shovels**, and all the **modern** conveniences in his **wardrobe** to dig himself out with? Now I want to ask you--if you got any **reasonableness** in you at all--what kind of a show would *that* give him to be a **hero**? Why, they might as well **lend** him the key and done with it. Picks and shovels--why, they wouldn't **furnish** 'em to a king."

"Well, then," I says, "if we don't want the picks and shovels, what do we want?"

"A couple of case-knives."

"To dig the **foundations** out from under that **cabin** with?"

Chinese Simplified

cabin: 小屋，船舱.
crippled: 瘫痪.
cry: 喊，叫，哭，哭泣.
dig: 挖掘.
dime: 一角银币，一角硬币.
foundations: 基础.
furnish: 供给，提供.
gnaw: 啃.
hero: 英雄.
hide: 躲藏，暗藏，掩饰，藏，隐瞒，隐藏.
hog: 猪.
kill: 打死，杀害，杀死.
knife: 刀子，刀，餐刀.
lend: 借出，借.
modern: 现今，现在，当前，现代的.
needed: 需要.
picks: 选择.
pitying: 同情.
prisoner: 犯人，罪犯，囚犯.
reasonableness: 合理性.
representing: 代表.
sack: 大袋子，开除.
settled: 安定.
shovels: 铁锨.
smuggle: 走私，私运.
steal: 偷窃，盗窃，偷，窃取.
till: 直到.
tools: 工具.
wardrobe: 衣厨，衣橱，衣柜.
watermelon: 西瓜.
woodpile: 柴堆.
yard: 码，厂，厂子，场地.

"Yes."

"**Confound** it, it's **foolish**, Tom."

"It don't make no **difference** how foolish it is, it's the *right* way--and it's the **regular** way. And there ain't no *other* way, that ever I heard of, and I've read all the books that gives any information about these things. They always **dig** out with a case-knife--and not through **dirt**, mind you; generly it's through **solid rock**. And it takes them weeks and weeks and weeks, and for ever and ever. Why, look at one of them **prisoners** in the **bottom dungeon** of the Castle Deef, in the **harbor** of Marseilles, that **dug** himself out that way; how long was *he* at it, you **reckon**?"

"I don't know."

"Well, guess."

"I don't know. A month and a half."

"*Thirty-seven year*--and he come out in China. *That's* the kind. I **wish** the bottom of *this* **fortress** was solid rock."

"*Jim* don't know **nobody** in China."

"What's *that* got to do with it? Neither did that other **fellow**. But you're always a-wandering off on a side issue. Why can't you **stick** to the main point?"

"All right--I don't care where he comes out, so he *comes* out; and Jim don't, either, I reckon. But there's one thing, anyway--Jim's too old to be dug out with a case-knife. He won't last."

"Yes he will *last*, too. You don't reckon it's going to take thirty-seven years to dig out through a *dirt* **foundation**, do you?"

"How long will it take, Tom?"

"Well, we can't resk being as long as we **ought** to, because it mayn't take very long for Uncle Silas to hear from down there by New Orleans. He'll hear Jim ain't from there. Then his next move will be to **advertise** Jim, or something like that. So we can't resk being as long **digging** him out as we ought to. By rights I reckon we ought to be a couple of years; but we can't. Things being so **uncertain**,

Chinese Simplified

advertise：登广告，标榜，刊登广告．
bottom：底部，屁股，底．
confound：惊讶，混淆．
difference：差异，差，差别，区别，分歧，分别，误差．
dig：挖掘．
digging：挖掘．
dirt：污垢．
dug：挖掘．
dungeon：地牢．
fellow：同伴，伙伴．
foolish：愚蠢的．
fortress：城堡．
foundation：基础，根据，依据．
harbor：港口，港湾，澳，海港，包藏，包庇．
nobody：没有人，没人．
ought：应该，活该．
prisoners：囚犯．
reckon：估计，计算．
regular：固定，正常，通常，端正，正规的，常例的，定期的，整齐的，有秩序的，正规，经常．
rock：岩石，簸荡，摇．
solid：固体，立体，固体的，坚硬，扎实，实心的，坚固的，坚实．
stick：棍，棒子，棍子，插入，棒，黏贴，手杖．
uncertain：渺茫，不肯定的．
wish：愿望，希望，意愿，祝，祝愿，志愿．

what I **recommend** is this: that we really **dig** right in, as **quick** as we can; and after that, we can *let on*, to **ourselves**, that we was at it thirty-seven years. Then we can **snatch** him out and **rush** him away the first time there's an **alarm**. Yes, I **reckon** that 'll be the best way."

"Now, there's *sense* in that," I says. "Letting on don't **cost** nothing; letting on ain't no **trouble**; and if it's any **object**, I don't mind letting on we was at it a **hundred** and **fifty** year. It wouldn't **strain** me **none**, after I got my hand in. So I'll mosey **along** now, and smouch a **couple** of case-knives."

"Smouch three," he says; "we want one to make a saw out of."

"Tom, if it ain't unregular and **irreligious** to sejest it," I says, "there's an old **rusty** saw-blade around **yonder** sticking under the **weather- boarding** behind the smoke-house."

He looked kind of **weary** and discouraged-like, and says:

"It ain't no use to try to **learn** you nothing, Huck. Run along and smouch the knives—three of them." So I done it.

Chinese Simplified

alarm：警报，惊动．
along：沿着，沿，一同．
boarding：围板．
cost：费用，花费，代价，价款，价钱是．
couple：一对，挂钩，连接，夫妇，一双．
dig：挖掘．
fifty：五十，半白．
hundred：百，佰．
irreligious：无宗教的．
learn：学，学习．
none：无，没有．
object：对象，物件，宾语，物体，物，事物．
ourselves：我们自己，我们．
quick：快，玲珑，敏捷的，迅速的．
reckon：估计，计算．
recommend：推荐，保送，引进．
rush：速行，匆匆．
rusty：腐蚀，生锈的．
snatch：夺取，攫取．
strain：拉紧，种，系，紧张，菌株，品系．
trouble：麻烦，难度，难处．
weary：疲劳，疲乏，疲倦的．
weather：天气．
yonder：那边．

CHAPTER XXXVI

TRYING TO HELP JIM

As soon as we reckoned **everybody** was **asleep** that night we went down the lightning-rod, and **shut ourselves** up in the lean-to, and got out our **pile** of fox-fire, and went to work. We cleared **everything** out of the way, about four or five **foot along** the middle of the **bottom log**. Tom said we was right behind Jim's **bed** now, and we'd **dig** in under it, and when we got through there couldn't **nobody** in the **cabin** ever know there was any **hole** there, because Jim's counter-pin **hung** down most to the ground, and you'd have to **raise** it up and look under to see the hole. So we **dug** and dug with the case-knives **till** most **midnight**; and then we was dog-tired, and our **hands** was blistered, and yet you couldn't see we'd done anything **hardly**. At last I says:

"This ain't no thirty-seven year job; this is a thirty-eight year job, Tom Sawyer."

He never said nothing. But he sighed, and **pretty** soon he **stopped digging**, and then for a good little while I knowed that he was **thinking**. Then he says:

"It ain't no use, Huck, it ain't a-going to work. If we was **prisoners** it would, because then we'd have as many years as we wanted, and no **hurry**; and we wouldn't get but a **few** minutes to dig, every day, while they was changing

Chinese Simplified

along：沿着，沿，一同.
asleep：睡着，睡着的.
bed：床，床铺.
bottom：底部，屁股，底.
cabin：小屋，船舱.
dig：挖掘.
digging：挖掘.
dug：挖掘.
everybody：每个人，各位.
everything：一切事物，应有尽有，一切，事事.
few：少数，很少.
foot：脚，足，步兵，英尺，呎.
hands：手.
hardly：几乎不，毫不，辛苦地.
hole：洞，漏洞，孔，穴，洞穴，窟窿.
hung：挂.
hurry：仓促，匆忙，赶忙.
log：圆形木材，圆木，木头.
midnight：午夜，半夜.
nobody：没有人，没人.
ourselves：我们自己，我们.
pile：一堆，桩，堆.
pretty：漂亮，美丽的，秀丽.
prisoners：囚犯.
raise：升起，提高，筹措，增加，抚育，举起.
shut：关闭.
stopped：停止.
thinking：思想，思维.
till：直到.

watches, and so our hands wouldn't get blistered, and we could keep it up right along, year in and year out, and do it right, and the way it **ought** to be done. But *we* can't **fool** along; we got to **rush**; we ain't got no time to **spare**. If we was to put in another night this way we'd have to **knock** off for a week to let our hands get well--couldn't **touch** a case-knife with them sooner."

"Well, then, what we going to do, Tom?"

"I'll tell you. It ain't right, and it ain't **moral**, and I wouldn't like it to get out; but there ain't only just the one way: we got to **dig** him out with the **picks**, and *let on* it's case-knives."

"*Now* you're *talking*!" I says; "your head gets **leveler** and leveler all the time, Tom Sawyer," I says. "Picks is the thing, moral or no moral; and as for me, I don't care shucks for the **morality** of it, nohow. When I start in to **steal** a nigger, or a **watermelon**, or a Sunday-school book, I ain't no ways particular how it's done so it's done. What I want is my nigger; or what I want is my watermelon; or what I want is my Sunday- school book; and if a pick's the handiest thing, that's the thing I'm a- going to dig that nigger or that watermelon or that Sunday-school book out with; and I don't give a **dead rat** what the authorities **thinks** about it nuther."

"Well," he says, "there's **excuse** for picks and letting-on in a case like this; if it warn't so, I wouldn't **approve** of it, nor I wouldn't **stand** by and see the **rules** broke--because right is right, and wrong is wrong, and a body ain't got no business doing wrong when he ain't **ignorant** and **knows** better. It might answer for *you* to dig Jim out with a pick, *without* any letting on, because you don't know no better; but it wouldn't for me, because I do know better. Gimme a case-knife."

He had his own by him, but I **handed** him **mine**. He flung it down, and says:

"Gimme a *case-knife*."

I didn't know just what to do--but then I thought. I scratched around amongst the old **tools**, and got a pickaxe and give it to him, and he took it and went to work, and never said a word.

He was always just that particular. Full of **principle**.

Chinese Simplified

approve：赞成，认证，赞同，认可，允许.
dead：死.
dig：挖掘.
excuse：包涵，借口，原谅.
fool：呆子，笨蛋，傻子，笨人，愚人.
handed：传递，有手的.
ignorant：愚昧，无知的，茫然.
knock：敲，敲撞.
knows：知道.
leveler：平等主义者.
mine：矿，我的，矿山，矿井.
moral：道德.
morality：道德.
ought：应该，活该.
pick：掐，采摘，挑选，挑，鹤嘴锄，采，选择.
picks：选择.
principle：原理，原则，道理.
rat：老鼠，鼠.
rules：条例，规程，守则，裁定，规则.
rush：速行，匆匆.
spare：备用，饶恕.
stand：站住，主张，架子，站立，耐，站，架.
steal：偷窃，盗窃，偷，窃取.
thinks：想.
tools：工具.
touch：触摸，笔锋，触，联系，碰，接触.
watermelon：西瓜.

So then I got a **shovel**, and then we picked and shoveled, turn about, and made the **fur** fly. We **stuck** to it about a half an hour, which was as long as we could stand up; but we had a good deal of a hole to show for it. When I got up stairs I looked out at the window and see Tom doing his level best with the lightning-rod, but he couldn't come it, his hands was so **sore**. At last he says:

"It ain't no use, it can't be done. What you **reckon** I better do? Can't you think of no way?"

"Yes," I says, "but I reckon it ain't regular. Come up the stairs, and let on it's a lightning-rod."

So he done it.

Next day Tom **stole** a pewter **spoon** and a **brass candlestick** in the house, for to make some pens for Jim out of, and six tallow candles; and I **hung** around the nigger **cabins** and laid for a chance, and stole three **tin plates**. Tom says it wasn't enough; but I said nobody wouldn't ever see the plates that Jim throwed out, because they'd fall in the dog-fennel and jimpson weeds under the window-hole--then we could tote them back and he could use them over again. So Tom was **satisfied**. Then he says:

"Now, the thing to study out is, how to get the things to Jim."

"Take them in through the hole," I says, "when we get it done."

He only just looked **scornful**, and said something about nobody ever heard of such an **idiotic** idea, and then he went to **studying**. By and by he said he had **ciphered** out two or three ways, but there warn't no need to decide on any of them yet. Said we'd got to post Jim first.

That night we went down the lightning-rod a **little** after ten, and took one of the candles along, and **listened** under the window-hole, and heard Jim **snoring**; so we **pitched** it in, and it didn't **wake** him. Then we whirled in with the pick and shovel, and in about two hours and a half the job was done. We **crept** in under Jim's bed and into the cabin, and pawed around and found the candle and lit it, and stood over Jim **awhile**, and found him looking **hearty** and healthy, and then we **woke** him up **gentle** and **gradual**. He was so glad to see us he most

Chinese Simplified

awhile: 一会儿.
brass: 黄铜.
cabin: 小屋，船舱.
candle: 蜡烛.
candles: 蜡烛.
candlestick: 烛台，蜡台.
ciphered: 密码.
crept: 爬行.
fur: 毛，软毛.
gentle: 轻松，文雅的，斯文，柔和.
gradual: 逐渐的.
hearty: 诚恳，热诚的.
hung: 挂.
idiotic: 白痴般，愚蠢的.
listened: 听.
lit: 点燃.
pitched: 沥青.
plates: 盘子.
reckon: 估计，计算.
satisfied: 满意，乐意，心满意足的.
scornful: 轻视，轻视的.
shovel: 铲子，铲，铁锨.
snoring: 打鼾.
sore: 疼痛，疮，疼痛的.
spoon: 匙，调羹.
stole: 偷了.
stuck: 黏贴.
studying: 学习.
tin: 锡，罐头.
wake: 醒来，醒觉.
woke: 醒觉.

cried; and called us **honey**, and all the **pet** names he could think of; and was for having us **hunt** up a cold-chisel to cut the **chain** off of his **leg** with right away, and **clearing** out without losing any time. But Tom he showed him how unregular it would be, and set down and told him all about our plans, and how we could **alter** them in a minute any time there was an **alarm**; and not to be the **least afraid**, because we would see he got away, *sure*. So Jim he said it was all right, and we set there and **talked** over old times **awhile**, and then Tom asked a lot of questions, and when Jim told him Uncle Silas come in every day or two to **pray** with him, and Aunt Sally come in to see if he was **comfortable** and had **plenty** to eat, and both of them was kind as they could be, Tom says:

"*Now* I know how to **fix** it. We'll send you some things by them."

I said, "Don't do nothing of the kind; it's one of the most **jackass** ideas I ever struck;" but he never paid no attention to me; went right on. It was his way when he'd got his plans set.

So he told Jim how we'd have to **smuggle** in the rope-ladder **pie** and other large things by Nat, the nigger that fed him, and he must be on the **lookout**, and not be **surprised**, and not let Nat see him open them; and we would put small things in uncle's coat-pockets and he must **steal** them out; and we would **tie** things to aunt's apron-strings or put them in her apron-pocket, if we got a chance; and told him what they would be and what they was for. And told him how to keep a **journal** on the **shirt** with his blood, and all that. He told him everything. Jim he couldn't see no sense in the most of it, but he allowed we was white folks and knowed better than him; so he was **satisfied**, and said he would do it all just as Tom said.

Jim had plenty corn-cob pipes and **tobacco**; so we had a right down good sociable time; then we crawled out through the **hole**, and so home to bed, with hands that looked like they'd been chawed. Tom was in high **spirits**. He said it was the best **fun** he ever had in his life, and the most intellectural; and said if he only could see his way to it we would keep it up all the rest of our lives and leave Jim to our children to get out; for he believed Jim would come to like it better and better the more he got used to it. He said that in that way it could be strung out

Chinese Simplified

afraid: 危惧，恐怕，害怕．
alarm: 警报，惊动．
alter: 更改，变更，修改，改变，改．
awhile: 一会儿．
chain: 链，链子，连锁．
clearing: 清除．
comfortable: 舒服，舒服的．
fix: 安装，奠定，固定，修理．
fun: 娱乐．
hole: 洞，漏洞，孔，穴，洞穴，窟窿．
honey: 蜂蜜，蜜，蜜糖．
hunt: 打猎，狩猎．
jackass: 笨蛋．
journal: 日志，通报．
least: 最少，至少，最少的．
leg: 腿，脚．
lookout: 眺望，伸出窗口观看．
pet: 宠物．
pie: 馅饼．
plenty: 丰富，许多．
pray: 祈祷．
satisfied: 满意，乐意，心满意足的．
shirt: 衬衫，衬衣．
smuggle: 走私，私运．
spirits: 精神．
steal: 偷窃，盗窃，偷，窃取．
surprised: 惊讶．
talked: 谈话．
tie: 不分胜负，打结，束缚，轨枕，绑，领带．
tobacco: 烟草．

to as much as **eighty** year, and would be the best time on record. And he said it would make us all **celebrated** that had a hand in it.

In the morning we went out to the **woodpile** and chopped up the **brass candlestick** into **handy sizes**, and Tom put them and the pewter **spoon** in his **pocket**. Then we went to the nigger cabins, and while I got Nat's notice off, Tom shoved a piece of candlestick into the middle of a **corn-** pone that was in Jim's **pan**, and we went along with Nat to see how it would work, and it just worked **noble**; when Jim bit into it it most mashed all his teeth out; and there warn't ever anything could a worked better. Tom said so himself. Jim he never let on but what it was only just a piece of rock or something like that that's always getting into **bread**, you know; but after that he never bit into nothing but what he jabbed his **fork** into it in three or four places first.

And whilst we was a-standing there in the dimmish light, here comes a couple of the hounds **bulging** in from under Jim's bed; and they kept on **piling** in **till** there was **eleven** of them, and there warn't hardly room in there to get your breath. By jings, we **forgot** to **fasten** that lean-to door! The nigger Nat he only just hollered "Witches" once, and keeled over on to the floor amongst the dogs, and begun to **groan** like he was **dying**. Tom jerked the door open and flung out a **slab** of Jim's **meat**, and the dogs went for it, and in two seconds he was out himself and back again and **shut** the door, and I knowed he'd fixed the other door too. Then he went to work on the nigger, coaxing him and petting him, and asking him if he'd been imagining he saw something again. He raised up, and blinked his eyes around, and says:

"Mars Sid, you'll say I's a **fool**, but if I didn't b'lieve I see most a million dogs, er devils, er some'n, I wisht I may die right heah in dese **tracks**. I did, mos' sholy. Mars Sid, I *felt* um--I *felt* um, sah; dey was all over me. Dad **fetch** it, I **jis'** wisht I could git my han's on one er dem witches jis' wunst--on'y jis' wunst--it's all I'd **ast**. But mos'ly I wisht dey'd lemme 'lone, I does."

Tom says:

Chinese Simplified

ast：虹志电脑.
brass：黄铜.
bread：面包.
bulging：膨胀.
candlestick：烛台，蜡台.
celebrated：着名，著名.
corn：玉蜀黍，包谷，玉米.
dying：不行了，垂死，垂死的.
eighty：八十.
eleven：十一.
fasten：绑住.
fetch：拿，取，带来.
fool：呆子，笨蛋，傻子，笨人，愚人.
forgot：忘记.
fork：叉，叉子.
groan：呻吟，哼.
handy：灵巧，便当，顺手，方便的，简便.
jis：日本工业标准.
meat：肉.
noble：高贵，高贵的，贵族.
pan：平锅.
piling：打桩，打桩工程，桩材.
pocket：口袋，衣袋，兜儿，窟窿.
shut：关闭.
sizes：大小.
slab：木板，石片，板皮，扁坯，石板.
spoon：匙，调羹.
till：直到.
tracks：轨道.
woodpile：柴堆.

"Well, I tell you what I think. What makes them come here just at this **runaway** nigger's breakfast-time? It's because they're **hungry**; that's the **reason**. You make them a **witch pie**; that's the thing for *you* to do."

"But my lan', Mars Sid, how's I gwyne to make 'm a witch pie? I doan' know how to make it. I hain't ever hearn er sich a thing b'fo'."

"Well, then, I'll have to make it myself."

"Will you do it, honey?--will you? I'll wusshup **de** groun' und' yo' **foot**, I will!"

"All right, I'll do it, **seeing** it's you, and you've been good to us and **showed** us the runaway nigger. But you got to be **mighty careful**. When we come around, you **turn** your back; and then **whatever** we've put in the **pan**, don't you let on you see it at all. And don't you look when Jim **unloads** the pan--something might **happen**, I don't know what. And above all, don't you *handle* the witch-things."

"*Hannel* 'm, Mars Sid? What *is* you a-talkin' 'bout? I wouldn' **lay** de **weight** er my **finger** on um, not f'r ten hund'd thous'n **billion** dollars, I wouldn't."

Chinese Simplified

billion: 万亿.
careful: 小心, 仔细, 不苟, 慎重, 周密, 小心的, 精细, 细心, 细致.
de: 可选择丢弃.
finger: 手指, 指头.
foot: 脚, 足, 步兵, 英尺, 呎.
handle: 柄, 把手, 把柄, 处理, 辫子, 耳子, 把子, 弄, 对付, 加以, 处置.
happen: 发生.
hungry: 饥饿, 饿, 饥饿的.
lay: 产卵, 安放, 放, 凡俗.
mighty: 伟大, 强势, 强大的.
pan: 平锅.
pie: 馅饼.
reason: 理由, 道理, 原因, 缘故, 缘由, 情理.
runaway: 逃亡者, 跑道.
seeing: 有鉴于.
showed: 展示.
turn: 转动, 转弯.
unloads: 卸货.
weight: 重量, 体重, 包袱, 衡量, 衡, 分量, 砝码, 重担, 使加权.
whatever: 无论如何, 无论何事, 不拘, 任何.
witch: 巫婆, 女巫.

CHAPTER XXXVII

JIM GETS HIS WITCH **PIE**

That was all **fixed**. So then we went away and went to the rubbage-pile in the back **yard**, where they keep the old **boots**, and **rags**, and pieces of bottles, and wore-out **tin** things, and all such **truck**, and scratched around and found an old tin **washpan**, and **stopped** up the **holes** as well as we could, to **bake** the pie in, and took it down **cellar** and **stole** it full of **flour** and started for **breakfast**, and found a couple of shingle-nails that Tom said would be **handy** for a **prisoner** to **scrabble** his name and **sorrows** on the **dungeon walls** with, and **dropped** one of them in Aunt Sally's apron-pocket which was hanging on a chair, and t'other we **stuck** in the band of Uncle Silas's hat, which was on the **bureau**, because we heard the children say their pa and **ma** was going to the **runaway** nigger's house this morning, and then went to breakfast, and Tom dropped the pewter **spoon** in Uncle Silas's coat-pocket, and Aunt Sally wasn't come yet, so we had to wait a little while.

And when she come she was hot and red and cross, and couldn't hardly wait for the **blessing**; and then she went to **sluicing** out **coffee** with one hand and cracking the handiest child's head with her **thimble** with the other, and says:

"I've hunted high and I've hunted low, and it does beat all what *has* become of your other shirt."

Chinese Simplified

bake：烤，烘，焙烧，烘烤，焙．
blessing：祝福．
boots：靴子．
breakfast：早餐，早饭，早点．
bureau：局，处．
cellar：地下室，地窖．
coffee：咖啡．
dropped：落下．
dungeon：地牢．
fixed：固定，确定，一定，固定的．
flour：面粉，白面，粉．
handy：灵巧，便当，顺手，方便的，简便．
hat：帽子．
holes：洞．
ma：妈，马，文学硕士．
pa：爸爸．
pie：馅饼．
prisoner：犯人，罪犯，囚犯．
rags：碎布．
runaway：逃亡者，跑道．
scrabble：涂写．
sluicing：泄水．
sorrows：悲哀．
spoon：匙，调羹．
stole：偷了．
stopped：停止．
stuck：黏贴．
thimble：顶针，缝纫用的顶针．
tin：锡，罐头．
truck：卡车．
walls：墙壁．
yard：码，厂，厂子，场地．

My heart fell down amongst my **lungs** and livers and things, and a hard piece of corn-crust started down my **throat** after it and got met on the road with a **cough**, and was **shot** across the table, and took one of the children in the eye and **curled** him up like a fishing-worm, and let a **cry** out of him the size of a warwhoop, and Tom he turned kinder blue around the **gills**, and it all amounted to a considerable state of things for about a **quarter** of a **minute** or as much as that, and I would a **sold** out for half price if there was a bidder. But after that we was all right again--it was the **sudden surprise** of it that knocked us so kind of cold. **Uncle** Silas he says:

"It's most **uncommon curious**, I can't understand it. I know **perfectly** well I took it *off*, because--"

"Because you hain't got but one *on*. Just ***listen*** at the man! I know you took it off, and know it by a better way than your wool-gethering memory, too, because it was on the clo's-line yesterday--I see it there myself. But it's gone, that's the long and the short of it, and you'll just have to change to a red flann'l one **till** I can get time to make a new one. And it 'll be the third I've made in two years. It just **keeps** a body on the **jump** to keep you in **shirts**; and whatever you do **manage** to *do* with 'm all is more'n I can make out. A body 'd think you *would* learn to take some sort of care of 'em at your time of life."

"I know it, Sally, and I do try all I can. But it oughtn't to be **altogether** my **fault**, because, you know, I don't see them nor have nothing to do with them **except** when they're on me; and I don't believe I've ever lost one of them *off* of me."

"Well, it ain't *your* fault if you haven't, Silas; you'd a done it if you could, I **reckon**. And the shirt ain't all that's gone, nuther. Ther's a **spoon** gone; and *that* ain't all. There was ten, and now ther's only nine. The **calf** got the shirt, I reckon, but the calf never took the spoon, *that's* certain."

"Why, what else is gone, Sally?"

"Ther's six ***candles*** gone--that's what. The rats could a got the candles, and I reckon they did; I **wonder** they don't walk off with the whole place, the way

Chinese Simplified

altogether：总共，一共.
calf：小牛，犊.
candles：蜡烛.
cough：咳，咳嗽.
cry：喊，叫，哭，哭泣.
curious：有好奇心，好奇，好奇的.
curled：卷曲.
except：除了，除了之外.
fault：故障，过失，缺点，毛病，断层，短处，缺陷.
gills：腮.
jump：跳，跳跃.
keeps：保持.
listen：听，倾听.
lungs：肺脏.
manage：符合，管理，处理.
minute：分钟，详细，分，微小的，渺小.
perfectly：完美，完美地.
quarter：四分之一.
reckon：估计，计算.
shirt：衬衫，衬衣.
shot：射击.
sold：卖了.
spoon：匙，调羹.
sudden：突然，急剧，突然的.
surprise：使吃惊，惊奇，惊骇.
throat：嗓子，喉咙，喉头，咽喉.
till：直到.
uncle：叔叔，伯伯，叔父，大爷，老大爷，姑夫.
uncommon：稀有，稀有的.
wonder：奇迹，惊奇.

you're always going to stop their **holes** and don't do it; and if they warn't fools they'd sleep in your hair, Silas--*you'd* never find it out; but you can't lay the *spoon* on the rats, and that I know."

"Well, Sally, I'm in **fault**, and I **acknowledge** it; I've been **remiss**; but I won't let to-morrow go by without **stopping** up them holes."

"Oh, I wouldn't **hurry**; next year 'll do. Matilda Angelina Araminta *Phelps*!"

Whack comes the **thimble**, and the child **snatches** her claws out of the sugar-bowl without fooling around any. Just then the nigger woman steps on to the **passage**, and says:

"Missus, dey's a **sheet** gone."

"*A sheet* gone! Well, for the land's sake!"

"I'll stop up them holes to-day," says Uncle Silas, looking sorrowful.

"Oh, *do* shet up!--s'pose the rats took the *sheet*? *Where's* it gone, Lize?"

"Clah to **goodness** I hain't no **notion**, Miss' Sally. She wuz on de clo'sline yistiddy, but she done gone: she ain' dah no mo' now."

"I **reckon** the world *is* coming to an end. I *never* see the beat of it in all my born days. A **shirt**, and a sheet, and a spoon, and six can--"

"Missus," comes a young yaller **wench**, "dey's a **brass** cannelstick miss'n."

"Cler out from here, you **hussy**, er I'll take a **skillet** to ye!"

Well, she was just a-biling. I **begun** to lay for a chance; I reckoned I would **sneak** out and go for the **woods till** the weather **moderated**. She kept a-raging right along, running her **insurrection** all by herself, and everybody else **mighty meek** and **quiet**; and at last Uncle Silas, looking kind of **foolish**, fishes up that spoon out of his **pocket**. She stopped, with her mouth open and her hands up; and as for me, I wished I was in Jeruslem or somewheres. But not long, because she says:

"It's *just* as I expected. So you had it in your pocket all the time; and like as not you've got the other things there, too. How'd it get there?"

Chinese Simplified

acknowledge：认知，承认.
begun：开始.
brass：黄铜.
fault：故障，过失，缺点，毛病，断层，短处，缺陷.
foolish：愚蠢的.
goodness：美德.
holes：洞.
hurry：仓促，匆忙，赶忙.
hussy：轻佻的女子.
insurrection：暴动，起义.
meek：谦顺的.
mighty：伟大，强势，强大的.
moderated：适中.
notion：观念.
passage：通道，通路，通过.
pocket：口袋，衣袋，兜儿，窟窿.
quiet：安静，寂静，安定，安生，沉静，宁静的.
reckon：估计，计算.
remiss：怠慢的，疏忽的，迟缓的.
sheet：片，一张，床单，纸张.
shirt：衬衫，衬衣.
skillet：长柄锅.
snatches：攫取.
sneak：潜行，潜入.
spoon：匙，调羹.
stopping：停止.
thimble：顶针，缝纫用的顶针.
till：直到.
wench：乡下姑娘，女仆.
whack：重打.
woods：树林，森林.

"I reely don't know, Sally," he says, kind of **apologizing**, "or you know I would tell. I was a-studying over my **text** in Acts Seventeen before breakfast, and I **reckon** I put it in there, not **noticing**, meaning to put my Testament in, and it must be so, because my Testament ain't in; but I'll go and see; and if the Testament is where I had it, I'll know I didn't put it in, and **that** will show that I **laid** the Testament down and took up the **spoon**, and--"

"Oh, for the land's **sake**! Give a body a rest! Go 'long now, the whole **kit** and biling of **ye**; and don't come nigh me again **till** I've got back my peace of mind."

I'd a heard her if she'd a said it to herself, let alone speaking it out; and I'd a got up and obeyed her if I'd a been dead. As we was **passing** through the setting-room the old man he took up his hat, and the **shingle- nail** fell out on the floor, and he just **merely** picked it up and laid it on the mantel-shelf, and never said nothing, and went out. Tom see him do it, and remembered about the spoon, and says:

"Well, it ain't no use to send things by *him* no more, he ain't reliable." Then he says: "But he done us a good turn with the spoon, anyway, without knowing it, and so we'll go and do him one without *him* knowing it--stop up his rat-holes."

There was a **noble** good lot of them down **cellar**, and it took us a whole hour, but we done the job **tight** and good and **shipshape**. Then we heard steps on the **stairs**, and blowed out our light and **hid**; and here comes the old man, with a **candle** in one hand and a **bundle** of stuff in t'other, looking as **absent**-minded as year before last. He went a mooning around, first to one rat-hole and then another, till he'd been to them all. Then he stood about five minutes, **picking** tallow-drip off of his candle and thinking. Then he turns off slow and dreamy towards the stairs, saying:

"Well, for the life of me I can't remember when I done it. I could show her now that I warn't to **blame** on account of the rats. But never mind-- let it go. I reckon it wouldn't do no good."

And so he went on a-mumbling up stairs, and then we left. He was a **mighty** nice old man. And always is.

Chinese Simplified

absent-minded: 大意，心不在焉的，茫然的.
apologizing: 道歉.
blame: 责备，咎，非难，责任，罪，责怪，归咎.
bundle: 捆，包裹，包，包扎，束，把.
candle: 蜡烛.
cellar: 地下室，地窖.
hat: 帽子.
hid: 躲藏.
kit: 工具.
laid: 放.
merely: 仅仅，只是，只，不过，单纯，只管，只顾.
mighty: 伟大，强势，强大的.
nail: 钉，指甲，钉子.
noble: 高贵，高贵的，贵族.
noticing: 注意到.
passing: 经过的，短暂的，目前的，及格的.
picking: 选择，投纬.
reckon: 估计，计算.
sake: 缘故.
shingle: 木瓦，屋顶板.
shipshape: 井然有序.
spoon: 匙，调羹.
stairs: 楼梯.
text: 课文，案文，正文，文字.
tight: 严格，严密，紧，紧的，严竣，狭隘.
till: 直到.
ye: 你们.

Tom was a good **deal bothered** about what to do for a **spoon**, but he said we'd got to have it; so he took a think. When he had **ciphered** it out he told me how we was to do; then we went and waited around the spoon-basket **till** we see Aunt Sally **coming**, and then Tom went to **counting** the spoons and laying them out to one side, and I **slid** one of them up my **sleeve**, and Tom says:

"Why, Aunt Sally, there ain't but **nine** spoons *yet*."

She says:

"Go 'long to your play, and don't bother me. I know better, I counted 'm myself."

"Well, I've counted them **twice**, Aunty, and I can't make but nine."

She looked out of all **patience**, but of course she come to count--anybody would.

"I **declare** to **gracious** ther' *ain't* but nine!" she says. "Why, what in the world--plague *take* the things, I'll count 'm again."

So I **slipped** back the one I had, and when she got done counting, she says:

"Hang the **troublesome** rubbage, ther's *ten* now!" and she looked huffy and bothered both. But Tom says:

"Why, Aunty, I don't think there's ten."

"You numskull, didn't you see me *count* 'm?"

"I know, but--"

"Well, I'll count 'm *again*."

So I smouched one, and they come out nine, same as the other time. Well, she *was* in a **tearing** way--just a-trembling all over, she was so **mad**. But she counted and counted till she got that addled she'd start to count in the **basket** for a spoon sometimes; and so, three times they come out right, and three times they come out **wrong**. Then she grabbed up the basket and slammed it across the house and knocked the **cat** galley-west; and she said cle'r out and let her have some **peace**, and if we come **bothering** around her again **betwixt** that and **dinner** she'd **skin** us. So we had the **odd** spoon, and **dropped** it in her apron-pocket

Chinese Simplified

basket: 篮，篮子，笼，淘箩，筐，笼子.
betwixt: 中间，在…之间.
bother: 烦扰，打扰，理会.
bothering: 打扰.
cat: 猫.
ciphered: 密码.
coming: 未来，到来.
count: 计数，伯爵，计算，有价值，认为.
deal: 处理.
declare: 宣布，陈述，声明，宣告.
dinner: 晚餐，正餐.
dropped: 落下.
gracious: 亲切，亲切的，有礼貌的.
mad: 狂，发怒，发狂，生气，疯狂的.
nine: 九.
odd: 奇怪，莫名其妙，零头，奇异的.
patience: 忍耐，忍受，耐心，耐性.
peace: 和平.
skin: 皮肤，剥皮.
sleeve: 袖子，衣袖.
slid: 滑行.
slipped: 滑落.
spoon: 匙，调羹.
tearing: 撕裂的.
till: 直到.
troublesome: 淘神，讨厌，麻烦，麻烦的，伤脑筋.
twice: 两次.
wrong: 不对，不平，错误的，错误.

whilst she was a- giving us our **sailing orders**, and Jim got it all right, along with her **shingle nail**, before **noon**. We was very well **satisfied** with this business, and Tom allowed it was worth twice the trouble it took, because he said *now* she couldn't ever count them **spoons** twice **alike** again to save her life; and wouldn't believe she'd counted them right if she *did*; and said that after she'd about counted her head off for the next three days he judged she'd give it up and **offer** to kill anybody that wanted her to ever count them any more.

So we put the sheet back on the line that night, and **stole** one out of her **closet**; and kept on putting it back and **stealing** it again for a couple of days till she didn't know how many sheets she had any more, and she didn't *care*, and warn't a-going to bullyrag the rest of her soul out about it, and wouldn't count them again not to save her life; she druther die first.

So we was all right now, as to the shirt and the sheet and the spoon and the **candles**, by the help of the **calf** and the rats and the mixed-up counting; and as to the **candlestick**, it warn't no **consequence**, it would blow over by and by.

But that **pie** was a job; we had no end of trouble with that pie. We fixed it up away down in the **woods**, and **cooked** it there; and we got it done at last, and very satisfactory, too; but not all in one day; and we had to use up three wash-pans full of **flour** before we got through, and we got **burnt** pretty much all over, in places, and eyes put out with the smoke; because, you see, we didn't want nothing but a **crust**, and we couldn't **prop** it up right, and she would always **cave** in. But of course we thought of the right way at last--which was to cook the **ladder**, too, in the pie. So then we laid in with Jim the second night, and **tore** up the sheet all in little strings and twisted them together, and long before **daylight** we had a lovely **rope** that you could a **hung** a person with. We let on it took nine months to make it.

And in the **forenoon** we took it down to the woods, but it wouldn't go into the pie. Being made of a whole sheet, that way, there was rope enough for forty **pies** if we'd a wanted them, and plenty left over for **soup**, or **sausage**, or anything you choose. We could a had a whole dinner.

Chinese Simplified

alike: 相同.
burnt: 烧伤的，烧过的，烧.
calf: 小牛，犊.
candles: 蜡烛.
candlestick: 烛台，蜡台.
cave: 洞穴，洞，穴.
closet: 壁橱.
consequence: 后果.
cooked: 煮熟.
crust: 面包皮，地壳.
daylight: 日光，白天.
flour: 面粉，白面，粉.
forenoon: 上午，午前.
hung: 挂.
ladder: 阶梯，梯子.
nail: 钉，指甲，钉子.
noon: 中午，正午，晌午.
offer: 捐助，开设，提供.
orders: 命令.
pie: 馅饼.
pies: 馅饼.
prop: 支撑，支柱.
rope: 绳索，绳子.
sailing: 航海术，航海，航行.
satisfied: 满意，乐意，心满意足的.
sausage: 香肠，腊肠.
shingle: 木瓦，屋顶板.
soup: 汤，羹汤.
spoon: 匙，调羹.
stealing: 偷垒，偷窃.
stole: 偷了.
tore: 撕扯.
woods: 树林，森林.

But we didn't need it. All we needed was just enough for the **pie**, and so we throwed the rest away. We didn't **cook** none of the **pies** in the **wash- pan**--afraid the **solder** would **melt**; but Uncle Silas he had a **noble brass** warming-pan which he thought considerable of, because it belonged to one of his ancesters with a long wooden handle that come over from England with William the Conqueror in the Mayflower or one of them early **ships** and was **hid** away up **garret** with a lot of other old pots and things that was **valuable**, not on account of being any account, because they warn't, but on account of them being relicts, you know, and we snaked her out, private, and took her down there, but she **failed** on the first pies, because we didn't know how, but she come up **smiling** on the last one. We took and lined her with **dough**, and set her in the **coals**, and **loaded** her up with **rag rope**, and put on a dough roof, and shut down the **lid**, and put hot embers on top, and stood off five foot, with the long handle, **cool** and comfortable, and in fifteen minutes she turned out a pie that was a satisfaction to look at. But the person that et it would want to **fetch** a couple of kags of toothpicks along, for if that rope **ladder** wouldn't **cramp** him down to business I don't know nothing what I'm talking about, and lay him in enough **stomach**-ache to last him till next time, too.

Nat didn't look when we put the **witch** pie in Jim's pan; and we put the three **tin plates** in the bottom of the pan under the vittles; and so Jim got everything all right, and as soon as he was by himself he busted into the pie and hid the rope ladder inside of his **straw tick**, and scratched some marks on a tin plate and throwed it out of the window-hole.

Chinese Simplified

brass：黄铜.
coals：煤.
cook：厨子，厨司，厨师，炊事员，烹调，煮，烹煮.
cool：凉，镇静，镇定，凉爽，凉爽的.
cramp：夹子，扒钉，钳.
dough：生面团.
failed：失败.
fetch：拿，取，带来.
garret：阁楼，顶楼.
hid：躲藏.
ladder：阶梯，梯子.
lid：盖子.
loaded：载入.
melt：溶化，融化，熔解.
noble：高贵，高贵的，贵族.
pan：平锅.
pie：馅饼.
pies：馅饼.
plates：盘子.
rag：破布，碎布.
rope：绳索，绳子.
ships：船只，船.
smiling：微笑的.
solder：焊料，焊.
stomach-ache：肚痛.
straw：稻草，吸管.
tick：壁虱，滴答声，勾.
tin：锡，罐头.
valuable：宝贵，有价值，有价值的.
wash：洗涤，洗刷，洗.
witch：巫婆，女巫.

CHAPTER XXXVIII

"HERE A CAPTIVE HEART BUSTED"

Making them pens was a distressid **tough** job, and so was the saw; and Jim **allowed** the **inscription** was going to be the toughest of all. That's the one which the **prisoner** has to **scrabble** on the **wall**. But he had to have it; Tom said he'd *got* to; there warn't no case of a state prisoner not scrabbling his inscription to **leave** behind, and his **coat** of **arms**.

"Look at Lady Jane Grey," he says; "look at Gilford Dudley; look at old Northumberland! Why, Huck, s'pose it *is* **considerble** trouble?--what you going to do?--how you going to get around it? Jim's *got* to do his inscription and coat of arms. They all do."

Jim says:

"Why, Mars Tom, I hain't got no coat o' arm; I hain't got nuffn but **dish** yer ole **shirt**, en you **knows** I got to keep de **journal** on dat."

"Oh, you don't understand, Jim; a coat of arms is very different."

"Well," I says, "Jim's right, **anyway**, when he says he ain't got no coat of arms, because he hain't."

Chinese Simplified

allowed：允许.
anyway：无论如何，反正.
arm：手臂，膀子，臂膀，臂，膀臂，胳膊，肩膀，武器.
arms：武器，武装，军备，兵戈，兵器，军火，兵戎.
coat：外套，上衣.
de：可选择丢弃.
dish：菜，碟.
inscription：题字，题词，铭刻.
journal：日志，通报.
knows：知道.
leave：别离，动身，离开，起身.
prisoner：犯人，罪犯，囚犯.
scrabble：涂写.
shirt：衬衫，衬衣.
tough：强硬，坚韧的.
wall：墙壁，墙.

"I reckon I knowed that," Tom says, "but you **bet** he'll have one before he goes out of this--because he's going out *right*, and there ain't going to be no **flaws** in his record."

So whilst me and Jim filed away at the pens on a brickbat **apiece**, Jim a-making his'n out of the **brass** and I making mine out of the **spoon**, Tom set to work to think out the coat of arms. By and by he said he'd **struck** so many good ones he didn't hardly know which to take, but there was one which he reckoned he'd decide on. He says:

"On the scutcheon we'll have a **bend** *or* in the dexter **base**, a saltire *murrey* in the fess, with a dog, couchant, for common charge, and under his foot a chain embattled, for **slavery**, with a chevron *vert* in a **chief** engrailed, and three invected lines on a **field** ***azure***, with the nombril **points rampant** on a dancette indented; **crest**, a **runaway** nigger, ***sable***, with his **bundle** over his shoulder on a bar **sinister**; and a couple of gules for supporters, which is you and me; **motto**, *maggiore fretta, minore otto*. Got it out of a book--means the more **haste** the less speed."

"Geewhillikins," I says, "but what does the rest of it mean?"

"We ain't got no time to **bother** over that," he says; "we got to **dig** in like all git-out."

"Well, anyway," I says, "what's *some* of it? What's a fess?"

"A fess--a fess is--*you* don't need to know what a fess is. I'll show him how to make it when he gets to it."

"Shucks, Tom," I says, "I think you might tell a person. What's a bar sinister?"

"Oh, I don't know. But he's got to have it. All the **nobility** does."

That was just his way. If it didn't suit him to explain a thing to you, he wouldn't do it. You might **pump** at him a week, it wouldn't make no difference.

He'd got all that coat of arms business fixed, so now he started in to **finish** up the rest of that part of the work, which was to plan out a **mournful** inscription--

Chinese Simplified

apiece: 各自，各自地.
azure: 天蓝色，蔚蓝色的.
base: 基础，基地，底，卑鄙，基，卑劣，卑下.
bend: 弯曲，弯折.
bet: 打赌，赌.
bother: 烦扰，打扰，理会.
brass: 黄铜.
bundle: 捆，包裹，包，包扎，束，把.
chief: 首席，首领，主要的.
crest: 鸡冠，冠子，鸟冠.
dig: 挖掘.
field: 领域，字段，田野，方面，场，平原，田地，田间的，野生的，田间.
finish: 完成，最后阶段，润饰，下场，结束.
flaws: 瑕疵.
haste: 匆忙.
motto: 座右铭.
mournful: 悲切，悲恸，悲恸的.
nobility: 贵族，高贵.
otto: 玫瑰油.
points: 点.
pump: 唧筒，泵.
rampant: 猖獗，嚣张，猛烈的，猖獗的.
runaway: 逃亡者，跑道.
sable: 黑貂.
sinister: 邪恶，邪恶的，不吉的.
slavery: 奴隶制度，奴隶制.
spoon: 匙，调羹.
struck: 敲打.

said Jim got to have one, like they all done. He made up a lot, and wrote them out on a paper, and read them off, so:

1. Here a **captive** heart busted. 2. Here a poor **prisoner**, forsook by the world and friends, fretted his **sorrowful** life. 3. Here a **lonely** heart broke, and a **worn** spirit went to its rest, after thirty-seven years of **solitary captivity**. 4. Here, **homeless** and **friendless**, after thirty-seven years of **bitter** captivity, perished a **noble stranger**, natural son of Louis XIV.

Tom's voice **trembled** whilst he was reading them, and he most broke down. When he got done he couldn't no way make up his mind which one for Jim to **scrabble** on to the wall, they was all so good; but at last he allowed he would let him scrabble them all on. Jim said it would take him a year to scrabble such a lot of **truck** on to the **logs** with a **nail**, and he didn't know how to make letters, besides; but Tom said he would **block** them out for him, and then he wouldn't have nothing to do but just follow the lines. Then pretty soon he says:

"Come to think, the logs ain't a-going to do; they don't have log walls in a **dungeon**: we got to **dig** the **inscriptions** into a rock. We'll **fetch** a rock."

Jim said the rock was worse than the logs; he said it would take him such a pison long time to dig them into a rock he wouldn't ever get out. But Tom said he would let me help him do it. Then he took a look to see how me and Jim was getting along with the pens. It was most **pesky tedious** hard work and slow, and didn't give my hands no show to get well of the **sores**, and we didn't seem to make no headway, hardly; so Tom says:

"I know how to **fix** it. We got to have a rock for the coat of arms and **mournful** inscriptions, and we can kill two birds with that same rock. There's a **gaudy** big **grindstone** down at the mill, and we'll smouch it, and **carve** the things on it, and file out the pens and the saw on it, too."

It warn't no slouch of an idea; and it warn't no slouch of a grindstone nuther; but we allowed we'd **tackle** it. It warn't quite **midnight** yet, so we cleared out for the mill, leaving Jim at work. We smouched the grindstone, and set out to roll her home, but it was a most nation tough job. Sometimes, do what we could, we

Chinese Simplified

bitter：苦，苦味，沉痛.
block：木块，街段，块，阻挡.
captive：俘虏.
captivity：囚禁.
carve：雕刻，雕塑.
dig：挖掘.
dungeon：地牢.
fetch：拿，取，带来.
fix：安装，奠定，固定，修理.
friendless：没有朋友的，无依无靠的.
gaudy：花哨，花里胡哨.
grindstone：磨石.
homeless：无家可归.
inscriptions：铭刻.
log：圆形木材，圆木，木头.
lonely：孤独，寂寞，孤独地.
midnight：午夜，半夜.
mournful：悲切，悲恸，悲恸的.
nail：钉，指甲，钉子.
noble：高贵，高贵的，贵族.
pesky：讨厌的.
prisoner：犯人，罪犯，囚犯.
scrabble：涂写.
solitary：孤独，独居的.
sores：疡.
sorrowful：悲痛，悲哀，哀愁，悲伤，悲伤的.
stranger：陌生人，异乡人，生人.
tackle：钓鱼用具，处理.
tedious：乏味，厌烦的.
trembled：发抖.
truck：卡车.
worn：穿.

couldn't keep her from **falling** over, and she come **mighty** near mashing us every time. Tom said she was going to get one of us, sure, before we got through. We got her half way; and then we was plumb played out, and most drownded with **sweat**. We see it warn't no use; we got to go and **fetch** Jim So he raised up his bed and **slid** the **chain** off of the bed-leg, and wrapt it round and round his neck, and we crawled out through our hole and down there, and Jim and me **laid** into that **grindstone** and walked her along like nothing; and Tom superintended. He could out-superintend any boy I ever see. He knowed how to do everything.

Our hole was pretty big, but it warn't big enough to get the grindstone through; but Jim he took the pick and soon made it big enough. Then Tom marked out them things on it with the **nail**, and set Jim to work on them, with the nail for a **chisel** and an iron **bolt** from the rubbage in the **lean-** to for a **hammer**, and told him to work **till** the rest of his **candle quit** on him, and then he could go to bed, and **hide** the grindstone under his **straw tick** and sleep on it. Then we helped him **fix** his chain back on the bed- leg, and was ready for bed ourselves. But Tom thought of something, and says:

"You got any **spiders** in here, Jim?"

"No, sah, thanks to **goodness** I hain't, Mars Tom."

"All right, we'll get you some."

"But **bless** you, **honey**, I doan' *want* none. I's afeard un um. I **jis'** 's soon have **rattlesnakes** aroun'."

Tom thought a minute or two, and says:

"It's a good idea. And I **reckon** it's been done. It *must* a been done; it stands to reason. Yes, it's a prime good idea. Where could you keep it?"

"Keep what, Mars Tom?"

"Why, a rattlesnake."

"De goodness **gracious alive**, Mars Tom! Why, if dey was a rattlesnake to come in heah I'd take en **bust** right out thoo dat **log** wall, I would, wid my head."

Why, Jim, you wouldn't be afraid of it after a little. You could **tame it**."

Chinese Simplified

alive：活着，活，活泼的，活着的.
bless：保佑，庇佑，祝福.
bolt：门栓，螺栓，枪栓.
bust：半身像，逮捕，破产.
candle：蜡烛.
chain：链，链子，连锁.
chisel：凿子，凿.
falling：落下的，落下.
fetch：拿，取，带来.
fix：安装，奠定，固定，修理.
goodness：美德.
gracious：亲切，亲切的，有礼貌的.
grindstone：磨石.
hammer：槌，锤.
hide：躲藏，暗藏，掩饰，藏，隐瞒，隐藏.
honey：蜂蜜，蜜，蜜糖.
jis：日本工业标准.
laid：放.
lean：倾斜.
log：圆形木材，圆木，木头.
mighty：伟大，强势，强大的.
nail：钉，指甲，钉子.
quit：退出，退离.
rattlesnake：响尾蛇.
reckon：估计，计算.
slid：滑行.
spiders：蜘蛛.
straw：稻草，吸管.
sweat：汗，出汗，流汗.
tame：驯服，驯服的.
tick：壁虱，滴答声，勾.
till：直到.

"*Tame* it!"

"Yes--easy enough. Every **animal** is **grateful** for **kindness** and **petting**, and they wouldn't *think* of hurting a person that pets them. Any book will tell you that. You try--that's all I ask; just try for two or three days. Why, you can get him so in a little while that he'll love you; and **sleep** with you; and won't stay away from you a **minute**; and will let you **wrap** him round your **neck** and put his head in your mouth."

"*Please*, Mars Tom--*doan'* talk so! I can't *stan'* it! He'd *let* me **shove** his head in my mouf--fer a **favor**, hain't it? I lay he'd wait a pow'ful long time 'fo' I ***ast*** him. En mo' en dat, I doan' *want* him to sleep wid me."

"Jim, don't act so **foolish**. A prisoner's *got* to have some kind of a **dumb** pet, and if a **rattlesnake** hain't ever been tried, why, there's more **glory** to be **gained** in your being the first to ever try it than any other way you could ever think of to **save** your life."

"Why, Mars Tom, I doan' *want* no sich glory. Snake take 'n **bite** Jim's **chin** off, **den** *whah* is de glory? No, sah, I doan' want no sich doin's."

"**Blame** it, can't you *try*? I only *want* you to try--you needn't keep it up if it don't work."

"But de trouble all *done* ef de snake bite me while I's a tryin' him. Mars Tom, I's willin' to **tackle** mos' anything 'at ain't onreasonable, but ef you en Huck fetches a rattlesnake in heah for me to **tame**, I's gwyne to *leave*, dat's *shore*."

"Well, then, let it go, let it go, if you're so bull-headed about it. We can get you some garter-snakes, and you can **tie** some buttons on their **tails**, and let on they're rattlesnakes, and I **reckon** that 'll have to do."

"I k'n stan' *dem*, Mars Tom, but blame' 'f I couldn' get along widout um, I tell you dat. I never knowed b'fo' 't was so much **bother** and trouble to be a prisoner."

"Well, it *always* is when it's done right. You got any rats around here?"

"No, sah, I hain't **seed** none."

Chinese Simplified

animal: 动物.
ast: 虹志电脑.
bite: 咬, 辣, 咬伤.
blame: 责备, 咎, 非难, 责任, 罪, 责怪, 归咎.
bother: 烦扰, 打扰, 理会.
chin: 下巴, 颏.
den: 窝.
dumb: 哑.
favor: 偏爱, 德, 赞成, 人情.
foolish: 愚蠢的.
gained: 获利, 赢得.
glory: 荣耀, 光荣, 辉煌.
grateful: 感谢, 感激的.
kindness: 仁慈, 好意.
minute: 分钟, 详细, 分, 微小的, 渺小.
neck: 颈项, 脖子, 颈.
pet: 宠物.
rattlesnake: 响尾蛇.
reckon: 估计, 计算.
save: 节约, 节省, 省得, 救, 援救, 挽救, 保存.
seed: 种子, 播种.
shove: 推.
sleep: 梦寐, 睡觉, 睡眠, 睡.
snake: 蛇.
tackle: 钓鱼用具, 处理.
tails: 尾巴.
tame: 驯服, 驯服的.
tie: 不分胜负, 打结, 束缚, 轨枕, 绑, 领带.
wrap: 包, 包裹.

"Well, we'll get you some **rats**."

"Why, Mars Tom, I doan' *want* no rats. Dey's de dadblamedest creturs to 'sturb a body, en **rustle** roun' over 'im, en **bite** his feet, when he's tryin' to sleep, I ever see. No, sah, gimme g'yarter-snakes, 'f I's got to have 'm, but doan' gimme no rats; I hain' got no use f'r um, skasely."

"But, Jim, you *got* to have 'em--they all do. So don't make no more **fuss** about it. Prisoners ain't ever without rats. There ain't no **instance** of it. And they **train** them, and **pet** them, and learn them **tricks**, and they get to be as sociable as flies. But you got to play music to them. You got anything to play music on?"

"I ain' got nuffn but a coase **comb** en a piece o' paper, en a juice-harp; but I reck'n dey wouldn' take no stock in a juice-harp."

"Yes they would. *they* don't care what **kind** of music 'tis. A jews-harp's **plenty** good enough for a rat. All **animals** like music--in a **prison** they **dote** on it. Specially, **painful** music; and you can't get no other kind out of a jews-harp. It always **interests** them; they come out to see what's the matter with you. Yes, you're all right; you're **fixed** very well. You want to set on your bed nights before you go to sleep, and early in the **mornings**, and play your jews-harp; play 'The Last Link is Broken'--that's the thing that 'll **scoop** a rat quicker 'n anything else; and when you've played about two minutes you'll see all the rats, and the snakes, and **spiders**, and things begin to feel **worried** about you, and come. And they'll just fairly **swarm** over you, and have a **noble** good time."

"Yes, *dey* will, I reck'n, Mars Tom, but what kine er time is *Jim* havin'? Blest if I kin see de **pint**. But I'll do it ef I got to. I reck'n I better keep de animals **satisfied**, en not have no trouble in de house."

Tom waited to think it over, and see if there wasn't nothing else; and **pretty** soon he says:

"Oh, there's one thing I **forgot**. Could you **raise** a **flower** here, do you reckon?"

"I doan know but maybe I could, Mars Tom; but it's tolable dark in heah, en I ain' got no use f'r no flower, nohow, en she'd be a pow'ful **sight** o' trouble."

Chinese Simplified

animals：动物.
bite：咬，辣，咬伤.
comb：梳，梳子.
dote：溺爱.
fixed：固定，确定，一定，固定的.
flower：花，花儿，华，花朵，开花.
forgot：忘记.
fuss：大惊小怪.
instance：例子，比方，实例.
interests：兴趣.
kin：亲属，骨肉.
mornings：早晨.
noble：高贵，高贵的，贵族.
painful：痛苦，痛苦的.
pet：宠物.
pint：品脱.
plenty：丰富，许多.
pretty：漂亮，美丽的，秀丽.
prison：监狱.
raise：升起，提高，筹措，增加，抚育，举起.
rat：老鼠，鼠.
rustle：瑟瑟.
satisfied：满意，乐意，心满意足的.
scoop：杓子，勺子，勺.
sight：视觉，景象，情景，目光，视力，视线.
spiders：蜘蛛.
swarm：蜂群，一群.
train：训练，火车，列车，乘务员，熏陶.
tricks：戏法，把戏.
worried：担心，不安，忧虑.

"Well, you try it, anyway. Some other **prisoners** has done it."

"One er dem big cat-tail-**lookin'** mullen-stalks would **grow** in heah, Mars Tom, I reck'n, but she wouldn't be wuth half de **trouble** she'd coss."

"Don't you believe it. We'll **fetch** you a little one and you **plant** it in the **corner** over there, and **raise** it. And don't call it mullen, call it Pitchiola--that's its right name when it's in a prison. And you want to water it with your **tears**."

"Why, I got **plenty spring** water, Mars Tom."

"You don't *want* spring water; you want to water it with your tears. It's the way they always do."

"Why, Mars Tom, I **lay** I kin raise one er dem mullen-stalks twyste wid spring water whiles another man's a *start'n* one wid tears."

"That ain't the idea. You *got* to do it with tears."

"She'll **die** on my han's, Mars Tom, she sholy will; kase I doan' skasely ever cry."

So Tom was stumped. But he studied it over, and then said Jim would have to **worry** along the best he could with an **onion**. He promised he would go to the nigger cabins and **drop** one, private, in Jim's coffee-pot, in the morning. Jim said he would "jis' 's soon have tobacker in his coffee;" and found so much **fault** with it, and with the work and **bother** of raising the mullen, and jews-harping the rats, and petting and flattering up the snakes and **spiders** and things, on top of all the other work he had to do on pens, and **inscriptions**, and journals, and things, which made it more trouble and worry and **responsibility** to be a prisoner than anything he ever **undertook**, that Tom most lost all **patience** with him; and said he was just loadened down with more gaudier **chances** than a prisoner ever had in the world to make a name for himself, and yet he didn't know enough to **appreciate** them, and they was just about wasted on him. So Jim he was sorry, and said he wouldn't **behave** so no more, and then me and Tom shoved for bed.

Chinese Simplified

appreciate: 涨价，感激，升值，欣赏.
behave: 举止，表现，行为.
bother: 烦扰，打扰，理会.
chances: 机会.
corner: 角落，隅，棱，角，转角.
die: 逝世，不讳，死.
drop: 落，水滴，衰退，掉落，降，点子.
fault: 故障，过失，缺点，毛病，断层，短处，缺陷.
fetch: 拿，取，带来.
grow: 生长，增长，成长，种植.
inscriptions: 铭刻.
kin: 亲属，骨肉.
lay: 产卵，安放，放，凡俗.
onion: 洋葱.
patience: 忍耐，忍受，耐心，耐性.
plant: 植物，安插，事业，种植，插.
plenty: 丰富，许多.
prison: 监狱.
prisoner: 犯人，罪犯，囚犯.
prisoners: 囚犯.
raise: 升起，提高，筹措，增加，抚育，举起.
responsibility: 责任.
spiders: 蜘蛛.
spring: 弹簧，泉，春天，绷簧，春季，水源，跳.
tears: 泪，泪水，眼泪.
trouble: 麻烦，难度，难处.
undertook: 从事.
worry: 担心，使烦恼，缠绕，担忧，心事，担，烦恼，着急.

CHAPTER XXXIX

TOM WRITES NONNAMOUS LETTERS

In the morning we went up to the **village** and **bought** a **wire** rat-trap and fetched it down, and unstopped the best rat-hole, and in about an **hour** we had **fifteen** of the bulliest kind of ones; and then we took it and put it in a safe place under Aunt Sally's bed. But while we was gone for **spiders** little Thomas Franklin Benjamin Jefferson Elexander Phelps found it there, and **opened** the door of it to see if the rats would come out, and they did; and Aunt Sally she come in, and when we got back she was a- **standing** on top of the bed raising Cain, and the rats was doing what they could to keep off the **dull** times for her. So she took and dusted us both with the hickry, and we was as much as two hours **catching** another fifteen or **sixteen**, drat that **meddlesome cub**, and they warn't the likeliest, nuther, because the first **haul** was the **pick** of the **flock**. I never see a likelier lot of rats than what that first haul was.

We got a **splendid stock** of **sorted** spiders, and bugs, and frogs, and **caterpillars**, and one thing or another; and we like to got a hornet's **nest**, but we didn't. The family was at home. We didn't give it right up, but **stayed** with them as long as we could; because we **allowed** we'd **tire** them out or they'd got to tire us out, and they done it. Then we got allycumpain and **rubbed** on the **places**, and was **pretty** near all right again, but couldn't set down **convenient**. And so

Chinese Simplified

allowed: 允许.
bought: 买了.
catching: 迷人的.
caterpillars: 履带.
convenient: 方便, 便利, 便当, 手, 方便的.
cub: 幼兽.
dull: 索然, 板滞, 沉闷的, 干燥, 拙, 深沉.
fifteen: 十五.
flock: 一群.
haul: 拖拉, 曳.
hour: 小时, 钟头, 钟点, 现在.
meddlesome: 多事, 多事的.
nest: 窝巢, 窝, 巢.
opened: 打开.
pick: 掐, 采摘, 挑选, 挑, 鹤嘴锄, 采, 选择.
places: 地方.
pretty: 漂亮, 美丽的, 秀丽.
rubbed: 摩擦.
sixteen: 十六.
sorted: 分类.
spiders: 蜘蛛.
splendid: 彪炳, 卓越, 辉煌, 灿烂的, 精彩, 辉煌的.
standing: 站立, 地位.
stayed: 停留.
stock: 存货, 股票, 股份, 库存.
tire: 疲倦.
village: 村庄, 农村, 乡村, 村子.
wire: 电线.

we went for the **snakes**, and grabbed a couple of **dozen garters** and house-snakes, and put them in a bag, and put it in our room, and by that time it was supper-time, and a rattling good honest day's work: and hungry?--oh, no, I **reckon** not! And there warn't a **blessed** snake up there when we went back--we didn't half **tie** the **sack**, and they worked out somehow, and left. But it didn't matter much, because they was still on the premises somewheres. So we judged we could get some of them again. No, there warn't no real **scarcity** of snakes about the house for a considerable **spell**. You'd see them **dripping** from the **rafters** and places every now and then; and they generly **landed** in your plate, or down the back of your neck, and most of the time where you didn't want them. Well, they was **handsome** and **striped**, and there warn't no **harm** in a million of them; but that never made no difference to Aunt Sally; she despised snakes, be the **breed** what they might, and she couldn't stand them no way you could **fix** it; and every time one of them flopped down on her, it didn't make no difference what she was doing, she would just lay that work down and light out. I never see such a woman. And you could hear her **whoop** to Jericho. You couldn't get her to take a-holt of one of them with the **tongs**. And if she turned over and found one in bed she would **scramble** out and lift a **howl** that you would think the house was **afire**. She **disturbed** the old man so that he said he could most wish there hadn't ever been no snakes created. Why, after every last snake had been gone clear out of the house for as much as a week Aunt Sally warn't over it yet; she warn't near over it; when she was setting thinking about something you could touch her on the back of her neck with a **feather** and she would **jump** right out of her **stockings**. It was very **curious**. But Tom said all women was just so. He said they was made that way for some reason or other.

We got a licking every time one of our snakes come in her way, and she allowed these lickings warn't nothing to what she would do if we ever **loaded** up the place again with them. I didn't mind the lickings, because they didn't amount to nothing; but I minded the trouble we had to lay in another lot. But we got them laid in, and all the other things; and you never see a **cabin** as blithesome as Jim's was when they'd all **swarm** out for music and go for him. Jim didn't like the **spiders**, and the spiders didn't like Jim; and so they'd lay for

Chinese Simplified

afire: 大为激动.
blessed: 幸福，幸福的.
breed: 品种，繁殖，饲养.
cabin: 小屋，船舱.
curious: 有好奇心，好奇，好奇的.
disturbed: 不安.
dozen: 一打，打.
dripping: 滴下.
feather: 羽毛.
fix: 安装，奠定，固定，修理.
garters: 吊袜带.
handsome: 英俊，慷慨的，英俊的.
harm: 伤害，损害，坏处，害处，祸害.
howl: 狂吠，号叫.
jump: 跳，跳跃.
landed: 着陆.
loaded: 载入.
rafters: 椽.
reckon: 估计，计算.
sack: 大袋子，开除.
scarcity: 缺乏，不足.
scramble: 攀登.
snake: 蛇.
spell: 拼写，咒语，符咒.
spiders: 蜘蛛.
stockings: 袜子，长统袜.
striped: 有条纹，有条纹的.
swarm: 蜂群，一群.
tie: 不分胜负，打结，束缚，轨枕，绑，领带.
tongs: 夹钳，铁子.
whoop: 呼叫声.

him, and make it **mighty** warm for him. And he said that between the **rats** and the snakes and the **grindstone** there warn't no room in bed for him, skasely; and when there was, a body couldn't sleep, it was so **lively**, and it was always lively, he said, because *they* never all **slept** at one time, but took turn about, so when the snakes was **asleep** the rats was on **deck**, and when the rats turned in the snakes come on watch, so he always had one **gang** under him, in his way, and t'other gang having a **circus** over him, and if he got up to **hunt** a new place the **spiders** would take a chance at him as he crossed over. He said if he ever got out this time he wouldn't ever be a **prisoner** again, not for a salary.

Well, by the end of three weeks everything was in pretty good shape. The **shirt** was sent in early, in a **pie**, and every time a rat bit Jim he would get up and write a little in his **journal** whilst the **ink** was fresh; the pens was made, the **inscriptions** and so on was all carved on the grindstone; the bed-leg was **sawed** in two, and we had et up the **sawdust**, and it give us a most **amazing stomach-ache**. We reckoned we was all going to die, but didn't. It was the most undigestible sawdust I ever see; and Tom said the same. But as I was saying, we'd got all the work done now, at last; and we was all pretty much **fagged** out, too, but mainly Jim. The old man had wrote a couple of times to the **plantation** below Orleans to come and get their **runaway** nigger, but hadn't got no answer, because there warn't no such plantation; so he allowed he would **advertise** Jim in the St. **Louis** and New Orleans **papers**; and when he mentioned the St. Louis ones it give me the cold **shivers**, and I see we hadn't no time to lose. So Tom said, now for the nonnamous letters.

"What's them?" I says.

"Warnings to the people that something is up. Sometimes it's done one way, sometimes another. But there's always somebody **spying** around that gives notice to the **governor** of the **castle**. When Louis XVI. was going to light out of the Tooleries a servant-girl done it. It's a very good way, and so is the nonnamous letters. We'll use them both. And it's usual for the prisoner's mother to change clothes with him, and she **stays** in, and he slides out in her clothes. We'll do that, too."

Chinese Simplified

advertise: 登广告，标榜，刊登广告.
amazing: 了不起，迷人的.
asleep: 睡着，睡着的.
castle: 城堡，城.
circus: 马戏团，杂技团，马戏.
deck: 甲板.
fagged: 累坏了的.
gang: 一群，帮.
governor: 州长.
grindstone: 磨石.
hunt: 打猎，狩猎.
ink: 墨水，墨水儿，篇幅.
inscriptions: 铭刻.
journal: 日志，通报.
lively: 活泼，热闹，生气勃勃，生气勃勃地，轻快.
louis: 路易斯.
mighty: 伟大，强势，强大的.
papers: 报纸.
pie: 馅饼.
plantation: 农园，种植园.
prisoner: 犯人，罪犯，囚犯.
rat: 老鼠，鼠.
runaway: 逃亡者，跑道.
sawdust: 木屑.
sawed: 锯.
shirt: 衬衫，衬衣.
shivers: 颤抖.
slept: 睡了.
spiders: 蜘蛛.
spying: 侦察.
stays: 停留.
stomach-ache: 肚痛.

"But looky here, Tom, what do we want to ***warn*** **anybody** for that something's up? Let them find it out for themselves--it's their lookout."

"Yes, I know; but you can't **depend** on them. It's the way they've acted from the very start--left us to do *everything*. They're so **confiding** and mullet-headed they don't take **notice** of nothing at all. So if we don't *give* them notice there won't be **nobody** nor nothing to **interfere** with us, and so after all our hard work and **trouble** this **escape** 'll go off **perfectly flat**; won't amount to nothing--won't be nothing *to* it."

"Well, as for me, Tom, that's the way I'd like."

"Shucks!" he says, and looked **disgusted**. So I says:

"But I ain't going to make no **complaint**. Any way that suits you suits me. What you going to do about the servant-girl?"

"You'll be her. You **slide** in, in the middle of the night, and **hook** that yaller girl's frock."

"Why, Tom, that 'll make trouble next morning; because, of course, she prob'bly hain't got any but that one."

"I know; but you don't want it but **fifteen** minutes, to carry the nonnamous letter and **shove** it under the **front** door."

"All right, then, I'll do it; but I could carry it just as **handy** in my own togs."

"You wouldn't look like a servant-girl *then*, would you?"

"No, but there won't be nobody to see what I look like, *anyway*."

"That ain't got nothing to do with it. The thing for us to do is just to do our ***duty***, and not **worry** about whether anybody *sees* us do it or not. Hain't you got no **principle** at all?"

"All right, I ain't saying nothing; I'm the servant-girl. Who's Jim's mother?"

"I'm his mother. I'll hook a **gown** from Aunt Sally."

"Well, then, you'll have to stay in the **cabin** when me and Jim leaves."

Chinese Simplified

anybody: 任何人.
cabin: 小屋，船舱.
complaint: 原告，牢骚，闲话，控诉，投诉.
confiding: 信任别人.
depend: 依赖，取决.
disgusted: 厌恶.
duty: 任务，义务，责任，关税，职责.
escape: 逃走，逃之夭夭，逃跑，逃避，逃脱，逃离，逃亡.
fifteen: 十五.
flat: 平坦，平板，平坦的，平的，居室.
front: 前面，正面，跟前，战线，阵地.
gown: 长袍，女装长袍.
handy: 灵巧，便当，顺手，方便的，简便.
hook: 钩，钩子.
interfere: 干涉，干扰，妨碍.
nobody: 没有人，没人.
notice: 通知，注意，布告，注意到，启事.
perfectly: 完美，完美地.
principle: 原理，原则，道理.
shove: 推.
slide: 滑落，滑行，滑.
trouble: 麻烦，难度，难处.
warn: 告诫，警告.
worry: 担心，使烦恼，缠绕，担忧，心事，担，烦恼，着急.

"Not much. I'll stuff Jim's clothes full of **straw** and lay it on his bed to **represent** his mother in **disguise**, and Jim 'll take the nigger woman's **gown** off of me and **wear** it, and we'll all **evade** together. When a **prisoner** of style escapes it's called an **evasion**. It's always called so when a king escapes, f'rinstance. And the same with a king's son; it don't make no difference whether he's a natural one or an **unnatural** one."

So Tom he wrote the nonnamous letter, and I smouched the yaller wench's **frock** that night, and put it on, and shoved it under the front door, the way Tom told me to. It said:

> Beware. Trouble is brewing. Keep a **sharp** lookout.
>
> UNKNOWN FRIEND.

Next night we **stuck** a picture, which Tom drawed in blood, of a **skull** and crossbones on the front door; and next night another one of a **coffin** on the back door. I never see a family in such a **sweat**. They couldn't a been worse scared if the place had a been full of **ghosts** laying for them behind everything and under the **beds** and **shivering** through the air. If a door banged, Aunt Sally she **jumped** and said "ouch!" if anything fell, she jumped and said "ouch!" if you happened to touch her, when she warn't **noticing**, she done the same; she couldn't face noway and be **satisfied**, because she allowed there was something behind her every time--so she was always a-whirling around **sudden**, and saying "ouch," and before she'd got **two**-thirds around she'd **whirl** back again, and say it again; and she was **afraid** to go to bed, but she dasn't set up. So the thing was working very well, Tom said; he said he never see a thing work more **satisfactory**. He said it showed it was done right.

So he said, now for the **grand bulge**! So the very next morning at the **streak** of **dawn** we got another letter ready, and was wondering what we better do with it, because we heard them say at **supper** they was going to have a nigger on watch at both **doors** all night. Tom he went down the lightning-rod to spy

Chinese Simplified

afraid: 危惧，恐怕，害怕.
beds: 床.
bulge: 胀起，肿胀.
coffin: 棺材，寿材.
dawn: 黎明.
disguise: 伪装，乔装.
doors: 门.
evade: 逃避，迴避，回避.
evasion: 逃避.
frock: 西式女衣.
ghosts: 鬼.
gown: 长袍，女装长袍.
grand: 堂皇，隆重，雄伟，盛大，宏大，大型的，宏伟.
jumped: 跳跃.
noticing: 注意到.
prisoner: 犯人，罪犯，囚犯.
represent: 代表.
satisfactory: 满意的，称心，圆满.
satisfied: 满意，乐意，心满意足的.
sharp: 尖锐，锐利，锋利的，锋利.
shivering: 颤抖.
skull: 头盖骨，头骨，头颅.
straw: 稻草，吸管.
streak: 斑纹，线条.
stuck: 黏贴.
sudden: 突然，急剧，突然的.
supper: 晚饭，晚餐.
sweat: 汗，出汗，流汗.
two-thirds: 三分之二.
unnatural: 不自然，不自然的.
wear: 穿带，穿.
whirl: 旋转，回旋.

around; and the nigger at the **back** door was **asleep**, and he **stuck** it in the back of his neck and come back. This letter said:

> Don't **betray** me, I wish to be your friend. There is a desprate **gang** of cut-throats from over in the Indian Territory going to **steal** your **runaway** nigger to-night, and they have been trying to **scare** you so as you will stay in the house and not **bother** them. I am one of the gang, but have got religgion and wish to **quit** it and lead an **honest** life again, and will betray the helish **design**. They will **sneak** down from northards, along the **fence**, at **midnight exact**, with a **false** key, and go in the nigger's **cabin** to get him. I am to be off a piece and **blow** a **tin horn** if I see any danger; but stead of that I will *ba* like a **sheep** soon as they get in and not blow at all; then whilst they are getting his **chains loose**, you **slip** there and **lock** them in, and can kill them at your leasure. Don't do anything but just the way I am telling you; if you do they will **suspicion** something and raise whoop-jamborcehoo. I do not wish any **reward** but to know I have done the right thing.
>
> UNKNOWN FRIEND.

Chinese Simplified

asleep: 睡着，睡着的.
ba: 文学士.
betray: 背叛，出卖.
blow: 吹，打击.
bother: 烦扰，打扰，理会.
cabin: 小屋，船舱.
chains: 连锁.
design: 设计，图案.
exact: 确切，精密，准确，正确的.
false: 假，虚伪，虚假.
fence: 篱笆，栅栏，栏位，栏.
gang: 一群，帮.
honest: 诚实，正直，清廉，刚正，坦白，正値，诚实的，体面，廉洁，深切.
horn: 角，犄角.
lock: 锁，撞锁.
loose: 松开，松弛的.
midnight: 午夜，半夜.
quit: 退出，退离.
reward: 报酬，酬劳，酬金，奖励，奖赏.
runaway: 逃亡者，跑道.
scare: 恐慌.
sheep: 羊，绵羊.
slip: 滑倒，溜走，溜.
sneak: 潜行，潜入.
steal: 偷窃，盗窃，偷，窃取.
stuck: 黏贴.
suspicion: 疑心，怀疑，嫌疑.
tin: 锡，罐头.
unknown: 未知，不得而知，不明，不见经传，未知的.

CHAPTER XL

A MIXED-UP AND SPLENDID RESCUE

We was **feeling pretty** good after **breakfast**, and took my **canoe** and went over the **river** a-fishing, with a **lunch**, and had a good time, and took a look at the **raft** and found her all right, and got home **late** to **supper**, and found them in such a **sweat** and **worry** they didn't know which end they was **standing** on, and made us go right off to **bed** the **minute** we was done supper, and wouldn't tell us what the **trouble** was, and never let on a word about the new **letter**, but didn't need to, because we knowed as much about it as **anybody** did, and as soon as we was half up **stairs** and her **back** was turned we **slid** for the **cellar** cubboard and **loaded** up a good lunch and took it up to our room and went to bed, and got up about half- past **eleven**, and Tom put on Aunt Sally's **dress** that he **stole** and was going to start with the lunch, but says:

"Where's the butter?"

"I **laid** out a hunk of it," I says, "on a piece of a corn-pone."

"Well, you *left* it laid out, then--it ain't here."

"We can get **along** without it," I says.

"We can get along *with* it, too," he says; "just you **slide** down cellar and **fetch** it. And then mosey right down the lightning-rod and come along. I'll go and

Chinese Simplified

along: 沿着，沿，一同.
anybody: 任何人.
ba: 文学士.
bed: 床，床铺.
breakfast: 早餐，早饭，早点.
canoe: 独木舟.
cellar: 地下室，地窖.
dress: 服装，打扮.
eleven: 十一.
feeling: 感觉，情绪，感情，情感，思绪.
fetch: 拿，取，带来.
laid: 放.
late: 晚，迟，迟慢，迟了，迟迟.
letter: 字母，信.
loaded: 载入.
lunch: 午餐，午饭.
minute: 分钟，详细，分，微小的，渺小.
pretty: 漂亮，美丽的，秀丽.
raft: 筏，木排，槎，桴.
river: 河，江，川，河流，条.
slid: 滑行.
slide: 滑落，滑行，滑.
stairs: 楼梯.
standing: 站立，地位.
stole: 偷了.
supper: 晚饭，晚餐.
sweat: 汗，出汗，流汗.
trouble: 麻烦，难度，难处.
worry: 担心，使烦恼，缠绕，担忧，心事，担，烦恼，着急.

stuff the **straw** into Jim's **clothes** to **represent** his mother in **disguise**, and be ready to *ba* like a **sheep** and **shove** soon as you get there."

So out he went, and down **cellar** went I. The hunk of **butter**, big as a person's **fist**, was where I had left it, so I took up the **slab** of **corn**- pone with it on, and blowed out my light, and started up **stairs** very stealthy, and got up to the main floor all right, but here comes Aunt Sally with a **candle**, and I clapped the **truck** in my **hat**, and clapped my hat on my head, and the next second she see me; and she says:

"You been down cellar?"

"Yes'm."

"What you been doing down there?"

"Noth'n."

"*Noth'n*!"

"No'm."

"Well, then, what possessed you to go down there this time of night?"

"I don't know 'm."

"You don't *know*? Don't answer me that way. Tom, I want to know what you been *doing* down there."

"I hain't been doing a single thing, Aunt Sally, I hope to **gracious** if I have."

I reckoned she'd let me go now, and as a generl thing she would; but I s'pose there was so many **strange** things going on she was just in a **sweat** about every little thing that warn't yard-stick straight; so she says, very **decided**:

"You just march into that **setting**-room and stay there **till** I come. You been up to something you no business to, and I lay I'll find out what it is before *I'm* done with you."

So she went away as I **opened** the door and **walked** into the setting-room. My, but there was a **crowd** there! Fifteen farmers, and every one of them had a **gun**. I was most **powerful sick**, and slunk to a chair and set down. They was setting around, some of them talking a little, in a low voice, and all of them

Chinese Simplified

ba: 文学士.
butter: 牛油，黄油.
candle: 蜡烛.
cellar: 地下室，地窖.
clothes: 衣服，服装，西装，件，衣裳.
corn: 玉蜀黍，包谷，玉米.
crowd: 人群.
decided: 决定.
disguise: 伪装，乔装.
fist: 拳头.
gracious: 亲切，亲切的，有礼貌的.
gun: 枪，炮，长枪.
hat: 帽子.
opened: 打开.
powerful: 强大，有力，强劲，强有力的.
represent: 代表.
setting: 排字，设定.
sheep: 羊，绵羊.
shove: 推.
sick: 生病.
slab: 木板，石片，板皮，扁坯，石板.
stairs: 楼梯.
strange: 奇怪，奇特，陌生，奇异的，生疏.
straw: 稻草，吸管.
stuff: 材料，填塞，职员.
sweat: 汗，出汗，流汗.
till: 直到.
truck: 卡车.
walked: 步行.

fidgety and **uneasy**, but trying to look like they warn't; but I knowed they was, because they was always taking off their **hats**, and putting them on, and **scratching** their heads, and changing their seats, and fumbling with their buttons. I warn't easy myself, but I didn't take my hat off, all the same.

I did wish Aunt Sally would come, and get done with me, and **lick** me, if she wanted to, and let me get away and tell Tom how we'd overdone this thing, and what a thundering hornet's-nest we'd got ourselves into, so we could stop fooling around straight off, and clear out with Jim before these **rips** got out of **patience** and come for us.

At last she come and begun to ask me questions, but I *couldn't* answer them straight, I didn't know which end of me was up; because these men was in such a fidget now that some was **wanting** to start right *now* and lay for them desperadoes, and saying it warn't but a few minutes to **midnight**; and others was trying to get them to hold on and wait for the **sheep- signal**; and here was Aunty pegging away at the questions, and me a- **shaking** all over and ready to **sink** down in my **tracks** I was that scared; and the place getting **hotter** and hotter, and the **butter** beginning to **melt** and run down my neck and behind my **ears**; and pretty soon, when one of them says, "*I'm* for going and getting in the **cabin** *first* and right *now*, and **catching** them when they come," I most dropped; and a **streak** of butter come a-trickling down my **forehead**, and Aunt Sally she see it, and turns white as a sheet, and says:

"For the land's **sake**, what *is* the matter with the child? He's got the brain-fever as **shore** as you're born, and they're **oozing** out!"

And everybody **runs** to see, and she **snatches** off my hat, and out comes the bread and what was left of the butter, and she grabbed me, and hugged me, and says:

"Oh, what a turn you did give me! and how glad and **grateful** I am it ain't no worse; for luck's against us, and it never **rains** but it pours, and when I see that **truck** I thought we'd lost you, for I knowed by the **color** and all it was just like your **brains** would be if--Dear, dear, whyd'nt you *tell* me that was what you'd

Chinese Simplified

brains：头脑，脑子，脑筋，脑袋，脑髓．
butter：牛油，黄油．
cabin：小屋，船舱．
catching：迷人的．
color：颜色，彩色．
ears：耳朵．
fidgety：烦躁．
forehead：前额，额，额头．
grateful：感谢，感激的．
hat：帽子．
hotter：热，热烈的．
lick：舔，舐．
melt：溶化，融化，熔解．
midnight：午夜，半夜．
oozing：渗出．
patience：忍耐，忍受，耐心，耐性．
rains：雨季，下雨．
rips：裂口．
runs：跑．
sake：缘故．
scratching：刮痕，抓．
shaking：摇动．
sheep：羊，绵羊．
shore：岸，滨，岸边，海岸，海滨．
signal：信号，手势，讯号．
sink：水槽，沉落，沈落，沉没．
snatches：攫取．
streak：斑纹，线条．
tracks：轨道．
truck：卡车．
uneasy：不安，担心，不安的．
wanting：缺少的，不足的．

been down there for, I wouldn't a cared. Now cler out to bed, and don't lemme see no more of you **till** morning!"

I was up **stairs** in a second, and down the lightning-rod in another one, and shinning through the dark for the lean-to. I couldn't hardly get my words out, I was so **anxious**; but I told Tom as quick as I could we must **jump** for it now, and not a minute to lose--the house full of men, **yonder**, with **guns**!

His eyes just blazed; and he says:

"No!--is that so? *Ain't* it **bully**! Why, Huck, if it was to do over again, I **bet** I could **fetch** two hundred! If we could put it off till--"

"**Hurry**! *Hurry*!" I says. "Where's Jim?"

"Right at your **elbow**; if you reach out your arm you can touch him. He's dressed, and everything's ready. Now we'll **slide** out and give the **sheep**-signal."

But then we **heard** the **tramp** of men coming to the door, and heard them begin to **fumble** with the pad-lock, and heard a man say:

"I *told* you we'd be too soon; they haven't come--the door is **locked**. Here, I'll lock some of you into the **cabin**, and you lay for 'em in the dark and kill 'em when they come; and the rest **scatter** around a piece, and listen if you can hear 'em coming."

So in they come, but couldn't see us in the dark, and most trod on us whilst we was hustling to get under the bed. But we got under all right, and out through the hole, **swift** but soft--Jim first, me next, and Tom last, which was **according** to Tom's orders. Now we was in the lean-to, and heard trampings close by outside. So we **crept** to the door, and Tom stopped us there and put his eye to the **crack**, but couldn't make out nothing, it was so dark; and **whispered** and said he would listen for the steps to get further, and when he nudged us Jim must **glide** out first, and him last. So he set his ear to the crack and **listened**, and listened, and listened, and the steps a-scraping around out there all the time; and at last he nudged us, and we slid out, and **stooped** down, not **breathing**, and not making the least noise, and **slipped** stealthy towards the **fence** in Injun file, and

Chinese Simplified

according: 根据.
anxious: 焦急, 巴不得, 担心, 焦虑的.
bet: 打赌, 赌.
breathing: 呼吸, 呼吸的, 微风.
bully: 欺负.
cabin: 小屋, 船舱.
crack: 裂缝, 精干, 崩裂, 爆裂, 裂开, 空隙.
crept: 爬行.
ear: 耳朵, 耳.
elbow: 肘, 手肘.
fence: 篱笆, 栅栏, 栏位, 栏.
fetch: 拿, 取, 带来.
fumble: 摸索.
glide: 滑翔, 滑行.
guns: 枪支.
hurry: 仓促, 匆忙, 赶忙.
jump: 跳, 跳跃.
listened: 听.
lock: 锁, 撞锁.
scatter: 分散, 散播, 驱散.
sheep: 羊, 绵羊.
slid: 滑行.
slide: 滑落, 滑行, 滑.
slipped: 滑落.
stairs: 楼梯.
stooped: 弯腰.
swift: 迅速的.
till: 直到.
tramp: 沉重脚步.
whispered: 耳语.
yonder: 那边.

got to it all right, and me and Jim over it; but Tom's britches catched fast on a **splinter** on the top **rail**, and then he hear the steps coming, so he had to pull **loose**, which **snapped** the splinter and made a noise; and as he **dropped** in our **tracks** and started somebody **sings** out:

"Who's that? Answer, or I'll shoot!"

But we didn't answer; we just unfurled our heels and shoved. Then there was a **rush**, and a ***bang, bang, bang***! and the **bullets** fairly whizzed around us! We heard them sing out:

"Here they are! They've broke for the river! After 'em, boys, and turn loose the dogs!"

So here they come, full **tilt**. We could hear them because they **wore boots** and **yelled**, but we didn't wear no boots and didn't yell. We was in the path to the **mill**; and when they got pretty close on to us we dodged into the **bush** and let them go by, and then dropped in behind them. They'd had all the dogs shut up, so they wouldn't **scare** off the robbers; but by this time somebody had let them loose, and here they come, making **powwow** enough for a million; but they was our dogs; so we stopped in our tracks **till** they catched up; and when they see it warn't nobody but us, and no **excitement** to offer them, they only just said howdy, and **tore** right ahead towards the **shouting** and clattering; and then we up-steam again, and whizzed along after them till we was nearly to the mill, and then **struck** up through the bush to where my **canoe** was tied, and hopped in and pulled for dear life towards the middle of the river, but didn't make no more noise than we was obleeged to. Then we struck out, easy and **comfortable**, for the island where my **raft** was; and we could hear them **yelling** and **barking** at each other all up and down the bank, till we was so far away the sounds got **dim** and died out. And when we stepped on to the raft I says:

"*Now*, old Jim, you're a free man again, and I **bet** you won't ever be a **slave** no more."

Chinese Simplified

bang：重击.
barking：叫声.
bet：打赌，赌.
boots：靴子.
bullets：子弹.
bush：灌木，布什，丛林.
canoe：独木舟.
comfortable：舒服，舒服的.
dim：阴暗，暗淡，暗淡的.
dropped：落下.
excitement：兴奋，刺激.
loose：松开，松弛的.
mill：磨子，磨坊.
powwow：巫师.
raft：筏，木排，槎，桴.
rail：铁路，轨道.
rush：速行，匆匆.
scare：恐慌.
shouting：呼喊.
sing：唱，歌唱，唱歌.
sings：唱.
slave：奴隶.
snapped：猛咬.
splinter：碎片.
struck：敲打.
till：直到.
tilt：倾斜，翘起，使倾侧.
tore：撕扯.
tracks：轨道.
wore：穿了.
yell：叫喊，呐喊.
yelled：叫喊.
yelling：叫声，叫喊.

"En a **mighty** good job it wuz, too, Huck. It 'uz planned beautiful, en it 'uz done beautiful; en dey ain't *nobody* **kin** git up a plan dat's mo' mixed-up en **splendid den** what dat one wuz."

We was all **glad** as we could be, but Tom was the gladdest of all because he had a **bullet** in the **calf** of his leg.

When me and Jim heard that we didn't feel so **brash** as what we did before. It was hurting him considerable, and **bleeding**; so we **laid** him in the **wigwam** and **tore** up one of the duke's shirts for to **bandage** him, but he says:

"Gimme the **rags**; I can do it myself. Don't stop now; don't **fool** around here, and the **evasion booming** along so **handsome**; man the sweeps, and set her **loose**! Boys, we done it elegant!--'deed we did. I wish *we'd* a had the **handling** of Louis XVI., there wouldn't a been no 'Son of Saint Louis, **ascend** to heaven!' wrote down in *his* **biography**; no, sir, we'd a whooped him over the *border*--that's what we'd a done with *him*--and done it just as **slick** as nothing at all, too. Man the sweeps--man the sweeps!"

But me and Jim was consulting--and thinking. And after we'd thought a minute, I says:

"Say it, Jim."

So he says:

"Well, den, dis is de way it look to me, Huck. Ef it wuz *him* dat 'uz bein' sot free, en one er de boys wuz to git shot, would he say, 'Go on en save me, nemmine 'bout a doctor f'r to save dis one?' Is dat like Mars Tom Sawyer? Would he say dat? You ***bet*** he wouldn't! *Well*, den, is *Jim* gywne to say it? No, sah--I doan' **budge** a step out'n dis place 'dout a *doctor*, not if it's forty year!"

I knowed he was white inside, and I reckoned he'd say what he did say--so it was all right now, and I told Tom I was a-going for a doctor. He raised considerable **row** about it, but me and Jim **stuck** to it and wouldn't budge; so he was for **crawling** out and **setting** the **raft** loose himself; but we wouldn't let him. Then he give us a piece of his mind, but it didn't do no good.

So when he sees me getting the **canoe** ready, he says:

Chinese Simplified

ascend：上升.
bandage：绷带.
bet：打赌，赌.
biography：传记，传，生平传记.
bleeding：渗色，出血.
booming：繁荣.
brash：胃灼热，无礼的，傲慢的.
budge：微微一动，改变态度，羔皮.
bullet：子弹.
calf：小牛，犊.
canoe：独木舟.
crawling：爬行.
den：窝.
evasion：逃避.
fool：呆子，笨蛋，傻子，笨人，愚人.
glad：高兴，高兴的.
handling：处理.
handsome：英俊，慷慨的，英俊的.
kin：亲属，骨肉.
laid：放.
loose：松开，松弛的.
mighty：伟大，强势，强大的.
raft：筏，木排，槎，桴.
rags：碎布.
row：一排，划，行.
setting：排字，设定.
slick：油头滑脑.
splendid：彪炳，卓越，辉煌，灿烂的，精彩，辉煌的.
stuck：黏贴.
tore：撕扯.
wigwam：帐篷，陋棚.

"Well, then, if you **re bound** to go, I'll tell you the way to do when you get to the **village**. Shut the door and **blindfold** the **doctor tight** and **fast**, and make him **swear** to be **silent** as the **grave**, and put a **purse** full of **gold** in his hand, and then take and **lead** him all around the back **alleys** and everywheres in the **dark**, and then **fetch** him here in the **canoe**, in a **roundabout** way amongst the **islands**, and **search** him and take his **chalk** away from him, and don't give it back to him **till** you get him back to the village, or else he will chalk this **raft** so he can find it again. It's the way they all do."

So I said I would, and left, and Jim was to **hide** in the **woods** when he see the doctor **coming** till he was **gone** again.

Chinese Simplified

alleys：胡同.
blindfold：蒙眼.
bound：限，边际，弹回，范围.
canoe：独木舟.
chalk：粉笔.
coming：未来，到来.
dark：暗，黑暗，夜.
doctor：医生，大夫，医师，博士.
fast：快，禁食，快速，迅速，速.
fetch：拿，取，带来.
gold：金，黄金.
gone：去.
grave：严重，庄重，坟墓，墓穴，深重.
hide：躲藏，暗藏，掩饰，藏，隐瞒，隐藏.
islands：岛屿，岛.
lead：领导，铅，带领，主角，率领.
purse：钱包，钱袋，囊.
raft：筏，木排，槎，桴.
re：再.
roundabout：曲线.
search：搜索，搜查，寻觅，寻找，找.
silent：无声，沉默的.
swear：立誓，发誓.
tight：严格，严密，紧，紧的，严竣，狭隘.
till：直到.
village：村庄，农村，乡村，村子.
woods：树林，森林.

CHAPTER XLI

"MUST 'A' BEEN SPERITS"

The doctor was an old man; a very **nice**, kind-looking old man when I got him up. I told him me and my **brother** was over on Spanish Island **hunting** **yesterday afternoon**, and camped on a **piece** of a **raft** we found, and about **midnight** he must a kicked his **gun** in his **dreams**, for it went off and **shot** him in the **leg**, and we wanted him to go over there and **fix** it and not say nothing about it, **nor** let **anybody** know, because we wanted to come home this **evening** and **surprise** the folks.

"Who is your folks?" he says.

"The Phelpses, down yonder."

"Oh," he says. And after a **minute**, he says:

"How'd you say he got shot?"

"He had a dream," I says, "and it shot him."

"**Singular** dream," he says.

So he **lit** up his **lantern**, and got his saddle-bags, and we **started**. But when he sees the **canoe** he didn't like the look of her--said she was big enough for one, but didn't look **pretty safe** for two. I says:

Chinese Simplified

afternoon: 下午，午后.
anybody: 任何人.
brother: 弟兄，兄弟.
canoe: 独木舟.
dreams: 梦想.
evening: 晚，黄昏，傍晚，晚上.
fix: 安装，奠定，固定，修理.
gun: 枪，炮，长枪.
hunting: 狩猎.
lantern: 灯笼.
leg: 腿，脚.
lit: 点燃.
midnight: 午夜，半夜.
minute: 分钟，详细，分，微小的，渺小.
nice: 和蔼，可亲，好，尼斯.
nor: 也不.
piece: 片，部分，一块，一片，块，部份，份.
pretty: 漂亮，美丽的，秀丽.
raft: 筏，木排，槎，桴.
safe: 安全，保险，安全的，稳妥，保险箱.
shot: 射击.
singular: 单数，单一的.
started: 开始.
surprise: 使吃惊，惊奇，惊骇.
yesterday: 昨天.

"Oh, you needn't be afeard, sir, she carried the three of us easy enough."

"What three?"

"Why, me and Sid, and--and--and *the guns*; that's what I mean."

"Oh," he says.

But he put his foot on the gunnel and **rocked** her, and **shook** his head, and said he reckoned he'd look around for a **bigger** one. But they was all locked and chained; so he took my **canoe**, and said for me to wait **till** he come back, or I could **hunt** around further, or maybe I better go down home and get them ready for the **surprise** if I wanted to. But I said I didn't; so I told him just how to find the **raft**, and then he started.

I **struck** an idea **pretty** soon. I says to myself, spos'n he can't **fix** that **leg** just in three **shakes** of a sheep's **tail**, as the saying is? spos'n it takes him three or four days? What are we going to do?--lay around there till he **lets** the **cat** out of the **bag**? No, sir; I know what *I'll* do. I'll wait, and when he comes back if he says he's got to go any more I'll get down there, too, if I **swim**; and we'll take and **tie** him, and keep him, and **shove** out down the river; and when Tom's done with him we'll give him what it's worth, or all we got, and then let him get **ashore**.

So then I **crept** into a lumber-pile to get some sleep; and next time I waked up the sun was away up over my head! I **shot** out and went for the doctor's house, but they told me he'd gone away in the night some time or other, and warn't back yet. Well, **thinks** I, that looks powerful bad for Tom, and I'll **dig** out for the **island** right off. So away I shoved, and turned the corner, and nearly rammed my head into Uncle Silas's **stomach**! He says:

"Why, *Tom*! Where you been all this time, you rascal?"

"I hain't been nowheres," I says, "only just **hunting** for the **runaway** nigger--me and Sid."

"Why, where ever did you go?" he says. "Your aunt's been **mighty** uneasy."

"She needn't," I says, "because we was all right. We followed the men and the **dogs**, but they outrun us, and we lost them; but we thought we heard them on

Chinese Simplified

ashore: 岸上，上岸.
bag: 袋子，袋，手提包，提包，囊.
bigger: 更大，较大.
canoe: 独木舟.
cat: 猫.
crept: 爬行.
dig: 挖掘.
dogs: 狗.
fix: 安装，奠定，固定，修理.
guns: 枪支.
hunt: 打猎，狩猎.
hunting: 狩猎.
island: 岛.
leg: 腿，脚.
lets: 让我们，让.
mighty: 伟大，强势，强大的.
pretty: 漂亮，美丽的，秀丽.
raft: 筏，木排，槎，桴.
rocked: 摇动，摇摆.
runaway: 逃亡者，跑道.
shakes: 摇动.
shook: 摇动.
shot: 射击.
shove: 推.
stomach: 胃，肚子.
struck: 敲打.
surprise: 使吃惊，惊奇，惊骇.
swim: 游泳.
tail: 尾巴，跟踪.
thinks: 想.
tie: 不分胜负，打结，束缚，轨枕，绑，领带.
till: 直到.

the water, so we got a **canoe** and took out after them and crossed over, but couldn't find nothing of them; so we cruised along up- **shore till** we got kind of **tired** and **beat** out; and tied up the canoe and went to **sleep**, and never waked up till about an **hour** ago; then we paddled over here to hear the news, and Sid's at the post-office to see what he can hear, and I'm a-branching out to get something to eat for us, and then we're going home."

So then we went to the post-office to get "Sid"; but just as I suspicioned, he warn't there; so the old man he got a letter out of the office, and we **waited awhile longer**, but Sid didn't come; so the old man said, come along, let Sid **foot** it home, or canoe it, when he got done fooling around--but we would **ride**. I couldn't get him to let me stay and wait for Sid; and he said there warn't no use in it, and I must come along, and let Aunt Sally see we was all right.

When we got home Aunt Sally was that **glad** to see me she **laughed** and cried both, and hugged me, and give me one of them lickings of hern that don't amount to shucks, and said she'd **serve** Sid the same when he come.

And the place was **plum** full of farmers and farmers' wives, to **dinner**; and such another clack a body never heard. Old Mrs. Hotchkiss was the **worst**; her **tongue** was a-going all the time. She says:

"Well, Sister Phelps, I've ransacked that-air **cabin** over, an' I b'lieve the nigger was **crazy**. I says to Sister Damrell--didn't I, Sister Damrell?--s'I, he's crazy, s'I--them's the very words I said. You all hearn me: he's crazy, s'I; everything **shows** it, s'I. Look at that-air **grindstone**, s'I; want to tell *me*'t any cretur 't's in his right mind 's a goin' to **scrabble** all them crazy things **onto** a grindstone, s'I? Here sich 'n' sich a person busted his heart; 'n' here so 'n' so pegged along for thirty-seven year, 'n' all that--natcherl son o' Louis **somebody**, 'n' sich everlast'n rubbage. He's plumb crazy, s'I; it's what I says in the fust place, it's what I says in the **middle**, 'n' it's what I says last 'n' all the time--the nigger's crazy--crazy 's Nebokoodneezer, s'I."

"An' look at that-air **ladder** made out'n **rags**, Sister Hotchkiss," says old Mrs. Damrell; "what in the name o' **goodness** *could* he ever want of--"

Chinese Simplified

awhile: 一会儿.
beat: 打，击败，拍击，敲打，拍子，敲.
cabin: 小屋，船舱.
canoe: 独木舟.
crazy: 发狂，疯狂，颠倒，疯狂的.
dinner: 晚餐，正餐.
eat: 吃.
foot: 脚，足，步兵，英尺，呎.
glad: 高兴，高兴的.
goodness: 美德.
grindstone: 磨石.
hour: 小时，钟头，钟点，现在.
ladder: 阶梯，梯子.
laughed: 笑.
longer: 较长的.
middle: 中央，中间，半中腰，中间的，中部，中央的.
onto: 到…上.
plum: 李子，梅.
rags: 碎布.
ride: 乘，骑，跨，坐.
scrabble: 涂写.
serve: 侍候，伺候，待候.
shore: 岸，滨，岸边，海岸，海滨.
shows: 显示.
sleep: 梦寐，睡觉，睡眠，睡.
somebody: 某人，有人.
till: 直到.
tired: 疲倦，疲乏，疲倦的.
tongue: 舌头，舌.
wait: 等待，等，伺候.
worst: 最坏的.

"The very words I was a-**sayin'** no **longer** ago th'n this **minute** to Sister Utterback, 'n' she'll tell you so **herself**. Sh-she, look at that-air **rag ladder**, sh-she; 'n' s'I, yes, *look* at it, s'I--what *could* he a-wanted of it, s'I. Sh-she, Sister Hotchkiss, sh-she--"

"But how in the nation'd they ever *git* that **grindstone** *in* there, ***anyway***? 'n' who **dug** that-air ***hole***? 'n' who--"

"My very *words*, Brer Penrod! I was a-sayin'--pass that-air sasser o' m'lasses, won't ye?--I was a-sayin' to Sister Dunlap, jist this minute, how *did* they git that grindstone in there, s'I. Without *help*, mind you-- 'thout *help*! *That's* wher 'tis. Don't tell *me*, s'I; there *wuz* help, s'I; 'n' ther' wuz a ***plenty*** help, too, s'I; ther's ben a ***dozen*** a-helpin' that nigger, 'n' I **lay** I'd **skin** every last nigger on this place but *I'd* find out who done it, s'I; 'n' **moreover**, s'I--"

"A *dozen* says you!--*forty* couldn't a done every thing that's been done. Look at them case-knife **saws** and things, how **tedious** they've been made; look at that bed-leg **sawed** off with 'm, a week's work for six men; look at that nigger made out'n **straw** on the bed; and look at--"

"You may *well* say it, Brer Hightower! It's jist as I was a-sayin' to Brer Phelps, his own self. S'e, what do *you* think of it, Sister Hotchkiss, s'e? Think o' what, Brer Phelps, s'I? Think o' that bed-leg sawed off that a way, s'e? *think* of it, s'I? I lay it never sawed *itself* off, s'I--somebody *sawed* it, s'I; that's my **opinion**, take it or leave it, it mayn't be no 'count, s'I, but sich as 't is, it's my opinion, s'I, 'n' if any body k'n start a better one, s'I, let him *do* it, s'I, that's all. I says to Sister Dunlap, s'I--"

"Why, **dog** my **cats**, they must a ben a house-full o' niggers in there every night for four weeks to a done all that work, Sister Phelps. Look at that shirt--every last **inch** of it kivered over with **secret** African writ'n done with **blood**! Must a ben a **raft** uv 'm at it right **along**, all the time, amost. Why, I'd give two dollars to have it read to me; 'n' as for the niggers that **wrote** it, I 'low I'd take 'n' **lash** 'm t'll--"

Chinese Simplified

along: 沿着，沿，一同.
anyway: 无论如何，反正.
blood: 血，血液，鲜血.
cats: 猫.
dog: 狗，犬.
dozen: 一打，打.
dug: 挖掘.
grindstone: 磨石.
hole: 洞，漏洞，孔，穴，洞穴，窟窿.
inch: 英寸.
ladder: 阶梯，梯子.
lash: 睫毛，鞭打，鞭挞，皮鞭，鞭笞.
lay: 产卵，安放，放，凡俗.
longer: 较长的.
minute: 分钟，详细，分，微小的，渺小.
moreover: 此外，而且，并且，另外，况且，又.
n: 安全理事会.
opinion: 意见，看法，意思，见解.
plenty: 丰富，许多.
raft: 筏，木排，槎，桴.
rag: 破布，碎布.
sawed: 锯.
saws: 锯.
secret: 秘密，机密.
self: 自己，自，自我，我.
skin: 皮肤，剥皮.
straw: 稻草，吸管.
tedious: 乏味，厌烦的.
wrote: 写了.

"People to *help* him, Brother Marples! Well, I **reckon** you'd *think* so if you'd a been in this house for a while back. Why, they've **stole** everything they could lay their hands on--and we a-watching all the time, mind you. They stole that **shirt** right off o' the line! and as for that **sheet** they made the **rag ladder** out of, ther' ain't no telling how many times they *didn't* **steal** that; and **flour**, and **candles**, and candlesticks, and spoons, and the old warming-pan, and most a thousand things that I disremember now, and my new **calico dress**; and me and Silas and my Sid and Tom on the **constant** watch day *and* night, as I was a-telling you, and not a one of us could catch **hide** nor hair nor sight nor sound of them; and here at the last minute, lo and **behold** you, they slides right in under our noses and fools us, and not only fools *us* but the Injun Territory robbers too, and actuly gets *away* with that nigger safe and sound, and that with **sixteen** men and twenty-two **dogs** right on their very heels at that very time! I tell you, it just bangs anything I ever *heard* of. Why, *sperits* couldn't a done better and been no smarter. And I reckon they must a *been* sperits--because, *you* know our dogs, and ther' ain't no better; well, them dogs never even got on the *track* of 'm once! You explain *that* to me if you can!--*any* of you!"

"Well, it does beat--"

"Laws **alive**, I never--"

"So help me, I wouldn't a be--"

"*House*-thieves as well as--"

"**Goodnessgracioussakes**, I'd a ben afeard to live in sich a--"

"'Fraid to *live*!--why, I was that scared I dasn't hardly go to bed, or get up, or lay down, or *set* down, Sister Ridgeway. Why, they'd steal the very--why, **goodness** sakes, you can **guess** what kind of a fluster I was in by the time **midnight** come last night. I hope to gracious if I warn't afraid they'd steal some o' the family! I was just to that pass I didn't have no **reasoning faculties** no more. It looks **foolish** enough *now*, in the **daytime**; but I says to myself, there's my two poor boys **asleep**, 'way up **stairs** in that **lonesome** room, and I **declare** to goodness I was that **uneasy** 't I crep' up there and locked 'em in! I *did*. And

Chinese Simplified

alive: 活着，活，活泼的，活着的.
asleep: 睡着，睡着的.
behold: 看见.
calico: 白布，白棉布.
candles: 蜡烛.
constant: 一贯，不变，不断，固定的，常量.
daytime: 白天，白昼，日间.
declare: 宣布，陈述，声明，宣告.
dogs: 狗.
dress: 服装，打扮.
faculties: 才能.
flour: 面粉，白面，粉.
foolish: 愚蠢的.
goodness: 美德.
gracious: 亲切，亲切的，有礼貌的.
guess: 猜测，臆测，猜谜儿，猜想，揣测，推测.
hide: 躲藏，暗藏，掩饰，藏，隐瞒，隐藏.
ladder: 阶梯，梯子.
lonesome: 寂寞，寂寞的.
midnight: 午夜，半夜.
rag: 破布，碎布.
reasoning: 推理.
reckon: 估计，计算.
sheet: 片，一张，床单，纸张.
shirt: 衬衫，衬衣.
sixteen: 十六.
stairs: 楼梯.
steal: 偷窃，盗窃，偷，窃取.
stole: 偷了.
uneasy: 不安，担心，不安的.

anybody would. Because, you know, when you get scared that way, and it **keeps** running on, and getting worse and worse all the time, and your **wits** gets to addling, and you get to doing all **sorts** o' **wild** things, and by and by you think to yourself, spos'n I was a boy, and was away up there, and the door ain't locked, and you--" She stopped, looking kind of wondering, and then she turned her head around **slow**, and when her eye **lit** on me--I got up and took a walk.

Says I to myself, I can explain better how we come to not be in that room this morning if I go out to one side and study over it a little. So I done it. But I dasn't go **fur**, or she'd a sent for me. And when it was late in the day the people all went, and then I come in and told her the **noise** and **shooting** waked up me and "Sid," and the door was locked, and we wanted to see the **fun**, so we went down the lightning-rod, and both of us got **hurt** a little, and we didn't never want to try *that* no more. And then I went on and told her all what I told Uncle Silas before; and then she said she'd **forgive** us, and maybe it was all right enough anyway, and about what a body might expect of boys, for all boys was a **pretty** harum-scarum lot as fur as she could see; and so, as long as no **harm** hadn't come of it, she judged she better put in her time being **grateful** we was **alive** and well and she had us still, stead of fretting over what was past and done. So then she kissed me, and patted me on the head, and **dropped** into a kind of a brown study; and pretty soon **jumps** up, and says:

"Why, lawsamercy, it's most night, and Sid not come yet! What *has* become of that boy?"

I see my chance; so I **skips** up and says:

"I'll run right up to town and get him," I says.

"No you won't," she says. "You'll stay right wher' you are; *one's* enough to be lost at a time. If he ain't here to **supper**, your **uncle** 'll go."

Well, he warn't there to supper; so right after supper uncle went.

He come back about ten a little bit **uneasy**; hadn't run across Tom's track. **Aunt** Sally was a good *deal* uneasy; but Uncle Silas he said there warn't no **occasion** to be--boys will be boys, he said, and you'll see this one turn up in the

Chinese Simplified

alive：活着，活，活泼的，活着的.
anybody：任何人.
aunt：伯母，姑妈，大娘，婶母，阿姨，姨妈，婶子.
dropped：落下.
forgive：包涵，包容，原谅，宽恕，饶恕.
fun：娱乐.
fur：毛，软毛.
grateful：感谢，感激的.
harm：伤害，损害，坏处，害处，祸害.
hurt：伤害，使受伤.
jumps：跳跃.
keeps：保持.
lit：点燃.
noise：噪音，噪声，响声，吵闹声，吵声.
occasion：时机，机会，场合，场面.
pretty：漂亮，美丽的，秀丽.
shooting：射击，猎场.
skips：跳跃.
slow：慢，缓慢，迟慢，迟钝，迟迟，迟缓.
sorts：种类.
supper：晚饭，晚餐.
uncle：叔叔，伯伯，叔父，大爷，老大爷，姑夫.
uneasy：不安，担心，不安的.
wild：野，猖披，猖獗，野生，野性的.
wits：智慧.

morning all sound and right. So she had to be **satisfied**. But she said she'd set up for him a while anyway, and keep a light burning so he could see it.

And then when I went up to bed she come up with me and fetched her **candle**, and tucked me in, and mothered me so good I felt mean, and like I couldn't look her in the face; and she set down on the bed and **talked** with me a long time, and said what a **splendid** boy Sid was, and didn't seem to want to ever stop talking about him; and kept asking me every now and then if I reckoned he could a got lost, or **hurt**, or maybe drownded, and might be laying at this **minute** somewheres **suffering** or dead, and she not by him to help him, and so the **tears** would **drip** down **silent**, and I would tell her that Sid was all right, and would be home in the morning, sure; and she would **squeeze** my hand, or maybe **kiss** me, and tell me to say it again, and keep on saying it, because it done her good, and she was in so much **trouble**. And when she was going away she looked down in my eyes so **steady** and **gentle**, and says:

"The door ain't going to be locked, Tom, and there's the window and the **rod**; but you'll be good, *won't* you? And you won't go? For *my* sake."

Laws **knows** I *wanted* to go bad enough to see about Tom, and was all intending to go; but after that I wouldn't a went, not for **kingdoms**.

But she was on my mind and Tom was on my mind, so I **slept** very **restless**. And **twice** I went down the rod away in the night, and **slipped** around front, and see her **setting** there by her candle in the window with her eyes towards the road and the tears in them; and I wished I could do something for her, but I couldn't, only to **swear** that I wouldn't never do nothing to **grieve** her any more. And the third time I waked up at **dawn**, and **slid** down, and she was there yet, and her candle was most out, and her old **gray** head was **resting** on her hand, and she was **asleep**.

Chinese Simplified

asleep: 睡着，睡着的.
candle: 蜡烛.
dawn: 黎明.
drip: 滴下，滴.
gentle: 轻松，文雅的，斯文，柔和.
gray: 灰色，灰.
grieve: 伤心，悼念，使伤心.
hurt: 伤害，使受伤.
kingdoms: 王国.
kiss: 吻，接吻，轻抚，轻触.
knows: 知道.
minute: 分钟，详细，分，微小的，渺小.
resting: 静止的.
restless: 不安，不安的.
rod: 棍子，棍.
satisfied: 满意，乐意，心满意足的.
setting: 排字，设定.
silent: 无声，沉默的.
slept: 睡了.
slid: 滑行.
slipped: 滑落.
splendid: 彪炳，卓越，辉煌，灿烂的，精彩，辉煌的.
squeeze: 压扁，压挤，榨.
steady: 稳定，坚定，平稳，平稳的.
suffering: 痛苦，熬煎，苦难.
swear: 立誓，发誓.
talked: 谈话.
tears: 泪，泪水，眼泪.
trouble: 麻烦，难度，难处.
twice: 两次.

CHAPTER XLII

WHY THEY DIDN'T HANG JIM

The old man was uptown again before **breakfast**, but couldn't get no **track** of Tom; and both of them set at the table **thinking**, and not **saying** nothing, and looking **mournful**, and their **coffee** getting **cold**, and not **eating** anything. And by and by the old man says:

"Did I give you the **letter**?"

"What letter?"

"The one I got **yesterday** out of the post-office."

"No, you didn't give me no letter."

"Well, I must a **forgot** it."

So he rummaged his pockets, and then went off somewheres where he had **laid** it down, and fetched it, and give it to her. She says:

"Why, it's from St. Petersburg--it's from Sis."

I **allowed** another **walk** would do me good; but I couldn't **stir**. But before she could break it open she **dropped** it and run--for she see something. And so did I. It was Tom Sawyer on a **mattress**; and that old **doctor**; and Jim, in *her* **calico** **dress**, with his **hands** tied behind him; and a **lot** of people. I **hid** the letter

Chinese Simplified

allowed：允许．
break：破坏，断，打破，犯，中断，破，裂．
breakfast：早餐，早饭，早点．
calico：白布，白棉布．
coffee：咖啡．
cold：冷，感冒，寒冷，寒，冷淡．
doctor：医生，大夫，医师，博士．
dress：服装，打扮．
dropped：落下．
eating：吃．
fast：快，禁食，快速，迅速，速．
forgot：忘记．
hands：手．
hid：躲藏．
laid：放．
letter：字母，信．
lot：地皮，批量，地段．
mattress：床垫．
mournful：悲切，悲恸，悲恸的．
saying：名言，说．
stir：轰动，搅拌，鼓动．
thinking：思想，思维．
track：跑道，径赛，径迹，轨道，行踪，履带，踪迹．
walk：行走，步行，走，走道，散步．
yesterday：昨天．

behind the first thing that come **handy**, and rushed. She flung herself at Tom, **crying**, and says:

"Oh, he's dead, he's dead, I know he's dead!"

And Tom he turned his head a little, and muttered something or other, which showed he warn't in his right mind; then she flung up her hands, and says:

"He's **alive**, thank God! And that's enough!" and she snatched a **kiss** of him, and **flew** for the house to get the bed ready, and **scattering orders** right and left at the niggers and everybody else, as fast as her **tongue** could go, every **jump** of the way.

I followed the men to see what they was going to do with Jim; and the old doctor and Uncle Silas followed after Tom into the house. The men was very huffy, and some of them wanted to **hang** Jim for an example to all the other niggers around there, so they wouldn't be trying to run away like Jim done, and making such a **raft** of trouble, and keeping a **whole** family scared most to death for days and nights. But the others said, don't do it, it wouldn't answer at all; he ain't our nigger, and his **owner** would turn up and make us pay for him, sure. So that **cooled** them down a little, because the people that's always the most **anxious** for to hang a nigger that hain't done just right is always the very ones that ain't the most anxious to pay for him when they've got their **satisfaction** out of him.

They cussed Jim considerble, though, and give him a **cuff** or two side the head once in a while, but Jim never said nothing, and he never let on to know me, and they took him to the same **cabin**, and put his own clothes on him, and chained him again, and not to no bed-leg this time, but to a big **staple drove** into the bottom **log**, and chained his hands, too, and both legs, and said he warn't to have nothing but **bread** and water to eat after this **till** his owner come, or he was sold at **auction** because he didn't come in a certain **length** of time, and filled up our hole, and said a couple of farmers with **guns** must stand watch around about the cabin every night, and a **bulldog** tied to the door in the **daytime**; and about this time they was through with the job and was tapering off with a kind of

Chinese Simplified

alive：活着，活，活泼的，活着的．
anxious：焦急，巴不得，担心，焦虑的．
auction：拍卖．
bread：面包．
bulldog：牛头犬，喇叭狗．
cabin：小屋，船舱．
cooled：凉爽．
crying：叫喊的，嚎哭的，显著的．
cuff：袖口．
daytime：白天，白昼，日间．
drove：驾．
flew：飞．
guns：枪支．
handy：灵巧，便当，顺手，方便的，简便．
hang：挂，悬挂．
hole：洞，漏洞，孔，穴，洞穴，窟窿．
jump：跳，跳跃．
kiss：吻，接吻，轻抚，轻触．
length：长度，长短，篇幅，长，一节，一段．
log：圆形木材，圆木，木头．
orders：命令．
owner：物主，业主，所有者，所有人，主人．
raft：筏，木排，桴，桴．
satisfaction：满意．
scattering：散射．
staple：钉书针，名产，主要成分．
till：直到．
tongue：舌头，舌．

generl **good**-bye cussing, and then the old doctor comes and takes a look, and says:

"Don't be no rougher on him than you're obleeged to, because he ain't a bad nigger. When I got to where I found the boy I see I couldn't cut the **bullet** out without some help, and he warn't in no condition for me to leave to go and get help; and he got a little worse and a little worse, and after a long time he went out of his head, and wouldn't let me come a-nigh him any more, and said if I chalked his **raft** he'd **kill** me, and no end of wild **foolishness** like that, and I see I couldn't do anything at all with him; so I says, I got to have *help* **somehow**; and the minute I says it out **crawls** this nigger from somewheres and says he'll help, and he done it, too, and done it very well. Of course I judged he must be a **runaway** nigger, and there I *was*! and there I had to **stick** right straight along all the rest of the day and all night. It was a **fix**, I tell you! I had a couple of patients with the **chills**, and of course I'd of liked to run up to town and see them, but I dasn't, because the nigger might get away, and then I'd be to **blame**; and yet never a **skiff** come close enough for me to **hail**. So there I had to stick plumb until **daylight** this morning; and I never see a nigger that was a better nuss or faithfuller, and yet he was **risking** his freedom to do it, and was all **tired** out, too, and I see **plain** enough he'd been worked main hard **lately**. I liked the nigger for that; I tell you, **gentlemen**, a nigger like that is worth a thousand dollars--and kind **treatment**, too. I had everything I needed, and the boy was doing as well there as he would a done at home--better, maybe, because it was so quiet; but there I *was*, with both of 'm on my hands, and there I had to stick **till** about **dawn** this morning; then some men in a skiff come by, and as good **luck** would have it the nigger was setting by the **pallet** with his head propped on his **knees** sound **asleep**; so I motioned them in quiet, and they **slipped** up on him and grabbed him and tied him before he knowed what he was about, and we never had no trouble. And the boy being in a kind of a flighty sleep, too, we muffled the oars and **hitched** the raft on, and towed her over very nice and quiet, and the nigger never made the least **row** nor said a word from the start. He ain't no bad nigger, gentlemen; that's what I think about him."

Chinese Simplified

asleep：睡着，睡着的.
blame：责备，咎，非难，责任，罪，责怪，归咎.
bullet：子弹.
chills：寒冷.
crawls：爬行.
dawn：黎明.
daylight：日光，白天.
fix：安装，奠定，固定，修理.
foolishness：愚蠢.
gentlemen：绅士.
good-**bye**：再会.
hail：冰雹，雹，雹子，欢呼.
hitched：蹒跚.
kill：打死，杀害，杀死.
knees：膝盖.
lately：近来，一向，最近.
luck：运气，幸运.
pallet：草荐，棘爪.
plain：平原.
raft：筏，木排，槎，桴.
risking：风险.
row：一排，划，行.
runaway：逃亡者，跑道.
skiff：小船，小艇.
slipped：滑落.
somehow：不知何故.
stick：棍，棒子，棍子，插入，棒，黏贴，手杖.
till：直到.
tired：疲倦，疲乏，疲倦的.
treatment：待遇，疗法，对待，治疗，处理.

Somebody says:

"Well, it sounds very good, doctor, I'm obleeged to say."

Then the others softened up a little, too, and I was **mighty thankful** to that old doctor for doing Jim that good turn; and I was glad it was **according** to my **judgment** of him, too; because I thought he had a good heart in him and was a good man the first time I see him. Then they all agreed that Jim had acted very well, and was **deserving** to have some notice took of it, and **reward**. So every one of them promised, right out and **hearty**, that they wouldn't cuss him no more.

Then they come out and locked him up. I hoped they was going to say he could have one or two of the **chains** took off, because they was **rotten** heavy, or could have **meat** and **greens** with his bread and water; but they didn't think of it, and I reckoned it warn't best for me to **mix** in, but I judged I'd get the doctor's **yarn** to Aunt Sally somehow or other as soon as I'd got through the breakers that was laying just ahead of me-- explanations, I mean, of how I **forgot** to mention about Sid being shot when I was telling how him and me put in that dratted night paddling around **hunting** the **runaway** nigger.

But I had plenty time. Aunt Sally she **stuck** to the sick-room all day and all night, and every time I see Uncle Silas mooning around I dodged him.

Next morning I heard Tom was a good deal better, and they said Aunt Sally was gone to get a **nap**. So I slips to the sick-room, and if I found him **awake** I reckoned we could put up a yarn for the family that would **wash**. But he was **sleeping**, and sleeping very **peaceful**, too; and **pale**, not fire- faced the way he was when he come. So I set down and **laid** for him to wake. In about half an hour Aunt Sally comes **gliding** in, and there I was, up a **stump** again! She motioned me to be still, and set down by me, and begun to **whisper**, and said we could all be **joyful** now, because all the **symptoms** was first-rate, and he'd been sleeping like that for ever so long, and looking better and peacefuller all the time, and ten to one he'd wake up in his right mind.

Chinese Simplified

according: 根据.
awake: 唤醒，觉醒，醒.
chains: 连锁.
deserving: 功过，赏罚.
forgot: 忘记.
gliding: 滑行的，下滑.
greens: 绿色.
hearty: 诚恳，热诚的.
hunting: 狩猎.
joyful: 欢喜，快乐的，欢喜的.
judgment: 判决，裁判，报应，判定，判断，裁.
laid: 放.
meat: 肉.
mighty: 伟大，强势，强大的.
mix: 混，混杂，糅，混合，掺混.
nap: 瞌睡.
pale: 苍白，苍白的.
peaceful: 安顿，安宁，安生，安谧，安静，和平的，沉静.
reward: 报酬，酬劳，酬金，奖励，奖赏.
rotten: 腐败的，腐朽.
runaway: 逃亡者，跑道.
sleeping: 睡眠，睡着.
stuck: 黏贴.
stump: 树桩，残肢.
symptoms: 症状.
thankful: 感谢，感谢的.
wake: 醒来，醒觉.
wash: 洗涤，洗刷，洗.
whisper: 耳语，低语.
yarn: 毛线.

So we set there watching, and by and by he **stirs** a bit, and opened his eyes very natural, and takes a look, and says:

"Hello!--why, I'm at *home*! How's that? Where's the raft?"

"It's all right," I says.

"And *Jim*?"

"The same," I says, but couldn't say it **pretty brash**. But he never noticed, but says:

"Good! Splendid! *Now* we're all right and safe! Did you tell Aunty?"

I was going to say yes; but she chipped in and says: "About what, Sid?"

"Why, about the way the **whole** thing was done."

"What whole thing?"

"Why, *the* whole thing. There ain't but one; how we set the **runaway** nigger free--me and Tom."

"Good land! Set the run--What *is* the child talking about! Dear, dear, out of his head again!"

"*No,* I ain't out of my *head*; I know all what I'm talking about. We *did* set him free--me and Tom. We **laid** out to do it, and we *done* it. And we done it **elegant**, too." He'd got a start, and she never checked him up, just set and stared and stared, and let him **clip** along, and I see it warn't no use for *me* to put in. "Why, Aunty, it cost us a power of work --weeks of it--hours and hours, every night, whilst you was all **asleep**. And we had to **steal candles**, and the **sheet**, and the **shirt**, and your **dress**, and spoons, and **tin plates**, and case-knives, and the warming-pan, and the **grindstone**, and **flour**, and just no end of things, and you can't think what work it was to make the **saws**, and pens, and **inscriptions**, and one thing or another, and you can't think *half* the **fun** it was. And we had to make up the **pictures** of **coffins** and things, and nonnamous letters from the robbers, and get up and down the lightning-rod, and **dig** the hole into the **cabin**, and made the **rope ladder** and send it in **cooked** up in a **pie**, and send in spoons and things to work with in your **apron** pocket--"

Chinese Simplified

apron：围裙，停机坪.
asleep：睡着，睡着的.
brash：胃灼热，无礼的，傲慢的.
cabin：小屋，船舱.
candles：蜡烛.
clip：夹子，回形针.
coffins：棺材.
cooked：煮熟.
dig：挖掘.
dress：服装，打扮.
elegant：高雅，文雅，优美，讲究的，优雅的.
flour：面粉，白面，粉.
fun：娱乐.
grindstone：磨石.
hole：洞，漏洞，孔，穴，洞穴，窟窿.
inscriptions：铭刻.
ladder：阶梯，梯子.
laid：放.
pictures：图画.
pie：馅饼.
plates：盘子.
pretty：漂亮，美丽的，秀丽.
rope：绳索，绳子.
runaway：逃亡者，跑道.
saws：锯.
sheet：片，一张，床单，纸张.
shirt：衬衫，衬衣.
steal：偷窃，盗窃，偷，窃取.
stirs：鼓动.
tin：锡，罐头.

"Mercy sakes!"

"--and **load** up the **cabin** with rats and snakes and so on, for company for Jim; and then you kept Tom here so long with the **butter** in his **hat** that you come near spiling the whole business, because the men come before we was out of the cabin, and we had to **rush**, and they heard us and let drive at us, and I got my share, and we dodged out of the path and let them go by, and when the dogs come they warn't interested in us, but went for the most noise, and we got our **canoe**, and made for the **raft**, and was all safe, and Jim was a free man, and we done it all by ourselves, and *wasn't* it **bully**, Aunty!"

"Well, I never heard the likes of it in all my born days! So it was *you*, you little rapscallions, that's been making all this trouble, and turned everybody's **wits** clean inside out and scared us all most to death. I've as good a **notion** as ever I had in my life to take it out o' you this very minute. To think, here I've been, night after night, a--*you* just get well once, you young scamp, and I lay I'll **tan** the Old Harry out o' both o' ye!"

But Tom, he *was* so **proud** and **joyful**, he just *couldn't* hold in, and his **tongue** just *went* it--she a-chipping in, and spitting fire all along, and both of them going it at once, like a **cat convention**; and she says:

"*Well*, you get all the **enjoyment** you can out of it *now*, for mind I tell you if I catch you meddling with him again--"

"Meddling with *who*?" Tom says, **dropping** his smile and looking **surprised**.

"With *who*? Why, the **runaway** nigger, of course. Who'd you reckon?"

Tom looks at me very **grave**, and says:

"Tom, didn't you just tell me he was all right? Hasn't he got away?"

"*Him*?" says Aunt Sally; "the runaway nigger? 'Deed he hasn't. They've got him back, safe and sound, and he's in that cabin again, on **bread** and water, and **loaded** down with **chains**, **till** he's claimed or sold!"

Tom rose square up in bed, with his eye hot, and his nostrils **opening** and **shutting** like **gills**, and **sings** out to me:

Chinese Simplified

bread：面包.
bully：欺负.
butter：牛油，黄油.
cabin：小屋，船舱.
canoe：独木舟.
cat：猫.
chains：连锁.
convention：公约，会议，习俗.
dropping：点滴，落下.
enjoyment：乐趣，享乐.
gills：腮.
grave：严重，庄重，坟墓，墓穴，深重.
hat：帽子.
joyful：欢喜，快乐的，欢喜的.
load：包袱，负载，装满，担子，装载，负荷，载重.
loaded：载入.
notion：观念.
opening：揭幕，口，打开，孔，开始.
proud：傲岸，骄矜，骄傲的，自豪的.
raft：筏，木排，槎，桴.
runaway：逃亡者，跑道.
rush：速行，匆匆.
shutting：关闭.
sings：唱.
surprised：惊讶.
tan：黄褐色，鞣，棕黄色.
till：直到.
tongue：舌头，舌.
wits：智慧.

"They hain't no *right* to **shut** him up! *shove*!--and don't you **lose** a **minute**. Turn him **loose**! he ain't no **slave**; he's as free as any cretur that **walks** this earth!"

"What *does* the child mean?"

"I mean every word I *say*, **Aunt** Sally, and if **somebody** don't go, *I'll* go. I've knowed him all his life, and so has Tom, there. Old Miss Watson died two months ago, and she was **ashamed** she ever was going to **sell** him down the **river**, and *said* so; and she set him free in her will."

"Then what on earth did *you* want to set him free for, **seeing** he was already free?"

"Well, that *is* a question, I must say; and just like women! Why, I wanted the ***adventure*** of it; and I'd a waded neck-deep in blood to-- **goodness alive**, *Aunt Polly*!"

If she warn't **standing** right there, just inside the door, looking as **sweet** and **contented** as an **angel** half full of **pie**, I wish I may never!

Aunt Sally **jumped** for her, and most hugged the head off of her, and cried over her, and I found a good enough place for me under the bed, for it was getting **pretty sultry** for us, seemed to me. And I peeped out, and in a little while Tom's Aunt Polly **shook** herself loose and stood there looking across at Tom over her spectacles--kind of **grinding** him into the earth, you know. And then she says:

"Yes, you *better* turn y'r head away--I would if I was you, Tom."

"Oh, deary me!" says Aunt Sally; "*is* he **changed** so? Why, that ain't *Tom*, it's Sid; Tom's--Tom's--why, where is Tom? He was here a minute ago."

"You mean where's Huck *Finn*--that's what you mean! I **reckon** I hain't **raised** such a scamp as my Tom all these years not to know him when I *see* him. That *would* be a pretty howdy-do. Come out from under that bed, Huck Finn."

So I done it. But not feeling **brash.**

Aunt Sally she was one of the mixed-upest-looking **persons** I ever see-- **except** one, and that was Uncle Silas, when he come in and they told it all to him.

Chinese Simplified

adventure：冒险，探险.
alive：活着，活，活泼的，活着的.
angel：天使，安琪儿.
ashamed：惭愧，羞愧，惭愧的.
aunt：伯母，姑妈，大娘，婶母，阿姨，姨妈，婶子.
brash：胃灼热，无礼的，傲慢的.
changed：改变.
contented：满意.
except：除了，除了之外.
goodness：美德.
grinding：磨的，磨削.
jumped：跳跃.
loose：松开，松弛的.
lose：丢失，丧失，失掉，遗失.
minute：分钟，详细，分，微小的，渺小.
persons：人.
pie：馅饼.
pretty：漂亮，美丽的，秀丽.
raised：凸起的，浮雕的.
reckon：估计，计算.
river：河，江，川，河流，条.
seeing：有鉴于.
sell：销售，游说，贩卖，出售.
shook：摇动.
shut：关闭.
slave：奴隶.
somebody：某人，有人.
standing：站立，地位.
sultry：闷热.
sweet：甜，甜食，糖果.
walks：步行.

It kind of made him **drunk**, as you may say, and he didn't know nothing at all the rest of the day, and preached a prayer-meeting **sermon** that night that gave him a rattling ruputation, because the **oldest** man in the world couldn't a **understood** it. So Tom's **Aunt** Polly, she told all about who I was, and what; and I had to up and tell how I was in such a **tight** place that when Mrs. Phelps took me for Tom Sawyer--she chipped in and says, "Oh, go on and call me Aunt Sally, I'm used to it now, and 'tain't no need to change"--that when Aunt Sally took me for Tom Sawyer I had to stand it--there warn't no other way, and I knowed he wouldn't mind, because it would be **nuts** for him, being a **mystery**, and he'd make an **adventure** out of it, and be **perfectly satisfied**. And so it turned out, and he let on to be Sid, and made things as **soft** as he could for me.

And his Aunt Polly she said Tom was right about old Miss Watson **setting** Jim free in her will; and so, sure enough, Tom Sawyer had gone and took all that **trouble** and **bother** to set a free nigger free! and I couldn't ever understand before, until that **minute** and that talk, how he *could* help a body set a nigger free with his bringing up.

Well, Aunt Polly she said that when Aunt Sally **wrote** to her that Tom and *Sid* had come all right and **safe**, she says to herself:

"Look at that, now! I might have expected it, letting him go off that way without **anybody** to **watch** him. So now I got to go and trapse all the way down the **river**, **eleven** hundred **mile**, and find out what that creetur's up to *this* time, as long as I couldn't seem to get any answer out of you about it."

"Why, I never heard nothing from you," says Aunt Sally.

"Well, I **wonder**! Why, I wrote you **twice** to ask you what you could mean by Sid being here."

"Well, I never got 'em, Sis."

Aunt Polly she turns around **slow** and **severe**, and says:

"You, Tom!"

"Well--*what*?" he says, kind of pettish.

Chinese Simplified

adventure: 冒险，探险.
anybody: 任何人.
aunt: 伯母，姑妈，大娘，婶母，阿姨，姨妈，婶子.
bother: 烦扰，打扰，理会.
drunk: 喝了，喝醉.
eleven: 十一.
mile: 英里.
minute: 分钟，详细，分，微小的，渺小.
mystery: 神秘.
nuts: 螺母.
oldest: 最年长的.
perfectly: 完美，完美地.
river: 河，江，川，河流，条.
safe: 安全，保险，安全的，稳妥，保险箱.
satisfied: 满意，乐意，心满意足的.
sermon: 传教.
setting: 排字，设定.
severe: 严重，严竣，严厉，严峻，剧烈，严肃的.
slow: 慢，缓慢，迟慢，迟钝，迟迟，迟缓.
soft: 柔软，柔和，柔软的.
tight: 严格，严密，紧，紧的，严竣，狭隘.
trouble: 麻烦，难度，难处.
twice: 两次.
understood: 明白.
watch: 观看，手表，监视.
wonder: 奇迹，惊奇.
wrote: 写了.

"Don t you what *me*, you **impudent** thing--hand out them **letters**."

"What letters?"

"*Them* letters. I be **bound**, if I have to take a-holt of you I'll--"

"They're in the **trunk**. There, now. And they're just the same as they was when I got them out of the office. I hain't looked into them, I hain't touched them. But I knowed they'd make **trouble**, and I thought if you warn't in no **hurry**, I'd--"

"Well, you *do* need skinning, there ain't no **mistake** about it. And I **wrote** another one to tell you I was **coming**; and I s'pose he--"

"No, it come **yesterday**; I hain't read it yet, but *it's* all right, I've got that one."

I wanted to **offer** to **bet** two dollars she hadn't, but I reckoned **maybe** it was just as **safe** to not to. So I never said nothing.

Chinese Simplified

bet: 打赌，赌.
bound: 限，边际，弹回，范围.
coming: 未来，到来.
hurry: 仓促，匆忙，赶忙.
impudent: 厚颜无耻.
letters: 信件，函件.
maybe: 或许，也许，或者，说不定，可能，不一定.
mistake: 错误，差错.
offer: 捐助，开设，提供.
safe: 安全，保险，安全的，稳妥，保险箱.
trouble: 麻烦，难度，难处.
trunk: 躯干，主干，树干.
wrote: 写了.
yesterday: 昨天.

CHAPTER XLIII

NOTHING MORE TO **WRITE**

The first time I catched Tom private I asked him what was his **idea**, time of the **evasion**?--what it was he'd planned to do if the evasion worked all right and he managed to set a nigger free that was already free before? And he said, what he had planned in his head from the start, if we got Jim out all **safe**, was for us to run him down the **river** on the **raft**, and have **adventures** plumb to the **mouth** of the river, and then tell him about his being free, and take him back up home on a **steamboat**, in style, and pay him for his **lost** time, and write **word ahead** and get out all the niggers around, and have them **waltz** him into **town** with a **torchlight procession** and a brass-band, and then he would be a **hero**, and so would we. But I reckoned it was about as well the way it was.

We had Jim out of the **chains** in no time, and when Aunt Polly and Uncle Silas and Aunt Sally found out how good he helped the **doctor nurse** Tom, they made a **heap** of **fuss** over him, and **fixed** him up **prime**, and give him all he wanted to **eat**, and a good time, and nothing to do. And we had him up to the sick-room, and had a high **talk**; and Tom give Jim **forty** dollars for being **prisoner** for us so **patient**, and doing it up so good, and Jim was **pleased** most to death, and busted out, and says:

Chinese Simplified

adventures: 冒险.
ahead: 前头, 前方, 前面的.
chains: 连锁.
de: 可选择丢弃.
doctor: 医生, 大夫, 医师, 博士.
eat: 吃.
evasion: 逃避.
fixed: 固定, 确定, 一定, 固定的.
forty: 四十.
fuss: 大惊小怪.
heap: 堆, 堆积.
hero: 英雄.
lost: 遗失.
mouth: 口, 嘴巴, 嘴, 吻.
nurse: 护士, 哺乳, 照料.
patient: 耐烦, 患者, 病号, 病员, 耐心, 忍耐, 病人.
pleased: 满意, 高兴的.
prime: 首要的.
prisoner: 犯人, 罪犯, 囚犯.
procession: 行列, 游行.
raft: 筏, 木排, 槎, 桴.
river: 河, 江, 川, 河流, 条.
safe: 安全, 保险, 安全的, 稳妥, 保险箱.
steamboat: 汽船, 轮船.
talk: 谈话, 报告, 言语, 谈.
torchlight: 手电筒.
town: 城镇, 城市, 市镇.
waltz: 华尔滋舞.
word: 字, 词, 单词, 誓言.
write: 撰写, 写, 编着, 写作, 写信给, 书写, 书写器, 写字, 作曲.

"*Dah,* now, Huck, what I tell you?--what I tell you up dah on Jackson islan'? I *tole* you I got a **hairy** breas', en what's de **sign** un it; en I *tole* you I ben **rich** wunst, en gwineter to be rich *agin;* en it's come true; en heah she is! *Dah,* now! doan' talk to *me*--signs is *signs,* **mine** I tell you; en I knowed **jis'** 's well 'at I 'uz gwineter be rich agin as I's a-stannin' heah dis minute!"

And then Tom he **talked** along and talked along, and says, le's all three **slide** out of here one of these nights and get an **outfit**, and go for **howling adventures** amongst the Injuns, over in the Territory, for a couple of weeks or two; and I says, all right, that suits me, but I ain't got no money for to buy the outfit, and I **reckon** I couldn't get **none** from home, because it's likely pap's been back before now, and got it all away from Judge Thatcher and **drunk** it up.

"No, he hain't," Tom says; "it's all there yet--six **thousand** dollars and more; and your pap hain't ever been back since. Hadn't when I come away, anyhow."

Jim says, **kind** of **solemn**:

"He ain't a-comin' back no mo', Huck."

I says:

"Why, Jim?"

"Nemmine why, Huck--but he ain't comin' back no mo."

But I **kept** at him; so at last he says:

"Doan' you 'member de house dat was float'n down de **river**, en dey wuz a man in dah, kivered up, en I went in en unkivered him and didn' let you come in? Well, **den**, you kin git yo' money when you wants it, kase dat wuz him."

Tom's most well now, and got his **bullet** around his **neck** on a **watch**-guard for a watch, and is always **seeing** what time it is, and so there ain't nothing more to write about, and I am **rotten glad** of it, because if I'd a knowed what a **trouble** it was to make a book I wouldn't a tackled it, and ain't a-going to no more. But I reckon I got to light out for the Territory **ahead** of the rest, because Aunt Sally she's going to **adopt** me and sivilize me, and I can't **stand** it. I been there before.

Chinese Simplified

adopt: 收养，采纳，抱养，采用.
adventures: 冒险.
ahead: 前头，前方，前面的.
bullet: 子弹.
den: 窝.
drunk: 喝了，喝醉.
glad: 高兴，高兴的.
hairy: 毛茸茸，多毛的，毛茸茸的.
howling: 咆哮的，啸声.
jis: 日本工业标准.
kept: 收存.
kin: 亲属，骨肉.
mine: 矿，我的，矿山，矿井.
neck: 颈项，脖子，颈.
none: 无，没有.
outfit: 旅行装备，装备.
reckon: 估计，计算.
rich: 富有，丰富，富有的，充实.
river: 河，江，川，河流，条.
rotten: 腐败的，腐朽.
seeing: 有鉴于.
sign: 符号，标记，署名，牌子，迹象，标志，签署，手势，旗.
slide: 滑落，滑行，滑.
solemn: 严肃，俨然，岸然，隆重，庄严的，庄重.
stand: 站住，主张，架子，站立，耐，站，架.
talked: 谈话.
thousand: 千.
trouble: 麻烦，难度，难处.
watch: 观看，手表，监视.

THE END

Yours **truly**,
Huck Finn

Chinese Simplified

truly: 真实地，未免，着实.

GLOSSARY

aboard：船上，在车，上
abreast：并肩，并排，并列
abroad：海外，国外，在国外，到国外，到处
absent：缺席，缺席的
absent-minded：大意，心不在焉的，茫然的
abuse：滥用，弊端，骂，虐待
abusing：滥用
accident：事故，不测，变故，失事，意外
accidents：事故
according：根据
account：帐户，账，帐，户口，重要性
accounts：据闻
ache：疼痛，酸痛，痛
acknowledge：认知，承认
acknowledging：承认
acquit：宣判无罪
acting：代理，临时的，代理的，行为
actions：作用，行动
acts：作用，法案
adage：格言
add：加，增加，增添
admirable：令人钦佩，令人钦佩的
admission：进场，承认
admitted：被承认了的
adopt：收养，采纳，抱养，采用
advance：进，前进，进军，进步
advantage：好处，裨益，优点
adventure：冒险，探险
adventures：冒险
advertise：登广告，标榜，刊登广告
advice：忠告，劝告，建议
advise：忠告，劝告，劝导，劝说
afflicted：使苦恼
afford：力足以做，负担得起
affront：泰然面对，冒犯，侮辱
afire：大为激动
afoot：徒步
afraid：危惧，恐怕，害怕
african：非洲的，非洲，非洲人的，非洲人
aft：在船尾
afternoon：下午，午后
afterwards：后来，然后，以后，此后，後，然後，后，过后，底下，此後，後来
aggravate：加剧，激怒，恼火
ago：前，之前，以前
agreement：协定，协议，契约，合约，同意
aground：在地上
ah：啊，哎呀
ahead：前头，前方，前面的
aiming：照准
air：空气，样子，晾
airy：通风，通风的
alarm：警报，惊动
alas：呜呼
alike：相同
alive：活着，活，活泼的，活着的
alleys：胡同
allow：容许，允许，任
allowed：允许
aloft：在高处
alone：独自，单独，单纯，单独地
along：沿着，沿，一同
alongside：并肩，在旁边
alter：更改，变更，修改，改变，改
altogether：总共，一共
amazing：了不起，迷人的
ambuscade：伏击，伏兵
ambush：埋伏，伏击
amen：阿们，阿门
america：美国
ammunition：弹药
amount：数量，量，数字，数目，数额
amusing：有趣，有趣的
angel：天使，安琪儿
angels：天使
animal：动物
animals：动物
ankle：脚踝，踝，脚脖子
ankles：脚脖子
answer：回答，解答，答案，答复，答，响应，适合，负责，符合
answered：回答
answering：回答
answers：回答
anxiety：焦急，忧虑，担
anxious：焦急，巴不得，担心，焦虑的
anybody：任何人
anyhow：无论如何，反正
anyway：无论如何，反正
anywhere：无论何处
apart：分别，分开
apiece：各自，各自地
apologizing：道歉
apple：苹果，蘋果
appointments：约会
appreciate：涨价，感激，升値，欣赏
approve：赞成，认证，赞同，认可，允许
apron：围裙，停机坪
argue：争辩，计较
aristocracy：贵族社会，贵族
ark：方舟
arm：手臂，膀子，臂膀，臂，膀臂，胳膊，肩膀，武器
armor：盔甲
arms：武器，武装，军备，兵戈，兵器，军火，兵戎
army：陆军，兵团，陆海空三军，部队，军，军队
arrangement：安排，布局，条理
arrive：抵达，到达，到
arriving：到达
arrows：箭
art：艺术，美术，功夫
article：文章，报导，本文
ascend：上升
ash：灰，灰烬
ashamed：惭愧，羞愧，惭愧的
ashes：灰烬
ashore：岸上，上岸
ask：问，询问
asks：问
asleep：睡着，睡着的
ass：驴子
ast：虹志电脑
astonished：诧异

astonishing：可惊，惊人，惊人的
astonishment：惊愕，惊讶
attend：出席，参加
attention：注意，注意力
attitude：态度，姿态，架势
attraction：吸引
auction：拍卖
auctioneer：拍卖人
audience：听众
aunt：伯母，姑妈，大娘，婶母，阿姨，姨妈，婶子
aunty：阿姨，老大娘，大妈
authorities：当局
average：平均，普通，平均的，通俗
awake：唤醒，觉醒，醒
awful：可怕，可怕的
awhile：一会儿
awkward：笨拙，尴尬，不得劲，拙，迟钝的
awning：雨篷
awry：歪
ax：斧头，削减
axe：斧子，斧，削减
azure：天蓝色，蔚蓝色的
ba：文学士
baby：婴儿，宝宝，宝贝，娃娃
backed：支撑
backs：支持
backwards：逆，逆向，向后
bacon：熏肉，咸肉，熏猪肉
bad：坏，糟糕，不良，不善，淘气，坏的
badly：非常的
bag：袋子，袋，手提包，提包，囊
baggage：行李
bagged：松弛下垂的
bait：饵，诱饵
bake：烤，烘，焙烧，烘烤，焙
balcony：阳台，阳
bald：光秃秃，兀，秃头的
baldhead：秃子
ball：球，舞会
balls：球
band：乐队，带，带子，绑带
bandage：绷带
bang：重击
bank：银行，岸
bar：酒廊，酒吧，柜台
bare：赤裸裸，赤裸的
barefooted：赤足，赤足的
bareheaded：光头
barely：仅仅，仅
bark：吠
barking：叫声
barn：谷仓，仓，马厩
barrel：桶，大桶
barrels：桶
base：基础，基地，底，卑鄙，基，卑劣，卑下
bashful：怕羞，怕羞的
basket：篮，篮子，笼，淘箩，筐，笼子
bath：沐浴，浴，冲凉，洗澡
baths：洗澡
baton：警棍，指挥棒
battle：斗争，战，战斗
battlements：堞
battles：战斗
bead：珠子，小珠
bear：熊，忍受，背负，忍耐，承担，担负，空头，堪
bearings：轴承
beast：野兽，动物
beat：打，击败，拍击，敲打，拍子，敲
beating：脉
beats：节奏
beautiful：漂亮，美，美丽，菲菲，锦绣，美丽的，秀丽，美观
beauty：美人，美丽，美
beaver：海狸，河狸
bed：床，床铺
bedclothes：被褥，床上用品
bedroom：卧室，卧房
beds：床
bedstead：床架
bedtime：就寝时间
bee：蜂，蜜蜂
beehive：蜂箱，蜂窝
beeswax：蜂蜡，蜜蜡
beforehand：预先，较早
beg：恳求，乞求，要求
begged：乞求
begging：行乞
begin：开始，开创，发起，掀起，兴办
beginning：开头，初，开端，开始
begins：开始
begun：开始
behave：举止，表现，行为
behold：看见
belch：嗝、嗳气，打嗝
bell：钟，铃
bellow：怒吼
bells：铃
belong：属于
below：下面，以下
belt：带，带子，地带，带儿
belted：束带的，装甲的
belting：带类
bench：长椅，长凳
bend：弯曲，弯折
beneath：在下方，之下，下面
bent：曲，弯，弯曲，弯折
berries：莓
berth：泊位，卧位，床位，卧铺
besides：此外，另外，除了，并且，再说，况且
bet：打赌，赌
betray：背叛，出卖
betwixt：中间，在…之间
beware：注意，留意
beyond：超越
bible：圣经，经典
bid：出价，企图，标，投标
bigger：更大，较大
biggest：最大
bile：胆汁
bilge：舱底
bill：法案，帐单，账单，发单
billion：万亿
biography：传记，传，生平传记
bird：鸟
birds：禽，禽类，鸟
birth：出生，起源，诞生，出身，开始
birthday：生日，诞辰，寿辰
biscuits：饼干
bit：位元，咬
bite：咬，辣，咬伤
bites：咬伤
bits：屑
bitter：苦，苦味，沉痛
bitters：苦味
blacker：黑色，黑人
blackest：黑人
blame：责备，咎，非难，责任，罪，责怪，归咎
blaming：责备
blank：空白，空白的，空
blanket：毛毯，被子
blankets：毛毯
blast：疾风，爆破，爆炸
bleed：流血
bleeding：渗色，出血
bless：保佑，庇佑，祝福
blessed：幸福，幸福的
blessing：祝福
blind：瞎，盲，百叶窗，盲目，盲的
blindfold：蒙眼
blister：水泡
block：木块，街段，块，阻挡
blood：血，血液，鲜血
blooded：纯种的
bloom：花开，开花
blossom：群花，花，开花
blow：吹，打击
blowing：吹
blows：打击
blubber：鲸脂
blue：蓝，蓝色，青
blue-black：深蓝色的
bluff：虚张声势，吹牛
board：木板，包饭，板，板子，板纸，牌匾，部，木版，委员会
boarding：围板
boards：纸板

boat：小船，船，帆船，乘务员
boats：船舶
bob：鲍勃
bodies：身体
bodkin：锥子
bogus：假的
bolt：门栓，螺栓，枪栓
bone：骨头，骨，骨法
bonnet：苏格兰帽，阀盖，无边有带的女帽
books：图书，书籍，书，篇
boom：景气，繁荣，吊杆，盛旺
boomed：繁荣
booming：繁荣
boot：长靴，靴子
boots：靴子
border：边界，边，疆界，边境，国界，缘
bored：无聊，沉闷的
born：出生，天生的
borrow：借
borrowing：借
boss：老板，上司，头子，浮雕
boston：波士顿
bother：烦扰，打扰，理会
bothering：打扰
bothersome：淘神，麻烦的，伤脑筋
bottle：瓶，瓶子
bottom：底部，屁股，底
bottoms：底
bought：买了
bounce：乱跳，退票，弹跳，跳，弹回
bound：限，边际，弹回，范围
bounden：义不容辞的，不可推卸
bow：弓
bowed：有弓的
bows：弓
box：箱，匣，包厢，拳击，拳打
boy：男孩，男孩子，男孩儿，小子
boys：哥儿，男孩
brace：支柱
brains：头脑，脑子，脑筋，脑袋，脑髓
branches：分支
brandy：白兰地
brash：胃灼热，无礼的，傲慢的
brass：黄铜
brave：勇敢，勇敢的，勇士
bray：驴叫声
bread：面包
break：破坏，断，打破，犯，中断，破，裂
breakfast：早餐，早饭，早点
breaks：中断
breast：奶子，乳房，胸，胸部
breasts：乳房
breath：气息，鼻息，呼吸，气流
breathe：呼吸
breathes：呼吸
breathing：呼吸，呼吸的，微风
breaths：呼吸
breed：品种，繁殖，饲养
breeze：和风
brick：砖，砖块
bricks：砖
bridge：网桥，桥梁，桥接器，桥，鼻梁
bridle：勒马缰绳
bright：聪明，光明，光亮，光明的，鲜明
bring：带，带来，携带
brings：带来
brisk：活泼，活泼的
broad：宽，宽广
broke：打破
broken：打破了
brother：弟兄，兄弟
brothers：兄弟，哥儿
brought：携带
brown：褐色，棕色，布朗
browsing：浏览
brush：刷，毛刷，洗刷，刷子，拂，擦
brute：畜，畜生
buck：雄鹿
bucket：水桶，桶
buckle：带扣，扣子
bud：芽，蓓蕾
budge：微微一动，改变态度，羔皮
bug：飞虫，错误，臭虫
build：建造，建立，兴建，筑，个子，造，建筑，建成，修筑，建
building：建筑物，建筑，房屋，建造
built：建了
bulge：胀起，肿胀
bulging：膨胀
bull：公牛
bulldog：牛头犬，喇叭狗
bullet：子弹
bullets：子弹
bully：欺负
bunch：束，串
bundle：捆，包裹，包，包扎，束，把
bundles：捆
bunker：暗堡，床位
bureau：局，处
buried：埋下
burnt：烧伤的，烧过的，烧
bush：灌木，布什，丛林
bushes：灌木
bust：半身像，逮捕，破产
busy：忙，繁忙，忙碌，占线，忙碌的
butt：臀部，屁股，枪托
butter：牛油，黄油
butterflies：蝴蝶
buttermilk：酪乳
butting：扎接
button：钮，扣子，按钮，钮扣，纽扣
buy：买，采买，购买
buying：购买
buys：购买
cabbage：甘蓝菜，包菜
cabin：小屋，船舱
cairo：开罗
calamity：危难，灾难，灾祸
calculating：工于心计的
calf：小牛，犊
calico：白布，白棉布
call：喊，称呼，叫，号召，召唤
camp：阵营，营，露营，安营
cancer：癌，癌症
candid：公正地
candle：蜡烛
candles：蜡烛
candlestick：烛台，蜡台
cane：手杖，甘蔗，杖，鞭打
cannibal：吃同类的动物，食人者
cannon：大炮
canoe：独木舟
canoes：独木舟
cap：便帽，帽子，套子，鸭舌帽
capital：首都，本钱，资本，本金
captain：队长，舰长，领队
captivated：如醉如痴
captive：俘虏
captivity：囚禁
carcass：残骸
careful：小心，仔细，不苟，慎重，周密，小心的，精细，细心，细致
carpenter：木匠
carpet：地毯
carry：搬运，输送，携带，进位
carrying：运送的，运输的
cart：手拉车，手推车
carve：雕刻，雕塑
cases：情况
cash：现金，现款，现钱
castle：城堡，城
cat：猫
catch：捕捉，捕捞，捕拿，捉
catching：迷人的
caterpillars：履带
catfish：鲇鱼
cats：猫
cattle：家畜，牛
caught：捉了
cautious：谨慎，仔细，慎重，警慎的
cave：洞穴，洞，穴
cavern：大地洞，大山洞
celebrated：着名，著名
cellar：地下室，地窖

cent：一分钱，分
century：世纪
certainly：一定，保管，当然，理所当然，岂不，肯定地
chain：链，链子，连锁
chains：连锁
chair：椅子
chairs：椅子
chalk：粉笔
chance：机会
chances：机会
changed：改变
changing：变化
channel：频道，通道，途径，海峡，渠
chap：家伙，皴裂
chapter：章节，章
character：性格，字，文字，特征，字符，色彩，字元
characters：人物，字符
charcoal：木炭，炭
charge：收费，控告，记帐，冲锋，指责，负荷
charging：收费，充电
charm：魅力，迷人
charts：图表
chase：追逐，驱赶
chasing：追逐
cheap：低廉，便宜的，便宜
cheek：脸颊
cheeky：不要脸的
cheer：喝采，叫好，欢呼
cheerful：愉快，愉快的
chest：胸部，箱，胸膛
chicken：鸡，小鸡
chickens：小鸡
chief：首席，首领，主要的
chile：智利
chills：寒冷
chilly：寒冷的
chin：下巴，颏
chip：碎片，芯片，晶片
chisel：凿子，凿
choose：挑选，选择，拣，推举，推选，选定，选取
chop：劈，剁，砍，伐
christmas：圣诞节，圣诞
christopher：克里斯托弗
chuckle：咯咯笑，暗笑
churning：搅乳，一次提制的奶油
chute：陡槽、滑道
cipher：暗号，密码，阿拉伯数字
ciphered：密码
circumstances：环境，情况，情形，境况，境地，形势，情景
circus：马戏团，杂技团，马戏
clan：氏族，家族
clap：拍手，拍
claw：爪
clay：泥土，黏土
clean：清洁，擦拭，乾净，刷，清洗，干净
cleanse：擦拭，洁净，清洗
clearing：清除
clerk：书记，营业员，办事员，职员
clever：高明，聪明的，伶俐，玲珑，机灵，巧妙，聪明
climb：爬，攀登
climbing：攀登，上升的
clip：夹子，回形针
clock：钟，时钟，钟表
close：关闭，闭合，密切，相近，结束，截止，亲密，关
closet：壁橱
cloth：布，布帛菽粟，布料
clothes：衣服，服装，西装，件，衣裳
clothesline：晒衣绳，晾衣绳
clothing：服装，装束，衣服
cloud：云
clouded：阴云密布的，有暗影的
clown：小丑
club：俱乐部，棍棒，棒子
clump：土块
cluttered：混乱
cluttering：混乱
coals：煤
coarse：粗劣，粗糙的，淫秽，粗鲁
coat：外套，上衣
coats：上衣
coax：哄
coffee：咖啡
coffin：棺材，寿材
coffins：棺材
col：山坳
cold：冷，感冒，寒冷，寒，冷淡
collar：硬领，衣领
collect：收藏，珍藏，收集，采集，捡，搜集
collected：收集成的，镇定的
collection：珍藏，汇编，收集，专集
college：学院
colonel：陆军上校
color：颜色，彩色
colors：颜色
comb：梳，梳子
comedy：喜剧
comes：来
comfort：安慰
comfortable：舒服，舒服的
coming：未来，到来
commence：着手，开始
common：通用，共同，公共，寻常，常规，平常，普通，一般，普通的，通俗
companionship：友谊
complain：抱怨，投诉，埋怨
complaint：原告，牢骚，闲话，控诉，投诉
complexion：气色，脸色，肤色
complicated：复杂，繁复，曲折，复杂的，疑难
compliment：道贺，祝贺，敬意
compliments：敬意
concern：关照，有关
concluded：结束
condition：条件，制约，状况，情况，地步
confidence：信心，自信
confidential：机密的
confiding：信任别人
conflict：冲突，争端，战争
confound：惊讶，混淆
congregation：集合
congress：国会，大会
connection：连接，相连，联系，联通，环节
conqueror：征服者
conscience：良心
consecutive：连续的
consequence：后果
consequences：后果，後果
consider：以为，考虑，考量
considerable：可观，相当多的
consideration：考虑，心眼，考量
considered：被尊重的，考虑过的
constant：一贯，不变，不断，固定的，常量
consumption：消耗量
contented：满意
continental：大陆的
contracted：收缩了的
contrary：相反，反而，相反的
contrive：设计
convenient：方便，便利，便当，手，方便的
convention：公约，会议，习俗
convince：说服
cook：厨子，厨司，厨师，炊事员，烹调，煮，烹煮
cooked：煮熟
cooking：烹调
cool：凉，镇静，镇定，凉爽，凉爽的
cooled：凉爽
copies：拷贝
corn：玉蜀黍，包谷，玉米
corner：角落，隅，棱，角，转角
corpse：尸体
correct：正确，拨正，不错，对，端正，纠正，对头，改正，对了
cost：费用，花费，代价，价款，价钱是
costs：成本，费用
costume：服装，衣服
cotton：棉花，棉
cough：咳，咳嗽

coughing：咳嗽
count：计数，伯爵，计算，有价值，认为
counterfeit：仿造，仿造的
county：郡，县
couple：一对，挂钩，连接，夫妇，一双
courage：勇气，胆子，胆量，精神
course：课程，经过，进程，路程，路线，学科，过程
cousin：表亲，表哥，堂表
cover：盖子，面儿，包罗，皮儿，采访，掩护，遮盖
covering：包层，衣子
cow：母牛，牛
coward：懦夫，胆小鬼
cows：母牛
crack：裂缝，精干，崩裂，爆裂，裂开，空隙
craft：手艺，狡诈，探测器，工艺
crafts：工艺
cramp：夹子，扒钉，钳
cramped：逼仄，难懂的
crash：粉碎，坠毁，相撞，毁坏，崩溃
craw：嗉子
crawl：爬，爬行
crawling：爬行
crawls：爬行
crazy：发狂，疯狂，颠倒，疯狂的
creation：创作，建立，创造
credit：信用，功劳
creep：爬行
creeps：爬行
creepy：毛骨悚然的
crept：爬行
crest：鸡冠，冠子，鸟冠
crew：人员，全体人员，包承组，工作人员
crime：罪行，犯罪
crippled：瘫痪
crockery：瓦器
cross：交叉，十字架，越过，相交，渡过，穿过
crossing：路口，横越，交叉点
crossings：横越
crowd：人群
crowded：拥挤的
crowding：人群，拥挤
crowds：人群
cruel：粗暴，残酷，残酷的，狠毒
crush：压碎，粉碎
crust：面包皮，地壳
cry：喊，叫，哭，哭泣
crying：叫喊的，嚎哭的，显著的
cub：幼兽
cuff：袖口
cup：杯，茶杯，杯子
cupboard：碗柜，柜子，橱
cure：治疗，防治，药，治愈，医治
curiosity：好奇心
curious：有好奇心，好奇，好奇的
curl：卷曲，卷发
curled：卷曲
curls：卷曲
curly：卷曲，卷曲的
current：潮流，现时，现在，这次，本届，当今，当前，当前的，水流，电流，现在的
curse：咒骂，诅咒，咒
curtain：布帘
custom：风俗，习惯，规矩，习俗
customary：习惯性，习惯性的
cut：采伐，切，刀口，伤口，割，截，剪切，切口
cypress：丝柏
dab：轻拍，少量，轻抚
dad：爸爸
dainty：纤巧，高雅，精致的
damp：潮湿，潮湿的
dance：舞蹈，舞会，跳舞，舞
dances：跳舞
dancing：跳舞
dandy：花花公子，纨绔子弟
danger：危险
dangerous：危险，危险的
dangers：危险
dangle：吊着，摇晃
dare：敢
dark：暗，黑暗，夜
darken：变暗，变黑
darkness：黑暗
darling：宝宝，宝贝，老公，老婆，打令
dart：镖，投射
dash：冲撞，猛冲，短跑
daughter：女儿，女孩儿，闺女
dauphin：法国皇太子
david：大卫
dawn：黎明
daybreak：黎明，破晓
daylight：日光，白天
daytime：白天，白昼，日间
dazzling：耀眼的，有声有色
de：可选择丢弃
deacon：执事
dead：死
deadly：死亡，致死，致命的
deal：处理
dear：亲爱，亲爱的，可爱的
debts：债务
deceive：欺骗，欺
decent：像样，合适，像样的，正经
decide：判定，决定，作主
decided：决定
deck：甲板
declaration：声明，宣言
declare：宣布，陈述，声明，宣告
deed：契据，行为
deep：深，深深，深刻，深厚，浓厚，深沉，奥秘
deeply：在深处，深深地
deer：鹿
delay：延迟，延期，耽搁，耽误，耽
deliberate：商讨，故意的，成心
delirium：神志昏迷，谵妄
den：窝
deny：驳斥，否认
depend：依赖，取决
descendant：后裔，後裔
deserve：应得
deserving：功过，赏罚
design：设计，图案
desperate：危急，非常的
despise：鄙视，轻视，不齿，鄙薄，蔑视，看不起
detective：侦探，暗探
devil：魔鬼，妖怪，鬼
diamonds：钻石
dictionary：字典，词典
die：逝世，不讳，死
difference：差异，差，差别，区别，分歧，分别，误差
difficulties：困难
difficulty：困难
dig：挖掘
digging：挖掘
dim：阴暗，暗淡，暗淡的
dime：一角银币，一角硬币
dinner：晚餐，正餐
dipper：舀水杓
directions：指导，说明，方向
directly：直接地，一头，索性
dirt：污垢
dirty：肮脏，脏脏，肮脏的，混浊
disappeared：不见了，消失
disappears：消失
disappoint：使失望，辜负
disappointed：败兴，失望的，惘
disciples：门徒
discourage：不鼓励
discover：发现，发觉，觉察
discovering：发现
discuss：商讨，商谈，讨论，商榷，洽谈
diseased：有病
disgrace：耻辱
disguise：伪装，乔装
disgusted：厌恶
disgusting：讨厌，令人恶心的，令人作呕的
dish：菜，碟
dismal：暗淡，忧郁的
disposition：意向，性格，脾气，安排，部署
dissatisfied：不满，不满意的
distance：距离

distinct：明显，不同，清楚，独特，独特的，清晰，鲜明
distracted：怅惘，心烦意乱的
distress：苦恼，悲痛
distressed：苦恼，哀伤
disturb：打扰，惊动，扰乱，干扰
disturbance：风波，骚动，干扰，骚乱
disturbed：不安
dive：潜水，跳水
dived：跳水
doctor：医生，大夫，医师，博士
doctoring：医生
dodge：躲闪，躲避
dog：狗，犬
dogs：狗
doings：做
doll：洋娃娃，玩偶
dollar：元
dolphin：海豚
domestic：国内，家里的
doors：门
dot：点，点缀，点子，圆点，嫁妆
dote：溺爱
double：双重，双，加倍
doubled：双，加倍努力
doubt：怀疑，疑
doubts：怀疑
dough：生面团
dove：鸽
downhearted：消沉，闷闷不乐的
dozed：打瞌睡
dozen：一打，打
dozing：打瞌睡
drafts：草案
drag：曳，拖拉，阻力，拖动
dragged：拖拉，拖曳
dragging：拖，拖动，拖曳
drank：喝了
draw：画，不分胜负，描，吸，拉
drawers：抽屉
drawing：图，图画，画儿，绘画，并条，图纸，画
dreadful：可怕，恐怖的
dream：梦寐，梦见，做梦，梦想
dreaming：梦见
dreams：梦想
dress：服装，打扮
dried：干燥的
drift：漂游，漂移，漂
drink：喝，饮用，饮，饮料
drinking：喝
drip：滴下，滴
dripping：滴下
drive：驱动器，精神，驾车，驾驶，志气，驾
driver：司机，开车人
droop：垂下
drop：落，水滴，衰退，掉落，降，点子
dropped：落下
dropping：点滴，落下
drove：驾
drown：使溺死，淹死，溺死
drowned：淹死
drug：药品，药物，药
drunk：喝了，喝醉
dry：索然，干燥，乾，干旱，乾燥
duck：鸭，鸭子
ducked：鸭
ducks：鸭
dug：挖掘
duke：公爵，公
dull：索然，板滞，沉闷的，干燥，拙，深沉
dumb：哑
dummy：假的，傀儡
dungeon：地牢
dusky：昏暗，昏暗的
dust：灰尘，土，尘，尘土，粉末
dusty：满身尘埃，沾尘的
duty：任务，义务，责任，关税，职责
dying：不行了，垂死，垂死的
eager：切望，踊跃，急切，渴望的
ear：耳朵，耳
earlier：一向，早些，早，先，较早时
earn：赚得，挣得
earnest：认真
ears：耳朵
ease：缓解，减轻，容易，悠，舒适
easier：更容易
east：东，东方
easy：容易，轻而易举，简易，安逸，便利，便当，容易的，纵横
eat：吃
eating：吃
eaves：屋檐
eavesdrop：窃听
edge：边缘，边，边沿，棱，沿儿
edgeways：从旁边
edging：边缘
educated：受过教育的
edward：爱德华
eggs：蛋
eight：八
eighty：八十
elbow：肘，手肘
elder：长老，较长
eldest：最年长，伯仲叔季，最年长的
elected：被选
elegant：高雅，文雅，优美，讲究的，优雅的
elephants：象
eleven：十一
emptied：空
empty：空，空洞
enamel：光漆，搪瓷
enchantment：魔法，迷惑
ending：结尾，结局，结束
ends：末端
endure：持久，忍受，忍耐
enemies：敌人
enemy：敌人
engagements：约会
engineer：工程师，策划
engines：发动机
english：英语，英国，英文，英国人
englishman：英国
enjoy：享有，享受，喜欢
enjoyment：乐趣，享乐
enter：进，进入，回车键，入
entire：整个，全部，全球，通通，总体，全体，全部的，完整的
entirely：完全，全部地
escape：逃走，逃之夭夭，逃跑，逃避，逃脱，逃离，逃亡
estate：地产，产业，园丘，房地产
estimation：估计
europe：欧洲
european：欧洲人，欧洲，欧洲的
evade：逃避，迴避，回避
evasion：逃避
evening：晚，黄昏，傍晚，晚上
everlasting：永久，永久的，永恒的
everybody：每个人，各位
everything：一切事物，应有尽有，一切，事事
exact：确切，精密，准确，正确的
exactly：刚好，就是，确切地，就，恰恰，可不是
examine：检查，核查，检验，考核，视察
example：例子，例题，榜样，例证，标兵，表率，模范，事例，典范，典型，典
except：除了，除了之外
excited：兴奋，兴奋的，兴高采烈，激昂的
excitement：兴奋，刺激
excuse：包涵，借口，原谅
expect：预期，期待
expected：预期
expense：花费，费用，支出
expenses：开支
explain：辩解，解释，申述，交代，澄清
explanation：说明，解释，解答
exploring：探索
exposed：暴露的，无掩蔽的
extra：额外，额外的
eye：眼睛，目，鼻儿
factory：工厂，厂房，厂家
facts：事实
faculties：才能
fagged：累坏了的

failed: 失败
failure: 失败
faint: 暗淡，隐约，昏厥，微弱
fainted: 昏厥
fair: 公平，博览会，清澈，公正，公道，展，直
fairly: 相当，比较，公平地
faith: 信心，信仰，信任，信念
fall: 跌落，落下，衰退，下跌，覆亡，沈落，跌倒，沉落
falling: 落下的，落下
false: 假，虚伪，虚假
families: 家庭
fancy: 花俏，想像力
farm: 农场，田间
farmer: 农人，农夫
farms: 农场
fashion: 时尚，方式，时装
fashioned: 方式
fast: 快，禁食，快速，迅速，速
fasten: 绑住
faster: 快些
fat: 档案分配区，肥，油脂，肥胖，脂肪
fate: 命运
fault: 故障，过失，缺点，毛病，断层，短处，缺陷
favor: 偏爱，德，赞成，人情
fear: 恐惧，忌惮，畏惧，生怕，害怕
feather: 羽毛
feathered: 有羽毛的
feathers: 翎毛，羽毛
feed: 饲料，哺养，哺育，喂养，饲养
feeling: 感觉，情绪，感情，情感，思绪
feelings: 感情，面子
feels: 感觉
feet: 英尺
fell: 采伐，伐，跌落
fellow: 同伴，伙伴
fence: 篱笆，栅栏，栏位，栏
fences: 栅栏
ferry: 摆渡，渡口，渡船，渡轮
fetch: 拿，取，带来
fetching: 迷人的
feud: 世仇
fever: 发烧，发热
feverish: 发烧的
few: 少数，很少
fiddle: 小提琴
fidgety: 烦躁
field: 领域，字段，田野，方面，场，平原，田地，田间的，野生的，田间
fifteen: 十五
fifth: 第五
fifty: 五十，半白
fight: 打，打仗，斗争，斗，打架，战斗，奋斗
fighting: 兵戈，战事，殴斗，战斗
fights: 战斗
file: 文件，档案，文档
fill: 添补，补足，装满，填满，填充
finally: 最后，到底，终于，最後，总算
finding: 发现物，发现
fine: 罚款，罚金，良好，要得，美好，精美，纤小，纤细，不赖，优美，美好的
finger: 手指，指头
finish: 完成，最后阶段，润饰，下场，结束
finished: 完结了的，完蛋了的
finn: 芬兰，芬兰人
fire: 火，射击，失火，火灾，发射，火力
fireplace: 壁炉
first-class: 第一流，第一流的
fish: 鱼，捕鱼
fishing: 钓鱼
fist: 拳头
fists: 拳头
fit: 合适，适应，适合，适
fix: 安装，奠定，固定，修理
fixed: 固定，确定，一定，固定的
fixing: 定影，固定
flabby: 松弛的，软弱，软弱的
flapping: 拍打
flash: 闪光，晃
flat: 平坦，平板，平坦的，平的，居室
flattery: 媚词
flaws: 瑕疵
fled: 逃离
flesh: 肉，血肉，肌肉
flew: 飞
flicker: 闪烁
fling: 扔丢
flitter: 飞来飞去
float: 漂浮
floating: 漂浮的，移动的，浮动的，飘浮
floats: 花车
flock: 一群
floor: 地板，地面
floored: 地板
floors: 地板
flour: 面粉，白面，粉
flower: 花，花儿，华，花朵，开花
flowers: 花
flutter: 飘扬，颤动，振翅
fluttering: 颤动
fly: 蝇，飞翔，苍蝇，飘扬，飞，飞行，飞跑
flying: 飞行，飞
fog: 雾
follow: 跟进，跟从，接着，跟随，遵照
fool: 呆子，笨蛋，傻子，笨人，愚人
foolish: 愚蠢的
foolishness: 愚蠢
foot: 脚，足，步兵，英尺，呎
footsteps: 脚步
force: 力，部队，力量，暴力，强迫，迫使，逼迫，动力
ford: 涉过
forehead: 前额，额，额头
forenoon: 上午，午前
forever: 永远，永久
forget: 忘记，忘，忘却
forgive: 包涵，包容，原谅，宽恕，饶恕
forgot: 忘记
fork: 叉，叉子
forks: 叉子
forlorn: 绝望，绝望的
forth: 向前
fortress: 城堡
fortune: 幸运，命运，运气
fortunes: 命运
forty: 四十
forty-five: 四十五，四十五个
forward: 向前，前言，在前，引言，前进的
foster: 养育，扶植，哺育，助长，养母，养父
fought: 打
foundation: 基础，根据，依据
foundations: 基础
fourteen: 十四
fourth: 第四，第四的
frame: 框，帧，架，画面，陷害，边框，诬陷，架子，框架
france: 法国，法兰西
frank: 坦率，率直，坦白的
fraud: 舞弊，骗局，作弊，欺骗
freedom: 自由
freight: 货物运输
french: 法国，法语，法文，法国的，法国人的，法语的
frenchman: 法国人
fresh: 新鲜，新鲜的，新
fret: 烦恼
friday: 星期五，周五
fried: 炸
friend: 朋友，熟人，友人
friendless: 没有朋友的，无依无靠的
friendly: 友好，友善，友好的，好客，友好地，和气
frock: 西式女衣
frog: 青蛙，蛙
front: 前面，正面，跟前，战线，阵地
frowning: 皱眉
fry: 用油炸
fumble: 摸索

fun：娱乐
funeral：葬礼
funerals：葬礼
funny：有趣的
fur：毛、软毛
furnace：熔矿炉、炉子、熔炉、极热的地方
furnaces：炉子
furnish：供给、提供
furnished：供给
fury：暴怒、怒火、愤怒、气愤
fuss：大惊小怪
gabble：叽里咕噜
gained：获利、赢得
gaining：赢得、增益
gal：姑娘
gallop：疾驰、飞奔
galloping：迅速发展的
game：游戏、把戏
gang：一群、帮
gap：差距、空白点、间隔、间隙
gaping：目瞪口呆
garden：花园
gardens：园林、花园
garret：阁楼、顶楼
garters：吊袜带
gasp：喘气、喘
gates：盖茨
gather：集合、聚集、采集、集聚、集会、召集、搜集、捡、聚会
gaudy：花哨、花里胡哨
gay：欢乐、快活、快乐的、基佬
gaze：凝视
gazing：凝视
geese：鹅
generous：大方、雍容大度、慷慨、慷慨的
gentle：轻松、文雅的、斯文、柔和
gentleman：绅士
gentlemen：绅士
george：乔治
ghost：鬼、鬼魂、幽灵
ghosts：鬼
gift：礼物、天赋、天才、禀赋、礼品
gifts：礼物
gills：腮
gin：杜松子酒、陷阱
gingerbread：姜饼
gingham：格子棉布、方格花布
girl：女孩、姑娘、女孩子
giving：慷慨、给予物
glad：高兴、高兴的
glance：一瞥、匆匆一看
glancing：粗略的
glare：强光、眩目的光、眩目
glares：眩目的光
glass：玻璃、杯子
glide：滑翔、滑行
gliding：滑行的、下滑
glimpse：一瞥，瞥见
gloomy：阴郁，暗淡、阴郁的
glorious：壮丽，辉煌、光荣的
glory：荣耀，光荣、辉煌
gloves：手套
glow：炽热，发光
gnaw：啃
gnawing：不断的苦痛，咬的
gobble：大吃，狼吞虎咽
god：神，上帝、老天爷
goes：去
goggles：护目镜
gold：金，黄金
gone：去
good-bye：再会
good-natured：和善、心眼好、性格好
goodness：美德
goose：鹅
gooseberry：醋栗、醋栗酒
gourd：葫芦
governor：州长
gown：长袍、女装长袍
gowns：长袍
grab：抓住，攫取，抓斗
grace：优雅，恩典，天恩、魅力，宽限
graceful：优雅，优美，优雅的，优美的
gracious：亲切、亲切的、有礼貌的
gradual：逐渐的
grain：谷类
grand：堂皇、隆重、雄伟、盛大、宏大、大型的、宏伟
grandmother：祖母，婆婆
granny：婆婆，老大娘
grass：草，青草
grassy：如草，长满草的
grateful：感谢，感激的
grave：严重，庄重，坟墓，墓穴，深重
graveyard：坟地，墓地
gray：灰色，灰
grease：油脂
greasy：泥泞的、油性的
greatest：莫大
great-grandfather：太公
greek：希腊语，希腊，希腊人，希腊语的
green：绿色，碧瓦，青，绿色的，未成熟的
greens：绿色
grief：哀思，哀痛，悲伤，忧伤
grieve：伤心，悼念，使伤心
grinding：磨的、磨削
grindstone：磨石
grit：粗砂，砂砾，沙子
groan：呻吟，哼
groaning：呻吟
ground：地、地面、地皮、理由、土地
grow：生长、增长、成长、种植
grub：蛆虫
grumble：抱怨、诉苦、发牢骚
guard：警卫、警备、把守、保守、守卫、防卫、警戒
guardian：监护人
guards：警戒
guess：猜测、臆测、猜谜儿、猜想、揣测、推测
gully：山沟、溪谷
gun：枪、炮、长枪
guns：枪支
gurgle：汩汩声、汩汩
gust：阵风、狂风
gutter：排水沟、沟、水槽、贫民区
hail：冰雹、雹、雹子、欢呼
hair：头发
hairy：毛茸茸、多毛的、毛茸茸的
half-way：半途
hall：厅、大厅、会堂、礼堂
halt：停止
halter：缰绳
ham：火腿
hammer：槌、锤
handbill：传单
handbills：传单
handcuffs：手铐
handed：传递、有手的
handkerchief：手帕、手绢
handle：柄、把手、把柄、处理、辫子、耳子、把子、弄、对付、加以、处置
handling：处理
hands：手
handsome：英俊、慷慨的、英俊的
handwritings：笔迹
handy：灵巧、便当、顺手、方便的、简便
hang：挂、悬挂
hanker：渴望
happen：发生
happened：发生
happening：事件、发生
happens：发生
happy：快乐、愉快、幸福、快活、美好、欢乐、高兴、快乐的、喜悦、舒畅、愉快的
harbor：港口、港湾、澳、海港、包藏、包庇
hard：硬、坚固、沉重、辛苦、艰苦、坚硬
harden：板结、使硬化、硬化
hardly：几乎不、毫不、辛苦地
hardness：硬度
hare：野兔、兔子
hark：倾听
harm：伤害、损害、坏处、害处、

祸害
harmless：无害，无害的
harp：竖琴
harrow：耙
harry：掠夺
hash：剁碎
haste：匆忙
hat：帽子
hatchet：斧头，斧子
haughty：傲慢，傲岸，骄矜，傲慢的
haul：拖拉，曳
headed：有头的
heading：标题，朝向
headline：标题
heads：头
healthy：健康的，健壮
heap：堆，堆积
hear：听见，听取，听
heard：听见
hearing：听力，听见
heart：心，心脏，中心，胸，内心
hearts：心
hearty：诚恳，热诚的
heat：热，暑气，热力，热气，加热，热量
heave：举起，波荡，喘气
heaven：天堂，天，天空
heavy：重，沉重，笨重，沈重，沉闷
heavy-hearted：心情沉重
hebrew：希伯来语，希伯来人，希伯来人的，希伯来语的，犹太
heel：脚跟，踵，踝部
heeled：有鞋后跟的
heirs：继承人
held：握住
hell：地狱
hello：你好，哈罗
helping：帮助人的，辅助的，帮助
helps：帮助
hence：因此，於是
hero：英雄
heroes：英雄
hers：她的
herself：她自己
hi：嗨
hid：躲藏
hide：躲藏，暗藏，掩饰，藏，隐瞒，隐藏
hiding：隐匿
higher：更高，高等
highest：最高
highland：高地
high-toned：调子高的，高尚的
hill：小丘，山坡，山岗，陵
hillside：山坡
hilltop：山顶
hind：后面的
hint：暗示
hire：雇，雇佣，雇用，招收，聘请，租，聘，聘用
history：历史，来历，过去的事，历史学
hit：袭击，命中，击中，打
hitch：拴住，蹒跚
hitched：蹒跚
hive：蜂房，蜂巢，蜂箱
hog：猪
hogwash：猪食，废话，空洞的作品
hoist：升起，吊车，举起
hold：握住，持有，把握，包容，认为，保持
hole：洞，漏洞，孔，穴，洞穴，窟窿
holes：洞
holiday：假日，节日，假期
holidays：每逢假日
hollow：凹陷，中空的，空心，空虚
holt：兽穴
holy：神圣，神圣的，神圣的东西
homeless：无家可归
homely：家常的
homesick：想家
honest：诚实，正直，清廉，刚正，坦白，正值，诚实的，体面，廉洁，深切
honey：蜂蜜，蜜，蜜糖
honor：荣誉，荣耀，尊严，面子，尊敬
hook：钩，钩子
hooker：妓女
hooks：钩
hooky：钩状
hop：跳跃，三级跳远
hope：期望，希望，指望
hoping：希望
horn：角，犄角
hornpipe：号笛
horrible：可怕，恐怖的
horse：马
horseback：马背
horseshoe：马蹄铁
hospitality：亲切，殷勤招待
hot：热
hotel：旅馆，酒店
hotter：热，热烈的
hottest：最热的，热烈的
hound：猎犬
hour：小时，钟头，钟点，现在
hours：小时
houses：房屋
howl：狂吠，号叫
howling：咆哮的，啸声
hub：中转站，集线器，中枢
hue：色调，色
hug：紧抱，拥抱
hugging：拥抱
hugs：拥抱
hum：哼，哼声，嗡嗡声，嗡嗡
human：人性，人类，人的
humble：谦逊，谦恭的
humbug：骗子
hump：驼背
hunched：肉峰
hundred：百，佰
hundreds：百
hung：挂
hungry：饥饿，饿，饥饿的
hunt：打猎，狩猎
hunting：狩猎
hurry：仓促，匆忙，赶忙
hurt：伤害，使受伤
husband：丈夫，爱人，老公
husky：壳的
hussy：轻佻的女子
hut：茅舍，棚屋
hymn：圣歌，圣诗
ice：冰
idiot：白痴，笨蛋，傻子
idiotic：白痴般，愚蠢的
idiots：白痴
ignorant：愚昧，无知的，茫然
illinois：伊利诺斯
illustrious：杰出，著名的
imaginary：虚构，虚构的
imitate：模仿
imitation：模拟，冒牌，模仿
immortal：不朽，不朽的，永垂不朽，神仙
impatient：不耐烦，无耐心的
imperative：必要的
impudent：厚颜无耻
inch：英寸
inches：英寸
indeed：的确，确实，果真
independence：独立
indian：印度人，印第安人，印第安语，印度的，印度
indifferent：冷淡，无关紧要，漠不关心的
infant：婴儿
infernal：地狱，地狱的
initial：开始，初步，最初，最初的
injured：受伤，受伤的，受损害的
ink：墨水，墨水儿，篇幅
inning：一局，轮到击球
innocent：无辜，无罪的，天真
inquire：查调，质问，询问
inscription：题字，题词，铭刻
inscriptions：铭刻
inshore：靠近海岸
inside：里面，内部，里，里头，秘密的，在里面，在内，之内，之中
insides：内部
instance：例子，比方，实例
instead：代替，反而
instinct：本能
insurrection：暴动，起义

interested：有兴趣，感兴趣的
interesting：有趣，有意思，有兴趣，好玩儿，吸引人的
interests：兴趣
interfere：干涉，干扰，妨碍
interpreted：解释执行
invent：编造，发明
invest：投资，投产
investigation：调查
invite：邀请
invited：约了
irish：爱尔兰，爱尔兰的，爱尔兰语
iron：铁，熨斗，鐵
irreligious：无宗教的
island：岛
islands：岛屿，岛
issue：发行，困难，散发，纠纷，议题，问题，颁布，颁发，发布，发出，课题
itch：发痒，痒
itching：痒的
jabber：磨嘴皮子
jack：小起重机，千斤顶，水手
jackass：笨蛋
jacket：夹克，上衣，短上衣，外套
jackson：杰克逊
jail：班房，监牢，监狱
jam：果酱，干扰
james：雅各书，詹姆士
jammed：挤满
jaw：颚，颌
jaws：咽喉，颌
jeans：牛仔裤
jest：玩笑，笑话，戏弄，戏谑
jewelry：首饰
jingle：叮铃
jingo：侵略主义，沙文主义
jis：日本工业标准
joggle：榫接
join：交接，加入，连结，结合，连接，使结合，参加，接合，接合点
joined：加入
joint：关节，接合，共同，联合，接合点
joke：笑话，玩笑，开玩笑
joker：家伙，爱开玩笑的人，诙谐者
jokes：笑林，笑话
joking：开玩笑的
jolly：痛快，开心的
jolt：颠簸，摇晃
jolted：摇晃
journal：日志，通报
journey：旅程，旅途，旅游，旅行
joy：乐趣，快乐，高兴，喜悦
joyful：欢喜，快乐的，欢喜的
judge：法官，裁判，判定，判断，审判员
judgment：判决，裁判，报应，判定，判断，裁
jug：细颈瓶，罐
juice：汁，汁液，液
jump：跳，跳跃
jumped：跳跃
jumps：跳跃
june：六月
juries：陪审团
kangaroo：袋鼠
keen：敏锐，渴望
keeping：保管，保持
keeps：保持
kept：收存
ketch：双桅船
kettle：水壶
key：钥匙，关键，题解，键，主要的
kick：踢
kill：打死，杀害，杀死
killed：被屠宰的，被杀死的
kills：杀死
kin：亲属，骨肉
kindness：仁慈，好意
king：国王，王
kingdom：王国
kingdoms：王国
kings：国王
kiss：吻，接吻，轻抚，轻触
kisses：吻
kit：工具
kitchen：厨房
knee：膝盖，膝
knees：膝盖
knife：刀子，刀，餐刀
knitting：编织
knob：把手，球形捏手，旋钮
knock：敲，敲撞
knot：结，打结，疙瘩，节
knots：节
knowing：博学的，知道
knows：知道
knuckles：关节
label：标签，取名
ladder：阶梯，梯子
ladies：女洗手间
lady：女士，夫人
lafayette：拉斐特
laid：放
lake：湖，湖泊
lamb：小羊，羔羊
lambs：小羊
lame：跛，跛足
lamp：灯
lan：区域网络，区域网路，本地网络，局域网
land：土地，着陆，陆地
landed：着陆
landing：着陆
lands：陆地
lane：小路，小巷，胡同
languages：语言
lanky：过分瘦长
lantern：灯笼
lap：一段行程，大腿，山坳，被包住
lash：睫毛，鞭打，鞭挞，皮鞭，鞭笞
latch：门闩
late：晚，迟，迟慢，迟了，迟迟
lately：近来，一向，最近
lath：板条
laugh：笑
laughed：笑
laughing：可笑的，笑
laughs：笑
lawsuit：诉讼，官司，讼诉案
lawyer：律师，法人
lay：产卵，安放，放，凡俗
layer：层，一层
lazy：懒惰，懒惰的
lead：领导，铅，带领，主角，率领
leading：领导
leads：铅
leaf：叶子，箔
leafy：多叶，多叶的
leak：漏洞，会漏，泄露，漏
lean：倾斜
leaned：倾斜
learn：学，学习
learned：有学问，博学，博雅，饱学
learning：学问，学术，学习
least：最少，至少，最少的
leather：皮革，皮
leave：别离，动身，离开，起身
leaves：离开
leavings：剩余物
lecture：报告，讲课，演讲
led：光二极管，领导
ledge：壁架，矿脉
left-hand：左手的
left-handed：左撇子
leg：腿，脚
lemonade：柠檬水
lend：借出，借
length：长度，长短，篇幅，长，一节，一段
lets：让我们，让
letter：字母，信
letters：信件，函件
leveler：平等主义者
liar：说谎者，撒谎者
lick：舔，舐
lid：盖子
lie：谎言，谎话，躺，撒谎，说谎
lies：谎言
lift：举起，开放，掀起，电梯，抬起
light：光，轻，灯，光纤，燃放，灯光，点燃，亮光
lighted：点燃
lighten：照亮，减轻
lighting：灯光，采光，照明

lightning: 闪电
lights: 灯火
liking: 爱好
limb: 肢，肢体
limber: 可塑
lineal: 直系，正统的，直系的
linen: 亚麻布
lines: 行数
lining: 衬里，衬，内褂
link: 连结，链路，相连，联通，链结，环节，连接，链接
lip: 唇，嘴唇，口头上的
lips: 嘴唇
liquor: 酒，酒精饮料，液体
list: 名单，列举，开列，目录，编目，列出，列表
listen: 听，倾听
listened: 听
listening: 听
listens: 听
lit: 点燃
litter: 残馀物，丢垃圾
live: 住，活，居住
lively: 活泼，热闹，生气勃勃，生气勃勃地，轻快
living: 活泼的
load: 包袱，负载，装满，担子，装载，负荷，载重
loaded: 载入
loading: 荷重
loads: 装载
loaf: 一块面，游荡
loafer: 浪子，游荡
loan: 贷款，借款，贷
lock: 锁，撞锁
locking: 锁紧
log: 圆形木材，圆木，木头
loll: 懒洋洋地倚靠
lone: 孤单，孤独
lonely: 孤独，寂寞，孤独地
lonesome: 寂寞，寂寞的
longer: 较长的
longest: 最长，最长的
lookout: 眺望，伸出窗口观看
looks: 样子，姿容，神态，看
loose: 松开，松弛的
loosing: 松开
loot: 抢掠
lord: 贵族，洛德，主人
lordship: 贵族身份
lose: 丢失，丧失，失掉，遗失
loss: 亏损，损失
lost: 遗失
lot: 地皮，批量，地段
loud: 高声，大声，大声的
louder: 较大声的
louis: 路易斯
lovely: 可爱，可爱的
low: 低，卑下，低廉，浅的，低的
low-down: 非常低的，下作
lowering: 昏暗的
luck: 运气，幸运
lucky: 幸运，幸运的，吉祥
lug: 拖拉
lumber: 木料，木材
lump: 块状，块，疙瘩
lunatic: 丧心病狂，疯子
lunch: 午餐，午饭
lungs: 肺脏
lying: 撒谎的
ma: 妈，马，文学硕士
mad: 狂，发怒，发狂，生气，疯狂的
magic: 魔术
magician: 魔术师，妖人，魔法师
magicians: 魔法师
mahogany: 桃花心木，红木
maid: 女佣，侍女，少女，姑娘
maim: 使残废
mainly: 主要地
majesty: 威严
majority: 多数，大多数
manage: 符合，管理，处理
manned: 由人操纵
manner: 方式，样子，态度，礼貌，神态，神气
manners: 礼貌
marble: 大理石
marched: 游行
marching: 游行
mare: 母马，牝马
mark: 标记，印，符号，标明，标识，迹，迹象，标志，成绩，马克，做记号
married: 已婚，已婚的
marry: 结婚
marseilles: 马赛
mary: 玛莉
mask: 面具
masked: 戴面具
mass: 群众
master: 主，大师，主人，主人翁，师傅，万事达，硕士
masterly: 巧妙地，巧妙的
match: 比赛，相配，对手，火柴，比拟，进军
mate: 伴侣，配偶，伙伴
materials: 物品，材料
mathematics: 数学
matter: 事情，事，物质，事项
matters: 事，事宜
mattress: 床垫
maybe: 或许，也许，或者，说不定，可能，不一定
meal: 餐，膳食，饭
meals: 膳食
meaning: 意义，意思，含义，含意，意味着
measles: 麻疹
meat: 肉
meddle: 干预，干涉
meddlesome: 多事，多事的
medicine: 药物，药品，医学，药剂，医药，药
meek: 谦顺的
meet: 遇见，见面，会合，会晤，聚会
meeting: 会议，集会，会晤，会见，聚会
mellow: 甜美多汁的
melt: 溶化，融化，熔解
member: 成员，议员，构件，会员，份子，团员
memory: 记忆，存储器，存储，记忆体，回忆
mention: 提到，提及
merchants: 商人
mere: 只有
merely: 仅仅，只是，只，不过，单纯，只管，只顾
mess: 杂乱，混乱
message: 信息，讯息，音信，消息
met: 遇见了
midday: 正午，中午
middle: 中央，中间，半中腰，中间的，中部，中央的
middling: 中级品
midnight: 午夜，半夜
mighty: 伟大，强势，强大的
mild: 温和的
mile: 英里
milk: 牛奶，乳
milking: 挤奶
mill: 磨子，磨坊
millions: 百万
mine: 矿，我的，矿山，矿井
minute: 分钟，详细，分，微小的，渺小
mire: 泥潭
miserable: 悲惨，凄惨，困苦，凄惨的
misery: 不幸
misfortune: 不幸，变故
mississippi: 密西西比
missouri: 密苏里
mist: 雾，薄雾
mistake: 错误，差错
mistaken: 错误，弄错
mister: 先生
misunderstood: 误会
mix: 混，混杂，糅，混合，渗混
mixed: 混合，混合的，错杂
moan: 悲叹
moat: 护城河
mob: 乌合之众，暴民
mocking: 嘲讽，嘲弄
moderated: 适中

modern：现今，现在，当前，现代的
monstrous：怪物似，似怪物的
month：月，月份
monthly：每月，单月
moon：月亮，月球，月
moonlight：月光
moral：道德
morality：道德
morals：道德
moreover：此外，而且，并且，另外，况且，又
mornings：早晨
mortar：臼，迫击炮
mortification：禁欲，坏疽
moses：摩西
moss：苔藓，苔
mostly：大多，多半，大部份
motto：座右铭
mournful：悲切，悲恸，悲恸的
mourning：追悼，丧
mouse：老鼠，滑鼠，鼠标器，鼠标
mouth：口，嘴巴，嘴，吻
mouthful：满口的
mouths：口
move：步骤，搬家，移动，一举，运动，感动，开动，移
moving：感动，动态，动人，活动，乔迁
mrs：夫人，太太
mud：泥，泥浆
muddled：糊涂，懵懂
muddy：泥泞的，混浊
muggins：蠢人
mules：骡子
multiplication：乘法，增加
mum：妈妈
mumble：嘀咕
mumps：流行性腮腺炎
murder：谋杀，杀人案件，杀害
murderer：凶手，杀人犯
muse：瞑想，沉思
music：音乐，民乐，曲子
myself：我自己
mysterious：神秘，莫名其妙，神秘的
mystery：神秘
n：安全理事会
nab：逮捕
nabob：富翁，大财主
nail：钉，指甲，钉子
naked：赤裸裸，裸体的
nap：瞌睡
narrow：狭窄，窄，逼仄，狭，小气，狭隘，狭窄的
nation：国家
native：土着，土生的，土著
natural：自然，天然，自然的，天生
naturally：自然，自然地
navigate：航行
near：近，靠近，接近，比邻
nearest：最靠近的
nearly：几乎，差不多，将近
near-sighted：近视的
neat：整齐，乾净，干净，平整，整洁的
necessity：必要性，必然，必需品，必需
neck：颈项，脖子，颈
needed：需要
needle：针，缝针
needles：针
needs：需要
needy：贫穷的
neighbor：邻居，比邻
neither：也不，二者，两者都不是
nest：窝巢，窝，巢
news：新闻，信息，消息
newspapers：报章，报纸
nice：和蔼，可亲，好，尼斯
nice-looking：好看
niece：侄女，甥女
nightcap：睡帽
nine：九
nineteen：十九
nip：咬，捏，掐
nobility：贵族，高贵
noble：高贵，高贵的，贵族
nobody：没有人，没人
nodding：点头
nods：点头
noise：噪音，噪声，响声，吵闹声，吵声
none：无，没有
nonsense：无聊，废话，屁话
noon：中午，正午，晌午
nor：也不
nose：鼻子
notice：通知，注意，布告，注意到，启事
noticing：注意到
notion：观念
nowhere：无处
nurse：护士，哺乳，照料
nuts：螺母
oak：橡树，橡
oar：桨
oath：誓言，誓词，宣誓
object：对象，物件，宾语，物体，物，事物
objections：反对
obsequies：丧礼
observer：观察者，观察家，观察员
occasion：时机，机会，场合，场面
ocean：海洋，洋
odd：奇怪，莫名其妙，零头，奇异的
odds：可能性，差距
ode：颂词
offer：捐助，开设，提供
offering：奉现，提供
officers：官员
ohio：俄亥俄
oilcloth：油布
oldest：最年长的
old-fashioned：过时，旧式的
one-horse：单马拉的
onion：洋葱
onto：到…上
oozing：渗出
opened：打开
opening：揭幕，口，打开，孔，开始
opinion：意见，看法，意思，见解
opportunity：机会，时机，机遇
opposed：反对的，对抗的，敌对的
opposite：相反，相对，对面，对立面，相反的
opposition：反对
oppression：压迫
oracle：神谕，预言者
ordering：排序，命令
orders：命令
ordinary：通常，普通，平常，寻常，一般，正常，普通的，正常的
orleans：奥尔良
ornery：低劣的
ostrich：鸵鸟
otto：玫瑰油
ought：应该，活该
ourselves：我们自己，我们
out-and-out：不折不扣
outer：在外，帮子，外部的
outfit：旅行装备，装备
outlandish：偏僻的，外国气派的，妄图
outrage：暴行，使愤慨
outrageous：不像话，残暴的，岂有此理
outside：外面，外表，表面，面儿，外来，外部的，外面的，外头，之外，外边
overboard：向船外
overcoat：大衣
overflow：溢出，泛滥，溢流
overhauling：大修，检查
owl：猫头鹰，枭
owls：猫头鹰
owned：拥有
owner：物主，业主，所有者，所有人，主人
ox：牛
pa：爸爸
pack：包装，包扎，包，背包
packed：挤得满满的
packing：包装
paddle：桨
padlock：挂锁
paid：支付
painful：痛苦，痛苦的

paint: 颜料，油漆，涂料，绘画
pair: 对，一对，双
palace: 宫殿，宫，皇宫
pale: 苍白，苍白的
pallet: 草荐，棘爪
pan: 平锅
panama: 巴拿马，科隆
panting: 气吁吁
pants: 裤子
paper: 纸，论文，纸张
papers: 报纸
paralysis: 瘫痪
parasol: 阳伞
parcel: 包裹，包，邮包
pardon: 赦免，包容，原谅，宽恕，饶恕
paris: 巴黎
parlor: 会客室
parrot: 鹦鹉
parrots: 鹦鹉
parson: 牧师
partly: 部分地
parts: 部件
pass: 隘口，及格，传递，度过，要隘
passage: 通道，通路，通过
passages: 通路
passengers: 旅客
passing: 经过的，短暂的，目前的，及格的
paste: 糊，软膏，粘贴，糊状物
pat: 轻拍，拍，恰好的，人为的
patch: 补缀，补丁，补
patent: 专利
path: 道，道路，路径，小径，走道
patience: 忍耐，忍受，耐心，耐性
patient: 耐烦，患者，病号，病员，耐心，忍耐，病人
pause: 暂停，停顿
paw: 爪子
paying: 有利的，合算的，支付的
pays: 支付
peace: 和平
peaceful: 安顿，安宁，安生，安谧，安静，和平的，沉静
peart: 快活的
peck: 啄
peddle: 贩卖，兜售，沿街叫卖，叫卖，零卖，挑卖
peep: 偷看，窥，张望
peg: 木钉，衣夹，栓
pen: 笔，栏圈，笔杆，笔杆子，栏位，栏，钢笔
pencil: 铅笔，笔套，笔帽
pendulum: 钟摆
pensive: 哀思，沉思的
perfect: 完美，完善，完美的，无话可说，完备
perfectly: 完美，完美地
performance: 性能，成绩，表演，表现，演出，完成，执行
perfumery: 香料店
persons: 人
persuade: 劝说，说服
pesky: 讨厌的
pet: 宠物
pew: 教堂长凳
philadelphia: 费城
phrenology: 骨相学
physician: 医生
piano: 钢琴
pick: 掐，采摘，挑选，挑，鹤嘴锄，采，选择
picked: 精选的
picking: 选择，投纬
pickles: 泡菜
picks: 选择
picnic: 野餐
picture: 图画，照片，图像，图片，画，画儿，拍摄，图象，像
pictures: 图画
pie: 馅饼
piece: 片，部分，一块，一片，块，部份，份
pies: 馅饼
pig: 猪
pigs: 猪
pike: 长枪，税关
pile: 一堆，桩，堆
piles: 痔，痔疮，堆
piling: 打桩，打桩工程，桩材
pilot: 飞行员，驾驶员，飞机师
pin: 别针，个人鉴别码
pinch: 捏，掐
pine: 松树
pins: 别针
pint: 品脱
pious: 虔诚的
pipe: 管，管子，筒，喉管
pirate: 海盗，剽窃
pistol: 手枪
pitch: 沥青，投，音调
pitched: 沥青
pitied: 同情
pitiful: 可怜，可怜的
pity: 怜悯，遗憾，哀怜，同情
pitying: 同情
pivot: 枢轴，支点，枢，枢纽
places: 地方
plain: 平原
plan: 计划，方案，规划，设计，主意，计画，擘画，打算，设计图
plank: 板，木板，木版，板子
plant: 植物，安插，事业，种植，插
plantation: 农园，种植园
plantations: 种植园
plate: 碟，盘子
plates: 盘子
platform: 平台，站台，平，主席台，主席
play: 表演，戏剧，游戏，玩，演出，戏，剧本，扮演，悬念，弹奏，奏
pleasant: 愉快，愉快的，舒适的
please: 请，使高兴
pleased: 满意，高兴的
pleasing: 愉快，愉快的，舒适的
pleasure: 欢乐，乐趣，愉快
plenty: 丰富，许多
plow: 犁，耕
pluck: 采摘，摘，勇气，采
plug: 插头，板烟，插
plum: 李子，梅
plunder: 掠夺，抢劫，抢夺
pocket: 口袋，衣袋，兜儿，窟窿
poetry: 诗，诗歌
pointed: 尖锐
pointing: 指，瞄准
points: 点
poke: 戳，拨开，插入
polished: 优美的，精练的，擦亮的
polite: 有礼貌，客气，有礼貌的，斯文，和气
pommel: 鞍头
ponderous: 笨重的
poor: 差，贫穷，穷，差劲，贫瘠，贫穷的，贫苦，困苦
popular: 流行，普及，受欢迎，民间，流行的
porch: 阳台，门廊
pore: 毛孔
pork: 猪肉
post: 职位，邮件，公告，柱，寄
potato: 马铃薯，土豆
pound: 磅，敲击
pour: 灌，奔流，倾倒，倒，注
powder: 粉，细粉
powerful: 强大，有力，强劲，强有力的
powwow: 巫师
practice: 演习，实际，操练，作法，练习，实践，实习
practiced: 熟练
prague: 布拉格
prairie: 大草原，草原
pray: 祈祷
prayer: 祷告，祈祷
preach: 传教，讲道，鼓吹
preacher: 传道者
preaching: 讲道法
precious: 宝贵，珍贵，贵重，宝贵的
premature: 为时过早，过早的，早熟的
prepared: 有准备的，准备好的，精制的
presence: 出席，面前
preserve: 保藏，保全，保留，维修

pressed: 压
pressing: 紧迫，逼人，迫切，紧迫的
pretty: 漂亮，美丽的，秀丽
previous: 前，以前，过去，先前的，过急的
price: 价钱，价格，代价，价目
pride: 自豪，骄傲
prime: 首要的
principal: 本金，主要，校长，首长
principle: 原理，原则，道理
print: 印刷，印，版画，打印
printer: 打印机，印刷者，印表机
printing: 印花，印刷，印数，印刷术
prison: 监狱
prisoner: 犯人，罪犯，囚犯
prisoners: 囚犯
private: 私人，私营，私人的，私有，士兵
privileged: 特权，有特权的
procession: 行列，游行
profit: 盈利，裨益，成果，收益，盈余，获利，利润，利益，盈馀
profitable: 有利可图，有利可图的
profits: 利润
progress: 进步，进展
project: 计划，项目，工程，规划，方案，专案，设计，投影
promise: 答应，约定，承诺，誓言，诺言，允诺
prompt: 提示，立刻，迅速的，敏捷的
pronounced: 明言
prop: 支撑，支柱
properly: 好好儿地，适当地
property: 财产，属性，特性，资产，财物，产业，地产
protect: 防守，保佑，保护，维护
protection: 保护，通行证
proud: 傲岸，骄矜，骄傲的，自豪的
prove: 证明
provisions: 食品
pry: 刺探
pudding: 布丁
pull: 拉，牵引
pulling: 拉
pump: 唧筒，泵
puncheon: 短柱
pup: 小狗
pure: 单纯，纯净的，纯洁，纯粹
purse: 钱包，钱袋，囊
push: 推
puts: 放
puzzled: 惑
quality: 品质，质量，质，高低，档次，特质，粗细，优质的
quarrel: 拌嘴，争吵，吵嘴，是非
quarrels: 争吵
quarrelsome: 喜欢吵架，喜爱争论的
quarry: 采石场
quarter: 四分之一
quarters: 住处，四分之一
queen: 女王，王后，皇后
queens: 女王
questions: 问题
quick: 快，玲珑，敏捷的，迅速的
quicksilver: 水银
quiet: 安静，寂静，安定，安生，沉静，宁静的
quietus: 平息
quilt: 棉被，被子
quit: 退出，退离
rabbit: 兔子，兔，野兔
rabbits: 野兔
race: 种族，竞赛，人种
rack: 网架，支架
racket: 球拍，拍子
rackety: 喧闹的
raft: 筏，木排，槎，桴
rafter: 椽
rafters: 椽
rafting: 放排
rafts: 木排
raftsman: 木排运送工人
rag: 破布，碎布
ragged: 破烂，衣著褴褛的
raging: 熊熊，狂怒，猛烈的，狂暴的，愤怒的
rags: 碎布
rail: 铁路，轨道
rails: 铁路，铁路股票，轨道
rain: 雨，下雨
rainbow: 虹
rained: 下雨
rains: 雨季，下雨
rainy: 下雨，多雨的
raise: 升起，提高，筹措，增加，抚育，举起
raised: 凸起的，浮雕的
raises: 加薪
ram: 公羊，随机存取存储器，灌输，撞
rampant: 猖獗，嚣张，猛烈的，猖獗的
ramrod: 推弹杆
ran: 跑
range: 范围，靶场，射程，牧场，区域，距离，围范
ranged: 排列
rank: 评价分类，身分，级别，等级，地位，排
ransom: 赎金
rascal: 小淘气，流氓
raspy: 易怒的
rat: 老鼠，鼠
rate: 比率，速度，率，速率，流量，等级
rattle: 发嘎嘎声，发出格格声响
rattlesnake: 响尾蛇
rave: 怒吼，谵，咆哮
raw: 生的，未加工的，阴冷的
re: 再
reach: 抵达，到达，抵，到
reached: 到达
reaching: 到达
reading: 读物，读数
reads: 阅读
ready: 就绪，愿意，准备，妥当
reason: 理由，道理，原因，缘故，缘由，情理
reasonable: 合理，合理的
reasonableness: 合理性
reasoning: 推理
receipt: 收据，收条
reckon: 估计，计算
recommend: 推荐，保送，引进
record: 记录，记载，档案，唱片，笔录，纪录
red: 红，红色，红色的
reddened: 变红
red-hot: 热烈的
referring: 参考
reform: 改革
reforming: 改革
regard: 看待，关系，认为，留意，注意，心意
regardless: 不管
region: 区域，地区，地域，一带，区，境
regular: 固定，正常，通常，端正，正规的，常例的，定期的，整齐的，有秩序的，正规，经常
regulations: 条例，规程，章程，规章
reins: 缰
relations: 关系
reliable: 可靠，确实，可靠的，稳当，稳妥
religion: 宗教
remember: 记忆，记得
remiss: 怠慢的，疏忽的，迟缓的
renowned: 闻名，大明鼎鼎，著名的，享有声誉
represent: 代表
representing: 代表
request: 要求，请求
require: 要求，要有，需要
rescue: 营救，抢救，搭救，拯救，挽救，救
resemblance: 相似，类似点，相似点，相似性，像
resigned: 忍从的
resolution: 决议，决心，决议案，分解
respect: 尊敬，方面，遵守，尊重
respectable: 可尊敬，可尊敬的
responsibility: 责任

rest：休息，安息，其余
resting：静止的
restless：不安，不安的
rests：休息
resurrection：复活
returns：返回
reveal：表露，暴露，透露，流露，走漏
reverend：应受尊敬的
revival：复苏，复兴
reward：报酬，酬劳，酬金，奖励，奖赏
rhyme：韵，押韵，压韵
rich：富有，丰富，富有的，充实
richard：理察
rid：摆脱
riddle：谜，谜语
ride：乘，骑，跨，坐
ridge：脊，屋脊，山脊，背脊
ridiculous：荒谬，荒谬的，岂有此理，可笑的
rigging：索具，帆具
rightful：正直的，合法的
rightly：正确地
rights：权力
ring：戒指，环，圈，篮圈，戒子，圈子，响铃，电话铃声
rip：扯裂，撕破，裂口
ripe：熟，成熟
rips：裂口
rise：升起，上升，上涨，兴起，增大
risking：风险
river：河，江，川，河流，条
rivers：河，河川
roads：道路
roast：焙烧，烘烤，烤，烤肉，烘，炙，烧烤
rob：抢劫
robber：强盗
robbery：掠夺，抢劫
robbing：抢劫
robinson：鲁滨逊
rock：岩石，簸荡，摇
rocked：摇动，摇摆
rocks：岩石
rocky：岩石的
rod：棍子，棍
rode：骑
roll：滚动，簸荡，卷
rolled：卷
rolling：滚动，旋转的，起伏的，波动的
roof：屋顶，顶部，顶板
rooms：房间
root：根，根本，根源
roots：根
rope：绳索，绳子
rose：蔷薇，玫瑰，升起
rot：腐坏，腐烂，腐化
rotten：腐败的，腐朽
rouge：胭脂
rough：粗暴，大概，粗糙，粗鲁
roundabout：曲线
rouse：唤醒
roused：激昂
row：一排，划，行
royal：皇家，女王的，王室的，王的
royalty：王权，版税
rub：摩擦，擦
rubbed：摩擦
rubbing：研磨，拓片，摩擦
rubbish：废物，垃圾，废话
rubs：摩擦
ruined：破败，毁坏
rule：统治，规则，规章，规矩，宰制，主宰，法则，尺子，尺，天下
rules：条例，规程，守则，裁定，规则
rumbling：隆隆响
runaway：逃亡者，跑道
rung：响铃
running：一连
runs：跑
rush：速行，匆匆
rustle：瑟瑟
rusty：腐蚀，生锈的
sable：黑貂
sack：大袋子，开除
sackful：满袋
sacred：神圣，神圣的
sad：悲伤，哀愁，不幸，哀伤，哀怨，悲伤的，悲哀的
saddle：鞍，鞍状物，马鞍
safe：安全，保险，安全的，稳妥，保险箱
safer：安全
sail：帆，帆船，航行，航海
sailing：航海术，航海，航行
saint：圣人，圣徒
sake：缘故
salable：有销路的
salary：薪水，薪金，工钱，待遇
sale：销路，销售
sales：销售，销售额，营收
salt：盐
sand：沙，沙子
sandy：有沙的
sarah：莎拉
sarcastic：讽刺的
sass：顶嘴
sat：坐了，星期六
satisfaction：满意
satisfactory：满意的，称心，圆满
satisfied：满意，乐意，心满意足的
saturday：星期六，周六
sausage：香肠，腊肠
save：节约，节省，省得，救，援救，挽救，保存
saves：节省
saving：节省
sawdust：木屑
sawed：锯
sawmill：锯木厂
saws：锯
saying：名言，说
scandalous：恶意中伤
scar：疤痕，痕，疤，瘢痕，伤痕
scarcity：缺乏，不足
scare：恐慌
scary：引起惊慌
scatter：分散，散播，驱散
scattered：零落，散播，散乱的，分散的
scattering：散射
scene：景色，场面，现场，实况，镜头，景象，幕，情景
scent：气味，嗅，香味
schoolhouse：校舍
science：科学，学，学术
scold：责骂
scoop：杓子，勺子，勺
scorched：焦
scornful：轻视，轻视的
scott：司克脱
scoundrel：无籁，坏蛋，无赖
scour：擦洗，擦亮，搜索
scrabble：涂写
scramble：攀登
scrambled：攀登，扰频
scrap：零头，剪报，报废，碎屑，废品
scrape：刮掉，削刮
scratch：抓伤，抓，搔刮
scratches：抓
scratching：刮痕，抓
scream：叫喊，呐喊，呼啸
screw：螺丝钉，螺钉
scripture：经文，手稿
scrubbing：擦洗
scrunch：碾碎
sea：海
sealing：密封
search：搜索，搜查，寻觅，寻找，找
season：季节，季，时节
seat：座位，位置，位子，席位，座
seats：座位
seconds：秒
secret：秘密，机密
secrets：秘密
section：部分，部，部门，段，股，部份，章节，阶段，科
security：安全，安全性
seed：种子，播种
seeing：有鉴于
seem：显得，看来，彷佛，好象
self：自己，自，自我，我

sell：销售，游说，贩卖，出售
selling：出售，卖的
send：派遣，派出，送，发送，寄，投，派
sending：发送
sent：送了
separate：脱离，另外，分别，分离，别
separated：分开
sermon：传教
serpent：蛇
servant：仆人，佣人，用人
serve：侍候，伺候，待候
sets：装置
setting：排字，设定
settle：奠定，安家落户，澄清，解决
settled：安定
seven：七
seventeen：十七
seventy：七十
severe：严重，严竣，严厉，严峻，剧烈，严肃的
sewed：缝
shabby：破旧，破旧的
shade：荫，荫凉，阴影，树阴
shadows：影子
shady：暧昧，背阴，不三不四，阴凉，阴凉的
shake：摇动，震动，摇，震荡，颤簸
shakes：摇动
shakespeare：莎士比亚
shaking：摇动
shaky：动摇不稳，震动的
shallow：粗浅，浅，鄙陋，浅的
shame：羞耻
shanty：棚屋
shape：形状，形式，外形，型状，形态，塑造，使成形，成形
share：部分，股，部份，股票，分享，共享，股份
shares：股
sharp：尖锐，锐利，锋利的，锋利
shave：刨，剃刮
shed：散出，棚子，流出，脱落
sheep：羊，绵羊
sheet：片，一张，床单，纸张
sheets：纸张
sheffield：谢菲尔德
shell：壳，部份，贝壳，贝，盖子，炮弹，剥，外壳
sheriff：郡治安官，行政司法长官
shin：外小腿，胫
shine：发光，发亮，照射，照耀，光
shines：发光
shingle：木瓦，屋顶板
shining：彪炳，发亮
shiny：发亮，闪亮，发亮的
ship：船
shipping：航运，装货，装运，海运，船舶
ships：船只，船
shipshape：井然有序
shirk：逃避，推卸
shirt：衬衫，衬衣
shiver：发抖，颤抖，哆嗦
shivering：颤抖
shivers：颤抖
shoal：浅滩
shook：摇动
shoot：射击，芽，射门
shooting：射击，猎场
shore：岸，滨，岸边，海岸，海滨
shores：岸
short：短，矮，小结，短暂
shortened：缩短
shot：射击
shotgun：猎枪
shots：射击
shoulder：肩，肩膀，担负
shoulders：肩，双肩
shout：叫喊，呼喊，呼唤，喊，喊叫
shouting：呼喊
shouts：呼喊
shove：推
shovel：铲子，铲，铁锹
shovels：铁锹
showed：展示
shows：显示
shrivel：起皱纹
shriveled：瘪
shroud：笼罩
shuck：壳
shut：关闭
shutter：百叶窗
shutting：关闭
sick：生病
sicken：使作呕
sickness：病，疾病
sideboard：餐具柜
sigh：叹息，叹气
sighs：叹息
sight：视觉，景象，情景，目光，视力，视线
sign：符号，标记，署名，牌子，迹象，标志，签署，手势，旗
signal：信号，手势，讯号
silent：无声，沉默的
silky：柔软光滑
silly：愚蠢，糊涂，愚蠢的，傻的，傻
silver：银，白银
simple：简单，简易，简略，简单的，单纯
simply：简直，只是，根本，简单地，高低，只管，只需，只顾
sin：罪恶，罪行
sing：唱，歌唱，唱歌
singing：歌咏，歌唱
single：单一，单独的，单身的，唯一的，选拔
sings：唱
singular：单数，单一的
sinister：邪恶，邪恶的，不吉的
sink：水槽，沉落，沈落，沉没
sinking：沉没
sir：先生，爵士
sister：姐妹
sisters：姊妹，姐妹
sitting：坐，开庭期间
situation：情况，形势，局面，局势，场合，事态，情形，气候，形式，状况
sixteen：十六
sixteenth：第十六，第十六的
sixty：六十
sixty-five：六十五
size：大小，尺寸，纤度，个子，个儿
sizes：大小
skiff：小船，小艇
skillet：长柄锅
skimming：撇沫
skin：皮肤，剥皮
skip：跳跃，跳过
skipping：跳跃，跳过
skips：跳跃
skull：头盖骨，头骨，头颅
sky：天空，天
skylight：天窗
slab：木板，石片，板皮，扁坯，石板
slam：猛撞，猛力关
slant：倾斜
slanted：倾斜
slanting：倾斜的
slap：掌击，拍
slave：奴隶
slavery：奴隶制度，奴隶制
sleep：梦寐，睡觉，睡眠，睡
sleepiness：睡意
sleeping：睡眠，睡着
sleepy：想睡，眼睡的
sleeve：袖子，衣袖
sleeves：袖子
slept：睡了
slick：油头滑脑
slid：滑行
slide：滑落，滑行，滑
slim：瘦长，纤细，苗条的
sling：弹弓，吊绳，背带，吊索
slip：滑倒，溜走，溜
slipped：滑落
slippers：拖鞋，便鞋
slobbers：口水
slogan：口号，标语
slope：倾斜，坡，采场，斜坡
slow：慢，缓慢，迟慢，迟钝，迟迟，迟缓

sluice：水闸
sluicing：泄水
slush：雪水，烂泥
sly：隐密，狡猾
smack：拍击，滋味
smart：高明，时髦的
smash：捣碎，粉碎，破碎
smell：嗅，臭，香味
smells：臭
smelt：熔炼，溶解
smile：微笑，笑容
smiling：微笑的
smoke：烟，抽烟，烟雾，硝烟，吸烟，熏
smoked：熏
smoking：冒烟，抽烟
smooth：平稳，润滑，光滑，平滑，通顺
smoothed：平滑的
smuggle：走私，私运
snack：小吃，快餐，点心
snag：故障，钉子，残干，根株
snake：蛇
snakeskin：蛇皮皮革
snap：折断，抢夺，猛咬
snapped：猛咬
snarls：缠结
snatch：夺取，攫取
snatches：攫取
sneak：潜行，潜入
sneaking：鬼鬼祟祟的
snoring：打鼾
snow：雪
snuff：鼻烟，用鼻子使劲吸
snug：舒适，舒适的
snuggled：偎依
soap：肥皂
sober：清醒，清醒的
socks：袜子，短袜
soft：柔软，柔和，柔软的
soften：变软，软化
sold：卖了
solder：焊料，焊
soldier：士兵，战士，军人，兵家
soldiers：兵员
sole：唯一，单一，唯一的，惟一，跖，鞋底
solemn：严肃，俨然，岸然，隆重，庄严的，庄重
solid：固体，立体，固体的，坚硬，扎实，实心的，坚固的，坚实
soliloquy：独白，自言自语
solitary：孤独，独居的
solomon：所罗门
somebody：某人，有人
somehow：不知何故
somewhere：某处
son：儿子
song：歌，歌曲，歌儿
sons：儿子
soon：不久，最近，眼看，快，近期，早，早日
sore：疼痛，疮，疼痛的
sores：疡
sorrowful：悲痛，悲哀，哀愁，悲伤，悲伤的
sorrows：悲哀
sorry：遗憾，对不起
sorted：分类
sorter：分类者
sorts：种类
soul：灵魂
souls：灵魂
sound：声音，音
sounds：声音
soup：汤，羹汤
sour：酸，酸味
soured：酸味
southern：南方的
sow：播种，播
spanish：西班牙语，西班牙文，西班牙，西班牙的
spare：备用，饶恕
spark：触发，火花
speak：说，讲
specially：专门，特殊
specimen：标本，样品，样本
speck：斑点，点子
spectacle：奇观，展示，景象
speculate：推测，猜测，思索
speculation：推测，思索
speech：演说，言语，报告
speeches：言论，演说
speed：速度，速率，奔驰，加速，进度
spell：拼写，咒语，符咒
spelling：拼字，斯佩林，拼写检查
spend：度过，花费，支出，耗费
spent：耗费了
spider：蜘蛛
spiders：蜘蛛
spin：纺，旋转
spinning：纺织，旋转
spirit：神，精神，灵魂，气概，白干儿，白乾儿
spirits：精神
spiritual：精神，心灵上，心灵上的
spite：恶意
splendid：彪炳，卓越，辉煌，灿烂的，精彩，辉煌的
splinter：碎片
split：均分，分裂，裂片，拆分，捧腹，裂开
splitting：极快的
spoke：辐条，说了
spool：线轴
spoon：匙，调羹
spoonful：一匙，满匙的
sport：运动
spot：斑点，点子，侦查
spotted：有斑点的
spread：扩散，流传，传播，散播，敷，撒
spreading：撒，散布，传播，展开，扩展
spring：弹簧，泉，春天，绷簧，春季，水源，跳
sprung：弹跳
spry：轻快
spun：旋转
spunk：引火木柴
spy：间谍，特务
spying：侦察
square：正方形，平方，四方形
squatting：蹲
squealing：啸声，振鸣声
squeeze：压扁，压挤，榨
squirm：蠕动
squirming：蠕蠕，蠕动
squirrels：松鼠
squirt：喷出
squirting：喷出
stack：堆，栈，垛，堆叠，堆积，堆置
stage：舞台，阶段，层次，发动，段
stagger：蹒跚，脚步蹒跚
staggered：交错
stairs：楼梯
stanchion：坚强，支柱，标柱
stand：站住，主张，架子，站立，耐，站，架
standing：站立，地位
standstill：瘫痪
staple：钉书针，名产，主要成分
staples：主要成分
starchy：含淀粉，古板的
stars：星
started：开始
starter：启动器，起动装置
starting：起步
starts：开始
starved：饥饿
stated：志明
statements：声明
stay：延缓，逗留，停留
stayed：停留
staying：停留
stays：停留
steady：稳定，坚定，平稳，平稳的
steal：偷窃，盗窃，偷，窃取
stealing：偷垒，偷窃
steam：蒸汽，热气，废气，蒸
steamboat：汽船，轮船
steep：险峻，峭壁，浸，泡，陡峭的
step：步骤，步伐，措施，一步，步调，步子，级，脚步，踏
steps：步骤

stern：严竣，严厉的，船尾
stick：棍，棒子，棍子，插入，棒，黏贴，手杖
sticks：棍
stiff：僵硬，板滞，僵硬的
stillness：静止，寂静
stilts：高跷
sting：刺，叮，螫
stir：轰动，搅拌，鼓动
stirring：活跃的，激动人心的，忙碌的
stirs：鼓动
stock：存货，股票，股份，库存
stockings：袜子，长统袜
stock-still：静止的
stole：偷了
stomach：胃，肚子
stomach-ache：肚痛
stood：站了
stool：凳，凳子
stoop：弯腰，门廊
stooped：弯腰
stooping：弯腰
stop：停止，终止，截止，站
stopped：停止
stopper：塞子，用塞子塞住
stopping：停止
stops：停止
store：商店，储藏，商号，贮藏，店铺
stores：商店，备用品
storm：暴风雨，暴风，风暴
storms：暴风雨
stormy：暴风雨的
story：故事，报导
stout：肥硕，强壮的
stow：装载
straight：直，海峡，迳直，直接，笔直，一直
strain：拉紧，种，系，紧张，菌株，品系
strange：奇怪，奇特，陌生，奇异的，生疏
stranger：陌生人，异乡人，生人
strangers：陌生人
straps：背带，带
straw：稻草，吸管
strawberries：草莓
stray：游荡，迷路
streak：斑纹，线条
stream：溪流，河流，流，小溪，川
street：街道，街，马路，大街，街头
streets：街道
strength：力量，力，强度，实力，力气，气力，浓度
stretch：张开，拉紧，伸展，伸
stretched：伸展
stretchers：担架
stretching：伸展
strike：罢工，打，敲打，敲，打击
strikes：打击
striking：引人注目，引人注目的
string：绳子，串，线，细线，弦
strip：长条，剥夺，剥，简易机场
striped：有条纹，有条纹的
stroke：笔锋，冲程，打击，行程，敲打，笔划
strong：轰轰烈烈，健全，霸道，坚强，强有力，强大，强烈，强大的，扎实，干，强烈的
stronger：较强
struck：敲打
struggles：奋斗
stuck：黏贴
studying：学习
stuff：材料，填塞，职员
stump：树桩，残肢
stunned：愕然
stupid：愚笨，笨拙，愚笨的
style：方式，风格，式样，样式，试样，笔调，模样，作风
sublime：崇高，崇高的
submit：提交，呈交
subscriptions：订阅
suck：吮吸，咂，吮
sudden：突然，急剧，突然的
suffer：受苦，蒙受，遭受，受到，遭到
suffering：痛苦，熬煎，苦难
sugar：糖
suit：适应，一套
suitable：得宜，适宜，适当，允当，合适，恰当，适当的，适
suited：适宜于
sultry：闷热
summer：夏天，夏季
sun：太阳，星期日，曝
sunday：星期日，星期天，礼拜天，周日，礼拜日
sundown：日落
sung：唱歌
sunk：沉没
sunset：日落，傍晚
sunshine：阳光
sunshiny：阳光照耀的
superintendent：监督人
supper：晚饭，晚餐
suppose：假使，猜想，假定
sure：肯定
surge：浪涌，大浪，波荡，波涛
surprise：使吃惊，惊奇，惊骇
surprised：惊讶
surprising：可惊
susan：苏珊
suspicion：疑心，怀疑，嫌疑
suspicions：怀疑
suspicious：可疑，可疑的
swallow：燕子，吞，咽
swamp：沼泽
swap：交换
swarm：蜂群，一群
swarmed：蜂涌
swear：立誓，发誓
sweat：汗，出汗，流汗
sweated：出汗
sweep：席卷，打扫，扫描
sweet：甜，甜食，糖果
sweet-scented：香味好的
swell：涨满，膨胀
swelled：膨胀
swelling：肿胀，增大，膨胀
swift：迅速的
swig：痛饮
swim：游泳
sword：剑
swords：剑
swore：立誓
swung：摇摆
sympathy：同情
symptoms：症状
tackle：钓鱼用具，处理
tag：标签，标记
tagging：加标签
tail：尾巴，跟踪
tails：尾巴
takes：拿，取走
takin：羚牛
tale：故事
talent：才能，天才，天资，才华
tales：候补陪审员召集令
talk：谈话，报告，言语，谈
talked：谈话
tall：高大的，高大
tame：驯服，驯服的
tan：黄褐色，鞣，棕黄色
tangle：纠缠
tanner：唐纳
tape：卷带，胶带，磁带，录音带
tar：焦油
tartar：牙垢，难对付的人，鞑靼，酒石，鞑靼人
tavern：客栈，酒馆
tea：茶，茶叶
teach：教，教导，讲课
teacher：教师，老师，教员，先生，导师，师长
tear：眼泪，撕破，撕
tearful：含泪的
tearing：撕裂的
tears：泪，泪水，眼泪
tedious：乏味，厌烦的
teeth：牙齿，牙
temperance：节制
tend：照料，倾向
tent：帐篷，帐蓬，篷帐
term：术语，学期，期限，项
terrible：可怕，糟糕，可怕的

territory：领土，版图，土地，疆土，领域，疆域
test：试验，测验，考验，检验
testament：遗嘱
texas：德克萨斯，得克萨斯
text：课文，案文，正文，文字
thank：感谢，谢谢
thankful：感谢，感谢的
thanks：感谢，谢谢
thatcher：茅屋顶
theater：剧场，戏剧，戏院，剧院
theatre：剧场
theatres：剧场
thee：你
thick：厚，密，浓厚
thicken：变厚
thickened：变厚
thicker：厚
thicket：丛林，灌木丛
thieving：偷
thighs：大腿
thimble：顶针，缝纫用的顶针
thin：薄，疏，细，淡
thinking：思想，思维
thinks：想
thirsty：渴的
thirteen：十三
thirty：三十
thomas：汤姆斯
thoughts：心头，感想
thousand：千
thrash：鞭打，击败
thread：线，线索，细线，运作
threaten：威胁
thrilling：毛骨悚然的
throat：嗓子，喉咙，喉头，咽喉
throw：扔，丢掉，丢，投
thump：重击
thunder：雷，雷声，打雷
tick：壁虱，滴答声，勾
ticket：票
tie：不分胜负，打结，束缚，轨枕，绑，领带
tight：严格，严密，紧，紧的，严竣，狭隘
till：直到
tilt：倾斜，翘起，使倾侧
tilted：倾斜的
timber：木料，木材，木头
timid：胆小，胆怯，胆怯的
tin：锡，罐头
tip：小费，尖端，尾端
tiptoe：趾尖，蹑手蹑脚
tiptop：拔尖儿，极好的，绝佳
tire：疲倦
tired：疲倦，疲乏，疲倦的
tiresome：使人疲惫的
title：锦标，标题，题目，称号，职称
tobacco：烟草
toe：脚趾
tolerable：可容忍，可容忍的
tomb：陵墓，坟墓
tombstone：墓碑
tomorrow：明天，未来，明日
ton：吨，公吨
tongs：夹钳，铗子
tongue：舌头，舌
tonight：今晚，今夜
tools：工具
tooth：牙齿
top：顶，盖，尖峰，顶端，顶部，树梢，最高的
torchlight：手电筒
tore：撕扯
torn：撕扯
touch：触摸，笔锋，触，联系，碰，接触
touches：接触
touching：动人
tough：强硬，坚韧的
tow：拖船，拖车，牵引，拖
town：城镇，城市，市镇
track：跑道，径赛，径迹，轨道，行踪，履带，踪迹
tracks：轨道
tract：地域
trade：贸易，商业，经贸
trader：商人
tragedian：悲剧演员
tragedy：悲剧
trail：线索，痕迹，形迹
train：训练，火车，列车，乘务员，熏陶
tramp：沉重脚步
trance：恍惚
trap：圈套，陷阱，阱
trash：垃圾，残馀物
travel：旅行，遨游，旅游，游历
traveled：旅客多的
traveler：旅客，旅游者，游客
treasure：爱护，爱惜，宝贝，宝物，宝贵，宝藏，珍惜
treat：对待
treatment：待遇，疗法，对待，治疗，处理
treats：对待
tree：树
trees：树木
tremble：发抖，哆嗦
trembled：发抖
trembling：发抖，发抖的
trial：审讯，测试
tribe：部落，部族
tribute：贡物
trick：手法，骗术，秘诀，欺骗，玩意儿，花样
tricks：戏法，把戏
trifling：些许，不重要的
trim：修剪，笔挺
trip：旅程，旅游，旅行，跟头，旅途
tripped：旅行
trot：快步跑，小跑
trouble：麻烦，难度，难处
troubles：坏处，麻烦
troublesome：淘神，讨厌，麻烦，麻烦的，伤脑筋
truck：卡车
true：真实，确实，确有其事，真正，属实，对头，真正的
truly：真实地，未免，着实
trunk：躯干，主干，树干
trust：信任，信赖，委托，信托，威信
trusts：信任
trusty：可信任，可信任的
truth：真理，实话
trying：难捱，设法
tub：浴盆，桶
tuck：挤进，塞进
tuesday：星期二，周二
tug：强拉，拖
tumble：跌倒，下跌，滚落，滚动
tumbles：跌倒
tumbling：摔倒
tune：调子，调
tunnel：隧道，地道
turn：转动，转弯
turner：车工
turnip：芜菁，萝卜
turnips：萝卜
turpentine：松节油
twelve：十二
twenty：二十
twice：两次
twig：嫩枝
twinkling：闪烁，闪烁的
two-thirds：三分之二
ugly：丑陋的，难看的，难看，丑恶，丑的
umbrella：雨伞，伞
uncertain：渺茫，不肯定的
uncle：叔叔，伯伯，叔父，大爷，老大爷，姑夫
uncomfortable：不舒适，不舒适的，拘束，别扭
uncommon：稀有，稀有的
underclothes：内衣裤
underneath：在下面，下面的
underside：下侧
understand：了解，明白，理解，领会
understood：明白
undertaker：承担人，殡仪馆
undertook：从事
undiscovered：未被发现，未知的
undisposed：未处理

uneasy: 不安，担心，不安的
unexpected: 意想不到，意外，不虞，突然，出现意外，没意料到的
unfavorable: 不利，不利的
ungrateful: 忘恩负义，忘恩负义的
unhitch: 解开
unities: 统一
unknown: 未知，不得而知，不明，不见经传，未知的
unless: 除非
unlikely: 不会，不可能
unloads: 卸货
unnatural: 不自然，不自然的
untie: 解开
upper: 帮子，上面的
uppish: 傲慢的
ups: 电供衡常器
upstairs: 楼上，在楼上
upwards: 向上地，向上
usual: 通常，寻常，一般的
vale: 再会
valid: 有效，有效的
valley: 山谷，峪，谷，流域，山沟
valuable: 宝贵，有价值，有价值的
value: 价值，值，宝贵，推崇，重视，估价，珍惜，计算结果
various: 各个，各式各样，数
vaults: 拱顶
veil: 面罩，面纱
venture: 冒险，敢
verse: 诗，韵文，诗节，散文
village: 村庄，农村，乡村，村子
villages: 村庄
vote: 投票，表决，表决权
voyage: 航行
wadding: 填塞物，填料，絮
wade: 在水步行，涉过，蹚
wages: 工资，待遇，工钱
wagon: 列车厢
wail: 哀号，哀泣，哀鸣，呜咽
wait: 等待，等，伺候
waiting: 等候，等待
wake: 醒来，醒觉
waking: 醒来，醒着的
walk: 行走，步行，走，走道，散步
walked: 步行
walking: 步态，步行
walks: 步行
wall: 墙壁，墙
wallowed: 喷出
walls: 墙壁
waltz: 华尔滋舞
wanting: 缺少的，不足的
wardrobe: 衣厨，衣橱，衣柜
warm: 暖，暖和，温暖，热烈，温暖的
warn: 告诫，警告
warning: 警报，鉴戒，警告
wars: 战争
wash: 洗涤，洗刷，洗
washes: 洗涤
washington: 华盛顿
waste: 荒芜，白费，浪费，糟蹋
wasting: 消耗
watch: 观看，手表，监视
watchman: 看守者，更夫
watermelon: 西瓜
waters: 水域
wave: 波浪，波，浪，浪头，浪潮，飘扬，摇，挥动
wax: 蜡
ways: 方法
weak: 衰弱，瘫软，脆弱，薄弱，虚弱，虚弱的，软弱，微弱
weaken: 削弱，弱化
weakening: 削弱
weapon: 武器
wear: 穿带，穿
weary: 疲劳，疲乏，疲倦的
weather: 天气
weaves: 编织
weaving: 编织
wednesday: 星期三，周三
wee: 细小
weeping: 垂枝的
weigh: 权衡，秤
weight: 重量，体重，包袱，衡量，衡，分量，砝码，重担，使加权
welcome: 欢迎，受欢迎，欢迎光临，受欢迎的，款待
wellington: 惠灵顿
wench: 乡下姑娘，女仆
west: 西，西面，西方
wet: 湿
whack: 重打
whale: 鲸鱼
whatever: 无论如何，无论何事，不拘，任何
wheel: 轮子，轮，车轮
whenever: 无论何时，每当
whereabouts: 行踪，下落，所在之处
wherever: 无论何处，哪里
whetstone: 磨刀石
whichever: 任何，视何者为
whip: 鞭打，鞭子，鞭
whirl: 旋转，回旋
whirls: 旋转
whiskers: 胡子
whisky: 威士忌酒
whisper: 耳语，低语
whispered: 耳语
whispers: 耳语
whistler: 吹口哨的人
whistling: 吹口哨，吹笛
whitest: 苍白的
whoever: 无论何人
whoop: 呼叫声
whose: 谁的
wicked: 邪恶，邪恶的，恶性
wide: 宽阔，广阔，开阔，宽广的，宽广
widow: 寡妇
wife: 妻子，太太，爱人，媳妇儿，妻，老婆
wig: 假发
wigwam: 帐篷，陋棚
wild: 野，猖披，猖獗，野生，野性的
wilderness: 荒野，荒地
william: 威廉
willing: 愿意，高兴，情愿的
willow: 柳树
wilt: 枯萎
win: 博得，赢得，胜，赢
wince: 退缩，因疼痛退缩
wind: 风，弯曲，上弦，缠绕
winding: 曲折，弯曲
window: 窗口，窗户，窗，窗子
windows: 视窗
winds: 风
wink: 眨眼，眨眼睛
winking: 眨眼
winner: 胜利者
winter: 冬天，冬季，冬
wipe: 拭，揩，擦掉，擦，擦去
wire: 电线
wise: 高明，明智的，英明
wish: 愿望，希望，意愿，祝，祝愿，志愿
wishing: 恭祝
wit: 风趣，机智，智慧
witch: 巫婆，女巫
witchcraft: 巫术
wits: 智慧
woe: 悲哀，悲痛
woke: 醒觉
won: 圜，胜
wonder: 奇迹，惊奇
wonderful: 奇妙，奇妙的
wont: 习惯
wood: 木，木材，木头
wooden: 木制，木制的
woodpile: 柴堆
woods: 树林，森林
woody: 木制的，木质的
woodyard: 堆木场
wool: 羊毛
woollen: 羊毛制的，毛织品
word: 字，词，单词，誓言
wore: 穿了
works: 作品，书籍，工作
worn: 穿
worried: 担心，不安，忧虑
worry: 担心，使烦恼，缠绕，担忧，心事，担，烦恼，着急
worse: 更坏，更糟

worsened：恶化
worst：最坏的
worth：价值，值，值得
wrap：包，包裹
wrapping：包皮
wreck：破坏，摧毁，祸害，糟蹋
wrench：螺旋钳，扳子，扳手，扳钳
wrist：腕，腕部
write：撰写，写，编着，写作，写信给，书写，书写器，写字，作曲
writes：写
writing：篇章，笔墨，着述，写，写作
wrong：不对，不平，错误的，错误
wrote：写了
yard：码，厂，厂子，场地
yards：场地
yarn：毛线
yawl：双桅帆船，舰载杂用船，船载小艇
yawn：哈欠，打呵欠，呵欠
yawning：打呵欠
ye：你们
yell：叫喊，呐喊
yelled：叫喊
yelling：叫声，叫喊
yellow：黄，黄色
yesterday：昨天
yield：出产，产量
yonder：那边
younger：较年轻的
yours：你的
yourself：你自己
yourselves：你们自己

Made in the USA